AF594046

PLATE 1.

CALYPSO BULBOSA (PAGE 47).

[*Frontispiece*

A. W. Darnell

ORCHIDS FOR THE OUTDOOR GARDEN

A DESCRIPTIVE LIST OF THE WORLD'S ORCHIDS, FOR THE USE OF AMATEUR GARDENERS

Preface by

GORDON W. DILLON

Executive Secretary, American Orchid Society, Inc.

DOVER PUBLICATIONS, INC., NEW YORK

This Dover edition, first published in 1976, is an unabridged republication of the work originally published by L. Reeve & Co., Ltd., Ashford, Kent, in 1930. A new Introduction by Gordon W. Dillon has been specially prepared for this edition. The frontispiece was reproduced in full color in the original edition.

International Standard Book Number: 0-486-23406-1
Library of Congress Catalog Card Number: 76-23979

Manufactured in the United States of America
Dover Publications, Inc.
180 Varick Street
New York, N.Y. 10014

PREFACE
To The Dover Edition

When it was first published in 1930, *Orchids for the Outdoor Garden* by A. W. Darnell met with an enthusiastic reception. The horticultural press hailed it as "a book that has long been wanted." As seen by the reviewers, the work not only had promise of opening up a new section of horticulture by advocating the growing of orchids outdoors, but would also "prove of considerable value to the many amateurs already interested in the cultivation of Orchids under glass, for the detailed information contained in its pages indicates that many plants will probably succeed favourably under lower temperatures than those usually accorded them." It was welcomed, too, for the many new species it introduced to the enthusiasts who had grown thirsty for new orchids and new orchid books during the publication drought that, after the turn of the century, followed the flood of works such as Williams' *The Orchid Grower's Manual*, Watson's *Orchids: Their Culture and Management* and *The Manual of Orchidaceous Plants* by James Veitch & Sons. The year 1930 seemed an auspicious time for the realization of Darnell's hope that the rock and water gardens of the British Isles would soon abound with exotic orchids from many parts of the world.

That the "orchid cultural revolution" which Darnell expected his book to engender has yet to occur is due to external circumstances rather than to any shortcomings in the author's vision or in his work. The world plunged into the Great Depression, followed within the decade by World War II, and the ensuing years saw in Great Britain the rise of problems which shattered the very foundations upon which Darnell's hopes were based. Recently, however, factors have come to the fore which indicate that *Orchids for the Outdoor Garden* is a book that appeared a half century ahead of its time.

In 1930, the cultivation of orchids in England and Europe, as well as in the United States, was at a very high level of the art, but it was confined to the greenhouses of a small coterie of wealthy—or at least well-to-do—amateurs and an even smaller group of commercial growers and importers. Emphasis was on perfecting traditional techniques, not on experimentation; interest was focused upon the newest hybrids which were just beginning to appear in great variety and abundance; and purse-strings were loosened primarily to purchase superior forms of species and hybrids which might capture horticultural awards or win prizes when displayed in flower and garden shows.

Today, while many of these attitudes still persist, the orchid world itself has changed completely. The number of enthusiasts has multiplied a thousandfold, and interest in these plants is expanding with ever-increasing intensity. At the same time, the growing of orchids has broadened in a hundred ways undreamed of just a few decades ago. Orchids are grown by housewives, doctors, businessmen, retired colonels and young children just becoming aware of the world around them. Orchids are grown for flowers, for specimen plants, for awards, for fun and for the inner satisfaction to be gained by cultivating plants.

Orchids are grown in greenhouses, in lath houses and on glassed-in porches. Indoors, orchids are grown in Wardian cases, on windowsills, under fluorescent lights in simple frames or in more elaborate basement rooms. And orchids are grown outdoors.

Particularly within the United States, the art of growing orchids outdoors has prospered. In the subtropical climates of Florida, Texas, California and Hawaii, an outdoor orchid garden such as Darnell envisioned is a not infrequent occurrence, although the orchids used are, for the most part, not those he suggested for British gardens. In more temperate areas of the Atlantic States, parts of the South, coastal regions of California and in the Pacific Northwest. native orchids have been successfully transplanted to naturalistic gardens. Orchid growers of many years' experience are turning to unusual species for their hobby collections, and novice growers, unhampered by tradition or experience, are experimenting with different species and methods, often with outstanding success. It is as if the orchid world anticipated by Darnell had finally arrived, nearly fifty years late.

Thus it is a happy circumstance that this reprint edition of *Orchids for the Outdoor Garden* is being published at this time. It should not only meet with an enthusiastic reception once again, but should also prove to be "a book that has long been wanted." Even more, it should truly open up a new horticultural pursuit, the growing of exotic—that is, non-native—orchids in outdoor gardens.

It should be noted that *Orchids for the Outdoor Garden* confines itself to a selection of orchids which, in the opinion of Mr. Darnell, are suitable for growing in the British Isles or, in the case of the epiphytic orchids, in the warmer western and southwestern counties of Great Britain. Many sections of the United States, of course, have climates roughly comparable to that of the British Isles, while in many others, where temperatures are more extreme, protective measures and special growing techniques can provide similar conditions. Thus many of the species described in this work are potentially suitable for outdoor growing in some parts of the United States.

The book treats of 977 species distributed among 117 separate genera, their native habitats ranging from Europe, Siberia, Japan, China, India, tropical Asia, Australia, New Zealand and the Pacific Islands into North America and Mexico, with a few species extending into tropical America. Many of the genera are considered as being comprised of tropical orchids, but Mr. Darnell has gleaned the more hardy species for his book. The bulk of the species are terrestrial in habit, but a small number are epiphytic; it is not known whether any of the latter have been successfully acclimated to the British Isles. Among the epiphytic orchids described are species of the genera *Bulbophyllum, Bulleya, Cirrhopetalum, Coelogyne, Cymbidium, Dendrobium, Earina, Eulophia, Galeola, Liparis, Mystacidium, Oberonia, Pleione, Saccolabium* and *Sarcochilus.*

It must be remembered that the classification of the Orchid Family was then —as it still is today—unstable and subject to differing interpretations. Nomenclature used by Mr. Darnell, while carefully adapted, was not definitive, and with the many changes since 1930, the orchid specialist will take exception to some of the generic and specific concepts used. Nevertheless, the average reader should have little difficulty in learning the accepted identity of most of the orchids discussed.

Readers living in the cooler areas of the United States will already be familiar with some of the orchids described, for these are native to the United States. Chief among these are the cypripediums, such as *Cypripedium acaule, C. arietinum, C. calceolus, C. californicum, C. candidum, C. fasciculatum, C. guttatum, C. hirsutum (= C. calceolus* var. *pubescens), C. montanum, C. parviflorum (= C. calceolus* var. *pubescens), C. passerinum* and *C. reginae.* Many of these have been successfully cultivated in native orchid gardens in the northeastern United States, although each species appears to have its special sensitivities to any change in environment. Still, some of these native cypripediums were transplanted into England as far back as the late 1700's.

The cypripediums have showy flowers, but not all United States native orchids are so blessed. *Aplectrum shortii (= A. hyemale)* and *A. spicatum (= A. hyemale),* and the even less decorative *Tipularia unifolia (= T. discolor),* will make interesting additions to a native orchid garden or bog garden but will hardly beckon to the eye of any non-orchid-minded gardener.

Arethusa bulbosa, on the other hand, is a beautiful native species which not only will delight the eye with its single large rose-purple flower (occasionally there are two) as it thrives in the bog garden, but it will please the botanical historian as being one of the few species of orchids known to Carolus Linnaeus, the father of modern botany, and in fact was named by him.

There are numerous other North American orchids which Darnell considered as being adaptable to the British gardens, such as species of *Corallorhiza, Pogonia, Listera, Liparis, Epipactis, Microstylis (= Malaxis), Orchis, Spiranthes* and *Habenaria,* among others. A number of such species actually had been, over the years, introduced into cultivation in England, especially in botanical gardens such as at Kew. Many, however, had never been attempted, while others had been introduced without success.

Quite a few of the orchids native to the British Isles are, of course, identical to, or closely related to, the orchid species of North America. The same holds true for some of the orchids of Europe, many of which have been studied intensively by botanists and horticulturists for several generations and adapted to cultivation. Somewhat surprising is Darnell's inclusion of many terrestrial orchids from Africa, China, Japan, Australia and New Zealand. He reasoned that a number of them are members of the same genera as are found in Europe and, since they come from temperate climes, logically can be expected to adapt to new but similar environments. Many species of *Habenaria* are found in temperate regions of Africa, as well as in China and Japan, along with species of related genera, such as *Pecteilis, Platanthera, Herminium, Peristylus* and *Perularia,* genera often included in a broader concept of the genus *Habenaria. Spiranthes,* too, is a terrestrial genus with more than a score of species native to the United States, with its range embracing temperate and tropical areas in both hemispheres.

But *Disa* and its relatives *Forficaria, Monadenia* and *Herschelia* are strictly African, as are the genera *Disperis, Brachycorythis* and *Stenoglottis,* while the genus *Satyrium,* although chiefly African, has a few species ranging into Java, China and Australia. The successful introduction of these into outdoor gardens in Europe or America would open a whole new dimension in the orchid-growing art.

So, too, would the successful adaptation of the many fascinating orchid genera from Australia, for what could be more delightful than to bloom such treasures as are to be found in the genera *Thelymitra, Diuris, Caladenia, Prasophyllum* or *Pterostylis,* which combine to account for more than 300 of the orchid species of Australia?

The key to the great treasure house of orchids for the outdoor garden is concealed in the phrase "successful adaptation," for although many of the orchids suggested by Darnell have climatic requirements not too difficult to achieve, many terrestrial orchids appear to have highly recondite needs that have yet to be defined. The simple transplantation of a native orchid from its natural habitat to a presumably similar man-made environment is often hazardous, the plant expiring within two or three years after the transplanting has appeared to be a success. How much more difficult will it be to take a *Disa* from the tablelands of South Africa and have it flourish in a garden in San Francisco?

Fortunately, there are many favorable factors today which were not present in 1930. Jet planes, for example, make rapid transport of plants possible. Plant physiology has made tremendous strides in the past fifty years. The germination of seed of many orchid genera has become a routine procedure. Interest in the study and growing of terrestrial orchids is increasing, with many hobbyists and botanical gardens maintaining collections of terrestrial orchids which only a few years ago would have seemed impossible. But much remains to be done.

Three areas of developmental activity must be pursued. First, comprehensive ecological studies of terrestrial orchids in their natural habitats must be undertaken so that the detailed requirements of each species can be known more precisely. Second, there must be a broad program to investigate the techniques for germinating by artificial means the seed of those genera and species which as yet have resisted such attempts. Third, the growing to maturity of seedlings of these species must be accomplished in laboratories and greenhouses until such efforts become routinely successful.

In this way the highly important conservation of such species in their native lands can be assured, while the interests of orchid hobbyists may be served. In so doing, we will add to our general knowledge and understanding of the Orchid Family. Equally important, perhaps, is that we will have paid proper tribute to A. W. Darnell, whose efforts and foresight gave us *Orchids for the Outdoor Garden.*

GORDON W. DILLON
Executive Secretary
American Orchid Society, Inc.
Botanical Museum of Harvard University
Cambridge, Massachusetts 02138

INTRODUCTION

In the following pages the author has endeavoured to give a complete descriptive list (as far as it is possible with the present available information) of all the species of Orchids suitable for outdoor culture in the British Isles, either generally, or in the more genial climate of the western counties only. The possession of a well-appointed rock garden, however small, with its moraine, "dripping well," boggy nooks, pools and variety of soils and aspects, enables the flower lover to bring together in a comparatively limited space, and grow to perfection, a vast number of both beautiful and interesting plants which hitherto could only be grown in districts where local conditions suited their exacting requirements. Among the innumerable floral treasures from all parts of the temperate regions which now furnish our rock and water gardens, the vast family of Orchids is very poorly represented, despite the fact that many which are suitable for general cultivation outdoors in this country are quite as interesting and beautiful as the popular tropical species; except for a few species of *Orchis* and *Cypripedium* they are rarely seen outside our largest Botanic Gardens. Considering the fact that a large number of the species enumerated in the following pages are frequently found growing in company with many of the most cherished denizens of our rock and water gardens in their native habitats, there seems little reason for their rarity in cultivation. Possibly they are somewhat more exacting in their cultural requirements than many other plants, but when once their likes and dislikes are understood they can be made to flourish for years with ordinary attention.

In order to make this work as complete as possible, and useful as a Book of Reference, the author has, apart from the comparatively few species in commerce and in cultivation in public and private gardens, included a very large number of species which have yet to be introduced into cultivation in this country. It may be of interest to state the methods by which the author has arrived at his decision to include a given species in this work, if little or nothing is known from cultural experiences as to the ability of such given species to withstand low temperatures.

The lowest temperature to which a plant can be exposed in cultivation, and yet survive and flourish, depends upon such circumstances as the latitude of its habitat north and south of the equator, altitude above sea-level, whether its native country be insular or continental, etc.

Fortunately for the author's purpose the modern horticultural and botanical plant collector invariably records the conditions under which the plant grows, including the altitude above sea-level and the exact locality of its habitat, and it is a comparatively easy task to ascertain from easily accessible meteorological data the mean and very frequently the minimum temperature to which a plant is subjected in its native country. In cases where the plant under consideration is a native of uninhabited mountains or mountain ranges for which no temperature records exist, the mean annual temperature of the nearest station to their base and the limit of perpetual snow on their summit or the limit calculated for that latitude if insufficiently lofty, have been used to arrive at the mean annual temperature of the locality the plant inhabits. This is allowing 1° fall in temperature for every 1000 feet of ascent from such station and 1° rise in temperature for every 1000 feet of descent from the limit of perpetual snow or isothermal of 32° F., which is nearly accurate for most parts of the world except in exceptional circumstances, such as occur in some hot valleys and mighty ravines in the Eastern Himalayas, the Alps of China and Persia, also in the mountains of tropical and subtropical Mexico, Central and South America, where they are so enclosed by mountains or so narrow that the thermometer never falls to freezing point although they are situated many thousands of feet above sea-level.

In conclusion, all Orchids native in districts at sea-level in the cool temperate regions, or growing on the mountains of the warm temperate, subtropical and tropical regions where the mean annual temperature is below 48° F. if the district is insular, and below 50° F. if it is continental, are considered by the author to be sufficiently hardy for outdoor culture throughout the British Isles, with the exception of species from the high tablelands of Mexico, Venezuela, Peru, Bolivar, parts of Central Africa, Southern Asia and Australasia, where the climate, although giving an annual reading of 48° F., is even more equable than ours.

Species native in insular localities with a mean annual temperature of 50° F., or if continental 55° F., have been deemed hardy enough for culture outdoors in the western and south-western maritime counties of Great Britain with the above exceptions. All Orchids inhabiting localities with a higher mean annual temperature than specified above have been considered too tender for culture outdoors in the British Isles, unless known to be otherwise from cultural experiments.

It will be noticed by the cultivators of Orchids that a number of their favourite epiphytal species which they grow in an orchid house have been included in this work as suitable for outdoor culture in the warmer and more humid parts of the British Isles. This may be explained by the fact that most mountains in tropical, subtropical and the warm temperate regions under conditions governed mainly by (1) the amount of moisture that is precipitated on their sides, (2) the latitude in which they are found, and

(3) proximity to the ocean, are clothed (from the base to a certain elevation above sea-level depending mainly on their distance from the equator) with a dense forest of evergreen trees, which is the home of most of the epiphytal Orchids. If the mountain or range of mountains attains sufficient elevation above sea-level the evergreen forest or " rain-forest " of the botanist gradually gives place to a forest of deciduous trees belonging to genera found in the cold temperate regions of the earth. A considerable number of the more robust epiphytal species spread from the " rain-forests " upwards far into the forest of deciduous trees and are frequently found on oaks, willows, beeches and birches in the cool temperate zone of the mountains, indeed a few epiphytal species ascend higher and are found on the knarled branches of trees in the " elfin wood " on the edge of the alpine zone. Several epiphytal Orchids which the author considers are too tender for experimental outdoor culture in the British Isles have been cultivated with complete success on the branches of trees in the open air in the South of France, Italy and South-Western Cape Colony without any protection from frost. All the epiphytal Orchids described in the following pages are found under similar climatic conditions to those which prevail in the warmer western and south-western counties of the British Isles, and there is no reason why they should not succeed in the outdoor garden in a sheltered humid spot on the trunks or branches of oaks, willows, etc., where they are clothed with a vigorous growth of the Polypody fern, firmly fixed among the decaying rhizomes and protected with a few spruce or yew branches overhead during frosty weather.

The nomenclature adopted for this work is for the most part that of the *Index Kewensis*, supplemented, where thought advisable, by the views of eminent European botanists, and is believed to be as up-to-date as it is possible to make it in these days of conflicting opinions.

The most frequently met with synonyms will be found printed in italics below the generic and specific names, but in order to avoid over-crowding the body of the work the less frequently used and more obscure synonyms have been included only in the general Index to Species. In order to make the general descriptions of the various species as concise as possible, simple scientific terms have been used, full explanation of which will be found in the Glossary. In most cases, except where they are necessary to distinguish the various species, descriptions of the sexual organs of the plant have been omitted as being of little interest to the majority of cultivators, and only the most salient features of the plant described.

In forming an opinion as to the decorative or garden value of a species, where access to the living plant has been unobtainable, authoritative coloured and uncoloured drawings and illustrations have been resorted to. In cases where these do not exist herbarium specimens have proved helpful. A knowledge of the conditions under which a plant flourishes in its native country is a useful, though by no means infallible, guide to its treatment in cultivation.

The cultural indications of plants that have yet to be introduced into cultivation are based on the information given in field notes and on the herbarium labels of collectors, supplemented by knowledge of the geological formation of the district in which it grows.

A large number of botanical works and periodical publications have been consulted in cases where plants have yet to be introduced into cultivation; among many others the following may be mentioned: The Colonial Floras (such as "Flora of Tropical Africa," "Flora Capensis," "Flora of British India," "Flora Australiensis," "Flora of New Zealand," "Flora of Tasmania"), Curtis' *Botanical Magazine*, Paxton's *Magazine of Botany*, *The Botanical Register*, *Kew Bulletin of Miscellaneous Information*, *Notes from the Botanic Gardens Edinburgh*, *Botanical Magazine of Tokyo*, Cheesman's "Manual of the New Zealand Flora, Camus, A., "Monographie des Orchidees de l'europe" and "Iconographie des Orchidees de l'europe"; Feede, F., "Repertorum novarum specierium regeni vegetabilis"; Engler, A., *Botanische Jahrbücher*; the *Botanische Zeitung*; *Revue génèrale de Botanique*; Lindley's "Genera and Species of Orchidaceous Plants"; Kränzlin's "Orchidacearum Genera et Species"; Britton's "Manual of the Flora of Northern United States and Canada"; Small's "Flora of the South-Eastern United States"; Henry's "Flora of Southern British Columbia"; Piper's "Flora of Washington"; Coulter's "Manual of Botany of the Central Rocky Mountains," etc.

In the short generic descriptions the number of species contained in the genus has been brought up to date and is believed to be approximately correct.

A. W. Darnell.

Hampton Wick,
1930.

ILLUSTRATIONS

PLATE 2.

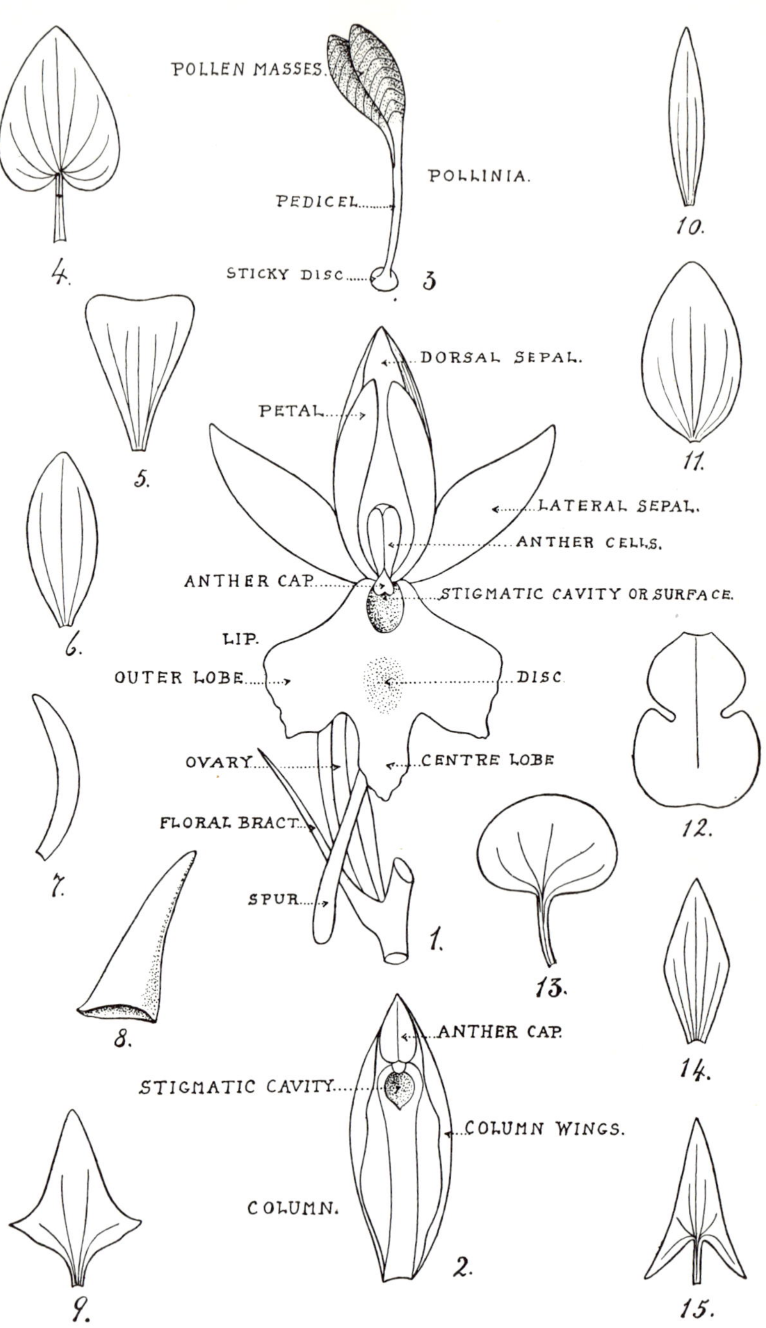

STRUCTURAL PLATE.

PROPAGATION

PROPAGATION BY SEED

Orchids, with but few exceptions, are incapable of self-fertilization and require the agency of insects to carry the pollen from flower to flower to enable them to produce good seed. The reproductive organs of an Orchid are borne on the column, a somewhat stout fleshy process in the centre of the blossom (Pl. 2, Fig. 2); the pollen is usually produced in rounded wax-like masses and in most of the species is contained in the pollinia, a thin membrane tapering to a slender stalk with a sucker-like disc at the base and frequently lobed at the tip (Pl. 2, Fig. 3). The pollen-masses are produced in a cell or cells at the apex of the column and are generally covered with a thin membranous scale known as the anther cap (Pl. 2, Figs. 1 and 2) which falls or is brushed off by a visiting insect when the pollen is ripe. Below the pollen cells on the face of the column is a deep, or at times very shallow, depression, furnished when in a fit state for fertilization with a sticky secretion; this cavity is called the stigmatic cavity or stigmatic surface and takes the place in Orchids of the stigma or pistil of other plants (Pl. 2, Figs. 1 and 2). When the pollen-masses are ripe the disc on the foot-stalk of the pollinia becomes glutinous and is usually exposed. In a state of nature the disc comes in contact with the head or thorax of an insect in search of nectar (which most Orchids secrete at the base of the column), and adhering firmly the pollinia is withdrawn from its cells and projects from the head or body of the insect like minute horns. On visiting another blossom the insect in its endeavour to secure the nectar rubs the ripe pollen masses on the sticky stigmatic surface, where they adhere, thus fertilizing the ovary. The column, pollinia and stigmatic surface differ remarkably in shape in the various genera, and in many species there is no sticky disc on the pollinia. In such cases a little sticky fluid is secreted by the column just below the anther cell and above the stigmatic cavity; when this secretion comes in contact with the head or body of an insect it causes the pollen masses to adhere when they are forcibly brushed against.

Beside our native species there are several from the cool temperate regions of the northern hemisphere that set fertile seed abundantly without the help of artificial fertilization (when in a flourishing state in the outdoor garden in this country). When the atmospheric conditions are suitable numbers of seedlings, springing from self-sown seed, may frequently be found near the parent plant and if these are protected from slugs and supplied with moisture they will form flowering plants in from two to six years. The majority of exotic Orchids, however, seem to need the services of the insects of their native countries and rarely produce seed in this country unless artificially fertilized. To the flower lover who possesses a well-established and healthy specimen of the species he desires to increase by seed, the author recommends the following plan, which has proved quite satisfactory. Select a perfect and fully developed flower from the inflorescence of the plant it is desired shall be the pollen parent and remove the floral segments, leaving only the column on the top of the ovary. Then with the aid of a sharply pointed piece of hard wood remove the anther cap if present; this should expose the base of the pollinia. The point of the wood should now be dipped in the stigmatic cavity so that it may become well smeared with the viscid secretion found therein, and then applied to the base of the pollinia, which will be found to adhere to the point of the stick and may be easily withdrawn from the cell. The flower selected to be the seed parent should be perfect and fully developed; the pollinia should now be very gently inserted into the stigmatic cavity—or applied to the stigmatic surface, as the case may be—of the seed parent, taking care not to bruise or injure it in any way or the resulting capsule may be found to contain nothing but chaff-like scales in the place of fertile seeds with plump nuclei. The above operations are best performed with the aid of a pocket lens. Care should be taken to ensure that the pollen is perfectly ripe, which may be ascertained by the presence of the sticky secretion on the base of the pollinia or near the mouth of the anther cell above the stigmatic cavity, which in the seed parent should also be sticky enough to cause the pollen masses to adhere firmly when they are applied to it. A few hours after the ripe pollen has been applied the flower withers and the stigmatic cavity closes, or if shallow, curves inwards, thus preventing the removal of the pollen by insects or rain. In the majority of the hardy species the ovary reaches full size in from six to ten weeks, when care should be taken to secure the minute seeds before they are scattered, as in some species the capsule frequently bursts whilst it is still green and fleshy. The seed may be sown as soon as it is ripe, or kept until the spring of the year; if possible it is advisable to examine a sample of the seed with a microscope, for it is waste of time to sow the seed unless the nucleus can be distinctly seen through the shining reticulated seed coat, for many Orchids have an irritating habit of producing plump capsules of nothing but chaff-like scales, however carefully the fertilizing process is performed. Considerable success can be obtained under suitable weather conditions by sowing the seed around the parent plant, but it is perhaps more satisfactory to prepare a slightly raised, well-drained bed of compost similar to that in which the parent plant flourishes, only more finely graded. It is advisable if the compost contains any quantity of loam, especially if the seed is that of a moisture-loving species, to mix a quantity of chopped sphagnum-moss with it in order that more moisture may be retained. As Orchid seed requires light to enable it to germinate, the seed bed should be in an open spot, but where the direct rays of the sun do not strike it; the seeds may be scattered evenly over the bed after it has been saturated with water. The bed should now be covered with a ventilated hand-light and kept closed until germination has taken place; moisture should be given when required in the form of a dust-like spray in order that the seeds may be disturbed as little as possible, and from now onwards the soil surface should never be allowed to become dry. The seeds of many hardy Orchids germinate in a month or six weeks if sown as soon as they are ripe, others require a year or more to produce the minute spherical bodies on the surface of the soil which denotes that growth is taking place; more air should be admitted as the tiny leaf develops, but adequate protection from frost should be given during their first winter. When the seedlings are large enough to handle they may be transferred to their permanent quarters and carefully tended until they are well established. The various species differ greatly in the length of time they take to form flowering plants from seed, for instance several *Disas* blossom in eighteen months or two years from the germination of the seed, whilst some members of the genus *Orchis* require six or more years to become sufficiently robust to flower. The seed beds for marsh Orchids should be made on a lower level than those for the seeds of meadow and woodland species, so that more moisture may be secured and retained. Seeds of those species which grow in decaying vegetable debris should be sown around the parent plant and not in seed beds, as they need the aid of minute fungi to enable them to germinate; these are found in the soil around the parent plant.

PROPAGATION BY DIVISION

Orchids with a tuberous rootstock produce tiny tubers beside the parent tuber or on the ends of fleshy roots or stolons; these small tubers or offsets offer a ready means of increase and may be safely separated from the parent plant when the leaves are turning yellow. Care should be taken that they are not bruised or cut, and it is also essential that they should be kept out of the ground as short a while as possible.

Those species whose root systems consist of creeping rhizomes or stolons may be dug up when at rest and cut into pieces with several roots and a bud, exactly in the same manner as one would propagate a German Iris.

The propagation of epiphytal species would probably need heat and should not be attempted out of doors. If the cultivator is fortunate enough to establish such a species it should be left severely alone and not even allowed to produce seed, as this tends to weaken even robust plants.

PROTECTION

Orchids with root systems of soft tubers, fleshy fibres, stolons and rhizomes should be left undisturbed in the ground throughout the winter, and the exotic species should have protection from frost and excessive wet. One of the best ways to this end is to pile a cone of dry material, such as cocoa-nut fibre refuse, cork dust, peat or ashes, over the crowns when at rest and cover them with a ventilated hand light. Another good method is to place the cone of dry material over the crown and cover it with a quantity of furze or holly trimmings to the depth of a foot or more and thatch with straw or some waterproof material secured with old fish netting well pegged down to prevent the covering being disturbed by high winds. Terrestrial evergreen species may be protected in frosty weather by a hand light or a box-like covering of canvas supported by stout stakes.

IMPORTATION

In these days so many people (if they are not among the fortunate ones with the time and means to travel abroad), have relatives and friends tea planting, fruit farming, cattle rearing, etc., in the localities where many of the plants are found, who would be only too glad to collect and forward specimens through the post. Such is the tenacious hold on life of Orchids with a root system of tubers or rhizomes that specimens properly packed have been six months in transit and yet have lived and flourished when planted under suitable conditions. Orchids with tubers of firm consistency or with stout rhizomes may be safely dug up when the leaves have died down, freed of dead stems and foliage, packed in dry peat or moss in small wooden boxes with lids that are easily detachable, and sent by the most speedy route through the post. Those with soft fleshy tubers, slender rhizomes or stolons should be packed in moss freshly gathered, or they may be dug up when they have produced a leaf or two if medium-sized specimens are chosen so that all the fleshy roots are secured without damage (which is very important), packed in freshly gathered moss in a shallow wooden box with a thin lining of cotton-wool, and sent through the post in the usual manner. Epiphytal species may be sent to this country in exactly the same manner, but it is advisable to pack them on the spot direct from the trees and rocks on which they grew. In attempts to establish epiphytal Orchids on trees and rocks in this country only seedlings, or better still freshly-imported plants, should be tried, as cultivation for any length of time in an Orchid house renders the chance of acclimatising the plant very slender.

GLOSSARY

ACULEATE : terminating in a sharp prickle-like point.
ACUMINATE : tapering to a point.
ACUTE : pointed.
AGGLUTINATE : adhering, as with glue.
ALTERNATE : leaves, etc., produced one above the other on opposite sides of the stem.
AMPLEXICAUL : stem clasping.
ANCIPITOUS : double.
ANTERIOR : front.
ANTHER : the upper part of the stamen which holds the pollen.
APICULATE : furnished with a little point.
APPRESSED : pressed close to the stem.
ARCUATE : bent, curved.
ARISTATE : having awns.
ARTICULATE : having swollen nodes or joints.
ASCENDING : when a stem is prostrate at the base and then erect.
AURICLE : an ear-like lobe.
AURICULATE : with two small ear-like lobes at the base.
AXIL : the angle between a leaf and the stem from which it springs.
AXILLARY : growing from the angle between a leaf and the stem.

BICARINATE : with two narrow keels.
BICONVEX : twice convex with a slight ridge between.
BIDENTATE : with two teeth.
BIFID, 2-FID : cleft into two lobes or segments.
BILOBED : two-lobed.
BIPARTITE, 2-PARTITE : deeply cleft to near the base into two lobes.
BITUBERCULATE : with two tubercles side by side.
BLADE : the broad, flat portion of a leaf or floral segment.
BRACT : a small leaf subtending the flowers or on the flower-stem (Pl. 2, Fig. 1).
BULLATE : blister-like, very deeply wrinkled.

CALCARATE : spur-like.
CALLUS, CALLI : a wart-like body, wart-like bodies.
CANALICULATE : with small channels or canals.

CAPITATE : gathered together in the form of a head.
CAPSULE : a seed pod.
CARINATE : ridged or keeled.
CAULINE : leaves on the stem.
CILIA : hair-like processes on the margins of leaves, etc.
CILIATE : fringed with hair-like processes.
CIRCINATE : rolled on the axis, so that the apex is the centre.
CLAVATE : club-shaped.
CLAW : the stalk of a floral segment.
COLUMN : the portion of an Orchid blossom bearing the united stamens and pistil (Pl. 2, Fig. 2).
CONDUPLICATE : folded so that the left and right halves are in contact.
CONNATE : joined together.
CONNIVENT, CONNIVING : converging.
CONVOLUTE : rolled or twisted one within the other lengthwise.
CORDATE : heart-shaped (Pl. 2, Fig. 4).
CORIACEOUS : leathery, thick but not fleshy.
CORM : the solid, thickened, basal portion of the stem of some herbs.
CORYMBOSE : clustered, in the manner of the blossoms of the Elderberry.
CRENATE, CRENULATE : with rounded teeth on the margin.
CRISTATE : having a crest of hairs.
CUCULLATE : hood-like.
CUNEATE : wedge-shaped (Pl. 2, Fig. 5).
CUNIFORM : shaped like a wedge.
CUSPIDATE : terminating in a tooth-like point.
CYMBIFORM : boat-shaped.

DECIDUOUS : shedding of foliage when at rest.
DECUMBENT : trailing but erect at the tip.
DENTATE : toothed like a saw.
DEPRESSED : vertically flattened.
DISC, DISK : the central portion of the middle lobe of the lip (Pl. 2, Fig. 1).
DISTICHOUS : leaves so arranged in two rows that the first is directly below the third.
DIVARICATE : widely divergent.
DORSAL SEPAL : the odd sepal opposite the lip in Orchids (Pl. 2, Fig. 1).

EARED : with small ear-like lobes.
EBRACTEATE : wanting a subtending bract to the flowers.
ELLIPTIC, ELLIPSOID : oval-shaped (Pl. 2, Fig. 6).
EMARGINATE : having a triangular notch at the tip.
ENSIFORM : sword-shaped.

ENTIRE : with a continuous uncut margin.
EPIPHYTE, EPIPHYTIC : a plant which grows on others but is not a parasite.
EROSE : having the margin irregularly notched.
EXSERTED : protruding beyond the mouth of the blossom.

FALCATE : sickle-shaped, hooked (Pl. 2, Fig. 7).
FASCICLE, FASCICULATE : leaves arranged in a bundle or tuft.
FILIFORM : thread-like.
FIMBRIATE : fringed at the margin.
FLABELLATE, FLABELLIFORM : fan-shaped.
FLAGELLATE : whip-like.
FUSIFORM : spindle-shaped.
FURFURACEOUS : covered with scales or scurf, like bran.

GALEA, GALEATE : a helmet-shaped blossom-segment, helmet-shaped (Pl. 2, Fig. 8).
GIBBOUS : pouch or bag-like.
GLABROUS : smooth, without hairs.
GLANDS : secreting cells.
GLANDULAR-HAIRY : hairs bearing a gland at the tip.
GLAUCOUS : covered with grey bloom like a grape.

HASTATE : halberd-shaped, triangular with diverging basal lobes (Pl. 2, Fig. 9).
HISPID : having stiff bristly hairs.
HYALINE : transparent.

IMBRICATE : placed one over the other like tiles on a roof.
INFUNDIBULIFORM : funnel-shaped.
INVOLUTE : where the margins are rolled inwards.

LABELLUM : the lip or segment of the flower opposite the dorsal sepal.
LACINIATE : jaggedly fringed.
LAMELLÆ : thin plates on the disc of the lip, like the " gills " of a mushroom.
LANCEOLATE : lance-shaped (Pl. 2, Fig. 10).
LATERAL SEPALS : the two sepals placed between the dorsal sepal and lip (Pl. 2, Fig. 1).
LAX : loose, not crowded.
LIGULATE : strap-shaped.
LIMB : the blade or broad part of a floral segment.
LINEAR : narrow, like a blade of grass.
LIP : usually the lowermost segment of the Orchid blossom (Pl. 2, Fig. 1).

MEMBRANOUS : thin, papery.
MUCRONATE : tipped with a sharp horny point.

NAVICULAR : boat-shaped.
NODE : the joint in a stem, usually somewhat swollen.

OBCORDATE : inversely heart-shaped.
OBLANCEOLATE : inversely lance-shaped.
OBLONG : longer than broad.
OBOVATE : egg-shaped, with the broad end at the tip.
OBPYRIFORM : inversely pear-shaped.
ORBICULAR : rounded.
OVARY : the portion of the plant containing the seeds (Pl. 2, Fig. 1).
OVATE : egg-shaped, with the narrow end at the top (Pl. 2, Fig. 11).
OVOID : broadly elliptical.

PALMATE : shaped like an open hand.
PANDURATE : fiddle-shaped (Pl. 2, Fig. 12).
PANICLE, PANICULATE : a raceme with branching stalks.
PAPILLÆ : minute wart-like elevations.
PAPILLOSE : covered with minute warts.
PECTINATE : comb-like.
PEDICEL : the flower-stalk.
PELTATE : when the stem is placed in the centre of the leaf.
PENICILLATE : furnished with bundles of short pencil-like hairs.
PENTADACTYLOUS : divided into five finger-like segments.
PERIANTH : a flower with one set of floral segments like a lily.
PETALS : the two inner segments of an Orchid blossom (Pl. 2, Fig. 1).
PETIOLE : the leaf-stalk.
PETIOLATE : having a distinct leaf-stalk, not sessile.
PILOSE : when clothed with rather long hairs.
PLAITED : folded like the ridges and depressions of a palm leaf.
PLICATE : plaited, folded.
PLUMOSE : plume-like, feathery.
POLLEN : the dust-like granules on the anther.
POLLINIA : a process bearing the pollen masses, with a gummy disk (Pl. 2, Fig. 3).
POLYDACTYLOUS : divided into many finger-like segments.
PORRECT : extended horizontally.
PROCUMBENT : trailing flat upon the ground.
PSEUDO-BULB : the solid bulb-like body which takes the place of a stem.
PUBESCENT, PUBERULOUS : downy.

QUADRATE : square.

RACEME : when flowers with a stalk are borne along a simple stem.

RADICAL : said of leaves which spring from the root.
RENIFORM : kidney-shaped (Pl. 2, Fig. 13).
RESUPINATE : upside down.
REVOLUTE : rolled outward, backward or downward.
RHIZOME : a thickened underground stem.
RHOMBOID, RHOMBOIDAL : lozenge or diamond-shaped (Pl. 2, Fig. 14).
RINGENT : open mouthed.
RUGOSE : wrinkled.
RUNCINATE : when the lateral lobes are curved backwards.

SACCATE : bag or pouch-like.
SAGITTATE : shaped like an arrow-head, with the lobes downwards (Pl. 2, Fig. 15).
SAPROPHYTE : a plant which lives on decaying vegetable matter.
SCAPE : the stem which bears the flowers.
SCARIOUS : like very thin pieces of horn.
SECUND : when flowers all face one way on the flower-stem.
SEPALS : the three outer segments of an Orchid blossom.
SERRATE : with regular pointed teeth, like a saw.
SERRULATE : with minute pointed teeth.
SESSILE : seated or stemless.
SETÆ : a bristle.
SETIFORM : having the form of a bristle.
SHEATHS : bracts which clasp the stem closely for two-thirds of their length.
SIMPLE : unbranched.
SINUS : a hollow or notch.
SPATHA, SPATHACEOUS : like the trumpet-shaped portion of an Arum Lily.
SPATHULATE : shaped like a spatula or a battledore.
SPIKE : when sessile flowers are produced along a simple or undivided stem.
SPUR : when the lower part of a floral segment is prolonged into a spur (Pl. 2, Fig. 1).
SQUAMIFORM : scale-like.
STAMINODE : a stamen without an anther.
STELLATE : arranged like the points of a star.
STIGMATIC CAVITY : a sticky cavity in the column of an Orchid (Pl. 2, Figs. 1 and 2).
STIPITATE : having a stalk.
STOLON : a basal branch rooting at the joints.
STRIATE : having slightly raised parallel longitudinal lines.
SUBULATE : awl-like.

TERETE : cylindrical and tapering.
TERRESTRIAL : growing on or in the earth.
TOOTHED : cut into tooth-like segments.

TRIDENTATE, 3-DENTATE : with three tooth-like segments.
TRIFID, 3-FID : divided into three lobes or segments.
TRICUSPIDATE : with three narrow, sharp points.
TRUNCATE : when the end is cut off square.
TUBER : when the root is thickened into a mass like a potato.
TUBERCLES : small elongated wart-like bodies with a stalk.
TURBINATE : top-shaped.

UMBLE : when stalked flowers spring from one point and reach the same level.
UNGUICULATE : when the base of a floral segment is narrow.
UNILATERAL : one-sided.

VENTRICOSE : when a floral segment is inflated.
VERRUCOSE : covered with little knobs or wart-like bodies.
VILLOUS : covered with long soft hairs.

WHORLED : arranged like the spokes of a wheel.
WINGED COLUMN : when the column is furnished with wings (Pl. 2, Fig. 2).

ORCHIDS FOR THE OUTDOOR GARDEN

ACERAS, R. Brown

Four species of curious deciduous terrestrial herbs with erect leafy stems terminating in a long loose spike of very quaint blossoms. The plants are by no means showy and are therefore of little use in decorative gardening but should prove interesting to lovers of nature's marvellous handiwork. The root system consists of two tubers, sessile on the base of the underground portion of the stem, with a few stout fleshy roots springing from the junction of the tubers and stem; the larger tuber supplies the nourishment for the developing growth and then perishes, the smaller tuber continues to increase in size and eventually becomes strong enough to produce a flower-stem. All four species are found in open places in hilly districts usually on calcareous soils. One is scattered over most of Europe and the others are natives of Western Asia. Propagation by division or separation of the tubers, and by seed.

1. ACERAS AFFINIS, Boiss

Himatoglossum affine, Schltr. *Loroglossum affine*, G. Camus.

Root: a large ovoid or oblong tuber. **Stem:** $1\frac{1}{2}'$–$2\frac{1}{4}'$ tall, fairly stout and leafy. **Leaves:** mostly cauline, oblong lanceolate, pointed, smaller upwards, 3″–4″ long. **Spike:** about 8″ long, lax, many-flowered. **Flowers:** about $\frac{7}{8}''$ long; sepals and petals oblong, blunt, forming a narrow hood over the column; lip 3-lobed; outer lobes linear-oblong; centre lobe narrowly linear, deeply bifid at the tip, about six times as long as the lateral lobes; spur cone-shaped, curved, short. *March to June.*

An interesting leafy species of tall spire-like habit with loose spikes of curious blossoms having a remarkably long centre lobe to the lip. The petals and sepals vary from white to dull purple and the lip is green and red. The plant is found in rather dry calcareous soils in pastures and on the borders of woods in Asia Minor, Kurdistan and Mesopotamia. It may be grown in an open sunny spot in well-drained calcareous loam. *A. Bolleana* (Siehe) is closely allied to this species.

2. ACERAS ANTHROPOPHORA, R. Br.

A. anthropomorpha, Sm. *A. anthropomorphum*, Pers. *Orchis anthropophora*, All. *Loroglossum anthropomorphum*, A. Rich. *L. brachyglottis*, Rich.

Root: of 2 ovoid or oblong tubers ¾″ long, one sessile and the other usually shortly stalked. **Leaves:** basal, about 6 in number, oblong or oblong-lanceolate, sheathing, 2″–5″ long. **Scape:** ¾′–1½′ tall, slender, naked, often slightly flexuous. **Spike:** 4″–8″ long, rather dense, many-flowered. **Flowers:** about ⅝″ long; dorsal sepal ovate, pointed; lateral sepals ovate-lanceolate, pointed; petals linear-lanceolate, much smaller than the sepals, all forming a galea over the column; lip 3-lobed; outer lobe linear or filiform; centre lobe bifid with a minute tooth in the sinus. *April to June.*

An extremely quaint native plant known as the Man Orchis. It is quite interesting, but is of no decorative value. The blossoms are green with a pale brown lip with a cream centre. It is found on chalky hillsides and dry pastures over Southern and Central Europe as far west as Eastern England. The plant forms several remarkable hybrids with members of the genus Orchis, many of which are more showy than the type; they may be grown in a well-drained spot in the rock garden in calcareous loam.

3. ACERAS FORMOSA, Lindl.

Himatoglossum formosum, C. Koch. *Orchis formosa*, Stev. *O. mutabilis*, Stev.

Root: an ovoid or globose tuber. **Stem:** 2′–2½′ tall, rather slender, leafy. **Leaves:** basal and cauline, lanceolate, pointed, degenerating into bracts upwards, 3″–5″ long. **Spike:** about 12″ long, lax, many-flowered. **Flowers:** about 1¼″ long; sepals broadly oblong, blunt; petals rhomboid, slightly shorter than the sepals, forming a loose narrow hood over the column with the sepals; lip 3-lobed; outer lobes narrowly oblong, margins crenulate and undulate; centre lobe linear, shallowly bilobed at the tip; spur cylindrical, curved, ½″ long. *April to June.*

The blossoms of this handsome and curious plant closely resemble those of *A. affinis* in shape, with the exception of the centre lobe of the lip, which is very much shorter. The sepals and petals are greenish-purple and the lip is rose colour tinted with green, with a white, green-spotted disc. The plant is found in calcareous soils in open situations on the mountains of North-Eastern Asia Minor and the Caucasus. In cultivation it may be grown in calcareous loam in full sun.

ACIANTHUS, R. Brown

Dwarf, deciduous terrestrial plants numbering 24 species; all have a weak root system consisting of a few fairly stout fleshy white fibres and two (rarely more) irregular fleshy tubers, about the size and shape of culinary peas, terminal on the stoutest fibres. A slender almost thread-like stem is produced by the larger tuber, clothed at its base by a solitary rounded leaf and terminating in a few-flowered spike of exceedingly quaint blossoms. The various species are thinly dispersed over Eastern Australia, Tasmania, the northern Island of New Zealand and the Kermadec Islands. The leaf-soil used in their cultivation should consist of partially decayed oak and beech leaves and should be of a loose flaky nature. Propagation by imported tubers and seeds when available.

4. ACIANTHUS CAUDATUS, R. Br.

Root: of small irregular tubers. **Stem:** 3″–6″ tall, very slender, almost filiform. **Leaf:** basal or nearly so, ovate, deeply cordate, ¾″–1″ long. **Spike:** short, of 1–3 blossoms. **Flowers:** 1½″ long; dorsal sepal filiform, broader below; lateral sepals filiform, shorter than the dorsal sepal; petals lanceolate, pointed, much shorter than the sepals; lip oblong-lanceolate, pointed, short, with 2 basal calli and a few papillæ on the disc. *October.*

An exceedingly quaint little plant with a solitary bright green rounded leaf and from one to three comparatively large deep purple-red blossoms with very slender segments. The plant grows in cool moist shady woods in New South Wales and Tasmania, reaching an elevation of 3000 feet on the mountains, where it is exposed to over 15° of frost during the winter for considerable periods. It should be given a cool moist root-run in nearly pure leaf-soil in a sheltered part of the rock garden. *See Plate 3 facing page 22.*

5. ACIANTHUS EXSERTUS, R. Br.

Root: of small irregular tubers. **Stem:** 3″–6″ tall, very slender. **Leaf:** solitary, ovate or orbicular, deeply cordate, frequently wavy, 1¼″ long. **Raceme:** short, of 3–6 blossoms. **Flowers:** ½″ long; dorsal sepal lance-shaped, narrow, incurved, concave; lateral sepals almost subulate; petals lanceolate, half as long as the sepals; lip oblong-lanceolate with 2 calli at the base and with or without a few papillæ down its centre. *October.*

A fragile little species of very delicate tinting. The solitary bright yellowish-green leaf is somewhat like that of the Ivy and clasps the flower-stem. The blossoms are quaintly shaped and are of a pale pink colour shaded with crimson, the lip being reddish-brown. It grows in damp shady woods in New South Wales, Victoria, South Australia and Tasmania where it is exposed to over 15° of frost for short periods during the winter in some of its more elevated habitats. In cultivation it should be grown under the same conditions as the foregoing species.

6. ACIANTHUS OBLONGUS, Schltr.

Cyrtostylis oblonga, Hook. f.

Root: of tubers on the ends of long fibres. **Stem:** very slender. **Leaf:** solitary, oblong or oblong-cordate, blunt, 1″ long, cordate or rounded at the base. **Scape:** 1″–3″ tall, bearing from 1–3 blossoms. **Flowers:** nearly ½″ across; sepals equal in size, narrowly linear; petals slightly shorter than the sepals, also narrowly linear; lip equalling the sepals in length, linear-oblong, blunt, with 2 small glands at its base. *August to October.*

A pretty little plant for the alpine house with a solitary bright green leaf, translucent stem, and green, pink-tinted blossoms with a purplish lip. This very delicate and fragile plant is found growing in almost pure leaf-soil in shady woods in the North Island and northern part of the South Island of New Zealand at sufficient elevation to ensure its hardiness in the warmer parts of Great Britain. In cultivation the conditions under which it grows in its native habitat should be copied as far as possible: *A. rotundifolius* and *A. macrophylla*, both from the northern Island of New Zealand, differ but little from the above species.

7. ACIANTHUS RENIFORMIS, Schltr.

Cyrtostylis Huegelii, Endl. *C. reniformis*, R. Br. *Caladenia reniformis*, Reichb. f.

Root: of small ovoid tubers on fleshy, white fibres. **Leaf:** solitary, radical, orbicular-cordate or reniform, sessile, ¾″–1½″ across. **Scape:** 1″–6½″ tall, bearing from 1–5 blossoms on short stems. **Flower:** about ⅞″ long; dorsal sepal linear or linear-lanceolate; lateral sepals very narrowly linear, short; petals very narrowly linear, shorter than the lateral sepals; lip strap-shaped, with recurved margins. *August to October.*

A fragile little plant with a translucent stem and a pale green kidney-shaped leaf. The stem bears a few comparatively large quaintly-shaped, pale green and pink blossoms, with a lilac-pink tongue-like lip having a crimson band down its centre fading to bright yellow towards the tip. It should prove a delightful addition to the alpine house. In nature it is found in rather dry soil in open situations amongst short herbage throughout the greater part of Australia, reaching an elevation of between 3000 and 4000 feet on the mountains and should therefore be quite hardy in all but the colder parts of Great Britain. A compost of fibrous loam in an open sunny spot is indicated.

8. ACIANTHUS SINCLAIRII, Hook. f.

Root: of tubers on the end of long white fibres. **Stem:** slender, juicy. **Leaf:** solitary, broadly cordate, deeply 2-lobed at the base, $\frac{1}{2}''$–$1''$ long. **Scape:** $1''$–$3''$ tall. **Raceme:** of from 2–6 flowers. **Flowers:** $\frac{1}{4}''$ across; dorsal sepal broadly linear-subulate, aristate; lateral sepals linear-subulate, also aristate; petals small, lanceolate or ovate-lanceolate, thickened at the tip and with 2 glands at the base. *May to October.*

The small green blossoms of this species have very little garden value, but as the plant is very dwarf it should prove of interest in a pan in the alpine house. It is common in moist shady woods throughout the North Island of New Zealand and is also found in the Kermadec Islands. It reaches sufficient elevation in its native country to ensure its hardiness in the warmer parts of Great Britain. It may be grown in a moist shady spot in the rock garden in leaf-soil, loam and sand.

9. ACIANTHUS VIRIDIS, Hook. f.

Root: of very small elongated tubers. **Stem:** $2''$–$3''$ tall, very slender, almost filiform. **Leaf:** solitary, orbicular, cordate at the base, $\frac{1}{2}''$ long. **Spike:** short, of 1–3 blossoms which are nearly sessile. **Flowers:** about $\frac{1}{2}''$ across; dorsal sepal erect, galeate, much incurved, tapering at both ends; lateral sepals, linear, blunt, as long as the dorsal sepal; petals, linear, very short; lip rhomboidal, concave, wavy, with 2 basal calli. *May to September.*

A very tiny plant of no decorative value but interesting to lovers of curious specimens for the alpine house. It has from one to three rather widely-separated green and pink blossoms on a slender succulent stem clasped about half-way up with a small bright green rounded leaf. It grows in damp shady woods in Tasmania and is by no means common and is easily overlooked. In nature it is subjected to as much as 12° of frost for short periods during its winter rest. It may be grown in damp leaf-soil in a shady corner of the rock garden.

ADENOCHILUS, Hooker, fils.

A genus of but 2 species of very slender terrestrial herbs of dwarf habit, with somewhat stout, fleshy wandering underground stems with numerous short blunt hairy roots springing from the lower surface; small tubers form on the ends of the underground stems and so perpetuate the species. The small leaf is placed about the middle of the stem and is usually oblong or ovate and of a rich green colour, the green and pink blossom is solitary and terminal and is of little or no decorative value. The two species are found in shady forest country in loose leaf-soil beneath the shade of trees, in New Zealand, Southern Australia and Tasmania. One is sufficiently hardy for experimental culture in the rock garden in the warmer part of the kingdom. Propagation by imported roots and tubers.

10. ADENOCHILUS GRACILIS, Hook. f.

Root: a rather long creeping underground stem emitting very short hairy fibres. **Stem:** slender, smooth, 5″–10″ tall. **Leaf:** solitary, ovate or ovate-oblong, pointed, ½″–1″ long, placed about midway on the stem with a close sheath some distance above it. **Flower:** solitary, terminal, about ⅝″ long, suberect; dorsal sepal ovate, pointed, very concave; lateral sepals, lanceolate very pointed; petals erect, narrowly lanceolate or linear-lanceolate, narrower and shorter than the sepals; lip much recurved and deeply concave, 3-lobed; outer lobes broad, erect; centre lobe narrowly linear, pointed; disc with numerous stipitate calli. *November to January.*

A very slender plant with a bright green leaf about the middle of the stem and a solitary blossom of no great decorative value, with green sepals, green and pink petals and white lip with red spots and yellow warts. It is found in shady forests and reaches an elevation of 2500 feet on the mountains of New Zealand. It may be tried outdoors in the rock garden in mild localities in a shady spot in loose leaf-soil.

AMITOSTIGMA, Schlechter

About 14 or 15 species of dwarf, fragile terrestrial plants allied to the genera Gymnadinia, Habenaria and Orchis. The majority are rarely more than six inches tall and bear a solitary narrow leaf below the middle of the very slender flexuous stem. The blossoms are generally small and few in number and are borne in loose racemes which are one-sided in some species. In habit and leaf they very much resemble some species of Habenaria, but the flowers are those of an Orchis. One or two species produce tiny bulbs in the leaf-axils and among the floral bracts; these might no doubt be used as a means of increase. The plants inhabit bogs in open country, frequently at considerable elevations on the mountains. In cultivation they should have their fleshy and tuberous roots buried in wet sphagnum moss and a small portion of fibrous peat, in an open sunny spot in the bog garden. Propagation by imported tubers.

11. AMITOSTIGMA BASIFOLIATUS, Schltr.

Orchis basifoliata, Schltr. *Peristylus tetralobus*, var. *basifoliatus*, Finet.

Root: of 1 or 2 irregular tubers about ½″ across. **Stem:** 5″–8″ tall, very slender, sinuous, with a solitary leaf some distance below the middle and a small spatha-like sheath near the root. **Leaf:** lanceolate, pointed, about 1¾″ long. **Raceme:** fairly lax, of 6–10 blossoms. **Flowers:** about ½″ long;

dorsal sepal erect, ovate; lateral sepals oblique, ovate, blunt; petals subrhomboid, blunt, forming a galea with the dorsal sepal; lip 3-lobed; outer lobes oblong blunt; centre lobe wedge-shape, bifid at the tip; lobes rounded, blunt, diverging. *July.*

A delightful little plant for alpine house decoration. The slender thread-like stem bears a loose raceme of pretty snow-white blossoms with a few purple markings at the base of the lip. It is found in open places in very boggy situations on the mountains of Western Yunnan, Western China, at 8500 feet above sea-level. It may be tried outdoors in very warm and sheltered localities in the bog garden in peat and growing sphagnum-moss, in full sun.

12. AMITOSTIGMA FABERI, Schltr.

Habenaria Faberi, Rolfe. *Gymnadenia Faberi*, Rolfe.

Root: of 2 globose tubers. **Leaf:** solitary, lanceolate, pointed, sessile, about 1″ long. **Scape:** 2″–3″ tall, slender, bearing 1–2 blossoms. **Flowers:** about $\frac{3}{16}$″ across; sepals elliptic-oblong, blunt; petals similar but narrower; lip 4-lobed; lobes oblong, subequal; spur small, club-shaped. *May to July.*

A minute green-flowered species, interesting from a botanical point of view only. It grows in damp rocky places on Mount Omei in Szechuan, Western China, at 9000 feet above sea-level. It should be quite hardy in the southern and western counties of Britain in the rock garden, planted in fibrous peat and moss on a damp sandstone rock.

13. AMITOSTIGMA KEISKEI, Schltr.

Root: an oblong or cylindrical tuber about 1″ long. **Stem:** about 4″ tall, slender, with a solitary leaf below and a few small sheaths above. **Leaf:** broadly linear, concave, about $2\frac{1}{2}$″ long, placed below the middle of the stem. **Spike:** loose, of 1–3 blossoms. **Flowers:** about $\frac{1}{4}$″ across; dorsal sepal elliptic-ovate, blunt; lateral sepals obliquely ovate, blunt, longer than the dorsal sepal; petals ovate, oblique, blunt, connivent; lip cuneate at the base, 3-lobed; outer lobes ligulate-oblong, blunt; centre lobe ligulate, slightly bifid at the tip; spur clavate-oblong, short, carried horizontally. *June and July.*

A delightful little plant for the alpine house. It has a slender sinuous stem bearing a few small white blossoms shaded with pale violet. It is found in boggy places on the mountains in Central Japan. It should be quite hardy in the rock or bog garden in a wet place in living sphagnum-moss and peat.

14. AMITOSTIGMA KINOSHITAI, Schltr.

Gymnadenia Kinoshitai, Makino. *G. gracilis* var. *angustifolia*, Makino.

Root: an oblong tuber with several long roots above it. **Stem:** very slender and slightly flexuous, clothed with a solitary leaf, and 1 or 2 bracts near the raceme. **Leaf:** linear, sometimes very narrow, somewhat channelled, pointed, 1½″–2″ long, placed below the middle of the stem. **Spike:** of 1–3 blossoms, secund. **Flowers:** about $\frac{3}{16}$″ across and $\frac{5}{16}$″ long; dorsal sepal broadly ovate, blunt; lateral sepals obliquely ovate, blunt; petals obliquely ovate, blunt; lip unguiculate at the base, wedge-shaped, deeply 3-lobed; outer lobes oblong, blunt; centre lobe large, wedge-shaped, cleft; spur short, cylindrical, blunt. *May to July.*

A delicate little plant with a very slender thread-like stem clothed with one leaf and bearing a few small white or lilac blossoms tinted with purple. It is found in bogs on the mountains of Central Japan and may be grown outdoors in Great Britain under the same conditions as the preceding species.

15. AMITOSTIGMA PINGUICULA, Schltr.

Gymnadenia Pinguicula, Reichb. f.

Root: of globose tubers about ½″ in diameter. **Stem:** about 6″ tall. **Leaves:** basal, 1 or 2 in number, cordate, ovate-oblong, pointed, about 2″ long. **Scape:** with 1 bract near the middle. **Spike:** ¾″–1½″ long, few or many-flowered. **Flowers:** about ⅝″ long; sepals and petals conniving, forming a galea over the column; lip unguiculate, nearly square, deeply cleft into 2 narrow lobes; disc with many small warts on its surface; spur cylindrical, incurved, ⅜″ long. *May to July.*

A pretty little plant for alpine house decoration with spikes of lilac, white or pale purple blossoms of considerable dimensions in comparison to the size of the plant. It is found in damp or marshy places on the mountains of Hupeh and Ningpo, Central China, and should be quite hardy in the western and southern counties of Great Britain, in a damp open spot of the rock garden in peat, loam and sphagnum-moss.

16. AMITOSTIGMA TETRALOBUM, Schltr.

Orchis tetraloba, Schltr. *Peristylus tetralobus*, Finct.

Root: of 2 very small irregular tubers with a few thick roots above them. **Stem:** 6″–10″ tall, very slender and thread-like, usually curved, with a leaf just below the middle and a small close sheath at its base. **Leaf:** suberect lanceolate, pointed, about 1½″ long. **Raceme:** of about 8 blossoms, loose. **Flowers:** ⅜″ long; dorsal sepal erect, ovate, blunt; lateral sepals ovate, blunt, spreading; petals narrowly ovate, forming a galea with the dorsal sepal; lip 3-lobed; outer lobes narrowly oblong, blunt, incurved; centre lobe truncate, bifid; lobes diverging. *May and June.*

A very slender plant bearing a loose raceme of small pale rose or purplish-rose-coloured blossoms on a sinuous thread-like stem; a gem for the alpine house. It is found in moist stony meadows on the mountains of Western Yunnan, Western China, at from 7500–9000 feet above sea-level. It may be tried outdoors in the warmer parts of Britain under the same conditions as *A. basifoliatus.*

ANOCHILUS, Rolfe

Two deciduous terrestrial plants whose root system consists of a small ovoid tuber attached to the base of the underground portion of the stem, with a few short white fleshy roots above it, this tuber shrivels when the seed capsules ripen and if the plant is in a vigorous healthy state one or more tubers are produced to replace the dead one. The flower-stems are fairly stout and are clothed with oblong sheathing leaves numerous at the base, and terminating in a dense oblong spike of rather small soberly-tinted blossoms of little decorative value. The plants should, however, prove of interest to lovers of curious plants. Both are confined to Cape Colony, in the Central and Western Divisions, where they inhabit rather dry spots, usually in poor sandy or rocky soils, and where they are subjected to great changes of temperature; they should be well supplied with water when in active growth and kept as dry as possible when at rest. Propagation by imported tubers and seeds when obtainable.

17. ANOCHILUS FLANAGANII, Rolfe

Pterygodium Flanaganii, Bolus

Root: a small sessile tuber. **Stem:** stout, erect. **Leaves:** cauline, ovate or ovate-oblong, sheathing and imbricate at the base, 2″–4″ long. **Scape:** 9″–12″ tall. **Spike:** 2″–3″ long, dense. **Flowers:** about ½″ across; dorsal sepal elliptic-oblong, blunt; lateral sepals obliquely ovate, concave, joined at the base to the dorsal sepal; petals ovate, obliquely decurved, conduplicately folded; lip oblong, broadly unguiculate, erect and recurved, downy; appendage broadly elliptic or suborbicular. *October to December.*

This is by no means a showy plant, but the curious smoky-grey colouring of its leaves and flowers, with the exception of the conspicuous dark maroon lip, should render it an object of interest in the rock garden or alpine house. It grows in rather dry, exposed rocky places at Broughton, near Molteno, in the Molteno Division of Cape Colony, at 6300 feet, and should be perfectly hardy in Great Britain if it can be induced to rest during our winter. A gritty loam in full sun is indicated.

18. ANOCHILUS INVERSUM, Rolfe

Ophrys inversa, Thunb. *Pterygodium inversum*, Sw.

Root: a small oval tuber. **Stem:** stout, erect. **Leaves:** cauline, oblong, from a broad sheathing base, 3″–6″ long. **Scape:** $\frac{3}{4}$′–1$\frac{1}{2}$′ tall. **Spike:** oblong, 4″–6″ long, dense. **Flowers:** over $\frac{5}{8}$″ across; dorsal sepal elliptic-oblong, with a short reflexed apex; lateral sepals obliquely ovate-oblong, blunt, conduplicately folded at the base, spreading; petals obovately suborbicular, blunt, conduplicately folded and concave near the base; lip broadly unguiculate, limb obovate-flabellate; appendage oblong, bilobed. *October and November.*

Although the blossoms of this species are of fair size, they are too soberly coloured to have any decorative value; they are greenish-yellow with brown stripes on the lip and at times on the petals. It grows in rocky and sandy ground, frequently in dry spots in Cape Colony and Little Namaqualand, where it reaches its greatest elevation at Lily Fontein at 4000 feet and is exposed to 12° or more of frost during its resting period in the winter. A gritty loam in full sun is indicated.

ANTHOGONIUM, Lindley

This genus consists of a solitary deciduous terrestrial plant with a shortly creeping rhizome emitting a few slender fleshy fibres and bearing several ovoid pseudo-bulbs on its surface. The leaves, from one to three in number, are lanceolate and plaited, they are narrowed into slender stalks and spring from the top of the pseudo-bulbs. The blossoms, which somewhat resemble those of the Aloe, are produced in simple or branched racemes and are quite interesting and decorative. The plant is found in the mountainous parts of Eastern India and Western China and may be propagated by division of the rhizome with one or two pseudo-bulbs and a few roots, and also by seeds when procurable.

19. ANTHOGONIUM GRACILE, Lindl.

A. Griffithii, Reichb. f.

Root: of slender fibres. **Pseudo-bulbs:** ovoid, $\frac{1}{2}$″–$\frac{3}{4}$″ long, bearing from 1–3 leaves. **Leaves:** narrowly lanceolate, 6″–10″ long, on narrow stalks. **Scape:** $\frac{1}{2}$′–1$\frac{1}{4}$′ tall, slender. **Raceme:** branched or simple, fairly dense. **Flowers:** $\frac{3}{4}$″–1″ long; sepals joined into a narrow cylinder, swollen at its base and free at the tip; the dorsal sepal is linear and straight, the lateral sepals are oblong and revolute; petals included, linear; lip narrow at the base, with a flabelliform blade. *September.*

A dainty and desirable plant with racemes of tubular rose-coloured blossoms with bright red spots on the lip; the ovary and tiny bracts are also prettily tinted. The plant usually grows on dry grassy mountain slopes and on moss-covered rocks in Eastern India and Western China, reaching an elevation of 8000 feet above sea-level. It should prove sufficiently hardy for outdoor culture in this country in the warm western counties, in good well-drained loam in a sunny part of the rock garden.

APLECTRUM, Nuttall

Two species of handsome terrestrial Orchids of erect, somewhat robust habit. The root system consists of numerous rather small tubers connected together by fibres that render them at times almost coralloid; the solitary rounded yellow-green leaf is produced the previous season to the flower-stem, usually in late autumn and winter, whilst the flower-stem appears in early summer. The blossoms are large and brightly coloured and are borne in long racemes subtended by small bracts. Both species are confined to North America, where they inhabit cool shady woodlands and grow in rich vegetable soil. Propagation by separation of the young tubers and by seeds which are freely produced in a state of nature.

20. APLECTRUM SHORTII, Rydb.

Root: a series of small tubers often connected together by fibres. **Leaf:** solitary, broadly oval-obovate, frequently as much as 2¾″ wide. **Scape:** 1′–2′ tall, stout, sheathed at its base with loose inflated sheaths. **Raceme:** 3″–6″ long, few-flowered. **Flowers:** about ¾″ across; sepals and petals broadly linear to lanceolate, very blunt; lip oblong, undulate on the margins, somewhat swollen at the base. *June.*

This handsome species is very closely related to the following species, but is usually a more robust plant. The solitary large yellowish-green leaf is followed the next season by a stout almost naked scape bearing a raceme of fairly large purplish blossoms with dull yellow markings on the lip. It is found in wooded country, usually in leaf-soil, in Kentucky, and is very rare and local. It may be cultivated outdoors in the warmer parts of Great Britain in a damp shady part of the rock garden in leaf-soil, fibrous loam and sand.

21. APLECTRUM SPICATUM, Walt.

A. hyemale, Nutt. *Cymbidium hyemale,* Pursh. *Corallorhiza hiemalis,* Nutt.

Root: a chain of small corms or tubers each representing a season's growth. **Leaf:** solitary, developed in the autumn and lasting until spring, elliptic, pointed, erect, narrowed at the base into a winged stalk, 2″–8″ long. **Scape:** ¾′–2′ tall, usually clothed with 3 lanceolate scales and springing from beside the leaf. **Raceme:** 2″–6″ long, few-flowered. **Flowers:** about $\frac{5}{8}$″ across; sepals and petals linear or linear-spathulate, pointed; lip narrowly oblong, undulate or crenulate, column curved. *May and June.*

A pretty orchid well worthy of cultivation; it produces racemes of brownish-yellow and purple blossoms on tall almost naked stems. In its native habitat it grows in shady woods, usually in rich vegetable soil, although in mountainous situations it may be found in poor stony soil. It ranges from Quebec to Ontario and southwards to the mountains of Georgia and California. It is quite hardy in Great Britain in good sandy leaf-soil in a shady spot in the rock garden.

ARETHUSA, Linnæus

This genus, as now constituted, contains but one species, it is a rather dwarf terrestrial plant of slender erect habit with a small underground bulb or tuber which produces a slender sheath-clothed stem bearing a solitary blossom of considerable beauty. The grassy leaf is produced after the blossom has faded and continues green after the capsules have scattered their seeds. In a state of nature it is found in peat bogs in eastern North America and is somewhat difficult to establish in Great Britain. In its native country the winters are very cold and long, but are not broken by mild spells such as we experience during normal winters in Great Britain and which are so detrimental to the roots of plants that are normally quite dormant during that period in their northern homes. Propagation by separation of the tubers and by seeds.

22. ARETHUSA BULBOSA, Lindl.

Root: corm-like, about $\frac{3}{4}$″ across. **Stem:** slender, scape-like, 4″–12″ tall. **Leaves:** usually reduced to sheathing scales except the basal one, which is linear in shape and from 4″–6″ long. **Flowers:** about $1\frac{1}{2}$″ long, usually solitary, rarely more, subtended by 2 small unequal bracts; sepals linear or oblong, erect, lateral ones curved; petals similar but shorter than the sepals; lip diverging, dilated towards the apex, where it is usually toothed or fringed, the upper surface crested or bearded. *May and June.*

A very delightful little plant with a slender sheath-clothed stem bearing one, rarely two, large rosy-purple blossoms with crimson and purple blotches and three snowy white hairy lines on the lip. A perfect plant for alpine house culture. It grows in peat bogs and mossy swamps from Newfoundland to the mountains of North Carolina and Indiana. It is quite hardy in Great Britain in the bog garden in peat and growing sphagnum-moss.

ARUNDINA, Blume

About 9 species of beautiful terrestrial plants of erect rigid habit, with a short stout rhizome producing slender rounded stems clothed with narrow distichous leaves deeply ribbed and of a bright green colour. The blossoms are borne in simple or branched racemes and are usually some shade of red. The various species are found in open spots, usually fully exposed to the sun, in dry soils in India, China and the East Indian Islands. Only one of them is sufficiently hardy for outdoor culture in Great Britain and this should only be tried in very warm sheltered localities in full sun. The rhizomes should be planted at least 3″ below the surface of the soil and should have protection in the winter from frost and wet. Propagation by division of the rhizome in large healthy plants only.

23. ARUNDINA CHINENSIS, Blume

A. affinis, Griff. *A. Philippii*, Reichb. f. *Cymbidium Meyeri*, Reichb. f.

Root: a short stout rhizome. **Stem:** 8″–12″ tall, fairly stout, erect, leafy. **Leaves:** distichous, linear, spreading and recurved, 4″–7″ long. **Raceme:** 1″–3″ long, few-flowered. **Flowers:** nearly $2\frac{3}{4}$″ across; sepals lanceolate, pointed, spreading; petals ovate-oblong, pointed; lip oblong, large, with at times obscure outer lobes, crisped; disc with 5 thickened lamellate nerves. *August.*

A very beautiful plant with erect leafy stems and racemes of from five to seven very large blossoms varying from white to rose-lavender, bright purple and rich red; the lip is usually bright yellow below the middle. The plant inhabits dry open pasture lands at from 7000–9000 feet above sea-level in Southern and Western China and is also found in Eastern India. Plants collected from the greatest altitude should be hardy in the western and southern counties of Britain in a well-drained spot of the rock garden in good fibrous loam and sand.

ASARCA, Lindley

A genus of about 15 species of South American terrestrial Orchids, 7 of which may be safely recommended for outdoor culture in the British Isles. They are very closely allied to the genus Chloræa and are, by some authorities, considered to belong to that genus. Most of the species are of robust habit, varying from 9″ to nearly 6′ in height, and are frequently bare of leaves at their flowering period, no doubt in many cases due to the arid situations in which they are found. The blossoms of most species are large, and many are attractively coloured, in a few cases the bracts are brightly tinted. The difficulty found in acclimatising many Chilian plants in this country is that the vegetative season is at its most active period during our winter; retardation as practised with Lily of the Valley rhizomes might prove of use. Propagation by imported tubers and by seeds when they can be procured.

24. ASARCA ACUTIFLORA, Poepp.

A. verrucosa, A. Rich. *Gavilea acutiflora*, Poepp.

Root: a cluster of tuber-like fibres. **Stem:** up to 2′ tall, slender, leafy below, sheathed above. **Leaves:** 4 in number, oblong-lanceolate, pointed, about 4″ long. **Spike:** loose, of 6–8 blossoms. **Flowers:** about 1″ across; dorsal sepal oblong-lanceolate, tapering to a tail-like point; lateral sepals similar but with longer points; petals oblong, pointed, sparsely verrucose below; lip 3-lobed; outer lobes large, rounded, strongly veined; centre lobe smaller, ovate, covered with depressed tubercles from the base.

November and December.

A pretty plant with rather large sulphur-yellow blossoms having bright green tips to the sepals and green tubercles on the lip. It is found in Araucaria forests on the Andes of Antuco and Curico in Central Chile at nearly 5000 feet above sea-level and should be hardy over the greater part of the kingdom in a half-shady spot in the rock garden in loose loam and leaf-soil.

25. ASARCA APPENDICULATA, Phil.

Root: a cluster of long, stout fusiform tubers. **Stem:** from $1\frac{1}{2}'$–$3\frac{1}{4}'$ tall, stout, leafy below, sheath-clothed above. **Leaves:** 5–6 in number, oblong, 4″–8″ long, shrivelling before the flowers expand. **Spike:** 6″–9″ long, of as many as 15 blossoms. **Flowers:** about $\frac{7}{8}''$ across; dorsal sepal oblong-lanceolate, concave, pointed; lateral sepals ovate, convolute and contorted at the tip; petals oblong, oblique, blunt, verrucose down the centre; lip 3-lobed; outer lobes subquadrate, rounded at the tip, with 2 rows of hooked tubercles; centre lobe linear or narrowly triangular, thickened at the tip; disc with club-shaped papillæ. *November and December.*

A very robust plant with medium-sized white blossoms with green, fleshy tips to the sepals. It is found in thin woods in Central Chile and Patagonia and should be sufficiently hardy for outdoor culture over the greater part of the kingdom in a sheltered spot in the rock garden in sandy loam and leaf-soil.

26. ASARCA COMMERSONII, Hook. f.

Chloræa Commersonii, Brong. *Serapias lutea*, Pers.

Root: a cluster of very stout tuber-like roots. **Stem:** 1′–2′ tall, leafy below. **Leaves:** oblong or oblong-lanceolate, blunt, upper leaves pointed, degenerating into sheaths above, about 4″ long. **Spike:** short, dense, few-flowered. **Flowers:** about $\frac{5}{8}''$ across; dorsal sepal lanceolate, pointed; lateral sepals lanceolate, prolonged into a tail-like appendage at the tip; petals unguiculate at the base, lanceolate, pointed, short; lip 3-lobed; outer lobes ovate or obcordate, almost falcate, with naked discs; centre lobe oblong-lanceolate with numerous tubercles on the disc and 2 or 3 short hairy ridges near the base of the lip. *August and September.*

A tall leafy species with rather small white blossoms spotted with green. It is not quite so desirable as many of its brethren, and is found in the evergreen beech woods of Southern Chile and Fuegia. It should prove perfectly hardy in this country in a shady part of the rock garden in leaf-soil and loam.

27. ASARCA GLANDULIFERA, Poepp.

Chloræa Volucris, Lindl.

Root: a cluster of thickened fibres. **Stem:** up to 2′ tall, clothed at the base with a few rose-coloured sheaths; the leaves are unknown. **Spike:** up to 8″ long, many-flowered. **Flowers:** about $\frac{3}{4}$″ across; dorsal sepal oblong, rounded at the tip; lateral sepals obliquely oblong, subfalcate, with a thick club-shaped tip; petals ovate-oblong, blunt, verrucose below the middle; lip 3-lobed; lateral lobes semiorbicular, with from 2–4 crescent-shaped hairy ridges; centre lobe linear or narrowly triangular. *October to December.*

An extremely beautiful plant with numbers of rather large rose-coloured blossoms subtended by leafy bracts of the same colour. It grows in wet places on the Andes, Central Chile, and is also found in swamps and bogs near the banks of the Rio Chico, Chubut, Patagonia. Plants collected from the latter locality should be quite hardy in Britain in the bog garden or on the banks of a stream or pond, in good rich soil.

28. ASARCA KINGII, Hook. f.

Root: of thickened fleshy fibres. **Stem:** about 12″ tall, leafy below. **Leaves:** radical, lanceolate, pointed, up to 6″ long. **Spike:** from 2″–4″ long, of 6–8 blossoms. **Flowers:** about $\frac{5}{8}$″ across, mixed with membranous bracts; dorsal sepal lanceolate, with a membranous point; lateral sepals shortly unguiculate, oblong-lanceolate or lanceolate; petals similar but shorter; lip shortly unguiculate, oblong, undivided, membranous, with thickened centre nerves. *August and September.*

This plant produces rather slender leafy stems and short spikes of rather small white and green blossoms of a thin paper-like texture. It is found in evergreen beech woods near Port Famine in the Straits of Magellan and should be perfectly hardy in Great Britain in a fairly damp half-shady spot in the rock garden in leaf-soil and loam.

29. ASARCA ODORATISSIMA, Poepp.

A. sulphurea, Phil. *Gavilea odoratissima*, Poepp.

Root: of thick fusiform fibres. **Stem:** $1\frac{1}{4}'$–5′ tall, very stout and fleshy, leafy below, sheath-clothed above. **Leaves:** basal, oblong, degenerating upwards into sheaths, 6″–8″ long. **Spike:** 4″–12″ long, many-flowered. **Flowers:** about $\frac{5}{8}''$ across; dorsal sepal ovate-oblong, pointed; lateral sepals obliquely oblong, thickened and tail-like at the tip; petals ovate, pointed; lip deeply 3-lobed; outer lobes semiorbicular, diverging; centre lobe oblong or rounded-triangular, tip thickened, blunt; disc with 5 rows of dense papillæ.

August to November.

A very robust species with long spikes of rather small blossoms with green sepals and lip, and white petals. It is found in rocky places in damp situations in the provinces of Antuco, Chillan, San Jago and Valdivia in Central Chile. It may be tried outdoors in the warm western counties in a damp spot in half shade, in rich leaf-soil and loam.

30. ASARCA PARVIFLORA, Poepp.

Cymbidium bicristatum, Poepp.

Root: a cluster of fusiform tubers on the ends of stout fibres. **Stem:** 15″–18″ tall, leafy at the base, clothed with distant sheaths upwards. **Leaves:** oblong or elliptic, withering before the blossoms are produced. **Spike:** 4″–6″ long, few or many-flowered, flowers usually distant. **Flowers:** about $\frac{3}{4}''$ across; dorsal sepal lanceolate-oblong, pointed, concave; lateral sepals linear, twisted, thickened, involute, blunt; petals oblong, blunt, with tubercles at the base; lip 3-lobed; outer lobes rounded; centre lobe oblong, blunt, much narrower than the outer lobes; disc and base of the lip with tubercles on the upper surface.

December.

A small-flowered species with loose spikes of fair-sized prettily tinted blossoms, the sepals are green with black tips, the petals are yellow and the lip is orange. It is found in a variety of situations in Central Chile, and may be tried outdoors in the milder parts of the kingdom in a damp half-shady spot in leaf-soil and loam.

AVICEPS, Lindley

The sole representative of this genus is one of the few Orchids adapted to inhabit an arid situation where the range of temperature is extreme over short periods. The root system consists of two or more small rounded tubers, the larger one of the two shrivels as soon as the seed capsules are perfected, the smaller one eventually becomes mature, produces a flower-stem and dies; fresh tubers are produced each vegetative season. The plant cannot be said to be of any decorative value but is well worth growing on account of its curious flowers and habit. It is confined to western Cape Colony and is found in desert country in rocky soil that is supplied with a certain amount of moisture during its growing season. It may be tried outdoors in the warm western counties fully exposed to as much sunshine and heat as possible and protected overhead by a pane of glass when at rest. Propagation by imported tubers and by seeds when procurable.

31. AVICEPS PUMILA, Lindl.

Satyrium pumilum, Thunb. *Diplecthrum pumilum*, Pers.

Root: of elliptic-ovoid tubers. **Stem:** stout. **Leaves:** basal, tufted, ovate, fleshy, $\frac{3}{4}''$–$1\frac{3}{4}''$ long, degenerating upwards into bracts. **Scape:** $1\frac{1}{4}''$–$4''$ tall. **Spike:** congested, very short, few-flowered. **Flowers:** about $\frac{3}{4}''$ long; sepals and petals united into a fleshy segment about $\frac{1}{2}''$ long by $\frac{1}{4}''$ broad; lip galeate, elliptic-ovate; spur very broadly saccate, short. *October*.

A very curious species with congested heads of Stapelia-like blossoms scarcely rising above the tuft of oval spreading grey-green leaves. The segment formed by the united sepals and petals is sepia-brown in colour, covered with numerous tiny white warts; lip yellow with numerous transverse streaks and spots. The blossoms emit a putrid odour. It is found in moist rocky and sandy soils in western Cape Colony and Little Namaqualand, where it reaches its greatest elevation near Lily Fontein at 5000 feet and is exposed to 15° or 20° of frost in the winter. A moist sandy loam in full sun is indicated.

BARTHOLINA, R. Brown

Very beautiful dwarf deciduous terrestrial plants numbering 3 species. Their root systems are very fragile and delicate, consisting of 2, or if the plant is in robust health more, tiny pea-like tubers on the ends of short fleshy fibres. The slender wiry flower-stems are clothed with long hairs and terminate in a solitary delicately-tinted blossom with erect narrow sepals and petals and a very large fan-shaped lip cut into numerous narrow segments. All the species are closely allied and are found in damp or fairly dry places amongst short herbage, and at times in the shade of dwarf shrubs, in south-eastern and south-western Cape Colony. Only one species is found at sufficient altitude in its native country to give reasonable hope that it may prove hardy in the warmer parts of Britain. Propagation by tubers removed from robust plants where more than two are produced, and seeds which are freely produced by the plants in their native habitat.

32. BARTHOLINA PECTINATA, R. Br.

B. Burmanniana, Ker. *Arethusa ciliaris*, Linn. *Orchis Burmanniana*, Linn. *O. pectinata*, Thunb.

Root: of 2 small ovoid tubers. **Leaf:** radical, solitary, horizontal, sessile, broadly cordate or orbicular, with a cordate base, ½″–1″ long. **Scape:** 2″–9″ tall, erect, densely hairy, bearing a solitary blossom. **Flower:** over 1¼″ across; dorsal sepal cucullate, lanceolate, rather pointed, downy; lateral sepals linear-oblong, downy, erect; petals lanceolate-linear, pointed, ⅓ as long as the sepals; lip spreading, fan-shaped, divided below the middle into many narrow segments; spur curved, narrowly conical, ⅜″ long.

October to December.

An extremely quaint and at the same time very beautiful plant with a very large blossom out of all proportion to the size of the tiny bright green leaf; the sepals are light green and the petals and lip are lilac or light purple. It is found in fairly damp places amongst stone and dwarf herbage, in south-western Cape Colony, where at Du Toits Kloof in the Worcester Division it attains an altitude of 4000 feet and is exposed to 12° of frost for short periods. It should be grown in peat and fibrous loam in a damp sunny spot in the rock garden.

BIPINNULA, Commers

A small genus numbering some 8 species of very beautiful terrestrial plants from South America, where they range from Uruguay to Argentina and Central Chile. Four species are found at sufficient elevation in their native countries to give reasonable hope that they may prove hardy in the western and southern counties of Great Britain. They are usually somewhat stout, leafy plants, the leaves in some cases withering before the flowers are perfected; the large blossoms with their remarkable plumose lateral sepals are produced in few- or many-flowered spikes, and vary from white and green to pink and yellow, they are frequently decorated with dark brown or black markings. The various species grow in localities subjected to great variation with regard to rainfall; in some cases they do not receive more than 6″ during the whole of their vegetative season. Propagation by imported roots.

33. BIPINNULA MONTANA, Arech.

Root: of clavate fusiform fleshy fibres, 1″–1½″ long. **Stem:** 6″ tall, clothed with imbricating sheaths. **Leaves:** in a basal rosette, lanceolate, pointed, about 3″ long, soon withering. **Spike:** loose, of 3–6 blossoms. **Flowers:** about 1″ across; dorsal sepal ovate-lanceolate, concave, pointed; lateral sepals linear-lanceolate, deflexed, tapering to a blunt point with a long feathery plume at the tip; petals ovate, blunt, incurved; lip ovate-oblong, broadly bilobed at the tip and recurved, margins crenate and strongly toothed; disc with 6 densely hairy ridges down its centre. *November.*

A charming little plant with a basal rosette of lance-shaped leaves and a few-flowered spike of large white blossoms lined and blotched with dark brown or black. It is found at sufficient elevations on the mountains of Uruguay to give reasonable hope that it may succeed outdoors in the milder parts of Great Britain in the rock garden in a compost of loam and leaf-soil.

34. BIPINNULA PHILIPPORUM, Kränzl.

Root and foliage unknown, probably resembling those of *B. plumosa.* **Spike :** of about 10 blossoms subtended by white, oblong-lanceolate bracts. **Flowers :** about $3\frac{1}{2}''$ across and $1\frac{1}{2}''$ long; dorsal sepal oblong-lanceolate, pointed; lateral sepals similar but narrower, ending in a long feathery plume; petals similar to the dorsal sepal; lip 3-lobed; outer lobes rounded; centre lobe large, rounded, strongly toothed on the margins; outer lobes with 3 rows of pointed calli on their surface; centre lobe with a few scattered calli on the disc. *September and October.*

This species has very large blossoms of a rich rose colour and should prove a very welcome addition to our gardens. It is found in rocky places on the mountains of Central Chile in the province of Curico, and should prove quite hardy in the warmer parts of the kingdom in a fairly open spot of the rock garden in sandy loam and leaf-soil.

35. BIPINNULA PLUMOSA, Lindl.

Root: of thickened fibres. **Stem:** about 2′ tall, stout, leafy. **Leaves:** lanceolate, pointed, about 6″ long, degenerating upwards into spatha-like bracts. **Spike:** of 6–8 blossoms, mingled with lanceolate bracts. **Flowers:** nearly 4″ across the plumose sepals, and $1\frac{3}{4}''$ long; dorsal sepal lanceolate, concave, pointed; lateral sepals lanceolate, ending in a long feathery plume; petals lanceolate, forming a galea with the dorsal sepal; lip shortly unguiculate, ovate-cordate, tapering to a point, margins cut into blunt teeth, long towards the point; disc with 7 rows of curved calli.

October and November.

A robust handsome species having very large blossoms with rich but pale green sepals and petals and a white lip with green calli. It is found in thinly-wooded localities on the mountains of Central Chile in the provinces of Curico and Santiago at 4000–5000 feet above sea-level. It may be tried outdoors in the warmer parts of the kingdom under the same conditions as the preceding species.

36. BIPINNULA VOLKMANNII, Kränzl.

Root: a cluster of thick fusiform fibres. **Stem:** 12″–15″ tall, leafy below. **Leaves:** oblong or oblanceolate, about 4″ long. **Scape:** clothed with a few distant sheaths. **Spike:** of 2–3 widely separated blossoms. **Flowers:** about $1\frac{3}{4}''$ across and 1″ long; dorsal sepal lanceolate, pointed; lateral sepals lanceolate, tapering to a blunt point, thinly plumose on the margins near the tip; petals oblong lanceolate, forming a galea with the dorsal sepal; lip shortly unguiculate, obscurely 3-lobed or oblong and dilated at the tip, hairy; disc furnished with a crescent-shaped patch of rounded calli. *November.*

A pretty species with 2 or 3 large yellow blossoms on a dwarf leafy stem. It is found in the dry pinewoods of the province of Nahuelbuta in Central Chile at sufficient elevation on the mountains to warrant a trial in the outdoor garden in the warmest parts of the kingdom. It should be grown in a dry sunny spot in pine leaf-soil and fibrous loam.

BLETILLA, Lindley

Bletia, Ruiz et Pav. **Gyas,** Salisb. **Thiebautia,** Colla.

About 25 species of handsome, epiphytal and terrestrial plants of erect, slender habit. Their root systems consist of globular pseudo-bulbs on short rhizomes, or in the terrestrial species, of globular or ovoid depressed tubers. The leaves are usually grass-like and plicate; the blossoms are borne in loose racemes and are frequently large and decorative, in colour they vary from white to rose, purple and crimson. The plants are found in tropical America, China and Japan; only one is sufficiently hardy for outdoor culture in this country. Propagation by separation of the tubers or pseudo-bulbs and by seeds, which are freely produced in their native countries.

37. BLETILLA STRIATA, Reichb. f.

Bletia hyacinthina, R. Br. *Limodorum striatum*, Thunb.

Root: a depressed tuber. **Stem:** about 12″ tall, slender, erect. **Leaves:** basal and cauline, linear-lanceolate to lanceolate, about 9″ long. **Raceme:** 4″–6″ long, of about 6 blossoms. **Flowers:** about $1\frac{1}{2}''$ across, drooping; dorsal sepal and lateral sepals ovate-lanceolate or lanceolate, pointed, spreading; petals similar but smaller and narrower; lip unguiculate, 3-lobed; outer lobes oblong, blunt, erect, concave; centre lobe bilobed; lobes rounded, slightly reflexed. *April to September.*

A beautiful terrestrial Orchid with erect flower-stems clothed with grassy leaves and racemes of large rosy purple blossoms. The plant is usually found in dry soil on the margins of thickets in China and Japan; it reaches its greatest elevation of 10,000 feet on the mountains of Western Yunnan. It is quite hardy in Great Britain in a sheltered half-shady spot in the rock garden in well drained loam and leaf-soil.

BRACHYCORYTHIS, Lindley

Handsome leafy spire-like deciduous plants numbering 26 species, with root stocks emitting numerous fusiform or ovoid tubers buried about three inches below the surface of the soil; the stems are robust and are clothed with many, rather small, leaves gradually degenerating into bracts upwards. The blossoms are produced in a long dense spike and are in many species very handsome and brightly coloured. All the hardy species are well worth growing in the choice border or rock garden. They are confined to Africa and Madagascar, where they are found in damp, usually open situations. In cultivation, as they are strong growing plants, they should have a good rich compost of somewhat heavy fibrous loam and leaf-soil with some sharp sand; the roots should be protected from prolonged frost. Propagation by offsets from strong plants, and also by seeds.

38. BRACHYCORYTHIS OVATA, Lindl.

Platanthera ovata, Schltr.

Root: of thick fusiform tubers. **Stem:** densely leafy, $\frac{3}{4}'$–$1\frac{1}{2}'$ tall. **Leaves:** cauline, very numerous, ovate or lanceolate-ovate, pointed, sessile, $1\frac{1}{2}''$–$2''$ long, decreasing upwards into bracts. **Raceme:** leafy, dense, $4''$–$9''$ long. **Flowers:** about $\frac{1}{2}''$ across; dorsal sepal broadly elliptic-oblong, somewhat cucullate, blunt; lateral sepals obliquely falcate-ovate, ascending; petals obliquely ovate, longer than the dorsal sepal; lip suberect from a curved base, ovate-oblong, shortly 3-dentate at the apex; disc with a narrow keel. *October to January.*

A pretty plant of robust spire-like habit with very numerous blossoms of fair size with purple or lilac sepals, petals and lip; the latter has a yellow keel and a few yellow spots scattered on its surface. It grows in grassy places on elevated plains and mountain slopes in eastern Cape Colony, Griqualand East, Natal and the Transvaal, where on the Mauch Berg near Lydenburg at 5800 feet it probably reaches its greatest altitude and is exposed to over 15° of frost during the winter. It should be grown in full sun in a rich, fairly moist, fibrous loam.

39. BRACHYCORYTHIS PLEISTOPHYLLA, Reichb. f.

Root: of very thick fleshy fibres. **Stem:** densely leafy, $1\frac{1}{4}'$–$2\frac{1}{4}'$ tall. **Leaves:** oblong-lanceolate or ovate-lanceolate, very pointed, degenerating into bracts above and sheaths below, $1''$–$2''$ long. **Raceme:** about $3\frac{1}{2}''$ long, many-flowered. **Flowers:** nearly $\frac{1}{2}''$ across; dorsal sepal ovate, rather pointed; lateral sepals semiovate, pointed; petals broadly ovate, blunt; lip elliptic-ovate, bilobed, lobes oblong, blunt; disc with a pair of erect linear calli near its base. *November to January.*

The blossoms of this species are of fair size and are tinted with white, pink and lilac; they are borne in a rather short dense raceme on the leafy stem. It is perhaps not quite so desirable a plant as the following species. In its native country it grows in open, wet situations such as marshes, stream sides, etc., and is found in Portuguese East Africa and British Central Africa, where on Mount Mlanje at 7000 feet it is subjected, during its resting period, to over 12° of frost. Culture as for other damp-loving species.

40. BRACHYCORYTHIS PUBESCENS, Harv.

Platanthera Brachycorythis, Schltr. *Peristylus hispidulus* var. *minor*, Rendle

Root: of elongated finger-like tubers. **Stem:** densely leafy, very downy, 1′–2′ tall. **Leaves:** cauline, ovate-lanceolate, sessile, $\frac{3}{4}''$–$1\frac{1}{2}''$ long, decreasing into short sheaths below and into bracts above. **Raceme:** 3″–8″ long, dense. **Flowers:** about $\frac{1}{2}''$ across; dorsal sepal concave, elliptic oblong, blunt; lateral sepals obliquely semiovate, falcately ascending, blunt; petals semi-ovate-oblong, blunt and oblique; lip 3-lobed; side lobes rounded; centre lobe broadly triangular; the whole lip suberect and subsaccate at the base; disc carinate. *November and December.*

This is quite an ornamental plant and has long spires of pretty white or flesh-coloured blossoms with a purple, yellow-spotted lip. The whole plant is thickly clothed with fine down. It grows in damp grassy places in woods and in marshes from British East Africa to Natal and the Transvaal, where near Lydenburg at 5000 feet it is exposed to over 12° of frost during its winter rest. It should be given a rich soil beside a pond or stream, in full sun.

BROWNLEEA, Harvey

This genus comprises 13 species of beautiful deciduous terrestrial plants allied to and very much like the Disas. The root consists of an ovoid tuber attached to the base of the underground portion of the stem; when the plant is in a robust healthy state two or more tubers are produced. The erect stems are usually not very leafy, the leaves being generally narrow; the blossoms, which are large and decorative in many of the species, are borne in long many-flowered spikes and are delicately tinted. All are natives of Africa, the majority being found in the southern portion of the continent. They are found in a variety of situations, usually in moist soil, several being almost alpine plants. The imported tubers should be planted at a depth of at least four inches and should be protected from severe and prolonged frost by a mulching of dry leaves, they may be increased by seeds when these can be procured.

PLATE 3.

ACIANTHUS CAUDATUS.

PLATE 4.

BROWNLEEA CŒRULEA.

41. BROWNLEEA ALPINA, N. E. Br.

Disa alpina, Hook. f. *D. Preussii*, Kränzl.

Root: of a small sessile tuber. **Stem:** fairly stout. **Leaves:** cauline, broadly linear or linear-lanceolate, tapering to a point and decreasing upwards into bracts, 3″–9″ long. **Scape:** $\frac{3}{4}$′–2′ tall. **Spike:** 1$\frac{1}{4}$″–3″ long. **Flowers:** erect, dense, about $\frac{1}{4}$″ across; dorsal sepal galeate; lateral sepals subfalcate-oblong, margins incurved; petals narrow, forming a galea with the dorsal sepal; lip linear, blunt, minute. *March to May.*

A tiny-flowered species, pretty but of little or no garden value; its blossoms are white and pink and are borne in narrow crowded spikes on long stems clothed with a few grassy leaves. It grows in damp rocky places on the Cameroon Mountains in the Cameroons, West Africa, at 8000 feet, where it is exposed to over 12° of frost for short periods during the winter or resting time. In cultivation it may be grown in moist fibrous loam and peat in an open part of the rock garden.

42. BROWNLEEA CŒRULEA, Harv.

Disa cœrulea, Reichb. f.

Root: a sessile tuber. **Stem:** rather slender. **Leaves:** cauline, ovate or elliptic-ovate, 2″–6″ long, decreasing upwards into bracts. **Scape:** $\frac{1}{2}$′–1$\frac{1}{2}$′ tall. **Spike:** 1″–3″ long, lax, many-flowered. **Flowers:** about $\frac{3}{4}$″ across; dorsal sepal galeate, ovate-lanceolate, somewhat recurved; spur cylindrical, slightly curved, about 1″ long; lateral sepals elliptic-lanceolate; petals oblong-lanceolate, oblique; lip very short, linear. *March.*

A very beautiful species, with large lilac-blue blossoms spotted with purple, borne on slender sheathed stems clothed with three or four spreading rich green leaves. It grows in rather shady spots in the hilly districts of eastern Cape Colony, Tembuland, Natal and the Transvaal, where it probably reaches its greatest altitude near Barberton at 5000 feet and is there subjected to 15° to 20° of frost during its resting period in the winter. It should be grown in a sheltered spot in damp peat, leaf-soil and loam.

43. BROWNLEEA GALPINII, Bolus

Root: a sessile tuber. **Stem:** slender. **Leaves:** cauline, linear-lanceolate or lanceolate, 2″–4″ long, sessile. **Scape:** 1$\frac{1}{2}$′ –2$\frac{1}{4}$′tall. **Spike:** subcapitate, dense. **Flowers:** over $\frac{3}{8}$″ across; dorsal sepal galeate, lanceolate, somewhat recurved near the apex; spur cylindrical, slightly curved, $\frac{3}{16}$″ long; lateral sepals oblong-lanceolate; petals oblong, oblique, very undulate on the outer margin; lip linear, minute. *March.*

The blossoms of this species are too small in comparison to the other parts of the plant to have any decorative value; they are white with a few purple spots on the petals. It inhabits moist mountain slopes in short herbage in Griqualand East, Natal, Transvaal and the Orange Free State, where it reaches its greatest elevation on Mont aux Sources at 8000 feet and should be perfectly hardy in Britain if it can be induced to rest during our winter. A moist peat and loam is indicated. The variety *major* (Bolus) has larger blossoms.

44. BROWNLEEA MONOPHYLLA, Schltr.

Root: a sessile tuber. **Stem:** slender. **Leaves:** cauline, narrowly-lanceolate or linear, about 2″ long. **Scape:** 6″–7″ tall, bearing one or two flowers. **Flowers:** about ¾″ across; dorsal sepal linear-lanceolate, galeate, recurved; spur cylindrical, nearly straight, 1½″ long; lateral sepals oblong-lanceolate; petals obliquely lanceolate-oblong, upper margins undulate; lip linear, minute, erect. *May.*

The beautiful snow-white blossoms of this species, with their long slender spur and delicate flower-stem clothed with one or two narrow leaves, should prove very attractive in a pot or pan in the alpine house. It grows on the grass-covered ledges of rocks near the summit of Mopedis Peak on Mont aux Sources in the Orange Free State at an elevation of 8000 feet, and should be perfectly hardy in Great Britain could it be induced to rest during our winter. It should be grown in moist fibrous loam on a ledge in the rock garden.

45. BROWNLEEA NELSONII, Rolfe

Root: a sessile tuber. **Stem:** rather slender. **Leaves:** cauline, lanceolate or lanceolate-oblong, sessile, 2″–3½″ long. **Scape:** about 8″ tall. **Spike:** oblong, rather lax, of about nine blossoms. **Flowers:** about ⅝″ across; dorsal sepal galeate, ovate-lanceolate; spur cylindrical, somewhat curved, about $\frac{3}{16}$″ long; lateral sepals elliptic-ovate; petals ovate-lanceolate, oblique; lip minute, 3-lobed, erect; centre lobe narrow. *March.*

This is a pretty species with medium-sized rosy purple blossoms on a dwarf stem clothed with two or three suberect deep green leaves. It should make a delightful rock garden or alpine house plant. It grows on the grassy slopes of hills near Barberton in the Transvaal at 5000 feet and is there exposed to over 15° of frost for short periods during the winter months. It should be grown in a well-drained spot in the rock garden in a sandy fibrous loam kept moist when the plant is in growth.

46. BROWNLEEA PARVIFLORA, Harv.

Disa parviflora, Reichb. f.

Root: a sessile tuber. **Stem:** rather slender. **Leaves:** cauline, lanceolate or oblong-lanceolate, sessile, 3″–5″ long. **Scape:** 1′–1½′ tall, clothed with two

41. BROWNLEEA ALPINA, N. E. Br.

Disa alpina, Hook. f. *D. Preussii*, Kränzl.

Root: of a small sessile tuber. **Stem:** fairly stout. **Leaves:** cauline, broadly linear or linear-lanceolate, tapering to a point and decreasing upwards into bracts, 3″–9″ long. **Scape:** $\frac{3}{4}$′–2′ tall. **Spike:** 1$\frac{1}{4}$″–3″ long. **Flowers:** erect, dense, about $\frac{1}{4}$″ across; dorsal sepal galeate; lateral sepals subfalcate-oblong, margins incurved; petals narrow, forming a galea with the dorsal sepal; lip linear, blunt, minute. *March to May.*

A tiny-flowered species, pretty but of little or no garden value; its blossoms are white and pink and are borne in narrow crowded spikes on long stems clothed with a few grassy leaves. It grows in damp rocky places on the Cameroon Mountains in the Cameroons, West Africa, at 8000 feet, where it is exposed to over 12° of frost for short periods during the winter or resting time. In cultivation it may be grown in moist fibrous loam and peat in an open part of the rock garden.

42. BROWNLEEA CŒRULEA, Harv.

Disa cœrulea, Reichb. f.

Root: a sessile tuber. **Stem:** rather slender. **Leaves:** cauline, ovate or elliptic-ovate, 2″–6″ long, decreasing upwards into bracts. **Scape:** $\frac{1}{2}$′–1$\frac{1}{2}$′ tall. **Spike:** 1″–3″ long, lax, many-flowered. **Flowers:** about $\frac{3}{4}$″ across; dorsal sepal galeate, ovate-lanceolate, somewhat recurved; spur cylindrical, slightly curved, about 1″ long; lateral sepals elliptic-lanceolate; petals oblong-lanceolate, oblique; lip very short, linear. *March.*

A very beautiful species, with large lilac-blue blossoms spotted with purple, borne on slender sheathed stems clothed with three or four spreading rich green leaves. It grows in rather shady spots in the hilly districts of eastern Cape Colony, Tembuland, Natal and the Transvaal, where it probably reaches its greatest altitude near Barberton at 5000 feet and is there subjected to 15° to 20° of frost during its resting period in the winter. It should be grown in a sheltered spot in damp peat, leaf-soil and loam.

43. BROWNLEEA GALPINII, Bolus

Root: a sessile tuber. **Stem:** slender. **Leaves:** cauline, linear-lanceolate or lanceolate, 2″–4″ long, sessile. **Scape:** 1$\frac{1}{2}$′ –2$\frac{1}{4}$′tall. **Spike:** subcapitate, dense. **Flowers:** over $\frac{3}{8}$″ across; dorsal sepal galeate, lanceolate, somewhat recurved near the apex; spur cylindrical, slightly curved, $\frac{3}{16}$″ long; lateral sepals oblong-lanceolate; petals oblong, oblique, very undulate on the outer margin; lip linear, minute. *March.*

The blossoms of this species are too small in comparison to the other parts of the plant to have any decorative value; they are white with a few purple spots on the petals. It inhabits moist mountain slopes in short herbage in Griqualand East, Natal, Transvaal and the Orange Free State, where it reaches its greatest elevation on Mont aux Sources at 8000 feet and should be perfectly hardy in Britain if it can be induced to rest during our winter. A moist peat and loam is indicated. The variety *major* (Bolus) has larger blossoms.

44. BROWNLEEA MONOPHYLLA, Schltr.

Root: a sessile tuber. **Stem:** slender. **Leaves:** cauline, narrowly-lanceolate or linear, about 2″ long. **Scape:** 6″–7″ tall, bearing one or two flowers. **Flowers:** about $\frac{3}{4}$″ across; dorsal sepal linear-lanceolate, galeate, recurved; spur cylindrical, nearly straight, $1\frac{1}{2}$″ long; lateral sepals oblong-lanceolate; petals obliquely lanceolate-oblong, upper margins undulate; lip linear, minute, erect. *May.*

The beautiful snow-white blossoms of this species, with their long slender spur and delicate flower-stem clothed with one or two narrow leaves, should prove very attractive in a pot or pan in the alpine house. It grows on the grass-covered ledges of rocks near the summit of Mopedis Peak on Mont aux Sources in the Orange Free State at an elevation of 8000 feet, and should be perfectly hardy in Great Britain could it be induced to rest during our winter. It should be grown in moist fibrous loam on a ledge in the rock garden.

45. BROWNLEEA NELSONII, Rolfe

Root: a sessile tuber. **Stem:** rather slender. **Leaves:** cauline, lanceolate or lanceolate-oblong, sessile, 2″–$3\frac{1}{2}$″ long. **Scape:** about 8″ tall. **Spike:** oblong, rather lax, of about nine blossoms. **Flowers:** about $\frac{5}{8}$″ across; dorsal sepal galeate, ovate-lanceolate; spur cylindrical, somewhat curved, about $\frac{3}{16}$″ long; lateral sepals elliptic-ovate; petals ovate-lanceolate, oblique; lip minute, 3-lobed, erect; centre lobe narrow. *March.*

This is a pretty species with medium-sized rosy purple blossoms on a dwarf stem clothed with two or three suberect deep green leaves. It should make a delightful rock garden or alpine house plant. It grows on the grassy slopes of hills near Barberton in the Transvaal at 5000 feet and is there exposed to over 15° of frost for short periods during the winter months. It should be grown in a well-drained spot in the rock garden in a sandy fibrous loam kept moist when the plant is in growth.

46. BROWNLEEA PARVIFLORA, Harv.

Disa parviflora, Reichb. f.

Root: a sessile tuber. **Stem:** rather slender. **Leaves:** cauline, lanceolate or oblong-lanceolate, sessile, 3″–5″ long. **Scape:** 1′–$1\frac{1}{2}$′ tall, clothed with two or three narrow sheaths. **Spike:** cylindrical, dense, 2″–4″ long. **Flowers:** $\frac{3}{16}$″ across; dorsal sepal galeate, ovate, rather incurved; spur stout, curved, minute; lateral sepals ovate-elliptic, united to the middle; petals obliquely ovate, joined to the dorsal sepal; lip linear, minute. *March.*

The tiny blossoms of this species have no horticultural value, they are white with a green spur and green nerves to the petals. It is found on moist mountain slopes amongst dwarf herbage in eastern Cape Colony and Transvaal where it reaches its greatest elevation on Woodbush Mountain at 6800 feet and where it is exposed to over 20° for considerable periods during the winter. It should be grown in a moist spot in fibrous loam, in full sun.

47. BROWNLEEA RECURVATA, Sond.

Disa recurvata, Reichb. f.

Root: a sessile tuber. **Stem:** rather slender. **Leaves:** cauline lanceolate or linear-lanceolate, sessile. **Scape:** 1′–$1\frac{1}{4}$′ tall. **Spike:** 2″–$3\frac{1}{2}$″ long, rather lax, usually many-flowered. **Flowers:** about $\frac{3}{4}$″ across; dorsal sepal galeate, ovate-lanceolate; spur cylindrical somewhat curved, blunt, $\frac{3}{8}$″ long; lateral sepals ovate-lanceolate; petals falcate-oblong, oblique, somewhat undulate on the outer margin; lip linear, minute, erect. *February to April.*

A handsome decorative plant with rather large pale pink blossoms that are sometimes streaked with purple, the conspicuous anther being reddish-brown. It is found in open grassy places on elevated plains and on the mountains in eastern Cape Colony, Tembuland and Basutoland, where, near Satsannas Peak in the Drakensberg Mountains, it attains its greatest elevation of 8750 feet and, could it be induced to rest during our winter, should be perfectly hardy in Great Britain. A good fibrous loam in full sun is indicated.

BULBOPHYLLUM, Thouin

Extremely bizarre evergreen epiphytal Orchids numbering some 1500 species whose root systems consist of a long or short creeping rhizome usually covered with thin chaffy scales. The somewhat leathery, oblong or lanceolate leaves usually spring from the top of the pseudo-bulbs, which are scattered over the rhizome and are well furnished with slender roots springing from their bases. The flower-stems are lateral and generally spring from the base of the pseudo-bulbs, and the weird blossoms have their segments elongated, twisted, fringed and cut into a variety of patterns; an attractive feature of many species is the mobile lip, which trembles at the slighest puff of air. The species are native in tropical and sub-tropical regions washed by the waters of the Pacific and Indian Oceans, the following species, however, are found at sufficient elevation in the southern and northern limits of their range to give hope that they may prove hardy in the warmest parts of the kingdom. They may be propagated by division, or rather separation, of the pseudo-bulbs, and also by seed.

48. BULBOPHYLLUM ELISÆ, F. Muell.

Cirrhopetalum Elisæ, F. Muell.

Root: a creeping rhizome, rather short. **Pseudo-bulbs:** $\frac{1}{2}''$ long, ovoid, deeply wrinkled and grooved. **Leaf:** solitary, narrowly oblong, contracted at the base, midrib prominent beneath, 1″–2″ long. **Raceme:** 6″–8″ long, dense, secund. **Flowers:** about $\frac{3}{4}''$ long; dorsal sepal lanceolate, short; lateral sepals linear-lanceolate, joined to the base of the column, forming a short pouch twice as long as the dorsal sepal; petals ovate-lanceolate, short; lip oblong, fleshy, erect or spreading, stalked. *October to January.*

A delicate and charming little species with numerous curious but beautiful blossoms with very attenuated segments. The sepals and petals are pink and white and the lip is bright purple; the foliage is rich green. It grows on the moss-covered trunks of trees and rock on the wooded slopes of the Blue Mountains of New South Wales, where it is exposed to 12° of frost for short periods during the winter. It may be tried on a damp moss-covered rock in a shady part of the rock garden in a small quantity of peat and sphagnum-moss.

49. BULBOPHYLLUM EUBLEPHARUM, Reichb. f.

Root: a creeping rhizome. **Pseudo-bulbs:** cylindrical, $1\frac{1}{2}''$–3″ long. **Leaf:** solitary, linear-oblong, 3″–8″ long, shortly stalked. **Scape:** $\frac{3}{4}'$–$1\frac{1}{2}'$ tall, clothed with about 4 sheaths. **Raceme:** 4″–6″ long, lax. **Flowers:** about $\frac{3}{8}''$ long; dorsal sepal ovate-lanceolate, concave, pointed; lateral sepals ovate, longer than the dorsal sepal; petals oblong, blunt, erosely fimbriate; lip stipitate, oblong-lanceolate, cordate at its base.

July to September.

Although the blossoms of this species are rather small it is quite a decorative plant. The long slender stem bears a loose raceme of white flowers flushed and speckled with pink, the lip is purple. It grows on moss-covered rock and on the trunks of trees in the forests of the Sikkim Himalaya at an altitude of from 7000–10,000 feet and is exposed to 15°–20° of frost for considerable periods during the winter. It may be grown in a shady humid part of the rock garden on a moss-covered limestone rock in peat and sphagnum-moss.

50. BULBOPHYLLUM EXIGUUM, F. Muell.

Dendrobium exiguum, F. Muell.

Root: a creeping rhizome. **Pseudo-bulbs:** $\frac{1}{4}''$–$\frac{1}{2}''$ long, ovoid or nearly globular, angular, deeply grooved. **Leaf:** solitary, from the apex of the pseudo-bulbs, oblong-linear or lanceolate, contracted at the base, with recurved margins and a prominent midrib beneath, $\frac{1}{2}''$–$1\frac{1}{2}''$ long. **Racemes:** 1″–2″ long with 2–4 blossoms, filiform. **Flowers:** about $\frac{3}{16}''$ long; dorsal sepal lanceolate, pointed; lateral sepals lanceolate, dilated at the base into a short broad pouch; petals lanceolate, half as long as the sepals; lip linear, channelled.

October to January.

This small species produces from two to four white, pink-tinted blossoms on a very slender flower-stem; they are much too small to have any decorative value but the plant should prove interesting in the alpine house. It grows in damp shady places, carpeting large rocks with its creeping roots, in Queensland and New South Wales where on the Blue Mountains at its greatest altitude it is exposed to 12° of frost for short periods during the winter. It may be tried on a damp rock in moss and peat in a shady humid part of the rock or bog garden.

51. BULBOPHYLLUM PYGMÆUM, Lindl.

Dendrobium pygmæum, Smith

Root: fibrous. **Pseudo-bulbs:** about the size of a garden pea. **Leaf:** solitary, linear-oblong, $\frac{1}{4}''$ long, grooved down the middle, sessile, leathery. **Scape:** about 1″ tall, bract-clothed. **Flower:** solitary, under $\frac{1}{8}''$ across; dorsal sepal ovate, convex; lateral sepals broadly ovate, pointed; petals linear-oblong, blunt, shorter than the sepals; lip ovate, blunt, with a ridge down its centre. *November to February.*

A very minute plant forming rich green patches on moss-covered tree trunks in its native home; the inconspicuous white and green blossoms have no decorative value. It is a common plant in the woodlands of the North and South islands of New Zealand and should make an interesting little plant on a moss-covered block of wood in the alpine house, or it might be grown on a rough-barked moss-covered tree trunk in a shady spot in the moist climate of the western seaboard of Great Britain, where it would be sufficiently hardy to withstand the winter.

52. BULBOPHYLLUM SHEPHERDII, F. Muell.

B. Schillerianum, Reichb. f. *Dendrobium Shepherdii*, F. Muell.

Root: a creeping rhizome clothed with scarious sheathing scales. **Pseudo-bulbs:** $\frac{1}{4}''$ long, very narrow. **Leaf:** solitary, linear, channelled, convex beneath, not keeled, thick and fleshy, 1″–2″ long. **Scape:** about $\frac{3}{8}''$ long, bearing a solitary blossom, with 1–2 sheathing scales at the base. **Flower:** $\frac{3}{16}''$ long; dorsal sepal broadly lanceolate at the base, tapering to a point; lateral sepals broadly ovate at the base, pointed at the apex; petals ovate-triangular, very minute; lip lanceolate, channelled, recurved.

October to January.

A very quaint little plant with tiny yellow blossoms on very short flower-stems springing from the base of the pseudo-bulbs, all over spreading roots. It is of no decorative value, but like its brethren should prove interesting in a pan in the alpine house. It grows on the trunks of trees and moss-covered rocks in New South Wales reaching its greatest altitude in the Blue Mountains, where it is exposed to 10° or 12° of frost for short periods during the winter. Culture the same as for the other species.

BULLEYA, Schlechter

This genus contains but one species; it is a curious yet attractive plant of epiphytal habit, with a short creeping rhizome bearing numerous crowded pseudo-bulbs; these usually produce two leaves from their tip. The flowers are borne in flattened spikes on thin wiry stems springing from between the two leaves on the top of the pseudo-bulbs. The flowers have somewhat long stalks and the whole inflorescence bears some resemblance to a spike of giant Totter-grass at first sight. Its nearest allies seem to be members of the genus Pholidota (Suide). In its native country it is found in forest lands on trees and rocks and is only suitable for culture outdoors in very mild and sheltered localities where in these it should have ample protection during the winter. Propagation by imported plants.

53. BULLEYIA YUNNANENSIS, Schltr.

Root: a short rhizome. **Pseudo-bulbs:** ovoid, laterally compressed, rough, crowded, about 1½″ long, bearing 2 leaves. **Leaves:** on long stalks, blade lanceolate, pointed, about 8″ long, stalks about 2″ long. **Scape:** 9″–15″ tall, slender, naked, from between the leaves. **Spike:** flattened, 4″–6″ long. **Flowers:** about ¾″ long; dorsal sepals ovate-oblong, pointed; lateral sepals ovate-oblong, oblique, pointed; petals elliptic-oblong, rather pointed, oblique; lip oblong and concave at the base, dilated into obscurely reniform lobes towards the tip, with 3 thickened nerves down its centre.

July and August.

A quaint yet desirable plant with flattened spikes of greenish-yellow blossoms. It is found on the moss-covered trunks of trees and on humus-covered boulders in mixed forest on the eastern flank of the Tali Range Western Yunnan, Western China, at from 8000–9000 feet above sea-level. It may be tried outdoors in Great Britain in warm sheltered localities on a moss-covered limestone rock with some oak or beech leaf-soil packed over its rhizome.

BURNETTIA, Lindley

This genus consists of a solitary species; it is a very dwarf and quite erect deciduous terrestrial plant. The underground portion of the plant consists of two or more rounded tubers about a quarter of an inch in diameter, sessile or on short somewhat fleshy fibres which are sometimes branched. The tubers are usually biennial, producing a leaf one vegetative season and a flower-stem the next and then perishing. The flower-stems are leafless, their place being taken by large spatha-like bracts, and the flowers are usually solitary, though at times as many as three are produced, they are interesting, though of no decorative value. The plant may be tried in a sheltered part of the rock garden in the warmer parts of Britain and should have its tubers buried abour three inches below the surface of the soil and protected from prolonged frost. Propagation by imported tubers.

54. BURNETTIA CUNEATA, Lindl.

Lyperanthus Burnettii, F. Muell. *Caladenia cuneata*, Reichb. f.

Root: of one or two pea-like tubers on the underground portion of the flower-stem. **Leaf:** solitary, ovate-lanceolate, pointed, $\frac{3}{4}''$ long, produced on a separate stem and withering before the flowers are produced. **Scape:** 2″–4″ tall, clothed with several sheathing scales. **Spike:** of 1–3 erect but much incurved blossoms. **Flowers:** $\frac{1}{2}''$ long; sepals and petals are lanceolate, rather concave, of nearly equal length; lip very broadly lanceolate, blunt, sometimes fringed, with a few small calli scattered on the disc.

December.

A tiny plant of little decorative value but of sufficient interest to warrant cultivation in a pan in the alpine house. The blossoms remain half open throughout their existence and are reddish-brown outside and pure white within. It is found in damp sandy soil at fairly low elevation in Tasmania, where it is rather local. It should be hardy enough for outdoor culture in the warmer parts of Great Britain. A damp sandy soil in a sheltered spot in the rock garden is indicated.

CALADENIA, R. Brown

A genus numbering about 60 species of very beautiful and delicate deciduous terrestrial plants, some of which are known as "Spider Orchids" in their native country from the fanciful resemblance of their blossoms to a huge hairy spider poised on the top of a slender grass-like stem; others may be likened to brilliant butterflies with outstretched wings hovering on spikes of grass. Their root systems are weak and consist of two or more rounded tubers either sessile or on slender fleshy fibres, the tubers shrivel and perish after flowering, fresh ones are produced each growing season to replace those that die, if the plants are in a healthy state. The leaves are grass-like and the blossoms, which are few in number, are usually large and ornamental. They range over the whole of Australia, being most numerous in the south-western portion of the continent and are also found in Tasmania, New Zealand and the Auckland Islands. Propagation by imported tubers and seeds which are quite freely-produced in their native countries.

55. CALADENIA CÆRULEA, R. Br.

Root: of few fleshy fibres and terminal oblong tubers. **Leaf:** solitary, cauline, linear or oblong-lanceolate, 3″–5″ long, fringed with silky hairs. **Scape:** 4″–6″ tall, hairy, with 2 sheathing bracts. **Flower:** solitary, about 1″ across; dorsal sepal narrowly oblong-lanceolate; lateral sepals oblong-lanceolate, all gland-dotted; petals narrowly oblong-lanceolate, slightly shorter than the sepals; lip 3-lobed; outer lobes broad, erect, blunt; centre lobe lanceolate, sometimes fringed; calli clavate, in 2 rows.

October and November.

A very dainty little plant suitable for alpine house culture. The erect flower-stem is clothed with a solitary, bright green, grassy leaf, and bears at its apex a comparatively large azure-blue blossom with deeper blue bands on the outer lobes of the lip. It grows in meadow and grasslands in open spots in New South Wales, Victoria and Tasmania, and should be sufficiently hardy for outdoor culture in the warmer parts of Great Britain. An open sunny spot amongst dwarf plants in a cool sandy soil is indicated.

56. CALADENIA CARNEA, R. Br.

C. alata, R.Br. *C. angustata*, Hook. f. *Arethusa castenata*, Sm.

Root: of a few ovoid tubers on fleshy fibres. **Leaf:** narrowly linear, 4″–9″ long, suberect. **Scape:** 6″–12″ tall, hairy. **Flowers:** in a loose raceme of 1–3, about $\frac{3}{4}$″ across; dorsal sepal lanceolate, erect; lateral sepals lanceolate, spreading, longer than the dorsal sepal; petals narrowly lanceolate, spreading, longer than the lateral sepals; lip 3-lobed; outer lobes broad, blunt, prominent; centre lobe lanceolate, margins undulate and at times fringed with calli; disc with 2 rows of calli or, in var. *quadriseriata*, with 4 rows.

October and November.

A charming little species with slender hairy stems bearing a solitary bright green, hairy, grass-like leaf and a raceme of from one to three dainty pink and white (pure white in the var. *alba*) blossoms, the lip is white, lined with crimson and its tip is yellow. It is common in a variety of situations both in wooded and grass country and is usually found in poor soils over the whole of Eastern Australia from Queensland to Tasmania. It should be quite hardy in the warmer parts of Great Britain. Culture as for the foregoing species.

57. CALADENIA CLAVIGERA, A. Cunn.

Root: of small oblong tubers on fleshy fibres. **Leaf:** sub-basal, oblong-linear or lanceolate, 2″–4″ long. **Scape:** 6″–12″ tall, slender, with a small bract below the middle, hairy. **Flowers:** about $1\frac{3}{4}''$ across, 1–2 in number fairly widely separated; dorsal sepal curved forward over the column and like the lateral sepals is lanceolate at the base tapering to a clavate tip, petals similar but without the clavate tip; lip 3-lobed; outer lobes rather broad; centre lobe lanceolate, at times crenulate near the base; calli in 4 rows down its centre. *November.*

A very quaint and beautiful species with large, brightly coloured, "spidery" blossoms. The sepals and petals are yellow, striped with crimson down their centres, the lip has yellow side lobes and a purple centre one. It should prove a highly interesting addition to the alpine house, where its curious blossoms could be carefully examined. It is usually found in thin forest land on sandy soil in New South Wales, Victoria and Tasmania and should prove hardy in the warmer parts of Great Britain. A compost of leaf-soil and sand in a damp half-shady spot in the rock garden is indicated.

58. CALADENIA CONGESTA, R. Br.

Root: of small irregular tubers on fleshy fibres. **Leaf:** sub-basal, narrowly linear, at times hairy, 6″–8″ long. **Scape:** 9″–12″ tall, downy, slender. **Flowers:** in a loose raceme of 2–3, about 1″ across; dorsal sepal narrowly lanceolate, curved forwards, concave; lateral sepals and petals narrowly lanceolate, of equal length; lip 3-lobed; side lobes rather long, erect and incurved; centre lobe narrowly lanceolate, recurved, longer than the side lobes, densely covered with thick blunt calli. *November.*

This species is closely allied to *C. carnea.* The blossoms are of a beautiful rose-pink colour, the lip is white tinted pink and is closely covered with bright purple warts. It is a decorative species and is well worth growing. It is found in open forest land, usually beneath the shade of Eucalypti, in New South Wales and Tasmania, where it is exposed to 12° of frost for short periods during its winter rest. It may be grown in the rock garden in a damp half-shady spot in leaf-soil and sand.

59. CALADENIA DEFORMIS, R. Br.

C. barbata, Lindl. *C. unguiculata,* Lindl.

Root: of very small ovoid tubers on short stout fibres. **Leaf:** sub-basal, linear, 2″–4″ long. **Scape:** 4″–8″ tall, slender, slightly hairy, bearing a solitary blossom. **Flower:** $1\frac{1}{4}''$ across; sepals and petals oblong or lanceolate, narrowed towards the tip, all of about equal length; lip obscurely 3-lobed, oblong, recurved, more or less fringed at the margin ; calli on the disc crowded and at times completely covering the recurved portion. *September and October.*

A very beautiful plant bearing a solitary, deep cobalt-blue blossom, paler beneath, with very regular segments giving a rounded blossom. The solitary hairy grass-like leaf is of a rich yellowish-green colour. It grows in open country in pastures and meadows and is a common plant in New South Wales, Victoria, Western Australia, Southern Australia and Tasmania. In its native habitat it is at times exposed to 12° of frost during the winter. A good fibrous loam in a fairly damp sunny spot is indicated. There is a white-flowered form which is rare.

60. CALADENIA FILAMENTOSA, R. Br.

C. denticulata, Lindl. *C. filifera*, Lindl.

Root: of small oblong tubers on thick white fibres. **Leaf:** subradical, oblong-linear or lanceolate, 2″–5″ long. **Scape:** 1′–1¾′ tall, clothed with 3–4 scale-like sheaths, densely hairy. **Raceme:** of 1–2 blossoms, widely separated on the stem. **Flowers:** about 3″ across; sepals almost filiform, slightly dilated at the base, tapering to a club-shaped tip, spreading, and covered beneath with glandular hairs ; petals similar, somewhat shorter ; lip obscurely 3-lobed, fringed at the margins, much recurved and with 2 rows of calli on its disc. *December.*

A strikingly quaint "spidery" species with one or two very deeply tinted blossoms at wide intervals on the slender hairy stem. The whole blossom is of a very deep crimson colour (pink in the form *pallens*) with a pale pink lip striped obliquely with crimson. It is very closely allied to *C. Patersonii* (R.Br.), and grows in thin forest lands mostly in poor soil in New South Wales, Southern and Western Australia and Tasmania and is exposed to 10° or 12° of frost for short periods during the winter. A compost of leaf-soil and sand in a fairly damp half-shady spot is indicated.

61. CALADENIA LATIFOLIA, R. Br.

C. elongata, Lindl. *C. mollis*, Lindl.

Root: of few ovoid tubers on short thick fibres. **Leaf:** subradical, oblong-lanceolate, 1½″–4″ long, hairy. **Scape:** 6″–12″ tall, slender, hairy, bearing 2–3 rather widely separated blossoms. **Flowers:** 1½″ across; dorsal sepal oblong-lanceolate, rather pointed; lateral sepals oblong-lanceolate, blunt, longer than the dorsal sepal ; petals lanceolate, shorter than the dorsal sepal ; lip deeply 3-lobed ; side lobes oblong, blunt ; centre lobe ovate or broadly lanceolate ; disc with calli in 2 converging rows. *September and October.*

A beautiful little plant with bright pink or rarely white blossoms from one to three in number carried horizontally on fairly stout stalks ; the flower-stem is hairy and bears a solitary bright green grassy leaf. It grows in the open and also in thin forest land on poor sandy soils in New South Wales, Victoria, Southern Australia, Western Australia and Tasmania. It should be quite hardy in all but the coldest parts of Great Britain. It should be given a fairly open position in the rock garden in a compost of leaf-soil and sand; *angustifolia, marginata* and *ochreata* are varieties.

62. CALADENIA LYALLII, Hook. f.

Root: of oblong tubers on long fleshy fibres. **Leaf:** basal, broadly linear, covered with spreading hairs, 2″–4″ long. **Scape:** stout, 4″–8″ tall, clothed with spreading hairs, frequently curved and bearing one or two blossoms. **Flowers:** 1″ across; dorsal sepal obovate-oblong, arched over the column; lateral sepals ovate-oblong, spreading, longer than the dorsal sepal; petals narrowly oblong; lip 3-lobed, broad; outer lobes rounded; centre lobe subulate, recurved, with a wavy margin and 2 glandular appendages at its base and 1 at its tip. *October and November.*

A beautiful little plant with a comparatively large pale pink blossom, considering the size of its leaf. Although usually but one is produced, in robust specimens they at times number two. It is very closely related to the Tasmanian *C. carnea* and grows in moist grassy places or swamps in low or elevated spots throughout New Zealand and the Auckland Islands and should be quite hardy in England; it may be grown in good soil on the banks of a pond or stream.

63. CALADENIA MENZIESII, R. Br.

C. macrophylla, R.Br. *Leptoceras macrophylla*, Lindl. *L. Menziesii*, Lindl. *L. oblonga*, Lindl.

Root: of small irregular tubers. **Leaf:** subradical, solitary, ovate-lanceolate or oblong-lanceolate, 1″–2″ long. **Scape:** 6″–9″ tall, slender, smooth or slightly hairy, bearing 1–2 flowers on long stalks. **Flowers:** $\frac{3}{4}$″ across; dorsal sepal lanceolate, concave, incurved; lateral sepals, falcate-lanceolate, slightly spreading; petals narrowly linear, at times filiform, quite erect, much longer than the sepals; lip ovate to orbicular, erect at the base, recurved at the tip; calli arranged in 2 or 4 rows. *October and November.*

A most delightful little species, the long erect petals giving the blossom a very quaint appearance. The flowers are produced on long stalks from the main stem and have lilac sepals, pink and crimson petals and a white, purple-striped lip. The solitary leaf is very broad and of a bright green colour. This species grows in damp soil in somewhat shady places in Victoria, Western Australia, Southern Australia and Tasmania, where it is quite frequent. It is sufficiently hardy for outdoor culture in the warmer parts of Great Britain in a damp sandy soil in half shade.

64. CALADENIA MINOR, Hook. f.

Root: of small oblong tubers on slender fleshy fibres. **Leaf:** basal, very narrowly linear, 1″–2″ long, hairy. **Scape:** 2″–8″ tall, slender, hairy, bearing 1, or rarely 2, blossoms. **Flowers:** $\frac{1}{2}$″ across; sepals narrowly linear, blunt; petals linear; lip 3-lobed, rather broad; outer lobes broadly ovate; centre lobe subulate, glandular at the margin; disc with a double row of stipitate glands down its centre. *December and January.*

A pretty slender little species with fair-sized bright but pale pink blossoms with rich purple bands on the outer lobes of the lip. The whole plant is covered with delicate spreading hairs. It seems, like our Bee Orchids, to grow in drier spots than most of its brethren, for it inhabits dry clay hills in the Northern and Southern Islands of New Zealand, where it is found as far south as Otago. It should be perfectly hardy in all but the bleakest parts of Great Britain. In cultivation the condition under which it grows in its native habitat should be copied as far as possible.

65. CALADENIA PATERSONII, R. Br.

C. pulcherrima, F. Muell.

Root: of fair sized oblong tubers on short stout fibres. **Leaf:** subradical, oblong-linear or lanceolate, hairy, 2″–6″ long. **Scape:** $\frac{3}{4}$′–2′ tall, slender, rather hairy, bearing 1–3 blossoms on fairly long stalks. **Flowers:** nearly 5″ in diameter; dorsal sepal and lateral sepals very narrow, almost filiform, dilated at the tip, covered with glandular hairs; petals similar to the sepals but not dilated at the tip; lip broadly ovate or ovate-lanceolate, usually divided into 3 rather broad lobes, margins fringed; calli numerous, arranged in 4 rows. *October and November.*

This elegant species is one of the largest flowered of the "spider orchids." The extremely attenuated segments of its blossoms are very remarkable; in ground colour they vary from greenish-white to yellow outside, and yellow to pink within; the lip is yellow and the disc is frequently of a rich purple hue. In habitat it varies very much and is most frequent in open forest lands in New South Wales, Victoria, Southern and Western Australia and Tasmania and is sufficiently hardy for outdoor culture in all but the coldest parts of Great Britain. A good sandy leaf-soil in half shade is indicated. *dilatata, pallida, Behrii* and *tentaculata* are varieties. *See Plate 5 facing page 78.*

66. CALADENIA SUAVEOLENS, Reichb. f.

C. sulphurea, A. Cunn. *Lyperanthus suaveolens.* R.Br. *L. sulphurea*, A. Cunn.

Root: of small ovoid tubers on short fleshy fibres. **Leaf:** subradical, linear or linear-lanceolate, 6″–8″ long, smooth. **Scape:** 9″–15″ tall, clothed with 2–3 sheathing scales. **Flowers** $1\frac{1}{2}$″ across, 2–6 in number, widely separated on the stem; dorsal sepal lanceolate, concave, pointed, incurved; lateral sepals and petals linear, spreading or recurved, nearly as long as the dorsal sepal; lip rather obscurely 3-lobed; outer lobes rounded, not prominent; centre lobe ovate-oblong, blunt, recurved; disc covered with papillæ in several rows. *September and October.*

A pretty and desirable species with more flowers to its stem than most of the other members of the genus; they are almost stalkless and nestle within sheathing bracts; in colour they vary from pink to pale yellow and nearly white, with crimson tinting on the lip. It is found in rather shady places, usually on poor soil, in New South Wales, Victoria and Tasmania, and should prove hardy in all but the coldest parts of Great Britain. It should be given a compost of leaf-soil and sand, in a half-shady spot.

67. CALADENIA TESTACEA, R. Br.

C. angustata, Lindl. *C. gracilis*, R.Br.

Root: of small ovoid tubers on short stout fibres. **Leaf:** subradical, linear, slightly hairy, 2″–4″ long. **Scape:** 6″–9″ tall, slender, slightly hairy, bearing from 1–3 blossoms. **Flowers:** about $1\frac{1}{4}$″ across; dorsal sepal lanceolate, erect; lateral sepals lanceolate, spreading, longer than the dorsal one; petals narrowly lanceolate, contracted at the base; lip 3-lobed; side lobes rather undeveloped, fringed; centre lobe lanceolate, recurved, fringed, with numerous calli on the disc in 4 crowded rows. *October and November.*

A pretty dwarf species very closely allied to *C. carnea*, with a slender stem, a narrow bright green grass-like leaf, and two or three pink and white blossoms, like butterflies, on the slender stalks. In nature it seems to prefer open grass-lands or poor soils in New South Wales, Victoria and Tasmania. It should be sufficiently hardy for outdoor culture over the greater part of Great Britain and should be given a compost of sandy fibrous loam in an open sunny position.

CALANTHE, R. Brown

Handsome leafy terrestrial plants of robust habit, either evergreen or deciduous. The root-stock is a short, rarely creeping, rhizome emitting numerous fleshy roots and is often furnished with large pseudo-bulbs. The leaves are usually lanceolate or oblong and plaited; the flower-stem, which is axillary, terminal or lateral, is usually fairly tall and terminates in a raceme of numerous small or medium-sized ornamental blossoms. They number about 210 species scattered over the tropical and sub-tropical countries of the whole world, a few being found in sufficiently high latitudes and at great enough elevation in their native homes to justify inclusion in this work. *Calanthes* being robust terrestrial plants require liberal treatment and should be grown mainly in rich fibrous loam with a little peat and sand in a fairly damp half-shady spot in the rock garden. Propagation by division of the rhizome when growth is commencing, and by seeds.

68. CALANTHE ALPINA, Hook. f.

Root: a short rhizome. **Stem:** very short. **Leaves:** plaited, cauline, elliptic-lanceolate, pointed, sessile, 4″–7″ long. **Scape:** 6″–12″; tall, stout. **Raceme:** 2″–4″ long, few-flowered. **Flowers:** over 1″ across, secund; sepals ovate-oblong, pointed, 5-nerved; petals elliptic-lanceolate, 3-nerved; lip suborbicular, very short, toothed and fringed. *July and August.*

A species of considerable beauty producing few-flowered racemes of large blossoms with yellow-green sepals, greenish-white petals and a white, purple-striped lip. It grows in damp rocky places in moist vegetable soil in the Sikkim Himalaya, where it reaches an altitude of 10,000 feet, and should therefore be hardy in all but the bleakest parts of Great Britain, in a damp half-shady spot in fibrous loam, peat and leaf-soil.

69. CALANTHE ARCUATA, Rolfe

Root: of few thick fleshy fibres. **Leaves:** narrowly lanceolate, narrow towards the base, shortly pointed, 8″–12″ long. **Scape:** about $1\frac{1}{2}$′ tall, fairly slender. **Raceme:** about 8″ long, lax. **Flowers:** about $1\frac{1}{2}$″ across; sepals lanceolate, pointed; petals linear or linear-lanceolate, pointed; lip 3-lobed; outer lobes oblong, toothed at the tip; centre lobe trowel-shaped, crenulate and undulate; spur semi-club-shaped, pointed. *June and July.*

A desirable though not brightly tinted plant with loose few-flowered racemes of fairly large purple and yellow blossoms. The plant is found in shady places on mountains near Hasingshan in the province of Hupeh, Central China, at sufficient elevation above sea-level to warrant an attempt to cultivate it outdoors in the warmest parts of Great Britain. Culture as for the following species.

70. CALANTHE BILOBA, Lindl.

Root: a short rhizome. **Stem:** short. **Leaves:** basal, plaited, broadly elliptic or oblong-lanceolate, narrowing into a long stalk, 8″–11″ long. **Scape:**

$1\frac{1}{2}'$–$2\frac{1}{2}'$ tall, stout, erect. **Raceme:** 4″–6″ long, lax-flowered. **Flowers:** about 1″ across; dorsal sepal ovate; lateral sepals broadly ovate, falcate, 5–7 nerved; petals oblong, pointed, 3-nerved; lip winged below with a very broad deeply 2-lobed blade; lobes broadly hatched-shaped or orbicular; spur short. *June to August.*

A very desirable Orchid producing tall downy spikes or racemes of rather large blossoms with pale purple petals and sepals and a pale pink lip. It grows in damp, rather shady places in rich soils in the Sikkim Himalaya where it reaches an altitude of 8000 feet above sea-level and should therefore be nearly hardy outdoor in a sheltered spot of the rock garden in good loam and leaf-soil in Western and Southern Britain.

71. CALANTHE BREVICORNU, Lindl.

Root: a stout fleshy rhizome. **Stem:** 4″–6″ tall, stout, leafy. **Leaves:** basal and cauline, plaited, oblong-lanceolate, sessile or stalked, 8″–12″ long. **Scape:** $\frac{3}{4}'$–$1\frac{1}{4}'$ tall, nearly smooth. **Raceme:** 4″–6″ long, few-flowered. **Flowers:** about $\frac{3}{4}''$ across; dorsal sepal broadly lanceolate; lateral sepals ovate-oblong, pointed, 5-nerved; petals oblong-lanceolate; lip 3-lobed; outer lobes falcate-oblong; centre lobe transversely oblong, retruse, waved; spur conical, very short. *June and July.*

A handsome plant with a few-flowered raceme of fairly large blossoms with spreading purple sepals, red-purple petals striped with golden-yellow, and a white and red lip. It grows in damp half-shady spots in rich soils in the Himalaya from Nepal to Sikkim at various elevations up to 8000 feet, where it is exposed to over 15° of frost during the winter. In cultivation it may be grown in a damp spot such as the banks of a pond, in rich soil.

72. CALANTHE CHLOROLEUCA, Lindl.

C. galeata, Lindl.

Root: a stout rhizome. **Stem:** 4″–6″ tall, stout, swollen at its base, and sheathed. **Leaves:** basal, elliptic, pointed, on long stalks, 6″–10″ long. **Scape:** 6″–10″ tall, stout. **Raceme:** few-flowered. **Flowers:** about $1\frac{1}{2}''$ across; dorsal sepal ovate-lanceolate, pointed; lateral sepals lanceolate, pointed, 5-nerved; petals narrowly-lanceolate, pointed, 3-nerved; lip 3-lobed; outer lobes small, oblong or rounded; centre lobe broadly obcordate or suborbicular, 2-lobed; spur stout, 1″ long. *June and July.*

Although this plant is not so brightly coloured as many of the other species, its large blossoms with their pale green red-striped sepals and petals and the yellow lip with its white outer lobes render it a desirable garden plant. It grows in damp places in rich soils in the Sikkim Himalaya where it attains an altitude of over 8000 feet and should therefore be nearly hardy in Southern and Western Britain in a damp spot in good fibrous loam and leaf-soil.

73. CALANTHE COELOGYNIFORMIS, Kränzl.

Root: a stout rhizome. **Stem:** about 9″ tall, clothed with 3 leaves and 1 or 2 basal sheaths. **Leaves:** oblong or oblong-lanceolate, pointed or blunt, thin, about 6″ long. **Raceme:** lax, bearing 3–5 blossoms. **Flowers:** about $1\frac{1}{2}$″ across; dorsal sepal and lateral sepals lanceolate, pointed and shortly contracted at the tip; petals narrowly lanceolate, pointed; lip suborbicular or very slightly 3-lobed, broader than long, crenulate and minutely toothed; spur short, blunt, curved. *July and August.*

A beautiful species with large pale green and white flowers with crimson or reddish-purple markings on the lip. It is found in damp shady places, frequently in thin forest lands, on the mountains of Eastern Tibet at 8000 to 10,000 feet above sea-level and should be sufficiently hardy for culture outdoors over the greater part of the Kingdom in a damp half-shady spot in fibrous peat, loam, and good leaf-soil.

74. CALANTHE DAVIDII, Franch

Root: a short rhizome emitting numerous fibres. **Stem:** 8″–9″ tall, fairly stout. **Leaves:** numerous, linear-lanceolate, pointed, smooth. **Raceme:** of 20–35 blossoms. **Flowers:** about $\frac{5}{8}$″ across; sepals and petals of equal length; sepals oblong, rather pointed; petals similar but narrower; lip 3-lobed; side lobes obliquely ovate; centre lobe divided into 2 ovate diverging lobes; disc lamellate. *July.*

A dwarf small-flowered species with narrow leaves and dense racemes of numerous rather small white and red flowers. It is quite a pretty and desirable plant. In a state of nature it grows in leaf-soil beneath the shade of trees in thin mountain woods in Western China. It may be grown outdoors in the warmer parts of the Kingdom in a sheltered half-shady spot in good oak or beech leaf-soil and loam.

75. CALANTHE DELAVAYI, Finet.

Root: a short rhizome emitting numerous thick fleshy fibres. **Stem:** very short. **Leaves:** cauline, elliptic-lanceolate, pointed, sessile, plaited, 6″–9″ long. **Scape:** 9″–16″ tall, stout. **Raceme:** 3″–6″ long, of few distant flowers. **Flowers:** about $1\frac{3}{8}$″ across, more or less secund; dorsal sepal erect, lanceolate, pointed, smooth; lateral sepals similar, with 7 nerves, oblique; petals narrower and smaller, with 5 nerves; lip rhomboid, truncate at the tip and toothed on the margins; spur cylindrical, clavate at the tip, retuse. *June and July.*

A pretty and desirable species having large rose and white blossoms with some deep rose-purple markings on the lip. It is found in moist spots in open pine forests in Yunnan, Western China, at 10,000 to 11,000 feet above sea-level and should be hardy over the greater part of the Kingdom in a damp half-shady spot in the rock garden, in loam and leaf-soil.

76. CALANTHE DISCOLOR, Lindl.

C. lurida, Dcne. *Alismorchis discolor,* O. Ktze.

Root: of stout white fibres from a thick root stock. **Leaves:** 2–3 in number, ovate or ovate-lanceolate, plaited, smooth, tapering into a sheathing stalk, $\frac{3}{4}'$–$1\frac{1}{2}'$ long. **Scape:** $\frac{3}{4}'$–$1\frac{3}{4}'$ tall, lateral, slender, flexuous, clothed with 2 or 3 distant bracts. **Raceme:** 4″–9″ long, of 12–20 blossoms. **Flowers:** about $1\frac{1}{4}''$ across, secund; sepals linear-lanceolate, pointed, spreading; petals similar only smaller, spreading; lip 3-lobed, almost fiddle-shaped; outer lobes small, oblong or lanceolate, curved outwards; centre lobe obovate, emarginate, with a small tooth at the apex; disc with 3 narrow lamellæ; spur short, blunt. *July*

A strikingly coloured species with large racemes of chocolate-brown or violet-rose blossoms with a white lip. It is found in fairly damp, grassy country in various parts of China and Japan. It should prove quite hardy in Great Britain in a sheltered sunny spot in the rock garden in fairly damp fibrous loam.

77. CALANTHE ELYTROGLOSSA, Reichb. f.

Root: a very stout rhizome. **Stem:** very short. **Leaves:** elliptic, ovate or lanceolate, stalked, 6″–10″ long. **Scape:** 2′–3′ tall, very robust, pubescent. **Raceme:** many-flowered. **Flowers:** $1\frac{1}{2}''$ across, on long stalks; dorsal sepal and lateral sepals oblong-lanceolate, pointed; petals narrowly oblong-lanceolate, 1-nerved; lip 3-lobed; outer lobes ovate, blunt; centre lobe broadly cuneately cordate; spur nearly 2″ long. *July and August.*

A very robust species with large but rather soberly coloured blossoms; they have green sepals, yellow petals and a white lip, and are thick and fleshy in substance, lasting a very long time in perfection. It is found in moist places such as the banks of streams in rich soils in the Sikkim Himalaya at elevations up to 8000 feet, where it is exposed to over 15° of frost in the winter when at rest. It may be grown outdoors in suitable localities on the banks of a pond or stream in a rich soil.

78. CALANTHE ENSIFOLIA, Rolfe

Root: of few thick fleshy fibres. **Leaves:** erect, straight, sword-shaped, pointed, $\frac{1}{2}'$–$1\frac{1}{2}'$ long. **Scape:** 2′–$3\frac{1}{2}'$ tall, erect, stout; **Raceme:** 6″–18″ long, loosely many-flowered. **Flowers:** $\frac{1}{2}''$ across; sepals elliptic-oblong, pointed, or rather blunt; petals elliptic-lanceolate, pointed; lip 4-lobed; outer lobes ovate-oblong, very blunt; centre lobes diverging, ovate, with numerous calli on the disc. *June and July.*

A very tall species with erect sword-shaped leaves and long many-flowered racemes of small yellow blossoms of no great decorative value. The plant inhabits damp rocky places, usually beneath the shade of trees, on the mountains of Szechuan and Hupeh in Western China. It should prove sufficiently hardy for culture outdoors in the warmer parts of Great Britain in a damp half-shady part of the rock garden in good rich loam and oak or beech leaf-soil.

79. CALANTHE FIMBRIATA, Franch

C. buccinifera, Rolfe

Root: a short stout rhizome furnished with thick fibrous roots. **Stem:** 9″–12″ tall, fairly stout. **Leaves:** basal, ovate or oblong, shortly pointed, 5″–7″ long. **Raceme:** short, of very few blossoms. **Flowers:** $\frac{3}{4}''$ across; sepals and petals subequal, narrowly lanceolate, tapering to long points; lip 3-lobed, lobes narrow, erosely fimbriate. *June.*

A beautiful plant with few-flowered racemes of large flowers with rich rose-purple sepals and petals and a rose-purple lip with purple markings on it. The plant is found on moss-covered boulders in dense shady pine forests in Western China at elevations of 11,000 feet above sea-level. It should prove hardy over the greater part of Great Britain in a shady spot in the rock garden in leaf-soil and peat.

80. CALANTHE HENRYI, Rolfe

Root: of several stout fleshy fibres. **Leaves:** elliptic or ovate lanceolate, shortly pointed, narrowing rapidly towards the base, 6″–10″ long. **Scape:** $1\frac{1}{4}'$–2′ tall, fairly stout. **Raceme:** about 8″ long, loosely many-flowered. **Flowers:** about $1\frac{1}{2}''$ across; sepals lanceolate, pointed; petals similar to the sepals only rather smaller; lip 3-lobed; outer lobes obliquely ovate-oblong, spreading; centre lobe oblong, dilated and blunt at the base; disc with 3 slender keels; spur slender, upcurved. *June to August.*

A beautiful plant with long many-flowered racemes of large white blossoms tinted with yellow. It is found in shady rocky places on the mountains of Hupeh in Western China, and may be tried outdoors in the warmer counties of Britain under the same conditions as the preceding species.

81. CALANTHE LAMELLOSA, Rolfe

Root: of rather thick fleshy fibres. **Leaves:** elliptic or obovate-elliptic, narrowing towards the base, shortly pointed, 9″–12″ long. **Scape:** about

$1\frac{1}{2}'$ tall, erect, rather slender. **Raceme:** about 6″ long, few-flowered. **Flowers:** about $1\frac{1}{2}''$ across; sepals lanceolate, pointed; petals similar but slightly smaller; lip 3-lobed; outer lobes rounded, oblong, blunt; centre lobe suborbicular, blunt; disc having down its centre 3 membranous lamellæ but little elevated above the surface; spur short, conical. *June and July.*

A beautiful species with few-flowered racemes of large white blossoms tinted with red and yellow. It grows on the mountains of Hupeh in Western China in half-shady places, frequently in rocky soil amongst vegetable debris. It may be tried outdoors in the warmer districts of Great Britain in good rich loam and oak or beech leaf-soil.

82. CALANTHE MEGALOPHA, Franch

Root: a short rhizome. **Stem:** 9″–17″ tall, leafy below, clothed with a few thin sheaths above. **Leaves:** basal, as many as 5 in number, oblong, pointed, smooth, 5″–7″ long. **Spike:** 3″–4″ long, lax, of 8–12 blossoms. **Flowers:** about $\frac{3}{4}''$ across; sepals ovate-lanceolate, shortly pointed, downy on the outside; petals oblong-linear, as long as the sepals; lip 3-lobed; outer lobes obovate; centre lobe transversely rhomboid. *June to August.*

A pretty species allied to *C. tricarinata* (Lindl.). The blossoms have white or pale pink sepals and petals, and a rose-pink or pale purple lip. It is found in thinly-wooded mountainous country in Western China at elevations of from 8000–9000 feet above sea-level. It should prove quite hardy in the warmer parts of Great Britain in a damp half-shady spot in good loam and leaf-soil.

83. CALANTHE NIPPONICA, Makino

C. trulliformis, King

Root: of hairy slender roots from a stout rhizome. **Stem:** 12″–15″ tall, erect, downy, with a bract about the middle. **Leaves:** sub-basal, 4–5 in number, lanceolate or oblong-lanceolate, 6″–8″ long. **Raceme:** 3″–5″ long, of 5–7 blossoms. **Flowers:** about $1\frac{1}{8}''$ across, dorsal sepal and lateral sepals oblong, blunt; petals oblong-lanceolate, blunt; lip 3-lobed; outer lobes obliquely ovate or rounded; centre lobe obovate-oblong with a sharp point; spur short, cylindric, curved downwards. *July to September.*

This species is not very attractively coloured, the rather large blossoms have yellowish-green sepals and petals, and a yellow lip. It is found in damp rocky places, mostly in the shade of a tree or shrub, on the mountains of the provinces of Shinano and Kaga, Japan, and should be quite hardy in Great Britain, in a damp shady spot in the rock garden, in oak and beech leaf-soil and good fibrous loam.

84. CALANTHE PLANTAGINEA, Lindl.

Root: a rather stout rhizome. **Stem:** 3″–10″ tall, clothed with long leaf-sheaths. **Leaves:** basal, plaited, elliptic-oblong, stalked, 8″–12″ long. **Scape:** $\frac{1}{2}$′–1$\frac{1}{4}$′ tall, downy. **Raceme:** fairly long, lax. **Flowers:** over 1$\frac{1}{4}$″ across; dorsal sepal and lateral sepals ovate-lanceolate, 3–5 nerved; petals oblong-lanceolate, pointed, 3-nerved; lip 3-lobed; lobes cuneate-obovate; spur slender, 1″ long. *April to August.*

A beautiful plant with a loose raceme of large white or pale lilac-coloured blossoms. It grows in damp rich soil in ravines and on the banks of streams in the Western Himalaya from Garwhal, where it reaches an altitude of 9000 feet above sea-level, to Nepal and Bhotan. It should be perfectly hardy outdoors in sheltered localities in all but the most exposed parts of Great Britain. It may be grown in a damp sunny spot in good fibrous loam and a little peat.

85. CALANTHE SIMILIS, Schltr.

Root: of fairly stout fibres from a short stock. **Leaves:** basal, 3 or 4 in number, elliptic, pointed and tapering to a short stalk, smooth, 6″–9″ long. **Scape:** 9″–12″ tall, erect or slightly flexuous, slender, with 1 or 2 pointed sheaths. **Raceme:** of 4–7 blossoms, secund, about 3$\frac{1}{2}$″ long. **Flowers:** about 1″ across; dorsal sepal and lateral sepals ovate-elliptic, pointed, spreading; petals linear-lanceolate, narrow and slightly curved at the tip, concave at the base; lip 3-lobed; outer lobes falcate-oblong, blunt; centre lobe large, narrowly unguiculate at the base, then suborbicular and pointed. *June.*

This plant produces slender one-sided racemes of pretty pink, white and green blossoms of fair size. It is found on wooded mountain slopes near Tong-tchou-an, Yunnan, Western China, and may be tried outdoors in the warmer parts of the Kingdom in a half-shady spot in good fibrous loam and oak leaf-soil.

86. CALANTHE TORIFERA, Schltr.

C. tricarinata, Maxim. *C. brevicornu* var. *megalopha*, Finet.

Root: of several somewhat fleshy fibres from a short stock. **Leaves:** usually 3 in number, elliptic, pointed, plicate, narrowed at the base into a short stalk, smooth, about 6″ long and 4″ wide. **Scape:** 12″–15″ long, erect or slightly flexuous, clothed with a few narrow sheaths. **Raceme:** lax, of 6–12 blossoms, about 6″ long. **Flowers:** about 1$\frac{1}{4}$″ across; dorsal sepal oblong, rather pointed; lateral sepals similar, oblique, spreading; petals narrowly lanceolate, pointed; lip 3-lobed, ovate at its base, where it is concave; outer lobes oblong, blunt; centre lobe suborbicular, margins undulate. *July and August.*

A pretty species with a fairly long loose raceme of fair-sized red and white blossoms; the large oval leaves are quite handsome. The plant inhabits pastures and borders of woods near Acmori, Nippon, Japan. It may be tried outdoors in Great Britain in warm localities in the rock garden in fibrous loam and rich leaf-soil.

87. CALANTHE TRICARINATA, Lindl.

C. occidentalis, Lindl.

Root: a stout rhizome. **Stem:** stout, 4″–8″ tall. **Leaves:** basal, sessile, oblong, pointed, 6″–10″ long. **Scape:** 1′–1½′ tall, stout, flowers lax, not numerous. **Flowers:** about 1½″ across; dorsal sepal and lateral sepals lanceolate, pointed, 7-nerved; petals narrowly lanceolate, 3-nerved; lip 3-lobed; outer lobes broadly oblong-falcate; centre lobe rounded or flabellate, retuse or bifid, waved. *May to August.*

This is quite a handsome species although somewhat soberly coloured. The sepals and petals are greenish-yellow and the lip is brown-purple. It grows in damp half-shady spots in vegetable soil in the Himalaya from Kashmir to Nepal and Japan, attaining an altitude above sea-level of 9000 feet, and should therefore be quite suitable for outdoor culture in all but the bleaker parts of Great Britain. It may be grown in the rock garden in a damp spot in good loam and leaf-soil.

88. CALANTHE UNDULATA, Schltr.

Root: a short rhizome emitting a few short filiform roots. **Stem:** 1′–1½′ tall, stout. **Leaves:** basal, spreading, usually 3 in number, elliptic, plicate, pointed, narrow at the base, deeply channelled, about 8″ long. **Spike:** lax, of 10 to 18 blossoms. **Flowers:** about 1¼″ across; dorsal sepal ovate, pointed; lateral sepals falcate-elliptic, rather pointed; petals obliquely ovate-spatulate, blunt, shorter than the sepals; lip 3-lobed; outer lobes subreniform, falcate, diverging, margins undulate; centre lobe reniform, bifid at the tip, margins undulate; disc with 3 crenulate and toothed lamellæ; base saccate. *June.*

Quite a handsome species with spikes of pretty blossoms with dull yellow petals and sepals, and a deep maroon-coloured lip and column. It is found in dry shady places amongst shrubs in valleys on the eastern flank of the Lichiang Range, Yunnan, Western China, at elevations of 9000–10,000 feet. It should be quite hardy in the warmer parts of Great Britain in loam and leaf-soil in a sheltered spot.

89. CALANTHE YUNNANENSIS, Rolfe

Root: of a few thick roots on a short rhizome. **Stem:** about 12″ tall. **Leaves:** 8″–12″ long, basal, 2–3 in number, elliptic or oblanceolate-oblong, pointed. **Raceme:** 5″–8″ long, of 7–12 blossoms. **Flowers:** about 1½″ across; sepals ovate-lanceolate, pointed; petals oblong-lanceolate, sharply pointed; lip shortly unguiculate, 3-lobed; lateral lobes reniform-orbicular, truncate; centre lobe transversely-oblong, emarginate rather undulate; base with 3 crenulate lamellæ; spur oblong, rather blunt, 1″–1½″ long. *June.*

A beautiful species with large creamy green-tinted blossoms with a lilac lip; they are pleasantly fragrant. It is found in somewhat dense mountain forests in Western Yunnan, Western China, at 8000–9000 feet above sea-level, and is therefore only suitable for outdoor culture in the warmer parts of the Kingdom in a sheltered shady spot, in good fibrous loam and oak or beech leaf-soil.

CALEANA, R. Brown

This genus consists of 3 quaint little plants with a few underground white fleshy fibres, the most robust of which terminate in rounded tubers about the size of a hedge nut. The smooth slender stems, which are clothed near the base by a grass-like leaf, terminate in a few curious, medium-sized blossoms placed upside down on their flower-stalks. They have little garden value and are found in well-drained, thinly-wooded country, at times at considerable elevation, in Queensland, New South Wales, Victoria, Western Australia and Tasmania. They may be tried outdoors in sheltered parts of Britain in a well-drained part of the rock garden in loam and leaf-soil. Propagation by imported tubers and by seeds when procurable.

90. CALEANA MAJOR, R. Br.

Caleya major, Endl.

Root: of small ovoid tubers. **Leaf:** subradical, solitary, linear or narrowly lanceolate, 2″–4″ long. **Scape:** ¾′–1¼′ tall, slender, with a solitary sheathing bract below the middle. **Spike:** loose, of form, 1–4 blossoms. **Flowers:** 1″ long; dorsal sepal narrowly linear, channelled, somewhat thick; lateral sepals narrowly linear, erect, pointed; petals very narrowly linear, almost filiform, shorter than the sepals; lip broadly oval or heart-shaped, the centre being inflated and hollow; column with broad petal-like wings. *December.*

An exceedingly quaint little plant with but few large weird-looking dark red or reddish-brown blossoms placed upside down on the slender flower-stem; the leaf, which is bright green tinted with red, is narrow and grass-like. It is a frequent plant in the open forest-lands in rather dry soil in Queensland, New South Wales, Victoria and Tasmania, ascending the mountains to over 2500 feet above sea-level and should therefore be fairly hardy over the greater part of the British Isles. A compost of leaf-soil and sand in a fairly sunny spot is indicated.

91. CALEANA MINOR, R. Br.

Root: of small ovoid tubers on short slender stems. **Leaf:** radical, narrowly linear, $1\frac{1}{2}''$–$2''$ long. **Scape:** about 6″ long, with at times a small bract below the middle. **Spike:** loose, of 1–3 blossoms. **Flowers:** about $\frac{5}{8}''$ long; dorsal sepal linear, sometimes dilated above the middle; lateral sepals and petals linear; lip linear, incurved, blade peltate and convex with tubercles on its surface; column with petal-like wings forming a broad sac or pouch. *November and December.*

This species is more delicate in its habit of growth than the preceding plant and is if anything more quaint when in blossom. The flowers are reversed on their stalks and are much smaller than those of *C. major* but are of the same dull red colour. It is found in thinly-wooded country in New South Wales and Tasmania and seems to be uncommon. It should prove sufficiently hardy in the warmer parts of Great Britain for culture in the open air. A sandy leaf-soil in a half-shady spot in the rock garden is indicated.

CALOCHILUS, R. Brown

Six species of stout, erect, leafy-stemmed Orchids with handsome spikes of medium-sized blossoms; all have their lips covered with brightly-coloured hairs. Their underground portions consist of one, or two or more (if the plant is in a robust healthy state) tubers, sessile on the base of the below-ground portion of the stem, on short, stout, fleshy fibres; they are like small potatoes in shape and shrivel after having produced a flowering stem and seed capsules. The stems are furnished with narrow leaves below, which degenerate upwards into leafy bracts. The plants are deciduous and their tubers are buried about two inches below the surface of the soil. They are confined to Eastern Australia and Tasmania, where they are usually found in open grassy places, and amongst very dwarf shrubs in mountainous districts. They may be grown outdoors in the mildest parts of Britain in a fairly damp spot in the rock garden. Propagation by imported tubers and seeds.

92. CALOCHILUS CAMPESTRIS, R. Br.

C. herbaceus, Lindl.

Root: of 1 or 2 fairly large ovoid tubers. **Leaf:** solitary, linear, 2″–4″ long, subradical. **Scape:** $\frac{3}{4}'$–$1\frac{1}{2}'$ tall, rather stout, clothed with 2–3 narrow leaf-like sheathing bracts. **Spike:** 3″–6″ long, with 3–7 widely separated blossoms. **Flowers:** $\frac{1}{2}''$–$1\frac{1}{4}''$ across; dorsal sepal very broadly lanceolate, concave; lateral sepals broadly lanceolate, spreading; petals broadly falcate, shorter than the sepals; lip ovate or obovate-oblong, the edges and whole surface covered with a long fringe of soft hair-like appendages.

November and December.

A tall, very handsome species which varies much in height, robustness, and size of blossom. The variety *grandiflora* has blossoms over $1\frac{1}{4}$ inches across. In the type they are pale green, tinted pink throughout, with the exception of the lip which is bright orange at the base and rich purple at the tip; the whole lip is covered with long purple hairs. It inhabits open grassy country in Queensland, New South Wales, and Tasmania, and is sufficiently hardy to stand the winter outdoors in the warmer parts of Great Britain. A good fairly moist fibrous loam in full sun is indicated.

93. CALOCHILUS PALUDOSUS, R. Br.

Root: of 2 large ovoid tubers. **Leaf:** subradical, linear, about 6″ long. **Scape:** 1′–$1\frac{1}{2}$′ tall, fairly stout, clothed with a few narrowly lanceolate sheath-like leaves or bracts. **Spike:** of 2–3 widely separated blossoms. **Flowers:** 1″–$1\frac{1}{2}$″ across; dorsal sepal very broadly lanceolate, rather blunt; lateral sepals lanceolate; petals broadly lanceolate, strongly veined; lip obovate, covered with long hairs except the tip, which is linear and flexuose.

October and November.

The blossoms of this species are interesting although not exactly showy; they are yellowish-green in ground colour with a purple tip to the lip which is covered with greenish-purple hairs. It is a native of the mountains of New South Wales, where it is found in damp grassy spots. It should prove sufficiently hardy for outdoor culture in the warmer parts of Great Britain and should be grown in an open sunny spot in a good moist fibrous loam and sand.

94. CALOCHILUS ROBERTSONII, Benth.

Root: of 2 large ovoid tubers. **Leaf:** subradical, broadly linear, 4″–6″ long. **Scape:** 1′–$1\frac{3}{4}$′ tall, stout, with 2–3 fairly large lanceolate sheaths on the upper portion. **Spike:** 3″–6″ long, fairly compact, of about 6 blossoms. **Flowers:** about $1\frac{1}{4}$″ across; dorsal sepal broadly lanceolate, concave; lateral sepals lanceolate, spreading; petals, falcate and pointed, shorter than the sepals; lip obovate-oblong, covered with long hair-like appendages except the tip which is smooth and shortly-pointed. *October and November.*

A handsome though somewhat dull-coloured plant of robust habit, with a stout stem and a spike of about half a dozen pale green blossoms with their lips covered with long purple and green hairs. It is found in moist open "heathy" spots on fairly elevated ground in Victoria, and does not appear to be very common. It should prove quite hardy in the warmer portions of Great Britain. A compost of fibrous peat and loam in a damp open situation is indicated.

CALYPSO, Salisbury

Two exquisitely beautiful terrestrial Orchids inhabiting high northern latitudes. Their root systems consist of ovoid ivory-white bulbs or tubers connected by fleshy, white coralloid roots. The somewhat fleshy stem is furnished with a solitary rich green, deeply-grooved leaf and is clothed with a few close sheaths. The blossom is terminal on the tip of the stem and resembles that of a *Cypripedium*. Both plants are found in somewhat shady woods of birch or pine, one in North America and Northern Europe and the other in Japan. The North American and European plant is accounted difficult to establish in Great Britain, the alternate frost and thaw of our normal winter exciting it into growth when it should be quite at rest. Propagation by separation of the bulbs and by seeds when available.

95. CALYPSO BULBOSA, Oakes

C. borealis, Salisb. *Cypripedium bulbosum*, Linn.

Root: a solid bulb with coralloid roots. **Leaf:** solitary, basal, broadly ovate, subcordate or rounded at the base, stalked, deeply veined, 1″–2″ long. **Scape:** 3″–6″ long, slender, clothed with from 1–3 membranous sheaths. **Flower:** solitary, drooping, about 1½″ long; sepals and petals linear-lanceolate, erect or spreading; lip inflated, saccate, with 2 short spurs below the apex and 3 ridges of papillæ near the mouth of the sac. *May and June.*

This little gem is certainly one of the most exquisite of the hardy Orchids; it produces a solitary deep green leaf and a slender bract-clothed stem bearing a solitary fragrant blossom having lilac petals and sepals striped with purple, and a large inflated lip striped and spotted with deep rose colour and variegated with yellow spots and blotches; there is a tuft of yellow or white hairs near the mouth and some brown markings inside. It is found in deep shady woods, and sometimes inhabits rather dry places in North America and Northern Europe. It may be grown in a cool shady part of the rock garden in light sandy peat and leaf-soil; it is a perfect plant for the alpine house.

96. CALYPSO SPECIOSA, Schltr.

C. bulbosa var. *japonica*, Makino

Root: an ovoid tuber with a few thick fleshy roots. **Leaf:** basal, solitary, ovate-elliptic, subcordate at the base, plicate, crisped on a short stalk, up to 2¾″ long. **Scape:** 8″ tall, slender, clothed with a few long sheaths. **Flower:** solitary, about 2″ long and 1½″ across; sepals and petals nearly equal in length, linear-lanceolate, pointed, spreading and ascending; lip inflated, pendant, fiddle-shaped, with 2 blunt spurs below the apex and numerous papillæ bordering the lower edge of the mouth. *June.*

This extremely beautiful plant was at one time considered to be a form of *C. bulbosa*; it has now been raised to specific rank by Dr. Schlechter. The blossoms have rose-coloured sepals and petals and a rosy-white lip fading to white near the base, where there are some dark lines; the tip and the dense beard around its mouth are bright yellow, the large winged column is rose-pink. The plant is found in shady woods, frequently at some elevation, on the mountains of the provinces of Suruga and Sagami, Japan. In cultivation it should succeed under the same cultural conditions as *C. bulbosa*.

CEPHALANTHERA, L. C. Richard

Leafy, rather handsome, deciduous terrestrial plants numbering about 12 species, with a short rarely creeping root stock, emitting numerous rather long fibres and erect wiry stems clothed with plaited lanceolate or oblong leaves, and loose few-flowered racemes of fair-sized blossoms, white, red or green in colour. The plants are usually found in woods and bushy places, and are thinly scattered over the northern temperate regions from England to Japan and southward to North Africa and the Himalaya. The plants are considered to be difficult to establish in gardens, this applies to our native species, which should be removed from the soil only when quite at rest. A compost of good fibrous loam and sharp sand is suitable for their cultivation, and most species are benefited by the addition of calcareous matter in some form. Propagation by division of large clumps and by seeds, which are freely produced in some seasons.

97. CEPHALANTHERA CHLOIDOPHYLLA, Reichb. f.

Epipactis chloidophylla, Wettst. *Limodorum chloidophylla*, O. Ktze. *Serapias chloidophylla*, Eaton.

Root: a slender creeping rhizome. **Stem:** 1′–1½′ tall, slender, somewhat leafy. **Leaves:** numerous, ovate-lanceolate below, lanceolate upwards, suberect, 2″–4″ long. **Raceme:** about 6″ long, lax, of over 12 blossoms. **Flowers:** about ⅝″ long; dorsal sepal lanceolate, pointed; lateral sepals lanceolate, pointed, oblique and spreading; petals broadly oblong, forming with the dorsal sepal a hood over the lip; lip ovate or oblong, narrow below, obscurely 3-lobed; centre lobe small. *May to July.*

A pretty leafy species from Japan, where it is found in thinly-wooded country. The slender wiry stems are clothed with several plaited lance-shaped leaves and terminate in a loose raceme of fairly large white blossoms tinged with red and green. The plant should be quite hardy in this country in a fairly damp half-shady spot in fibrous loam and leaf-soil.

98. CEPHALANTHERA CUCULLATA, Boiss.

C. epipactoides, Fisch. *C. kurdica*, Brom. *Epipactis cucullata*, Wettst.

Root: a creeping rhizome producing numerous short fleshy roots. **Stem:** $\frac{3}{4}'$ to $1\frac{1}{2}'$ tall, rather stout, sinuous, leafy to the top. **Leaves:** numerous, lowermost sheath-like, those on the stem oblong-lanceolate, becoming smaller upwards and passing into bracts amongst the blossoms, 2″–4″ long. **Spike:** 3″–7″ long, loosely few-flowered. **Flowers:** about $\frac{5}{8}''$ long; petals and sepals all lanceolate, forming a loose hood over the column; lips 3-lobed; outer lobes triangular blunt; centre lobe larger than the side lobes, heart-shaped, slightly incurved at the margin. *May and June.*

The blossoms of this species are rather too small and too few in number to give the plant much decorative value; they are yellowish-white in colour, and are produced in leafy spikes. The plant ranges from Greece to Persia and is found in wooded country. It may be grown under the same conditions as the following species.

99. CEPHALANTHERA ELEGANS, Schltr.

Root: a slender rhizome emitting numerous fine rootlets. **Stem:** $1'$–$1\frac{1}{4}'$ tall, slender, leafy, with a few sheaths at its base. **Leaves:** 5–6 in number, elliptic-lanceolate or lanceolate, smooth, suberect, $2''$–$3\frac{1}{2}''$ long. **Raceme:** about 6″ long, lax, of 10–15 blossoms. **Flowers:** about $\frac{1}{2}''$ long; dorsal sepal lanceolate, rather pointed; lateral sepals obliquely lanceolate, pointed; petals obliquely oblong-elliptic, blunt, forming with the sepals a loose hood over the column; lip ovate, 3-lobed; outer lobes ovate-triangular, oblique, blunt; centre lobe subreniform, short, rather blunt. *June and July.*

A slender leafy species with a long loose spike of rather small but dainty red and white blossoms of decorative value. It is found in grassy or thinly-wooded country in Hakodate, Japan. It should prove hardy in all but the coldest parts of Great Britain in the rock garden in good fibrous loam and leaf-soil. Its roots should be protected from very severe frost.

100. CEPHALANTHERA ERECTA, Bl.

Epipactis erecta, Wettst. *Limodorum erectum*, O. Ktze. *Serapias erecta*, Thbg.

Root: of 2 irregular tubers. **Stem:** 12″–15″ tall, slender, leafy below, sheath-clothed above. **Leaves:** cauline, usually 3 in number, ovate-lanceolate, plicate, stem-clasping, pointed, $1\frac{1}{2}''$ to 2″ long. **Raceme:** short, of about 8 blossoms. **Flowers:** about $\frac{3}{8}''$ long; dorsal sepal ovate-lanceolate, concave, pointed; lateral sepals similar but blunt; petals lanceolate, pointed; lip entire, more or less erect, ovate-lanceolate concave, pointed; spur saccate, very blunt, slightly curved. *May and June.*

An upright, somewhat slender species with short loose racemes of small green and white blossoms of no decorative value. The plant is found in damp grassy places in many parts of Japan and Northern China. It should be quite hardy in Great Britain in a damp spot in loam and peat.

101. CEPHALANTHERA FALCATA, Lindl.

C. platycheila, Reichb. f. *Epipactis falcata*, Sw. *Limodorum falcatum*, O. Ktze.

Root: a slender creeping rhizome furnished with many short rootlets. **Stem:** 9″–15″ tall, slender, leafy. **Leaves:** 4–6 in number, broadly lanceolate, plaited, smooth, suberect, 2″–3″ long. **Raceme:** about 6″ long, lax, of 9–18 blossoms. **Flowers:** $\frac{5}{8}$″ long; dorsal sepal lanceolate, pointed; lateral sepals similar to the dorsal sepal, spreading; petals oblong-elliptic, falcate, blunt, incurved; lip ovate, narrow below, 3-lobed; outer lobes ovate-triangular, diverging, blunt; centre lobe oblong, pointed. *May to July.*

A pretty plant with slender leafy stems bearing many-flowered racemes of fair-sized pure white or green-tinged white blossoms. This species inhabits shady places in sparely wooded localities on the mountains of Yunnan, Western China, at 9000–10,000 feet above sea-level. It should prove hardy in warm localities in a shady spot of the rock garden in loam and leaf-soil.

102. CEPHALANTHERA LONGIBRACTEATA, Bl.

Epipactis longibracteata, Wettst. *Limodorum longibracteatum*, O. Ktze. *Serapias longibracteata*, Eaton.

Root: a slender creeping rhizome. **Stem:** 12″–15″ tall, slender, sinuous, leafy. **Leaves:** 5–6 in number, broadly lanceolate and pointed below, degenerating upwards into long bracts among the flowers. **Raceme:** about 6″ long, lax, many-flowered. **Flowers:** about $\frac{1}{2}$″ long; dorsal sepal lanceolate, pointed; lateral sepals obliquely lanceolate, pointed; petals oblong-elliptic, forming a loose galea with the dorsal sepal; lip narrow below, ovate, pointed, with 3 hairy ridges down its centre. *May to July.*

The white and green blossoms of this species are half hidden by the long leaf-like bracts. It is found in bushy places and in woods of deciduous trees over the greater part of Japan and Korea. The plant should be quite hardy in Great Britain in a half-shady spot in the rock garden in loam and leaf-soil.

103. CEPHALANTHERA LONGIFOLIA, Fritsch.

C. acuminata, Lindl. *C. ensifolia*, Rich. *C. Xiphophyllum*, Reichb. f.

Root: of stout fleshy fibres. **Stem:** $\frac{1}{2}'$–$1\frac{1}{2}'$ tall, fairly stout. **Leaves:** oblong or lanceolate on the lower part of the stem, linear upwards, 3″–8″ long. **Raceme:** 4″ to 8″ long, lax, many-flowered. **Flowers:** about $\frac{3}{4}''$ long; sepals lanceolate, pointed; petals elliptic, blunt; lip small, erect below, embracing the column, recurved towards the tip. *April to June.*

A rather handsome native plant with erect stems bearing plaited leaves of a rich green colour, and a loose raceme of from six to twenty white blossoms with, at times, yellow markings on the lip. The plant and its forms are scattered over the whole of Europe, North Africa and Western temperate Asia, as far east as the Himalaya. The forms *citrina*, *gibbosa*, *longibracteata* and *pumila* are all worth growing. *C. Schulzei* (Nobis) is a hybrid between this species and *C. pallens*; it is intermediate between the two. All are perfectly hardy and may be grown in a shady part of the rock garden in good loam and leaf-soil.

104. CEPHALANTHERA MAIREI, Schltr.

Root: a slender stock with numerous fibrous rootlets. **Stem:** 6″–9″ tall, usually erect, leafy, sheathed at the base, smooth. **Leaves:** cauline, sub-erect, elliptic or elliptic-lanceolate, pointed, plaited, smooth, 2″–3″ long. **Raceme:** about 3″ long, usually dense, of 8–20 blossoms. **Flowers:** about 1″ long; dorsal sepal rhombeo-lanceolate, rather blunt; lateral sepals rhombeo-lanceolate, oblique, pointed; petals similar to the lateral sepals, all smooth, forming a loose hood over the column; lip concave, hood-like at the base and 3-lobed towards the tip; outer lobes obliquely triangular; centre lobe reniform with 3 thickened nerves down its centre. *June.*

A delicate and dwarf species with pretty snow-white blossoms in long, fairly dense racemes. It grows in woods in Western Yunnan, Western China, at elevations up to 8000 feet above sea-level, and should prove hardy in a shady spot in leaf-soil and fibrous loam.

105. CEPHALANTHERA PALLENS, Rich.

C. Damasonium, Druce. *C. grandiflora*, Bab. *Epipactis pallens*, Willd.

Root: a creeping rhizome emitting numerous thick fleshy roots about 1″ long. **Stem:** $\frac{3}{4}'$–2′ tall, stout, leafy, slightly sinuous. **Leaves:** numerous, ovate or ovate-lanceolate, degenerating into bracts among the blossoms, 2″–4″ long. **Spike:** 4″–8″ long, loose, few-flowered. **Flowers:** about $\frac{7}{8}''$ long; dorsal sepal ovate-lanceolate; lateral sepals lanceolate, slightly curved at the tip; petals similar to dorsal sepal; lip 3-lobed; outer lobes, small, triangular, blunt; centre lobe broadly elliptic with the disc covered with lines of fine hairs; the petals and sepals form a loose hood over the column.

May and June.

A rather handsome native plant with loose spikes of six or eight yellowish-white or cream-coloured blossoms of fair size. It is found in woods and thickets beneath the shade of deciduous trees throughout Europe as far as the Caucasus and Asia Minor. It may be grown in the rock garden in a shady spot in calcareous loam and leaf-soil. The varieties *alba, adenophora, Duffortii, ochroleuca* and the sub-species *comosa* and *maravignae* are worth cultivating.

106. CEPHALANTHERA RUBRA, Rich.

Epipactis rubra, All. *Serapias grandiflora,* Schm. *S. Helleborine,* Linn.

Root: of numerous black somewhat thick fibres 1″–2″ long, from a short stout creeping rhizome. **Stem:** $\frac{3}{4}$′–2′ tall, erect or slightly zig-zag, leafy to the top. **Leaves:** numerous, lanceolate, spreading, 2″–4″ long. **Spike:** 2″–4″ long, of from 6–12 blossoms. **Flowers:** $\frac{3}{4}$″ long; dorsal sepal lanceolate; lateral sepals lanceolate, tapering to a fine point; petals lanceolate also very pointed; lip cordate, small. *May and June.*

The blossoms of this native plant are pretty but remain half open throughout their existence; they are borne in a loose spike on leafy stems and are of a pinkish-red or pale violet-red colour with a white lip narrowly margined with red near the tip. The plant is found in open spaces in thickets and in woods, usually on chalk, over the whole of Europe and Asia Minor to Persia. It may be grown in the rock garden in a half-shady spot in chalky loam and leaf-soil; *albiflora* and *parviflora* are pleasing varieties.

CERATANDRA, Ecklon

This genus contains but one species, it is a rather dwarf, stout-stemmed, deciduous terrestrial plant, with large tuberous roots and numerous narrow spreading or suberect leaves and long spikes of many fair-sized blossoms of quite an ornamental character. The plant is found in mountainous districts in South-Western Cape Colony and is apparently rather scarce. It may be tried in the warmer districts in the western and southern counties outdoors in the rock garden in an open but sheltered spot in moist but well-drained fibrous loam, with a little fibrous peat or osmunda fibre. The tubers should be planted three or four inches below the surface of the soil, and should have protection from prolonged frost during our winter. Propagation by imported tubers and also by seeds when these are obtainable.

107. CERATANDRA CHLOROLEUCA, Eckl.

C. arata, Durand & Schinz. *C. auriculata*, Lindl. *Ophrys arata*, Linn. *Pterygodium atratum*, Sw. *Hippopodium atratum*, Harv.

Root: of fleshy tubers. **Stem:** rather stout, somewhat flexuous. **Leaves:** radical and cauline, linear, 1″–3″ long, numerous. **Scape:** $\frac{3}{4}$′–1′ long. **Spike:** 1″–6″ long, dense. **Flowers:** about $\frac{5}{8}$″ across; dorsal sepal oblong-lanceolate; lateral sepals ovate-oblong, concave; petals elliptic-lanceolate, conduplicately folded and concave; lip broadly unguiculate, limb broadly cordate with an ovate-oblong fleshy appendage near the middle, about $\frac{1}{8}$″ long.

October to January.

A rather curious species having fairly large blossoms with yellow-green sepals and bright yellow petals and lip. The long spikes of blossom are quite ornamental. It grows on elevated plains and grassy mountain slopes in Cape Colony, reaching its greatest altitude in Du Toits Kloof, in the Worcester Division, at 4000 feet altitude, where 12° of frost is registered in the winter. A good fibrous loam in full sun is indicated.

CERATANDROPSIS, Rolfe

Two species of beautiful deciduous terrestrial plants of stout erect habit with two or more fleshy tubers like small potatoes. Their stems are clothed with narrow suberect or somewhat spreading leaves, and the small or medium-sized blossoms are borne in shortly oblong or subcapitate spikes, mixed with narrowly linear bracts. They are found in open spots on elevated grassy flats and on the gently sloping sides of mountains in damp but well-drained spots, and appear to be confined to South-Western Cape Colony, where they are locally abundant. They may be tried in the open air in a sheltered but open part of the rock garden in the warmest parts of Britain, in a compost of sandy loam with some peat or osmunda fibre, and the tuber should never be allowed to shrink for want of moisture. Some form of protection in winter is desirable. Propagation by imported tubers and by seeds which are freely produced in South Africa.

108. CERATANDROPSIS GLOBOSA, Rolfe

Ceratandra globosa, Lindl. *C. parviflora*, Lindl.

Root: fleshy, tuberous. **Stem:** rather stout. **Leaves:** radical and cauline, linear, 2″–3″ long, numerous. **Scape:** $\frac{1}{2}$′–1$\frac{1}{4}$′ tall. **Spike:** $\frac{1}{2}$″–2″ long, dense. **Flowers:** under $\frac{1}{2}$″ across; dorsal sepal narrowly ovate; lateral sepals ovate-oblong, subconduplicately folded, blunt, spreading; petals broadly obliquely ovate, blunt; lip broadly unguiculate; limb broadly ovate-cordate, convex, blunt, broader than long. *October to December.*

Although the blossoms of this species are rather small, the dull red sepals and white petals and lip make a pretty contrast and give it some decorative value. It grows on elevated plains and grassy mountain slopes and summits in Cape Colony, probably reaching its greatest altitude in Du Toits Kloof at 4000 feet in the Worcester Division and is exposed to 12° of frost for short periods during its winter rest. It should be grown in moist sandy loam in a sheltered sunny spot.

109. CERATANDROPSIS GRANDIFLORA, Rolfe

Ceratandra grandiflora, Lindl.

Root: fleshy, tuberous. **Stem:** moderately stout. **Leaves:** radical and cauline, linear, $\frac{3}{4}''$–$1\frac{3}{4}''$ long, crowded. **Scape:** 6″–10″ tall. **Spike:** 1″–$2\frac{1}{2}''$ long, dense. **Flowers:** nearly 1″ across; dorsal sepal oblong-lanceolate; lateral sepals ovate-oblong, blunt, concave, incurved at the base; petals semiovate-oblong, oblique, prominently auriculate above the base, concave, conduplicately folded; lip broadly unguiculate; limb broadly cordate-ovate, convex, broader than long. *October and November.*

The large deep yellow blossoms of this species render it a very decorative and desirable plant for the rock garden or alpine house. It inhabits sandy open places amidst short herbage, both on the mountains and on elevated plains in Southern and Western Cape Colony, where it probably reaches its greatest elevation in Du Toits Kloof in the Worcester Division at 4000 feet, and where it is exposed to 12° of frost in the winter for short periods. A sandy loam in full sun is indicated.

CHILOGLOTTIS, R. Brown

A genus consisting of 7 species of deciduous terrestrial plants, usually of dwarf but stout habit. The root system consists of a short slender stock producing a few rather stout fleshy fibres of varying lengths, some of which terminate in small ovoid tubers, these form the next season's plants, for the old stock and tuber from which it was produced perish as soon as the seed capsules have ripened. The leaves vary in shape in the different species and are few in number, being placed near the base of the stem. The blossoms, which are usually of a decorative nature, are generally solitary on the apex of the stems. They are usually found in woods and shady places, mostly in a rich light soil, and are confined to South-Eastern Australia, Tasmania, New Zealand, the Auckland and Campbell Isles. They may be tried outdoors in Britain in sheltered spots in the rock garden, in good light soil. Propagation by imported tubers and by seeds when procurable.

110. CHILOGLOTTIS BIFOLIA, Hook. f.

Caladenia bifolia, Hook. f.

Root: of oblong tubers on short fleshy fibres. **Leaves:** radical, oblong, spreading, hairy, $\frac{3}{4}''$–$1\frac{1}{4}''$ long. **Scape:** 3″–5″ tall, stout, ebracteate. **Flower:** solitary, 1″ across; dorsal sepal linear-oblong, blunt, suberect; lateral sepals linear; petals linear, blunt, slightly shorter than the lateral sepals; lip nearly stemless, orbicular-ovate, with 2 short narrow lines of glands near the base.

December and January.

A delightful little species with a bright pink blossom perched " butterfly-like " on the tip of a bright green stem, clothed with two oblong rich green hairy leaves. It should prove very attractive in the alpine house. It is found in moist spots throughout New Zealand and the Auckland Islands, reaching its greatest altitude above sea-level on Mount Brewester at 5000 feet and should therefore be quite hardy in Great Britain. It should be grown in a good fibrous loam in a moist sunny spot.

111. CHILOGLOTTIS CORNUTA, Hook. f.

Root: of small tubers on long fibres. **Leaves:** linear-oblong, pointed, 1″–$1\frac{1}{2}''$ long. **Scape:** 2″–4″ tall, stout, lengthening as the capsule develops. **Flower:** solitary, about $\frac{1}{2}''$ across; dorsal sepal ovate-lanceolate, rather pointed; lateral sepals linear; petals ovate, erect, pointed, shorter than the sepals; lip trowel-shaped with a horn-like appendage at the base of the disc and a broader one on each side of it; there are also 3 flat tumid glands near by.

December and January.

This is a quaint little plant and is suitable for culture in a pan in the alpine house. It produces a rather stout stem clothed at its base by two bright green leaves covered with pretty reticulations, and a curiously constructed lurid purple blossom perched on the top of the stem. It is found in moss on the ground and at times on tree trunks, in shady places in the Auckland and Campbell Islands off New Zealand. It should be quite hardy in Great Britain and in cultivation the condition under which it is found in nature should be copied as far as possible.

112. CHILOGLOTTIS DIPHYLLA, R. Br.

Acianthus bifolius, R. Br. *Caladenia diphylla,* Reichb. f. *Epipactis reflexa,* Labill.

Root: of small tubers on fairly long stems. **Leaves:** radical, ovate-elliptic to oblong-lanceolate, pointed, contracted into a short stem, $\frac{3}{4}''$–$1\frac{1}{2}''$ long. **Scape:** 3″–6″ tall, bearing 2 sheathing bracts. **Flower:** solitary, $1\frac{1}{2}''$ across;

dorsal sepal cuneate, contracted towards the base; lateral sepals rounded, linear, very slender; petals lanceolate; lip obovate, contracted at the base into a long claw; calli covering the disc in 2 crowded rows.

April and May.

The leaves of this species closely resemble those of our Tway Blade Orchid. The large deep red blossom is solitary and is shaded with green on the backs of the sepals. It grows in woods and shady places in Queensland, New South Wales, Victoria and Tasmania and is exposed to over 12° of frost for short periods during the winter. It is suitable for outdoor culture in the warmer parts of Great Britain in a compost of leaf-soil and sand, in a damp half-shady spot in the rock garden. It is by no means showy.

113. CHILOGLOTTIS GUNNII, Lindl.

Caladenia Gunnii, Reichb. f.

Root: of small ovoid tubers on the tips of long fleshy fibres. **Leaves:** subradical, ovate-elliptical, 2 in number, pointed, contracted into a short stalk, about 2″ long. **Scape:** 3″–7″ long, very stout, with 1 sheathing bract. **Flower:** solitary, about 1½″ across; dorsal sepal ovate-oblong, rather pointed; lateral sepals narrowly linear or narrowly lanceolate, pointed; petals broadly lanceolate-falcate, nearly as long as the sepals; lip broadly ovate, pointed, on a very short claw; calli in 2 crowded rows. *October.*

This species is usually, although not always, more dwarf than the foregoing species and, like it, has dull red blossoms tinted green. It is of no great decorative value but should prove interesting in a pan in the alpine house. It grows in damp shady places on the mountains of Victoria and Tasmania, where it attains its greatest altitude above sea-level on Ben Lomond at 5000 feet, and is therefore quite hardy in Great Britain. A compost of peat and fibrous loam in a damp half-shady spot is indicated.

CHLORÆA, Lindley

Deciduous terrestrial plants numbering about 100 species, natives of South America, where they range from Southern Bolivia to Argentine, Uruguay throughout Chile to Terra del Fuego and the Falkland Islands, a few species extend to Patagonia. Most of the species are of a robust leafy habit; the foliage in a few species is wanting or has shrivelled before the flowers are perfected; this may be accounted for in some cases by the arid situations which they inhabit. The blossoms are produced in many- or few-flowered spikes and are in most cases large and showy, their sepals are frequently thickened and produced into stout tail-like appendages, which are usually tinted a different colour to the remainder of the segments. Like the genus Asarca many species are at the height of their growing season during our mid-winter months and are only suitable for very sheltered spots. Propagation by imported tubers and by seeds when procurable.

114. CHLORÆA ALPINA, Poepp.

Root: of numerous rounded or clavate fleshy fibres. **Stem:** about 9″ tall, fairly stout, leafy below, sheath-clothed above. **Leaves:** 5–6 in number, oblong, pointed, sheathing, decreasing into spatha-like sheaths above, 3″–4″ long. **Spike:** about 3″ long, of 3–5 blossoms. **Flowers:** about 2″ across, erect; dorsal sepal ovate-triangular, pointed; lateral sepals similar, but blunt; petals oblong, pointed; lip 3-lobed, narrow at the base; outer lobes oblong, rounded, large, veined; centre lobe oblong, incurved at the margin near the tip, where it is pointed; disc with 6 crenulate lines down its centre. *December.*

A beautiful and delicate plant with a few large white and green blossoms in a short spike. It is found in damp half-shady places among rocks on the Andes of Central Chile at Chillan and Antuco, where it reaches an elevation of 6000 feet. It should be quite hardy over the greater part of Great Britain in a damp half-shady spot in the rock garden in fibrous peat and loam.

115. CHLORÆA AURANTIACA, Lindl.

Asarca aurantiaca, Lindl.

Root: of numerous club-shaped fibres. **Stem:** about $2\frac{1}{2}'$ tall, rather slender, leafy at the base, sheathed above. **Leaves:** oblong, blunt, degenerating upwards into sheaths. **Spike:** 6″–9″ long, lax, many-flowered. **Flowers:** $1\frac{1}{4}''$ across; dorsal sepal lanceolate, pointed, concave; lateral sepals lanceolate, retuse at the tip; petals oblong, tip retuse; lip narrow below, 3-lobed; outer lobes oblong, blunt; centre lobe ovate-triangular with broad blunt teeth on the margin; upper surface with numerous thorn-like curved tubercles. *November.*

A species of considerable decorative value with rather large orange-coloured blossoms with some deeper coloured markings on the lip. It is found in thin woods on the mountains of Chillan and Concepcion in Central Chile. It should prove quite hardy in the western and southern counties of Britain in a fairly damp half-shady spot in beech leaf-soil and sand.

116. CHLORÆA AUREA, Phil.

Root: of numerous thickened fleshy fibres. **Stem:** $2'$–$2\frac{1}{2}'$ tall, leafy at the base, naked above. **Leaves:** basal, narrowly lanceolate, 6″–9″ long. **Raceme:** about 4″ long, of 10–15 blossoms. **Flowers:** 2″ across; dorsal sepal oblong or elliptic; lateral sepals ovate, blunt at the tip; petals ovate-oblong, blunt, with five lines of papillæ down the centre; lip unguiculate below, rounded, obscurely

3-lobed; outer lobes rounded, minutely dentate; centre lobe oblong, margin crenulate; disc with numerous thorn-like tubercles and blunt calli.

October to December.

A very handsome species with many-flowered racemes of large bright yellow blossoms with black tips to the lateral sepals and brown plates on the lip; the column is also brown. It is found on the mountains of Central Chile in thin woodlands and should be hardy in the warmer parts of the Kingdom in rather damp fibrous peat and leaf-soil, in a half-shady spot.

117. CHLORÆA BERGII, Hieron

Root: a cluster of clavate tubers 2″ long. **Stem:** fairly stout, 6″–9″ tall, clothed with a few bracts above and leafy below. **Leaves:** 3–4 in number, oblong, sheathing the stem, 2″–3″ long. **Flower:** solitary, nearly 2″ across and 1½″ long; sepals ovate, narrowing to a point; petals oblong, pointed, minutely toothed at the apex; lip ovate-oblong, bordered with a deep fringe of very numerous linear segments, and with a dense patch of hairs near its base.

October and November.

A beautiful plant with a fairly stout stem, leafy at its base, and bearing on the tip a large shining white blossom tinted with green and with thickened green nerves to its segments. The plant is found in open country amongst herbage on the mountains of Patagonia. It should prove quite hardy in most parts of Great Britain in a fairly damp open spot in the rock garden in peat and fibrous loam.

118. CHLORÆA BICALLOSA, Phil.

Root: a cluster of thickened fibres. **Stem:** about 12″ long, fairly stout. **Leaves:** reduced to a few narrowly lanceolate sheaths. **Spike:** of 10–12 scattered blossoms. **Flowers:** about ¾″ across; dorsal sepal ligulate, blunt; lateral sepals similar but narrower, thickened below, with the apical margin incurved; petals obovate-oblong, blunt, shorter than the sepals; lip oblong or elliptic, narrow at the base, where there are 2 erect ear-like lobes; disc with a crescent-shaped mass of small tubercles near the base. *January.*

The blossoms of this dwarf species are of a pale greenish-white colour with bright green tubercles on the lip. It is found in the Araucaria forest on the Andes of Chillan in Central Chile at sufficient elevation above sea-level to ensure its hardiness in the warmer parts of Great Britain in a half-shady spot in the rock garden in leaf-soil and loam.

119. CHLORÆA CALOPOGON, Phil.

Root: a cluster of large club-like much thickened fibres. **Stem:** up to 3′ tall, sheathed. **Leaves:** in the form of lanceolate sheaths. **Spike:** about

8″ long, few or many-flowered. **Flowers:** about 1½″ across; dorsal sepal oblong-ligulate, blunt; lateral sepals similar with incurved and minutely toothed margins near the tip, which is thickened; petals oblong, pointed; lip unguiculate, rounded, 3-lobed; outer lobes semi-oblong, minutely toothed; centre lobe suborbicular, toothed; disc and base with long thread-like tubercles on its surface. *December.*

A tall robust species with long spikes of large white flowers with green veins. It is found in the beech and conifer forests in the province of O'Higgins in Central Chile and should be sufficiently hardy for outdoor culture over the greater part of the Kingdom in a half-shady spot in leaf-soil and loam.

120. CHLORÆA CAMPESTRIS, Poepp.

C. Poeppigiana, A. Rich.

Root: a cluster of club-like fibres of considerable size. **Stem:** from ¾′ to 2′ tall, leafy below, sheath-clothed above. **Leaves:** oblong, pointed, 2″–3″ long, degenerating upwards into a few sheaths. **Spike:** of many congested blossoms. **Flowers:** 1″ across; dorsal sepal lanceolate, pointed; lateral sepals rectangular, diverging, narrow and somewhat thickened at the tip where the margins are incurved; petals oblong, blunt; lip oblong, ovate-oblong or subrhomboid, blunt at the tip, margins obscurely crenulate; disc furnished with numerous thorn-like tubercles. *November.*

This species produces a congested spike of fair-sized yellow blossoms with dark markings on the lip. It is found in mountain meadows in Central Chile at considerable elevation above sea-level and should be quite hardy over the greater part of the Kingdom in a damp sunny spot in fibrous loam.

121. CHLORÆA CHICA, Speg et Kränzl.

Root: a cluster of thickened fibres. **Stem:** about 4″ tall, slender, leafy below, sheath-clothed above. **Leaves:** linear-oblong, blunt, about 6″ long. **Spike:** short, of about 3 blossoms. **Flowers:** ⅝″ across; dorsal sepal oblong; lateral sepals ovate-oblong, not thickened, rather blunt; petals oblong, blunt, cuneate at the base, where the veins are thickened and downy; lip shortly unguiculate, simple, oblong, with numerous thorn-like tubercles in its upper left-hand corner, and a few short downy ridges below the middle on the right hand side. *March.*

An exceedingly dwarf species with a few large white and green blossoms. It should make a very charming addition to the alpine house in a pan of fibrous peat, loam and moss. It is found in damp boggy places on the banks of the Rio Chico in Patagonia and should be hardy in all but the bleakest parts of Great Britain.

122. CHLORÆA CHLOROSTICTA, Phil.

Root: a cluster of thickened fibres. **Stem:** 2′–2½′ tall, slender, leafy below, clothed with a few appressed sheaths above. **Leaves:** basal, narrowly lanceolate, pointed, 3″–4″ long. **Spike:** 6″–9″ long, lax, of 6–7 blossoms. **Flowers:** about 2″ across; dorsal sepal narrowly lanceolate, pointed, 3-nerved; lateral sepals linear, tip thickened, margins incurved, blunt; petals oblong-lanceolate, covered with minute papillæ; lip obscurely 3-lobed; lateral lobes rounded, very slightly crenulate; centre lobe suborbicular, furnished with long pointed teeth on the margin; disc with a few thorn-like tubercles and 3 thick hairy ridges down its centre. *November to January.*

A tall slender species with a long loose spike of very large white blossoms spotted with green. It is found in rocky soil in thin woods on the Andes of Linares in Central Chile and should prove nearly hardy in Great Britain in a half-shady spot in sandy loam and leaf-soil.

123. CHLORÆA CHOLILENSIS, Speg.

Root: a cluster of rather long fleshy fibres. **Stem:** 9″–12″ tall, leafy, rather slender. **Leaves:** few, sheathing, oblong, pointed, degenerating into bracts upwards, 3″–4″ long. **Flowers:** about 2″ across, 5 to 7 in number in a loose spike; dorsal sepal oblong, blunt; lateral sepals similar but connate at the base; petals narrowly oblong, smaller than the sepals; lip ovate, narrowed to the base, toothed on the margin and with numerous pointed tubercles on the disc. *November.*

A somewhat dwarf leafy plant with large green and white blossoms in a short spike. It is found in open grass lands in Patagonia and Southern Chile at considerable elevations on the mountains and should be quite hardy in Great Britain in a fairly damp sunny spot in the rock garden in fibrous peat and sandy loam.

124. CHLORÆA CHRYSANTHA, Poepp.

Root: a cluster of large club-like tubers or thickened fibres. **Stem:** 2′–2¾′ tall, rather slender, leafy at the base, clothed with a few distant sheaths above. **Leaves:** basal, 4–5 in number, oblong, pointed, 3″–5″ long, shortly stalked, degenerating into sheaths above. **Spike:** lax, of about 15 blossoms. **Flowers:** about 1¼″ across; dorsal sepal linear-lanceolate, pointed; lateral sepals similar but blunt and thickened at the tip; petals lanceolate, pointed, shorter than the sepals; lip narrow at the base, 3-lobed; outer lobes semi-oblong; centre lobe ovate-oblong, crenulate on the margin; disc and outer lobes with numerous fusiform tubercles. *October.*

A tall leafy species with loose spikes of numerous saffron-coloured blossoms with green tips to the lateral sepals and green tubercles on the lip. It is found in thin woodlands on the mountains of various parts of Southern and Central Chile and should be hardy in Britain under the same conditions as *C. bicallosa.*

125. CHLORÆA CHRYSOCHLORA, Phil.

Root: a cluster of thickened fleshy fibres. **Stem:** up to 20″ tall, leafy at the base, sheathed above. **Leaves:** basal, sheath-like, 3″–6″ long, degenerating into 6 sheaths on the scape. **Spike:** usually dense, of few or many flowers. **Flowers:** about $1\frac{3}{8}$″ across; dorsal sepal oblong-lanceolate, pointed; lateral sepals lanceolate, thickened and incurved at the tip; petals cuneate at the base then ovate-lanceolate, blunt, shorter than the sepals; lip very narrow at the base then ovate, obscurely 3-lobed; outer lobes rounded; centre lobe ovate with bluntly toothed margins, surface covered with numerous stalked warts. *November.*

This species produces fairly long spikes of rather large yellow or pale orange flowers with green warts on the lip. It is found in damp grassy places near Valdivia and Concepcion in Central Chile and should be sufficiently hardy for outdoor culture in the warm western counties in a sheltered spot in fibrous loam and leaf-soil.

126. CHLORÆA CRISPA, Lindl.

C. dasypogon, Phil. *Cymbidium luteum,* Willd.

Root: a cluster of horizontal club-like fleshy fibres. **Stem:** $1\frac{1}{2}$′–$2\frac{1}{4}$′ tall, slender, leafy at the base, sheath-clothed above. **Leaves:** oblong or lanceolate, 4″–6″ long. **Spike:** about 6″ long, lax or dense, of 10–20 blossoms. **Flowers:** $1\frac{3}{4}$″ across; dorsal sepal oblong, blunt; lateral sepals narrowly obovate-oblong, thickened at the tip; petals elliptic, blunt, with minute granules on the centre vein; lip unguiculate below, obscurely 3-lobed; outer lobe semi-ovate; centre lobe orbicular, crenulate, margin very slightly incurved; disc and outer lobes with numerous suberect thorn-like tubercles. *November.*

A rather tall species producing a fairly long spike of handsome yellow, green spotted blossoms. It is found in the mountainous parts of the provinces of Concepcion, Curico, Colchagua, O'Higgins and Valdivia in Central Chile and should be sufficiently hardy for outdoor culture in most parts of Great Britain in a somewhat damp half-shady spot in fibrous peat, loam and leaf-soil.

127. CHLORÆA CROCATA, Phil.

Root: a cluster of much-thickened fibres. **Stem:** $\frac{3}{4}$′–2′ tall, leafy below, sheath-clothed above. **Leaves:** basal, oblong, 2″–3″ long, degenerating into close sheaths above. **Spike:** of 12–15 flowers, dense. **Flowers:** $1\frac{1}{2}$″ across; dorsal sepal linear-lanceolate, pointed; lateral sepals linear with thickened tips; petals lanceolate with a few calli at the base; lip shortly unguiculate, 3-lobed; outer lobes rounded; centre lobe bluntly triangular, margins broadly and bluntly toothed, incurved at the tip; disc and outer lobes with large curved thorn-like tubercles on the surface. *December.*

This beautiful species produces a dense spike of large saffron-coloured blossoms with numerous green tubercles on the lip. It is found in rocky places among short herbage, and at times in pinewoods, on the Andes of Linares and Chillan in Central Chile. It should be hardy in most parts of Great Britain in a sheltered spot in well drained fibrous loam and leaf-soil.

128. CHLORÆA CUNEATA, Lindl.

C. obovata, Phil.

Root: of thick club-shaped tubers. **Stem:** up to 2′ tall, stout sheath-clothed. **Leaves:** in the form of narrow distant sheaths. **Spike:** 6″–9″ long, usually of many scattered blossoms. **Flowers:** nearly 2″ long; dorsal sepal oblong, blunt; lateral sepals linear, pointed; petals linear with thick fleshy veins; lip wedge-shaped, dilated, blunt and bluntly toothed at the tip; disc with 4 thickened hairy ridges on the outer margins.

November and December.

The large white and green blossoms of this robust species are very attractive, they are produced in long many-flowered spikes on stout stems. The plant is found in thin pinewoods on the mountains near Valdivia, Central Chile. It should prove sufficiently hardy for outdoor culture in the western and southern counties of Britain in a half-shady spot in leaf-soil and loam.

129. CHLORÆA CYLINDROSTACHYA, Poepp.

Root: a cluster of clavate fleshy fibres of considerable size. **Stem:** $1\frac{1}{2}$′–3′ tall, very stout, leafy below, sheathed above. **Leaves:** sheathing, 6″–9″ long, ovate-oblong or oblong pointed or blunt. **Spike:** about 9″ long, lax below, dense above, cylindrical, many-flowered. **Flowers:** about $\frac{3}{4}$″ across; dorsal sepal ovate-lanceolate concave, pointed; lateral sepals erect, with incurved margins and thickened tip, similar in shape to dorsal sepal; petals linear-lanceolate, incurved; lip oblong at the base, dilated and rounded, triangular at the tip where the edges curve under, margin and surface covered with oval tubercles; base with 5 wavy ridges down its centre.

December and January.

The blossoms of this species are greenish-yellow in colour with rich green markings on the lip. It is found in pinewoods on the Andes of Central Chile and Northern Patagonia. It should be generally hardy in Great Britain in a half-shady spot in the garden in leaf-soil and loam.

130. CHLORÆA DISCOIDES, Lindl.

Root: of numerous thickened fibres of considerable size. **Stem:** 12″ to 20″ tall, leafy at the base, sheathed above. **Leaves:** basal, ovate, pointed, 4″–9″ long, degenerating upwards into large imbricating sheaths. **Spike:** of 5–15 blossoms. **Flowers:** about 2″ across; dorsal sepal oblong-lanceolate, pointed; lateral sepals similar but blunt, thickened and twisted at the tip; petals oblong, pointed, naked, shorter than the sepals; lip 3-lobed; outer lobes large, rounded ear-like; centre lobe oblong, rounded at the tip, where there is a mass of tiny tubercles; disc with 7 wavy lamellæ and side-lobes with short lamellæ on their upper surfaces. *September and October.*

A tall white-flowered species of considerable decorative value. It is found in conifer and beech woods on the mountains of Chillan and Valparaiso, Central Chile. This plant should prove suitable for outdoor culture in the warmer parts of Great Britain in a shady spot in beech-leaf soil and loam.

131. CHLORÆA FALKLANDICA, Kränzl.

Root: a cluster of thickened fibres. **Stem:** up to 8″ tall, slender, sheath-clothed. **Leaves:** basal and cauline, oblong, pointed, 3″–3½″ long. **Raceme:** of 5 blossoms, lax. **Flowers:** about 1″ across; dorsal sepal oblong, concave, blunt; lateral sepals linear-oblong, narrower than the dorsal sepal, reticulate, thickened at the tip; petals oblong, blunt; lip unguiculate, simple, ovate, blunt, denticulate in the middle of the margin, slightly thickened and concave at the tip; disc with some short lamellæ towards its base, remainder of disc downy. *January.*

A dwarf species, suitable for alpine house cultivation. It has slender sheath-clothed flower-stems terminating in a lax, few-flowered spike of comparatively large green, yellow and white blossoms of considerable decorative value. The plant is found in open pasture land in various parts of East Falkland Island. It should be quite hardy in most parts of Great Britain in an open sunny spot in the rock garden in sandy loam and peat.

132. CHLORÆA FERRUGINEA, Speg.

Root: a cluster of cylindrical fibres 3″–5″ long. **Stem:** 12″–15″ tall, leafy below, sheathed above. **Leaves:** basal, oblong, blunt, 3″–4″ long, degenerating upwards into spatha-like sheaths. **Spike:** 3″–6″ long, loose, few-flowered. **Flowers:** about 2″ across; dorsal sepal erect, lanceolate, pointed; lateral sepals similar but thickened at the tip; petals oblong, pointed, spreading; lip narrow at the base, 3-lobed; outer lobes rounded-oblong, veined; centre lobe oblong, pointed, margin incurved at the tip; disc with 6 sinuous fleshy ridges. *January.*

A curious species with large reddish-brown blossoms and very pale green or white floral bracts. It is found on the shady banks of rivers in Central Patagonia and should be perfectly hardy in Great Britain in a shady part of the bog garden or on the banks of a stream in good rich soil.

133. CHLORÆA FONKII, Phil.

C. gymnoglossa, Phil.

Root: of numerous thickened fleshy fibres of considerable size. **Stem:** 9″–15″ tall, leafy. **Leaves:** linear or linear-lanceolate, erect, pointed, 4″–6″ long, degenerating into bracts among the blossoms. **Spike:** 2″–4″ long, bearing 3–5 blossoms. **Flowers:** about 1″ across; dorsal sepal oblong-lanceolate, pointed; lateral sepals similar but thickened and twisted at the tip; petals oblong, shorter than the sepals, strongly veined; lip ovate-triangular, lower two-thirds with long stalked tubercles on the surface and edges, upper third with numerous thorn-like tubercles on its surface.

December and January.

A comparatively dwarf species with short spikes bearing a few fair-sized green and white blossoms. It is found in evergreen woods near Valdivia and on many of the islands of the Chonos Archipelago, Southern Chile. It should be hardy over the greater part of the kingdom in a shady spot in the rock garden in beech and oak leaf-soil with plenty of sand.

134. CHLORÆA GAUDICHAUDII, Brongn.

Root: of very large finger-like fleshy tubers. **Leaves:** mostly radical, oblong, pointed, sheathing at the base, membranous, 4″–8″ long. **Scape:** 1′–2½′ tall, stout, clothed with several elongate-oblong sheaths. **Spike:** 4″–7″ long, lax, many-flowered. **Flowers:** 1¾″ across; dorsal sepal narrowly ovate, curved over the column; lateral sepals narrowly ovate, tapering into sharp points longer than the dorsal sepal; petals oblong, blunt; lip 3-lobed; outer lobes rounded, fringed; centre lobe oblong, covered with papillæ.

December and January.

A handsome plant with large bright yellow blossoms; the lip is deep yellow or orange with darker spots and green warts on the disc. The foliage is large and handsome, being of a pale blue-green colour tipped brown and spotted near the base with purple. It grows on heaths and in moist places in the Falkland Isles. It may be tried outdoors in the warmer parts of Britain in moist fibrous peat and loam, in full sun.

135. CHLORÆA GRANDIFLORA, Poepp.

Root: a cluster of thick clavate fibres of considerable size. **Stem:** usually under 12″ tall. **Leaves:** mostly basal, oblong-lanceolate, pointed, up to 3″ in length. **Spike:** of about 5 blossoms. **Flowers:** 2″–$2\frac{3}{4}$″ across; dorsal sepal narrowly ovate-oblong; lateral sepals similar, but thickened at the base, with incurved margins, and slightly twisted near the tip; petals oblong, blunt, narrower and shorter than the sepals; lip triangular with rounded corners and a blunt truncate tip, surface covered with rounded calli.

November to January.

A dwarf few-flowered species with short spikes of very large white blossoms of great decorative value. It grows in the subalpine regions of the mountains of the province of Antuco, Central Chile, and should be quite hardy in this country in an open sunny spot in sandy loam and leaf-soil. It should be well supplied with moisture when in full growth.

136. CHLORÆA HEMICHLORIS, Kränzl.

Root: of numerous large club-shaped tubers on thickened fibres. **Stem:** up to $2\frac{1}{2}$′ in height, stout, sheath-clothed. **Leaves:** in the form of spatha-like sheaths. **Spike:** rather dense, of 8–16 blossoms. **Flowers:** about $\frac{3}{4}$″ across; dorsal sepal oblong, pointed; lateral sepals linear, thickened and somewhat twisted at the tip; petals oblong, pointed, warted at the base; lip narrow at the base, oblong, slightly 3-lobed, apex recurved and covered with minute papillæ, surface with numerous stalked tubercles down the centre.

January.

This Patagonian species has a dense many-flowered spike of medium-sized yellowish-white blossoms with numerous green tubercles on the lip. It is found in moist grass land on the Andes of Central Patagonia reaching an elevation of 3000 feet. It should be quite hardy in Great Britain in good rich soil on the banks of a stream or pond.

137. CHLORÆA HOMOPETALA, Phil.

Root: a cluster of much thickened fibres. **Stem:** up to 18″ tall, stout, leafy below, sheathed above. **Leaves:** sheath-like, linear-lanceolate, more or less erect, up to 9″ in length. **Spike:** subcorymbose, of 8–15 blossoms. **Flowers:** about $2\frac{1}{2}$″ long; dorsal sepal oblong; lateral sepals oblong-lanceolate, pointed; petals similar but shorter; lip oblong-lanceolate, pointed, with 2 tiny rounded ear-like lobes at the base where there are 5 short hairy ridges.

November and December.

A very beautiful plant with numerous bright orange-coloured blossoms in a crowded spike. It inhabits rocky places in thin woodland on the mountains of Central Chile, and is frequently found in very arid situations. It should be quite hardy in most parts of the British Isles in a half-shady spot in the garden in sandy leaf-soil and a small portion of fibrous loam.

138. CHLORÆA HOOKERIANA, Speg.

Root: a cluster of thickened fleshy fibres. **Stem:** 9″–10″ tall, leafy below, clothed with a few sheaths above. **Leaves:** basal, oblong-lanceolate, pointed, 2″–3″ long. **Spike:** usually 3-flowered. **Flowers:** about 1½″ across; dorsal sepal linear, blunt; lateral sepals narrower, thickened at the margins; petals oblong, pointed; lip 3-lobed, narrow at the base; outer lobes rounded-oblong, veined; centre lobe narrowly ovate, pointed, with fleshy crenulate ridges down its centre extending to the base of the lip. *October to April.*

A somewhat dwarf species with a stout stem clothed below with a few bright green leaves and terminating in a few-flowered spike of large green and white blossoms. The plant is found in bushy places on stony soils and ranges from Central Chile through Patagonia to Fuegia, and should be quite hardy in this country in a well-drained gravelly soil in a half-shady spot in the rock garden.

139. CHLORÆA INCISA, Poepp.

Root: a cluster of club-shaped tubers on long fibres. **Stem:** 1½′–3′ tall, thick and fleshy, leafy above the base. **Leaves:** oblong or lanceolate, pointed, sheath-like, distant above. **Spike:** 4″–8″ long, usually few-flowered. **Flowers:** about 1½″ across; dorsal sepal oblong-lanceolate, pointed; lateral sepals linear, twisted near the tip, where they are thickened and blunt; petals oblong, blunt, shorter than the sepals; lip unguiculate below, rounded, obscurely 3-lobed; outer lobes rounded; centre lobe ovate with a slightly elevated and sharply-toothed margin; disc with numerous thorn-like tubercles curved and pointed. *December and January.*

A handsome green and white-flowered species of robust habit. It is found in dry almost arid situations in gravelly soil on the Andes from Nahuelbuta to Valdivia in Central Chile and should be hardy in all but the bleakest parts of the Kingdom in an open spot of the rock garden in gravelly soil.

140. CHLORÆA INCONSPICUA, Phil.

Root: of numerous clustered club-like fleshy fibres. **Stem:** about 12″ tall, fairly stout, leafy at the base, sheathed above. **Leaves:** lanceolate, pointed, 2″–2½″ long, degenerating upwards into bracts among the blossoms. **Spike:** of 2–5 blossoms, loose. **Flowers:** about 1⅛″ across; dorsal sepal lanceolate; lateral sepals lanceolate with a long thickened point; petals oblong, pointed, shorter than the sepals; lip oblong, thickened at the tip where the margin is incurved, surface with numerous stalked tubercles and 4 leaf-like lamellæ near the base, which is narrow. *January.*

A dwarf plant with a few-flowered spike of medium-sized pale green or white blossoms with deeper green markings. It is found in shady places on the mountains near Valdivia in Southern Chile. It should prove quite hardy in the warmer parts of Great Britain in a half-shady spot in the rock garden in sandy leaf-soil and loam.

141. CHLORÆA LAGUNÆ PACIS, Kränzl.

Root: a cluster of thickened fibres. **Stem:** about 9″ tall, sheathed. **Leaves:** basal, sheath-like, oblong, pointed, degenerating upwards into close sheaths, 2″–3″ long. **Spike:** subcapitate, few- or many-flowered. **Flowers:** about $\frac{3}{4}$″ across; dorsal sepal lanceolate, pointed; lateral sepals similar, not thickened at the tip but with a thick central nerve; petals lanceolate, reticulate, smaller than the sepals; lip obscurely 3-lobed; outer lobes semi-oblong, margins smooth; centre lobe orbicular, bluntly and strongly toothed on the margin; disc and outer lobes with numerous hooked and blunt tubercles. *November.*

This very dwarf Patagonian plant bears short crowded spikes of fair-sized pure white blossoms of considerable beauty. It inhabits rich lush pastures on the hilly shores of Lake Paz in Patagonia. It may be grown outdoors over the greater part of the Kingdom in a damp open spot in the rock garden in rich fibrous loam.

142. CHLORÆA LECHLERI, Lindl.

Root: a cluster of thick clavate fibres of considerable size. **Stem:** 15″–20″ tall, leafy below, sheathed above. **Leaves:** lanceolate, 2″–3″ long, degenerating upwards into narrow sheaths. **Spike:** of few flowers, rather dense. **Flowers:** about 1″ across; dorsal sepal oblong, pointed; lateral sepal oblong, suboblique, sometimes thickened at the tip, blunt; petals oblong, pointed, base warted, shorter than the sepals; lip oblong, blunt, narrow at the base; disc with 4–5 lines of depressed tubercles. *November.*

A tall somewhat slender species with dense few-flowered racemes of medium-sized yellow blossoms with bright green markings. It inhabits sandy meadows near Valdivia, Central Chile, and should be sufficiently hardy for outdoor culture in the warmer parts of Great Britain in a damp open spot in the rock garden in sandy loam.

143. CHLORÆA LEUCOJIFLORA, Kränzl.

Root: a cluster of thick fleshy fibres. **Stem:** about 9″ tall, rather stout, leafy below. **Leaves:** linear, degenerating upwards into narrow membranous sheaths, 2″–3″ long. **Spike:** lax, of 3–4 blossoms. **Flowers:** about $1\frac{1}{2}$″ across; dorsal sepal oblong, pointed, erect; lateral sepals narrowly oblong; petals linear-oblong, spreading; lip concave, narrow at the base, then slightly dilated broadening out into a lanceolate blade, blunt and slightly bifid at the tip; base with 3 short raised hairy ridges. *November and December.*

A dwarf species suitable for alpine house culture. It has few-flowered spikes of rather large white blossoms with strong green veinings. It is found in conifer and beech woods on the Andes of Chillan, Central Chile. In cultivation it should succeed outdoors in all but the bleakest parts of Great Britain in a half-shady spot in the rock garden in loam and leaf-soil.

144. CHLORÆA LONGIPETALA, Lindl.

Root: a cluster of much thickened fibres. **Stem:** 1′–1¼′ tall, rather stout, leafy below. **Leaves:** mostly basal, oblong, degenerating into oblong sheaths upwards, 3″–4″ long. **Spike:** of 5–8 somewhat crowded blossoms. **Flowers:** about 1¾″ across; dorsal sepal oblong; lateral sepals similar, but thickened at the tip; petals ovate-oblong, blunt, with thickened veins; lip ovate or obovate, slightly eared and narrowed at the base; disc with numerous short lamellæ of various lengths on its surface. *January.*

A beautiful species with large pure white blossoms in rather crowded spikes. It inhabits Araucaria forests on the Andes near Nahuelbuta, Central Chile, and should succeed outdoors in the warmer parts of the British Isles in a half-shady spot in the rock garden in sandy loam and leaf-soil.

145. CHLORÆA MAGELLANICA, Hook.

C. Bougainvilleana, Franch

Root: a cluster of thickened fibres. **Stem:** ¾′–1′ tall, leafy, stout. **Leaves:** cauline, variable, ovate, or ovate-oblong, those on barren shoots narrowly lanceolate or lanceolate-linear, about 4″ long. **Spike:** of 4–7 blossoms, loose. **Flowers:** about 2″ across; dorsal sepal ovate-lanceolate; lateral sepals similar but smaller; petals lanceolate-ovate, pointed, all spreading; lip obscurely 3-lobed; lobes rounded or ovate, crested on the upper surface. *December.*

A handsome and desirable plant with loose spikes of large blossoms with white sepals and petals tessellated with black markings, and a black lip. It is found in evergreen woods on the shores of the Straits of Magellan, Elizabeth Isle, and in Southern and Northern Patagonia. It should be quite hardy throughout the British Isles in a damp shady spot in beech leaf-soil and loam.

146. CHLORÆA MULTIFLORA, Lindl.

C. decipiens, Poepp. *C. Poeppigiana,* A. Rich.

Root: a cluster of club-like fibres of fair size. **Stem:** 9″–15″ tall, leafy below, clothed with 3–4 narrow pointed sheaths above. **Leaves:** lanceolate, pointed, 2″–3″ long. **Spike:** of 6–20 blossoms, rather dense. **Flowers:** about 1″ across; dorsal sepal oblong-lanceolate, pointed; lateral sepals ligulate, thickened at the tip where the margins are incurved; petals oblong, pointed, cuneate at the base; lip shortly unguiculate, variable in shape, simple or 3-lobed; outer lobes rounded; centre lobe oblong or triangular, crenulate; disc with thorn-like tubercles on its surface, frequently becoming leafy lamellæ towards its base. *September to February.*

The blossoms of this species vary from yellow to yellowish-white and pure white, more or less spotted with bright green. It is a very decorative plant, the blossoms being fairly large and numerous. The plant is found in half-shady spots among spare herbage on the mountains of Central Chile and should be hardy in the milder parts of Britain under the same conditions as *C. crispa.*

147. CHLORÆA NERVOSA, Phil.

Root: a cluster of clavate tubers. **Stem:** up to 1¾′ tall, stout. **Leaves:** reduced to a few pointed sheaths. **Scape:** naked below flowers. **Spike:** 3″–6″ long, few or many-flowered. **Flowers:** nearly 1¾″ across; dorsal sepal large, oblong, pointed; lateral sepals linear or narrowly lanceolate, thickened at the tip, reflexed; petals lanceolate, narrow below, with thickened nerves; lip 3-lobed; outer lobes rounded, small; centre lobe large, rounded, notched around the margin; disc with lamellæ of various lengths thickened towards the apex and tapering to the base. *January.*

A very beautiful plant with numerous large blossoms of a bright deep yellow colour with green veins. The plant inhabits sandy pastures and the borders of woods about Valdivia, Central Chile, and should be sufficiently hardy for culture outdoors in the warmer parts of the Kingdom in the rock garden in sandy loam and leaf-soil.

148. CHLORÆA NUDILABIA, Poepp.

Root: of numerous clavate fleshy fibres. **Stem:** ¾′–2¼′ tall, stout, leafy below, clothed with a few sheaths above. **Leaves:** several, oblong-lanceolate, 6″–9″ long. **Spike:** up to 9″ long, of 5–10 flowers. **Flowers:** about 2¼″ across and 2″ long; dorsal sepal oblong or oblong-lanceolate, pointed; lateral sepals similar but thickened at the base and more pointed; petals oblong, smaller than the sepals; lip 3-lobed; outer lobes very small, oblong, blunt; centre lobe ovate-oblong, narrow at the base, blunt at the tip. *January.*

An exceedingly beautiful plant with a tall stem bearing a long raceme of very large orange-coloured blossoms with some dark markings on the lip. It is found in stony places at a considerable elevation on the Andes of Central Chile. It should be quite hardy in Great Britain in an open spot in the rock garden in gritty peat and loam.

149. CHLORÆA PENICILLATA, Reichb. f.

Root: a cluster of thickened fibres. **Stem:** about 12″ tall, rather stout. **Leaves:** mostly basal, sheath-like, narrow, 1½″–2″ long. **Flower:** solitary, about 2″ across and 1¾″ long; sepals ligulate, rather blunt; petals linear, conniving over the column; lip cuneate at the base, then ligulate, dilated and recurved at the tip, densely hairy at the base. *January.*

A rather dwarf species with a moderately stout stem bearing a solitary white or pale yellow blossom of considerable size. It is a native of the country around Orange Harbour, Terra del Fuego, and is usually found in woods. The plant should be quite hardy in Great Britain in a damp half-shady spot in the rock garden in almost pure beech leaf-soil and sand.

150. CHLORÆA PHILIPPII, Reichb. f.

Root: of numerous club-like fleshy fibres. **Stem:** about 12″ tall, leafy at the base, sheathed above. **Leaves:** linear-lanceolate, few, 3″–4″ long. **Scape:** naked below the blossoms. **Spike:** of about 10 blossoms. **Flowers:** about 1″ across; dorsal sepal lanceolate; lateral sepals similar; petals oblong-lanceolate, pointed, conniving; lip narrow at the base, 3-lobed; outer lobes oblong, blunt; centre lobe oblong, rather blunt, with a tiny point; surface covered with numerous depressed tubercles. *November and December.*

A beautiful species of dwarf habit with a crowded spike of medium-sized white blossoms. The plant is found in thin woods on the mountains of the provinces of San Juan, San Jago de Chile and Valdivia, Central Chile. It should be quite hardy in the warmer parts of the Kingdom in a damp shady spot in the rock garden in beech leaf-soil and sand.

151. CHLORÆA PHŒNICEA, Speg.

Root: a cluster of clavate or filiform fleshy fibres 1″–2″ long and ¼″ thick. **Stem:** 2″–4″ tall, stout, smooth. **Leaves:** oblong or oblong-lanceolate, pointed, 2″–2½″ long. **Spike:** usually 2-flowered. **Flowers:** about 1¾″ across; dorsal sepal lanceolate, pointed; lateral sepals lanceolate, subfalcate, pointed; petals lanceolate, smaller than the sepals; lip trowel-shaped, pointed, covered with hooked tubercles and with 3 wavy lamellæ from the base to the middle. *November and December.*

An exquisite plant very suitable for alpine house culture. The very dwarf stem bears two very large blossoms of a bright cinnabar-red colour, well set off by the rich green leaves. It inhabits rocky, volcanic soils on the Andes of Tucuman in the Argentine, reaching an elevation of 9000 feet above sea-level. The plant should be quite hardy in Britain in the rock garden in damp loam and peat, with good drainage.

152. CHLORÆA PIQUICHEN, Lindl.

C. fimbriata, Phil. *Cymbidium virescens*, Willd.

Root: a cluster of much thickened fibres. **Stem:** 15″–20″ tall, stout and fleshy, leafy below, clothed with pointed sheaths above. **Leaves:** oblong, about 3″ long, degenerating into sheaths above. **Spike:** rather short, congested, of about 15 blossoms. **Flowers:** 2″ across; dorsal sepal oblong-lanceolate, concave, pointed; lateral sepals ligulate, twisted and thickened at the tip where they are downy; petals oblong, blunt, with numerous short downy lamellæ towards the base; lip shortly unguiculate, rhomboid or ovate, at times obscurely 3-lobed, margins sharply toothed below the middle; surface more or less covered with hooked tubercles and short hairy lamellæ.

October to January.

A handsome plant with white, or white and green, blossoms spotted with green. It inhabits evergreen beech woods on the mountains of Central Chile and is also found on the shores of Lake Nahuel, Huapi, in Patagonia. It should be more or less hardy in the rock garden in almost pure beech leaf-soil.

153. CHLORÆA PRODIGIOSA, Reichb. f.

C. odontoglossa, A. Rich.

Root: of numerous club-like thickened fibres. **Stem:** 2′–2½′ tall, leafy at the base, clothed with a few sheaths above. **Leaves:** 4–5 in number, linear-lanceolate or linear, 3″–4″ long. **Spike:** 4″–8″ long, laxly many-flowered. **Flowers:** about 1¾″ across; dorsal sepal oblong, pointed; lateral sepals linear, thickened at the tip; petals linear-lanceolate, pointed; lip obscurely 3-lobed or simple, unguiculate below, margins deeply serrate; disc with numerous thread-like tubercles on its upper surface. *February.*

A rather tall species with a loose few-flowered spike of very large white and green blossoms with green markings. The plant is found in evergreen woods in the provinces of Valdivia and Araucania, Central Chile. It should prove quite hardy in the warmer parts of Great Britain in a sheltered shady spot in the rock garden in leaf-soil and loam.

154. CHLORÆA REFLEXA, Phil.

Asarca bidentata, Poepp.

Root: of numerous clustered club-shaped fibres. **Stem:** 1½′–2′ tall, leafy at the base, sheathed above. **Leaves:** 4–5 in number, oblong, pointed, 2″–4″ long. **Spike:** of about 10 blossoms, loose. **Flowers:** about ⅝″ across; dorsal sepal oblong, hooded, blunt; lateral sepals linear, twisted and thickened at the tip; petals reflexed, obliquely rhomboid, with downy nerves; lip obovate, with 2 small tooth-like lobes about the middle, surface with 3 lamellæ in the centre near the base and 2 notched lamellæ on either side reaching nearly to the outer lobes. *December and January.*

This species produces spikes of rather small white and green blossoms on tall stems. It is found in shady places on the Andes of Antuco and Chillan, in Central Chile, and should be quite hardy in this country in a fairly damp half-shady spot in the rock garden in peat, loam and leaf-soil.

155. CHLORÆA RYPALOGLOSSA, A. Rich.

Root: of numerous thickened fibres. **Stem:** up to 2′ tall, stout, leafy. **Leaves:** lanceolate-oblong, pointed, degenerating upwards into sheaths, about 6″ long. **Spike:** at times 9″ long, many-flowered. **Flowers:** about $1\frac{1}{4}''$ across; dorsal sepal lanceolate, pointed; lateral sepals lanceolate at the base, thickened, blunt, and twisted at the tip; petals oblong-lanceolate, pointed; lip 3-lobed; outer lobes oblong, falcate; centre lobe oblong with the margins incurved at the base and tip; disc and centre lobe with 7 wavy lamellæ down their surfaces. *December.*

A beautiful species with tall stems bearing long many-flowered spikes of large white blossoms with green spots. It is found in half-shady places on the Andes of San Jago, Central Chile, and should be hardy in most parts of Great Britain in a fairly damp half-shady spot in the rock garden in loam and leaf-soil.

156. CHLORÆA SCEPTRUM, Reichb. f.

Root: of much thickened fibres of considerable size. **Stem:** up to 3′ tall, sheath-clothed below. **Leaves:** in the form of lanceolate sheaths. **Spike:** up to 12″ long, densely many-flowered. **Flowers:** about $1\frac{1}{2}''$ across; dorsal sepal lanceolate, pointed; lateral sepals similar; petals lanceolate, blunt, shorter than the sepals; lip shortly unguiculate, obscurely 3-lobed; outer lobes semi-oblong; centre lobe triangular, margins with strong blunt teeth; disc furnished with numerous thread-like tubercles. *December.*

A very tall species with long dense spikes of beautiful white blossoms with green markings. It inhabits half-shady places in damp spots on the Andes of the province of O'Higgins, Central Chile. The plant should succeed outdoors in the warmer parts of Great Britain in a damp half-shady spot in good rich loam and leaf-soil.

157. CHLORÆA SEMIBARBATA, Lindl.

C. Besseri, Reichb. f.

Root: a cluster of clavate tubers or thickened fibres. **Stem:** up to 2′ tall, leafy at the base, nearly naked above. **Leaves:** oblong-elliptic or obovate, blunt or shortly pointed, 2″–4″ long. **Spike:** about 4″ long, densely many-flowered. **Flowers:** about 2″ across; dorsal sepal oblong-lanceolate, blunt; lateral sepals linear, slightly thickened at the tip; petals ovate, blunt; lip shortly unguiculate, 3-lobed; outer lobes rounded, bluntly toothed; centre lobe suborbicular, toothed; disc with numerous upcurved thorn-like tubercles. *December.*

A very handsome species with a dense spike of very large blossoms of a rich yellow or orange colour. It is found in half-shady places on the Andes of Central Chile from Chillan to Valdivia. There are two subspecies—*Pearcei* (Kränzl.) with a different lip to the type, and *spectabilis* (Kränzl.) with white blossoms nearly 3 inches across. The type and its forms should be sufficiently hardy for outdoor culture in the warmer parts of the Kingdom in a damp spot in peat loam and leaf-soil.

158. CHLORÆA SPECIOSA, Poepp.

C. Gayana, A. Rich.

Root: a cluster of thickened fibres. **Stem:** 14″–17″ tall, stout, fleshy, leafy at the base, sheathed above. **Leaves:** oblong-lanceolate, pointed, 4″–6″ long, passing into long sheaths upwards. **Spike:** of 2–5 blossoms. **Flowers:** over $3\frac{1}{2}$″ across; dorsal sepal ovate-lanceolate; lateral sepals similar but longer, with a thickened tip, spreading; petals ovate, pointed, shorter than the sepals, reticulate; lip lanceolate, pointed, covered with thorn-like tubercles. *December and January.*

An exceedingly beautiful plant with a stout fleshy stem bearing a short few-flowered spike of very large white blossoms with green markings. There is a beautiful sterile form from Patagonia with rose-coloured veinings on the petals. The type is found in rocky places on the Andes of Central and Southern Chile and also those of Patagonia. The plant and its form should prove quite hardy in Great Britain in the rock garden in a fairly damp half-shady spot in leaf-soil and sandy loam.

159. CHLORÆA ULANTHOIDES, Lindl.

Root: of numerous club-like thickened fibres. **Stem:** $\frac{3}{4}$′–$2\frac{1}{2}$′ tall, stout, leafy below, sheathed above. **Leaves:** mostly basal, oblong or oblong-lanceolate, degenerating upwards into dense sheaths, 3″–8″ long. **Spike:** of 1–5 blossoms. **Flowers:** dorsal sepal ovate-oblong, retuse; lateral sepal linear, connate below; petals oblong-ovate, blunt, shorter than the sepals; lip very broad, 3-lobed; lobes deeply toothed; disc with 5 leaf-like lamellæ on its surface. *November.*

A tall stout species with a few-flowered spikes of large white blossoms with green veins. It is found in half-shady places on the Andes of the provinces of

Valparaiso, O'Higgins and Aconcagua, in Central Chile, and should be quite hardy in the warmer parts of the Kingdom in a damp half-shady spot in peat and leaf-soil.

160. CHLORÆA VERRUCOSA, Phil.

Root: of numerous thickened fibres. **Stem:** 18″–20″ tall, stout, leafy at the base, sheathed above. **Leaves:** lanceolate, pointed, up to 6″ long, degenerating into sheaths upwards. **Spike:** of about 6 erect blossoms. **Flowers:** about 2″ across; dorsal sepal lanceolate, rather pointed; lateral sepals similar but slightly hooked, thickened and twisted near the tip; petals oblong-lanceolate, pointed; lip broadly lanceolate, thickened at the tip, surface and edges lined with stalked tubercles or calli. *November and December.*

The large pale green blossoms of this species are quite ornamental; the tips of the sepals and the lower half of the lip are usually of a much deeper green than the remainder of the blossom. The plant is found in shady places on the Andes of Chillan, Central Chile, and should prove hardy in most parts of Great Britain in a damp shady spot in loam and leaf-soil.

161. CHLORÆA XEROPHILA, Kränzl.

Root: of cylindrical, much thickened fibres, about 2″ long. **Stem:** up to 12″ tall, stout. **Leaves:** cauline, lanceolate, pointed, sheathing, about 5″ long, soon withering. **Spike:** of 2–3 blossoms, crowded. **Flowers:** about $2\frac{1}{2}$″ across; dorsal sepal oblong, erect; lateral sepals narrowly oblong, convolute and thickened at the tip, reflexed; petals broadly ovate-oblong, shortly pointed; lip unguiculate, 3-lobed; outer lobes oblong, blunt, margin slightly thickened; centre lobe broadly oblong, blunt, margin crenulate; disc with 5 rows of crenulate lamellæ. *November.*

This species is closely allied to *C. ferruginea* (Speg.). The large green, white and yellow blossoms are borne on a stout leafy stem in the form of a subcapitate spike. It should prove a very decorative plant in the alpine house or rock garden in sandy loam and peat. The plant is found in arid pastures on the mountains of Patagonia and should be quite hardy in Great Britain.

CIRRHOPETALUM, Lindley

Exceedingly quaint and at the same time very beautiful dwarf evergreen epiphytal plants numbering about 150 species. The root-system consists of a long or short creeping rhizome which produces a number of fleshy fibrous roots. Pseudo-bulbs are usually present, they are scattered over the rhizome and bear one, or very rarely two, rather leathery oblong or lanceolate leaves. The blossoms are usually borne in whorls or umbels, the flowers being carried in a slightly drooping manner, all radiating like the spokes of a wheel from the top of the flexuous flower-stem. In many species the segments are cut and fringed in a most beautiful manner, others are entire and are nearly connate throughout their entire length, and resemble the bill of a duck. They range from China through India and the Malay Archipelago to the Mauritius. In cultivation they may be tried outdoors in Britain in warm humid localities, in a sheltered but light spot. Propagation by division of the pseudo-bulbs and rhizomes and also by seeds.

162. CIRRHOPETALUM BREVIPES, Hook. f.

Root: a long slender scandent suberect rhizome. **Pseudo-bulbs:** narrow, cylindrical, about $1\frac{1}{4}''$ long. **Leaf:** linear-oblong, pointed, 2″ long. **Scape:** $\frac{1}{2}''$–1″ long, clothed with a few minute sheaths. **Umbels:** of 3–4 blossoms. **Flowers:** about 1″ long; dorsal sepal broadly ovate, blunt, very small; lateral sepals falcate-lanceolate, pointed, not connivent; petals broadly ovate, rounded at the tip; lip linear, stalked. *September and October.*

A curious species producing a long slender ascending rhizome from which numerous small pseudo-bulbs, each bearing a solitary, narrow, deep green leaf, are produced; the exceedingly short scapes spring directly from the rhizome and bear three or four beautiful rose-pink blossoms in a cluster. It grows on mossy tree trunks in the Sikkim Himalaya from Yoksum to Jongri, reaching an elevation of 8000 feet above sea-level and should therefore be fairly hardy in Southern and Western Britain. It may be tried in living sphagnum-moss and peat on an apple stump in a warm humid spot.

163. CIRRHOPETALUM EMARGINATUM, Finet.

Root: a creeping rhizome emitting numerous fibrous rootlets. **Pseudo-bulbs:** pear-shaped, fairly crowded. **Leaf:** solitary, linear-ovate, blunt, shortly conduplicate, from the top of the pseudo-bulbs. **Scape:** 4″–6″ tall, naked, springing from the base of the pseudo-bulb. **Flowers:** about $1\frac{1}{4}''$ long, 2–3 in number, from the top of the scape; dorsal sepal cuneate-lanceolate, tip truncate, retuse; lateral sepals oblong, oblique at the base, caudate; petals subquadrate, narrow, erect, shorter than the sepals; lip erect, subtriangular, concave, margins revolute, tip recurved. *November.*

This dainty little Chinese species has short scapes with two to three rather large blossoms tinted with crimson-purple on a pale yellow ground, and are faintly fragrant. It is found on dry trees in shady places on the mountains of Western Yunnan, Western China, at 8000 to 9000 feet above sea-level. It may be tried outdoors in a sheltered position in the warm western counties of Great Britain in half shade on a sandstone rock in fibrous peat and oak leaf-soil.

164. CIRRHOPETALUM TRICHOCEPHALUM, Schltr.

Root: a short rhizome with numerous fibrous rootlets. **Pseudo-bulbs:** cylindrical, about 1″ long, bearing a solitary leaf. **Leaf:** narrowly oblong, blunt, cuneate towards the base, $1\frac{1}{2}$″–$2\frac{1}{2}$″ long. **Scape:** 3″–5″ long, slender, flexuous, clothed with 3–4 small sheaths and bearing numerous blossoms in a close head about $2\frac{1}{2}$″ through. **Flowers:** about 2″ across; dorsal sepal ovate towards the base, tapering from the middle to the tip into a slender tail; lateral sepals similar but oblique; petals ovate, oblique, somewhat blunt; lip oblong, cordate at the base, narrower towards the tip, with a double row of calli on the disc. *June to September.*

A delicate and beautiful plant with numerous quaint white or cream-coloured blossoms in a compact head on a slender stem springing from the base of a pseudo-bulb. The plant is found on moss-covered trees and rocks near Szemao, Western Yunnan, China, from 6000 to 10,000 feet above sea-level. It may be tried outdoors in Great Britain under the same conditions as the preceding species.

165. CIRRHOPETALUM VIRIDIFLORUM, Hook. f.

Root: a fairly stout creeping rhizome. **Pseudo-bulbs:** ovoid, about 1″ long. **Leaves:** 1 or 2, elliptic-lanceolate, rather pointed, 4″–6″ long. **Scape:** about 6″ long, slender. **Raceme:** 2″–4″ long, of many nodding blossoms. **Flowers:** nearly $\frac{3}{4}$″ long; dorsal sepal ovate, pointed, rather small; lateral sepals ovate-lanceolate, pointed, connivent to the tips; petals suborbicular, 1-nerved; lip short, narrowly oblong. *May to August.*

This species differs from those previously described in bearing racemes instead of umbels of blossoms; they are large, pale green throughout, with the exception of the purple lip, and in shape somewhat resemble the bill of a duck. Although of no great decorative value, this plant, like all the half-hardy species of the genus, should prove a most interesting subject for alpine house culture, in a pan of living sphagnum-moss and orchid peat. It grows on trees in the forests in various parts of the Himalaya up to 9000 feet, where it is exposed to 15° or more of frost during the winter.

166. CIRRHOPETALUM WALLICHII, Lindl.

Bulbophyllum muscicola, Reichb. f.

Root: a rather slender creeping rhizome. **Pseudo-bulbs:** varying from subglobose to club-shaped, about 1″ long. **Leaf:** elliptic-oblong, 2″–4″ long. **Scape:** about 6″ long, slender. **Umbels:** of few blossoms. **Flowers:** nearly $1\frac{1}{4}$″ long; dorsal sepal oblong, blunt, 3-nerved; lateral sepals linear-lanceolate, falcately incurved, pointed, 5-nerved, very much longer than the dorsal sepal; petals short, linear, rounded, 3-nerved; lip oblong, rather pointed, very small. *August to October.*

The blossoms of this little species vary from red-brown to yellow, with red markings. It should make a delightful specimen in the alpine house. In a state of nature it grows on mossy tree-trunks and rocks in various parts of the Himalaya from Nepal to Sikkim, attaining an elevation of 9000 feet above sea-level and should therefore be nearly hardy in Western and Southern Britain, in a damp spot on a moist limestone rock in living sphagnum-moss and peat.

CODONORCHIS, Lindley

A genus of but 3 terrestrial herbs with very beautiful blossoms. The root system consists of a branched fleshy underground stem creeping to some distance close to the surface of the soil; the stouter fibres terminate in small rounded tubers which give rise to new plants after the parent plant has perished and after the seeds have been scattered. These small pea-like tubers apparently take more than a year to become sufficiently strong to produce flower-stems. The slender succulent stem is clothed below the middle with a whorl of small rich green somewhat fleshy leaves, and terminates in a solitary blossom of great beauty. The plants are found in a variety of situations in Chile and the Falkland Islands. Protection from frost should be given in the winter by a hand-light. Propagation by imported tubers and by seeds.

167. CODONORCHIS LESSONII, Lindl.

Root: a slender underground stem emitting very short fleshy roots terminating in small pea-like tubers. **Stem:** fairly slender, juicy, clothed with a solitary sheath near the base. **Leaves:** cauline, in a whorl of 2–4, usually 3, broadly ovate, sessile or very shortly stalked, $\frac{1}{2}''$–$1\frac{1}{2}''$ long, situated about 3″ from the ground. **Scape:** with stem 4″–9″ tall, slender, naked, bearing a solitary blossom. **Flower:** $1\frac{1}{2}''$ across, suberect; sepals equal, broadly lanceolate, pointed, slightly concave; petals broadly ovate, blunt, converging, shorter than the sepals; lip entire, broadly lanceolate, margin incurved near the centre; disc and tip dotted with stalked glands or calli. *November and December.*

A delightfully dainty little plant with blossoms bearing a superficial resemblance to a snowdrop; they have white sepals and petals, the latter ornamented with several violet blotches, and a pink or white, yellow-tipped lip. The plant grows in meadows and on heaths in East and West Falkland Islands and, like some of our own Orchids, is plentiful one season and rare the next. Damp sandy peat should form a suitable compost.

168. CODONORCHIS POEPPIGII, Lindl.

Root: of small tubers on thick fleshy roots of varying lengths. **Stem:** stout, fleshy, sheath-clothed near the base. **Leaves:** 3–4 in number, rhomboid-ovate, shortly stalked, 1″–2″ long. **Scape:** with stem 6″–10″ tall, fairly stout, naked, bearing a solitary blossom. **Flower:** about 1½″ across, more or less erect; sepals equal, ovate-lanceolate, concave; petals somewhat similar, blunt, usually converging; lip entire, narrow below, rhomboid-ovate above, pointed, concave, recurved at the tip, centre furnished with numerous clavate glands on the disc. *January.*

A pretty plant with pale green and pink petals and sepals, and a purple lip with yellow and red warts on its upper surface. The plant is found in damp alpine woods on the Andes of Central Chile and should be quite hardy in all but the bleakest parts of the Kingdom, in a shady part of the rock garden, in damp beech leaf-soil and sand.

169. CODONORCHIS SKOTTSBERGII, Kränzl.

Root: of small oval tubers on stout fibres. **Stem:** about 12″ tall, flexuous, somewhat fleshy, rather stout. **Leaves:** 2 in number, subopposite, sessile or shortly stalked, suborbicular, about 1¼″ across, placed some 4″ up the stem. **Flower:** 1¾″ across, solitary, on a naked stem; dorsal sepal ovate-oblong, pointed; lateral sepals similar but narrower; petals ovate, blunt; lip unguiculate, 3-lobed; outer lobes rounded; centre lobe ligulate, blunt; lateral lobes downy; disc furnished with 2 irregular rows of cylindrical tubercles. *February.*

A beautiful Patagonian species with a fairly tall, flexuous stem clothed with two rounded leaves, and terminating in a solitary, slightly nodding, blossom tinted with white, rose and purple. The plant is found in grassy places near the banks of the Rio de las Minas, in Southern Patagonia. It should prove hardy in sheltered localities in Great Britain under the same cultural conditions as *C. Lessonii* (Lindl.).

CŒLOGYNE, Lindley

Beautiful epiphytal plants numbering about 210 species, all of which are evergreen; they have long or short creeping rhizomes with numerous pseudo-bulbs scattered on their surface. From the base of the pseudo-bulbs where they join the rhizome numerous fleshy roots are emitted. The leaves are usually solitary and spring from the top of the pseudo-bulbs; the bracts are long and are frequently conspicuous, in some species they are deciduous. The blossoms are generally produced in racemes which are frequently of considerable length, arching or pendulous; in a few species the blossoms are but two or three in number. The species described in the following pages are usually

PLATE 5.

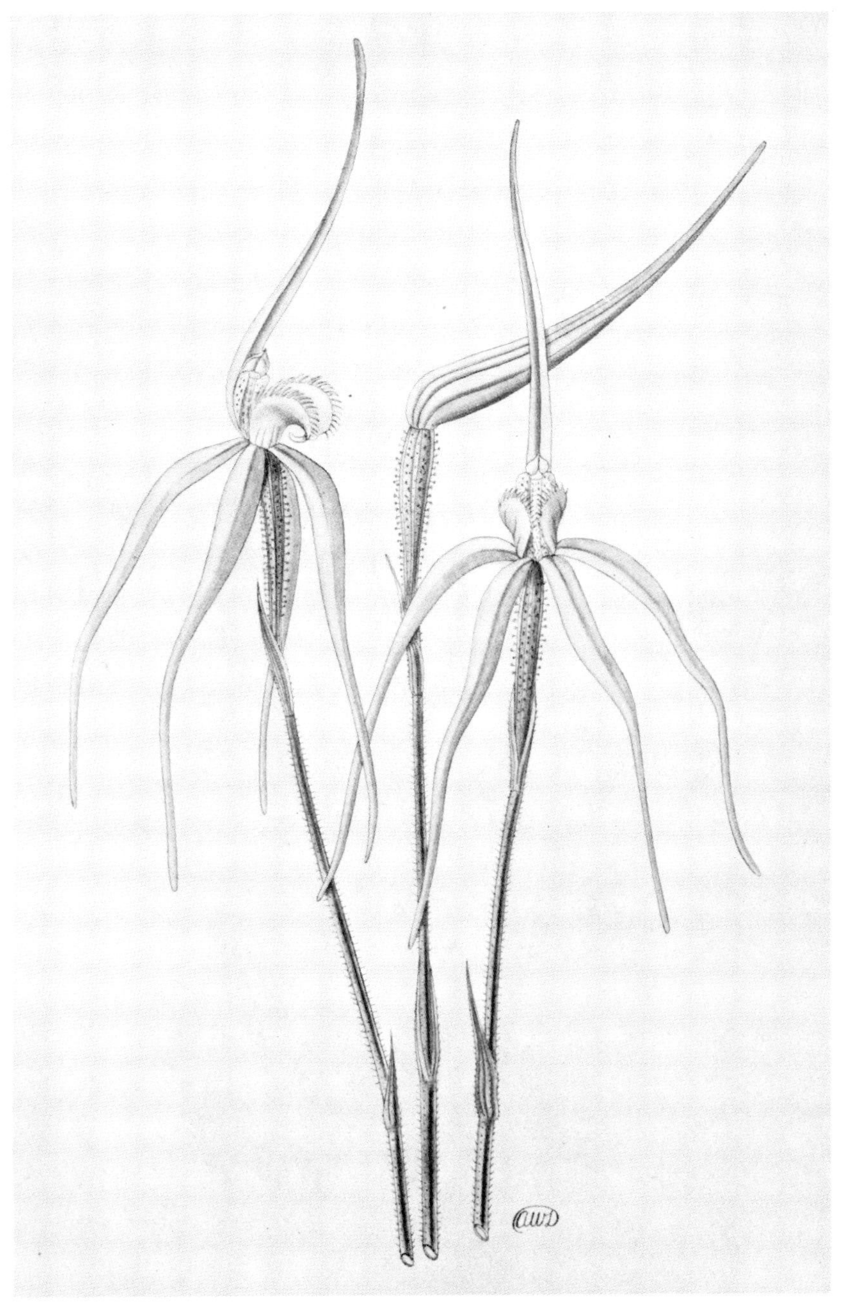

CALADENIA PATERSONII.

PLATE 6.

CŒLOGYNE CORYMBOSA.

found in living moss and vegetable debris on the branches of oaks, birches and rhododendrons, though at times they may be found on mossy rocks, and even on the ground. The plants are confined to Eastern Asia and are propagated by separation of the pseudo-bulbs with a portion of the rhizome.

170. CŒLOGYNE CORYMBOSA, Lindl.

Root: a rather stout creeping rhizome. **Pseudo-bulbs:** ovoid or subrhomboid, crowded, over 1½″ long. **Leaves:** elliptic-lanceolate, 4″–8″ long. **Scape:** 6″–12″ long, sheath-clothed to the first blossom. **Raceme:** long, erect or drooping, many-flowered. **Flowers:** nearly 3½″ across; sepals lanceolate, pointed; petals narrowly lanceolate, pointed; lip large, 3-lobed, but at times variable; outer lobes erose; centre lobe ovate or ovate-lanceolate; disc with 3 low ridges. *June and July.*

An exceedingly beautiful species producing a long crowded raceme of large fragrant blossoms. The sepals, petals and lip are pure white, the latter has four golden "eyes" bordered with orange and there are sometimes red markings on the side lobes. It grows on mossy trees and rocks in the Khasia Hills and Himalaya, frequently reaching an elevation of 11,000 feet; plants collected from such an altitude should be quite hardy in Great Britain on a mossy rock of tree fern stump, in a humid spot.

171. CŒLOGYNE OCHRACEA, Lindl.

Root: a creeping rhizome. **Pseudo-bulbs:** 1″–1½″ long, oblong, polished, crowded. **Leaves:** from tops of pseudo-bulbs, elliptic-lanceolate with fairly long stalks, 4″–7″ long. **Scape:** about 9″ long, erect or drooping. **Raceme:** bearing 6–8 blossoms. **Flowers:** about 1¾″ across; sepals linear-oblong, pointed; petals narrowly lanceolate; lip 3-lobed; outer lobes serrulate; centre lobe broadly ovate, pointed, base serrulate; disc 2-ridged. *May.*

A very handsome species closely resembling *C. corymbosa.* It has racemes of white blossoms with variable confluent orange, yellow and brown markings on the lip. The flower-stems spring from the undeveloped pseudo-bulbs beside the old ones. It grows on trees and moss-covered rocks on the Himalaya from Kumaon to Upper Assam and reaches an elevation of 9000 feet, where it is exposed to nearly 15° of frost during the winter. It may be tried outdoors in mild humid localities in a half-shady spot on a damp sandstone rock, in living sphagnum-moss and fibrous peat.

172. CŒLOGYNE ODORATISSIMA, Lindl.

C. angustifolia, A. Rich. *C. trifida*, Reichb. f.

Root: a creeping rhizome. **Pseudo-bulbs:** very variable, usually small, globose or ovoid, with hyaline sheaths. **Leaves:** from the apex of the pseudo-bulbs, elliptic-lanceolate, membranous, 2″–3″ long. **Scape:** springing from both the developed and undeveloped pseudo-bulbs, slender, 6″–9″ long. **Raceme:** of 2–3 flowers. **Flowers:** about $1\frac{1}{2}$″ across, sepals oblong-lanceolate, pointed; petals lanceolate; lip 3-lobed; outer lobes falcate-oblong, blunt; centre lobe orbicular, large; disc 3-ridged. *October to December.*

A delightful, sweet-scented species with a few-flowered raceme of large white blossoms with a yellow disc to the lip. It grows on the branches of large trees and moss-covered rocks in the forests on the Nilghiri Hills of Southern India at 8000 feet above sea-level and should therefore be sufficiently hardy for culture outdoors in the warmer parts of Great Britain, in sheltered humid spots on a sandstone rock in living sphagnum-moss and fibrous peat.

CORALLORHIZA, R. Brown

A genus containing about 20 species of leafless deciduous plants. They are terrestrial, and their roots resemble small pieces of coral; their erect reddish-brown or purple stems are clothed with a few small sheaths and terminate in a rather loose spike of few or many flowers; these are usually pink, purple and white, and are of no decorative value. The plants are known as Coral Roots in their native countries, and are saprophytes, living on the decaying remains of other plants. They usually inhabit moist shady places such as woods and thickets, and are frequently found in pinewoods. In introducing plants into the garden as large a portion as possible of the soil in which they are growing should be taken with the roots *in situ*, as the mycelium or white thread-like roots of the various fungi which are usually present in such soils may have something to do with their successful cultivation. Propagation by division of the roots.

173. CORALLORHIZA CORALLORHIZA, Karst.

C. innata, R. Br. *C. trifida*, Chatel. *C. Jacquemontii*, Dcne.

Root: a jointed coral-like rhizome. **Leaves:** reduced to a few sheathing scales. **Scape:** 4″–12″ tall, erect, slender. **Raceme:** 1″–4″ long, few-flowered. **Flowers:** about $\frac{1}{4}$″ long; sepals narrowly lanceolate to ovate-lanceolate, lateral ones deflexed; petals linear or linear-lanceolate, incurved, ascending; lip oblong, usually 3-lobed; outer lobes narrow, tooth-like; centre lobe retuse or pendulous, notched or toothed at the apex. *May to July.*

Like the greater number of its genus, this plant, though interesting, is devoid of any decorative value. The leafless stems and sheaths vary from pale yellow and light brown to pale purple in colour and are at times slightly tinged with green below. The blossoms vary from yellowish-green to dull purple, usually with a white lip blotched with purple. It grows among decaying leaves in damp woods in North America as far south as Georgia, and in Europe from Northern Italy to the Arctic regions and in Northern Asia as far south as Kashmir. The plant should be transferred to the rock garden with a large portion of the compost in which it is growing; it requires shade and moisture. The variety *ericetorum* has small yellowish-green blossoms.

174. CORALLORHIZA MERTENSIANA, Bong.

Root: a large coral-like rhizome. **Leaves:** reduced to a few small scales. **Stem:** 8″–16″ tall, rather slender, erect. **Raceme:** 2″–6″ long, laxly many-flowered. **Flowers:** about $\frac{3}{8}$″ long; dorsal sepal narrowly lanceolate, erect; lateral sepals similar but deflexed; petals linear, pointed; lip narrowly oblong, entire, with two small teeth at the base, where it narrows into a stalk; spur, stout, cylindrical, with upper half joined to the ovary, about $\frac{3}{16}$″ long.

July.

A very deeply-tinted species with a slender, dark red or purple stem and a long, many-flowered raceme of dull deep red blossoms. It is a curiosity, but of little decorative value, and grows in pine and spruce woods in Western North America from California to Alaska. It should be quite hardy in this country, in soil from a coniferous wood, planted in the shade of evergreen trees.

175. CORALLORHIZA MULTIFLORA, Nutt.

C. innata, Nutt.

Root: resembling a piece of coral. **Leaves:** reduced to a few lanceolate or linear scales. **Scape:** 8″–20″ tall, stout, usually erect. **Raceme:** 2″–8″ long, of 9 to 30 blossoms. **Flowers:** about $\frac{3}{8}$″ long; sepals linear or linear-oblong; petals oblong, shorter than the sepals; lip oblong, crenulate, 3-lobed; lobes rounded; column winged below. *July to September.*

This species produces a greater number of blossoms than any other member of the genus. The tall deep purple stem, with its long many-flowered spike of pale purple blossoms and conspicuous white, purple-spotted lips, is quite attractive. *C. occidentalis* is a slight variety from Western North America. The type and its form grow in decaying leaves and twigs in damp shady woodlands from Newfoundland to British Columbia and southward in the United States to Missouri and California. It should be quite hardy in Great Britain in a damp shady spot in the rock garden in decaying vegetable matter.

176. CORALLORHIZA ODONTORHIZA, Nutt.

Cymbidium odontorhizon, Pursh. *Ophrys corallorhiza*, Michx.

Root: composed of a number of short fleshy fibres, coral-like in shape. **Leaves:** reduced to several sheathing scales on the stem. **Scape:** 4″–12″

tall and at times zig-zag. **Raceme:** 1½″–4″ long, bearing from 10–20 flowers. **Flowers:** about 3/16″ long; sepals linear or linear-spathulate; petals broadly linear, about as long as the sepals; lip obovate or ovate-obovate, entire or irregularly toothed, contracted at the base, about as long as the petals; column with narrow wings. *July to September.*

This curious plant produces a leafless sheath-clothed stem of a light or deep purple colour throughout, and a fairly close raceme of very small pinkish-purple or dark purple blossoms, of but little decorative value. The plant, like all the other members of the genus, is a saprophyte, being found in moist shady woods growing in decaying leaves and twigs. It ranges from Massachusetts to Michigan and southward to Florida and Missouri. It should be quite hardy in Great Britain in a damp shady spot in the rock garden in decaying oak and beech leaves.

177. CORALLORHIZA STRIATA, Lindl.

C. Macraei, Gray

Root: a short, thick cluster of coral-like fibres. **Leaves:** reduced to a few narrow sheathing bracts. **Scape:** 9″–18″ tall, stout, nearly erect. **Raceme:** 2″–6″ long, many-flowered, lax. **Flowers:** about ½″ long, drooping; sepals and petals narrowly elliptic, spreading; lip ovate or obovate, usually entire, undulate, somewhat narrowed at the base, about as long as the petals; spur almost obsolete. *July and August.*

A stout robust species with purple flower-stems and racemes of from ten to twenty-five dull purple and brownish-crimson blossoms, very quaint but of no decorative value. It is found in damp woods, swampy places, rocky ground and bogs on the top of lofty mountains. It is spread over the whole of Canada and the United States as far south as New York, Michigan, Oregon and California. It may be grown in a damp shady part of the rock garden, in leaf-soil and moss.

178. CORALLORHIZA WISTERIANA, Conrad

Root: coral-like, branching; **Leaves:** reduced to several linear sheathing scales. **Scape:** 6″–15″ tall, erect or slightly zig-zag. **Raceme:** 1¼″–4″ long, of 6–15 flowers. **Flowers:** about ½″ long; sepals and petals subequal, linear or linear-lanceolate; lip broadly ovate, truncate, notched at the tip, narrowed into a stalk at the base; column strongly 2-winged at its base. *February to May.*

This species has rather larger blossoms than most of its brethren; the stem and sheaths are light or dark purplish-brown and the blossoms are purplish-pink with a white, crimson-spotted lip. It is an interesting though not very showy plant. In its native habitat it grows among decaying leaves in damp shady woods from Massachusetts to Ohio and southward to Florida and Texas. It should be quite hardy in Great Britain in a damp shady spot in the rock garden in decaying leaves.

CORYSANTHES, R. Brown

Nematoceras, Hook. **Calcearia,** Blume. **Corybas,** Salisb.

Very dwarf fragile deciduous terrestrial plants of weak habit. They number about 60 species, with creeping fleshy fibrous roots or underground stems terminating in small pea-like tubers which are quite numerous when the plants are in a healthy condition. The slender translucent stems are clothed near the middle with a rounded, stalked or sessile leaf, solitary, like the blossoms, which are quite large considering the size of the plant. The lip is very beautiful and is usually like the shell of a Nautilus, whilst the sepals and petals are very long and almost bristle-like. The flower-stalk lengthens considerably as the capsule ripens. The plants are found in damp shady spots either growing in moss on tree trunks or rocks, or in pure leaf-soil surfaced by moss, in New Zealand, Tasmania, Australia, the East Indian Islands and New Guinea. Propagation by imported tubers and by seeds, which are freely produced.

179. CORYSANTHES FIMBRIATA, R. Br.

C. pruinosus, Reichb. f. *Corybas fimbriatus*, Reichb. f.

Root: of small irregular tubers on fleshy, white fibres. **Stem:** about $1\frac{1}{2}''$ tall, translucent. **Leaf:** solitary, cauline, orbicular-cordate, about $1''$ in diameter. **Flower:** solitary, terminal, about $\frac{3}{4}''$ across; dorsal sepal, hooded, fairly large; lateral sepals and petals linear, small; lip shell-like, very concave, with inflexed, fringed margins; disc hairy down its centre.

July to September.

A tiny little plant rarely more than 2 inches in height, with a shell-like blossom, surrounded by a solitary pale green, somewhat fleshy leaf. It is too small to make much show in the rock garden, but should prove a very interesting addition to the alpine house, where its exquisite blossom may be examined more readily. In colour the blossom varies from deep red to violet-purple, with green shadings on the dorsal sepal. It is found in damp woods growing in moss on the surface of the soil in New South Wales, Victoria, Southern and Western Australia and Tasmania, and is exposed to 12° of frost for short periods during the winter. A rich leaf-soil in a moist shady spot is indicated.

180. CORYSANTHES MACRANTHA, Hook. f.

Nematoceras macrantha, Hook. f.

Root: of small tubers on stoutish fibres. **Stem:** fairly stout. **Leaf:** long stalked, solitary, oblong-orbicular, cordate or 2-lobed at the base, blunt, with a broad, thickened margin. **Scape:** 6″–10″ tall. **Flower:** solitary, about 3″ across, on short scape at the base of the petiole; dorsal sepal narrow and pointed; lateral sepals and petals very narrowly linear, almost filiform, 1″–2″ long; lip very broad, recurved, almost 2-lobed, strongly undulate.

October to December.

An extremely quaint and interesting plant (quite a little gem for the alpine house) with a fleshy, beautifully reticulated bright green leaf, translucent stems, and lurid purple blossoms, with a shell-like lip and spider-like sepals and petals; it is not uncommon in damp shady woods in the central part of the Northern Island and the whole of the South Island of New Zealand and the Auckland Islands. It should be hardy in South-Western Britain, and may be given a damp shady spot in almost pure leaf-soil and sand.

181. CORYSANTHES OBLONGA, Hook. f.

Nematoceras oblonga, Hook. f.

Root: of small tubers on long fleshy fibres. **Stem:** very slender, translucent, 2″ tall. **Leaf:** solitary, ovate-oblong, at times subcordate at the base, sessile, membranous, $\frac{3}{4}$″–1$\frac{1}{2}$″ long. **Flower:** solitary, $\frac{3}{4}$″ across; dorsal sepal narrowly linear; lateral sepals very narrowly linear; petals filiform; lip involute, broadly truncate, with a toothed margin.

September to November.

A very beautiful and delicate little plant, with a rich green leaf, like that of the Lesser Celandine, and a curious solitary flower of a lurid purple colour with a deep blood-red lip. A gem for the alpine house. It inhabits damp somewhat shady places in numerous localities in the North Island, and woods near Nelson and Otago in the South Island of New Zealand, and should prove hardy in the warmer parts of the Kingdom. It may be tried in damp leaf-soil and peat, in a shady part of the rock garden.

182. CORYSANTHES RIVULARIS, Hook. f.

Nematoceras rivularis, Hook. *Acianthus rivularis*, Hook. f.

Root: of small oblong tubers on stout fibres. **Stem:** 2″ tall, slender and translucent. **Leaf:** solitary, orbicular-ovate or ovate-cordate, often 2-lobed at the base, membranous, $\frac{3}{4}$″–1$\frac{1}{4}$″ across. **Flower:** 1″ across, solitary; dorsal sepal narrowly linear, pointed; lateral sepals narrowly linear or filiform;

petals filiform, $1\frac{1}{2}''$ long; lip involute, trowel-shaped, with undulate margins, recurved. *September to December.*

This little plant produces a large blossom for the size of its growth; it is of a reddish or lurid purple colour throughout. The bristle-like sepals reach a length of $1\frac{1}{2}''$ and project from the blossoms like the antennæ of an insect. It grows in moss on rocks and tree trunks, usually in shady ravines, throughout New Zealand, and is also found in the Auckland Islands. It should prove quite hardy in the warmer parts of Great Britain. It may be tried in the rock garden in a damp shady spot, on a moist moss-covered rock.

183. CORYSANTHES ROTUNDIFOLIA, Hook. f.

Nematoceras rotundifolia, Hook. f.

Root: of very small tubers on the ends of long fibres. **Stem:** very slender, translucent, $1''$–$1\frac{1}{2}''$ tall. **Leaf:** solitary, orbicular, cordate or 2-lobed at the base, sessile or shortly stalked, membranous, $\frac{1}{3}''$–$1''$ in diameter. **Flower:** solitary, $\frac{1}{3}''$ across, subsessile; dorsal sepal narrowly linear; lateral sepals very narrowly linear; petals filiform; lip involute, broadly truncate, with its margin coarsely toothed. *September to December.*

But for the more rounded leaf and smaller size, this quaint little species differs but very little from *C. oblonga*. The singular blossom is of a reddish-purple colour throughout and is almost stemless. All members of the genus should make very interesting plants for the alpine house. It grows in moss on tree trunks in woods in several parts of the North Island and at Nelson in the South Island of New Zealand; it is also found in the Auckland and Campbell Islands and is sufficiently hardy for culture outdoors in the warmer parts of Great Britain. Culture as for the foregoing species.

184. CORYSANTHES TRILOBA, Hook. f.

C. hypogæa, Col. *Nematoceras triloba*, Hook. f.

Root: of 2 small ovoid or oblong tubers on long fleshy fibres. **Stem:** $4''$–$8''$ tall, clothed with 1 leaf below the middle. **Leaf:** reniform or orbicular, more or less distinctly 3-lobed at the tip, centre-lobe pointed, cordate at the base, $\frac{1}{2}''$–$2''$ long. **Flower:** solitary, $\frac{1}{2}''$–$2''$ long; dorsal sepal obovate-spathulate, concave, narrow below; lateral sepals filiform, long; petals similar but narrower; lip shaped like the Nautilus shell with an undulate and recurved margin and a reflexed tip. *October to December.*

This comparatively large species should prove an interesting addition to the alpine house in a deep pan of fibrous peat, leaf-soil and sphagnum-moss. It is found in damp shady places mostly in wooded country in the North and South Islands of New Zealand and also Stewarts Island and reaches an elevation above sea-level of over 2000 feet. It should prove hardy in most parts of Great Britain under the same conditions as *C. fimbriata.*

CREMASTRA, Lindley

Hyacinthorchis, Blume

This genus contains four species of beautiful deciduous plants of terrestrial habit, with a large sessile tuber at the base of the flower-stem, being replaced annually by a fresh tuber, the old one perishing as soon as the seeds are perfected. The stout flower-stem is clothed at its base with a few large deeply-veined leaves, somewhat rounded in shape; the remaining part of the stem is clothed with several sheaths and ends in a spike or raceme of Hyacinth-like blossoms, all facing one way. The species are found in India, China, and Japan in shady situations. They may be grown outdoors in the milder parts of the Kingdom in shady spots of the rock garden or choice border, in good rich rather moist soil. They may be increased by division of the roots in strong specimens, and by seeds. The tubers should be planted at least 6 inches below the surface of the soil; protection from frost is desirable.

185. CREMASTRA LANCEOLATA, Schltr.

Pogonia lanceolata, King

Root: an irregular tuber. **Leaves:** subradical, lanceloate or ovate-lanceolate, plicate, almost sessile, 4″–8″ long. **Scape:** 1′–1½′ tall, stout, sheath-clothed. **Raceme:** 4″–6″ long, loose, many-flowered. **Flowers:** about 1″ long, usually more or less secund and nodding; sepals and petals united to the middle, forming a globular tube, with the 5 segments free towards the tip, where they are recurved; lip narrow, 3-lobed at the tip; lobes pointed; disc with a pointed appendage in its centre. *June and July.*

This Orchid has fairly long rather loose spikes of purple and green blossoms of some decorative value. It inhabits thin woodlands and other shady places in the Eastern Himalaya and Western Yunnan and Szechuan, Western China. It should be quite hardy in the warmer parts of the Kingdom in a sheltered shady spot in good leaf-soil and sand.

186. CREMASTRA MITRATA, A. Gr.

C. appendiculata, Makino. *C. Wallichiana*, Miq.

Root: a small irregular tuber. **Leaves:** basal, elliptic-ovate or elliptic-lanceolate, plicate, stalked, 4″–8″ long. **Scape:** 9″–15″ tall, fairly stout, sheath clothed. **Raceme:** 3″–5″ long, loosely many-flowered. **Flowers:** ¾″ long, secund; sepals and sepals united to the middle, forming a narrow tube, with the segments free, pointed and recurved at the tip; lip shallowly 3-lobed; lobes pointed; disc with a linear, pointed appendage. *June and July.*

This species is more dwarf and slender than the other members of the genus. The tubular purple blossoms are borne in many-flowered spikes and are quite decorative. It is found in shady places, usually in woodlands, over the whole of Japan from Yeso to Sikok, and should be quite hardy in Great Britain in a shady spot in the rock garden in good rich leaf-soil and sand.

187. CREMASTRA UNGUICULATA, Finet.

Oreorchis unguiculata, Finet.

Root: a short rhizome emitting numerous white fleshy roots. **Pseudo-bulbs:** erect, tuberous, ovoid or ovoid-globose, about 1″ long. **Leaves:** 2 in number, from the tip of the pseudo-bulbs, broadly lanceolate or oblong-lanceolate, about 6″ long, narrowing below into a short stalk. **Scape:** erect, up to about 18″ in length, clothed with 2 sheaths. **Raceme:** erect, of about 7–10 blossoms, 4″–6″ long. **Flowers:** about $1\frac{1}{2}$″ across; dorsal sepal linear-spathulate, tapering towards the apex; lateral sepals similar, slightly falcate; petals linear-spathulate, very slightly curved; lip deeply divided into 3 lobes; outer lobes linear-ligulate; centre lobe rhomboid-panduliform, margin minutely toothed. *June.*

A rather handsome species with brownish-yellow, purple-spotted blossoms with a white lip. It is found in half-shady places on the mountains of Yezo and Nippon, Japan, and should be perfectly hardy in Great Britain, in a damp half-shady spot in fibrous peat, leaf-soil and loam.

188. CREMASTRA WALLICHIANA, Lindl.

Hyacinthorchis variabilis, Blume

Root: an irregular tuber about 1″ in diameter. **Leaves:** radical, elliptic, plicate, shortly stalked, 6″–10″ long. **Scape:** 1′–2′ tall, stout, clothed with loose sheaths. **Raceme:** of fairly numerous, secund, pendulous blossoms. **Flowers:** about $1\frac{1}{2}$″ long, tubular; sepals and petals joined into a tube below, spreading and recurved above; lip linear, erect, dilated at the tip into 3 linear lobes, subsaccate at its base; disc with a tongue-shaped appendage in its centre. *July to August.*

The long purple Hyacinth-like blossoms are produced in racemes on tall, stout sheath-clothed stems, clothed at the base with a few broad leaves. It is found in shady woods from the Himalaya to Japan and should be perfectly hardy in all but the bleakest parts of Great Britain, in a damp shady portion of the rock garden, in a compost of fibrous loam and leaf-soil.

CRYPTOSTYLIS, R. Brown

Handsome deciduous terrestrial plants usually of robust habit. Their root system consists of a much thickened coral-like mass of white fleshy fibres near the surface of the soil. The erect flower-stems are clothed at their base with a few rather narrow deeply-veined leaves, and a few leaf-like sheaths higher up. The blossoms, which are rather handsome, are usually red and green, and quite large and decorative; they are borne in loose few-flowered spikes. The genus contains about 22 species native from Tasmania and Australia, through the Malayan Islands to Eastern India, only one of which is sufficiently hardy for culture outdoors in Britain. It should be given a sheltered spot and the roots must be protected from prolonged frost. Propagation by imported tubers and also by seeds when procurable.

189. CRYPTOSTYLIS LONGIFOLIA, R. Br.

C. subulata, Reichb. f. *Malaxis subulata*, Labille.

Root: a rhizome from which a few fleshy roots spring. **Leaves:** radical leaf-blade oblong or lanceolate, 2″–4″ long; petiole rigid, stout, 1″–3″ long. **Scape:** 1′–2′ tall, clothed with a few sheathing scales. **Spike:** 4″–8″ long, loose. **Flowers:** about $1\frac{3}{4}$″ across; dorsal sepal lanceolate, with incurved margins; lateral sepals narrowly lanceolate, with incurved margins; petals similar to the lateral sepals, pointed; lip broadly oblong or ovate-oblong, margins reflexed and with 2 small calli near the tip. *February.*

A very handsome robust plant, producing a stout stem terminating in a long spike of about half-a-dozen large, pale green and deep crimson blossoms placed upside down on their stalks. Two or three bright green spear-shaped leaves clothe the base of the stem. It grows in moist and swampy places on the mountains, as well as the lowlands, of the whole of Eastern Australia from Queensland to Tasmania and is exposed to 20° or more of frost for short periods during the winter. A rich soil on the banks of a pond or stream is indicated.

CYMBIDIUM, Swartz

A fairly large genus of handsome and popular Orchids numbering about 110 species. The majority are evergreen epiphytal plants (very few are terrestrial) and these are found on moss- and fern-clad rocks. The root system is well developed and consists of a short, stout stock and a tuft of thick fleshy roots. The stem is usually very short and is rarely elongated into a pseudobulb; it produces a tuft of long, narrow arching leaves and long, usually many-flowered, racemes of large blossoms of a decorative nature. The few species enumerated in the following pages may be tried outdoors, in very sheltered humid localities in the western counties of Britain, with reasonable hope of success, as they are found at high elevations in their native mountains, being exposed to occasional temperatures of 22° F. during the winter season. They are scattered over the tropical and sub-tropical regions of Asia and Africa. Propagation by division of large clumps and by seeds.

190. CYMBIDIUM FORRESTII, Rolfe

Root: a stout fleshy rhizome. **Leaves:** 6–7 in number, tufted, narrowly linear, minutely denticulate, 12″–15″ long. **Scape:** 6″–9″ long, clothed with a few sheaths. **Flowers:** 1–2 in number, from sheaths near the apex of the stem, about 1½″ across; dorsal sepal oblong, rather blunt; lateral sepals oblong, all spreading; petals similar, spreading; lip 3-lobed; outer lobes suborbicular, rounded at the tip; centre lobe suborbicular, undulate, concave. *February and March.*

This species has narrow grass-like leaves and short flower-stems clothed with sheathing bracts and terminating in one or two green or yellowish-green blossoms of no great decorative value. It is found in dry rocky pinewoods in Yunnan, South-Western China, at elevations up to 9000 feet, and should prove hardy in all but the bleakest parts of the Kingdom in a well-drained half-shady spot in the rock garden, in soil collected from beneath conifers.

191. CYMBIDIUM GRANDIFLORUM, Griff.

C. giganteum, Lindl. *C. Hookerianum*, Reichb. f.

Root: a cluster of stout fibres. **Stem:** very short and stout. **Leaves:** basal, broadly linear, ¾′–2′ long. **Scape:** 1′–3½′ tall, stout, usually decurved, clothed with loose deeply grooved sheaths. **Raceme:** lax, few-flowered. **Flowers:** about 4″ across, sepals and petals oblong-lanceolate, pointed; dorsal sepal incurved, lateral sepals reflexed; lip 3-lobed; outer lobes rounded, erect; centre lobe suborbicular, waved, crenate, ciliate; disc with 2 hairy crests between the side lobes. *August to October.*

A very handsome species with tufts of long sedge-like foliage and drooping racemes of from six to twelve very large sweet-scented blossoms with pale or yellowish-green sepals and petals, and a yellow or yellowish-green lip marked with red or brown. The plant is found in thickets and forests of mixed evergreen and deciduous trees, epiphytal on the branches of oaks, etc., in the Himalaya, and mountains of Western China, up to 9000 feet above sea-level. It may be tried outdoor in the warm western counties of the Kingdom in a sheltered spot on the branches of an oak, in vegetable debris, or under the same conditions as *C. longifolium*.

192. CYMBIDIUM LANCIFOLIUM, Hook. f.

C. Gibsonii, Paxt. *C. javanicum*, Blume.

Root: a tuft of very long thick and spongy fibres. **Stem:** 2″–6″ tall, fleshy, fusiform, almost pseudo-bulbus. **Leaves:** elliptic-lanceolate, on long slender stalks, 6″–10″ long. **Scape:** 4″–8″ tall, flexuous, bearing a few blossoms. **Flowers:** about 2″ across; sepals lanceolate, pointed; petals broadly lanceolate, pointed; lip 3-lobed; outer lobes narrow; centre lobe ovate, blunt; disc with 2 crests between the outer lobes. *July to September.*

A pretty dwarf species with a tuft of broad foliage and drooping spikes of about eight blossoms with green, yellow or white sepals, white petals with a pink midrib and a white lip spotted with red-purple. It grows in forest country in a variety of situations, on trees and moss-covered rocks, and in rich vegetable soils beneath the shade of trees, from Java, Malaya, Burma, Eastern India to China and Japan. It may be tried in the outdoor garden in the warmer parts of Britain, in a humid shady spot in the rock garden on a bank of lumpy fibrous loam and peat surfaced with growing sphagnum-moss.

193. CYMBIDIUM LONGIFOLIUM, Don.

C. erythrœum, Lindl. *Limodorum angustifolium*, Ham.

Root: a tuft of thick fleshy fibres. **Stem:** very short. **Leaves:** basal, narrowly linear, pointed, 2′–3′ long. **Scape:** 1′–2′ tall, suberect or recurved. **Raceme:** many-flowered, usually drooping. **Flowers:** about 2½″ across; sepals and petals linear-oblong or lanceolate, pointed; lip 3-lobed; outer lobes rounded erect; centre lobe broadly ovate or orbicular; disc covered with fine hairs. *July and August.*

A handsome robust species with a well-developed tuft of grass-like leaves and drooping flower-stems bearing many large fragrant flowers with pale green sepals and petals streaked with red or purple and a white or yellowish-green lip spotted with red. It grows on ledges and clefts in cliffs in wooded ravines in the Himalaya and South-Western China, reaching an elevation of 9000 feet in China. It may be tried outdoors in the warmer western and southern counties in a shady sheltered part of the rock garden in fibrous loam, peat, sand and small pieces of limestone.

194. CYMBIDIUM PUMILUM, Rolfe

Root: a cluster of thick fleshy fibres. **Pseudo-bulbs:** small, oval, bearing 3–5 leaves. **Leaves:** elongate-linear, rather pointed, recurved, 6″–12″ long. **Raceme:** 4″–5″ long, suberect, clothed at its base by a few lanceolate sheaths, many-flowered. **Flowers:** about 1¼″ across; sepals spreading, oblong, blunt;

petals narrowly elliptic-oblong, subconniving, rather blunt; lip suberect, 3-lobed; lateral lobes erect, oblong, blunt; centre lobe oblong, blunt, recurved; disc deeply grooved, with 2 obscure ridges down its centre. *August.*

A desirable species with long, deeply-grooved, grass-like foliage and short racemes of large blossoms with reddish-brown, yellow-margined sepals and petals, and a white lip with a bright yellow disc, there are a few reddish-brown spots on the centre lobe and some minute ones on the outer lobes. It is found on damp limestone rocks in vegetable debris at 8000–10,000 feet in Western Yunnan, Western China. It should succeed outdoors in the warmer parts of the Kingdom in a sheltered spot in leaf-soil and calcareous loam.

CYNORCHIS, Thouin

This genus contains 25 species of rather tall, slender deciduous terrestrial plants, which spring from bundles of fleshy roots that are often thickened into fusiform tubers. The oblong leaves, few in number, are placed near the base of the stem, which is either naked or clothed with a few bracts becoming very small and narrow when they mingle with the blossoms. The flowers of the few species that may be tried outdoors in Britain are for the most part small, although some of the tropical forms have very large and decorative blossoms of exceedingly quaint shapes. They are all natives of Africa, the greater number being indigenous to Madagascar, where the most curious species are found. They may be tried outdoors in very mild localities, in sheltered but sunny spots in the rock garden, in moist but well-drained fibrous peat and loam, and should have their roots protected in winter. Propagation by division and also by seeds.

195 CYNORCHIS ANACAMPTOIDES, Kränzl.

Root: a bunch of fleshy fibres. **Stem:** 9″–18″ tall, leafy below. **Leaves:** linear-lanceolate, attentuate below, 2″–4½″ long, few in number. **Raceme:** very short, dense. **Flowers:** about $\frac{3}{16}$″ across; dorsal sepal broadly ovate, pointed; lateral sepals suboblique, ovate-oblong; petals ovate-oblong, forming a hood with the dorsal sepal; lip entire, linear, rather blunt; spur subfiliform, about ⅛″ long. *September and October.*

The tiny pink- or rose-coloured blossoms of this species, although dainty and pretty, are too small to render the plant of any great garden value. The grass-like leaves spring from near the base of the stem. It grows amongst heather and other dwarf plants in open spots on Mount Ruwenzori in British East Africa at 10,000 feet, where it is subjected to 15° or 20° of frost for short periods when deciduous. It may be grown in a sunny part of the rock garden, in fairly damp fibrous peat and loam.

196. CYNORCHIS BUCHANANII, Rolfe

Root: of elongated tubers. **Stem:** 1′–1¼′ tall, sparely leafy below. **Leaves:** lanceolate-oblong, attenuate towards their base, glandular-pubescent above, 1½″–3″ long. **Raceme:** 1¼″–2″ long, dense. **Flowers:** ⅜″ across; dorsal sepal ovate, cucullate, rather blunt; lateral sepals obliquely ovate-oblong, rather blunt; petals falcate-oblong, blunt; lip entire, narrowly cuneate-oblong, blunt; spur cylindrical, ¼″ long. *August to October.*

This species produces a slender stem, clothed near its base with two or three bright green leaves with a few sheaths below them, and bearing at its apex a short narrow spike of small rose-pink blossoms, rather too small to be of much garden value. It is found in damp or marshy spots among rocks on the top of Mount Zomba in British Central Africa at 7000 feet and is there exposed to over 15° of frost during its deciduous period. In cultivation it may be grown in a sunny spot, in damp fibrous peat and sandy loam.

197. CYNORCHIS VOLKENSII, Kränzl.

Habenaria pleistadenia, Reichb. f.

Root: of oblong fleshy tubers. **Stem:** 9″–12″ tall, glandular-pubescent, clothed with a few acuminate sheaths. **Leaves:** basal, ovate-oblong or cuneate-oblong, suberect, 2″–4¼″ long. **Raceme:** 1″–4″ long, lax, many-flowered. **Flowers:** about ½″ across; dorsal sepal ovate, rather pointed; lateral sepals oblong-lanceolate, oblique, deflexed, rather blunt; petals ovate-oblong, oblique, rather blunt, forming a hood with the dorsal sepal; lip entire, linear-oblong, blunt, reflexed at the sides; spur cylindrical, very slightly thickened above, ¾″ long. *August to October.*

A delightful little species for alpine house culture having a loose spike of fairly large blossoms of a rich violet colour. The sheath-clothed stem has one or two oval leaves at its base. The plant is found on Mount Kilimanjaro in Tanganyika, among dwarf herbage in damp open rocky spots up to 10,000 feet, where it is exposed to 15° or 20° of frost when deciduous. In cultivation it should be treated in the same manner as the other half-hardy species.

CYPRIPEDIUM, Linnæus

Without question this genus of terrestrial herbs, which numbers about 100 species, contains some of the most beautiful Orchids that may be cultivated in the open air over the greater part of the British Isles. The majority are robust leafy plants with rather slender rhizomes or underground stems creeping horizontally not far from the surface of the soil and well furnished with fairly thick and short fibres. In some species no stems are produced, and the flower-stalks grow from between two large leaves springing from a bud on the rhizome;

most, however, have erect stems clad with handsome, deeply grooved, rich green leaves. The blossoms of some of the Chinese species are among the largest produced by any Orchid, frequently being over six inches across. The species are scattered over most parts of the northern hemisphere in a variety of habitats. Propagation by division of the rhizome when the plants are at rest, and by seeds which are freely produced by most species in their native habitats.

198. CYPRIPEDIUM ACAULE, Ait.

C. humile, Pursh. *Fissipes acaulis*, Small.

Root: of fleshy fibres. **Stem:** obsolete. **Leaves:** basal, usually 2 in number, occasionally with a small leaf on the scape; they vary from oblong-elliptic to ovate and at times nearly lanceolate, undulate, downy, 3″–9″ long. **Scape:** 4″–18″ tall, bearing 1 or very rarely 2 blossoms. **Flowers:** about 2½″ across by 2″ long; sepals oblong or lanceolate, pointed rather convex; petals narrower and longer than the sepals, at times twisted at the tip; lip inflated, ovoid or elliptic, split from the top to the bottom down the front; column 6-angled. *May to September.*

An exquisite plant with a pair of large rich green hairy leaves and a slender flower-stem bearing a very large blossom with very pale green sepals shaded with pink, deep rose-pink petals and a rose-pink lip veined with crimson and crested inside with silvery hairs. The lip is sometimes tinged with an exquisite lilac colour. The plant grows in damp pinewoods and the boggy margins of forest pools, usually in sandy soil and living moss, in North America from the Arctic Ocean to North Carolina. It may be grown in the rock garden in a shady spot in damp sandy peat, leaf-soil and living sphagnum-moss.

199. CYPRIPEDIUM AMESIANUM, Schltr.

Root: a shortly creeping rhizome emitting numerous matted fibrous roots. **Stem:** 1′–1½′ tall, fairly stout, erect or slightly flexuous, sparsely leafy. **Leaves:** usually 3 in number, elliptic, amplexicaule, pointed, covered with fine hairs, 3″–5″ long. **Flower:** usually solitary, about 2½″ across; dorsal sepal, oblong, pointed; laterals sepals oblong, connate beneath and shortly bifid at the tip; petals obliquely oblong-lanceolate, margin finely ciliate, slightly undulate on the inside; lip oval, inflated, large, projecting and slightly pendent; column elliptic-oblong, densely hairy around its base. *June and July.*

A handsome large-flowered species closely allied to *C. himalaicum*, generally with erect stems clothed with a few broad leaves and bearing solitary blossoms of a purplish-crimson colour mottled with a deeper tint. It is found in thickets and woodlands in Western Szechuan, China, reaching an elevation of 10,000 feet above sea-level. It should be quite hardy in Britain in a shady part of the rock garden in good fibrous peat and leaf-soil.

200. CYPRIPEDIUM ARIETINUM, R. Br.

Arietinum americanum, Bech. *Criosanthes borealis*, Rafin. *C. parviflora*, Rafin.

Root: a slender creeping rhizome with short fleshy fibres. **Stem:** 6″–12″ tall, very slender, leafy, downy. **Leaves:** cauline, usually 4 in number, elliptic or lanceolate, at times undulate, pointed, semi-erect, 2″–4″ long. **Flower:** solitary, about $\frac{5}{8}$″ across and $\frac{3}{4}$″ long, pendulous or horizontal; sepals lanceolate, lateral ones connate below the lip; petals linear, parallel with the pouch; lip or pouch, shaped like a sheep's head, broad at the base, narrowing to a blunt spur at the tip. *May to August.*

A quaint and delicate little plant with small but pretty blossoms; the petals and sepals are pale yellowish-green with crimson veins, the pouch is white with red or pink tessellations on the front and yellow and red markings on the hairy inner surface. It grows on raised ground or hummocks in tamarack or cedar swamps, and is locally abundant in Eastern North America from Quebec to Manitoba, and southward to New York and Minnesota. It is quite hardy in Great Britain, but appears to be difficult to establish. A raised part of the bog garden in peat and moss is indicated.

201. CYPRIPEDIUM BARDOLPHIANUM, W. W. Sm.

Root: a widely creeping rhizome well furnished with fibrous rootlets. **Stem:** $2\frac{1}{2}$″–3″ tall, slender, bearing 2 leaves. **Leaves:** smooth, oblong-lanceolate, rounded at the tip, about 2″ long. **Flower:** solitary, about 1″ across; dorsal sepal elliptic ovate, blunt; lateral sepals connate beneath the lip, elliptic ovate, pointed, bifid at the tip; petals lanceolate, spreading, about as long as the sepals; lip oval, bullate and frequently deformed, inflated. *June and July.*

A very curious little species with small blossoms having an orange-coloured lip covered with irregular warts, and pale green sepals and petals. The blossoms are reported to have an unpleasant odour. The plant grows in shady mountain woods in mossy leaf-soil in Kansu, Western China, and is frequently found growing in company with *C. luteum*, it should be quite hardy in Britain in a shady spot in the rock garden in loose leaf-soil and fibrous loam.

202. CYPRIPEDIUM CALCEOLUS, Linn.

C. cruciatum, Dulac. *Calceolus marianus*, Crantz. *C. alternifolius*, St. L.

Root: a creeping horizontal rhizome with short fleshy fibres. **Stem:** 1′–$1\frac{3}{4}$′ tall, stout, leafy, hairy. **Leaves:** cauline, 4–6 in number, ovate-lanceolate, hairy, 3″–6″ long. **Flower:** usually solitary, rarely 2 in number, $2\frac{1}{2}$″–$3\frac{1}{2}$″

across, subtended by a bract; dorsal sepal erect lanceolate, tapering to a point; lateral sepals connate beneath the lip and bifid at the tip; petals ribbon-like, pointed and much twisted; lip egg-shaped, inflated, corrugated, hairy or nearly smooth; column dilated, petal-like. *May and June.*

A very beautiful native plant with large, curiously-shaped flowers with dark or chestnut-brown sepals and petals and a rich yellow lip. It grows in woodlands, most frequently on calcareous soils, throughout Europe and Northern Asia from England to China. There are several beautiful forms such as *album* with white and *fulvum* with pale yellow blossoms; *Atsmorii* from Japan, with slender stems bearing large pale blossoms; *major* with blossoms over 4″ across; *viridiflorum* with yellowish-green blossoms; *mandschuricum* with large richly-coloured flowers. There is a beautiful hybrid between *C. calceolus* and *C. macranthum* known as *Barbeyi*, it has vinous red sepals and petals with yellow bases, and a vinous red lip. The type and its forms may be grown in a shady spot in the rock garden in calcareous loam and leaf-soil.

203. CYPRIPEDIUM CALIFORNICUM, A. Gray

Root: a creeping rhizome. **Stem:** 1′–2¼′ tall, stout, leafy, hairy. **Leaves:** numerous, ovate or elliptic below, narrowing upwards and passing into bracts amongst the blossoms, 2″–4″ long. **Flowers:** from 5–10 in number, 1″ across and 1¼″ long; dorsal sepal ovate, pointed; lateral sepals oblong, connate beneath the lip; petals narrowly oblong or lanceolate, frequently falcate at the tip; lip oval, inflated, mouth almost closed; column suborbicular. *May.*

This species differs from most of its brethren in producing a leafy spike of blossoms which are quite pretty and decorative, although rather small. The sepals and petals are tawney yellow and the lip is white, slightly stained with pink and obscurely spotted with brown. The plant grows in damp, thin woodlands and on open damp moors in Western North America from Northern California to Oregon. It may be grown outdoors in the milder parts of Great Britain in the rock garden in damp peat and leaf-soil, and should have some protection to its roots in frosty weather.

204. CYPRIPEDIUM CANDIDUM, Muhlenb.

Root: of long, somewhat fleshy fibres. **Stem:** 6″–21″ tall, leafy above and sheathed below. **Leaves:** 3–4 in number, elliptic or lanceolate, pointed, at times narrowing upwards, 3″–5″ long. **Flower:** solitary, about 2″ across and the same measurement in length, usually more or less drooping; sepals lanceolate, lateral ones connate below the lip; petals linear-lanceolate or linear, usually somewhat spirally twisted; lip egg-shaped, mouth open, inflated, but flatter than in most species; column lance-shaped. *May to July.*

A beautiful and desirable species with delicate tintings. It produces a close growth of rather stout, erect, leafy stems topped by fairly large blossoms with green or greenish-brown sepals and petals, and a white lip with rich yellow markings which occasionally occupy nearly the whole of its surface. The plant inhabits bogs and wet meadows in the Eastern United States from New York and New Jersey to Minnesota and southward to Nebraska. It is quite hardy in this country and may be grown in a cool spot in the bog or rock garden in peat, leaf-soil and moss.

205. CYPRIPEDIUM CORDIGERUM, Don.

Root: of stout fibres. **Stem:** $\frac{3}{4}'$–2′ tall, stout or slender, often downy, leafy. **Leaves:** subradical and cauline, varying from nearly orbicular to lanceolate, usually pointed, 3″–6″ long. **Flower:** solitary, nearly 4″ across the petals, subtended by a large leafy bract; sepals ovate-lanceolate, spreading; petals narrowly lanceolate, pointed, spreading; lip oblong, inflated. *July.*

This beautiful plant is very closely related to *C. calceolus* and is possibly an Indian form of that plant; it is quite distinct for horticultural purposes. Several leafy stems are produced, each terminating in very large blossoms having green and white sepals and petals and a large "baggy" white lip with hairy orange markings on the inside. It grows in thinly-wooded country and also in shady places amongst rock in the Himalaya from Kashmir to Kumaon, reaching an elevation of 11,000 feet. It may be treated like *C. calceolus* in cultivation.

206. CYPRIPEDIUM CORRUGATUM, Franch

Root: A shortly-creeping horizontal rhizome. **Stem:** 7″–12″ tall, leafy, stout. **Leaves:** oblong, pointed, margins ciliate, 4″–5″ long. **Flower:** solitary, subtended by a large bract, nearly 4″ across the petals; dorsal sepal ovate-oblong, pointed; lateral sepals ovate, connate beneath the lip, bifid at the tip; petals ovate-lanceolate, pointed; lip obovate or rotund, strongly corrugated or bullate, mouth small, sac inflated; column ovate-cordate, pointed, large. *June.*

This species is very closely related to *C. tibeticum* (King). It is a handsome species with very large blossoms with green petals and sepals suffused with reddish-brown and veined with purple, and a deep purple-maroon lip with very dark veinings. It grows in open mountain meadows and on the margins of pine forests in Western Yunnan, Western China, at an elevation of 10,000–11,000 feet and should be quite hardy in Britain in a half-shady spot in the rock garden in leaf-soil and fibrous loam; *obtusa* (Franch) is a more robust form.

207. CYPRIPEDIUM DEBILE, Reichb. f.

C. cardiophyllum, Franch

Root: a slender creeping rhizome. **Stem:** 6″–12″ long, slender, smooth, curving in a semicircle with the weight of the blossom. **Leaves:** 2 in number, opposite, nearly smooth, cordate-triangular, very pointed and undulate, nearly sessile, placed about the centre of the stem, $1\frac{1}{2}$″–2″ long. **Flower:** solitary, about $1\frac{1}{2}$″ across and $\frac{3}{4}$″ long, with a small bract some distance below the blossom; dorsal sepal lanceolate, pointed, curving over the column; lateral sepals lanceolate, connate beneath the lip; petals broadly lanceolate, spreading; lip shaped exactly like a moccasin, with an inflated corrugated toe. *June and July.*

A delicate and pretty little plant with a solitary drooping blossom on the tip of a curved stem, and with pale green sepals and petals and a white, brown-blotched lip. It grows in thinly-wooded country in China and Japan, reaching an elevation of over 5000 feet in the latter country. It may be grown in the rock garden in a damp shady spot in peat and leaf-soil, and should be protected during severe frost.

208. CYPRIPEDIUM EBRACTEATUM, Rolfe

Root: a horizontally creeping rhizome furnished with fibrous rootlets. **Leaves:** 2 in number, suberect, ovate-orbicular, rather pointed, 4″–$4\frac{1}{2}$″ long. **Scape:** 6″–8″ tall, slender or fairly stout, covered with minute down. **Flower:** solitary, about $1\frac{3}{4}$″ across; dorsal sepal elliptic-ovate, rather pointed; lateral sepals ovate-lanceolate, connate beneath the lip, pointed; petals lanceolate, pointed; lip elliptic-oblong, blunt, saccate; column ovate-oblong. *June.*

A curious species with the habit of *C. japonicum* (Thunb.). It has a large greenish-yellow blossom more or less covered with deep purple and maroon markings. In a state of nature it is found in dry shady spots in pine forests in Western Yunnan, Western China, at from 9000–11,000 feet. It should prove hardy in Great Britain in a shady part of the rock garden in soil collected from beneath conifers.

209. CYPRIPEDIUM ELEGANS, Reichb. f.

Root: a short branching rhizome. **Stem:** 1′–$1\frac{1}{2}$′ tall below the leaves, very hairy. **Leaves:** orbicular-ovate or oblong, 1″–2″ long, subopposite, about $1\frac{1}{2}$″ below the blossom. **Flower:** solitary, about 1″ across, subtended by an ovate bract; dorsal sepal oblong-lanceolate, pointed, curved forward; lateral sepals oblong, short, spreading; petals ovate, pointed; lip short, almost orbicular, inflated; mouth triangular. *July.*

A pretty, rather small-flowered species, very closely allied to *C. japonicum.* It produces a rather tall stem clothed at the top by two small leaves and bearing a solitary blossom with greenish-yellow sepals and petals striped with red, and a greenish-yellow lip strongly suffused with rich ruby-red. It is found in stony places on the margins of thickets in the Sikkim Himalaya and Eastern Tibet. It may be tried outdoors in this country under the same conditions as *C. japonicum.*

210. CYPRIPEDIUM FARRERI, W. W. Sm.

Root: a short slender rhizome with numerous fibrous rootlets. **Stem:** 6″–8″ tall, slender. **Leaves:** 2 in number, placed some distance up the stem, ovate-lanceolate, rather pointed, thin, margins fringed with minute hairs. **Flower:** solitary, about 3″ across; dorsal sepal ovate, rather blunt; lateral sepals connate beneath the lip, ovate-lanceolate, bifid at the tip; petals linear-lanceolate, twisted, spreading; lip flask-shaped or subglobular, mouth small. *June.*

A dwarf, delicate plant of considerable beauty, with very large blossoms, in proportion to its stature, these have greenish-yellow sepals and petals lined with maroon, and a glossy, cream-coloured or pale yellow lip lined internally with maroon; they are pleasantly fragrant. The plant is found on wooded shady limestone cliffs in loose leaf-soil above Siku in Yunnan, Western China, at from 8000–9000 feet above sea-level. A damp shady spot in the rock garden in a loose calcareous leaf-soil and fibrous peat is indicated.

211. CYPRIPEDIUM FASCICULATUM, Kellogg

C. pusillum, Rolfe

Root: a creeping rhizome emitting short fibres. **Stem:** 6″–12″ tall, stout, hairy. **Leaves:** 2 in number, sessile, opposite, below the middle of the stem, ovate or elliptic, pointed, undulate on their margins, plaited, hairy below, 2″–3″ long, usually suberect. **Flowers:** 3–4 in number, about 1″ across, almost umbellate; dorsal sepal and lateral sepals subequal, lanceolate, pointed, the latter are connate and bifid at the tip; petals lanceolate, pointed, spreading; lip small, oval, margins of the mouth corrugated, incurved; column large, 3-lobed. *May and June.*

A very quaint little plant with small, but quite pretty blossoms with pale green or yellowish-green sepals and petals and a yellowish-green lip with a brownish-purple margin. It is found in damp soil in thin woods, and on the margins of thickets, etc., in California. It may be grown outdoors in the warmer districts of Great Britain in a damp half-shady spot in the rock garden in peat and leaf-soil; its roots should be protected from frost in the winter.

212. CYPRIPEDIUM FASCIOLATUM, Franch

Root: a stout horizontally creeping rhizome. **Stem:** 9″–16″ tall, fairly stout, downy above. **Leaves:** cauline, about 3 in number, oblong, about 4½″ long, covered with minute hairs. **Flower:** solitary, about 4½″ across; dorsal sepal ovate, pointed; lateral sepals ovate-lanceolate, connate beneath the lip, bifid at the tip; petals linear or linear-lanceolate, twisted towards the tip; lip short, globular, with a contracted mouth; column oblong. *June.*

A very beautiful species with a large blossom with dull yellow sepals and petals veined and streaked with purple, and a purplish-rose coloured lip veined with a deeper tint; at times specimens are found of a reddish-purple colour with almost black veinings. The plant is found in dry open spots in pinewoods in Yunnan, Western China, at from 7000–11,000 feet above sea-level. It should be quite hardy over the greater part of Britain in a well-drained, half-shady spot in the rock garden in peat and leaf-soil.

213. CYPRIPEDIUM FRANCHETII, Rolfe

Root: a shortly creeping rhizome with a few fibrous rootlets. **Stem:** ¾′–1¼′ tall, fairly stout, erect, leafy, very hairy above. **Leaves:** 3–5 in number, elliptic or elliptic lanceolate, plaited, rather blunt, 2″–3½″ long. **Flower:** usually solitary, about 1¾″ across, subtended by a large leafy bract; dorsal sepal ovate-lanceolate, pointed, generally arching over the column; lateral sepals connate under the lip; petals lanceolate, slightly incurved at the tip, pointed, oblique; lip oval, inflated, large, with the veins so deeply indented as to render its surface bullate, mouth ovate, small. *June.*

This beautiful plant is very closely allied to *C. macranthum*, but has a more hairy stem and leaves. The solitary blossom is of a beautiful rosy-purple colour throughout, with deep crimson-purple veinings. The plant grows in thin forest of conifers and deciduous trees in Szechuan and Western Hupeh, Western China, reaching an elevation of 7300 feet above sea-level. It may be grown outdoors in this country under the same conditions as *C. fasciolatum.*

214. CYPRIPEDIUM GUTTATUM, Sw.

C. orientale, Spreng. *C. variegatum*, Georyi. *C. Calceolus* var. *variegatum*, Falk.

Root: a very long and slender creeping rhizome with fleshy fibres springing from the nodes. **Stem:** 6″–12″ tall, rather slender, very hairy. **Leaves:** 2 in number, ovate or lanceolate, plaited, hairy, sessile, 3″–4″ long. **Flower:** usually solitary, 1¼″ across and 1½″ long; dorsal sepal elliptic or nearly sub-orbicular, very convex, ribbed, projecting over the column; lateral sepals connate below the lip, narrowly oblong, bifid at the tip ; petals narrowly oblong or linear, spreading, with incurved tips ; lip large, inflated, almost heart-shaped, mouth small ; column small, cordate. *June and July.*

An exceedingly dainty little species with large hairy leaves, and fair-sized white blossoms covered with large crimson-purple spots and blotches ; the sepals and petals are sometimes unspotted. There are several forms such as *latifolium,* a more robust plant ; *Redowskii* from North-Eastern Russia with almost pure white blossoms ; and *Yatabeanum* from Japan with flowers having yellowish-green sepals shaded with purple-brown, white petals blotched with purple-brown, and a yellow lip blotched with reddish- or purple-brown. The type and its forms are found on the margins of swamps and pools, and in damp places in birch forests growing in leaf-soil, from North-Eastern Russia through Siberia to North-Western Canada. It may be grown in a cool shady spot in the rock garden in birch leaf-soil, peat and sphagnum-moss.

215. CYPRIPEDIUM HENRYI, Rolfe

C. chinense, Franch

Root : a horizontally creeping rhizome with fibrous roots. **Stem :** $1\frac{1}{2}'$–$2'$ tall, leafy, downy. **Leaves :** several, elliptic or elliptic-oblong, plicate, pointed, $4''$–$8''$ long. **Flowers :** 2–4 in number, about $3\frac{1}{2}''$ across, each subtended by a leaf-like bract ; dorsal sepal ovate-lanceolate, pointed ; lateral sepals ovate, connate beneath the lip, bifid at the tip ; petals linear-lanceolate, pointed ; lip ovoid or subglobose, inflated, $\frac{3}{4}''$ long. *June.*

A beautiful, delicately tinted species closely allied to *C. cordigerum* (Don). The sepals and petals are pale greenish-yellow and the lip is very pale yellow, or nearly white. It is found in woods and bushy places in Hupeh and Szechuan in Western China and should be quite hardy in Great Britain in a sheltered shady spot in the rock garden in fibrous loam and oak leaf-soil.

216. CYPRIPEDIUM HIMALAICUM, Rolfe

Root : a creeping rhizome emitting short stout fibres. **Stem :** $\frac{1}{2}'$–$1\frac{1}{2}'$ tall, slender, usually slightly curved, leafy above, clothed with a few sheaths or scales below. **Leaves :** usually 4 in number, ovate or lanceolate, plaited, edges of lower-most undulate, margins ciliate, $2''$–$3''$ long. **Flower :** solitary, about $1\frac{1}{2}''$ across and $1''$ long ; dorsal sepal very broadly ovate or oblong, convex, forming a hood over the column ; lateral sepals connate below the lip, bifid at the tip ; petals narrowly lanceolate, oblique at the tip, pointing downwards ; lip almost spherical, much inflated, corrugated, opening small. *May to July.*

This beautiful species was, until recently, confounded with *C. macranthum*; it has large "baggy" blossoms with pale greenish-yellow sepals and petals prettily striped with deep red, and a maroon-purple lip with the opening bordered with white, the inner surface being yellowish-green spotted with red. In a state of nature the plant grows on the borders of woods and thickets, usually in rocky situations in the Himalaya and Western China, reaching an elevation of over 12,500 feet in the Himalaya. It is quite hardy in Great Britain, and may be grown in a half-shady spot in damp leaf-soil, fibrous loam and sand mingled with a few large pieces of sandstone.

217. CYPRIPEDIUM HIRSUTUM, Mill

C. pubescens, Willd. *C. parviflorum*, Ait.

Root: of long, somewhat stout fibres. **Stem:** $\frac{3}{4}'$–$2\frac{1}{4}'$ tall, stout, leafy, downy, erect. **Leaves:** cauline, oblong or elliptic, sessile, sheathing at the base, pointed, downy, 3″–6″ long. **Flowers:** up to $3\frac{1}{2}''$ across the petals, 1–3 in number on the top of the stem; sepals ovate or lanceolate, lateral ones connate beneath the lip; petals narrowly linear, pointed, usually much twisted in a spiral manner; lip fairly large, inflated, bladder-like; column long-triangular. *April to June.*

This beautiful species produces clumps of tall leafy stems, each bearing from one to three blossoms with yellowish-green or fawn, purple-striped sepals and petals, and a bright yellow lip with greenish-purple or ruby-red lines and spots; the inside of the sac near the top is lined with glistening white hairs. This plant is found in dry woods, open, arid moraines in the alpine regions, margins of swamps and wet places on the prairies, etc. It thrives in cultivation in a cool shady spot (but perhaps produces more flowers in the open) in a compost of fibrous peat, leaf-soil and a little loam. It is a native of North America from Newfoundland to British Columbia, south to Georgia.

218. CYPRIPEDIUM IRAPEANUM, Lav et Lese

C. splendidum, Scheid.

Root: a creeping rhizome emitting numerous, somewhat fleshy, fibres. **Stem:** 1′–$1\frac{3}{4}'$ tall, slender, leafy. **Leaves:** cauline, several, ovate, pointed, stem-clasping at the base, 4″–6″ long, spreading or suberect. **Flower:** usually solitary, frequently over 5″ across the petals; dorsal sepal broadly ovate, pointed, bending over the column slightly; lateral sepals connate beneath the lip; petals ovate or oblong, over 2″ long; lip ovate, much inflated, nearly 2″ long. *August.*

This magnificent plant much resembles *C. hirsutum* in habit and blossom and is perhaps a southern form of it. The slender stems are clothed with handsome pale green foliage and usually bear a solitary blossom with rich, bright yellow sepals and petals, and bright but deep yellow lip with a few crimson blotches near its mouth. The plant is found in half-shady places, usually on a rocky sub-soil in Central Mexico at 5000 feet above sea-level. It may be grown outdoors in the milder parts of the kingdom in fibrous peat and leaf-soil in a damp shady spot.

219. CYPRIPEDIUM JAPONICUM, Thunb.

Root: a branched creeping rhizome emitting a mass of fairly stout fibrous roots. **Leaves:** 2 in number, springing from a bud on the rhizome, suberect, very broadly ovate, plicate, about 6″ long. **Scapes:** 1 or 2 in number, about 12″ tall, slender, leafless, hairy, springing from between the pair of leaves. **Flower:** about $3\frac{3}{4}$″ across and $2\frac{3}{4}$″ long; solitary, terminate, subtended by a large leafy bract, dorsal sepal ovate, large, bending over the column; lateral sepals connate beneath the lip; petals lanceolate; lip ovate, inflated, about $2\frac{1}{2}$″ long, split like that of *C. acaule* for two-thirds of its length down the face. *May and June.*

A remarkably beautiful "Lady's Slipper," resembling in habit *C. acaule.* The huge, solitary blossom is very nearly 4 inches across the spreading petals which, together with the sepals, are pale green with some small crimson spots at the base; the lip is white, marbled with pink, and is very massive. It is found in shady woods in Japan and China. It may be grown in a shady part of the rock garden in damp loam and leaf-soil, and should be protected from severe frost during the winter.

220. CYPRIPEDIUM KNIGHTÆ, A. Nels.

Root: a horizontally creeping rhizome with fibrous roots from the nodes. **Stem:** 1″–3″ long, thinly clothed with long hairs. **Leaves:** 2 in number, nearly opposite, ovate, blunt, 2″–3″ long, springing from the base of the scape. **Scape:** $1\frac{1}{2}$″–4″ tall, usually naked, covered with glandular hairs. **Flowers:** 2 or 3 in a cluster at the top of the scape, about $\frac{5}{8}$″ across and $\frac{3}{4}$″ long; dorsal sepal ovate-lanceolate, pointed; lateral sepals similar but united nearly to the tip; petals ovate, pointed, spreading; lip inflated, saccate, elliptic, mouth deeply infolded; column elliptic. *June and July.*

A quaint little species with a very restricted habitat. It closely resembles *C. fasciculatum* (Kellogg) from California. The blossoms are brownish-purple or deep purple throughout, except the lower part of the lip which is greenish-yellow. The plant is found in half-shady places on the mountains of Medicine Bow in Colorado, and Wyoming in the United States. In cultivation it may be treated like the above-mentioned species.

221. CYPRIPEDIUM LANUGINOSA, Schltr.

Root: a shortly-creeping rhizome with slender fibrous rootlets. **Stem:** 6″–10″ tall, rather slender, erect, covered where clasped by the leaf base with dense woolly hairs. **Leaves:** usually 3 in number, elliptic, pointed, plaited, sheathing at the base, downy on the under-side and margins, 3″–4½″ long. **Flower:** solitary, about 2½″ across, carried horizontally on the stem; dorsal sepal elliptic-ovate, pointed, erect; lateral sepals elliptic, pointed, connate beneath the lip, not bifid; petals obliquely lanceolate, pointed, spreading; lip oblong-ovoid, inflated; mouth narrowly oblong, densely downy at the base; column hastate-lanceolate. *August.*

This pretty dwarf species is very like *C. himalaicum* in both habit and flower. It inhabits mountain woodlands in Kouytcheou, Western China, and should be quite hardy in the warmer parts of Great Britain in a half-shady spot in the rock garden in good fibrous peat, leaf-soil and chopped sphagnum-moss.

222. CYPRIPEDIUM LUTEUM, Franch

Root: a stout creeping rhizome. **Stem:** 9″–18″ tall, erect, stout, downy, clothed with small sheaths below, leafy to the apex above. **Leaves:** ovate, sheathing, pointed, plaited, downy, 5 or 6 in number, 2½″–9″ long. **Flower:** solitary, terminal, 2½″–3½″ across; dorsal sepal ovate, convex, arching over the column; lateral sepals joined beneath the lip, pointed; petals ovate, pointed, narrower than the dorsal sepal; lip or pouch ovate, inflated. *June.*

The foliage and stems of this beautiful plant are covered with a brownish down. The solitary blossom has deep, clear yellow sepals and petals and a yellow lip, usually sparely spotted or blotched with orange-brown. It is a decorative and desirable plant and grows on the margins of thin woods and thickets usually in rather damp places in a variety of soils, in South-Western China at elevations up to 11,000 feet above sea-level. It should be quite hardy in Britain in a cool shady spot in calcareous loam and leaf-soil.

223. CYPRIPEDIUM MACRANTHUM, Sw.

C. macranthon, Sw. *C. macranthos*, Sw.

Root: a creeping horizontal rhizome furnished with numerous fleshy fibres. **Stem:** 1′–1½′ tall, usually very stout and downy. **Leaves:** several, ovate to lanceolate-elliptic, pointed, downy, undulate, amplexicaul, 3″–6″ long. **Flowers:** 1–2 in number, 3″ across and 2½″ long; dorsal sepal ovate, concave, usually curving over the column; lateral sepals connate beneath the lip, bifid at the tip; petals variable in shape, usually linear-lanceolate, spreading, drooping slightly but rarely twisted; lip large, inflated, egg-shaped, corrugated around the mouth. *June and July.*

This handsome plant has stout leafy stems bearing one or two "baggy" blossoms of a rose-purple or salmon colour, frequently tessellated with dark purple. There is a beautiful white form and several hybrids between it and *C. Calceolus*, such as *ventricosum* or *ventricosa*, *ventricosum luteum*, *v. album* and *v. roseum*, all are worth growing. The type and its forms are found in openings and on the margins of birch woods frequently in rocky soil, in northern and sub-arctic Europe and Asia. The plant is quite hardy in Great Britain but is difficult to flower. A half-shady spot in rich loam and leaf-soil is suitable for its culture.

224. CYPRIPEDIUM MARGARITACEUM, Franch

Root: a creeping horizontal rhizome. **Stem:** obsolete. **Leaves:** radical, 2 in number, oblong, opposite or sub-opposite, shortly pointed, about 5″ long. **Scape:** rarely more than 8″ long, erect. **Flower:** solitary, about 2″ across, without a subtending bract; dorsal sepal oblong; lateral sepals narrowly oblong; petals oblong-lanceolate, pointed; lip ovate, pointed, inflated, mouth large; column ovate-oblong. *June.*

This curious species produces two large, deeply-grooved, dark green leaves sprinkled with large purple-maroon blotches and covered with purple hairs beneath. The scape springs from between the pair of leaves and bears a solitary blossom of a very brittle wax-like consistency; the sepals and petals are yellowish-green spotted with purple, and the lip is pale yellow, spotted with purple and covered with purplish glandular hairs. It is found in nearly pure limestone, in moist places in pine woods, in North-Western Yunnan at 11,000 feet above sea-level and should be hardy in Britain in a damp spot in the rock garden, in stony calcareous loam with some pine leaf-soil.

225. CYPRIPEDIUM MICRANTHUM, Franch

Root: a short rhizome emitting numerous rootlets. **Stem:** very short, not more than $\frac{3}{4}$″ long. **Leaves:** radical, 2 in number, subopposite, oblong, shortly pointed, about 4″ long. **Scape:** about $3\frac{1}{2}$″ tall, densely hairy, bearing a solitary blossom without a subtending bract. **Flower:** about $2\frac{1}{2}$″ across; dorsal sepal ovate-oblong, pointed, or lanceolate-oblong; lateral sepals lanceolate-oblong, connate beneath the lip, bifid at the tip; petals ovate, smooth, pointed; lip obovate, inflated, mouth large; column cordate. *June.*

A quaint species rather closely allied to *C. margaritaceum* (Franch) and *C. ebracteatum* (Rolfe). It produces a short hairy flower-stem from between the two large deep green leaves, ending in a solitary blossom with yellowish-green sepals and petals and a yellowish-green lip with some purple markings. It is found in thin, mixed woodlands in Szechuan, Western China, and should succeed outdoors in Great Britain in mild sheltered localities in a half-shady spot in the rock garden in oak leaf-soil and loam.

226. CYPRIPEDIUM MICROSACCOS, Kränzl.

Root: a creeping rhizome. **Stem:** 12″–18″ tall, leafy, downy, erect. **Leaves:** broadly oblong, shortly pointed, 9-nerved, up to 6″ long. **Flowers:** usually 2 in number, about 2½″ across, subtended by large bracts; sepals lanceolate, pointed, lateral ones connate beneath the lip and bifid for half their length; petals narrow, slightly twisted; lip shortly unguiculate, rounded-obovate, inflated, ⅝″ long; column obovate. *June.*

This Siberian species is closely allied to our native *C. Calceolus.* It produces tall leafy stems clothed with large downy leaves and one or two blossoms with pinkish-brown sepals, purple-brown petals and a yellow lip. It is found near the banks of the river Tirma in the province of Primorski, Siberia, and should be quite hardy in this country under the same cultural treatment as *C. Calceolus.*

227. CYPRIPEDIUM MONTANUM, Dougl.

C. occidentale, Watson

Root: a creeping rhizome emitting numerous fleshy fibres. **Stem:** 9″–24″ tall, fairly stout, clothed with about 4 hairy leaves which clasp the stem at their base. **Leaves:** sessile, very broadly lanceolate or oblong, deeply ribbed, undulate on their margins, rather smooth, 2″–5″ long. **Flowers:** from 1 to 4 in number, about 3″ across and 4″ in length, lateral and terminal; dorsal sepal large, lanceolate, drawn out to a long twisted point; lateral sepals connate beneath the lip, lanceolate, bifid at the tip; petals linear, very long and narrow, spirally twisted, spreading or quite pendulous; lip usually pendulous, inflated, oblong, mouth large; column small. *May and June.*

A quaint yet very beautiful species with leafy stems bearing blossoms remarkable for their long petals; the sepals and petals are greenish-yellow shaded with purple and brown; the lip is white with purple veinings and red markings inside; the small column is yellow, spotted with red. It grows in damp marshy soil on the margins of mountain lakes, swamps, damp open woods, etc., in Western North America from British Columbia to California. It is quite hardy in Great Britain in a sheltered half-shady spot in the rock garden in damp fibrous peat, loam and leaf-soil, with plenty of water in the summer. *See Plate 7 facing page 122.*

228. CYPRIPEDIUM PARVIFLORUM, Salisb.

C. Calceolus, Michx. *C. parvulum,* Fedde.

Root: of long, somewhat fleshy fibres. **Stem:** 1′–2′ tall, fairly stout, erect or sometimes zig-zag. **Leaves:** cauline, elliptic or ovate, pointed, 3″–6″ long.

Flowers: from 3″–4″ across the petals, from 1–3 in number, on the top of the stem; sepals lanceolate or oblong-lanceolate, lateral, connate beneath the lip; petals narrowly linear, twisted; lip or pouch bladder-like, much inflated. *April to June.*

This delightful plant is very closely allied to *C. pubescens*, or *hirsutum* as it is now called, and is frequently mistaken for that plant; it differs in having smaller blossoms, with the lip a much deeper shade of yellow and often marked and suffused with reddish-purple. To add to its attractions the blossoms are fragrant. It grows on the mossy banks of alpine streams, in damp wood and cedar swamps over Eastern North America from Newfoundland to Georgia. It is quite hardy in Great Britain in a cool shady spot in the rock garden in damp fibrous peat, leaf-soil and sphagnum-moss.

229. CYPRIPEDIUM PASSERINUM, Rich.

Root: a creeping rhizome emitting fleshy fibres. **Stem:** 9″–12″ tall, stout, succulent, leafy, sheath-clothed below. **Leaves:** suberect, ovate or lanceolate, pointed, sessile, undulate on the margins and deeply ribbed, 2″–6″ long. **Flowers:** 1–2 in number, $\frac{3}{4}$″–1$\frac{1}{8}$″ long and about the same across; dorsal sepal broadly elliptic, projecting over the column; lateral sepals ovate, connate beneath the lip; petals oblong, blunt, spreading; lip nearly spherical, much inflated, about $\frac{5}{8}$″ long; column triangular. *June to August.*

Although the blossoms of this species are smaller than those of most of the other species, it is quite a desirable little plant for the alpine house or rock garden; the flowers have pale green sepals and petals, and a white or pale magenta lip spotted with bright red or deep magenta; column yellow, spotted crimson. It grows in wet sandy places, on the margins of rivers, lakes, spruce swamps, moist places in pine woods, and ascends the mountains to considerable elevations in Western North America. It should be hardy in Great Britain in a damp spot in the rock garden in good leaf-soil and sharp sand.

230. CYPRIPEDIUM PLECTROCHILUM, Franch

C. plectrochilon, Franch

Root: a slender creeping rhizome with short fleshy fibres. **Stem:** 6″–12″ tall, slender, leafy, downy. **Leaves:** cauline, lanceolate, undulate, pointed, suberect, 2″–4″ long. **Flower:** solitary, $\frac{3}{4}$″ across, usually pendulous; sepals ovate, bluntly pointed; petals linear, much longer than the sepals; lip inflated above, tapering to a point at the tip, mouth small. *May to July.*

A curious yet attractive plant very closely allied to *C. arietinum* (R. Br.) from North America, but considered a good species by Dr. R. Schlechter, the eminent German authority on Orchids. The plant produces a slender somewhat leafy stem terminating in a solitary blossom with brownish-green sepals and petals, and a pink lip veined with purplish-green and tipped with yellowish-green. It grows in dry shady places in pine forests in North-Western Yunnan and Szechuan, Western China, at 9000 to 11,000 feet above sea-level. It should prove hardy over the greater part of the Kingdom in a well-drained spot in the rock garden in soil collected from beneath the shade of conifers.

231. CYPRIPEDIUM PULCHRUM, Ames & Schltr.

Root: a very short rhizome with long fibrous rootlets. **Stem:** 8″–10″ tall, fairly stout, erect, very sparely leafy. **Leaves:** usually 2 in number, elliptic, lowermost blunt, uppermost pointed, margins minutely ciliate, 2″–3½″ long. **Flower:** solitary, about 2¾″ across, carried suberect; dorsal sepal ovate, shortly pointed, with minute wool at its base; lateral sepals ovate, connate beneath the lip, bifid at the tip; petals obliquely oblong, shortly pointed, spreading; lip subglobose, inflated, mouth shortly oval, densely downy at the base; column ovate-oblong, blunt, cordate at the base. *June and July.*

A dwarf sturdy little plant with large elliptic leaves and rather stout stem bearing a solitary blossom closely resembling that of *C. himalaicum* both in shape and colouring. It is found in moist shady places in Western Szechuan in woodlands, reaching an elevation of 8000 feet above sea-level. In cultivation it should succeed under the same conditions as *C. lanuginosum.*

232. CYPRIPEDIUM REGINÆ, Walt.

C. album, Ait. *C. canadense,* Michx. *C. spectabile,* Salisb.

Root: of long fleshy fibres. **Stem:** 1′–3′ tall, stout, leafy to the top. **Leaves:** cauline, ovate or elliptic, pointed, frequently undulate, plaited, downy, 3″–8″ long. **Flowers:** 1–4 in number, about 3½″ across and 3¾″ long; sepals oblong or ovate, lateral sepals connate beneath the lip; petals narrowly oblong or lanceolate, spreading; lip about 2″ long, elliptic or oblong, inflated, pendulous; column cordate. *May and June.*

The Moccasin Flower is probably the finest and most desirable of all the hardy Orchids. Under congenial conditions it produces sturdy clumps of handsome foliage up to 3 feet in height, each stem bearing from one to four very large blossoms with white sepals and petals and a white, pale pink or pale purple lip with rose-pink or purple markings; there is also a very beautiful pure white form. The plant grows in damp woods, cedar and tamarack swamps, peat bogs, etc., in Eastern North America from Nova Scotia to Ontario and southward to Georgia. It should be grown in a cool shady spot in the rock garden or border, in good rich loam, leaf-soil and sand.

233. CYPRIPEDIUM SPECIOSUM, Rolfe.

Root: a creeping horizontal rhizome. **Stem:** 8″–16″ tall, rather stout, leafy, covered with fine hairs. **Leaves:** cauline, few in number, ovate below, becoming broadly lanceolate or oblong on the upper part of the stem, covered with fine hairs, 2″–6″ long. **Flower:** solitary, 3″ across and 3½″ long; dorsal sepal very broadly ovate or orbicular, slightly incurved at the tip; lateral sepals oblong-lanceolate, connate beneath the lip, bifid at the tip; petals large, lanceolate, pointed, drooping; lip oval or suborbicular, large, inflated, almost smooth, mouth small; column cordate. *May to July.*

An exquisitely beautiful species with handsome pale green hairy foliage, and large, solitary blossoms with white or flesh-coloured sepals and petals veined with rose-crimson and spotted with deep crimson at the base, and a white or flesh-pink lip with crimson veinings and a crimson line around the pure white edge of the lip. The column is heart-shaped and is white with a yellow line down its centre. The plant is widely scattered throughout the wooded districts of Japan and was formerly confounded with *C. macranthum.* It is hardy in Great Britain and may be grown like the above species in the rock garden in a good rich fibrous loam.

234. CYPRIPEDIUM THUNBERGII, Bl.

Root: a rather stout creeping rhizome. **Stem:** 1′–1½′ tall, stout, leafy. **Leaves:** cauline, numerous, ovate-oblong amplexicaul, pointed, deeply grooved, 4″–6″ long. **Flower:** usually solitary rarely 2 in number, over 3″ across and 3″ long, subtended by a large leaf-like bract; dorsal sepal lanceolate, pointed, erect; lateral sepals narrowly lanceolate, connate beneath the lip, bifid at the tip; petals narrowly lanceolate, spreading; lip inflated, saccate, ovate, blunt; column hastate, pointed. *June and July.*

A beautiful and desirable species with leafy stems bearing large blossoms of a rosy-purple tint throughout, with beautiful reticulations in a deeper tint on the lip. It is found in half-shady places such as the margins of woods, etc., in various parts of Japan. It is quite hardy in Great Britain in a half-shady spot in the rock garden in peat, loam and leaf-soil.

235. CYPRIPEDIUM TIBETICUM, King

C. macranthon var. *corrugatum*, Franch

Root: a stout creeping rhizome. **Stem:** 3″–18″ tall, stout, erect. **Leaves:** 3, rarely 4, in number, 2½″–6″ long, ovate or oblong, pointed, undulate, plaited, sheathing at the base, nearly smooth on the surface, margins fringed with hairs. **Flower:** solitary, slightly nodding, 3½″–6″ across; dorsal sepal ovate, pointed, convex, arching over the column; lateral sepals joined beneath the lip, bifid at the tip; petals elliptic, sometimes waved at their margins, usually extended parallel with the pouch; lip inflated, rounded, corrugated. *July and August.*

This handsome plant probably possesses larger blossoms than any other hardy Orchid. Stout stems clothed with rich green foliage spring from the root, each bearing one huge blossom with its sepals and petals covered with reddish-purple tessellations on a paler ground; the lip is rich maroon-purple. The plant grows among short herbage on the high alpine moorlands of Western China and Tibet, reaching an altitude of over 12,000 feet. It may be grown in an exposed spot in the rock garden in a cool, moist, but well-drained root-run of fibrous loam, peat and leaf-soil.

236. CYPRIPEDIUM VAGANUM, Cockl. and Baker

Root: of fleshy fibres. **Stem:** 1′–1½′ tall, sparely leafy. **Leaves:** cauline, not numerous, lanceolate, pointed, strongly veined, 3″–5″ long. **Flowers:** 1 or 2 in number, about 3″ across; dorsal sepal oblong-lanceolate; lateral sepals lanceolate, connate beneath the lip, bifid at the tip; petals narrow, linear twisted; lip oval, much inflated, laterally compressed, downy at the base; column triangular. *June.*

A pretty plant very closely allied to, and perhaps only a form of, *C. parviflorum.* The blossoms have yellowish-green, purple-shaded sepals and petals, and a bright yellow lip speckled with dull red within and towards the apex outside; the flowers are slightly fragrant. The plant has a very restricted habitat, it is confined to Sapello Canyon Las Vegas Range at about 8000 feet above sea-level in New Mexico. From such an altitude it should be quite hardy in Great Britain under the same treatment as *C. parviflorum.*

237. CYPRIPEDIUM WARDII, Rolfe

Root: a creeping rhizome emitting fleshy fibrous roots. **Stem:** 6″–9″ tall, sheathed at the base, sparely leafy. **Leaves:** generally 3 in number, almost sessile, elliptic or elliptic-lanceolate, rather pointed, 2″–3½″ long. **Flower:** solitary, about 1½″ across, subtended by a leafy bract; dorsal sepal elliptic-ovate, pointed; lateral sepals connate beneath the lip, ovate-elliptic, concave; petals rhomboid-oblong, blunt, rather spreading; lip ovoid or nearly globose; column elliptic. *June.*

A pretty little species closely allied to *C. guttatum*, differing, however, from that species in its differently-shaped sepals and petals. It has white or pale purple blossoms spotted with deep purple and is found on limestone cliffs in dense shady forest lands at Kun-a-tong in South-East Tibet at 10,000 feet above sea-level. In cultivation it should prove quite hardy in the warmer parts of Britain in a damp shady spot in the rock garden in peat and calcareous loam.

238. CYPRIPEDIUM WILSONII, Rolfe

Root: a horizontally creeping rhizome with fibrous rootlets. **Stem:** 12″–15″ tall, stout, leafy, downy. **Leaves:** sheathing, elliptic or ovate-elliptic, pointed, plicate, hairy with minute down, 3″–6″ long, 2″–5″ across. **Flower:** solitary, about 6″ across; dorsal sepal ovate, very pointed; lateral sepals narrowly ovate, connate beneath the lip, slightly bifid; petals narrowly oblong, pointed, spreading; lip oval, inflated, corrugated at the mouth. *June.*

A very handsome species whose huge blossoms are at times larger than those of *C. tibeticum*. The sepals and petals are yellow in ground colour, striped with chocolate, and the lip is pale yellow with chocolate spots. It grows in densely shady woods between Wantung and Mosimien in Szechuan, Western China, at 7300 feet above sea-level and may be tried outdoors in the rock garden in the warmer parts of the Kingdom in nearly pure oak or beech leaf-soil and sand.

239. CYPRIPEDIUM YUNNANENSE, Franch

Root: a horizontally creeping rhizome. **Stem:** about 12″ tall, leafy, sparely downy above. **Leaves:** cauline, 3–4 in number, oblong or oblong-lanceolate, pointed, 3″–4″ long, hairy below. **Flower:** solitary, terminal, 2½″ across, subtended by a large lanceolate, pointed, bract; dorsal sepal oblong, shortly pointed; lateral sepals ovate; petals narrowly ovate, pointed; lip ovate, inflated; column cordate, pointed. *June and July.*

A very beautiful species with solitary blossoms on the top of stout leafy stems; they have white sepals and petals, striped with purple, and a rose-purple lip deeply veined with purple. The plant is found in rather dry situations in pine forests in Yunnan, Western China, and should be sufficiently hardy for culture outdoors over the greater part of Britain. It may be planted in the rock garden, in a half-shady spot in soil collected from beneath the shade of conifers.

DACTYLOSTALIX, Reichenbach fils.

Pergamena Reichb. f.

This genus was created for a very curious little terrestrial Orchid from Japan. It has the habit and appearance of a Calypso and the lip of an Orchis. The root system consists of a fairly stout underground stem creeping at no great distance from the surface of the soil; the succulent stem bears a comparatively large rich green leaf which is deeply grooved by nine longitudinal veins exactly similar to the leaf of *Calypso bulbosa*. The blossom is large considering the size of the plant, which does not usually exceed five inches in total height. It inhabits mountain forests in its native country and is rare and local. Propagation by imported roots.

240. DACTYLOSTALIX RINGENS, Reichb. f.

Pergamena uniflora, Finet. *Calypso japonica*, Maxim.

Root: a rather stout horizontally creeping rhizome emitting a few fibrous roots. **Stem:** 5″–6″ tall, slender, sheathed at the base, bearing a solitary leaf. **Leaf:** elliptic, pointed, narrowed at the base into a short stalk, plicate, 2½″–3½″ long. **Scape:** clothed with 2 sheaths, bearing a solitary blossom. **Flower:** slightly nodding, about ¾″ long; dorsal sepal broadly lanceolate; lateral sepals lanceolate, suberect, 7-nerved; petals narrowly ovate, pointed, 3-nerved; lip narrow at the base then broadly ovate, sub-trilobed; lobes rounded, toothed. *June.*

A pretty little plant with a pale green and lilac-pink blossom on a slender stalk clothed with a solitary bright green leaf. It is found in the forests of Kayashimve, Japan, at 4500 feet above sea-level and should be quite hardy in Great Britain in a damp shady spot in the rock garden in beech and oak leaf-soil and sand.

DENDROBIUM, Swartz

A genus of over 1500 species of very beautiful and deservedly popular plants of epiphytal, or rarely terrestrial, habit. Their root systems consist of a long or short creeping rhizome, well supplied with fleshy roots in the majority of species. The long jointed stems are sometimes very slender and hang down like bunches of whipcord from the branches of the trees on which they grow, at other times they are swollen between the nodes, forming a chain of elongated pseudo-bulbs. They are evergreen or deciduous and the leaves are very variable in shape. The beautiful blossoms are produced in racemes, or at times singularly, from the nodes on the upper part of the stem. The plants are found on moss- and fern-clad trees in humid forests, on sun-baked rocks and on dry banks from Japan southward through China to India, Malaya, New Guinea, Australia and New Zealand. Propagation by cuttings of the stems, division of the rhizomes and by seeds.

241. DENDROBIUM ÆMULUM, R. Br.

Root: a creeping rhizome emitting a few long white fibres. **Stems:** 3″–12″ long, round, rather thick and at times tapering towards the base, springing from small pseudo-bulbs. **Leaves:** ovate or oblong, 2″–4″ long, near the apex of the stem. **Racemes:** 2″–3″ long, in the axils of the leaves, 1–3 in number. **Flowers:** about 1½″ across, 3–7 to a raceme; sepals narrowly lanceolate to broadly linear, striate, basal spur short, broad, recurved; petals narrowly linear, as long as the sepals; lip short, 3-lobed; side lobes broad, short, pointed; centre lobe ovate, very wavy, tip recurved.

May and June.

An interesting and pretty species with jointed, rounded, thick, deep green stems, with a tuft of about three smooth deep green somewhat leathery leaves near the tip, and racemes of about half a dozen rather large cream-coloured blossoms with pink lines on the lip. It grows on moss-covered trees and rocks, in damp shady places in Queensland and New South Wales where on the Blue Mountains it attains sufficient elevation to give reasonable hope that it may be hardy enough for outdoor culture in South-Western England, on a damp mossy rock in a humid shady spot.

242. DENDROBIUM BULLEYI, Rolfe

Root: of several fleshy fibres. **Stems:** 10″–12″ tall, clustered, subcylindric, sheaths covered with fine black hairs. **Leaves:** few, lanceolate, or ovate-lanceolate, bilobed at the tip, leathery, about 2″ long. **Raceme:** short, of from 1–3 blossoms, from the axils of the leaves on the upper part of the stem. **Flowers:** about 1″ across; dorsal sepal lanceolate-elliptic, erect; lateral sepals triangular, pointed; petals elliptic-lanceolate, pointed, spreading; lip ovate, shortly 3-lobed at the tip; outer lobes large, rounded; centre lobe short, toothed. *September.*

A soberly-coloured yet attractive species well worth cultivating. The blossoms have yellowish-white sepals and petals and a reddish-orange lip with dark veinings. It is found on dry shady banks in pine woods in Western Yunnan, Western China, at 9000 feet above sea-level and may be tried outdoors in sheltered localities in the rock garden in a compost of sandy loam and oak leaf-soil in half-shade.

243. DENDROBIUM CLAVATUM, Linde

Callista clavata, O. Ktze.

Root: of few fleshy fibres. **Stem:** $1\frac{1}{2}'$–$2\frac{1}{2}'$ tall, stout, slightly club-shaped, about $\frac{5}{8}''$ thick. **Leaves:** few, linear-oblong, blunt, leathery, 3″–5″ long. **Racemes:** 2″–3″ long, few-flowered. **Flowers:** 2″–$2\frac{1}{2}''$ across, thick and glossy; sepals linear-oblong; petals suborbicular; lip shortly convolute at the base, blade transversely oblong and downy, margin recurved and irregularly toothed. *July and August.*

A very handsome species producing numerous racemes of large ochre-yellow blossoms, with a paler lip blotched with blood-red in the centre; they are borne on the leafless stems. It is found on dry ledges and crevices in cliffs in the Himalaya, Khasia Hills, and mountains of Western Yunnan, reaching an elevation of 9000 feet above sea-level. Plants collected from such altitudes should prove sufficiently hardy for culture outdoors in the warmer parts of Britain, in a crevice of a sandstone rock in a sunny spot of the rock garden.

244. DENDROBIUM CUNNINGHAMII, Lindl.

D. biflorum, A. Rich.

Root: of thickened whitish fibres, epiphytic. **Stem:** tufted, slender, pendulous, polished, branched, 1′–2′ long. **Leaves:** cauline, broadly linear, 1″–1½″ long, numerous. **Racemes:** axillary, slender, 2- or many-flowered, ½″–1¼″ long. **Flowers:** ¾″ across; dorsal sepal narrowly lance-shaped; spur conical, short; lateral sepals broadly lance-shaped; petals oblong, blunt, equalling the sepals in length; lip 3-lobed; centre lobe broader than long, wavy, blunt; lateral lobes small. *December and January.*

A beautiful species with branching racemes of fairly large pale rose-coloured blossoms, beautifully contrasted by the pale green foliage and purplish stems. It is found on the moss-covered branches of large trees, and also on damp rocks, and is abundant in the woodlands throughout the North and South Islands of New Zealand. It grows at sufficient elevation in its native country to ensure its complete hardiness in the warmer parts of Great Britain. It may be tried on a damp moss-covered rock, sunk in a shady part of the bog garden.

245. DENDROBIUM LONGICORNU, Lindl.

D. flexuosum, Griff.

Root: of fleshy fibres on a short rhizome. **Stem:** 6″–12″ tall, rather slender, flexuous, with swollen internodes. **Leaves:** linear-lanceolate, unequally and bluntly 2-lobed at their tips, 2″–3″ long. **Flowers:** 2″ long, lateral and terminal; sepals lanceolate, not keeled, pointed; lateral sepals swollen and funnel-shaped at the base; petals narrowly lanceolate; lip 3-lobed; outer lobes rounded; centre lobe smaller than the outer lobes, orbicular, fringed; disc with 3-crenate ridges. *September and October.*

A beautiful plant with slender, flexuous jointed stems bearing numerous large white blossoms on short stems from the leaf axiles. It grows on trees and moss-covered rocks in forests and ravines in the Khasia and Naga Hill, and in the Himalaya from Nepal to Bhotan, reaching an elevation of 8000 feet above sea-level in Sikkim. It should be quite hardy in Southern and Western Britain outdoors, in a sheltered humid spot on a block of sandstone or apple stump, in living sphagnum-moss and peat.

246. DENDROBIUM MACRAEI, Lindl.

D. flabellum, Reichb. f. *D. nodosum*, Dalz. *D. pardalinum*, Reichb. f. *D. Rabanii*, Lindl. *Desmotrichum fimbriatum*, Blume.

Root: an annulate creeping rhizome. **Stems:** 2′–3′ long, pendulous, springing from fusiform pseudo-bulbs 2″–2½″ long. **Leaves:** linear-oblong blunt, sessile, 4″–8″ long. **Flowers:** about 1″ long, on stalks ¾″–1″ long, 2–3 to a stalk; dorsal sepal erect, linear-lanceolate; lateral sepals similar but swollen at their base into a short cone; petals narrowly linear-lanceolate; lip 3-lobed; outer lobes oblong, blunt; centre lobe small, crenulate and crisped, with 2 diverging lobules; disc between the outer lobes with 2 fleshy crests.

August and September.

A striking and handsome species with long pendulous stems over which are scattered numerous pseudo-bulbs from the apex of which spring sessile leaves and short racemes of two or three blossoms. The flowers are white, with the side lobes of the lip sprinkled with small red spots. It grows on the branches of trees in humid forests from Eastern Himalaya, where it reaches 8000 feet, to Ceylon and Java, and may be treated like *D. longicornu.*

247. DENDROBIUM PUGIONIFORME, A. Cunn.

D. pungentifolium, F. Muell.

Root: a creeping rhizome on the surface, emitting slender roots. **Stems:** rather slender, much branched, rooting at the nodes and covered with chaffy scales when young. **Leaves:** on short joints from the axils of the scales, ovate or ovate-oblong or ovate-lanceolate, tapering to a sharp point, ¾″–1¾″ long. **Racemes:** short, few-flowered. **Flowers:** about ⅝″ across; dorsal and lateral sepals lanceolate; spur at their base straight, blunt, ¼″ long; petals linear, as long as the sepals; lip broadly ovate-triangular, with a narrow base, much undulated; disc with 3 raised lines on its surface.

October to December.

A plant of but little decorative value, with prostrate creeping stems clothed with a few deep green leathery leaves and a few racemes of white, green and red blossoms springing from the creeping stem. It is found on moss-covered trees and rocks in woods and shady ravines in Queensland and New South Wales, and should be sufficiently hardy for culture outdoors in the sheltered valleys of South-Western England and Ireland on a moss-covered tree or rock, in a warm humid spot, with some peat over the roots.

248. DENDROBIUM SPECIOSUM, Sm.

Root: of few fleshy fibres springing from nodes on the creeping stem. **Stems:** very thick and fleshy, 6″–12″ long. **Leaves:** towards the apex of the stem, distichous, ovate or oblong, leathery, 3″–6″ long. **Raceme:** 9″–15″ long, terminal, many-flowered. **Flowers:** about $\frac{3}{4}$″ across; dorsal sepal lanceolate, slightly spreading or erect; lateral sepals similar, incurved; petals lanceolate, slightly spreading; lip 3-lobed; outer lobes short and broad; centre lobe broader than long, blunt. *September to November.*

This species is probably one of the most desirable of the sub-hardy species. It produces long racemes of fairly large blossoms with pale yellow sepals and petals and a white lip decorated with a few purple spots and blotches. It is found in shady places on moss- and fern-clad rocks in Queensland, New South Wales and Victoria where on the Nangatta Mountains it probably attains its greatest elevation above sea-level. Plants collected from the latter locality should succeed outdoor in Western and Southern Britain in a humid sheltered spot in peat and sphagnum-moss on a sandstone rock in shade.

249. DENDROBIUM STRIOLATUM, Reichb. f.

D. teretifolium, Lindl. *D. Milliganii*, F. Muell.

Root: a creeping rhizome emitting long white fibres. **Stem:** lax, fairly stout, branched, 6″–18″ long. **Leaves:** terminal or distant, terete, usually curved, fleshy, 1″–4″ long. **Scape:** solitary, short, 1- or 2-flowered, from the axils of the leaves. **Flowers:** over 1″ across; dorsal sepal narrowly lanceolate, basal spur short; lateral sepals lanceolate; petals narrowly lanceolate, almost linear; lip dilated in the middle into 2 broad lobes with a centre lobe ovate-oblong in shape with undulate margins and a recurved tip. *September and October.*

A pretty species with long, much branched drooping stems clothed with a bunch of rounded leaves at their tips from which springs a terminal flower-stem bearing one or two white blossoms with a few reddish-brown markings. It grows on moss-covered rocks and trees in shady places both in the lowlands and mountains of New South Wales, Victoria and Tasmania and is probably the hardiest of the southern species. It may be tried in a warm humid locality on a moss-covered tree or rock in the open air with some peat and sphagnum-moss over its roots.

DERŒMERIA, Reichenbach fils.

Dwarf deciduous terrestrial plants with roots composed of several oblong, ovoid or fusiform tubers, often of considerable size; they are usually sessile on the undergound position of the stem and have a few short fleshy roots above them. The large rounded leaves frequently shrivel up before the flowers are perfected; they spring from the base of the flower-stem, which is frequently very hairy and is clothed with numerous, often imbricating, sheaths.

The blossoms are borne in cylindrical or one-sided racemes and are usually small and of little decorative value. The genus numbers about 9 species and they are confined to tropical Africa and Arabia. The following species are found at sufficient altitude above sea-level to justify their inclusion in this work. They may be tried outdoors in Britain in all but the most exposed places, but it may be necessary to protect their tubers during the winter in some districts. Propagation by imported tubers and by seeds when procurable.

250. DERŒMERIA ACUMINATA, Rendle

Root: of fairly large oblong or ovoid tubers. **Leaf:** solitary, broadly orbicular, 1½″ across, withering before the blossoms appear. **Scape:** about 6″ tall, smooth, clothed with numerous triangular-lanceolate sheaths. **Raceme:** about 2½″ long, lax, many-flowered. **Flowers:** about ¼″ across; dorsal sepal and lateral sepals ovate or ovate-oblong, rather pointed; petals ovate, at times with a small tooth on either side below the apex; lip cymbiform, eared at its base; spur straight, ⅛″ long. *January and February.*

A plant of little or no decorative value but of interest for the alpine house. It has a narrow raceme of about eighteen small greenish-yellow and white blossoms borne on a short rather stout sheath-clothed stem. It grows in somewhat dry grassy places on rocky soils in the mountainous parts of British East Africa and Abyssinia, where, on Mount Edda Girges at 7000 feet above sea-level, it is exposed to over 15° of frost when at rest. A good fibrous sandy loam in full sun is indicated.

251. DERŒMERIA MONTIGENA, Rolfe

Holothrix montigena, Ridl.

Root: an oblong or ovate tuber of fair size. **Leaves:** very broadly rounded, amplexicaule, 1½″–2″ broad. **Scape:** fairly stout, 5″–8″ tall, downy at its base, smooth above, clothed with several pointed sheaths. **Raceme:** 1″–2″ long. **Flowers:** secund, about ¼″ across; dorsal sepal and lateral sepals ovate, rather blunt; petals spathulate, blunt; lip suborbicular, with its apex obscurely 3-lobed; spur narrowly conical, slightly curved, very short. *February.*

A dwarf white-flowered species of little decorative value but of interest for the alpine house. The blossoms are produced in a one-sided raceme on a rather stout sheath-clothed flower-stem which is leafy when bearing blossoms. The plant is found in dry spots among dwarf bushes at Gafat in Abyssinia at 8400 feet above sea-level, and is quite hardy in all but the most exposed parts of Great Britain. It should be grown in leaf-soil and loam in a half-shady spot.

252. DERŒMERIA PRÆCOX, Rendle

Holothrix præcox, Reichb. f.

Root: a rather large oblong tuber. **Leaf:** solitary, broadly orbicular, nearly 2″ across, withering before the flowers are produced. **Scape:** about 1′ tall, slender, clothed with many triangular, pointed sheaths. **Raceme:** about 4″ long. **Flowers:** about $\frac{1}{2}$″ across, secund; dorsal sepal and lateral sepals triangular, the latter shorter than the former; petals oblong, recurved at the tip which is prolonged into a thread or divided into several threads in the upper flowers; lip oblong, boat-shaped, apex deflexed; spur filiform. *January to April.*

This plant is of but little decorative value, the greenish-white blossoms are, however, very quaintly formed and it should prove of value to lovers of interesting plants; the blossoms are produced in one-sided racemes on slender flower-stems. It grows in rocky soil beneath the shade of trees near Debra Erki, in Abyssinia, at 9400 feet above sea-level and is quite hardy in Great Britain. In this country it may be grown under the same conditions as the former species.

253. DERŒMERIA SCHIMPERI, Rolfe

Holothrix Schimperi, Reichb. f.

Root: a rather small ovoid or oblong tuber. **Leaf:** solitary, orbicular-reniform, $1\frac{1}{4}$″ broad. **Scape:** 5″–9″ tall, clothed with numerous pointed sheaths. **Raceme:** 2″–4″ long, with the blossoms arranged in a spiral manner. **Flowers:** about $\frac{3}{8}$″ across; dorsal sepal and lateral sepals lanceolate-triangular; petals ligulate, toothed at the apex; lip cymbiform, at times subtrilobed at the tip; spur arcuate, pointed, short. *March and April.*

Like those species already described, this plant is only of interest to lovers of curious, apart from decorative, subjects. The greenish-white blossoms are borne in a twisted raceme like those of most species of Spiranthes, which it much resembles both in flower and mode of growth. It grows in shady places amongst rocks and in wooded ravines on the mountains of Abyssinia at sufficient elevation above sea-level to ensure its complete hardiness in all but the bleakest parts of Great Britain. Sandy leaf-soil and a half-shady situation will meet its requirements.

254. DERŒMERIA SQUAMATA, Reichb. f.

Holothrix squamata, Reichb. f. *Peristylus squamatus*, Hochst. *Spiranthes abyssinica*, Hochst.

Root: a fairly large ovoid or oblong tuber. **Leaf:** solitary, orbicular, broad, about 2″ across, withering before the flowers are produced. **Scape:**

4″–5″ tall, stout, clothed with numerous long ovate-lanceolate sheaths. **Flowers:** several, on stalks of varying lengths, $\frac{1}{4}$″ across sepals; dorsal and lateral sepals ovate or ovate-oblong, blunt; petals ovate-oblong, blunt, slightly longer than the sepals; lip broadly oblong, blunt, undivided; spur conical, blunt. *February to April.*

A dwarf species with green and white flowers suitable for alpine house culture, they have no decorative value. The plant grows in dry meadows and fields in various parts of elevated regions in Abyssinia, reaching an altitude above sea-level that should ensure its hardiness in all but the bleakest parts of Great Britain. In cultivation it may be grown in an open sunny spot, in a heavy loam.

255. DERŒMERIA UNIFOLIA, Reichb. f.

Holothrix unifolia, Reichb. f. *Peristylus unifolius,* Hochst.

Root: a fusiform or ovate tuber. **Leaves:** orbicular, cordate, rather pointed, $1\frac{1}{2}$″–2″ across. **Scape:** 4″–5″ tall, bristly, the upper half clothed with sessile, triangular, pointed sheaths. **Raceme:** about $1\frac{3}{4}$″ long, cylindrical. **Flowers:** about $\frac{3}{8}$″ across, secund; dorsal sepal and lateral sepals ovate, pointed; petals cuneate, ovate, pointed; lip oblong, with its apex divided into 5 minute lobes; spur cylindrical, rather short.

March to May.

Like many of the other members of the genus this species produces its cylindrical racemes of greenish-yellow blossoms after the basal leaves have withered, which is probably accounted for by the dry sun-baked nature of its habitat. It grows in dry open meadows and agricultural land near Debra Eski in Abyssinia at 9300 feet above sea-level, where it is exposed to over 20° of frost when at rest. In cultivation a good rich heavy loam in full sun is indicated.

DIPODIUM, R. Brown

This genus contains 12 species of handsome deciduous terrestrial plants of erect habit, some are quite leafless, the place of the leaves being taken by sheathing and frequently imbricating bracts. The root is composed of thick, almost tuberous, fibres and is buried quite near the surface of the soil. The flower-stem is stout and is usually richly tinted; it bears a long spike or raceme of pretty blossoms which are brightly coloured and remain in good condition for a long time. Most of the plants, which are found in woods and forest beneath the shade of trees, are saprophytes and probably some are parasites. The species range from Malaya to Australia and some are also found in the islands of the Pacific. The plants should be imported with some of the soil in which they are growing and if possible planted over the roots of some species of Eucalyptus in damp leaf-soil and sand. Propagation by imported tubers and seed.

256. DIPODIUM PUNCTATUM, R. Br.

Dendrobium punctatum, Sm.

Root: of thick, almost tuberous fibres. **Scape:** 1′–2′ tall, leafless, clothed with a few sheathing scales, imbricate below, more scattered upwards. **Raceme:** 4″–9″ long, fairly dense. **Flowers:** about $1\frac{1}{4}''$ in diameter; dorsal sepal, lateral sepals and petals oblong-lanceolate, of nearly equal length; lip 3-lobed; outer lobes narrow and erect; centre lobe ovate or obovate-oblong; disc with raised hairy lines; basal pouch short. *March.*

A very handsome and desirable plant of robust habit, with a tall bract-clothed stem frequently of a rich purple colour and a hyacinth-like spike of large pale crimson blossoms, which are usually spotted and blotched with purple. It is found, generally speaking, in moist stony ground at the roots of Eucalypti over nearly the whole of Australia. It ascends the mountains to an elevation of over 4000 feet in Victoria and is exposed to over 15° of frost for short periods during the winter. The plant is probably parasitical and may be tried in the warmer parts of Britain, planted at the roots of some of the hardy Eucalypti.

DISA, Bergen

The majority of the 150 or more species which constitute this genus are highly ornamental and desirable plants; they are deciduous or sub-evergreen terrestrial herbs with tuberous and stoloniferous root systems, the tubers usually perish after the seeds have ripened, fresh tubers being produced each vegetative season if the plants are in a thriving condition. The leaves, which appear with or before the flower-stem, are variously shaped, radical or cauline, and are at times produced on separate growths. The leaves on the flower-stems are reduced to sheaths. The blossoms are corymbose, racemose or in loose or dense cylindrical spikes, rarely solitary. The floral bracts are usually narrow. In a state of nature the plants are found in a great variety of situations where their flowers are exposed to the sun and their roots are in a cool moist soil which is at times of a heavy nature. They are confined to Africa and Madagascar. Propagation by separation of the tubers and division of the stolons and also by seed.

257. DISA ACONITOIDES, Sond.

Root: tuberous, sessile, terrestrial. **Stem:** moderately stout. **Leaves:** radical, linear-oblong, 3″–5″ long; cauline leaves lanceolate-oblong, 1″–3″ long, reduced to bracts upwards, all suberect. **Scape:** $\frac{3}{4}'$–2′ tall, sheath-clothed. **Spike:** 3″–8″ long, lax. **Flowers:** $\frac{1}{2}''$ across; dorsal sepal galeate, erect, broadly ovate; spur conical, $\frac{1}{4}''$ long; lateral sepals oblique, ovate; petals falcate, constricted below, dilated above; lip elliptic-spathulate, convex.

October to December.

This is rather a pretty plant with its long, narrow, loose spikes of small white or lilac blossoms, sprinkled with small light purple spots, and borne on erect leafy stems. It inhabits moist grassy places in Eastern Cape Colony, Natal, Orange Free State and the Transvaal, and attains its greatest altitude on the Elands Spruit Mountains at 7000 feet, where the thermometer falls to the zero point (F.) for short periods during its resting season. It requires a cool moist root run in fibrous loam and full exposure to the sun.

258. DISA BRACHYCERAS, Lindl.

D. tenella var. *brachyceras*, Schltr.

Root: tuberous, sessile. **Stem:** slender. **Leaves:** numerous, suberect, linear, curved, $\frac{1}{2}''$–$1\frac{1}{4}''$ long. **Scape:** slender, 2″–4″ tall. **Spike:** dense, $\frac{1}{3}''$–$1\frac{1}{2}''$ long. **Flowers:** $\frac{1}{4}''$ across; dorsal sepal galeate, broadly ovate; spur broadly saccate, minute; lateral sepals ovate-oblong; petals rhomboid-ovate, narrowing upwards; lip linear, blunt. *August.*

This tiny species is too small to make any show in the rock garden, but the closely-packed spikes of little yellow and white blossoms set off by their neat foliage should prove attractive in the alpine house. It is found in damp stony places in the hilly districts and elevated plains in Western Cape Colony, reaching its greatest altitude on the Cold Bokkeveld in the Ceres Division at 3500 feet, a region where 15° of frost are frequently registered for short periods during the winter. It should be grown in a compost of sandy peat and loam in a sunny sheltered spot, and kept saturated when in growth. It is only suitable for outdoor culture in Western and Southern Britain.

259. DISA CAPRICORNIS, Reichb. f.

D. gladioliflora, Bolus

Root: tuberous, sessile. **Stem:** slender. **Leaves:** radical, grass-like, 3″–8″ long. **Scape:** sheath-clothed, 10″–15″ tall. **Spike:** many-flowered, lax, $2\frac{1}{2}''$–4″ long. **Flowers:** $\frac{5}{8}''$ across; dorsal sepal galeate, ovate-oblong; spur slender, curved, $\frac{3}{16}''$ long; lateral sepals oblong; petals falcate-oblong, with a short rounded basal lobe in front; lip spathulate-ovate, obtuse.

November and December.

A pretty species with rather short loose spikes of fair-sized hooded, rose-coloured blossoms on a slender sheath-clothed flower-stem with a tuft of bright green grassy leaves at its base. It is found on grassy mountain slopes, usually where there are outcrops of rock, in Southern Cape Colony and Griqualand East, where on the Insizwa Mountains at 6900 feet it attains its greatest elevation above sea-level. At such altitudes the thermometer frequently touches the zero point (F.) for short periods during the winter. It should be given a gritty fibrous peat, in full sun, and plentifully supplied with water when in leaf.

260. DISA CEPHALOTES, Reichb. f.

Root: of sessile tubers. **Stem:** rather slender. **Leaves:** cauline, few, linear-lanceolate, 3″–8″ long. **Scape:** 6″–18″ tall, sheath-clothed. **Spike:** dense, many-flowered, subcapitate or shortly oblong, $\frac{1}{2}$″–1″ long. **Flowers:** $\frac{3}{8}$″ long; dorsal sepal galeate, broadly oblong or ovate, margin incurved; spur cylindrical, curved, nearly $\frac{1}{2}$″ long; lateral sepals broadly ovate-oblong, flat; petals broadly ovate, oblique; lip linear-oblong, blunt.

January and February.

A dainty and delicate plant with a dense head of white blossoms spotted with purple. It grows in stony places in the mountainous districts of Eastern Cape Colony, Orange Free State, Tembuland and Natal, where it attains its greatest elevation above sea-level on the grass-covered slopes of stony hills near Van Reenen at 7000 feet. It should be hardy in all but the bleakest parts of Great Britain in a damp fibrous peat in full sun.

261. DISA CHRYSOSTACHYA, Sw.

D. gracilis, Lindl.

Root: tuberous, sessile. **Stem:** often very stout. **Leaves:** numerous, ligulate-linear or linear-oblong below, oblong above, passing into bracts, 9″–12″ long. **Scape:** $1\frac{1}{4}$′–$3\frac{1}{4}$′ tall, clothed with imbricate sheaths. **Spike:** 6″–18″ long, dense, cylindrical. **Flowers:** $\frac{1}{4}$″ long; dorsal sepal galeate, elliptic-obovate; spur inflated, elliptic-oblong, $\frac{3}{16}$″ long; lateral sepals elliptic, blunt; petals obovate, blunt; lip linear. *November and December.*

This is a very robust and rather handsome plant with its long cylindrical spikes of rather small blossoms with orange-coloured sepals and yellow petals and lip. It inhabits marshy districts and is common throughout nearly the whole of South Africa, where it can find conditions to suit its requirements. It reaches its greatest altitude at Oliviers Hoek in Natal at 5000 feet, where it is exposed to 15° or more of frost for periods during the winter. It should be planted in a rich soil on the banks of a pond or stream or in the bog garden. Some fibrous peat should be mixed with the compost.

262. DISA COOPERI, Reichb. f.

Root: of sessile tubers. **Stem:** very stout. **Leaves:** cauline, 1″–3″ long, ovate-oblong, on stem; radical leaves, 4″–16″ long, lanceolate, springing from a distinct bud. **Scape:** $1\frac{1}{4}$′–2′ tall, clothed with broad imbricate sheaths. **Spike:** 6″–10″ long, dense, many-flowered. **Flowers:** nearly 1″ across; dorsal sepal galeate, very broadly ovate; spur ascending, curved, about $1\frac{1}{2}$″ long; lateral sepals ovate, obtuse; petals broadly oblong; lip broadly rhomboid-ovate, crenulate. *December and January.*

A very beautiful and most desirable plant, with large rose-pink blossoms with a yellow lip; the flowers are of great substance and lasting power. It grows on the margins of marshes and rivers in the Orange Free State, Transvaal, Basutoland, Swaziland, Natal and Griqualand East; it reaches its greatest altitude between Swaziland and Carolina at 6900 feet where it is subjected to 25° of frost during its resting period. At this elevation it is somewhat dwarf. It should be grown on the banks of a pond or stream or in the bog garden, in good soil composed of fibrous peat and fibrous loam surfaced with sphagnum-moss. *See Plate 8 facing page 123.*

263. DISA CRASSICORNIS, Lindl.

D. macrantha, Hemsl. *D. megaceras*, Hook. f.

Root: a sessile tuber. **Stem:** very stout. **Leaves:** radical and cauline, oblong-lanceolate, fleshy, 3″–12″ long. **Scape:** 1′–3′ tall, sheath-clothed. **Spike:** 4″–10″ long, dense or somewhat lax. **Flowers:** $1\frac{3}{4}$″ across; dorsal sepal galeate, broadly ovate; spur curved, stout, $1\frac{3}{4}$″ long; lateral sepals narrowly ovate, oblique; petals broadly ovate, oblique; lip oblong-lanceolate, blunt. *November.*

This fine plant is certainly one of the most beautiful members of the genus. The very large fragrant yellow or cream-coloured blossoms with their pale purple spots are very decorative. It grows in clefts of rocks and in moist places, sometimes in shade, on the mountains of Natal and Griqualand East and also in Eastern Cape Colony; here it probably attains its greatest elevation above sea-level on the Witteberg Range at Aliwal North, at 8000 feet, where the thermometer frequently falls to zero F. for short periods during the winter. It should succeed in the border or rock garden in strong fibrous loam and peat kept reasonably moist during the summer.

264. DISA CYLINDRICA, Sw.

D. bracteata, Lindl. *Satyrium cylindricum*, Thunb. *Monadenia bracteata*, Durand & Schinz

Root: of oval tubers. **Stem:** stout, leafy, 6″–12″ tall. **Leaves:** numerous, oblong, $1\frac{1}{2}$″–4″ long, decreasing upwards into bracts. **Raceme:** dense, cylin-

PLATE 7.

CYPRIPEDIUM MONTANUM.

PLATE 8.

DISA COOPERI.

drical, 1″–4½″ long. **Flowers:** under ½″ long; dorsal sepal galeate, ovate-oblong; spur saccate, oblong, minute; lateral sepals ovate-oblong, recurved; petals obliquely ovate; lip linear-oblong, recurved. *October to December.*

Although this is by no means a decorative plant, the small dull yellow blossoms in their dense cylindrical spikes and the neat suberect leafage of the flower-stem should appeal to lovers of interesting plants apart from decorative value. It is found in moist rocky ground and clefts in damp rocks, usually in shade, in South-Western Cape Colony and attains its greatest altitude on the mountains of the George Division above Montague Pass at 4000 feet, where it is subjected to over 10° of frost for short periods when deciduous. It may be given a compost of gritty fibrous peat and loam, in a sheltered half-shady bay in the rock garden and kept saturated when in growth. It is only suitable for outdoor culture in the warmer Southern and Western counties of Britain.

265. DISA DECKENII, Reichb. f.

D. kilimanjarica, Rendle; *D. polygonoides*, Kränzl.

Root: an ovoid tuber. **Stem:** stout. **Leaves:** radical and cauline, strap-shaped, decreasing upwards into leaf-like bracts, 2″–8″ long. **Scape:** 6″–12″ tall, smooth, fairly stout. **Spike:** 1″–2″ long, dense. **Flowers:** ⅜″ across; dorsal sepal galeate, ovate, blunt; spur slender, ¼″ long; lateral sepals ovate, pointed, widely spreading; petals narrowly lanceolate, rather pointed; lip linear-lanceolate, pointed. *August.*

Although the blossoms of this species are small their brilliant crimson or red-mauve colouring should render the plant a striking object in the rock garden. It grows in moist or marshy spots on the slopes of Kilimanjaro in Tanganyika, East Africa at an elevation of 10,000 feet above sea-level and may therefore be considered an alpine plant. It should prove quite hardy in Great Britain, in a raised part of the bog garden or in a damp spot in the rock garden, in fibrous sandy peat and loam.

266. DISA DRACONIS, Sw.

Orchis Draconis, Linn. *Satyrium Draconis*, Thunb.

Root: a sessile tuber. **Stem:** rather stout. **Leaves:** 3″–9″ long, sub-radical, few, linear or oblong-linear. **Scape:** 1′–1¾′ tall, sheath-clothed. **Spike:** 2″–5″ long, usually many-flowered. **Flowers:** 1½″ across; dorsal sepal subgaleate, obovate or obovate-oblong, somewhat reflexed; spur filiform, 2¼″ long; lateral sepals oblong, spreading; petals oblong or subfalcate-oblong, recurved; lip linear, obtuse. *November and December.*

The large straw-coloured blossoms are very pretty and are well set off by the rich green grassy foliage. It is a very desirable garden plant and is found in damp rocky soil on the mountains of Western Cape Colony and Little Namaqualand and attains its greatest altitude at Lily Fountein (5000 feet), where it is exposed to 15° or more of frost for considerable periods during its winter rest. It should be grown in full sun in a compost of gritty peat and leaf-soil, and should never be dry even when it is at rest.

267. DISA FRAGRANS, Schltr.

Root: a sessile tuber. **Stem:** stout. **Leaves:** 2″–3½″ long, few, cauline, reduced upwards into sheaths. **Scape:** ½″–¾″ tall, sheath-clothed. **Spike:** 2″–4″ long, oblong, dense. **Flowers:** about ⅜″ across; dorsal sepal galeate, elliptic-oblong; spur somewhat clavate, ¼″ long; lateral sepals oblong, blunt; petals subspathulate-oblong, blunt; lip spathulate-linear, blunt.

February and March.

Although the pink or whitish, purple-spotted blossoms are too small to be of any use in decorative gardening, it should prove an attractive little plant for a deep pan in the alpine house. It is confined to stony places clothed with but scant herbage, on or near the summits of high mountains in Natal, Griqualand East, Transvaal and the Orange Free State, where on the western face of Mont aux-Sources it reaches an elevation of 9000 feet and is nowhere found below 6500 feet. It should be perfectly hardy in Great Britain could its resting period be made to coincide with our winter. A gritty peat with moisture is indicated.

268. DISA FRIGIDA, Schltr.

D. cephalotes, Kränzl. partly

Root: a sessile tuber. **Stem:** rather slender. **Leaves:** 2¼″–4″ long, subcauline, few, linear. **Scape:** 5″–10″ tall, clothed with two or three narrow sheaths. **Spike:** 1″–2″ long, lax. **Flowers:** ⅜″ across, dorsal sepal galeate, broadly ovate; spur slender, curved, ⅛″ long; lateral sepals oblong; petals obliquely ovate; lip subspathulate-linear. *November and December.*

This Orchid probably reaches a greater altitude in South Africa than any other species. The blossoms are usually rose colour, though sometimes white, and are too small to be of any decorative value. It should make a welcome addition to the alpine house. It grows in rocky ground amongst low herbage on the summit of Mont aux-Sources, on the Orange Free State side of the mountain, where the zero F. point is frequently reached during its resting period. It should be given a compost of gritty fibrous loam and peat in full sun and kept moist when in growth.

269. DISA GALPINII, Rolfe

Root: a sessile tuber. **Stem:** stout. **Leaves:** cauline, 1″–2″ long, oblong, reduced upwards into bracts. **Scape:** about $1\frac{1}{2}$′ tall, sheath-clothed. **Spike:** 5″ long, subcylindrical, dense. **Flowers:** $\frac{3}{8}$″ across; dorsal sepal galeate, broadly ovate; spur clavate, over $\frac{1}{2}$″ long; lateral sepals oblong, blunt; petals broadly oblong, oblique; lip oblong, blunt. *November to January.*

Although the fleshy, hooded blossoms of this species, with their long spurs, are rather small, their numbers and bright red tint give some decorative value to the plant. It is found on the banks of streams in the Maclear District of Griqualand East at 5600 feet altitude, where the thermometer falls to 10° F. for short periods during the winter months. This plant should be grown in the bog garden or on the banks of a stream or pond, where its roots may be cool and moist and its blossoms fully exposed to the sun, in a good rich loam and peat.

270. DISA GLANDULOSA, Burch.

Root: a sessile tuber. **Stem:** rather stout. **Leaves:** radical, spathulate or ovate-lanceolate, glandular-pubescent, $\frac{1}{2}$″–1″ long. **Scape:** 3″–7″ tall, sheath-clothed, pubescent. **Spike:** $\frac{1}{2}$″–1″ long, compact. **Flowers:** $\frac{1}{2}$″ across; dorsal sepal galeate, ovate; spur rather stout, $\frac{1}{4}$″ long; lateral sepals elliptic-oblong, blunt; petals somewhat oblique, ovate-oblong, blunt; lip obovate-oblong, blunt. *December and January.*

This is a pretty rather dwarf species with about a dozen rose-pink, hooded blossoms borne on the downy sheath-clothed flower-stem which rises from a tuft of rich green, somewhat spreading, leaves. It should make a delightful subject for alpine house culture. It is found in clefts in wet rocks on or near the summits of the mist-shrouded mountains of South-Western Cape Colony and attains its greatest elevation at Lowrys Pass in the Stellenbosch Division at 4200 feet and is there exposed to 12° of frost during the winter. It should be grown in moist "lumpy" peat, loam and lumps of sandstone.

271. DISA HAMATOPETALA, Rendle

Root: an ovoid or oblong tuber. **Stem:** slender. **Leaves:** linear-filiform, sub-basal, 4″–6″ long. **Scape:** 6″–18″ tall, smooth, clothed with numerous membranous sheaths. **Spike:** of 1–7 flowers, lax. **Flowers:** about $\frac{1}{8}$″ across; dorsal sepal galeate, ovate; spur stout and blunt, $\frac{3}{16}$″ long; lateral sepals oblong, concave, blunt, rather spreading; petals broad at the base, narrow in the middle, dilated and toothed at the apex; lip broadly oblong, deeply fringed. *August and September.*

A beautiful plant bearing in well-grown specimens about half-a-dozen large blue and purple blossoms in a loose raceme or spike on a slender sheath-clothed flower-stem. In its native habitat the leaves wither away before the blossoms are perfected. It grows in elevated regions in open grassy places, liable to inundation during the rainy season, in various parts of Tanganyika, East Africa and British Central Africa, where on Mount Zomba it reaches an elevation of 7000 feet above sea-level. Hardy in sheltered districts in moist fibrous peat and loam.

272. DISA LÆTA, Reichb. f.

D. hircicornis, Schltr. partly. *D. Culveri*, Schltr.

Root: a sessile tuber. **Stem:** stout. **Leaves:** 4″–9″ long, linear or linear-oblong, radical. **Scape:** $1\frac{1}{4}$′–$1\frac{1}{2}$′ tall, sheath-clothed. **Spike:** 3″–4″ long, oblong, dense. **Flowers:** over $\frac{5}{8}$″ across; dorsal sepal galeate, broadly triangular-ovate; spur cylindrical, curved near the base, $\frac{3}{8}$″ long; lateral sepals ovate-oblong; petals narrowly ovate-oblong; lip subspathulate-linear, rather blunt. *November and December.*

The white or pale pink blossoms are of medium size and would make the plant a decorative subject for the stream-side or bog garden. It grows in marshes and swamps, reaching its greatest altitude near Botsabelo, near Middleburg, in the Transvaal, at 4800 feet, where the thermometer frequently falls to 20° F. for short periods during its resting season. It is also found in Natal. It should be grown in a good rich loam on the banks of a stream or pond, or in the bog garden; the blossoms should be exposed to the sun.

273. DISA MACOWANII, Reichb. f.

D. versicolor, Schltr., partly.

Root: a sessile tuber. **Stem:** stout. **Leaves:** radical, elongate-linear, fleshy, 6″–11″ long; cauline leaves ovate-oblong, $1\frac{1}{2}$″–3″ long, fleshy. **Scape:** 1′–$1\frac{3}{4}$′ tall, sheath-clothed. **Spike:** 4″–9″ long, cylindrical, very dense. **Flowers:** $\frac{3}{8}$″ across; dorsal sepal galeate, broadly ovate; spur nearly straight, $\frac{1}{4}$″ long; lateral sepals obliquely ovate, spreading; petals obliquely ovate, rather blunt; lip subspathulate-oblong. *December to February.*

This stout leafy species, with its rather small pink blossoms with hooded dorsal sepal and spreading lateral sepals growing in long many-flowered poker-like spikes, should make an attractive subject for the bog garden. It grows in wet or swampy places on the summits of mountains or on the plains in Eastern Cape Colony, Orange Free State, Transvaal, Natal and Griqualand East, where on the Insizwa Range it reaches an elevation of 6500 feet and is subjected to 25° of frost. It should be grown in a damp spot in good loam and fibrous peat.

274. DISA MARLOTHII, Bolus

Root: a sessile tuber. **Stem:** rather slender. **Leaves:** 1″–2½″ long, radical, numerous, lanceolate or oblong-lanceolate. **Scape:** 5″–10″ tall, sheath-clothed. **Spike:** short, 1–6-flowered. **Flowers:** nearly ¾″ in diameter; dorsal sepal subgaleate, ovate-orbicular, subtruncate; spur conical, ¾″ long; lateral sepals broadly oblong; petals falcate-oblong; lip oblong. *January.*

A decidedly decorative species with medium-sized bright rose-pink blossoms with small deep carmine spots on the dorsal sepal and petals. The neat rather slender stem and somewhat spreading rich green foliage adds to its attractions. It grows in damp stony or sandy places on the high mountains of Western Cape Colony, attaining its greatest altitude on the Skurjdeberg Range in the Ceres Division at 6000 feet, and, could its growth be retarded so that its deciduous period coincided with our winter, should be perfectly hardy in Great Britain. A moist sandy peat and full exposure to the sun is indicated.

275. DISA MICROPETALA, Schltr.

Root: a sessile tuber. **Stem:** stout. **Leaves:** ¾″–3″ long, radical and cauline, linear, numerous. **Scape:** 6″–9″ tall. **Spike:** 2½″–5″ long, dense, many-flowered. **Flowers:** about $\frac{3}{16}$″ across; dorsal sepal galeate, broadly ovate; spur oblong, curved, minute; lateral sepals ovate or ovate-oblong, blunt; petals linear or falcate-linear, blunt; lip linear-oblong, blunt.
October to January.

The tiny yellowish-white blossoms of this species, although copiously produced in long spikes, are of but little decorative value. It is suitable for a pot or pan in the alpine house. It grows in South-Western Cape Colony on moist grassy mountain slopes and attains its greatest altitude on the mountains near Genadendal in the Caledon Division at 4800 feet, where it is exposed to over 20° of frost for fairly long periods when deciduous. It may be grown in the bog garden in fibrous peat and loam in full sun.

276. DISA MONTANA, Sond.

D. pulchra var. *montana,* Schltr.

Root: a sessile tuber. **Stem:** stout, leafy. **Leaves:** 3″–6″ long, ensiform, rigid. **Scape:** 1½′–2′ tall. **Spike:** about 3″ long, lax, many-flowered. **Flowers:** nearly ¾″ across; dorsal sepal galeate, broadly ovate; spur very narrowly conical, ⅜″ long; lateral sepals ovate-oblong, oblique; petals narrowly ovate-triangular, pointed; lip oblong, blunt.
November to January.

This is a decidedly decorative plant with medium-sized, hooded, rosy-red blossoms borne on a tall upright leafy flower-stem. It is found in moist grassy places on high mountains in Griqualand East and Eastern Cape Colony on the Winterberg Range in the Queenstown Division, where it reaches its greatest altitude of 6000 feet and should be perfectly hardy in Great Britain, if its vegetative season could be retarded. It may be grown in the bog garden or in a damp spot in a compost of fibrous peat and loam kept saturated when the plant is in full growth.

277. DISA NEGLECTA, Sond.

D. lineata, Bolus

Root: a sessile tuber. **Stem:** fairly stout. **Leaves:** radical, linear-lanceolate, about $3\frac{1}{2}''$ long; cauline leaves linear, $1\frac{1}{2}''$–$3''$ long. **Scape:** $4''$–$7''$ long, clothed with a few sheaths below. **Spike:** $1\frac{1}{2}''$–$2\frac{1}{2}''$ long, oblong, rather dense, many-flowered. **Flowers:** over $\frac{3}{8}''$ in length; dorsal sepal very broadly ovate, galeate, with a narrow mouth; spur obsolete; lateral sepals oblong, slightly concave; petals semiovate-oblong, oblique; lip ovate-lanceolate, concave. *November and December.*

The blossoms of this species have their segments so converging that they remain in a half-closed state even when fully developed; they are dull yellow with purple-lined and spotted sepals and a purple stain on the middle of the lip, and are too small to have any decorative value. It is found on moist mountain slopes amongst short herbage in South-Western Cape Colony, reaching its greatest altitude on the Outeniqua Mountains above Montague Pass in the George Division at 4000 feet, where it is exposed to 12° of frost in the winter. It should be grown in sandy peat in an elevated spot in the bog garden.

278. DISA NERVOSA, Lindl.

Root: a sessile tuber. **Stem:** slender. **Leaves:** cauline, $4''$–$8''$ long, linear or narrowly oblong-linear, rather fleshy. **Scape:** $1\frac{1}{2}'$–$2'$ tall, sheath-clothed. **Spike:** $4''$–$6''$ long, oblong, rather dense. **Flowers:** nearly $1\frac{1}{2}''$ across; dorsal sepal galeate, oblong or elliptic-oblong, margins incurved; spur cylindrical, curved, $\frac{3}{4}''$ long; lateral sepals oblong, blunt; petals falcate-oblong, blunt; lip filiform, thickened at the apex. *November to February.*

A very beautiful plant with large deep pink or rosy-purple blossoms in fairly long spikes. It grows amongst grass and short herbage in stony or rocky places in elevated districts in Pondoland and Natal, where it reaches its greatest altitude at Van Reenen, 6000 feet, and is exposed to 25° of frost for short periods during the winter. It should be given a compost of sandy peat and loam mixed with lumps of sandstone and should be kept moist when in growth.

279. DISA OREOPHILA, Bolus

Root: tuberous, sessile. **Stem:** slender. **Leaves:** radical and cauline, numerous, narrowly linear, 3″–8″ long. **Scape:** 6″–9″ tall, sheath-clothed. **Spike:** 2″–3″ long, rather lax, many-flowered. **Flowers:** about ½″ across; dorsal sepal galeate, ovate-oblong; spur cylindrical, ⅜″ long; lateral sepals ovate-oblong, with a long slender dorsal apiculus; petals broadly oblong, with a large rounded basal lobe; lip spathulate. *January and February.*

This is a pretty dwarf species suitable for alpine-house culture; it has rather small pale pink blossoms with small crimson spots on the sepals. It grows in rocky stony ground amongst short herbage, mostly in elevated regions, in the Orange Free State, Tembuland, Natal and Griqualand East, where it reaches its greatest altitude on Mount Currie at 7500 feet, the temperature frequently falling to the zero F. point during the winter. It should be grown in full sun in a gritty peat and loam.

280. DISA OVALIFOLIA, Sond.

D. pallidiflora, Bolus

Root: a sessile tuber. **Stem:** very stout. **Leaves:** radical, few, broadly elliptic or suborbicular, fleshy, 1″–1¾″ long. **Scape:** 6″–8″ tall, sheath-clothed. **Spike:** 1½″–3″ long, oblong, rather dense, many-flowered. **Flowers:** ¾″ across; dorsal sepal galeate, funnel-shaped; spur cylindrical, slender, ½″ long; lateral sepals oblong, somewhat spreading, concave; petals falcate-oblong, incurved; basal lobe rounded; lip linear-oblong, blunt, fleshy. *September and October.*

A desirable dwarf species with rather large white blossoms with the hood drawn out like a long funnel. It is hardly dainty enough for the alpine house, but should prove of use for the rock garden. It is found in stony ground amongst dwarf herbage, and also in rocky places where there is moisture, in South-Western Cape Colony and probably reaches its greatest elevation on the Cold Bokkeveld near Gydouw at 3500 feet and is there subjected to 12° of frost in winter. It should be given a moist fibrous peat and loam in the sun. It is only suitable for outdoor culture in the warmer Western counties.

281. DISA PATULA, Sond.

D. stenoglossa, Bolus; *Monadenia lydenbergensis*, Kränzl.

Root: a sessile tuber. **Stem:** stout. **Leaves:** cauline, 2″–5″ long, lanceolate or ovate-lanceolate, reduced upwards. **Scape:** 9″–18″ tall. **Spike:** 2″–6″ long, dense or sometimes lax. **Flowers:** over ¾″ across; dorsal sepal galeate, broadly oblong, somewhat incurved at the margins; spur cylindrical, curved, $\frac{5}{8}''$ long; petals obliquely ovate-oblong, blunt; lip linear.

December to February.

The pink or rose-coloured blossoms of this pretty plant are at times spotted and lined with purple, and being of a good size they are of value for garden decoration. It inhabits damp, grassy, stony places on mountain slopes and is found in Eastern Cape Colony, Transvaal and Natal, where at Oliviers Hoek at 5000 feet it attains its greatest altitude and is exposed to a winter temperature of 15° F. for short periods. It should be grown in a compost of fibrous peat, loam and grit, kept saturated when in active growth and never very dry even when it is at rest. The plant is only suitable for outdoor culture in South-Western Britain.

282. DISA PORRECTA, Sw.

D. Zeyheri, Sond.

Root: a sessile tuber. **Stem:** moderately stout. **Leaves:** radical, 5″–7″ long, elongate-linear, numerous. **Scape:** $1'$–$1\frac{1}{2}'$ tall, sheath-clothed. **Spike:** $2''$–$3\frac{1}{2}''$ long, oblong, rather dense. **Flowers:** over $\frac{5}{8}''$ across; dorsal sepal galeate, very broadly ovate, undulate; spur narrowly conical, upcurved, slender, $1\frac{1}{4}''$ long; lateral sepals elliptic-suborbicular, concave; petals nearly quadrate, blunt; lip oblong or lanceolate-oblong. *January to March.*

This is a very beautiful plant with fairly large blossoms of a deep rich vermilion colour, they are rather fleshy and have conspicuously long spurs to the hooded dorsal sepals. It grows in poor stony soil amidst scant herbage on the hills and mountains of Transkei, Basutoland and Eastern Cape Colony, where in the Koudeveld Mountains in the Graaff Reinet Division it probably reaches its greatest altitude at 4450 feet and is exposed to 15° or 20° of frost during its resting period. A gritty loam in full sun is indicated.

283. DISA PULCHELLA, Hochst.

Root: a small ovoid sessile tuber. **Stem:** fairly stout. **Leaves:** radical and cauline, lanceolate to elliptic-oblong, pointed, gradually decreasing upwards in length, 3″–4″ long. **Scape:** smooth, 6″–15″ tall. **Spike:** $1\frac{1}{2}''$–$4\frac{1}{2}''$ long, dense. **Flowers:** about $\frac{1}{2}''$ across; dorsal sepal galeate, oblong or suborbicular; lateral sepals oblong or cuneate-oblong, blunt; petals oblong, dilated at the apex, eared at the base; lip linear-oblong, lanceolate or spathulate-obovate, keeled down its margin. *August and September.*

As its scientific name implies, this is a pretty little plant with white or cream-coloured purple-spotted blossoms in a fairly long spike on a slender flower-stem. It is found in moist grassy places and on the banks of streams in various places in Abyssinia and probably reaches its greatest elevation above sea-level on Debra Tabor at 8500 feet, where it is exposed to over 20° of frost during its deciduous period. A compost of fibrous peat and loam in a damp sunny spot is indicated.

284. DISA PULCHRA, Sond.

Root: a sessile tuber. **Stem:** rather stout. **Leaves:** cauline, 3″–8″ long, linear or oblong-linear, numerous, reduced upwards into bracts. **Scape:** $1\frac{1}{2}'$–$2\frac{1}{4}'$ tall. **Spike:** 5″–10″ long, somewhat lax, many-flowered. **Flowers:** over 2″ across; dorsal sepal galeate, elliptic or elliptic-lanceolate; spur cylindrical, $\frac{3}{4}''$ long; lateral sepals elliptic-lanceolate, pointed; petals lanceolate or narrowly ovate-lanceolate; lip ovate or elliptic-ovate. *December.*

An exquisite plant with very large pink or rose-coloured blossoms of great substance, growing in long spikes on stems clothed with neat rich green leafage. It is certainly one of the most beautiful of the whole genus. It inhabits grassy open slopes on the mountains of Eastern Cape Colony, Orange Free State, Swaziland, Griqualand East and Natal, where at Emangweni it reaches its greatest elevation at 7000 feet. Plants collected from this altitude should prove perfectly hardy in Great Britain if their resting period could be made to coincide with our winter. It should be given a moist fibrous peat and loam in full sun.

285. DISA RHODANTHA, Schltr.

Root: a sessile tuber. **Stem:** stout. **Leaves:** radical, in short tufts, lateral, linear or oblong-linear, 4″–8″ long; cauline leaves oblong-linear. **Scape:** $1'$–$1\frac{3}{4}'$ tall, sheath-clothed. **Spike:** 2″–6″ long, oblong, dense. **Flowers:** about $\frac{5}{8}''$ across; dorsal sepal galeate, broadly triangular-ovate; spur strongly curved, $\frac{5}{8}''$ long; lateral sepals obliquely ovate-oblong; petals oblong-lanceolate; lip spathulate-oblong, blunt. *November to January.*

A pretty and desirable species with medium-sized rose-coloured blossoms in long many-flowered spikes borne on leafy stems. This plant is a swamp lover, being found in such habitats in elevated districts in the Transvaal, Griqualand East and Natal and probably reaches its greatest altitude in a swamp near Nottingham Road at 5000 feet, where it is subjected to well over 20° of frost during the winter when it is deciduous. It should be given a good rather heavy soil in the bog garden or on the banks of a stream or pond.

286. DISA SANGUINEA, Sond.

D. Huttonii, Reichb. f.

Root: a sessile tuber. **Stem:** stout. **Leaves:** cauline, oblong-lanceolate, imbricate, somewhat fleshy, 1″–3″ long. **Scape:** $1'$–$1\frac{1}{4}'$ tall, sheath-clothed.

Spike: $\frac{3}{4}''$–$1\frac{1}{4}''$ long, very dense. **Flowers:** over $\frac{1}{4}''$ across; dorsal sepal galeate, broadly ovate or semihemispherical; spur oblong, small; lateral sepals broadly oblong, carinate; petals falcate-linear, hidden within the hooded sepal; lip rhomboid-ovate with a small dew-drop-like gland at the tip. *November and December.*

Although the blossoms of this plant are rather small, they are brilliantly coloured and densely crowded on the flower-stems, somewhat resembling at a distance a tiny red-hot poker plant; they are bright crimson outside and pale rose within. It grows in moist stony places on the mountains of Eastern Cape Colony, attaining its greatest altitude on the Winterberg Range in the Fort Beaufort Division at 4000 feet, where it is exposed to over 12° of frost during the winter for short periods. A moist gritty loam in full sun is indicated. This species is only suitable for outdoor culture in the warmer counties.

287. DISA SANKEYI, Rolfe

Root: a sessile tuber. **Stem:** rather stout. **Leaves:** cauline or subradical, oblong or linear-oblong, somewhat fleshy, $2''$–$3\frac{1}{2}''$ long, reduced in length upwards. **Scape:** $5''$–$7''$ tall, sheath-clothed. **Spike:** $1\frac{1}{2}''$–$3''$ long, oblong, dense. **Flowers:** about $\frac{1}{2}''$ across; dorsal sepal subgaleate, ovate-oblong, blunt; spur linear or subclavate, short; lateral sepals oblong, blunt, spreading; petals obovate-oblong, suboblique; lip linear-oblong, blunt. *November to January.*

A plant with fair-sized green and purple fragrant blossoms of but little decorative value. It is sufficiently dwarf and compact to make an interesting addition to the alpine house. It grows in open grassy places on the highlands near Harrismith in the Orange Free State at about 6000 feet above sea-level, where it is subjected to over 20° of frost for considerable periods during its winter rest (May to August). It should be grown in a good moist fibrous loam in a position exposed to the sun's rays.

288. DISA SAXICOLA, Schltr.

Root: a sessile tuber. **Stem:** rather slender. **Leaves:** cauline, lanceolate or linear-lanceolate, few, $2''$–$5''$ long. **Scape:** $6''$–$10''$ long, clothed with one or two narrow sheaths. **Spike:** $1\frac{1}{2}''$–$3''$ long, somewhat lax, many-flowered. **Flowers:** over $\frac{3}{8}''$ across; dorsal sepal galeate, broadly ovate, blunt; spur subcylindrical, $\frac{1}{2}''$ long; lateral sepals broadly oblong, blunt; petals broadly falcate-oblong, dilated at the base in front; lip spathulate. *December.*

This dwarf compact species, with its suberect foliage and small white purple-spotted blossoms, is more suited to the alpine house than the decorative garden, for its blossoms are not showy. It grows in the clefts of rocks and at times on trees in the highlands of Nyasaland, Transvaal and Swaziland, where it probably reaches its greatest elevation on the Devil's Bridge Mountains at 5000 feet and is exposed to over 15° of frost during its resting period. It should be grown in moist fibrous peat and sand in half-shade. It is only suitable for outdoor culture in South-Western Britain.

289. DISA STACHYOIDES, Reichb. f.

D. gracilis, Krauss; *D. hemisphærophora*, Reichb. f.

Root: a sessile tuber. **Stem:** rather stout. **Leaves:** cauline, lanceolate or oblong-lanceolate, fleshy, few, 1″–2″ long. **Scape:** 6″–12″ tall, clothed with a few sheaths. **Spike:** 1½″–4½″ long, cylindrical, dense. **Flowers:** about ⅜″ across; dorsal sepal galeate, oblong, margins involute; spur stout, nearly straight, ¼″ long; lateral sepals oblong, concave, blunt; petals broadly ovate, oblique; lip oblong, blunt or pointed. *October to January.*

The blossoms of this species are rather too small to have much decorative value although it should make a welcome addition to the alpine house; they have deep pink or purple sepals and pale pink or lilac petals and lip. It inhabits stony and rocky ground mostly on high mountains in Transvaal, Orange Free State, Tembuland, Griqualand and Natal, where on the Drakensburg Range at 6000 feet it is subjected to over 25° of frost during its resting period. A compost of fibrous peat and gritty loam is indicated, in full sun.

290. DISA STAIRSII, Kränzl.

D. Gregoriana, Rendle; *D. Wissmannii*, Kränzl.

Root: an ovoid sessile tuber. **Stem:** stout, smooth. **Leaves:** strap-shaped or lanceolate, pointed, gradually degenerating into clasping sheaths. **Scape:** about 2′ tall. **Spike:** 3″–4″ long, somewhat lax. **Flowers:** nearly ¾″ across; dorsal sepal galeate, suborbicular, blunt; spur slender, ¾″ long; lateral sepals oblong, blunt, spreading; petals falcate-oblong, free, rather blunt; lip cuneate-oblong, blunt. *August to October.*

This species probably attains a greater elevation above sea-level than any other African Orchid, being found in wet and boggy ground on the slopes of the higher mountains in British East Africa and Tanganyika, East Africa. It is of robust habit and bears fairly long spikes of white and pink blossoms loosely arranged. It reaches its greatest elevation on Mount Ruwenzori at 12,000 feet and should therefore be quite hardy in Great Britain in the bog garden, or in peat and loam on the banks of a stream.

291. DISA STRICTA, Sond.

Root: a sessile tuber. **Stem:** rather slender. **Leaves:** cauline, linear, numerous, 2″–6″ long. **Scape:** 9″–18″ tall, clothed with leaf-like sheaths.

Spike: 1″–3″ long, cylindrical, dense. **Flowers:** about ⅜″ across; dorsal sepal galeate, broadly ovate, subcompressed; spur broadly conical, blunt, ¼″ long; lateral sepals ovate oblong or broadly elliptic-oblong, blunt; petals falcate-linear, subobtuse; lip broadly elliptic-oblong, blunt.

November and December.

The small purple blossoms of this species are of but little decorative value and like so many of its brethren it is a lover of the open wind-swept slopes and summits of the lofty mountains of its native countries. It is found in Eastern Cape Colony, Tembuland and Griqualand East, where on the rough stony summits of the Insizwa Range at 6800 feet it probably reaches its greatest elevation. Here the thermometer frequently falls to the zero F. point in the winter. It may be grown in peat, loam and small pieces of sandstone in full sun.

292. DISA TENELLA, Sw.

Orchis tenella, Linn. *Satyrium tenellum*, Thunb.

Root: a sessile tuber. **Stem:** rather slender. **Leaves:** radical and cauline, linear, flexuous, numerous, 1″–2¼″. **Scape:** 3″–5″ tall. **Spike:** ½″–2″ long, rather dense, many-flowered. **Flowers:** under a ¼″ across; dorsal sepal galeate, broadly ovate, inflexed at the margin; spur narrowly conical, short; lateral sepals broadly oblong; petals broadly ovate or rhomboid-ovate; lip spathulate. *August to October.*

A dwarf species with pinkish-purple and at times yellow and white blossoms, too small to be of much decorative value. It would probably make a good alpine house plant. It grows in sandy soil amongst short herbage in South-Western Cape Colony and probably reaches its greatest elevation on the Cold Bokkeveld at 3500 feet, where it is exposed to 12° of frost during the winter for short periods. It may be given a moist sandy soil in full sun in the rock garden or a pan of the same compost in the alpine house. It is only suitable for outdoor culture in the warmest parts of Britain.

293. DISA THODEI, Schltr.

Root: a sessile tuber. **Stem:** moderately stout. **Leaves:** cauline, oblong, pointed, rather thin, 2″–3″ long. **Scape:** 12″ tall, sheath-clothed. **Spike:** about 2″ long, of about 6 lax blossoms. **Flowers:** about 1″ across; dorsal sepal galeate, broadly ovate; spur cylindrical, straight, ¾″ long; lateral sepals narrowly ovate; petals ovate, pointed; lip oblong-lanceolate, pointed.

September to December.

A very beautiful and desirable species with large submembranous purple or pale pink blossoms on stems clothed with rich green leafage. It grows on the grassy banks of streams on the slopes of the Caledon Range in the

Orange Free State at 7900–8300 feet, at which altitude it is exposed to a temperature that frequently reaches the zero point F. during its deciduous period. It should be grown in good peat on the banks of a stream or pond, or in an elevated spot in the bog garden in full sun.

294. DISA TRIPETALOIDES, N.E. Br.

D. venosa, Lindl. *D. excelsa*, Sw. *Orchis tripetaloides*, Linn. *Satyrium excelsum*, Thunb.

Root: a sessile tuber. **Stem:** moderately stout. **Leaves:** radical, in a tufted rosette, lanceolate or oblong-lanceolate, $1\frac{1}{4}''$–$4''$ long. **Scape:** $9''$–$18''$ tall, sheath-clothed. **Spike:** $2''$–$5''$ long, lax, many-flowered. **Flowers:** about $\frac{3}{4}''$ across; dorsal sepal galeate, broadly ovate or orbicular-ovate; spur broadly conical or oblong, $\frac{3}{8}''$ long; lateral sepals ovate-oblong or ovate-elliptic; petals falcate-oblong, blunt; lip linear or oblong-linear, blunt. *January.*

A pretty species with medium-sized blossoms, pale pink or white in ground colour with carmine spots on the sepals. In the variety *aurata*, Bolus, they are of a uniform bright yellow throughout. It is a desirable garden plant and grows in its native habitat on the wet banks of streams and on moist mountain slopes in Natal and Cape Colony, where on the banks of rivulets above Montagu Pass in the George Division at 4000 feet it probably reaches its greatest altitude and is exposed to 12° of frost during winter. A good sandy peat on the banks of a stream or pond should suit its requirements.

295. DISA TYSONII, Bolus

Root: a sessile tuber. **Stem:** rather stout. **Leaves:** cauline, ovate-lanceolate, numerous, fleshy, sheathing at the base, $2''$–$4\frac{1}{2}''$ long, decreasing upwards. **Scape:** $9''$–$15''$ tall. **Spike:** $3''$–$4''$ long, oblong, dense. **Flowers:** over $\frac{1}{2}''$ across; dorsal sepal galeate, very broadly ovate, blunt; spur upcurved, oblong, blunt, $\frac{3}{16}''$ long; lateral sepals broadly ovate-elliptic, blunt; petals falcate-oblong, blunt; lip ovate-oblong, convex, blunt.

November to January.

Although the blossoms of this plant are on the small side and by no means brilliantly coloured, their light green sepals, white petals and yellow lip provides a combination of tints somewhat unusual in the genus and gives it some claim on our consideration. It is found on grassy mountain slopes in Cape Colony and Griqualand East, where it attains its greatest elevation on the Insizwa Range at 6800 feet and should be perfectly hardy in Great Britain if it could be induced to rest during the winter. A good fibrous loam in full sun is indicated.

296. DISA UNIFLORA, Berg.

D. grandiflora, Linn. *D. Barellii* Reydt. *Satyrium grandiflorum*, Thunb.

Root: a sessile tuber. **Stem:** leafy, stout. **Leaves:** lanceolate or elongate linear, spreading, 3″–8″ long. **Scape:** 1′–2½′ tall, sheath-clothed. **Spike:** of 1 to 5 flowers. **Flowers:** nearly 4″ across; dorsal sepal galeate, broadly ovate; spur narrowly conical, ½″ long; lateral sepals broadly ovate, abruptly pointed; petals obovate or obovate-oblong, with incurved apex; lip linear-lanceolate.

January to March.

The huge, brilliant scarlet blossoms of this species with the dark veinings on the dorsal sepal and the yellow or orange-markings on the lip, give it without doubt the distinction of being the most beautiful of all the terrestrial Orchids that should succeed under suitable conditions outdoors in the warmest parts of Great Britain. It grows on the peaty banks of mountain pools and streams amongst reeds and grasses in Cape Colony where, in Du Toit's Kloof in the Worcester Division at 4000 feet, 12° of frost is registered in the winter. Plants collected from such an altitude should succeed outdoors in very sheltered situations in the Western counties of Britain; it is very moist for the greater part of the year and is never dry even when at rest, these conditions should be imitated in cultivation.

297. DISA VAGINATA, Harv.

D. modesta, Reichb. f.

Root: a sessile tuber. **Stem:** rather stout. **Leaves:** basal, subsessile, lanceolate or ovate-lanceolate, smooth and fleshy, ½″–1¼″ long. **Scape:** 3″–7″ tall, clothed with resin-dotted sheaths. **Spike:** 1½″ long, few-flowered. **Flowers:** about ⅜″ across; dorsal sepal galeate, ovate; spur slender, about ¼″ long; lateral sepals broadly oblong, blunt; petals falcate-oblong, concave towards the tip; the lip obovate-oblong, truncate.

November to January.

The small pale pink, green-lipped flowers of this species have some decorative value for the rock garden or alpine house. It is a compact neat plant and is found in its native country on damp cliffs both in clefts and on the surface amidst short herbage. It is confined to South-Western Cape Colony, where it attains its greatest elevation on the Drakenstein Mountains in the Paarl Division at 4000 feet and is exposed to 10° or 12° of frost for short periods during the winter. It should be grown in fibrous peat and loam, in a moist spot in the rock garden. It is only suitable for culture outdoors in the warmer Western counties of Britain.

298. DISA VASSELOTII, Bolus

Root: a sessile tuber. **Stem:** moderately stout. **Leaves:** radical, tufted, linear or lanceolate-oblong, $\frac{1}{2}''$–$1\frac{1}{4}''$ long. **Scape:** 3″–7″ tall, clothed with a few sheaths. **Spike:** 1″–2″ long, subcorymbose, few-flowered. **Flowers:** over $\frac{3}{8}''$ across; dorsal sepal galeate, broadly ovate, obtuse; spur conical-oblong, $\frac{1}{4}''$ long; lateral sepals elliptic-ovate, obtuse; petals falcate-oblong, crenulate, obliquely acute; lip subspathulate-linear, blunt. *November to January.*

A dwarf species with rather small white blossoms of but little decorative value. It would probably prove of interest in a pan in the alpine house. It inhabits moist grassy mountain sides in Eastern Cape Colony, where on the mountains near Knysna in the Knysna Division it probably attains its greatest altitude at 4000 feet and is at times exposed to 10° or 12° of frost for short periods during the winter. It should be given a moist spot in the rock garden in a good fibrous loam and peat.

299. DISA ZOMBICA, N.E. Br.

Root: an ovoid sessile tuber. **Stem:** stout, leafy. **Leaves:** produced on a separate shoot beside the flower-stem, ovate or lanceolate, rather pointed, $1\frac{1}{2}''$–2″ long. **Scape:** $1\frac{1}{2}'$–2′ tall, smooth. **Spike:** 6″–7″ long, rather dense. **Flowers:** about $1\frac{1}{4}''$ across; dorsal sepal erect, with a channelled claw and broad hood; spur pendulous, clavate; lateral sepals spreading upwards, oblong, blunt, concave at the apex; petals spathulate-lanceolate, blunt, eared at the base; lip linear, blunt. *August to October.*

A handsome large-flowered robust plant producing a long leafless flower-stem from beside a tuft of oval leaves, and bearing a long somewhat dense spike of white and rose-pink blossoms. It grows in damp and marshy places, frequently in rocky soil, on the top of Mount Zomba in Nyasaland, in British Central Africa at 7000 feet, where it is exposed to 12° or 15° of frost for short periods. A soil of fibrous peat and loam in a boggy spot is indicated.

DISPERIS, Swartz

Delicate little plants with erect slender stems; they are terrestrial and deciduous and resemble a dwarf small-flowered Disa in habit. The root system consists of sessile ovoid, oblong or fusiform tubers buried about two inches below the surface of the soil. The leaves are small, ovate or oblong, solitary or alternate and are sometimes in opposite pairs. The blossoms which are small are at times solitary, but are more frequently in loose few-flowered spikes; they are too small to make any show in the outdoor garden, but should prove attractive in the alpine house in deep pans of fibrous peat, sphagnum-moss, a little loam and some small pieces of charcoal with plenty of crocks as drainage. The various species, which number about 70, are most numerous in South Africa and spread eastward to Madagascar, Southern India and New Guinea. Propagation by imported tubers and by seeds when procurable.

300. DISPERIS ALLISONII, Rolfe

Root: of oval tubers. **Stem:** moderately stout. **Leaves:** basal, oblong or ovate-oblong, sheathing at the base, 1″ long. **Scape:** about 10″ tall. **Spike:** 4″ long, rather lax. **Flowers:** about $\frac{5}{8}$″ across; dorsal sepal galeate, triangular, deflexed; lateral sepals oblong-lanceolate, spreading, with a short conic-oblong sac about the middle; petals falcate-oblong, outer margin undulate; lip broadly unguiculate, limb pandurate, appendage triangular-lanceolate, cucullate, $\frac{3}{16}$″ long. *October to January.*

A pretty plant with medium-sized bright carmine-rose blossoms on stout stems, clothed at the base with about four suberect leaves. It grows in moist rocky soil amongst short herbage at Olivier's Hoek in Natal at 5000 feet, where it is subjected to over 15° of frost for short periods during the winter months. It should be grown in a moist fibrous loam in a sunny spot in the rock garden or border and is only suitable for outdoor culture in very warm spots.

301. DISPERIS ANOMALA, Schltr.

Root: a small oval tuber. **Stem:** straight, slender, puberulus below. **Leaves:** cauline, lanceolate, amplexicaul, $\frac{3}{4}$″–1″ long. **Scape:** 6″ tall. **Spike:** few-flowered. **Flowers:** nearly $\frac{3}{4}$″ across; dorsal sepal galeate; lateral sepals obliquely lanceolate, with a small sac about the middle; petals obliquely subfalcate-lanceolate, cohering with the dorsal sepal; lip narrowly unguiculate, limb peltate, narrowly linear, bifid at the apex; appendage boat-shaped, lanceolate, curved. *November to January.*

A dainty plant with a slender stem bearing two or three fair-sized pure white blossoms, the dark green leaves which clothe the stem are three in number. It should make a very desirable plant for the alpine house. It grows amongst short grass in damp spots near Nottingham Road in Natal at 5000 feet, where it is exposed to over 15° of frost for short periods during the winter. It should be grown in a sunny spot in damp fibrous loam in the rock garden and is only suitable for outdoor culture in warm localities.

302. DISPERIS ANTHOCEROS, Reichb. f.

Root: a small oblong tuber. **Stem:** rather slender. **Leaves:** cauline, subcordate-ovate, sessile or subsessile, $\frac{3}{4}$″–1$\frac{3}{4}$″ long. **Scape:** 3″–8″ tall. **Spike:** short or subcorymbose. **Flowers:** about $\frac{5}{8}$″ across; dorsal sepal with a short broadly triangular limb and a narrow conic-oblong galea; lateral sepals spreading, obliquely ovate, with a short broad subconical sac below the middle; petals broadly ovate-oblong, cohering with the dorsal sepal; lip narrowly unguiculate, ovate-oblong, conduplicate, very short and reflexed; appendage bilobed, recurved. *October to January.*

A pretty plant with delicate white blossoms spotted with lilac, growing on a slender stem furnished with two nearly opposite bright green oval leaves, like those of our Tway-blade; from one to five flowers are produced. It grows in grassy places in wooded country in Natal and the Transvaal, where it probably attains its greatest altitude on Woodbush Mountain at 6650 feet and is there subjected to over 20° of frost during the winter. A compost of leaf-soil and loam in half-shade is indicated.

303. DISPERIS BICOLOR, Rolfe

Root: a small sessile tuber. **Stem:** slender. **Leaves:** cauline, ovate-lanceolate, $\frac{3}{4}''$–1″ long. **Scape:** about 6″ tall. **Spike:** few-flowered. **Flowers:** $\frac{5}{8}''$ across; dorsal sepal with a broadly triangular apiculate deflexed limb, galea broadly conical; lateral sepals elliptic-oblong, spreading, with a narrowly oblong sac about the middle; petals obovate-elliptic, outer margins sinuat-undulate; lip broadly unguiculate, limb navicular, reflexed; appendage linear, blunt, about $\frac{3}{16}''$ long. *October to January.*

A dainty little plant with a slender stem bearing two leaves near its base and at its apex one or two blossoms with purple hoods and yellow lips and petals. It should prove a welcome addition to the alpine house. It is found in moist spots amongst short herbage at Olivier's Hoek in Natal at 5000 feet, where it is exposed to over 15° of frost for short periods during its resting season in the winter. It should be grown in good fibrous loam in a moist spot in full sun and is only suitable for outdoor culture in warm sheltered localities.

304. DISPERIS CARDIOPHORA, Harv.

Root: of oval tubers. **Stem:** rather stout, smooth. **Leaf:** solitary, subradical, sessile, amplexicaul, suborbicular, $\frac{1}{2}''$–1″ long. **Scape:** 4″–9″ tall. **Spike:** 1″–3″ long, distichous, secund, rather dense. **Flowers:** $\frac{3}{8}''$ across; dorsal sepal with a short triangular limb and a subglobose galea; lateral sepals falcate-oblong, with a short broad conical sac about the middle; petals obliquely ovate-oblong, cohering to the dorsal sepal; lip broadly unguiculate, limb ovate, reflexed; appendage broadly oblong, erect, about $\frac{1}{8}''$ long.

October to January.

This plant is not very decorative, it has rather small white and green blossoms with dull purple tips to the petals, in dense one-sided spikes on stems clothed with a solitary rounded leaf. It grows on grassy mountain slopes in Cape Colony, Transvaal and Natal, where it probably reaches its greatest elevation near Van Reenen at 5500 feet and is there exposed to over 20° of frost during the winter. It should be grown in moist fibrous loam in full sun.

305. DISPERIS CONCINNA, Schltr.

Root: a small oval tuber. **Stem:** slender, smooth. **Leaves:** cauline, alternate, oblong-lanceolate, sessile, $\frac{1}{3}''$–$\frac{1}{2}''$ long. **Scape:** 5″–10″ tall. **Spike:** short, rather lax. **Flowers:** $\frac{1}{2}''$ across; dorsal sepal galeate, with an obtuse rounded sac nearly as long as the limb; lateral sepals oblong below, narrowed above, with a large oblong sac about the middle; petals falcate-lanceolate, oblique; lip narrowly unguiculate, limb ovate-oblong, conduplicate, blunt; appendage broadly subpandurate-oblong, keeled, about $\frac{1}{8}''$ long.

January.

A pretty, slender stemmed species, bearing from one to three rose-coloured blossoms of fair size, the stem is clothed with three bright green leaves. It should prove useful for alpine house culture. It grows in marshes and damp grassy places in the Transvaal and Natal, where it reaches its greatest elevation on the Mohlamba Range at 6000 feet and should be hardy in Southern Britain. A rich moist loam and peat is indicated, in full sun.

306. DISPERIS COOPERI, Harv.

Root: an oval tuber. **Stem:** moderately stout, fairly straight. **Leaves:** cauline, alternate, sessile, ovate or ovate-lanceolate, 1″–$1\frac{1}{2}''$ long. **Scape:** 9″–15″ tall. **Spikes:** 3″–4″ long, rather lax, many-flowered. **Flowers:** $\frac{5}{8}''$ across; dorsal sepal galeate, suborbicular, globose, with an oblong mouth; lateral sepals spreading, broadly ovate-lanceolate with a short broadly conical sac about the middle; petals falcate-lanceolate, cohering to the dorsal sepal; lip broadly unguiculate, limb cucullate, ovate; appendage subulate-lanceolate, cucullate, $\frac{1}{4}''$ long. *February to April.*

A rather dull-coloured species of but little decorative value, with a fairly long spike of green blossoms having a purple lip and purple spots on the margins of the petals; the stem is clothed with from two to four suberect leaves. It grows on the open grassy windswept plains, on the top of the Drakensburg Range near Nelson's Kop in the Orange Free State, at 8000 feet and should be quite hardy in Britain could it be induced to rest during our winter. A good fibrous peat in full sun is indicated.

307. DISPERIS FANNINIÆ, Harv.

Root: an oval tuber. **Stem:** rather slender. **Leaves:** cauline, cordate ovate, much narrowed above, amplexicaul, $\frac{3}{4}''$–$3\frac{1}{4}''$ long. **Scape:** 6″–18″ tall.

Spike: few-flowered, lax. **Flowers:** over $\frac{3}{4}''$ across; dorsal sepal with a triangular deflexed limb and a broadly saccate blunt galea; lateral sepals spreading, falcate-obovate, with short broadly oblong sacs about the middle; petals broadly falcate-obovate, with 2 prominent rounded lobes on the outer margin and cohering to the dorsal sepal; lip linear, dilated near the middle, bent; appendage cucullate, blunt, $\frac{1}{8}''$ long. *February to April.*

The large white blossoms of this species are at times tinged with purple and have raised purple dots on the petals; they are very decorative and are borne on slender stems, clothed with very rich green leaves, of from one to four in number. It grows in thin woods in Griqualand East, Natal, Orange Free State and Transvaal, where it probably reaches its greatest elevation on Woodbush Mountain at 6550 feet and is subjected to over 20° of frost for short periods in the winter. A compost of leaf soil and loam in half-shade is indicated.

308. DISPERIS FLAVA, Rolfe

Root: of ovoid tubers. **Stems:** moderately slender and smooth. **Leaves:** cauline, lanceolate, spreading, $\frac{3}{4}''$–$1''$ long. **Scape:** about $5''$ tall, bearing 2 flowers at its apex. **Flowers:** nearly $\frac{3}{4}''$ across; dorsal sepal with a narrowly triangular deflexed limb and a broadly saccate galea; lateral sepals spreading, obliquely ovate, with a large oblong sac below the middle; petals falcate-lanceolate, outer margin slightly undulate; lip broadly unguiculate, limb ovate-lanceolate, deflexed, cucullate; appendage broadly oblong, blunt, about $\frac{1}{8}''$ long. *January to April.*

A beautiful rather large flowered species with a moderately slender stem clothed with two bright green leaves and two yellow blossoms with orange tipped hoods. It grows in damp places amongst short grass at Olivier's Hoek in Natal at 5000 feet, where it is exposed to 15° or more of frost for short periods during the winter months. A damp spot in full sun in a good fibrous peat is indicated.

309. DISPERIS GALERITA, Reichb. f.

Root: a very small ovoid tuber. **Stem:** fairly stout. **Leaves:** cauline, ovate-oblong, sessile, alternate, $\frac{1}{2}''$–$1''$ long. **Scape:** $3''$–$6''$ tall. **Raceme:** of 3 flowers, loose. **Flowers:** about $\frac{1}{2}''$ across; dorsal sepal galeate, apex incurved, pointed, prolonged behind into a blunt sac, oblong; lateral sepals semi-ovate, rather pointed, oblique, spreading; petals falcate-oblong, obliquely pointed, united to the margins of the dorsal sepal; lip subulate-lanceolate, with a pair of rounded ears at its base; appendage linear, thickened at the tip. *August.*

This little species should make an attractive addition to the alpine house in a dwarf pot or pan. The blossoms are rose-purple in colour and are borne on a leafy stem. It is a lover of moist grassy places on the mountains of Abyssinia, where on Debra Tabor at 8500 feet it probably attains its greatest altitude above sea-level and is exposed to over 20° of frost for short periods when deciduous. A moist spot in full sun in a compost of peat and loam is indicated.

310. DISPERIS GRACILIS, Schltr.

D. Wealii, Kränzl.

Root: an ovoid tuber. **Stem:** slender, smooth. **Leaves:** cauline, oblong-lanceolate, alternate, sessile, smooth, $\frac{3}{4}''$–1″ long. **Scape:** $\frac{1}{2}'$–$1\frac{1}{4}'$ tall, bearing from 1–4 blossoms. **Flowers:** about $\frac{1}{2}''$ across; dorsal sepal galeate, ovate, broadly saccate, with a broad mouth; lateral sepals spreading, falcate-oblong, with oblong obtuse sacs below the middle; petals falcate-oblong, cohering with the dorsal sepal; lip broadly unguiculate, limb oblong-lanceolate; appendage ovate, narrowed upwards, somewhat cucullate, $\frac{3}{16}''$ long.

September to December.

This is a pretty but by no means showy species. The blossoms are pure white and are produced on tall wand-like stems clothed near the base with about three bright green leaves. It grows in marshes on Woodbush Mountain in Northern Transvaal at 6500 feet and is exposed to 20° of frost for short periods during its winter rest. It should be grown in a raised part of the bog garden, in fibrous peat and sphagnum-moss, in full sun.

311. DISPERIS KERMESINA, Rolfe

Root: of oval tubers. **Stem:** moderately slender. **Leaves:** cauline, ovate-lanceolate, sheathing at base, $\frac{3}{4}''$–$1\frac{1}{4}''$ long. **Scape:** 9″–15″ tall. **Spike:** 2″–$5\frac{1}{2}''$ long, lax. **Flowers:** about $\frac{1}{2}''$ across; dorsal sepal with a short triangular deflexed limb and a conic-oblong blunt galea; lateral sepals elliptic-oblong, spreading, concave, with a short conic-oblong sac about the middle; petals falcate-obovate, outer margins obscurely undulate; lip narrowly unguiculate, limb subpandurate-oblong; appendage linear, blunt, about a $\frac{1}{4}''$ long.

December to February.

A delicate and pretty plant, with medium-sized carmine blossoms in long spikes, on slender stems clothed with two bright green leaves. It grows in damp places amongst short herbage at Olivier's Hoek in Natal at 5000 feet above sea-level, where it is exposed to over 15° of frost for short periods during its resting season. It should be grown in fibrous peat in a moist spot exposed to full sun and is only suitable for outdoor culture in the warmest part of Britain.

312. DISPERIS KILIMANJARICA, Rendle

Root: a very small ovoid tuber. **Stem:** slender. **Leaves:** cauline, cordate, pointed, sessile, alternate, about $\frac{1}{2}''$ long. **Scape:** about 3″ tall. **Flowers:** nearly $\frac{1}{2}''$ across; dorsal sepal galeate, pointed, terminating in an obscure sac behind; lateral sepals obliquely ovate, calcarate near the inner margins; petals linear, united at their margins to the dorsal sepal forming a hood; lip oval, narrowing towards its base where there is an elongated spur.

August to October.

A very tiny plant quite suitable for alpine house culture. The slender flower-stem bears a solitary white, purple-spotted blossom with a bract at its base; the stem is clothed with two bright green heart-shaped leaves. It grows on open moist rock-strewn mountain slopes at an elevation of over 10,000 feet on Kilimanjaro in Tanganyika, East Africa and increases by tubers formed on the tips of the long fleshy stolons. It may be grown in a damp open spot in fibrous peat and light loam.

313. DISPERIS LINDLEYANA, Reichb. f.

Root: of small ovoid tubers. **Stem:** moderately slender, smooth. **Leaf:** cauline, solitary, broadly cordate, amplexicaul, $1\frac{1}{4}''$–$2\frac{1}{4}''$ long. **Scape:** 6″–12″ tall. **Spike:** usually of 3 blossoms. **Flowers:** about $\frac{5}{8}''$ across; dorsal sepal galeate, with a broadly triangular deflexed apex and a conical blunt sac; lateral sepals falcate-ovate, spreading, with a very short broad truncate sac about the middle; petals falcate-oblong, outer margins undulate, cohering with the dorsal sepal; lip broadly unguiculate, limb subpandurate-linear, tip sharply deflexed; appendage ovate-oblong, fleshy and papillose at the apex, $\frac{1}{4}''$ long. *December.*

This is a quaint plant with fairly large, cream-yellow blossoms, thinly sprinkled with green dots and a hairy purple patch on the petals. It grows in thin woods and ravines on mountains in Natal, Transvaal and Eastern Cape Colony, where on the Kaga Berg in the Bedford Division at 4500 feet it is exposed to 15° of frost for short periods during the winter. It should be grown in leaf-soil and sand in a half-shady spot.

314. DISPERIS MACOWANII, Bolus

Root: a small oval tuber. **Stem:** slender, slightly downy. **Leaves:** cauline, broadly cordate-ovate, amplexicaul, minutely hairy, 4″–7″ long. **Scape:** 3″–6″ tall with 1 flower. **Flower:** $\frac{3}{8}''$ across; dorsal sepal with a triangular limb and a broadly conical blunt sac; lateral sepals obliquely obovate-oblong with a short broadly oblong sac near the apex; petals falcate-lanceolate, with an undulate margin and cohering to the dorsal sepal; lip narrowly unguiculate, limb subrhomboid, reflexed, very short; appendage linear-lanceolate, blunt, recurved at the apex. *December to March.*

This pretty little plant is suitable for the alpine house but of little value for garden decoration. The solitary blossom is of a bluish-white colour with a few green dots on the petals. It grows in moist places mostly in the shade in Cape Colony and Natal, where near Van Reenen in Natal at 7000 feet it is exposed to sufficient degrees of frost to ensure its complete hardiness in the British Isles, if it can be induced to rest during our winter. A compost of leaf-soil and loam is indicated.

315. DISPERIS MEIRAX, Reichb. f.

Root: a very small ovoid tuber. **Stem:** rather stout. **Leaves:** cauline, ovate or ovate-oblong, pointed, the lowest one sheath-like, about $\frac{3}{4}''$ long. **Scape:** about 3″ tall. **Raceme:** loose, of 2–3 blossoms. **Flowers:** about $\frac{1}{4}''$ across; dorsal sepal galeate, with rounded lateral margins; lateral sepals obliquely semiovate, conduplicate-concave, united by their infolded inner margins; petals broadly falcately semiovate, very oblique, with a rounded basal margin united to the dorsal sepal; lip ovate-oblong, narrow at the base, appendage oblong, slightly toothed at the apex. *April and May.*

A very dwarf species with a stout short stem, bearing three small oval leaves and a raceme of two or three yellowish-green blossoms. It is found in damp half shady places on the mountains of Abyssinia probably reaching its greatest elevation above sea-level on Debra Eski at 8500 feet where it experiences 20° or more of frost during its resting period. A good fibrous loam in a damp spot is indicated.

316. DISPERIS MICRANTHA, Lindl.

Root: a small oval tuber. **Stem:** rather slender, smooth. **Leaves:** cauline, broadly cordate, amplexicaul, $\frac{3}{4}''$–$1\frac{1}{2}''$ long. **Scape:** 5″–7″ tall. **Spike:** short, lax. **Flowers:** about $\frac{3}{16}''$ across; dorsal sepal with a triangular limb, deflexed, and a broadly saccate galea; lateral sepals obliquely ovate-oblong, spreading, with a short broadly conical blunt sac above the middle; petals obliquely falcate-ovate, cohering with the dorsal sepal; lip narrowly unguiculate, limb reflexed, with 2 short diverging lobes; appendage broadly oblong, blunt, downy. *March.*

This species is of but little decorative value; the small blossoms are pink and green, two to five in number, on short slender stems clothed with two or three leaves. It grows in damp shady places in the mountainous regions in Cape Colony and Transvaal, where it reaches its greatest elevation on Woodbush Mountain at 5500 feet and is there exposed to 12° of frost for short periods during the winter. It should be grown in a moist half shady spot, in leaf-soil and loam.

317. DISPERIS NELSONII, Rolfe

Root: of small oval tubers. **Stem:** slender, smooth. **Leaves:** cauline, broadly ovate, subsessile, opposite, $1\frac{1}{2}''$–$1\frac{3}{4}''$ long, rather thin in texture. **Scape:** 6″–8″ tall, bearing 1–2 flowers. **Flowers:** over $\frac{5}{8}''$ across; dorsal sepal with a triangular deflexed limb and a broadly saccate galea; lateral sepals obliquely falcate-elliptic, spreading, with a very broad oblong sac below the middle; petals elliptic-oblong, somewhat constricted in the middle and slightly crenulate below; lip narrowly unguiculate, limb ovate, reflexed; appendage bipartite, with subclavate lobes, $\frac{1}{8}''$ long.

September to January.

A pretty little plant with medium-sized pink or rose-coloured flowers in pairs on slender stems clothed with two bright green leaves. It grows in damp half-shady spots on Woodbush Mountains in the Transvaal at 5500 feet and is there exposed to 12° of frost for short periods during its winter rest. It should be given a moist half-shady spot in the rock garden in leaf-soil and good loam and is only suitable for outdoor culture in very warm localities.

318. DISPERIS OXYGLOSSA, Bolus

Root: a small oval tuber. **Stem:** slender, smooth. **Leaves:** cauline, elliptic or oblong-lanceolate, sessile, $\frac{3}{4}''$–$1\frac{1}{2}''$ long. **Scape:** 6″–12″ tall. **Spike:** lax, bearing 2–3 blossoms. **Flowers:** nearly $\frac{3}{4}''$ across; dorsal sepal galeate, oblong-lanceolate; lateral sepals spreading, falcate-lanceolate, with an oblong sac below the middle; petals obliquely lanceolate, cohering with the dorsal sepal; lip linear, unguiculate at the base; appendage erect, linear, winged at the base.

October to January.

This is rather a pretty plant, with large purple blossoms having green warts on the petals; from two to three are borne on slender stems clothed with three suberect leaves. It inhabits moist grassy places on the mountains or elevated plains in Eastern Cape Colony, Tembuland, Griqualand East and Natal. It reaches its greatest elevation on the summit of the Insizwa Mountains in Griqualand East, where it is exposed to over 20° of frost during the winter. A moist fibrous loam and peat is indicated.

319. DISPERIS STENOPLECTRON, Reichb. f.

Root: a small ovoid tuber. **Stem:** moderately stout. **Leaves:** cauline, ovate or ovate-lanceolate, cucullate, sessile, 1″–2″ long. **Scape:** 9″–12″ tall. **Spike:** 2″–4″ long, lax. **Flowers:** nearly $\frac{3}{4}''$ across; dorsal sepal galeate, broadly ovate; lateral sepals spreading, obliquely elliptic-lanceolate, with a conic-oblong sac below the middle; petals obliquely falcate-oblong, constricted in front about the middle, cohering with the dorsal sepal; lip broadly unguiculate, limb pandurate-oblong with an incurved margin and conical teeth below; appendage subulate-linear. *February and March.*

A plant of no high decorative value, with rather large green and purple blossoms numbering from six to ten, on a fairly stout stalk clothed with from two to four deep green leaves. It grows on mountain slopes with underground moisture, in Eastern Cape Colony and Griqualand East, where it reaches its greatest altitude on the slopes of Mount Currie at 5000 feet and is there subjected to 12° of frost during the winter. A moist fibrous peat is indicated.

320. DISPERIS TYSONII, Bolus

Root: an ovate tuber. **Stem:** slender, rather flexuous. **Leaves:** cauline, lanceolate or ovate-lanceolate, sessile, alternate, $\frac{1}{3}''$–$1''$ long. **Scape:** $6''$–$15''$ tall. **Spike:** $1''$–$4\frac{1}{2}''$ long, lax, somewhat secund. **Flowers:** $\frac{3}{8}''$ across; dorsal sepal galeate, ovate, with an obtuse sac as long as the limb; lateral sepals spreading, obliquely elliptic-lanceolate, falcately curved, concave, with an obtuse sac above the middle; petals falcate-ovate, oblique; lip narrowly unguiculate, limb ovate or ovate-lanceolate, prominently bituberculate at the base; appendage subulate, thin, narrowed and then subclavate. *January to March.*

This is a rather pretty plant with small pink blossoms in long spikes on slender stems clothed with from three to five leaves. It grows in moist grassy places on the mountains of Cape Colony, Transvaal, Tembuland, Natal and Griqualand East, where on Satsannas Peak it reaches an elevation of 9300 feet and should be perfectly hardy in Great Britain if it could be induced to rest during our winter. A compost of fibrous peat and sand in a moist sunny spot is indicated.

321. DISPERIS VILLOSA, Sw.

Arethusa villosa, Linn.

Root: a very small oval tuber. **Stem:** downy, moderately slender. **Leaves:** cauline, ovate or cordate, velvety, $\frac{1}{3}''$–$\frac{3}{4}''$ long. **Scape:** $1\frac{1}{2}''$–$6''$ tall, bearing 1 or rarely 2 blossoms. **Flowers:** $\frac{3}{8}''$ across; dorsal sepal with a broadly triangular limb and a rounded blunt galea; lateral sepals obovate, spreading, with a broadly conical obtuse sac close to, and exceeding, the apex; petals broadly falcate-lanceolate, with undulated outer margins and cohering to the dorsal sepal; lip narrowly unguiculate, limb very short, cucullate; appendage lanceolate-oblong, cucullate. *August to October.*

This is not a very decorative plant, it has rather small dull canary-yellow blossoms in ones or twos, on short slender stems clothed with two deep green leaves. It is suitable for the alpine house and grows in moist grassy or rocky places on the mountains of Cape Colony reaching its greatest elevation near Zwartbosch Kraal in the Clanwilliam Division at 5000 feet, where it is exposed to over 20° of frost during the winter. A moist fibrous peat and loam is indicated.

322. DISPERIS VIRGINALIS, Schltr.

D. Kerstenii, Schltr.

Root: a small oval tuber. **Stem:** smooth, rather slender. **Leaves:** cauline, broadly ovate, sessile, $\frac{3}{4}''$–$1\frac{3}{4}''$ long. **Scape:** 5″–9″ tall, bearing one or two blossoms. **Flowers:** about $\frac{1}{2}''$ across; dorsal sepal with a triangular deflexed apex and a broadly conical blunt galea; lateral sepals spreading, obliquely obovate-oblong, with a conical subacute sac above the middle; petals obliquely falcate-rhomboid, almost 2-lobed, with an ample rounded lobe in front near the base; lip narrowly unguiculate, limb minute, reflexed; appendage 4-lobed, recurved. *November to February.*

A species of but little horticultural value, with small white flowers to the number of one or two on slender stems clothed with a pair of oval leaves. It grows in thin woods on Woodbush Mountains in the Transvaal at 7300 feet, where it is exposed to over 20° of frost for considerable periods during its winter rest. It may be grown in good loam and leaf-soil in a moist half-shady spot.

323. DISPERIS WEALII, Reichb. f.

Root: a small ovoid tuber. **Stem:** slender, smooth. **Leaves:** cauline, elliptic or oblong-lanceolate, sessile, alternate, smooth, $\frac{1}{2}''$–$\frac{3}{4}''$ long. **Scape:** 6″–8″ tall. **Spike:** lax, of 1–5 blossoms. **Flowers:** $\frac{5}{8}''$ across; dorsal sepal with a triangular pointed limb and an obtuse rounded sac; lateral sepals oblong-lanceolate, very pointed, hooked at the apex with an oblong blunt spur above the middle, spreading; petals broadly falcate-lanceolate, front margins somewhat undulate; lip broadly unguiculate, limb ovate, cucullate; appendage ovate. *March and April.*

A dainty little species with fair-sized white blossoms barred transversely with bright green; they are borne on slender stems clothed with three suberect leaves. It grows in marshes on the summits of high mountains in Eastern Cape Colony, Griqualand East, Natal and the Orange Free State, where near Harrismith at 7500 feet it reaches its greatest altitude and should be quite hardy in Britain if it could be induced to rest during the winter. A good soil in the bog garden is indicated.

DIURIS, Smith

Twenty-five species of delightful deciduous terrestrial Orchids. They are of erect habit with roots of fairly large irregular tubers which are replaced annually, for each tuber shrivels as soon as it has produced ripe capsules of seeds. The leaves are grass-like and few in number and are usually placed near the base of the stem, which is sometimes hairy. The flowers are in a loose raceme and are at times solitary, they are never very numerous, their segments are spreading, the lateral sepals are generally very narrow and are deflexed below the lip, like the crossed blades of a pair of scissors. All should make delightful additions to the alpine house in pans of moist fibrous peat, loam and charcoal. They are mainly marsh plants, being found on the banks of streams, edges of swamps, wet grass land, etc., over the whole of Australia and Tasmania. Propagation by separation of the tubers and also by seeds when available.

324. DIURIS LONGIFOLIA, R. Br.

D. porrifolia, Lindl. *D. corymbosa*, Lindl.

Root: of fair-sized oblong tubers on thick white fibres. **Leaves:** sub-radical, narrowly or broadly linear, 3″–8″ long. **Scape:** 9″–18″ tall, slender, smooth, bearing from 3–5 blossoms on stalks of varying lengths. **Flowers:** 1″–1½″ across; dorsal sepal ovate or triangular, slightly incurved and concave; lateral sepals linear, dilated above the middle; petals oval or oblong-elliptical, with a long claw; lip 3-lobed from the base; side lobes very broadly cuneate or obliquely obovate; centre lobe contracted into a claw.

September and October.

An interesting and at the same time decorative species, with fair-sized blossoms of a dull yellow or buff colour suffused with orange-red, the lateral sepals are dull green and the lip is red or purple with a broad yellow zone. It grows in moist grassy places both in the mountains and lowlands of Victoria, Southern Australia, Western Australia and Tasmania. It should be quite hardy in all but the most bleak parts of Great Britain and should be grown in damp fibrous loam in full sun.

325. DIURIS MACULATA, Sm.

D. pardina, Lindl. *D. curvifolia*, Lindl.

Root: of small oblong tubers on short fleshy fibres. **Leaves:** subradical, narrowly linear; lowermost 6″ long, others degenerating upwards into bracts. **Scape:** 9″–12″ tall, slender, bearing 3–6 blossoms. **Flowers:** about ¾″ across, on long stalks, secund; dorsal sepal ovate-oblong, concave; lateral sepals very narrow, crossed over one another below the lip; petals ovate, on a long claw; lip 3-lobed; outer lobes and centre lobe almost of equal length, outer lobes diverging, centre one very broad at the tip. *October.*

A very variable species of slender habit, with bright green grass-like leaves and loose racemes of quaint little bright yellow blossoms spotted and blotched with rich red-brown. In shape and colouring they bear a striking resemblance to those of some species of Oncidium from South America. It is found in pastures, thin woods and forest land over the greater part of Eastern Australia from Queensland to Tasmania and should be quite hardy in all but the coldest parts of Great Britain. A cool moist compost of fibrous loam and leaf-soil is indicated.

326. DIURIS PALUSTRIS, Lindl.

Root: of small oblong tubers on slender fibres. **Leaves:** radical and cauline, very narrowly linear, lowermost about 3″ long, decreasing in length upwards. **Scape:** 4″–6″ tall, slender, bearing from 1–4 blossoms. **Flowers:** about $\frac{5}{8}$″ across; dorsal sepal ovate-oblong, erect, slightly concave; lateral sepals strap-shaped, projecting below the lip, $\frac{3}{4}$″ long; petals ovate, very blunt; lip short, 3-lobed; side lobes large, rounded; centre lobe broad, emarginate. *December.*

This plant very much resembles *D. maculata*, but is smaller. It bears from one to four blossoms on stalks of varying lengths; the dorsal sepal, petals and lip are bright yellow in ground colour, but this is almost obscured by large purple spots and blotches; the lateral sepals are dull green, edged with brown. The plant is found in damp or swampy places amongst grasses in Victoria, Southern Australia and Tasmania and ascends the mountains to over 3000 feet and should be quite hardy in all but the coldest parts of Great Britain. It should be given a good fibrous loam in a damp sunny spot in the rock garden.

327. DIURIS PEDUNCULATA, R. Br.

D. lanceolata, Lindl. *D. Behrii*, Schltr.

Root: of small ovoid tubers on rather long fleshy fibres. **Leaves:** basal, linear to narrowly linear, 4″–6″ long, reduced in length upwards. **Scape:** slender, 6″–9″ tall, bearing 1–2 blossoms on stalks of varying length. **Flowers:** about $\frac{5}{8}$″ across; dorsal sepal short, heart-shaped, concave; lateral sepals linear; petals elliptical, stipitate, equalling the sepals in length; lip 3-lobed; lateral lobes curved, rather narrow and at times toothed; centre lobe ovate-rhomboid, four times the length of the lateral lobes. *October.*

A dainty grassy-leaved species with slender stems bearing one or perhaps two pale yellow blossoms with brownish tinting towards the base of the segments. Like all its brethren it should make a pretty addition to the alpine house. It is a lover of damp and marshy places in open spots, both on the mountains and lowlands of the whole of Eastern Australia from Queensland to Tasmania and should be quite hardy in all but the bleakest parts of Great Britain. A damp spot in a good rich soil in the rock garden should suit it.

328. DIURIS PUNCTATA, Sm.

D. elongata, Sw. *D. lilacina*, F. Muell.

Root: of rather large oblong tubers on stout fibres. **Leaves:** sub-basal, 2 in number, linear, 3″–6″ long. **Scape:** 1′–2¼′ tall, rather stout, clothed with a few sheathing bracts and bearing 2–3 blossoms on stalks of varying length. **Flowers:** nearly 2″ across; dorsal sepal broadly ovate-oblong; lateral sepals very narrow, nearly 2″ long, deflexed below the lip; petals broadly elliptic-oblong; lip divided to the base into 3-lobes; outer lobes oblong-falcate, usually crenulate; centre lobe obovate-oblong, longer than the lateral ones.

October and November.

An exceedingly handsome robust species, with stout stems bearing from two to three large blue or purple blossoms with dark dottings or punctations. There is a form known as *longissima* with lateral sepals over 3″ long, and a dwarf form (*minor*) with smaller flowers. The plant grows in moist grassy places both on the mountains and in the lowlands of New South Wales and Victoria, where it reaches an elevation which ensures its hardiness in this country. A good rich soil in a moist sunny spot is indicated.

329. DIURIS SULPHUREA, R. Br.

D. oculata, F. Muell.

Root: of small ovoid tubers on long fibres. **Leaves:** subradical, narrowly linear, 2″–4″ long, decreasing upwards into bracts. **Scape:** 9″–15″ tall, rather slender, bearing from 2–5 blossoms. **Flowers:** about ¾″ across; dorsal sepal narrowly ovate, concave, opening out upwards; lateral sepals narrowly linear-lanceolate; petals broadly lanceolate, contracted into a claw at the base; lip 3-lobed from its base; side lobes broad, more or less toothed and undulated; centre lobe very broadly lanceolate, twice as long as the side lobes.

November.

A pretty plant with a long slender stalk clothed at its base with two narrow bright green grassy leaves; the blossoms are from two to five in number and face alternate ways on the stem, they are sulphur-yellow in ground colour, more or less blotched with brown or brownish-purple. It grows in moist grassy places and marshes in New South Wales, Victoria, South Australia and Tasmania and should be perfectly hardy in all but the most exposed parts of Great Britain. A damp fibrous loam in an open sunny spot is indicated.

EARINA, Lindley

This genus consists of 10 tufted evergreen epiphytal plants of erect rigid habit; they have numerous thick white fleshy roots which anchor the plants

PLATE 9.

DIURIS SULPHUREA.

PLATE 10.

EULOPHIA HIANS.

to the moss-covered branches of the trees on which they grow. The leaves are distichous, tufted, narrowly linear, decreasing in length on the flattened flower-stems and degenerating into bracts amongst the blossoms, which are borne in terminal simple or branched spikes or panicles. The blossoms are small and are of no great decorative value. The plants are found on the branches of trees and on moss and fern-clad rocks in the temperate rain forests of New Zealand, frequently attaining considerable elevation above sea-level. They may be tried outdoors in humid sheltered localities, on a damp moss-covered and fern-clad rock, or on a block of apple wood with some peat or osmunda fibre packed round their roots. Propagation by imported plants and by seeds when procurable.

330. EARINA AUTUMNALIS, Hook. f.

E. suaveolens, Lindl.

Root: of creeping, thick white fibres, epiphytic. **Stem:** stout, slightly compressed, leafy. **Leaves:** radical and cauline, narrowly linear, 2″–3½″ long, rigid, distichous, numerous. **Scape:** 1′–1½′ tall. **Panicle:** short, stiff, distichously branched. **Flowers:** ¼″ across, numerous; dorsal and lateral sepals broadly oblong, spreading; petals ovate, spreading; lip broad, obscurely 3-lobed, retuse. *March to June.*

The white purple-spotted blossoms of this species are too small and too few in number to have much decorative value. It grows on moss-covered rocks and clefts in the branches of large trees in the North and South Islands of New Zealand, where it is not uncommon and reaches sufficient elevation in the uplands to ensure its complete hardiness in the warmer parts of Great Britain. It may be grown on a moss-covered rock kept saturated, or in fibrous peat and sphagnum-moss, in an elevated spot in the bog garden. It should be protected from severe frost.

331. EARINA MUCRONATA, Lindl.

Root: of thick white fibres, epiphytic. **Stem:** slender, leafy. **Leaves:** radical and cauline, narrowly linear or strap-shaped, distichous, 4″–6″ long, numerous. **Scape:** 1′–3′ tall. **Panicle:** slender, sparingly branched. **Flowers:** widely separated, ¼″ across; dorsal and lateral sepals linear-oblong, nearly of equal length; petals linear-oblong, spreading; lip deeply 3-lobed, lateral lobes incurved. *October to December.*

A plant of but little decorative value, the small white blossoms with their purple-spotted lips are not very freely produced. It grows on trees and moss-covered rocks and is common throughout the North and South Islands of New Zealand, attaining sufficient altitude above sea-level to ensure its complete hardiness in the warmer parts of Great Britain. It may be grown in fibrous peat and sphagnum-moss in a raised part of the bog garden or on a damp moss-covered rock. The plant should be protected by a handlight during the winter.

EPHIPPIANTHUS, Reichenbach fils.

A genus containing but one species. It is a very fragile little terrestrial deciduous herb and is very closely related to some members of the genus Liparis and like them inhabits damp mountain forests, its slender root ramifies amongst the decaying leaves and other vegetable debris. In importing the wood-loving species it is very necessary to lift them in as large a quantity of soil as possible in order that the minute fungi may be imported as well, for without these fungi the plants seem to be unable to produce sound seed or to succeed in cultivation for any length of time.

332. EPHIPPIANTHUS SACHALINENSIS, Reichb. f.

E. Schmidtii, Reichb. f.

Root: a slender filiform rhizome. **Stem:** very slender, about 6″ tall, with 1 perfoliate leaf at its base. **Leaf:** deeply cordate-ovate, blunt, shortly stalked, about 1″ long. **Scape:** naked, bearing from 2–5 blossoms. **Flowers:** about $\frac{1}{4}$″ across; sepals oblong, blunt; petals ligulate, slightly shorter than the sepals; lip unguiculate, oblong, obscurely lobed, blunt; disc with erect, frequently bilobed, calli near its base. *July and August.*

A dwarf species with a solitary bright green leaf with deeper green reticulations and a slender few-flowered spike of rather small green and purple blossoms. It is of no decorative value but should prove interesting in a pan of peat, leaf-soil and sphagnum-moss in the alpine house. It is usually found in damp mountain forests in various parts of Eastern Siberia and Japan, frequently at as much as 6000 feet above sea-level. It should prove quite hardy in this country in a damp shady spot in the rock garden.

EPIPACTIS, R. Brown

Helleborine, Hill

Erect, leafy, deciduous terrestrial plants numbering 28 species, with creeping rhizomes sometimes of considerable length, well furnished with fibrous roots. The leafy stems which rise from the nodes frequently attain considerable height and are clothed with large ovate or lanceolate, deeply veined leaves degenerating on the upper part of the stem into leaf-like bracts. These subtend the blossoms which are borne in loose one-sided racemes and are of fair size but somewhat soberly coloured, and consequently not very decorative. The various species, which range over most of the temperate regions of the northern hemisphere, are usually found in damp soils in wooded districts and also at considerable elevation on the mountains. All, but with very few exceptions, are quite hardy in Britain and may be grown in a damp spot in the rock garden in half-shade. Propagation by division of the rhizomes and also by seed.

333. EPIPACTIS AFRICANA, Rendle

Root: a stout creeping rhizome. **Stem:** erect, stout, leafy, covered with minute rust-coloured hairs. **Leaves:** cauline, ovate or ovate-oblong, subobtuse, amplexicaul, decreasing upwards into bracts, lowest 3″ long. **Scape:** $1\frac{1}{4}'$–2′ tall. **Raceme:** 3″–6″ long, loose. **Flowers:** about $\frac{3}{4}''$ long; dorsal sepal lanceolate, pointed; lateral sepals broadly ovate, with an oblique base, and a narrowly falcate apex; petals ovate, subfalcate, pointed; lip with basal part narrowly oblong and apex broadly ovate, at its base are 2 linear-oblong staminoides. *August to October.*

The dull green and red blossoms of this species although of fair size are of but little decorative value. It is found in damp peaty soil amongst heather, on the Ruwenzori Range in British East Africa at an elevation of 10,000 feet above sea-level and is therefore quite hardy in Southern Britain. A compost of fibrous peat and loam in a damp half-shady spot should suit it.

334. EPIPACTIS ATRORUBENS, Schult.

E. atropurpurea, Raf. *E. media*, Fries. *E. ovalis*, Bab. *E. rubiginosa*, Gaud.

Root: of thick fleshy fibres about 2″ long, from a short rhizome. **Stem:** 9″–21″ tall, sparely leafy, frequently sinuous, hairy. **Leaves:** few, ovate, clasping the stem, degenerating into scales below, 1″–2″ long, sheathing the stem, alternate. **Spike:** 3″–5″ long, frequently one-sided, loose, of about a dozen blossoms. **Flowers:** about $\frac{1}{2}''$ long; dorsal sepal ovate-lanceolate; lateral sepals lanceolate, curved at the tip; petals lanceolate, usually twisted obliquely at the tip; lip divided into 2 distinct portions, basal portion rounded, apical half cordate, crenulate, pointed. *June and July.*

A native species with sinuous stems frequently tinted with purple and clothed with deep green leaves. The blossoms are borne in a loose spike and are of no great decorative value; they have dull purple sepals and petals and a dark red lip and are half closed and drooping; in some specimens the blossoms are green. The plant is found in half shady places over the whole of Europe and Western Asia as far as Persia. It may be grown in a shady spot in the rock garden in leaf-soil and loam.

335. EPIPACTIS CONSIMILIS, Wall

E. amœna, Ham. *E. veratifolia*, Boiss

Root: a slender creeping rhizome, emitting stout fleshy fibres. **Stem:** erect, rather slender, downy above, 1′–2′ tall. **Leaves:** lanceolate, sessile, plaited, 4″–7″ long. **Raceme:** lax-flowered. **Flowers:** about $1\frac{1}{2}$″ across, on long stalks; sepals ovate-lanceolate, pointed; petals lanceolate, pointed; lip rather large, narrowly oblong at the base, lanceolate and recurved towards the tip. *June to August.*

This species bears large green and purple blossoms in a loose few-flowered raceme; they are by no means showy but are quite interesting; the handsome plaited foliage is of a rich green colour. It grows in shady rocky places usually on damp limestone in hilly districts from Syria to the Himalaya and should be quite hardy in Great Britain in a damp shady spot in the rock garden, in calcareous loam and a little leaf-soil.

336. EPIPACTIS GIGANTEA, Doug.

E. americana, Lindl.

Root: of stout fibres. **Stem:** 1′–$3\frac{3}{4}$′ tall, erect or zig-zag, leafy. **Leaves:** radical and cauline, ovate on the lower part of the stem, lanceolate or ovate-lanceolate above, sessile and stem clasping, 4″–6″ long. **Raceme:** of several widely separated blossoms. **Flowers:** about $1\frac{1}{4}$″ across; sepals and petals ovate to lanceolate, pointed, spreading; lip concave below with erect margins, ovate and petal-like towards the tip with thickened veins. *July to September.*

A very tall leafy species with rather large green purple-veined blossoms of no great decorative value. It is found in Western North America from British Columbia to California and Texas in damp shady places, in dry coniferous wood, etc., and should be quite hardy in Great Britain in the Western and Southern counties in a shady part of the herbaceous border in good loam and leaf-soil.

337. EPIPACTIS HELLEBORINE, Crantz

E. Dalhousiæ, Wight; *E. latifolia*, All. *E. macrostachya*, Lindl. *Helleborine latifolia*, Druce

Root: a short creeping rhizome. **Stem:** 1′–3′ tall, stout. **Leaves:** cauline, orbicular, ovate-lanceolate or lanceolate, margins hairy. **Raceme:** usually long, secund. **Flowers:** $\frac{1}{2}$″–$\frac{3}{4}$″ long; sepals ovate-lanceolate; petals lanceolate; lip small oblong, tip somewhat recurved. *April to July.*

A native plant of but little garden value with long drooping racemes of green and purple blossoms. There are several forms such as *herbacea* (greenish-white), *intrusa* (pale green), *purpurata* or *violacea* (yellowish-green and purple), *Thomsonii* (green and pale purple) and *viridiflora* (yellowish-green). The type and its forms are scattered over various parts of Europe and temperate Asia as far east as Japan and southward to the Himalaya, where one form reaches an elevation of 11,000 feet. They may be grown in a cool shady spot in the rock garden in leaf-soil and loam as they are woodland plants.

338. EPIPACTIS LONGIFOLIA, Thbg.

Root: a creeping rhizome emitting numerous fibres. **Stem:** 1′–2′ tall, fairly stout, leafy. **Leaves:** cauline, 5–6 in number, lanceolate, deeply channelled, pointed, sheathing at the base, 3″–6″ long. **Raceme:** short, loose, of 12–14 blossoms. **Flowers:** about ½″ long; dorsal sepal broadly ovate, blunt, erect; lateral sepals ovate, blunt; petals narrowly ovate, more pointed than the sepals; lip trowel-shaped, blunt, retuse, suberect; spur, conical, very short. *July to September.*

The small green and purple blossoms of this species are of no decorative value; they remain half closed throughout their existence. The plant is found on the margins of woods and thickets in various parts of Japan and Korea. It should be quite hardy in Great Britain in a half-shady spot in leaf-soil and loam.

339. EPIPACTIS MICROPHYLLA, Sw.

E. Helleborine var. *microphylla*, Reichb. f. *E. latifolia* var. *microphylla*, D.C. *Serapias microphylla*, Ehrh.

Root: a short rhizome emitting numerous stout fleshy fibres 1″ or 2″ long with clavate tips. **Stem:** ¾″ to 1¾″ tall, erect or slightly sinuous, hairy, clothed with numerous leaves resembling scales. **Leaves:** ovate, pointed, spatha-like, pressed close to the stem, ½″–1″ long. **Spike:** 2″–4″ long, lax, few-flowered. **Flowers:** ⅜″ long; dorsal sepal ovate, pointed; lateral sepals lanceolate, falcate at the tip; petals similar but smaller; lip narrow at the base, broad and petal-like at the tip with 2 ridges at the base of the disc. *June.*

A slender plant with a long stem clothed with pale green leaves which are frequently pressed close to the stem, and a loose spike of about six or nine blossoms with green and pink sepals and petals and a bright green lip; they are drooping and are of little decorative value. It is found in damp shady places both in the highlands and lowlands of Middle and Southern Europe and is quite hardy in Britain in a damp shady spot in leaf-soil and loam.

340. EPIPACTIS PALUSTRIS, Crantz.

E. longifolia, Linn. *Helleborine palustris*, Schrank; *Cymbidium palustre*, Swartz; *Serapias Helleborine* var. *palustris*, Linn.

Root: a short stout rhizome with numerous fleshy fibres. **Stems:** 9″–24″ tall, rather slender, leafy. **Leaves:** lanceolate, alternate, fairly numerous, becoming smaller upwards, sheathing below, 2″–4″ long. **Spike:** 3″–5″ long, loosely many-flowered. **Flowers:** about ⅝″ long; dorsal sepal lanceolate, curving over the ovary; lateral sepals lanceolate, narrow and curved at the tip; petals ovate, large; lip divided into 2 distinct portions, the lower half concave and small, upper half broad and petal-like. *June and July.*

A pretty native plant with erect stems clothed with pale green foliage, and loose spikes of medium-sized blossoms with rose-pink sepals and petals tinted with green; the large lip has the upper half pink and the lower half white. There are several forms such as *ericetorum*, *ochroleuca*, *salina*, and *silvatica*. The type and its forms are found in moist meadows and marshes, usually in calcareous soils, from Great Britain to Japan, the Himalaya and Persia; it is also found in North Africa; they may be grown in an open spot in the bog garden or on the banks of a stream or pond in good calcareous loam.

341. EPIPACTIS PAPILLOSA, Franch

Helleborine papillosa, Druce; *Limodorum papillosum*, O. Ktze.

Root: a thick underground creeping stem furnished with stout rootlets. **Stem:** fairly stout, erect, leafy, covered with minute down, 1′–2¼′ tall. **Leaves:** cauline, 5–6 in number, broadly lanceolate, pointed, deeply channelled, suberect, 4″–6″ long, minutely downy. **Raceme:** of 10–12 blossoms, loose. **Flowers:** about ½″ long; dorsal sepal broadly ovate, blunt; lateral sepals ovate, blunt; petals narrowly ovate, pointed; lip narrow below, broad and petal-like at the tip, oricular, pointed, crenulate, suberect; spur short, conical. *June and July.*

This species produces a short raceme of rather small purple and green blossoms of but little decorative value. It is found over the whole of Northern Japan and Korea in cool shady woods, usually of deciduous trees. It should prove perfectly hardy in Great Britain in a shady part of the garden in cool oak leaf-soil and sand.

342. EPIPACTIS ROYLEANA, Lindl.

Cephalanthera Royleana, Regel

Root: a fleshy creeping rhizome. **Stem:** 1′–2′ tall, fairly stout. **Leaves:** varying from lanceolate to orbicular, margins hairy, 4″–7″ long. **Raceme:**

6″–10″ long, lax-flowered. **Flowers:** about 1″ across; sepals ovate-lanceolate, pointed; petals lanceolate, smaller than the sepals; lip 3-lobed; outer lobes rounded, erect or incurved; centre lobe tongue-like, pointed.

July and August.

A leafy species, very closely allied to, if not identical with, *E. americana.* It has tall flexuous stems clothed with distant lance-shaped leaves, and long racemes of blossoms varying from pale green with a yellow or red lip to dark purple maroon throughout, and is quite a handsome plant. It is usually found in poor dry soil on the margins of pine forests frequently on limestone formations, from Asia Minor to the Himalaya and Western China, reaching an elevation of over 12,000 feet above sea-level, and is therefore quite hardy in Great Britain in shady spots in stony calcareous loam.

343. EPIPACTIS TANGUTICA, Schltr.

Root: a shortly creeping rhizome. **Stem:** 9″–15″ tall, rather slender, sparely leafy. **Leaves:** few in number, ovate or elliptic, narrower upwards, degenerating into leafy bracts amongst the blossoms, $1\frac{1}{2}''$–$2\frac{1}{2}''$ long. **Raceme:** of 6–10 blossoms, rather lax, 6″ long. **Flowers:** about $\frac{3}{8}''$ long; dorsal sepal ovate, shortly pointed, downy on the back; lateral sepals obliquely ovate; petals ovate, blunt, oblique towards the tip; all forming a loose hood over the column; lip divided into 2 parts, basal semiglobose with thickened nerves; apical subreniform, shortly pointed, with a few calli on its upper surface.

June to August.

This species closely resembles *E. latifolia* (All.) in the shape of its blossoms which are dull purple, tinted with green, and are of but little garden value. It is found in wooded country in Western Kan-su, North-Western China, and in Tibet. It should be perfectly hardy in Britain in a damp half-shady spot in the rock garden in peat and leaf-soil.

344. EPIPACTIS YUNNANENSIS, Schltr.

Root: a creeping rhizome with fibrous rootlets. **Stem:** $1'$–$1\frac{1}{4}'$ tall, erect, sparely leafy, downy upwards. **Leaves:** 4–5 in number, oblong or ovate-elliptic, rather blunt, smooth, $1\frac{1}{2}''$–$2\frac{1}{2}''$ long. **Raceme:** about 6″ long, laxly many-flowered. **Flowers:** about $\frac{3}{4}''$ long; dorsal sepal elliptic, concave, rather pointed; lateral sepals elliptic, obliquely pointed, all downy on the outer surfaces; petals obliquely ovate-lanceolate, pointed, smooth, forming with the sepals a loose open hood over the column; lip oblong-ovate at the base, expanded at the tip into a short, truncate, petal-like lobe with some small calli near its base. *August and September.*

A slender species with sparely leafy stems and long loose racemes of reddish-purple blossoms of some decorative value. It is found on thinly wooded mountains near Tong-tchouan, North-Eastern Yunnan, in Western China. It should prove quite hardy in Britain in a damp spot in calcareous loam and leaf-soil.

EPIPOGUM, Swartz

This genus contains about 10 species of erect leafless herbaceous plants of terrestrial habit; they are saprophytes living on decaying vegetable matter. Their roots which are composed of short thick coralloid fibres are buried just below the surface of the mass of leaves and twigs in which they grow. The stout, sometimes beautifully tinted, stems are clothed with a few scale-like bracts; the flowers are interesting and quite pretty and are borne in loose racemes. The plants are found in fairly damp shady places frequently in rocky soils, growing in rotting vegetable debris. Possibly they may derive some form of nourishment from the bacteria and mycelia of fungi usually present in such soils. The plants are widely scattered over most parts of the Old World; only two species are sufficiently hardy for outdoor culture, one of which is a native. Propagation by imported roots.

345. EPIPOGUM GMELINII, Rich.

E. aphyllum, Swartz; *Satyrium Epipogium*, Linn.

Root: a number of short, thick, fleshy, coral-like fibres. **Stem:** 4″–8″ tall, often very stout and swollen at the base, clothed with 1–2 short appressed sheaths. **Raceme:** loose, of 3–6 blossoms. **Flowers:** about 1″ across; sepals and petals narrowly lanceolate, subequal, margins involute; lip oblong or ovate, 3-lobed; outer lobes small, oblong; centre lobe larger, with lines of glandular warts; spur at the base of the lip thick and broad.

July to September.

A very curious native plant not wanting in quaint beauty. It is leafless, the stout stem and sheaths are yellowish-brown in colour, tinted with pink; the comparatively large blossoms are pale yellow or pink, often spotted with a deeper tint, the lip is white or very pale pink with rows of red warts down its centre. It grows among rotting leaves and twigs in damp shady places in Europe and Northern Asia, reaching its southern limit in the Himalaya at 8500 feet. It may be grown in a damp shady spot in the rock garden in pure leaf-soil.

346. EPIPOGUM JAPONICUM, Makino

E. aphyllum var. *japonicum*, Makino; *Galera japonica*, Makino

Root: of ovoid tubers, about $\frac{3}{4}$″ long. **Leaves:** obsolete. **Stem:** about 8″ tall, erect, fleshy, clothed with from 2–5 adpressed sheaths placed some distance apart. **Raceme:** lax, of from 1–7 blossoms. **Flowers:** nodding, about $1\frac{1}{4}''$ across; sepals and petals subequal, narrowly ovate; lip entire, large, subhorizontal, triangular, deeply concave, thick and fleshy, with a few obscure rows of minute papillæ on its upper surface; spur pendulous, oblong, slightly compressed and obscurely 2–4-lobed at the tip.

September and October.

This quaint plant produces a dwarf, stout, pale yellow stem minutely spotted with purple and clothed with purple-tinted sheaths. The nodding blossoms are pale yellow with numerous minute spots and stripes on their segments. It is found in shady forests in the province of Shimotsuke, Japan, and is very rare. In cultivation it would probably succeed in the rock garden in a shady spot in decaying beech and oak leaves.

ERIOCHILUS, R. Brown

Delightful miniature deciduous terrestrial plants numbering 7 species. Their root system is formed of several pea-like tubers on long or short white roots; each tuber, after having produced a flower-stem, perishes and is replaced by one or more young tubers if the plant is in a flourishing condition. The slender hairy stem bears a solitary ovate or lanceolate leaf at the base and ends in a few-flowered spike of delicately tinted curiously constructed blossoms, each blossom being subtended by a short oval bract. Only one species is at all suitable for permanent planting outdoors in Britain, the others—*E. dilatatus*, *E. multiflorus*, *E. scaber* and *E. tenuis*—are all natives of Western Australia and are probably too tender for outdoor culture in this country. The various species are usually found in rather dry soil in open situations and are confined to Australia. Propagation by imported tubers and by seeds.

347. ERIOCHILUS AUTUMNALIS, R. Br.

E. cucullatus, Reichb. f. *Epipactis cucullata*, Labill.

Root: of small ovoid tubers on short white fibres. **Leaf:** solitary, radical, ovate, pointed, about $1\frac{1}{4}''$ long, usually shrivelling before the flowers are perfected. **Scape:** $3''$–$6''$ tall, slender, bearing 2–3 rather widely separated blossoms. **Flowers:** about $\frac{3}{4}''$ long; dorsal sepal narrowly lanceolate, pointed, erect or slightly incurved; lateral sepals elliptic-lanceolate, very pointed, very narrow at the base; petals linear or linear-spathulate; lip 3-lobed; lateral lobes minute; centre lobe ovate-oblong, recurved. *September.*

An exceedingly interesting little plant with delicately tinted insect-like blossoms poised on the slender stems. The dorsal sepal is pink inside and green outside; the lateral sepals are pink, the lip is green spotted with red and is covered with golden hairs. The whole plant is covered with white red-tipped glandular hairs. A gem for the alpine house. It is fairly common in open situations in rather poor dry soils over the whole of Eastern Australia and should be quite hardy in the more sheltered parts of Great Britain. A sandy loam in an open sunny spot in the rock garden is indicated.

EULOPHIA, R. Brown

Many members of this genus, which numbers over 390 species, are of decorative value; they are for the most part deciduous terrestrial plants, although a few are epiphytal and evergreen with distinct pseudo-bulbs. The majority, however, have narrow sword-shaped leaves springing in a tuft from creeping underground stems, which are frequently thickened at the nodes into fleshy or woody tubers, often of considerable size, these give rise to new plants. The lax racemes of small, medium-sized, or at times large, blossoms are usually some shade of yellow or purple. The various species are widely scattered over the warm temperate regions of the Old World, being most abundantly represented in Africa; they are usually found in open grassy country and many grow at sufficient altitude above sea-level in their native countries to give reasonable hope that they may prove hardy in Britain. Propagation by imported tubers and seed when obtainable.

348. EULOPHIA ABYSSINICA, Reichb. f.

Orthochilus abyssinicus, Hochst.

Root: a stout creeping rhizome. **Leaves:** basal, lanceolate or oblong-lanceolate, rather pointed, 6″–12″ long, reduced at the base into a sheathing petiole. **Scape:** $1\frac{1}{2}'$–$1\frac{3}{4}'$ tall, clothed with a few sheaths. **Raceme:** 4″–6″ long, many-flowered. **Flowers:** over an inch across; sepals broadly ovate, pointed; petals elliptic-ovate, pointed; lip 3-lobed; outer lobes very broadly oblong, blunt; centre lobe suborbicular, blunt; disc with 2 keels down its centre; spur oblong, blunt, small. *April to June.*

A handsome robust species with a long raceme of large white and green blossoms on a tall sheath-clothed flower-stem. It grows in wet meadows and swamps both in the lowlands and on the mountains in several districts in Abyssinia. In cultivation it should be sufficiently hardy for culture outdoors in Southern Britain, in the bog garden or on the banks of a stream or pond in rich soil.

349. EULOPHIA ACULEATA, Spreng.

E. capensis, Bolus; *E. odontoglossa*, Reichb. f. *E. pedicellata*, Spreng. *E. plicata*, Bolus; *E. plicatum*, Harv. *Cymbidum aculeatum*, Sw.

Root: a rather stout creeping rhizome, irregularly thickened between the nodes. **Stem:** fairly stout. **Leaves:** radical, linear or linear-lanceolate,

$\frac{1}{4}''$–$1\frac{1}{2}''$ long. **Scape:** 3″–18″ tall, sheath-clothed. **Raceme:** subcapitate or oblong, $2\frac{1}{2}''$ long, dense. **Flowers:** $\frac{3}{4}''$ across; sepals subconnivent, oblong or oblong-lanceolate; petals broadly elliptic, blunt; lip 3-lobed, as broad as long; centre lobe triangular-oblong; outer lobes broadly oblong, all slightly undulate; spur obsolete. *November to February.*

A pretty plant with fairly large cream-coloured or yellow flowers on stems of varying lengths, clothed near the base with one or two bright green leaves. It is found on the mountains in moist grassy places in Tembuland, Transvaal and Cape Colony, where on the Bosch Berg in the Somerset Division at 4800 feet it is at times exposed to over 20° of frost when at rest. A compost of moist fibrous peat and loam in full sun is indicated.

350. EULOPHIA ÆMULA, Schltr.

Root: a creeping, stout rhizome, thickened at the nodes. **Leaves:** in a fascicle of 4–5, narrowly linear, 6″–18″ long. **Scape:** 9″–21″ long, sheath-clothed. **Raceme:** lax, many-flowered. **Flowers:** nearly $\frac{3}{4}''$ across; sepals lanceolate-oblong, subequal; petals elliptic-oblong, pointed; lip 3-lobed; side lobes oblong; centre lobe obovate or rounded, obtuse, longer than the side lobes; disc with 3–5 crested nerves; spur clavate, slightly curved, $\frac{1}{8}''$ long. *December to February.*

Quite a pretty plant with rather large light and deep purple flowers in short racemes, on slender sheath-clothed flower-stems rising from the close tuft of bright green grassy leaves. It is found on grassy hill and mountain slopes in Cape Colony, Tembuland, Swaziland, Natal, Orange Free State, Bechuanaland and the Transvaal, where near Botsabelo at 5000 feet it is exposed to over 15° of frost for short periods during its winter rest. It should be grown in a somewhat moist fibrous loam in a sunny spot in the rock garden and is only suitable for Southern and Western gardens.

351. EULOPHIA ALIWALENSIS, Rolfe

Root: a creeping rhizome thickened at the nodes. **Leaves:** very immature at flowering time, linear, in fascicles of 3–4, 6″–12″ long. **Scape:** $1\frac{1}{2}'$ tall, clothed with about 3 lanceolate sheaths. **Raceme:** about 4″ long, of about $\frac{1}{2}$ a dozen blossoms. **Flowers:** about $\frac{3}{4}''$ long; sepals subconnivent, elliptic-oblong; petals elliptic, much broader than the sepals; lip 3-lobed, broadly elliptic; side lobes broadly rounded; centre lobe suborbicular, with 7–9 crested veins; spur subclavate, nearly straight, slender, $\frac{1}{6}''$ long. *November to January.*

This is a rather sombre species with fairly large blossoms of yellowish-brown colour outside and pale purple within, they are borne in racemes of from seven to nine blossoms on a slender sheath-clothed stem which springs from beside the tuft of undeveloped leaves. It grows in dry, flat, grassy ground at Elands Hoek in the Aliwal North Division of Cape Colony at 4550 feet, where it is exposed to nearly 20° of frost for short periods when it is deciduous. It should be grown in fibrous loam in an open sunny spot.

352. EULOPHIA BAKERI, Rolfe

Root: a stout creeping rhizome. **Leaves:** in a tuft, elongate-lanceolate, attenuated at the base, 6″–8″ long. **Scape:** 9″–15″ tall. **Raceme:** lax, of 6–8 blossoms. **Flowers:** over 1″ across; sepals oblong-lanceolate; petals ovate-elliptic, longer than the sepals and twice as broad; lip ovate-elliptic, 3-lobed; side lobes narrow with rounded apex; front lobe broadly elliptic or suborbicular; disc with 5–7 thickened fringed keels; spur oblong, over $\frac{1}{6}$″ long. *October to December.*

A beautiful decorative plant with large pale pink or lilac blossoms on a slender bract-clothed stem rising from a tuft of lance-shaped leaves. It should make a delightful subject for rock garden decoration. In its native habitat it grows in rocky soil and is confined to high rocky ridges near Johannesburg in the Transvaal at 5000 feet, where it is subjected to 15° or 20° of frost for short intervals during its deciduous period in the winter months. It should be given a gritty fibrous loam in an open sunny spot in the rock garden.

353. EULOPHIA BARBATA, Spreng.

E. ovalis, Lindl. *E. Dregeana,* Bolus; *Serapias capensis*, Linn. *Limodorum barbatum,* Thunb.

Root: of subglobose tubers, joined by tough fibres. **Leaves:** in a tuft, narrowly ensiform or linear, pointed, 4″–10″ long. **Scape:** compressed, 6″–12″ long, clothed with numerous lanceolate, imbricate sheaths. **Raceme:** 3″–4″ long, many-flowered. **Flowers:** $\frac{3}{4}$″ long; sepals oblong-lanceolate; petals elliptic-oblong, about twice as broad as the sepals; lip broadly elliptic, 3-lobed; side lobes short, broadly rounded; centre lobe broadly rounded, blunt; disc with 3–5 thickened fringed keels; spur oblong, blunt, over $\frac{1}{6}$″ long. *November to January.*

A delicately tinted plant with half closed blossoms having green sepals and white petals and lip. It should make a beautiful addition to the rock garden. It grows in a variety of situations, but is most frequently found in moist sandy spots both in the lowlands and on the mountains in Natal, Griqualand East and Cape Colony, where on the summit of the Bosch Berg at 5000 feet it is exposed to 20° or more of frost during its resting period in the winter. A moist sandy loam in full sun is indicated.

354. EULOPHIA BICALLOSA, Hook. f.

Bletia bicallosa, Don

Root: a thick rhizome, swollen at the nodes. **Leaves:** undeveloped at flowering time, narrowly sword-shaped, 6″–10″ long. **Scape:** about $1\frac{1}{2}'$ tall, erect, rounded, scaly. **Raceme:** elongate, of 6–8 blossoms. **Flowers:** about $\frac{3}{4}''$ across; sepals elliptic-oblong, pointed; petals shaped like the sepals only smaller; lip 3-lobed; outer lobes rounded, somewhat erect; centre lobe suborbicular, crisped. *June to August.*

Quite a decorative plant with long racemes composed of from six to eight widely separated blossoms of a pale straw-colour or greenish-white; it is leafless when in blossom. It grows in moist rocky places and in thinly wooded ravines in the Himalayas of Nepal up to 8000 feet above sea-level. It may be tried outdoors in Southern and Western Britain in a damp spot in the rock garden in good loam and leaf-soil, to which has been added a little calcareous matter in some form.

355. EULOPHIA BILAMELLATA, Schltr.

Root: a creeping rhizome thickened at the nodes. **Leaves:** tufted, linear, blunt, 2″–4″ long. **Scape:** about 1′ tall, clothed with loose, broadly ovate sheaths. **Raceme:** lax, many-flowered. **Flowers:** about 1″ across; dorsal sepal lanceolate; lateral sepals somewhat spreading, obliquely ovate-lanceolate; petals oval, narrowed at the base, thickened at the apex; lip obscurely 3-lobed, concave, smooth; side lobes very short, bluntly truncate; centre lobe ovate, rounded at the apex, margins undulate; disc with 2 short parallel keels; spur pyramidal, incurved, blunt at the apex, $\frac{1}{4}''$ long. *November to January.*

This species has large yellow and green blossoms in a loose raceme on a slender sheath-clothed flower-stem, springing from a tuft of about half-a-dozen grassy leaves. It grows on rocky hills and mountain sides amongst grass in Natal, Swaziland and the Transvaal, where, near Barberton, it reaches an elevation of 5000 feet and is exposed to over 15° of frost during the winter. A gritty fibrous loam in full sun is indicated. This species is only suitable for outdoor culture in Southern and Western Britain.

356. EULOPHIA BRACHYSTYLA, Schltr.

Root: a small rhomboid-oblong depressed rhizome. **Leaves:** radical, in fascicles of 2–4, linear, 6″–10″ long. **Scape:** $\frac{3}{4}'$–$1\frac{1}{4}'$ long, slender, flexuous. **Raceme:** 2″–3″ long, lax, many-flowered. **Flowers:** about $\frac{1}{2}''$ long; sepals oblong, 5-nerved; petals broadly obovate-oblong, blunt, twice as broad as the sepals, with several nerves; lip 3-lobed; outer lobes obliquely oblong, blunt; inner lobe oblong, blunt; disc with 3–5 hairy keels; spur subcylindrical, $\frac{1}{8}''$ long. *November and December.*

A rather small-flowered species that produces its raceme of blossoms before the leaves are developed; the slender stem bears under a dozen pale violet flowers in a loose raceme. It is found in rocky places amongst short herbage on the Insizwa Range in Griqualand East, South Africa, at 6800 feet. Plants collected from the above altitude should be perfectly hardy in Great Britain if they can be induced to rest during our winter months. It should be given a gritty loam in a sunny spot in the rock garden.

357. EULOPHIA CALANTHOIDES, Schltr.

Root: a stout woody rhizome thickened at the nodes. **Leaves:** in a fascicle, ensiform or elongate-lanceolate, conduplicate at the base, $\frac{1}{2}'$–$1\frac{1}{4}'$ long. **Scape:** 1′–2′ tall, sheath-clothed. **Raceme:** 4″–8″ long, somewhat dense, many-flowered. **Flowers:** over $1\frac{1}{2}''$ across; sepals linear-lanceolate or oblong-lanceolate, very pointed; petals elliptic-oblong, over twice as broad as the sepals; lip broadly elliptic, 3-lobed; side lobes broadly rounded; front lobe, elliptic-oblong; disc with 3–7 slightly thickened veins crested towards the base; spur slender, curved, blunt, $\frac{1}{4}''$ long. *December and January.*

This is a beautiful plant with large cream-coloured blossoms in rather dense racemes on slender sheath-clothed stems springing from beside a tuft of seven or eight sword-shaped, strongly veined leaves. It grows in moist grassy places in the Transvaal, Orange Free State and Natal, and probably reaches its greatest elevation near Van Reenen in Natal at 6000 feet and is there subjected to 20° or more of frost during its resting period. A good fibrous loam in a moist spot is indicated.

358. EULOPHIA CAMPESTRIS, Wall.

E. hemileuca, Lindl. *E. ramentacea*, Lindl. *E. rupestris*, Lindl. *Bletia Dabia*, Don; *Dipodium ramentaceum*, Ham. *Limodorum dubium*, Ham. *L. ramentaceum*, Rox.

Root: an irregular tuber of considerable size. **Leaves:** undeveloped at flowering time, elliptic-lanceolate, radical 3″–6″ long. **Scape:** $\frac{1}{2}'$–$1\frac{1}{2}'$ tall, stout or slender, clothed with a few subappressed sheaths. **Raceme:** subsecund, many-flowered. **Flowers:** about $1\frac{1}{2}''$ across; sepals linear-lanceolate, pointed, 5–7-nerved; petals oblong-lanceolate, 3–5-nerved; lip cuneate-obovate or oblong, 3-lobed; outer lobes short; centre lobe orbicular or oblong, crenulate; disc with 3 thickened central nerves; spur conical or subclavate, about $\frac{3}{8}''$ long. *May.*

A pretty plant with racemes of large blossoms of pale green or yellow pink-striped sepals and petals and a purple and green lip. It grows in open grassy country both in the lowlands and highlands over Afghanistan, India and parts of Burma. It may be grown outdoors in the warmer parts of Great Britain in a sunny spot, in good rich fibrous loam in a fairly moist position.

359. EULOPHIA COOPERI, Reichb. f.

Root: a stout woody thickened rhizome. **Leaves:** in a fascicle, ensiform, with imbricate sheaths at the base, 2″–5″ long. **Scape:** 6″–9″ tall, clothed with several large spathaceous sheaths. **Raceme:** subcorymbose, dense. **Flowers:** nearly 1″ long; sepals oblong-lanceolate, pointed; petals elliptic-lanceolate, broader than the sepals; lip 3-lobed, broadly elliptic; side lobes broad with a rounded apex; centre lobe nearly as broad as long, rounded; disc with 5–7 verrucose keels, slightly hairy in front; spur broadly oblong.

December to February.

A large-flowered though not very showy species, with green sepals and purple petals and lip to its blossoms which are borne in a spray-like raceme on a slender stem springing from beside a bunch of four or five bright green leaves that are immature at flowering time. It grows in grassy spots near Harrismith in the Orange Free State at 6500 feet and should be perfectly hardy in the warmer parts of Great Britain if it could be induced to rest during our winter. A moist fibrous loam is indicated and full sun.

360. EULOPHIA CORALLORRHIZIFORMIS, Schltr.

Root: a creeping rhizome thickened at the nodes. **Leaves:** narrowly linear, 4″–6″ long, erect. **Scape:** 9″–12″ tall, clothed with a few spathaceous sheaths below. **Raceme:** $1\frac{1}{2}$″–3″ long, rather lax, many-flowered. **Flowers:** $\frac{3}{8}$″ long; sepals subconnivent, oblong-lanceolate, pointed; petals broadly oblong-lanceolate; lip 3-lobed, half as long as the sepals; outer lobes shortly and broadly oblong, diverging; inner lobe suborbicular with 7 rows of rather long, erect, closely arranged papillæ; spur oblong, $\frac{1}{10}$″ long.

November to February.

This is not a very showy plant on account of its blossoms remaining in a half-closed state; they are yellow in colour and are borne in lax racemes on slender stems which, with the young leaves, spring from a papery sheath. It inhabits marshes in the Transvaal and probably reaches its greatest elevation near Donkerhoek at 4900 feet, where it is exposed to 12° of frost for short periods during its winter rest. It should be grown in the bog garden in peat loam and sand mixed with sphagnum-moss, and is only suitable for outdoor culture in the warmer parts of Britain.

361. EULOPHIA ENGLERI, Rolfe

Root: a stout rhizome thickened at the nodes. **Leaves:** in a tuft, elongate-linear, 4″–6″ long. **Scape:** about 1′ tall, clothed with several lanceolate sheaths. **Raceme:** lax. **Flowers:** about $\frac{3}{4}$″ across; sepals oblong or elliptic-oblong; petals broadly elliptic, as long as the sepals; lip strongly 3-lobed, shorter than the petals; outer lobes broad, with rounded apex; centre lobe broadly orbicular, broader than long; disc covered with a mass of very prominent, short, fleshy papillæ, terminating behind in 5 verrucose keels; spur clavate, scarcely $\frac{1}{6}$″ long. *October to January.*

A somewhat dwarf species with a slender sheath-clothed flower-stem bearing a raceme of about nine fairly large yellow and purple blossoms. The leaves are very immature at flowering time. It grows among stones on the Klip River Mountain in the Transvaal at 6000 feet and is there exposed to over 20° of frost when at rest in the winter. A gritty rough fibrous loam in a sunny spot is indicated.

362. EULOPHIA EXPLANATA, Lindl.

Dipodium scariosum, Ham.

Root: a thick tuber-like rhizome. **Leaves:** very undeveloped at flowering time; elliptic-oblong, short. **Scape:** 4″–8″ tall, rather stout, clothed at its base with a few short sheaths. **Raceme:** loose, of 10–12 blossoms. **Flowers:** about 1$\frac{1}{4}$″ across; sepals oblong-ovate, rather pointed; petals broadly elliptic, 5-nerved; lip subpanduriform, base saccate with spreading nerves; disc with 2 thick crenate lamellæ, midrib thickened and warted towards the truncate tip; spur conical. *May.*

A low growing plant which is nearly leafless at its flowering period. The rather large blossoms have yellow or purplish-yellow spreading segments, and are quite decorative. It grows in grassy valleys in North-Western India and the Nepal Himalaya and reaches sufficient elevation to ensure its hardiness in the warmer and more sheltered parts of the Kingdom, in a sunny spot in the rock garden, in good fibrous loam.

363. EULOPHIA FABERI, Rolfe

Root: a stout creeping rhizome thickened at the nodes into ovoid tubers. **Leaves:** probably like those of *E. campestris* (Wall.). **Scape:** 1′–1$\frac{1}{4}$′ tall, sheathed at the base with spatha-like sheaths. **Raceme:** about 4″ long, few-flowered. **Flowers:** about 1″ across; sepals linear-oblong, abruptly pointed; petals similar to the sepals; lip oblong, 3-lobed; outer lobes short, blunt, obscurely crenulate; centre lobe rounded, undulate; disc with 3 lamellæ down its centre; spur cylindrical. *April.*

A species closely allied to *E. campestris* (Wall.) with a few-flowered raceme of medium-sized blossoms having brownish-pink sepals and petals and a pink lip with dark markings. It is found in dry stony ground in valleys on the mountains of Yunnan, Western China, at 7600 feet above sea-level and may be tried outdoors in Great Britain in mild sheltered localities in a good fibrous loam in full sun.

364. EULOPHIA FLANAGANII, Bolus

Root: a rather slender woody rhizome thickened at the nodes. **Leaves:** in a fascicle, linear-ensiform, 9″–12″ long. **Scape:** $1\frac{1}{4}$′–$1\frac{1}{2}$′ tall, flexuous, clothed with about 4 sheaths low down. **Raceme:** lax, one-sided, many-flowered. **Flowers:** $\frac{3}{8}$″ across; sepals lanceolate-oblong, spreading; petals oblong, deflexed above the lip, twice as broad as the sepals; lip porrect, 3-lobed, cuneate; side lobes short; centre lobe quadrate, slightly retuse; disc with a cluster of pointed setiform papillæ below the apex, and 3 rows of shorter ones below that; spur ovate, $\frac{1}{12}$″ long. *November to January.*

Although the blossoms of this species are small they are borne in racemes of nearly two dozen, and are rather attractively coloured; the sepals are a livid glaucous green, the petals are pale lilac bordered with purple, the lip is pale lilac with a purple margin. It grows on grassy mountain slopes in Eastern Cape Colony and probably reaches its greatest elevation at Elands Hoek in the Aliwal North Division at 4500 feet, where it is exposed to 15° of frost when at rest. A good moist fibrous loam is indicated.

365. EULOPHIA FOLIOSA, Bolus

E. Reichenbachiana, Bolus; *E. aculeata*, Bolus; *E. Buchananii*, Durand et Schinz; *Cymbidium Buchananii*, Reichb. f. *Cyrtopera foliosa*, Lindl.

Root: a creeping rhizome, stout, and irregularly thickened at the nodes. **Leaves:** in a fascicle, linear-lanceolate or elongate-lanceolate, 4″–18″ long. **Scape:** 6″–18″ tall, sheath-clothed. **Raceme:** 2″–3″ long, dense. **Flowers:** $\frac{5}{8}$″ across; dorsal sepal oblong-lanceolate; lateral sepals broadly oblong-lanceolate; petals elliptic or elliptic-lanceolate; lip strongly 3-lobed; outer lobes broadly oblong, diverging; centre lobe suborbicular, larger than the side lobes; disc with several rows of small papillæ; spur obsolete.

November to February.

This species has green blossoms with a purple lip; they are borne in a rather dense raceme on a sheath-clothed flower-stem, springing from a bunch of about four leaves; it is not a very decorative plant. It grows on grassy mountain slopes in the Transvaal, Orange Free State, Griqualand East and Natal, where it probably reaches its greatest elevation at Van Reenens at 6000 feet and is exposed to over 20° of frost during the winter. A good damp fibrous loam in full sun is indicated.

366. EULOPHIA FRAGRANS, Schltr.

Root: a thickened creeping rhizome. **Leaves:** in a fascicle, linear, pointed, 3″–6″ long. **Scape:** 1′–1¼′ tall, clothed with numerous short cucullate sheaths. **Spike:** dense, subcorymbose or oblong, few-flowered. **Flowers:** nearly 1½″ across; sepals lanceolate, pointed, subequal; petals ovate, pointed, twice as broad as the sepals; lip 3-lobed; side lobes short, pointed; front lobe ovate, blunt, twice as long as the side lobes; disc with about 6 thickened subcristate nerves; spur short, conical. *October to January.*

This handsome plant has about half-a-dozen very large whitish-yellow blossoms in an oblong spike on a slender stem clothed with hooded papery sheaths. The leaves are not produced until after the blossoms are passed. It grows in damp grassy places on hill sides near Heidelberg in the Transvaal at 5000 feet, where it is exposed to over 15° of frost in the winter during the period of rest. It should be grown in the rock garden in damp fibrous loam in full sun and is only suitable for outdoor culture in mild sheltered localities.

367. EULOPHIA HERBACEA, Lindl.

E. brachypetala, Lindl. *E. albiflora*, Edgw. *Limodorum bicolor*, Roxb.

Root: a thickened rhizome, tuber-like. **Leaves:** often produced after the blossoms have faded, linear-lanceolate, many-nerved, 6″–8″ long. **Scape:** 2′–3′ tall, stout, clothed with large pointed sheaths. **Raceme:** short, of 8–10 blossoms. **Flowers:** nearly 2¾″ across; sepals linear-lanceolate, pointed; petals elliptic or lanceolate, blunt; lip ovate-oblong; outer lobes small, rounded; centre lobe ovate-oblong; disc with many fimbriate nerves. *July.*

A variable species with regard to the tintings of its blossoms. It is a very handsome and decorative plant, with very large flowers having green sepals, white or cream-coloured petals with purple nerves, and a white lip with yellow nerves. It is found in grassy places on the Himalaya and on the mountains of other parts of India up to 7000 feet above sea-level and may be grown outdoors in the warmer parts of Great Britain in a sunny sheltered spot in the rock garden, in good loam and leaf-soil kept reasonably moist.

368. EULOPHIA HIANS, Spreng.

E. clavicornis, Lindl. *E. emarginata*, Lindl. *E. platypetala*, Krauss; *Limodorum hians*, Thunb. *Satyrium hians*, Linn.

Root: a very stout, woody, creeping rhizome irregularly thickened at the nodes. **Leaves:** in a fascicle, narrowly ensiform, conduplicate, prominently veined, 3″–6″ long. **Scape:** 6″–15″ tall, sheath-clothed below. **Raceme:** 2″–3″ long, lax, many-flowered. **Flowers:** ¾″ across; sepals narrowly oblong, spreading; petals elliptic-oblong, blunt, twice as broad as the sepals; lip 3-lobed; side lobes oblong, small, diverging; front lobe broadly obovate or obcordate; disc with 3–5 thickened keels, papillose in front; spur narrowly clavate, $\frac{1}{4}''$ long. *December to February.*

A rather pretty plant with fairly large blossoms of brownish-yellow sepals and pink or lilac petals and lip; they are borne in loose racemes on sheath-clothed stems which spring from beside a tuft of about four rather immature leaves. It is a common plant throughout South Africa and probably reaches its greatest elevation at Kokstad in Griqualand East at 5100 feet, in short grass. It should be grown in fibrous loam and will stand 25° of frost when at rest. *See Plate 10 facing page 151.*

369. EULOPHIA HUTTONII, Rolfe

Root: a stout woody rhizome much thickened at the nodes. **Leaves:** in a fascicle, elongate-linear, closely veined, 6″–12″ long. **Scape:** 6″–15″ tall, clothed with numerous lanceolate, imbricate sheaths. **Raceme:** 1″–3″ long, rather dense. **Flowers:** about $\frac{3}{4}''$ across; sepals elliptic-lanceolate or oblong-lanceolate; petals elliptic-oblong, rather broader than the sepals; lip broader than long, 3-lobed; side lobes broadly oblong with a rounded apex, diverging; centre lobe suborbicular or broadly oblong, rounded at the apex, with 3 prominent strongly crested keels from the middle to the apex; spur obsolete. *October to January.*

This species has very little decorative value; it has dull brown or red blossoms on a slender sheath-clothed stem springing from beside a tuft of three or four bright green leaves. It grows on damp grassy mountain slopes in Cape Colony, Orange Free State, Natal and Griqualand East, where it probably reaches its greatest elevation near Kokstad at 5000 feet and is exposed for short periods during the winter to over 15° of frost. It should be given a damp fibrous loam in full sun.

370. EULOPHIA INÆQUALIS, Schltr.

Root: a stout creeping rhizome. **Leaves:** in a fascicle, linear-oblong, rather spreading, 2″–4″ long. **Scape:** stout, 6″–15″ tall, with about 3 short spathaceous sheaths. **Raceme:** lax, few- or many-flowered. **Flowers:** $\frac{5}{8}''$ across; sepals oblong-lanceolate, subequal; petals ovate-oblong, almost twice as broad as the sepals; lip 3-lobed; outer lobes oblong, short; inner lobe rounded, concave, with crenulate undulate margin; disc with 2 crested keels at the base and numerous papillose crests in the centre; spur clavate, short. *November to February.*

Rather a pretty plant with yellow blossoms and dull purple sepals; they are borne on slender sheath-clothed stems springing from a tuft of three or four narrow deep green leaves. It is found in grassy places in Natal and probably reaches its greatest elevation near Ladysmith at 4200 feet, where it is subjected to over 10° of frost for short periods during the winter when it is deciduous. It should be grown in a damp spot fully exposed to the sun in a good fibrous loam and is only suitable for outdoor culture in very warm, sheltered localities.

371. EULOPHIA LATIPETALA, Rolfe

Root: a creeping rhizome thickened at the nodes. **Leaves:** in a spreading tuft, broadly linear-oblong, attenuate, conduplicate at the base, 4″–12″ long, with 2 or 3 exterior sheaths. **Scape:** about a foot tall, stout, clothed with numerous sheaths. **Raceme:** somewhat dense, about 3″ long. **Flowers:** over 1″ across; sepals ovate-oblong; petals broadly ovate, nearly twice as broad as the sepals; lip 3-lobed; side lobes broadly rounded, short; centre lobe suborbicular-oblong, blunt; disc with 3–5 somewhat thickened keels; spur very short, subconical. *October to February.*

This is a desirable species and has large creamy white blossoms in from six- to twelve-flowered racemes, on stout flower-stems rising from a tuft of about half-a-dozen prominently veined leaves. It is found in open grassy spots in thin woodland on Woodbush Mountain in the Northern Transvaal at 5800 feet, where it is exposed to over 15° of frost during the winter for short periods. It should be grown in a mixture of fibrous loam and leaf-soil, in an open sunny spot, and is only suitable for outdoor culture in the warmer Western counties.

372. EULOPHIA LAXIFLORA, Schltr.

Root: a thickened creeping rhizome. **Leaves:** in a fascicle, narrowly linear, very pointed, 6″–10″ long. **Scape:** 9″–15″ tall, subflexuous, clothed with many appressed membranous sheaths. **Raceme:** lax, many-flowered. **Flowers:** $\frac{1}{2}$″ long; sepals oblong-lanceolate; petals oblong, pointed; lip oblong, 3-lobed; outer lobes oblong, blunt; inner lobe subquadrate, blunt, with 5 thickened densely papillose nerves extending along the disc to near the base; spur cylindric, incurved, blunt, about $\frac{3}{16}$″ long.

December to February.

The blossoms of this species are too small to have much decorative value; they are pale creamy yellow in colour, marked with purple lines, and are borne in lax racemes of a dozen or more on slender sheath-clothed stems rising from a tuft of about four bright green leaves. It grows in damp grassy places in the Transvaal, Orange Free State, Natal and Eastern Cape Colony, where at Aliwal North at 4200 feet it is exposed to over 20° of frost for short times during its resting period. A damp fibrous loam in full sun is indicated.

373. EULOPHIA LEONTOGLOSSA, Reichb. f.

E. lissochiloides, Krauss

Root: of subglobose tubers about $\frac{3}{4}''$ broad. **Leaves:** in a fascicle, linear or lanceolate-linear, 4″–15″ long. **Scape:** 4″–12″ long, clothed with a few lanceolate sheaths. **Spike:** congested or rarely oblong, drooping, 1″–2″ long. **Flowers:** nearly $\frac{3}{4}''$ long; sepals lanceolate-oblong, subconnivent; lip 3-lobed; side lobes oblong, blunt, somewhat divergent, short; front lobe elliptic oblong, blunt; disc with 5 obscured keels below, papillose all over in front; spur oblong or subclavate, blunt, $\frac{1}{6}''$ long. *October to February.*

The half-closed blossoms of this species vary from greenish-buff to yellow, pink, and white and are borne in a very congested spike on a flexuous stem springing from a bunch of two or three grassy leaves. It is pretty but not of any great decorative value. It grows on grassy hill slopes in the Transvaal, Orange Free State, Griqualand East and Natal, where near Van Reenen it reaches its greatest elevation of 6000 feet, and is exposed to over 20° of frost during the winter. A damp fibrous loam is indicated.

374. EULOPHIA MELEAGRIS, Reichb. f.

Root: a stout creeping rhizome: **Leaves:** in a fascicle, linear-oblong or elongate-lanceolate, membranous, 6″–12″ long. **Scape:** stout, 1′–1½′ tall, clothed with several spathaceous, lanceolate sheaths. **Raceme:** 6″ long, loosely many-flowered. **Flowers:** about $\frac{5}{8}''$ across; sepals oblong, rather broader towards the apex, more or less spreading and rather fleshy; petals suborbicular-oblong, half as long as the petals; lip 3-lobed; outer lobes obliquely semiovate; front lobe oblong, pointed; disc with 3 prominent keels, markedly crenulate in front; spur cylindrical, rather stout, blunt, somewhat curved. *November to March.*

This species has almost bell-shaped glaucous green, purple-spotted blossoms of fair size, borne on a stout flower-stem in a long loose raceme, the prominently veined leaves are produced in a bunch of about half-a-dozen. It grows in grassy places amongst shrubs in Eastern Cape Colony and Griqualand East, where at Fort Donald it reaches its greatest elevation of 5000 feet and is subjected to 20° of frost for short periods during the winter. It should be grown in leaf-soil and loam in half-shade.

375. EULOPHIA NIGRICANS, Schltr.

Root: a creeping rhizome thickened into tubers at the nodes. **Leaves:** basal, linear, 4″–8″ long. **Scape:** 1′–1½′ tall, densely covered with membranous cucullate, pointed sheaths. **Spike:** lax, many-flowered. **Flowers:** nearly 1¼″ in diameter; sepals lanceolate, subequal; petals broadly lanceolate; lip

3-lobed; outer lobes subtriangular, short, pointed; inner lobe ovate-oblong, blunt; disc verrucose or with short papillæ; spur short, conical.

November to January.

The blossoms of this species though large are not very decorative on account of their sombre tints of glaucous green and dull dark purple; they are borne on sheath-clothed stems furnished at the base with two deep green leaves. It grows in grassy rocky places near Heidelberg in the Transvaal at an elevation of 4700 feet and is there exposed to 12° of frost for short times during its resting period in the winter. It should be grown in sandy loam in full sun and kept well supplied with water during its vegetative period. The plant is only suitable for outdoor culture in warm sheltered localities.

376. EULOPHIA OLIVERIANA, Bolus

Cyrtopera Oliveriana, Reichb. f.

Root: a creeping rhizome, stout and thickened at the nodes. **Leaves:** in a fascicle, ensiform-linear, 6″ long. **Scape:** 1′–2′ tall, sheath-clothed. **Raceme:** 3″–6″ long, compact or rather loose, many-flowered. **Flowers:** $\frac{3}{4}$″ across; sepals elliptic or elliptic-oblong, blunt; petals broadly elliptic, rather broader than the sepals; lip 3-lobed; side lobes suborbicular, narrowed behind; front lobe oblong or narrowly oblong, blunt; disc convex with 3–5 thick, fleshy, verrucose keels; spur very short and conical.

December and January.

A rather large-flowered though not very decorative species with yellow, brown-tinted blossoms in long racemes on stout sheath-clothed stems; the bunch of four or five leaves is rather small at flowering time. It grows on rocky or grass-covered mountain slopes in Eastern Cape Colony, Griqualand East, Natal, Orange Free State and the Transvaal, where on the Elands Spruit Mountains at 6800 feet it probably reaches its greatest elevation and should be quite hardy in the warmer parts of Great Britain if it can be induced to rest during our winter. A good fibrous loam is indicated.

377. EULOPHIA PETERSII, Reichb. f.

E. longepedunculata, Rendle; *E. Schrimperiana,* A. Rich. *Epidendrum Schrimperianum,* Hochst. *Galeandra Petersii,* Reichb. f.

Root: a creeping rhizome clothed with horny imbricate scales. **Leaves:** strap-shaped, narrowed above, falcate, 1′–1½′ long. **Scape:** 3′–5′ tall, springing from a swollen base or pseudo-bulb 3″ long, sheath-clothed. **Panicle:** loose, at times simple, 6″–15″ long. **Flowers:** nearly 2″ across; sepals oblong-lanceolate, rather pointed; petals oblong, blunt, slightly shorter than the sepals; lip obscurely 3-lobed; outer lobes elliptic-oblong, undulated; centre lobe elliptic-oblong, nearly quadrate, undulated; disc with an undulated lamellæ down its centre; spur clavate-oblong, incurved, $\frac{1}{4}''$ long.

March to July.

A very handsome species of tall robust habit with numerous very large cream-coloured and purple blossoms. It grows in marshes in Arabia, Tanganyika, East Africa and Abyssinia, where it reaches an elevation of over 7000 feet above sea level and should be quite hardy in Southern Britain on the banks of a pond or stream in rich heavy soil.

378. EULOPHIA REHMANNII, Rolfe

Root: a creeping rhizome thickened at the nodes. **Leaves:** in a spreading tuft, linear-oblong, attenuate and conduplicate at the base, 4″–6″ long. **Scape:** $1\frac{1}{2}'$ tall, clothed with 2 or 3 sheaths. **Raceme:** dense, of about 12 flowers. **Flowers:** $1\frac{1}{4}''$ across; sepals lanceolate, pointed; petals elliptic-ovate, 3 times as broad as the sepals; lip 3-lobed, ovate; side lobes broadly rounded, short; centre lobe ovate; disc covered with crenulate slightly thickened keels; spur clavate, slender, $\frac{1}{4}''$ long. *October to January.*

An attractive plant with large yellowish-white blossoms in a fairly long raceme, on slender flower-stems springing from a bunch of six or eight spreading grassy leaves. It grows in open grassy spots in woods on Woodbush Mountains at 6000 feet, in the Northern Transvaal and is there exposed to over 15° of frost for short periods during its winter rest. It should be grown in full sun in a good rather damp fibrous loam in the rock garden.

379. EULOPHIA ROBUSTA, Rolfe

E. Dregeana, Schltr.

Root: a creeping rhizome thickened at the nodes: **Leaves:** in a fascicle, ensiform or elongate-linear, 4″–12″ long, with several exterior sheaths at the base. **Scape:** 9″–18″ tall, stout, sheath-clothed. **Raceme:** 3″–6″ long, rather dense, many-flowered. **Flowers:** nearly $1\frac{1}{4}''$ across; sepals oblong-lanceolate or attenuated from a broader base; petals elliptic-oblong or ovate, twice as broad as the sepals; lip 3-lobed, broadly ovate; outer lobes broadly rounded; centre lobe broadly elliptic or rounded; disc with 5–7 thickened veins verrucose behind with scattered crests in front; spur oblong, rather stout.

December to February.

A very handsome plant with large yellow blossoms in which the petals and lip are sometimes pink, sometimes white, the flower-stem springs from a bunch of from four to six recurving grassy leaves. It grows on rough grassy mountain slopes in Natal, Griqualand East, Transvaal, Orange Free State and Basutoland, where in the Drakensburg at 8000 feet it reaches its greatest elevation and should be quite hardy in Great Britain if it can be induced to rest during our winter. A gritty peat in full sun is indicated.

380. EULOPHIA SANGUINEA, Hook. f.

Cyrtopera sanguinea, Lindl. *C. rufa*, Thw.

Root: an irregular tuber. **Leaves:** developed after the flowers have faded, elliptic-oblong, rather short. **Scape:** 6″–10″ tall, stout, clothed with loose sheaths. **Raceme:** loose, of from 6–12 blossoms. **Flowers:** 1½″ across; sepals ovate-lanceolate, pointed; petals elliptic, shorter than the sepals, pointed, many-nerved; lip short, 3-lobed; outer lobes rounded; centre lobe orbicular or ovate; disc with many crenulate nerves. *July to October.*

A deeply coloured species producing a leafless sheath-clothed flower-stem terminating in a loose raceme of large blossoms with pale green or yellow sepals and petals, and a white, pink or pale green lip with a red-purple or brown centre. It is found in open rocky places among short herbage in the Eastern Himalaya and Khasia Hills and is only suitable for outdoor culture in the warmest and most sheltered districts of the Kingdom; it may be planted in a sheltered sunny nook in the rock garden in good loam and leaf-soil kept fairly moist the whole year round.

381. EULOPHIA SANKEYI, Rolfe

Root: a stout rhizome thickened at the nodes. **Leaves:** in a fascicle, oblong-linear, 4″–6″ long, with a few short basal sheaths. **Scape:** about 9″ tall, rather stout, clothed with a few broadly oblong-lanceolate sheaths. **Raceme:** 4″ long, somewhat lax. **Flowers:** about 1″ across; sepals ovate-lanceolate, dorsal broader than the lateral; petals ovate, twice as broad as the sepals; lip 3-lobed, rather short, ovate; side lobes short, rounded at the apex; centre lobe broadly ovate; somewhat undulate; disc with 5–7 thickened verrucose keels at the base beyond the middle; spur oblong, ⅛″ long.
October to January.

A beautiful plant with many large creamy white blossoms in a raceme on a stout sheath-clothed stem rising from a bunch of three or four narrowly lance-shaped, bright green leaves. It grows amongst grass in stony places on the hills near Harrismith in the Orange Free State at an elevation of 6500 feet and is exposed to over 25° of frost for short periods during the winter. A good gritty fibrous loam is indicated.

382. EULOPHIA SHUPANGÆ, Kränzl.

Cyrtopera Shupangæ, Reichb. f.

Root: of elongated woody tubers. **Leaves:** basal, elongate-lanceolate or linear-lanceolate, petiolate, 1′–1½′ long. **Scape:** 2′–5′ tall, clothed with pointed, imbricate sheaths. **Raceme:** 3″–6″ long, many-flowered. **Flowers:** nearly 1½″ across; sepals lanceolate-oblong, pointed; petals oblong, pointed;

lip 3-lobed; outer lobes triangular-oblong, rather blunt; centre lobe broadly oblong or obovate-oblong, blunt; disc densely hairy in front; spur oblong, very short. *August to November.*

A handsome species of tall robust habit, with a long raceme of large yellow blossoms having a patch of long orange-coloured hairs on the centre of the lip. It grows on the banks of rivers and streams, also in marshes on the mountains, in Tanganyika, East Africa and British Central Africa, where on the top of Mount Zomba in peat marshes at 7000 feet above sea-level it probably attains its greatest altitude and is there exposed to 12° or 15° of frost during its period of rest. A rich peaty soil in the bog garden or on the banks of a pond or stream is indicated.

383. EULOPHIA STENANTHA, Schltr.

Root: a very stout swollen rhizome. **Leaves:** in a fascicle, linear, 3″–6″ long. **Scape:** about 10″ tall, clothed with numerous erect pointed sheaths. **Spike:** corymbose, many-flowered. **Flowers:** nearly $1\frac{1}{4}$″ across; sepals lanceolate, subequal; petals obliquely oblong-lanceolate, rather broader than the sepals; lip 3-lobed, cuneate at the base; outer lobes very small; centre lobe large, ovate, blunt, crenulate-undulate at the margin; disc with central nerves thickened from the base, papillose-verrucose in front; spur short, blunt. *November to January.*

This is a beautiful species with many large cream and purple blossoms in a loose spike rising from a tuft of narrow bright green leaves. It grows on stony cliffs on the Elands Spruit Mountains in the Transvaal at an elevation of 7000 feet above sea-level and should be perfectly hardy in Great Britain if it could be induced to rest during our winter. It should be grown in stony fibrous loam in full sun and kept well supplied with water when in growth. It should prove a good moraine plant.

384. EULOPHIA SUBINTEGRA, Rolfe

Root: a thickened rhizome. **Leaves:** in a tuft, elongate-lanceolate, plicate, 9″–12″ long. **Scape:** slender, 1′–$1\frac{1}{2}$′ tall, sheath-clothed below. **Raceme:** about 4″ long, lax. **Flowers:** nearly $1\frac{1}{4}$″ across; sepals linear-lanceolate; petals oblong or elliptic-oblong, over twice as broad as the sepals; lip elliptic, broader than the petals, entire or subentire; disc with 7–9 slightly thickened keels below, terminating in numerous nerves above, slightly downy; spur oblong, curved, blunt, $\frac{1}{6}$″ long. *December and January.*

A desirable plant with a loose spike of large blossoms of buff, brown-tinted sepals, and yellow petals and lip, the foliage is well developed and strongly nerved. It grows in damp grassy places at Oliviers Hoek in Natal at 5000 feet, where it is exposed to 15° or more of frost for short periods during its winter rest. It should be grown in a moist open spot fully exposed to the sun, in a compost of fibrous peat and loam. It is only suitable for outdoor culture in warm sheltered localities.

385. EULOPHIA THOMSONII, Rolfe

Root: of elongated woody tubers. **Leaves:** elongate-linear, about 6″ long. **Scape:** about 1′ tall, slender. **Raceme:** dense, subcapitate. **Flowers:** about 1″ across; sepals ovate-oblong, pointed; petals elliptic-oblong, pointed; lip 3-lobed; outer lobes broadly rounded, blunt; centre lobe broadly suborbicular; disc with about 5 hairy keels at the base, downy in front; spur conical, minute. *October to February.*

A dwarf species with rather large green and white blossoms in an almost rounded head on a slender flower-stem. It is found in marshes and on the banks of streams in British Central Africa on the plateaus between Lakes Nyasa and Tanganyika at elevations up to 8000 feet above sea-level. It should be quite hardy in all but the bleaker parts of Great Britain in a rich soil in the bog garden or on the banks of a stream or pond.

386. EULOPHIA TRANSVAALENSIS, Rolfe

Root: a stout rhizome thickened at the nodes. **Leaves:** tufted, linear or linear-lanceolate, 9″–12″ long: **Scape:** 9″–15″ tall, sheath-clothed. **Raceme:** about 4″ long, rather lax. **Flowers:** about $\frac{3}{4}$″ across; sepals broadly oblong; petals ovate-oblong, broader than the sepals; lip 3-lobed, broadly ovate, nearly as long as the sepals; side lobes broadly rounded; centre lobe nearly quadrate, rather broader than long; disc with 5–7 thickened veins bearing several stout papillæ in front, extending to the base as 3 slightly verrucose keels; spur clavate, nearly straight, $\frac{1}{6}$″ long. *November to January.*

This species has medium-sized greenish-brown and white blossoms to the number of about half-a-dozen in a rather loose raceme on a slender sheath-clothed stem springing from a tuft of narrow leaves. It grows in moist grassy places between the Devil's Kantoor and Pretoria at 6000 feet, where it is exposed to over 20° of frost for short periods during the winter. It should be grown in moist fibrous loam in full sun.

387. EULOPHIA VIOLACEA, Reichb. f.

Root: a stout rhizome thickened at the nodes. **Leaves:** in a fascicle, linear, 1″–4″ long. **Scape:** stout, about 1′ tall, clothed with 4 narrow sheaths. **Raceme:** about 3″ long, lax. **Flowers:** about $\frac{3}{4}$″ across; sepals oblong, pointed; petals ovate, blunt, agglutinated to the back of the column, broader than the sepals; lip 3-lobed, quadrate; side lobes rounded; centre lobe large, quadrate, obtuse angled, emarginate; disc with mid nerve, principal side nerves crested; spur cylindrical, subemarginate, $\frac{1}{4}''$ long.

November to February.

A handsome plant with about ten rather large blossoms of a deep purple or violet colour throughout. It should make a welcome addition to rockeries in the warmer parts of Great Britain. It grows in moist grassy places in Eastern Cape Colony and probably reaches its greatest elevation near Grahamstown in the Albany Division at 5000 feet, where it is exposed to 15° or 20° of frost for short periods during its winter rest. A damp fibrous loam in full sun is indicated.

388. EULOPHIA ZEYHERI, Hook. f.

E. bicolor, Reichb. f. *E. Zeyheriana*, Schltr.

Root: a stout woody rhizome thickened at the nodes. **Leaves:** in a fascicle, 9″–18″ long, elongate-lanceolate or linear-lanceolate, with 2 or 3 ovate-lanceolate sheaths at the base. **Scape:** stout, $1'$–$1\frac{3}{4}'$ tall, clothed with several loose spathaceous sheaths. **Raceme:** very short and dense. **Flowers:** over $1\frac{1}{2}''$ across; sepals and petals ovate-lanceolate or elliptic-oblong; lip 3-lobed, broadly elliptic; outer lobes broadly rounded; centre lobe suborbicular, blunt, very broad; disc with 10–13 slightly thickened veins bearing numerous long slender filaments; spur oblong, blunt, $\frac{1}{4}''$ long. *November to January.*

This species is probably the most handsome of the genus. It has very large yellow blossoms with a deeper yellow disc and purple side lobes, and handsome bright green deeply veined foliage. It grows in open grassy country, frequently on mountain slopes, in the Transvaal, Natal and Griqualand East, where it probably reaches its greatest elevation at 5000 feet and is exposed to over 15° of frost during its winter rest. A good fibrous loam in a damp sunny spot is indicated. It is only suitable for warm sheltered localities.

EVOTA, Rolfe

Three species of slender deciduous terrestrial plants of considerable horticultural merit, with a short rootstock furnished with thick fleshy tuber-like roots. The narrow grass-like leaves are few in number and are more numerous towards the base of the stem; they decrease in size upwards and degenerate into bracts among the blossoms, which are usually large and handsome and borne in a loose few-flowered spike or raceme. All the species that are known are confined to South-Western Cape Colony, where they are found amongst grass and reeds, mostly in damp places that are supplied with underground water. They should make very charming alpine-house plants in deep pans of fibrous peat or osmunda fibre with growing sphagnum-moss and a little fibrous loam. In cultivation they should have plenty of moisture when they are in full growth and should never be quite dry. Propagation by imported roots and by seeds from the same source.

389. EVOTA BICOLOR, Rolfe

Ceratandra bicolor, Sond. *C. Harveyana*, Sond.

Root: fleshy, thick. **Stem:** rather slender, flexuous. **Leaves:** radical and cauline, linear, broadening and sheathing at the base, 6″–18″ long. **Scape:** 4″–9″ tall. **Spike:** 1″–2¼″ long, lax, of 1–8 blossoms. **Flowers:** nearly 1″ across; dorsal sepal elliptic-lanceolate, blunt; lateral sepals obliquely and broadly ovate, spreading; petals obliquely cuneate-obovate, crenulate; lip broadly unguiculate, limb oblong, divergently bilobed, crenulate, with a falcately curved bipartite appendage. *October to December.*

A large-flowered handsome species with yellowish-green sepals, pale yellow petals and a yellow lip with some red stripes down its centre. It is sufficiently dwarf for alpine-house decoration and is found amongst grass and thatching reeds on mountain slopes in South-Western Cape Colony and reaches its greatest elevation on the Skurjde Berg in the Cere Division at 5000 feet and should be hardy in Great Britain. A fibrous loam and peat in full sun is indicated.

FORFICARIA, Lindley

This genus contains but one species, it is an erect deciduous terrestrial herb with a tuft of narrow grass-like leaves springing from the base of the flower-stalk which is slender and sheathed with some leaf-like bracts. The blossoms are borne in a loose, many-flowered spike and are not very ornamental. Like so many terrestrial Orchids this species has a root system of one or more irregular tubers which shrivel after the flowers are passed and if the plant is in a healthy condition several smaller ones have formed around the old one; these in time give rise to flower-stems. The plant is found in grassy places on the sides of hills and in stony rocky ground in South-Western Cape Colony and is only fit for culture outdoors in Britain in sunny spots in the warm Western counties; it requires plenty of water when in full growth and should have its roots protected in winter. Propagation by imported tubers and seed.

390. FORFICARIA GRAMINIFOLIA, Lindl.

Disa Forficaria, Bolus

Root: an irregular tuber. **Stem:** rather slender. **Leaves:** radical, narrowly linear, 6″–8″ long, rather numerous. **Scape** 1′–1½′ tall, sheath-clothed. **Spike:** 3″–6″ long, rather lax, many-flowered. **Flowers:** dorsal sepal broadly ovate, saccate behind; lateral sepals obliquely ovate-lanceolate; petals falcate-oblong, the upper half narrow, recurved, ciliate; lip subreniform, rather recurved, obscurely 3-lobed, ciliate. *October to April.*

The blossoms of this plant are about half an inch in length and have pale yellow sepals and red-purple petals and lip; they are few in number and are borne in a slender spike springing from the grassy foliage. It is of no great decorative value and grows in its native habitat on stony and grass-covered hill sides in South-Western Cape Colony, where in Du Toits Kloof in the Worcester Division at 4000 feet it is exposed in the winter to 12° of frost for short periods. It should be grown in a fairly moist gritty loam in full sun.

GALEOLA, Loureiro

A genus of 26 very curious terrestrial or epiphytal Orchids with an elongated rhizome emitting stout fibres. The stems are erect and sometimes comparatively short but more frequently very long, and twining to a considerable height; they are usually clothed with small scales in the place of leaves, although some of the species do produce small leaves. The blossoms are produced in loose panicles or racemes and are generally very handsome. In some species the stems are branched and the clusters of flowers hang down. All inhabit forest country and are scattered over India, Malaya and Northern Australia; with the following exceptions they are too tender for outdoor culture in Britain. The plants under consideration should be well protected from frost during the winter. Propagation by imported root and by seeds when these can be procured.

391. GALEOLA FABERI, Rolfe

Root: a stout branching rhizome. **Leaves:** obsolete. **Stem:** 1′–2½′ tall, fairly stout, clothed with a few ovate, blunt, fleshy sheaths. **Panicle:** loosely branched, branches clothed with rust-coloured hairs. **Flowers:** about 1¼″ long; sepals and petals oblong-linear, rather blunt; lip elliptic, crisped and undulate, with elevated papillose crenulate veins on the disc.

July to September.

A quaint yet beautiful plant very closely allied to the following species, from which it may be distinguished by the narrower segments of its blossoms; these are produced in a loose rounded panicle and are of a rich yellow or orange colour. It is found in woods on Mount Omei in Szechuan, Western China, at an elevation of 7000 feet above sea-level and may be tried outdoors in Great Britain under the same conditions as the following species.

392. GALEOLA LINDLEYANA, Reichb. f.

Cyrtosia Lindleyana, Hook. f. *Erythorchis Lindleyana*, Reichb. f.

Root: an elongate, tortuous, pale red rhizome about 1½″ in diameter, emitting stout unbranched fibres. **Stem:** unbranched, erect, 2′–3′ tall, clothed with clasping, oblong, blunt, sheaths. **Panicle:** loosely branched, branches horizontal. **Flowers:** about 1″ long; sepals broadly ovate-oblong, strongly ribbed dorsally; petals broadly ovate, tip obtuse, crenate; lip nearly hemispherical, toothed and fringed, very hairy on the inner surface.

July to October.

A very remarkable and at the same time beautiful plant with erect sheath-clothed brownish-purple stems and horizontal sprays of almost globular yellow blossoms; it is very unlike an Orchid. It is a native of the Himalaya, Naga and Khasia mountains up to elevations of 7000 feet above sea-level and is found in thin forest and wooded ravines growing probably as a saprophyte on the decaying leaves and twigs, like our native *Epipogum.* It may be tried outdoors in the warm humid Western counties in a shady spot in decaying leaves and peat.

GASTRODIA, R. Brown

Of twenty-six erect, leafless, deciduous, terrestrial species, parasitical on the roots of various plants. The rootstock is swollen into a very thick oblong rhizome with numerous stout roots ending in fibrous sucker-like processes which attach themselves to the roots of the plants with which the parasite grows. Their stems are usually very stout, erect and of a golden-brown or purplish colour, smooth and clothed with a few short sheaths or scales. The blossoms are borne in loose racemes and although not brightly coloured are interesting and of some decorative value. The plants are found in wooded districts growing in vegetable debris over the roots of trees and shrubs in Eastern India, Malaya, Eastern Australia and New Zealand. No doubt the best method of introducing them into this country would be to secure the plants when at rest with as large a portion as possible of its host; failing this the rhizomes may be tried over the roots of a willow, in leaf-soil.

393. GASTRODIA CUNNINGHAMII, Hook. f.

Root: thick, fleshy and tuberous, sometimes 1½′ long. **Stem:** stout, scale-clothed. **Leaves:** none. **Scape:** 1′–2′ tall. **Raceme:** 6″–10″ long, fairly dense. **Flowers:** fleshy, ½″ long; sepals united into a tube to near their tips, where they are slightly reflexed; petals smaller than the sepals, united to them at the base with their tips reflexed and projecting; lip included within the sepals, linear oblong with crenulate margins. *November to January.*

The dull green, white-spotted blossoms of this species have no decorative value; they are produced in racemes of from ten to twenty blossoms on stout brownish-purple flower-stems. It is not uncommon in damp shady woods growing at the base of tree trunks in pure leaf-soil in the North and South Islands of New Zealand at sufficient elevation to ensure its complete hardiness in this country south of the Trent. In cultivation the conditions under which it grows in nature should be copied as nearly as possible.

394. GASTRODIA ELATA, Blume

Root: a large oblong jointed tuber, parasitic by a small fibrous base to the roots. **Leaves:** obsolete. **Scape:** $\frac{3}{4}'$–2′ tall, stout, clothed with a few short blunt sheaths. **Raceme:** loose, many-flowered. **Flowers:** about $\frac{3}{4}''$ long; sepals and petals united forming a tube, swollen in the middle, slit above and showing the stalked, ovate-oblong lip which is furnished with 2 fleshy oblong or reniform calli. *July to September.*

A tall leafless parasite with a brownish-purple stem and a loose raceme of numerous Aloe-like blossoms of a dull yellow or brown outside, white inside and with a white lip. It is a quaint and not unattractive plant and might be tried in pure leaf-soil over the roots of a poplar or willow in a sheltered locality, and should prove generally hardy in Great Britain. It is widely scattered in woods from Tibet through China to Japan.

395. GASTRODIA GRACILIS, Blume

Root: an irregular tuber-like rhizome with numerous stout fibres. **Stems:** 6″–12″ tall, somewhat slender, clothed with several oblong scales in place of leaves. **Racemes:** 2″–4″ long, usually loose, many-flowered. **Flowers:** about $\frac{5}{8}''$ long; sepals and petals united forming a globose tube divided towards the apex into 5 more or less equal ovate segments and slit up the centre on the upper side; lip ovate-oblong or oblong-lanceolate, crisped on the margin, narrow below. *June to September.*

This plant is very closely related to *G. elata,* but may be distinguished from that species by its more slender habit and the shape of its lip. It produces a slender scale-clothed stem of a pale brown tint and a loose raceme of yellowish-brown and white blossoms. It is found in damp shady places growing over the roots of trees in various parts of Japan. It may be grown in a shady spot over the roots of a deciduous tree in good leaf-soil.

396. GASTRODIA MINOR, Petrie

Root: an irregular fleshy tuber. **Stem:** 8″–15″ tall, very slender, clothed with a few oblique, sheathing scales in the place of leaves. **Raceme:** 1″–3″ long, of 3–5 blossoms. **Flowers:** about $\frac{1}{2}''$ long; dorsal sepal, lateral sepals and petals united, forming a globular blossom split to about the middle into 5 rounded, ovate, undulated segments; lip oblong, blunt, with an incurved margin and 2 ridges down its centre, about as long as the other segments. *January.*

A quaint slender plant with an amber-brown, unspotted stem clothed with a few yellowish-brown scales and a few-flowered raceme of pale greenish-brown blossoms, tipped with greyish-white. It is of botanical interest only and is found in damp woods near Otago in the South Island of New Zealand. It should be hardy in the warmer parts of the Kingdom in a damp-shady spot in the rock garden, in oak or beech leaf-soil.

397. GASTRODIA OROBANCHOIDES, Benth.

Gamoplexis orobanchoides, Falc.

Root: a large ellipsoid or oblong, jointed tuber, parasitic by a small fibrous base to the roots. **Leaves:** obsolete. **Scape:** 9″–24″ tall, usually very stout, clothed with short truncate sheaths. **Raceme:** loose, many-flowered. **Flowers:** about $\frac{3}{4}$″ long; sepals and petals united, forming a tube slit above; lip sessile, ovate, blunt, recurved. *August and September.*

This species very much resembles *G. elata* (Blume); it has the same tall leafless stem clothed with greenish-yellow, purple-marked sheaths and swollen tubular blossoms of a greenish-purple or brownish-purple outside and dull white or pale green within. It is interesting though by no means decorative and grows in a state of nature in vegetable debris over the roots of forest trees in the Himalaya from Kashmir to Garwhal, reaching an altitude of 9000 feet, and is sufficiently hardy for culture outdoors in all but the bleakest parts of this country under the same conditions as the preceding species.

398. GASTRODIA SESAMOIDES, R. Br.

Root: a very thick oblong irregular rhizome, emitting a few stout roots. **Leaves:** none, their place being taken by a few pointed, sheathing scales. **Scape:** 1′–1$\frac{1}{2}$′ tall, sheathed with the above-mentioned scales. **Raceme:** 1″–6″ long, fairly dense. **Flowers:** about $\frac{3}{4}$″ in length; dorsal sepal, lateral sepals and petals united into a 5-lobed tube; lip slightly 3-lobed, trowel-shaped, much undulated, with 2 longitudinal raised lines on its disc. *November to January.*

A curious but at the same time rather attractive species with a stout, erect yellowish-brown stem clothed with a few olive-brown scales and bearing a raceme of twenty or thirty Heath-like blossoms yellow-brown outside and pure white within; the lip is white with golden markings. The plant has a superficial resemblance to a Broom Rape and like those plants is a parasite. It appears to grow in a variety of situations from dry rocky ground to humid forest lands over nearly the whole of Eastern Australia and is hardy enough for culture out of doors in the warmer parts of Great Britain. It should be planted in sandy soil over the roots of a forest or fruit tree in a sheltered spot.

PLATE 11.

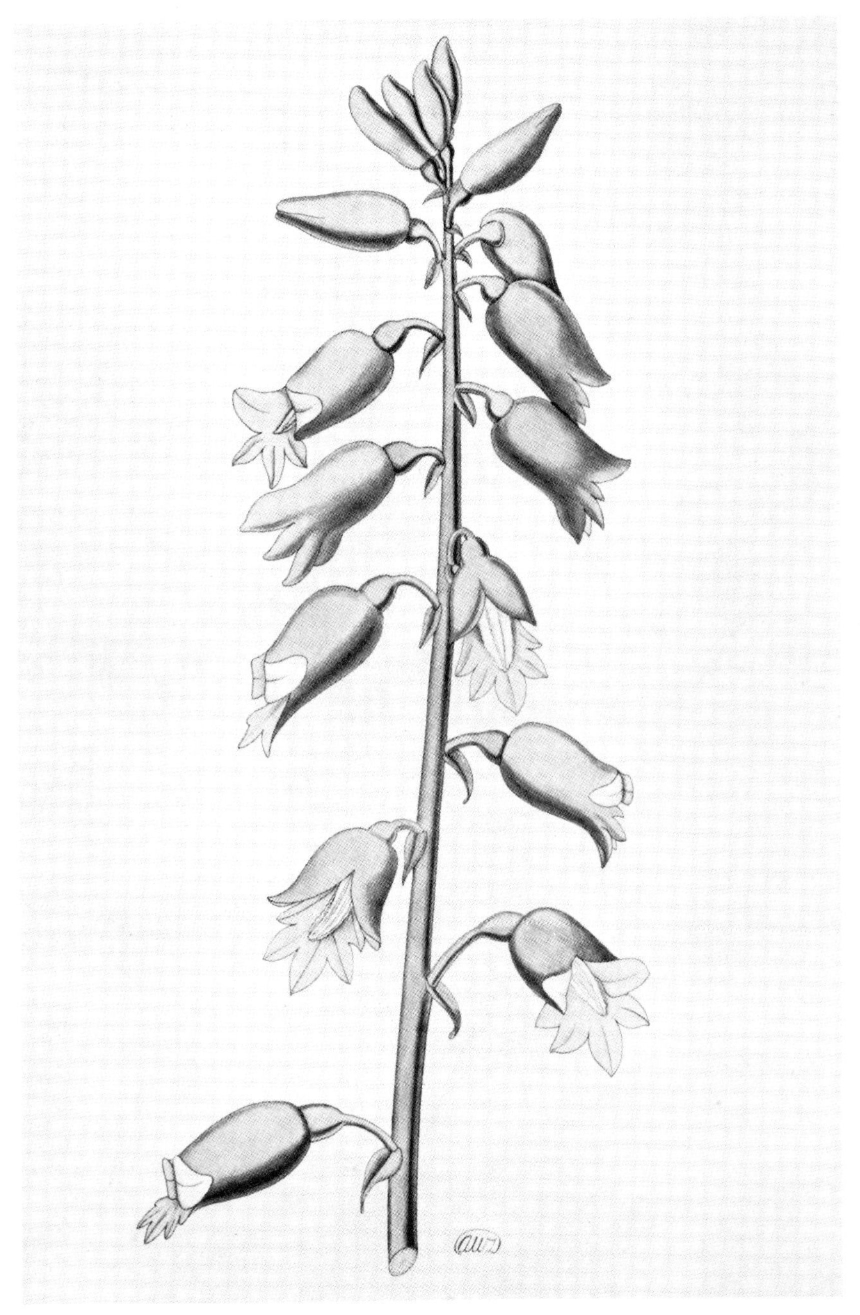

GASTRODIA SESAMOIDES.

PLATE 12.

HABENARIA TETRAPETALA.

399. GASTRODIA VIRIDIS, Makino

Root: a large tuber with annular rings and numerous fibrous roots. **Stem:** $\frac{3}{4}$′–$2\frac{1}{2}$′ tall, fairly stout, clothed with a few short, blunt sheaths. **Raceme:** 3″–10″ long, loose, many-flowered. **Flowers:** about $\frac{3}{4}$″ long; sepals and petals united, forming a tube inflated in the middle and slit down the upper side, ending in 5 more or less equal, ovate, pointed lobes; lip unguiculate below, ovate-oblong, pointed, crisped, with 2 calli at the base. *July and August.*

This species very much resembles *G. elata* in habit and form but is readily distinguished from that species by its decidedly green blossoms and more greenish-brown stem and scales. It is found in mountain woodlands in Central and Southern Japan growing over the roots of forest trees in vegetable debris; it should be quite hardy in Great Britain under the same conditions as *G. elata.*

GLOSSODIA, R. Brown

Beautiful deciduous terrestrial plants numbering but 5 species; the underground portions consist of a short stock with several white fleshy fibres and two or more tubers on the ends of the stoutest fibres; these are small and somewhat irregular in shape. The slender hairy flower-stem is clothed at its base by a solitary oblong or lanceolate hairy leaf, below which is a membranous sheath. The flower-stem is naked except for a small bract about the middle and a similar bract at the base of each blossom. The flowers, which are solitary or in pairs on the top of the stems, are very beautiful and somewhat resemble those of the Spring Star-flower (*Brodiæa uniflora*). The plants are found in open country usually in poor but rather moist sandy soils and are confined to Australia and Tasmania. They may be grown outdoors in Britain in sheltered localities in the rock garden. A sunny position should be chosen for them in damp sandy peat and loam. Propagation by imported roots and by seeds when procurable.

400. GLOSSODIA MAJOR, R. Br.

Caladenia major, Reichb. f.

Root: of small ovoid tubers on stout white fibres. **Leaf:** solitary, radical, oblong or lanceolate, 1″–2″ long, hairy on its margins. **Scape:** 6″–12″ tall, fairly stout, covered with glandular hairs and clothed with 1–2 bracts; it bears 1–2 blossoms on stems of unequal length. **Flowers:** $1\frac{1}{2}$″ across; sepals and petals of equal length, oblong-lanceolate, blunt; lip ovate biconvex, rounded, surface covered with long hairs. *October and November.*

A very beautiful plant with regular Ixia-like blossoms varying in colour from mauve to reddish-purple; the lip is bright mauve with a large patch of glistening white hairs covering the greater part of its surface. A gem for the alpine house. It grows in open sunny spots in poor sandy soil over the whole of Eastern Australia from Queensland to Tasmania and is very common. It should be quite hardy in all but the most exposed parts of Great Britain. An open sunny spot in the rock garden in a sandy loam should meet its requirements.

401. GLOSSODIA MINOR, R. Br.

Caladenia minor, Reichb. f.

Root: of very small ovoid tubers on short white fibres. **Leaf:** solitary, radical, lanceolate, $\frac{1}{2}''$–$1''$ long. **Scape:** $3''$–$5''$ tall, hairy, slender, bearing 1 blossom, very rarely 2. **Flower:** about $1''$ across; dorsal sepal, lateral sepals, and petals of almost equal length, oblong-lanceolate, blunt; lip triangular, $\frac{1}{3}$ the length of the sepals; disc covered with long hairs, biconvex.

October to January.

A miniature representation of the preceding species except for a few small differences. The slender stem is covered with reddish glandular hairs and bears a small lance-shaped bright green leaf at its base. The blossom is considerably smaller than that of *G. major,* and is of a rich purple-blue colour with a large patch of snow-white hairs on its rather small lip. It should prove a very beautiful addition to the alpine house. It is found in Queensland, New South Wales and Victoria under the same conditions as *G. major* and should be accorded the same conditions in cultivation.

GOODYERA, R. Brown

Dwarf, deciduous or evergreen terrestrial plants numbering 95 species. They have creeping rhizomes which emit thick fleshy fibres that ramify amongst the decaying leaves of their native woodlands. The slender stems are generally clothed with neat and beautifully reticulated foliage which is frequently decorated with silvery markings. The blossoms are borne in slender one-sided racemes and with but few exceptions are too small to be of any decorative value. Most of the species should make charming alpine-house plants in shallow pans of leaf-soil, peat and growing sphagnum-moss. The majority of them are found in woodlands usually beneath the shade of conifers; they are scattered over the Northern Hemisphere but are nowhere very abundant. The various species that are suitable for outdoor culture may be grown in the rock garden in peat and leaf-soil in a shady position. Propagation by division of the rhizomes in spring.

402. GOODYERA FUSCA, Hook. f.

Ætheria fusca, Lindl. *Cystorchis fusca,* Benth.

Root: a dense tuft of thick fleshy fibres. **Stem:** $6''$–$12''$ tall, stout. **Leaves:** radical, broadly ovate, revolute, rather pointed, leathery and shortly stalked.

Spike: secund, dense, many-flowered. **Flowers:** about $\frac{3}{8}''$ across; dorsal sepal narrowly oblong, blunt, 1-nerved; lateral sepals ovate-oblong, 3-nerved; petals falcate, swollen at the base; lip deeply pouched, with a decurved beak, strongly ridged within. *August and September.*

A very robust species very closely allied to our *G. repens* but very much larger. It bears dense one-sided spikes of blossoms of a greenish-white colour tinted with purple; they are half hidden by the large leafy bracts; it is of little garden value although the foliage is quite handsome. The plant grows in moss in woods and on damp fern-clad rocks in the Himalaya, reaching an altitude of 14,000 feet, and is a true alpine plant. It is evergreen and is perfectly hardy in Great Britain in a cool moist shady spot in the rock garden in sphagnum-moss and peat with a few lumps of limestone.

403. GOODYERA HENRYI, Rolfe

Epipactis Henryi, Eaton

Root: a creeping rhizome furnished with rather fleshy fibres. **Stem:** 6″–12″ tall, decumbent at the base then erect, leafy. **Leaves:** ovate, narrowed into a sheath-like stalk, clasping at the base. **Spike:** 1″–$1\frac{1}{4}''$ long, many-flowered. **Flowers:** about $\frac{5}{8}''$ across; sepals ovate-oblong, blunt, concave; petals oblong-lanceolate, rather pointed, 1-nerved; lip ovate, blunt, concave and saccate at its base, downy on the disc. *July to September.*

A comparatively large-flowered species closely allied to *G. foliosa* (Lindl.). It produces a short many-flowered spike of white and pale green blossoms of some decorative value. The plant grows in shady places on the mountains of Hupeh, Western China, at sufficient elevation above sea level to ensure its hardiness in Western and Southern Britain, in a shady part of the rock garden in loam and leaf-soil.

404. GOODYERA MENZIESII, Lindl.

Peramium Menziesii, Morang. *Spiranthes decipiens*, Hook. f.

Root: of several stout, shortly creeping fibres. **Stem:** 8″–16″ tall, stout, glandular-pubescent, clothed with a few scales. **Leaves:** mostly basal, ovate-lanceolate, pointed at the tip, tapering at the base, $1\frac{1}{2}''$–$2\frac{1}{2}''$ long. **Spike:** 2″–6″ long, many-flowered. **Flowers:** about $\frac{3}{8}''$ long, not secund; sepals and petals forming a concave, ovate-lanceolate galea, usually with a long recurved tip; lip ovate, swollen at the base. *August.*

This plant is probably the most robust member of the genus. It bears a tall slender spike of small green and white blossoms and is clothed at the base with rather small deep green leaves, which are frequently blotched and reticulated with white. It is of no great garden value and inhabits damp mossy woods in North America from Quebec to British Columbia and Southward to Minnesota, California and Arizona. It may be grown in the rock garden or cool shady border, in a compost of peat and leaf-soil.

405. GOODYERA OPHIOIDES, Rydb.

Goodyera repens of American Authorities not of R. Brown. *Peramium ophioides*, Rydb.

Root: slightly creeping, of fleshy fibres. **Stem:** including scape 4″–9″ tall, leafy. **Leaves:** alternate, lanceolate-ovate or ovate, abruptly contracted into a sheathing stalk, about $3\frac{3}{4}$″ long. **Raceme:** spike-like, 2″–4″ long. **Flowers:** about $\frac{3}{16}$″ long, secund; sepals and petals conniving forming a galea with short recurving tips; lip saccate, with a recurved tip. *July to September.*

The tiny white or greenish-white blossoms of this plant are of no decorative value, but the rich green leaves are prettily blotched and spotted with silvery white along the cross veins. It should make a pretty foliage plant for the alpine house. In a state of nature it grows in damp woods, forests and cedar swamps, usually in moss-covered soil in Canada and the Eastern United States, as far south as North Carolina and Colorado and is perfectly hardy in Great Britain in damp leaf-soil, loam, and sphagnum-moss, in a half-shady spot in the rock garden.

406. GOODYERA PUBESCENS, R. Br.

Peramium pubescens, MacM. *Neottia pubescens*, Pursh. *Satyrium repens*, Michx.

Root: a cluster of thick fleshy fibres. **Stem:** including spike 3″–8″ tall, leafy, more or less downy. **Leaves:** several, mostly basal, ovate or oblong-elliptic, smooth, contracted into sheathing stalks, $\frac{3}{4}$″–2″ long. **Spike:** cylindrical, 3″–6″ long, dense. **Flowers:** nearly $\frac{1}{4}$″ long; sepals ovate rather pointed; petals oblong, pointed; lip saccate, blunt at the tip. *July and August.*

This dwarf plant has but little to recommend it except its pretty deep green, white-marbled leaves, for the tiny white or pink flowers are too small to be of any decorative value. It grows in dry woods both on rich and poor soils from Newfoundland to Florida and westward to Minnesota. It may be grown in the alpine house or outdoors in the rock garden, in an elevated shady spot in leaf-soil and sand, for it is perfectly hardy.

407. GOODYERA REPENS, R. Br.

Peramium repens, Salisb.

Root: a shortly creeping rhizome with a few fleshy fibres. **Stems:** 6″–12″ tall, rather slender, clothed with a few pointed scales. **Leaves:** near the base of the stem, ovate, tapering into sheathing stalks, $\frac{1}{2}''$–$1\frac{1}{4}''$ long. **Spike:** 2″–4″ long; blossoms 9 to 18 in number. **Flowers:** about $\frac{1}{4}''$ long, secund; dorsal sepal and petals conniving forming on oval galea over the column; lateral sepals ovate, blunt, shorter than the dorsal sepal; lip saccate, with a narrow recurved or spreading apex. *July and August.*

A native plant with pretty rich green leaves blotched with pale green and elegantly reticulated; the flowers are small and of a greenish-white colour. The plant is of botanical interest only and is found in moist woods and forest throughout the Northern and Arctic regions of the Northern Hemisphere. It may be grown in a damp shady spot in the rock garden in peat, leaf-soil and sphagnum-moss and makes a pretty foliage plant in a pan in the alpine house.

408. GOODYERA SCHLECHTEDALIANA, Reichb. f.

G. japonica, Bl. *G. similis*, Bl. *Georchis Schlechtedaliana*, Reichb. f.

Root: a shortly creeping rhizome. **Stem:** 3″–7″ tall, slender, sparely leafy below. **Leaves:** basal, few in number, ovate, on fairly long stalks, $\frac{3}{4}''$–$1\frac{1}{2}''$ long. **Spike:** $\frac{3}{4}''$–$2\frac{1}{2}''$ long, few or many-flowered. **Flowers:** about $\frac{3}{16}''$ long, secund; dorsal sepal ovate, forming a galea with the petals; lateral sepals ovate, pointed, spreading; petals ovate-lanceolate; lip saccate with a narrow apex. *June and July.*

This little species should make an attractive alpine house plant on account of its pleasantly fragrant flowers which are of the usual pale green colour so common to most members of the genus. It is found in stony soil in pine forests on the mountains of Yunnan, Western China, at 11,000 feet above sea-level. The plant should be quite hardy in all but the bleakest parts of Great Britain in a well-drained half-shady spot in the rock garden in pine leaf-soil.

409. GOODYERA SECUNDIFLORA, Lindl.

Root: a stout, short, tuber-like, creeping rhizome. **Stem:** 6″–10″ tall, erect, glandular downy above. **Leaves:** few, sub-radical ovate or rarely elliptic, pointed, shortly stalked, $1\frac{1}{2}''$–2″ long. **Spike:** 2″–3″ long, secund, lax-flowered. **Flowers:** about $\frac{1}{2}''$ across, pubescent; sepals ovate, 1 nerved, dorsal slightly narrower than the lateral; petals subfalcate, crenate on the outer edges, 1-nerved; lip saccate, with a short beak, lamellate on the disc. *July and August.*

This rather robust species has one-sided spikes of white blossoms, and rich green leaves with silvery markings. It is a desirable plant for alpine house decoration. In a state of nature it grows in mossy woods and on damp fern-clad rocks from Eastern India (11,000 feet) to China and is perfectly hardy in this country in a cool moist spot in the rock garden in sphagnum-moss, peat and leaf-soil.

410. GOODYERA TESSELLATA, Lodd.

Peramium tessellatum, Rydb.

Root: of creeping, thick, fleshy fibres. **Stem:** 6″ to 9″ tall, rather slender. **Leaves:** mainly basal, ovate or oblong-lanceolate, $\frac{3}{4}$″–1$\frac{1}{2}$″ long. **Spike:** about 1$\frac{1}{2}$″ long, bearing from 6–18 blossoms. **Flowers:** nearly $\frac{3}{8}$″ long; sepals and petals conniving forming a galea with a recurved tip; lip less saccate and less recurved than that of *P. repens*. *August.*

A delicate little plant with a stiff upstanding stem, clothed at its base with small dark green leaves which are frequently blotched with white; the small green and white blossoms are quite pretty. It is found in damp woods in vegetable soil and moss, in Eastern North America from Newfoundland to Manitoba and southward to New York. It may be grown in the rock garden in a cool shady spot in leaf-soil and peat. It should make a pretty addition to the alpine house as a foliage plant.

411. GOODYERA VITTATA, Benth.

Georchis vittata, Lindl.

Root: a rather stout creeping rhizome. **Stem:** 4″–6″ tall, leafy nearly up to the spike. **Leaves:** subradical, ovate, fleshy, 1$\frac{1}{2}$″–3″ long. **Spike:** 2″–3″ tall, flowers subsecund. **Flowers:** about $\frac{5}{8}$″ across; dorsal sepal oblong-lanceolate, pointed; lateral sepals ovate, pointed; petals oblong-lanceolate, falcate, 3-nerved; lip pouched, terminating in a long beak with 2 lamellæ on the disc. *July to September.*

A very beautiful plant with spikes of white, pink-tipped blossoms and handsome rich green foliage with silvery veinings. It should make a very welcome addition to the rock garden or alpine house. It grows on damp mossy soil and in moss on the trunks of trees, also on damp rocks, in the Sikkim Himalaya, reaching an elevation of 9000 feet above sea-level and should be perfectly hardy in all but the bleakest parts of Great Britain in a damp shady spot in the rock garden in sphagnum-moss and peat with a few lumps of sandstone buried in it.

412. GOODYERA YUNNANENSIS, Schltr.

Root: a prostrate stem-like rhizome with many fibrous rootlets. **Stem:** about 12″ tall, slender, sheath-clothed. **Leaves:** about 6 in number, basal, spreading, elliptic or lanceolate-elliptic, cuneate at the base, shortly stalked, smooth, $\frac{3}{4}$″–1$\frac{1}{2}$″ long. **Raceme:** about 4″ long, densely many-flowered, secund. **Flowers:** about $\frac{3}{8}$″ across; dorsal sepal narrowly ovate, rather pointed; lateral sepals narrowly ovate, oblique, all downy at the base on the back;

petals very narrowly oblong, oblique, forming with the sepals a galea over the column; lip subglobose or helmet-shaped, with 4 obscure parallel hairy ridges down its centre. *July.*

The blossoms of this species resemble those of our native *G. repens* being green in colour and of no decorative value. It is found in shady places among rocks on the mountains near Tong-tchuan, Yunnan, at about 8000 feet above sea-level. It may be grown in a shady spot in the rock garden in calcareous leaf-soil and sand.

GYMNADENIA, R. Brown

A genus of about 15 species of delicate terrestrial plants related to the genus *Habenaria*. Most of them are decidedly pretty and well worth cultivating. The root system consists of two or more tubers at the base of the stem with a few fleshy roots above them. The somewhat juicy stems are clothed below with a few bright green leaves and terminate in a spike of pretty blossoms varying from pink to purple and at times white. The majority being dwarf plants they are well suited to alpine house culture in pans of wet peat and sphagnum-moss. The various species are scattered over Europe and Northern Asia from Great Britain to Japan and are also found in North Africa; they are, with but few exceptions, confined to damp grass lands in open country. Propagation by separation of the tubers and by seeds which are freely produced by the various species in a state of nature.

413. GYMNADENIA ALBIDA, Rich.

Bicchia albida, Parlat. *Cœloglossum albidum*, Hartm. *Orchis albida*, Scop. *Habenaria albida*, Swartz; *Peristylus albidus*, Lindl.

Root: of several short, much thickened fibres. **Stem:** $\frac{3}{4}'$–$1\frac{1}{2}'$ tall, leafy, tapering from base to summit. **Leaves:** few, oblong or lanceolate, pointed, degenerating upwards into bracts, 1″–4″ long. **Spike:** 1″–3″ long, spire-like, many-flowered but not very dense. **Flowers:** about $\frac{3}{16}''$ long, secund or subunilateral; dorsal sepal ovate; lateral sepals lanceolate curved; petals oblong, all forming a loose galea over the column; lip triangular in outline, divided into 3 subequal tooth-like lobes. *July and August.*

A rather slender Orchid with a sparely leafy stem and a short spike of very small green and white blossoms of no decorative value. It is a native plant and is usually found in mountain pastures over the whole of Northern Europe and on the more lofty ranges of Central and Southern Europe. There is one form known as *tricuspis* which differs but little from the type; both may be grown in the rock garden in a fairly damp sunny spot in peat and fibrous loam.

414. GYMNADENIA CALCICOLA, W. W. Sm.

Root: of 2 globose tubers, about $\frac{1}{2}''$ in diameter. **Stem:** $2''$–$8''$ tall, usually erect, bearing 2 leaves near the base. **Leaves:** varying from lanceolate to oblong-lanceolate or nearly linear, $1\frac{1}{2}''$–$3''$ long. **Spike:** about $1\frac{1}{2}''$ long, of 6–12 blossoms. **Flowers:** about $\frac{5}{8}''$ across; sepals subequal, obliquely lanceolate, rather pointed; petals linear, as long as the sepals; lip 3-lobed; outer lobes linear; centre lobe linear, longer than the outer lobes; spur cylindrical, incurved, thickened at the tip, about $\frac{1}{4}''$ long. *June to August.*

A delicate and dainty little plant with comparatively large rose-coloured blossoms which are sweetly fragrant. It is found in rather dry limestone grassland in Yunnan, Western China, reaching elevations of 13,000 feet above sea-level, so should be quite hardy in Great Britain in an open sunny spot in the rock garden in calcareous sandy loam. It is allied to *G. pseudo-diphylax* and may prove a form of that species.

415. GYMNADENIA CAMPTOCERAS, Rolfe

Habenaria camptoceras, Rolfe

Root: of 2 rather large globular tubers. **Leaves:** 2 in number, ovate, pointed, subopposite, $\frac{3}{4}''$–$1\frac{1}{2}''$ long. **Scape:** naked, slender, $3''$–$4''$ tall, bearing from 1–3 blossoms. **Flowers:** about $1\frac{1}{4}''$ across; dorsal sepal ovate, blunt or pointed; lateral sepals similar but hooked; petals simple, linear, forming a galea over the column; lip cuneate, rhomboid, 3-lobed; lateral lobes obovate-oblong, blunt; centre lobe oblong, blunt, margin crenulate; spur slender, curved, inflated at the tip, blunt, $1''$ long. *July to September.*

A very delightful little plant with a short slender flower-stem bearing from 1–3 very large lilac pink or pale purple blossoms. It should prove a gem for alpine house culture. In a state of nature it is found on open grassy cliffs in Western Szechuan near the Tibetan border at elevations of from 9000–13,500 feet. It should prove quite hardy in Great Britain in a sunny spot in the rock garden in sandy, fibrous loam.

416. GYMNADENIA CONOPEA, R. Br.

G. transsilvanica, Schur. *Orchis conopsea*, R. Br. *O. ornithis*, Jacq. *O. setacea*, Gilib. *Habenaria conopea*, Franch. *Satyrium conopseum*, Whalby

Root: of 2 palmately lobed tubers, $1''$–$1\frac{1}{2}''$ long. **Leaves:** mainly basal, few in number, linear-lanceolate, suberect, $2''$–$4''$ long. **Scape:** $\frac{3}{4}'$–$2'$ tall, slender, clothed with a few sheath-like bracts. **Spike:** $2''$–$3''$ long, rather loose, many-flowered, cylindrical. **Flowers:** about $\frac{3}{8}''$ long exclusive of the spur; dorsal sepal oblong, blunt; lateral sepals lanceolate, curved, spreading; petals lanceolate, curved, smaller than the sepals, forming a galea over the column with the dorsal sepal; lip usually wedge-shaped, shallowly 3-lobed at the tip; spur cylindrical, curved, $\frac{1}{2}''$–$\frac{3}{4}''$ long. *June to August.*

A delightful little native species with loose spikes of pink, lilac, pale purple or pure white, scented blossoms with very long curving spurs. The subspecies *densiflora* (Dictr.) is an extremely beautiful plant; other forms are *alpina, clavata, crenulata, comigera, inodora, monticola, ornithis, sibirica, ussuriensis* and *yunnanensis*. It also produces many beautiful natural hybrids with members of the genus *Orchis*. The type and its forms are found over the greater part of Europe and temperate Asia as far as Japan; they may be grown in open spots in the rock garden in fairly moist fibrous loam. In a state of nature they inhabit heaths, pastures, mountain meadows, etc.

417. GYMNADENIA CRASSINERVIS, Finet

Root: of irregular finger-like or fusiform tubers. **Stem:** stout, 4″–6″ long, erect. **Leaves:** usually 5 in number, 2 uppermost sheath-like, oblong-lanceolate, suberect, 3″ long. **Spike:** about $1\frac{1}{2}''$ long, more or less pyramidal, very dense, many-flowered. **Flowers:** about $\frac{3}{8}''$ long; dorsal sepal oblong, blunt; lateral sepals ovate-lanceolate, pointed; petals ovate, margins sub-serrate, all with stout thickened nerves; lip cuneate, 3-lobed; outer lobes semi-rotund; centre lobe blunt-triangular; spur incurved, very blunt, $\frac{1}{4}''$ long. *July and August.*

A dwarf, leafy little species suitable for alpine house culture in a pan of peat, loam and chopped sphagnum-moss. It has very dense pyramid-shaped spikes of small pink or pale lilac-coloured flowers. It is found in moorland pastures on the mountains of Yunnan, Western China, and should be sufficiently hardy for culture outdoors over the greater part of the Kingdom in a sunny spot in the rock garden in damp peat and loam.

418. GYMNADENIA CUCULLATA, Reichb. f.

Root: of 2 globose tubers, one about $\frac{1}{2}''$ across and the other much smaller. **Leaves:** 2 in number, usually opposite, basal, ovate, about $1\frac{1}{2}''$ long. **Scape:** 6″–9″ tall, slender, curved, naked or clothed with a solitary bract. **Spike:** 1″–$2\frac{1}{2}''$ long, loose, usually few-flowered, secund. **Flowers:** about $\frac{3}{8}''$ long; dorsal sepal narrowly oblong; lateral sepals and petals narrowly lanceolate or linear, all conniving and forming a galea with a recurved tip over the column; lip wedge-shaped, divided into 3-lobes, linear or lanceolate, the centre one the largest; spur-curved, stout, $\frac{1}{8}''$ long. *July and August.*

A very quaint little plant with a slender stem bearing a one-sided spike of small but very pretty pink, lilac or pale purple blossoms like little helmets. It should prove a welcome addition to the alpine house; there is a subspecies known as *purpurea* (Schur.). The plant is found in damp open spots usually in mountainous country from Germany throughout Russia and Siberia to China. It may be grown in the bog garden in peat and loam.

419. GYMNADENIA DECIPIENS, Schltr.

G. Vidalii, Franch. *Neolindleya decipiens*, Kränzl. *Platanthera decipiens*, Lindl.

Root: of large oblong or ovoid tubers. **Stem:** 8″–20″ tall, very leafy, thick and fleshy. **Leaves:** 5–6 in number, oblong or suborbicular, 3″–4″ long. **Spike:** 4″–6″ long, usually many-flowered. **Flowers:** about ⅜″ across; dorsal sepal, lateral sepals and petals narrowly ovate, pointed; lip cuneate, with 3 teeth at the tip; spur small, conical, incurved. *July and August.*

A plant of little or no decorative value with yellowish-green blossoms in long, many-flowered spikes. It grows in damp boggy soil in open situations in Siberia, Kamchatka, and Japan and should, of course, be quite hardy in Great Britain in the bog garden or on the banks of a stream in peat and rich loam.

420. GYMNADENIA DELAVAYI, Schltr.

Root: of 2 palmately lobed tubers. **Stem:** about 9″ tall, rather leafy. **Leaves:** 4–5 in number, cauline, ligulate-lanceolate, pointed, 3″–4″ long. **Spike:** about 2½″ long, cylindrical, densely many-flowered. **Flowers:** about ⅝″ long; dorsal sepal oblong, concave, blunt; lateral sepals obliquely oblong, blunt; sepals similar but smaller; lip broadly rhomboid-cuneate, 3-lobed; outer lobes short, rounded; centre lobe longer, nearly square, very blunt; spur filiform, pointed, pendulous, about ⅝″ long. *July and August.*

A most delightful little plant with dense spikes of bright pink or rich red blossoms of considerable size in comparison to the stature of the plant. It is found in open situations on the sides of mountains in damp soil in Yunnan, Western China, at 11,000 feet above sea-level and should be quite hardy in Great Britain, in an open spot in the rock garden in damp calcareous loam and peat.

421. GYMNADENIA FRIVALDII, Grisco

G. Frizaldszkyana, Hampe. *Habenaria densiflora*, Schur. *H. transsilvanica*, Schur.

Root: of 2 oblong-palmately lobed tubers about ¾″ long. **Leaves:** few in number, cauline and basal, oblong-lanceolate, degenerating upwards into bracts, 1″–3″ long. **Scape:** 6″–15″ tall, slender, clothed with a few bracts towards the top. **Spike:** 1″–2″ long, cylindrical, dense, many-flowered, slender. **Flowers:** about ⅜″ long not including the spur; dorsal sepal ovate-oblong; lateral sepals broadly lanceolate, curved; petals similar only narrower, conniving, forming a galea over the column; lip cuneiform, 3-lobed, lobes rounded, centre one the smallest; spur filiform, curved, about $\frac{5}{8}''$ long.

June to August.

A pretty slender species with small but dainty lilac or white blossoms. It is found in grassy places in the alps of Hungary and Roumania. The plant may be grown in a damp sunny spot in the rock garden in good calcareous loam and sand.

422. GYMNADENIA GRAMINIFOLIA, Reichb. f.

Poneorchis graminifolia, Reichb. f.

Root: of 2 irregular tubers. **Leaves:** basal and cauline, linear suberect, 2″–4″ long. **Scape:** $\frac{3}{4}'$–$1\frac{1}{2}'$ tall, slender, clothed with a few narrowly linear sheaths. **Spike:** short, congested, many-flowered. **Flowers:** about $\frac{3}{8}''$ across and the same in length exclusive of the spur; dorsal sepal oblong, rather blunt; lateral sepals somewhat similar, spreading; petals lanceolate, forming a galea with the dorsal sepal over the column; lip cuneate, obscurely 3-lobed, lobes rounded; spur cylindrical, curved, blunt, $\frac{3}{8}''$ long. *May to July.*

A slender grassy-leaved species allied to *G. conopea* (R. Br.) with somewhat dense clusters of small lilac-pink or rosy-red blossoms with a comparatively short spur. It is found in damp grasslands both in the highlands and lowlands of Japan. It should be quite hardy in Great Britain in a damp spot in the rock garden or in the bog garden in loam and peat.

423. GYMNADENIA HIMALAYICA, Schltr.

Root: of 2 tubers divided into 4 fusiform lobes. **Stem:** 18″–20″ tall, fairly stout, leafy. **Leaves:** 5–7 in number, oblong-ligulate or lanceolate, pointed or blunt, about 6″ long. **Spike:** $3\frac{1}{2}''$–$4\frac{1}{2}''$ long, cylindrical, densely many-flowered. **Flowers:** about $\frac{1}{2}''$ long; dorsal sepal oblong, erect, concave; lateral sepals obliquely oblong, blunt, spreading; petals obliquely ovate, blunt; lip cuneate, 3-lobed; outer lobes obliquely triangular, blunt; centre lobe broadly triangular, blunt; spur filiform, pointed, pendulous, $\frac{1}{2}''$ long.

July and August.

A beautiful and desirable plant with a tall somewhat leafy stem terminating in a long dense spike of pretty blossoms of a violet-rose colour. It is found in damp soil at the head of the Varul valley in the North-Western Himalaya at between 12,000 and 15,000 feet above sea-level. It should be perfectly hardy in Great Britain in the bog garden or on the banks of a pond in good rich soil.

424. GYMNADENIA MONOPHYLLA, Ames and Schltr.

Root: of 2 subglobose tubers. **Stem:** 3″–5″ tall, slender, erect or slightly flexuous. **Leaf:** radical, narrowly lanceolate, sheathed at the base, $1\frac{1}{2}$″–2″ long. **Raceme:** 1″–$1\frac{1}{2}$″ long, densely many-flowered, secund. **Flowers:** about $\frac{3}{8}$″ long; dorsal sepal lanceolate, pointed, erect; lateral sepals lanceolate, falcate at the tip; petals subfalcate-linear, pointed, forming a loose galea over the column with the lateral sepals; lip deeply 3-lobed, cuneate at the base; outer lobes linear, blunt; centre lobe broadly strap-shaped, blunt; spur swollen at the base, incurved, $\frac{3}{16}$″ long. *August.*

A dainty little plant very suitable for alpine house culture in a deep pan of damp sandy fibrous peat and sphagnum-moss. It produces a dense spike of small bright red blossoms on a slender stem clothed at its base by a solitary grassy leaf, and is found in the Alpine regions of North-Western Szechuan, China, at 12,000 feet above sea-level, growing in dwarf herbage.

425. GYMNADENIA ODORATISSIMA, Reichb. f.

G. erubescens, Zucc. *G. suaveolens,* Reichb. f. *Orchis odoratissima,* Linn. *O. conospea,* Asso. *Satyrium odoratissimum,* Whalen.

Root: of 2 irregular tubers divided at the tip into 2–4 finger-like lobes about $1\frac{1}{4}$″ long. **Leaves:** mainly basal, linear or linear-oblong, pointed, degenerating into small bracts on the upper part of the stem, 3″–8″ long. **Scape:** 9″–15″ tall, rather slender, frequently flexuous. **Spike:** 2″–4″ long, cylindrical, dense, often sinuous. **Flowers:** about $\frac{1}{4}$″ long; dorsal sepal ovate; lateral sepals lanceolate; petals lanceolate, slightly curved, smaller than the sepals, all form an open galea over the column; lip cuneate, 3-lobed; lobes ovate, centre one the largest; spur cylindrical, curved, $\frac{1}{4}$″ long.
June and July.

A slender plant with a cylindrical spike of many small pale lilac, pale purple or white blossoms, they are pretty but too small to have much garden value. It is found in damp meadows and marshes both in the lowlands and on the mountains over the greater part of Europe. There are several forms such as *borealis, carpatica, oxyglossa,* and *Retzdorffii.* The plant produces many natural hybrids with members of the genera *Orchis, Nigritella,* and *Platanthera.* They may be grown in the rock garden in damp loam or in the bog garden in peat and loam.

426. GYMNADENIA ORCHIDIS, Lindl.

G. cylindrostachya, Lindl. *G. violacea,* Lindl. *Habenaria Orchidis,* Hook. f. *Platanthera Orchidis,* Lindl.

Root: a rather large ovoid tuber. **Stem:** 1′–2′ tall, stout, leafy. **Leaves:** oblong or linear-oblong, erect, pointed, sheathing, 2″–6″ long. **Spike:** 2″–6″

long, subcylindric, very dense. **Flowers:** about $\frac{3}{8}''$ across; dorsal sepal elliptic, spreading; lateral sepals, oblong; petals rhombic-orbicular; lip cuneately obovate, lobes very short; spur slender, short. *July.*

This species produces cylindrical spikes of many crowded pink or white blossoms and is well worth growing. It is found in grassy openings in pine forests, usually in damp places from the Western Himalaya to Western China, reaching an elevation of 12,000 feet above sea-level and should be perfectly hardy in Great Britain in a damp half-shady spot in the rock garden in soil collected from pine woods.

427. GYMNADENIA PSEUDO-DIPHYLAX, Kränzl.

Root: of 2 small irregular tubers. **Stem:** $2\frac{1}{2}''$–$6''$ tall, rather slender, erect. **Leaves:** 1 or 2 in number, ovate-oblong, placed near the base of the stem. **Scape:** smooth, slender, clothed with one or two bracts. **Spike:** $\frac{3}{4}''$–$2''$ long, loose, few-flowered. **Flowers:** about $\frac{3}{8}''$ long; dorsal sepal narrowly oblong, blunt; lateral sepals lanceolate, pointed; petals lanceolate or linear, all conniving and forming a hood over the column; lip cuneate, 3-lobed; outer lobes linear; centre lobe lanceolate, larger than the outer lobes; spur thick, short and blunt. *September.*

A very dwarf species suitable for culture in the alpine house. It has a few-flowered spike of pale rosy-purple or rosy-red blossoms on a slender stem clothed at its base with two small rich green leaves. It is found in shady spots on the grassy banks of streams in North-Western Yunnan at over 10,000 feet above sea-level. An open sunny spot in the bog garden in peat and moss is indicated.

HABENARIA, Willdenow

A very large genus containing well over 1000 species of deciduous terrestrial Orchids varying in height from a few inches to four or more feet. Their root system consists of sessile oval or rounded tubers which in a few species are broadly lobed; there are usually a few white fleshy roots springing from the stem just above the tubers. The stems are erect and generally leafy; the leaves vary from oblong to lanceolate and linear, degenerating into narrow bracts amongst the blossoms which are borne in long dense, or few-flowered, spikes or racemes. Although the majority are of little horticultural value there are many that are exceedingly chaste and beautiful with long racemes of large, butterfly-like pure white blossoms. The plants are widely scattered throughout the temperate and tropical regions of the whole world, and are generally found in wet soils. Propagation by separation of the tubers and also by seeds. The genus *Platanthera* is included in *Habenaria* by some authors.

428. HABENARIA ACHALENSIS, Kränzl.

Root: of small ovoid or oblong tubers on fairly long fibres. **Stem:** 1′–2′ tall, erect, rounded or angular, leafy below, sheathed above. **Leaves:** lanceolate, stem-clasping, erect, pointed, membranous, 3″–5″ long, decreasing in size upwards. **Raceme:** 3″–6″ long, few or many-flowered. **Flowers:** about $\frac{3}{8}$″ across; dorsal sepal ovate, pointed; lateral sepals obliquely ovate, pointed, deflexed; petals very deeply bilobed; lobes linear, outer one falcate at the tip; lip deeply 3-lobed; outer lobes linear, deflexed; centre lobe ligulate; spur filiform, clavate at the tip. *February.*

This South American species produces racemes of rather small white or pale green blossoms of but little decorative value. It is found on the banks of pools and rivers and also in marshes on the mountains near La Plata. It should be sufficiently hardy for culture outdoors in the warmest parts of the Kingdom in the bog garden or in good soil on the banks of a pool or stream.

429. HABENARIA AITCHISONII, Reichb. f.

H. brachyphylla, Aitch.

Root: tuberous, thick and fleshy. **Stem:** $\frac{3}{4}$′–1$\frac{1}{2}$′ tall, very variable in size and stoutness. **Leaves:** opposite, orbicular, cuspidate, inserted above the base of the stem, 1″–3″ long. **Spike:** 3″–6″ long, rather slender, dense, clothed with a few small sheaths. **Flowers:** about $\frac{1}{2}$″ across; dorsal sepal oblong-ovate, erect; lateral sepals oblong-ovate, spreading; petals equalling the sepals in length, ovate-lanceolate; lip straight, deeply divided almost to the base into 3 narrow segments; spur filiform, about $\frac{1}{4}$″ long. *August.*

This species produces a long one-sided spike of rather small pale green blossoms and is not of any great decorative value. It grows in damp rocky places among grass and short herbage from Afghanistan to Sikkim, reaching an elevation of 12,000 feet and is therefore quite hardy in Great Britain. It may be grown in the bog garden in peat and sphagnum-moss kept moist the whole year round.

430. HABENARIA ALTIOR, Rendle

Root: of ovoid tubers. **Stem:** about 1$\frac{1}{4}$′ tall, leafy below the middle. **Leaves:** radical and cauline, linear-lanceolate, pointed, stem-clasping, degenerating upwards into bracts, 2″–3″ long. **Raceme:** ovate, densely packed with blossoms. **Flowers:** about $\frac{5}{8}$″ across; dorsal sepal narrow at its base, spathulate at the tip; lateral sepals very obliquely ovate; petals, divided to near the base into 2 lobes, the upper lobe is filiform and the lower one lanceolate-subulate, both are hairy; lip deeply 3-lobed; outer lobes linear, rather pointed; centre lobe similar only blunt; spur dilated in the centre and somewhat twisted, $\frac{3}{4}$″ long. *September.*

A pleasing species with fair-sized pale green and white blossoms in a dense short raceme. It grows in boggy soil on the exposed slopes of Mount Kilimanjaro in Tanganyika, East Africa at 10,000 feet above sea-level and should therefore be hardy in all but the most exposed parts of Great Britain under the same conditions as the following species.

431. HABENARIA ANGUICEPS, Bolus

Root: of large ovoid-oblong tubers. **Stem:** $\frac{1}{2}'$–$\frac{3}{4}'$ tall, leafy. **Leaves:** oblong-lanceolate, degenerating upwards into bracts, sessile, fleshy, 1″–1$\frac{1}{4}$″ long. **Raceme:** about 3″ long, fairly broad, dense. **Flowers:** about $\frac{3}{8}$″ across; dorsal sepal concave, broadly ovate, blunt; lateral sepals obliquely semiovate-oblong, blunt; petals semiovate-oblong, blunt; lip linear-oblong, fleshy, blunt; spur fairly thick, swollen at the apex, about $\frac{3}{8}$″ long.

December to February.

A species of no great decorative value, with medium-sized pale green and white blossoms in oblong racemes on leafy stems. It is sufficiently dwarf for alpine house culture and is found in a state of nature in damp grassy places and the borders of marshes in Eastern Cape Colony, Natal and the Orange Free State where at Harrismith (7000 feet) it probably attains its greatest altitude and should be perfectly hardy in Great Britain if it could be induced to rest during our winter. A rich fibrous loam on a pond side is indicated.

432. HABENARIA ANISOPTERA, Reichb. f.

Root: of ovoid or oblong tubes. **Stem:** stout, leafy, 1′–1$\frac{1}{2}$′ tall. **Leaves:** radical and cauline, numerous, ovate, pointed, amplexicaul, largest 4$\frac{1}{2}$″ long, decreasing upwards into bracts. **Raceme:** nearly 5″ long, many-flowered. **Flowers:** $\frac{1}{2}$″ across; dorsal sepal triangular, pointed, small; lateral sepals oblong, pointed, very large; petals triangular, pointed, margins minutely ciliate; lip very deeply 3-lobed; outer lobes linear, pectinate outside; centre lobe linear, pointed; spur cylindrical, 2″ long. *May and June.*

A quaint species with a long cylindrical raceme of curious rather small green blossoms on a very leafy stem. It is found in marshes on Debra Tabor in Abyssinia at 8500 feet above sea-level and should therefore be hardy in Great Britain in sheltered localities in a rich loamy soil on the banks of a pond or stream.

433. HABENARIA ANTENNIFERA, A. Rich.

H. leptobrachiata, Ridl.

Root: an ovate tuber. **Stem:** $\frac{3}{4}'$–1′ tall, leafy below, sheath-clothed above. **Leaves:** radical and cauline, ovate-lanceolate or ovate-oblong, rather pointed, 2$\frac{1}{2}$″–4″ long. **Raceme:** 3$\frac{1}{2}$″–4$\frac{1}{2}$″ long, many-flowered. **Flowers:**

nearly $\frac{1}{2}''$ across; dorsal sepal small, oblong-lanceolate, blunt, recurved at its apex, margins fringed; lateral sepals reflexed, semiovate-oblong, pointed; petals very deeply divided into 2 lobes; outer lobe ligulate, blunt, fringed; inner lobe linear-lanceolate, twice as long as the outer lobe; lip 3-lobed; outer lobes filiform; centre lobe linear, longer than the side lobes; spur cylindrical below, clavate above, $\frac{3}{8}''$ long. *September.*

A dwarf leafy species with rather small pale green and white blossoms of but little decorative value. It grows on the borders of woods and in damp half-shady places in Abyssinia, probably attaining its greatest elevation above sea-level on Jan Meda at 8500 feet and should be quite hardy in Great Britain in a sheltered half-shady spot in damp leaf-soil and fibrous loam.

434. HABENARIA ARIETINA, Hook. f.

H. pectinata, Lindl.

Root: a large oblong tuber, frequently irregular. **Stem:** 1′–2′ tall, stout, very leafy. **Leaves:** ovate-lanceolate, upper ones all sheathing. **Spike:** 3″–7″ long, dense, many-flowered. **Flowers:** about 2″ across; dorsal sepal lanceolate, erect; lateral sepals ovate-lanceolate, spreading; petals linear-falcate, blunt; lip about as long as the sepals, divided into 3 narrow long lobes; outer lobes lacerate to the middle or inner margin; centre lobe linear; spur subclavate, $\frac{5}{8}''$ long. *August.*

A handsome plant with large green and white blossoms with a much cut lip. It should make an attractive addition to the bog or water garden in a good rich soil. It grows in marshes and wet grassy spots in the Himalaya and Khasia Hills, reaching an elevation of 10,000 feet, and is therefore hardy in all but the bleakest parts of Great Britain.

435. HABENARIA ATTENUATA, Hook. f.

Root: an ovoid tuber. **Stem:** 1′–1$\frac{1}{4}$′ tall, sparely leafy. **Leaves:** cauline, oblong or oblong-linear, 1$\frac{1}{2}$″–3″ long. **Raceme:** 2$\frac{1}{2}$″–5″ long, somewhat loose. **Flowers:** under $\frac{1}{4}''$ across; dorsal sepal broadly ovate, concave, blunt; lateral sepals ovate-oblong, rather blunt; petals broadly ovate, blunt; lip 3-lobed; outer lobes linear, blunt, spreading; centre lobe linear-oblong, a little longer than the outer lobes, whole lip fleshy; spur slender, thickened in the middle, $\frac{1}{2}''$ long. *July to September.*

This species has very small pale green blossoms of no decorative value. It grows in marshes and wet rocky ground in the alpine regions of the Cameroon Mountains in the Cameroons, West Africa at 10,000 feet above sea-level, and should therefore be quite hardy in Great Britain in the bog garden or on the banks of a pond or stream in fibrous peat and loam.

436. HABENARIA BEESIANA, W. W. Sm.

Root: of 2 narrowly oblong tubers. **Stem:** 4″–12″ tall, slender, erect, with 2–3 leaves near the base and a few sheaths upwards. **Leaves:** suberect, linear, pointed, smooth, 1½″–3″ long. **Spike:** 3″–5″ long, rather laxly many-flowered. **Flowers:** about ¼″ across; dorsal sepal ovate, blunt, erect; lateral sepals deflexed, oblong, blunt; petals obliquely ovate-lanceolate, blunt; lip deeply divided into 3-lobes, lobes linear, centre one the longest; spur cylindrical, incurved. *August.*

The green blossoms of this species are too small to be of any horticultural value. It is found in dry openings in thin woods in Western Yunnan, Western China, at elevations up to 10,000 feet above sea-level, and should prove hardy in all but the coldest parts of Great Britain in a half-shady spot in the rock garden in sandy loam and leaf-soil. It is allied to *H. Forrestii* and may prove a form of that species.

437. HABENARIA BRACTEOSA, Hochst.

Root: a small ovoid tuber. **Stem:** ¾′–1′ tall, leafy. **Leaves:** cauline, oblong-lanceolate or elliptic-lanceolate, pointed, decreasing upwards into bracts, 2″–4″ long. **Raceme:** 4″–5″ long, many-flowered. **Flowers:** about ¼″ across; dorsal sepal ovate-oblong, blunt, downy at its apex; lateral sepals oblong, blunt; petals subobliquely ovate-oblong, blunt; lip 3-lobed, base broad; outer lobes oblong, blunt; centre lobe broadly oblong, blunt; spur filiform, 1″ long. *May to July.*

The small green and white blossoms of this species have spurs very long in proportion to their size. It is of no great decorative value for the garden. In its native habitats in Abyssinia and Tanganyika, East Africa it grows in mountain marshes and other wet places and should be quite hardy in Southern Britain in the bog garden in a peaty soil.

438. HABENARIA BULLEYI, Rolfe

Root: of 2 oblong tubers about ¾″ long. **Stem:** 1′–2′ tall, bearing 3 leaves and sheathed at the base. **Leaves:** cauline, linear, rather blunt, 2″–3″ long. **Raceme:** about 4½″ long, lax, many-flowered. **Flowers:** about ½″ across; dorsal sepal ovate-oblong, blunt, rather fleshy; lateral sepals similar, spreading; petals oblong, rather blunt; lip narrow, divided into 3 narrowly linear-oblong pointed lobes; spur oblong, somewhat incurved. *September.*

The green blossoms of this Chinese plant are too small to have any horticultural value. It is found on barren mountain pastures in Western Yunnan, Western China, at from 7000–8000 feet above sea-level and should prove hardy in all but the most exposed parts of Great Britain in an open position in the rock garden, in damp calcareous loam and peat.

439. HABENARIA CARDIOCHILA, Kränzl.

Root: a rather large ovoid or oblong tuber. **Stem:** $1\frac{1}{4}'$–$1\frac{3}{4}'$ tall, very leafy above, clothed with several loose sheaths below. **Leaves:** cauline, oblong-lanceolate, pointed, amplexicaul, erect, 4″–5″ long. **Raceme:** 4″–5″ long, cylindrical, dense. **Flowers:** over $\frac{1}{4}''$ across; dorsal sepal oblong, pointed; lateral sepals ovate, pointed, oblique, connivent; petals oblong, apex rounded; lip 3-lobed, with a pandurate or cordate base with 2 rounded ears; outer lobes linear falcate, recurved; centre lobe broadly linear, apex rounded, blunt; spur cylindrical, pendulous, about $\frac{1}{2}''$ long. *June and July.*

A fairly stout leafy species bearing a cylindrical raceme of small white blossoms of little decorative value. It is found in damp places on the highlands and mountains of Abyssinia and is sufficiently hardy for culture outdoors in the warmer parts of Britain in the bog garden or in peat on the banks of a stream or pond.

440. HABENARIA CASSIDEA, Reichb. f.

Bonatea cassidea, Sond. *B. Darwinii*, Weale.

Root: of ovoid tubers. **Stem:** 1′–$1\frac{1}{2}'$ tall, slender, leafy. **Leaves:** cauline, linear or linear-oblong, pointed, thin, 3″–6″ long, reduced to lanceolate sheaths upwards. **Raceme:** 3″–6″ long, dense. **Flowers:** about $\frac{5}{8}''$ across; dorsal sepal elliptic-oblong, rather hooded; lateral sepals oblong-lanceolate, oblique; petals 2-lobed; outer lobes narrowly lanceolate; inner lobe broadly lanceolate, pointed, short; lip 3-lobed to the base; outer lobes broadly lanceolate, pointed; centre lobe elongate-linear, longer than the outer lobes; spur cylindrical, $\frac{3}{4}''$ long. *October to December.*

This species produces long racemes of pale green and white blossoms on slender stems clothed with narrow leaves and sheaths. It grows in damp spots in woods and shady places in Eastern Cape Colony, probably reaching its greatest elevation above sea-level on the Kaga Berg in the Bedford Division at 4000 feet. It should be quite hardy in the warmer parts of Great Britain in a damp shady spot in fibrous loam and leaf-soil.

441. HABENARIA CEPHALOTES, Lindl.

Root: a large ovoid tuber. **Stem:** 6″–8″ tall, rather stout, sheathed above. **Leaves:** often subradical, broadly oblong-lanceolate, 3″–5″ long. **Spike:** cylindrical or oblong, crowded. **Flowers:** about $\frac{1}{2}''$ across; dorsal sepal very broadly ovate; lateral sepals obliquely ovate; petals broadly ovate, almost saccate; lip cuneately obovate, deeply 3-lobed; outer lobes fimbriate; centre lobe broad; spur cylindrical, rather short.

July to September.

The dense cylindrical spikes of medium-sized green and white blossoms are of some decorative value; they are borne on a stout stem which is leafy below and sheath-clothed above. It grows on open grassy mountain sides in the Nilghiri and Travancore Hills at 8000 feet in Southern India. It may be grown outdoors in Great Britain in all but the most exposed counties in a damp sunny spot in the rock garden, in a good loamy soil.

442. HABENARIA CERATOPETALA, A. Rich.

Root: an oblong tuber. **Stem:** $\frac{3}{4}'$–$1\frac{1}{2}'$ tall, fairly stout and leafy. **Leaves:** cauline, elliptic to oblong, rather blunt, numerous, 1″–4″ long. **Raceme:** 2″–9″ long, dense. **Flowers:** about $\frac{3}{4}''$ across; dorsal sepal cucullate, elliptic-oblong, blunt; lateral sepals falcate-oblong, pointed, slightly oblique at the apex; petals very deeply 2-lobed; upper lobe linear-filiform; inner lobe over an inch long, broader than the upper lobe, much curved or circinnate at the tip; lip divided into 3 linear lobes narrowed above; spur filiform, clavate above, 3″ long. *August to October.*

A handsome plant with large "spidery" green and white blossoms in a long many-flowered raceme on a stout leafy stem. It grows on the banks of streams and rivers in the highlands of Abyssinia and reaches an elevation of 8000 feet above sea-level, so is hardy in all but the bleakest parts of Great Britain. It should be grown in a rich soil on the banks of a stream or pond.

443. HABENARIA CILIOSA, Lindl.

Root: of oblong tubers. **Stem:** $1\frac{1}{4}'$–$1\frac{3}{4}'$ tall, leafy. **Leaves:** linear-oblong or oblong-lanceolate, reduced upwards into bracts and downwards into sheaths at the base of the stem, rather fleshy, pointed, 2″–4″ long. **Raceme:** 2″–5″ long, dense. **Flowers:** about $\frac{1}{2}''$ across; dorsal sepal broadly ovate or ovate-oblong, blunt, fringed; lateral sepals obliquely ovate or ovate-oblong, blunt, fringed; petals obliquely semiovate-oblong, blunt; lip 3-lobed; side lobes linear-oblong, blunt; centre lobe linear blunt, all fleshy; spur $\frac{3}{4}''$ long. *January and February.*

The pale green blossoms of this species, although interesting, are of but little value for garden decoration; they are borne in fairly long oblong racemes on stout leafy stems, the fleshy rich green leaves are usually barred with black. It grows in damp or marshy places in Transkei, Tembuland, Griqualand East and Natal, where at N'kandhla at 5000 feet it is exposed to over 15° of frost for short periods during the winter. It should be grown in rich loam on a pond side in full sun and is only suitable for culture outdoors in warm localities.

444. HABENARIA CLARENCENSIS, Rolfe

H. prœalta, Lindl.

Root: an oblong tuber $1\frac{1}{2}''$ long. **Stem:** $\frac{1}{2}'-2\frac{1}{2}'$ tall, leafy. **Leaves:** cauline, oblong-linear, pointed, $1\frac{1}{2}''-10''$ long. **Raceme:** $2''-12''$ long, of many flowers. **Flowers:** about $\frac{1}{4}''$ across; dorsal sepal ovate-oblong, blunt; lateral sepals suboblique, ovate oblong, rather blunt; petals ovate, blunt, rather shorter than the sepals; lip 3-lobed, from a broad base; outer lobes oblong, blunt, spreading; centre lobe ovate-oblong, blunt; spur filiform, $\frac{1}{2}''$ long. *September.*

A tall wand-like plant with long racemes of small closely-packed green and white blossoms of very little decorative value. The plant is confined to wet rocky places on the top of Clarence Peak in the island of Fernando Po off the West Coast of Africa at an elevation of 10,000 feet and should be quite hardy in all but the coldest parts of Great Britain in a raised part of the bog garden in fibrous peat and growing sphagnum-moss.

445. HABENARIA CLARKEI, Kränzl.

Root: of 2 oval tubers about $\frac{1}{2}''$ long. **Leaves:** 2 in number, radical, cordate, reticulate, subopposite, about $\frac{3}{4}''$ long. **Scape:** naked, slender, $2''-3''$ long. **Raceme:** of 2–3 blossoms. **Flowers:** about $\frac{1}{2}''$ across; dorsal sepal ovate, pointed, hooded; lateral sepals ovate, pointed; petals deeply bilobed; lobes narrowly triangular; lip deeply divided into 3 linear lobes; lateral lobes recurved at the tip, narrower than the central one; spur cylindrical, flattened at the back, clavate at the tip, blunt, about $\frac{1}{2}''$ long. *August.*

This Himalayan plant is not of much garden value. It produces a short flower-stem bearing two or three comparatively large green and white blossoms, and would no doubt prove an interesting little plant in the alpine house in a pan of fibrous peat and chopped sphagnum-moss kept very moist.

446. HABENARIA CLAVATA, Reichb. f.

Bonatea clavata, Lindl.

Root: of large oblong tubers. **Stem:** $\frac{3}{4}'-2\frac{1}{2}'$ tall, stout, leafy. **Leaves:** oblong or elliptic-oblong, sessile, submembranous, $2''-4\frac{1}{2}''$ long, decreasing upwards into bracts and downwards into sheaths at the base. **Raceme:** $4''-8''$ long, rather dense. **Flowers:** $\frac{3}{4}''$ across; dorsal sepal elliptic-ovate, rather blunt; lateral sepals obliquely falcate-obovate; petals 2-lobed; upper lobe linear; lower lobe subfiliform, falcate, twice as long as the upper lobe; lip 3-lobed, lobes narrowly linear, curved; spur filiform, thick at the tip, $1\frac{1}{2}''$ long. *January to March.*

A pretty and desirable plant with rather large green and white or green and yellow blossoms in long racemes on stout leafy stems. It is frequent in damp spots or swamps over nearly the whole of Eastern South Africa and probably attains its greatest altitude above sea-level (6650 feet) at Belfast in the Transvaal and should be sufficiently hardy for outdoor culture in all but the bleakest parts of Great Britain if it could be induced to rest during our winter. A rich soil on a pond side is indicated.

447. HABENARIA COMBUSTA, Ridl.

Root: an ovoid tuber $\frac{3}{4}''$ long. **Stem:** $4''$–$8''$ tall, very sparely leafy and clothed with a few basal sheaths below. **Leaves:** cauline, oblong or oblong-linear, pointed, $1\frac{1}{4}''$–$3\frac{3}{4}''$ long. **Raceme:** $1\frac{1}{4}''$–$2''$ long, dense. **Flowers:** about $\frac{3}{8}''$ across; dorsal sepal ovate, pointed; lateral sepals ovate, oblique, erect; petals ovate-oblong, very blunt, as long as the dorsal sepal; lip 3-lobed, cordately eared at its base; outer lobes linear-falcate, blunt; centre lobe broadly linear, twice as long as the outer lobes; spur saccate-oblong, very short. *August and September.*

The dwarf habit of this species recommends it for alpine house culture; although the green and white blossoms are small they are pretty. It is found on Mount Guna in Abyssinia in wet and swampy places at an elevation of 10,000 feet and is therefore quite hardy in Great Britain. It should be grown in peat and loam in a wet sunny spot in the rock garden.

448. HABENARIA CORNUTA, Lindl.

Root: of ovoid tubers. **Stem:** $1'$–$1\frac{1}{2}'$ tall, stout, leafy. **Leaves:** elliptic-oblong or oblong-lanceolate, rather leathery, $1\frac{1}{2}''$–$4''$ long, becoming smaller upwards. **Raceme:** $3''$–$5''$ long, dense. **Flowers:** about $\frac{5}{8}''$ across; dorsal sepal elliptic-ovate; lateral sepals obliquely semiovate, rather blunt, spreading; petals cleft into 2-lobes at the tip; upper lobe narrowly linear; lower lobe incurved, twice as long as the upper lobe; lip divided into 3 tapering lobes; spur $\frac{1}{2}''$ long. *October to December.*

This is a pretty plant and has fair-sized green and white blossoms in long dense racemes on stout stems clothed with numerous deep green leaves. It is a marsh-loving plant and is also found on the banks of rivers in Kaffirland, Transkei, Griqualand East, Transvaal and Natal, where near Charlestown at 6000 feet above sea-level it is exposed to over 20° of frost for short periods during its winter rest. In cultivation it should be given a sunny position beside a pond or stream, in rich loam.

449. HABENARIA CULTRATA, A. Rich.

Root: an oblong tuber. **Stem:** stout, up to $2\frac{1}{2}'$ tall, leafy below. **Leaves:** cauline, oblong or elliptical, about $9''$ long. **Raceme:** about $6''$ long, dense.

Flowers: about $\frac{5}{8}''$ across; dorsal sepal oblong, pointed, cucullate, small; lateral sepals oval, much larger than the dorsal sepal; petals very deeply 2-lobed and densely pilose; upper lobe linear-lanceolate, minute; lower lobe falcate, broad at the base, twice as long as the upper one; lip 3-lobed; outer lobes linear-filiform; centre lobe broadly linear, twice as long as the outer lobes; spur filiform below, clavate above, $\frac{3}{4}''$ long. *October.*

A tall robust species with the lower half of the tall stem furnished with numerous oblong leaves; the blossoms, which are white and green in colour, are produced in a long raceme, they are pretty but of no great decorative value. It grows in bogs and marshes on the north side of Mount Semayata in Abyssinia at 8500 feet and should be quite hardy in Southern Britain in the bog garden or on the banks of a pond.

450. HABENARIA CULTRIFORMIS, Kränzl.

Root: an ovate tuber. **Stem:** $2\frac{1}{2}'$–$2\frac{3}{4}'$ tall, leafy. **Leaves:** cauline, oblong, pointed, plicate, canaliculate, subdistichous, about $3\frac{1}{2}''$ long. **Raceme:** 6″–8″ long, lax, many-flowered. **Flowers:** about $\frac{5}{8}''$ across; dorsal sepal oblong, small; lateral sepals broadly oblong, rather larger than the dorsal one; petals very deeply 2-lobed; outer lobe narrowly linear, curved; inner lobe caudate, from a rounded base; lip 3-lobed, lobes linear, centre one very blunt; spur cylindrical, $\frac{3}{4}''$ long. *September and October.*

A rather striking species with long leafy stems and loose racemes of fair-sized white blossoms shaded green at the base. It should make a pretty addition to the bog garden in peat and growing sphagnum-moss. In a state of nature it grows in boggy soil and other wet places on the mountains of Abyssinia, reaching an elevation of over 7500 feet above sea-level near Amba Sea, and should be quite hardy in Southern Britain.

451. HABENARIA DAVIDII, Franch.

H. pectinata var. *Davidii*, Finet

Root: of 2 oblong tubers. **Stem:** 1′–2′ tall, fairly stout, very leafy. **Leaves:** very crowded at the base, rounded, becoming broadly lanceolate and stem-clasping upwards, pointed, erect, 3″–4″ long. **Raceme:** erect, of 8–12 rather crowded blossoms. **Flowers:** about $\frac{1}{2}''$ across and $1\frac{1}{4}''$ long; sepals and petals narrowly ovate, pointed, fringed on their margins; lip divided for two-thirds of its length into 3 linear segments; outer lobes deeply fringed; centre lobe entire; spur cylindrical, thickened at the tip, pendulous, nearly 3″ long. *July.*

The dull yellow blossoms of this species whilst by no means showy are quite large and beautifully fringed. The plant is found in moist mountain meadows in Western China at from 9000–10,000 feet above sea-level and should be hardy in most parts of Britain in the bog garden or on the banks of a pond or stream, in good loam and peat.

452. HABENARIA DECORATA, Hochst.

Root: an oblong or ovoid tuber. **Stem:** 6″–9″ tall, fairly stout, leafy. **Leaves:** cauline, ovate-lanceolate to oblong-lanceolate, pointed, 1″–3″ long. **Raceme:** short, loose. **Flowers:** over $\frac{5}{8}$″ across; dorsal sepal ovate, blunt, pubescent; lateral sepals ovate-oblong, suboblique, pointed; petals sub-obliquely ovate-oblong, rather blunt; lip deeply 3-lobed; outer lobes sub-falcate-oblong, divaricate with the tip, split into 5 filiform segments; centre lobe triangular-linear, rather blunt; spur cylindrical, $1\frac{1}{4}$″ long. *September.*

A dainty dwarf species, very suitable for alpine house culture. It has neat deep green foliage and a raceme of from two to seven quite large white and pale green blossoms on its dwarf stem. It grows in boggy places on a few of the high mountains of Abyssinia, reaching its greatest elevation above sea-level on Mount Guna at 10,000 feet and is therefore quite hardy in this country in the bog garden in peat and sphagnum-moss.

453. HABENARIA DELAVAYI, Finet

H. yunnanensis, Rolfe

Root: of 2 small ovoid or oblong tubers. **Stem:** slender, smooth, sheath-clothed, 12″–18″ tall. **Leaves:** cauline and basal, few or many, degenerating upwards into sheaths, 2″–4″ long. **Spike:** 2″–6″ long, few or many-flowered. **Flowers:** about $\frac{1}{4}$″ across; dorsal sepal lanceolate, pointed; lateral sepals narrowly lanceolate, pointed; petals linear-lanceolate, pointed; lip very deeply 3-lobed; lobes fringed; centre lobe linear, pointed; spur pendulous, thickened at the tip. *June and July.*

This species is rather a pretty plant and has many-flowered spikes of small blossoms with green sepals and petals and a white lip. The blossoms are faintly fragrant. It is found in dry open pasture land in Western Yunnan, Western China at elevations of from 8000–9000 feet above sea-level and should be hardy in the milder parts of the Kingdom in an open well-drained spot in the rock garden in fibrous loam.

454. HABENARIA DICERAS, Schltr.

Root: of oblong tubers. **Leaves:** basal, 2 in number, suborbicular, opposite, pointed, about 2″ long. **Scape:** 10″–14″ tall, round, covered with minute down. **Spike:** 3″–5″ long, densely many-flowered. **Flowers:** about $\frac{1}{2}$″ across; dorsal sepal ovate, erect, blunt; lateral sepals falcate-ovate, erect, blunt, reflexed; petals lanceolate-ligulate, blunt, erect; lip deeply divided into 3 segments; outer segments linear-subulate; centre one similar, deflexed; spur narrowly cylindrical, slightly dilated at the tip, about $\frac{1}{4}''$ long. *October.*

This species produces a Plantain-like spike of rather small yellowish-green blossoms of no decorative value. It is found in dry shady situations in pine forests in Western Yunnan, Western China, at elevations of from 9000–10,000 feet above sea-level. It should be quite hardy over the greater part of the Kingdom in a well-drained, half-shady spot in the rock garden in soil collected from beneath the shade of conifers.

455. HABENARIA DIGITATA, Lindl.

H. trinervia, Wight; *Bonatea benghalensis*, Griff. *B. herbacea*, Wall. *B. punduana*, Lindl.

Root: an ovoid tuber. **Stem:** 1′–2′ tall, leafy. **Leaves:** varying from orbicular to lanceolate, pointed, 2″–5″ long. **Raceme:** 4″–7″ long, many-flowered. **Flowers:** about $\frac{3}{4}''$ across; dorsal sepal suborbicular; lateral sepals ovate, pointed; petals divided into 2 segments, the upper one being the broader; lip divided nearly to the base into 3 linear segments; spur subclavate, at times inflated. *July.*

This species has large pale green blossoms in long many-flowered racemes on tall leafy stems. It is an interesting but not showy plant. In a state of nature it grows in damp open clearings in woods among grasses and other herbage on the mountains of India, reaching sufficient altitude in the Himalaya to ensure its hardiness in the open in the Western and Southern counties of Great Britain in a moist spot in the rock garden in a good loamy soil.

456. HABENARIA DIPHYLLA, Dalz.

H. Jerdoniana, Wight; *H. Sutleri*, Reichb. f. *Liparis diphyllos*, Nimmo; *Platanthera canarensis*, Lindl.

Root: a rather large ovoid tuber. **Stem:** slender, 4″–10″ tall, clothed with many small sheaths. **Leaves:** radical, orbicular-cordate, thinly fleshy, 1″–2″ long. **Raceme:** 2″–4″ long, narrow, many-flowered. **Flowers:** about $\frac{1}{2}''$ across; dorsal sepal ovate, blunt; lateral sepals oblong, blunt; petals linear, as long as the sepals; lip divided almost to the base into 3 linear segments, the centre one being shorter than the others; spur inflated, pointed, about $\frac{1}{2}''$ long. *July and August.*

A slender plant with rather small pale green blossoms in a long many-flowered raceme on a slender stem clothed with many small bracts or sheaths which continue among the blossoms. It grows in damp open grassy places in various parts of India, reaching an elevation of about 7000 feet in the North-

Western Himalaya and should be quite hardy in Western and Southern Britain in a damp sunny spot in the rock garden in a good loamy compost.

457. HABENARIA DIPLONEMA, Schltr.

Root: of globose tubers. **Leaves:** basal, 2 in number, suborbicular, spreading, reticulate, about ¾″ long. **Scape:** 3″–7″ tall, slender, round, covered with minute down. **Raceme:** 1″–3″ long, of 6–14 blossoms, subsecund. **Flowers:** about ⅜″ across; dorsal sepal ovate, blunt, erect; lateral sepals obliquely elliptic, blunt, deflexed; petals subfalcate-ovate, dilated on the outer margins, erect or oblique; lip deeply divided into 3 segments; outer segments filiform; centre one linear-ligulate, rather pointed; spur clavate, incurved, ¼″ long. *August.*

The faintly fragrant, pale green blossoms are too small to be of any decorative value. The plant has its leaves decorated by numerous white reticulations. It is found in shady, dry situations on the ledges of cliffs in Western Yunnan at from 10,000–12,000 feet above sea-level and should be quite hardy in the rock garden in a half-shady well-drained position, in peat and loam.

458. HABENARIA DREGEANA, Lindl.

Root: of ovoid tubers. **Leaves:** radical, broadly cordate-orbicular, fleshy, sessile, spreading horizontally, 1″–1¾″ long. **Scape:** ½′–1¼′ tall, sheath-clothed. **Raceme:** 1½″–4″ long, dense. **Flowers:** about ⅜″ across; dorsal sepal ovate, rather pointed; lateral sepals obliquely semi-ovate-oblong; petals divided at their base into 2 lobes; upper lobe falcate, oblong, pointed, slightly toothed, lower lobe linear, diverging, much shorter than the upper lobe; lip 3-lobed; centre lobe linear-oblong; side lobes linear or filiform, diverging, shorter than the centre lobe; spur slender, ⅜″ long *December to February.*

A plant of some decorative value with small green blossoms in rather long racemes on a sheath-clothed flower-stem furnished at its base with two fleshy deep green leaves. It grows in moist spots in mountain marshes and on river banks in Eastern Cape Colony, Griqualand East, Natal, Orange Free State and the Transvaal, where near Belfast at 6500 feet altitude it is exposed to 20° or more of frost during the winter. A rich soil on the banks of a pond or stream is indicated.

459. HABENARIA DUCLOUXII, Rolfe

Root: of 2 ovoid-oblong tubers about ⅜″ long. **Stem:** 4″–10″ tall, hollow, sheathed at the base and bearing 2–3 leaves. **Leaves:** cauline, spreading, narrowly linear, pointed, 2″–3″ long. **Raceme:** 2″–3″ long, lax, few-flowered. **Flowers:** about $\frac{3}{16}$″ across; dorsal sepal ovate-oblong, blunt; lateral sepals similar, conniving with the dorsal sepal; petals narrowly ovate-oblong, blunt; lip very deeply divided into 3 lobes; outer lobes very narrow, curved upwards; centre lobe oblong, blunt, fleshy; spur subglobose, minute.

September.

The pale green blossoms of this little plant are too small to be of any decorative value. It inhabits damp barren moorland on the western slopes of the Tsan-shan Range in Western Yunnan, Western China, at from 9000–10,000 feet above sea-level and is probably quite hardy in this country in an open spot in the rock garden, in damp sandy peat.

460. HABENARIA FALCICORNIS, Bolus

H. Bilabrella, Kränzl. *H. Mundtii*, Kränzl. *H. tetrapetala*, Reichb. f. *Bonatea Bilabrella*, Lindl. *B. minor*, Mund. *B. tetrapetala*, Lindl. *Bilabrella falcicornis*, Burch. *Orchidea falcicornis*, Burch.

Root: of large potato-like tubers. **Stem:** 1′–3′ tall, stout, leafy. **Leaves:** linear-oblong, rather leathery, gradually decreasing upwards into imbricating sheaths, $2\frac{1}{2}$″–8″ long. **Raceme:** 3″–9″ long, dense. **Flowers:** about $\frac{1}{2}$″ across; dorsal sepal elliptic-oblong, blunt; lateral sepals broadly and obliquely semiovate; petals 2-lobed; upper lobe linear; lower lobe broadly ovate, 5 times as long as the upper lobe; lip divided into 3 linear lobes to the base; spur linear, $1\frac{1}{2}$″ long. *November to January.*

This is a very robust species but its white or green and white blossoms are too small in proportion to its leafy growth to render the plant of much decorative value. It is a common plant in its native habitat, where it grows in marshes and swamps. It is found in Cape Colony, Natal and Griqualand East, where at Kokstad at 5000 feet it is exposed to over 15° of frost for short periods during the winter. A rich soil beside a pond or stream is indicated.

461. HABENARIA FLAGELLIFERA, Makino

Cœloglossum flagelliferum, Maxim.

Root: of 2 ovoid tubers. **Stem:** 9″–15″ tall. **Leaves:** lanceolate, basal and cauline, reduced upwards into bracts, about 3″ long. **Raceme:** 3″–4″ tall, slender, lax, of few or many blossoms. **Flowers:** about $\frac{1}{4}$″ long; dorsal sepal ovate-lanceolate; lateral sepals similar but longer, at times oblong-lanceolate; petals ovate oblique; lip 3-lobed; outer lobes flagellate-filiform, longer than the centre lobe, which is oblong-lanceolate and blunt; spur short, clavate, retusely bifid at the tip. *July to September.*

The rather small greenish blossoms of this species are of but little decorative value; they are borne in a fairly long raceme on a slender leafy stem. It is found in damp places on mountains in the province of Tosa, Shikoku, Japan.

It should be quite hardy in all but the bleakest parts of Great Britain, in the bog garden or on the banks of a stream or pond, in good loam and peat.

462. HABENARIA FOLIOSA, Reichb. f.

H. polyphylla, Kränzl. *Bonatea foliosa*, Lindl. *Orchis foliosa*, Sw.

Root: of large oblong tubers. **Stem:** ½′–1½′ tall, stout, densely leafy. **Leaves:** ovate-oblong or oblong, sessile, rather fleshy, becoming smaller upwards, imbricate, 1″–3″ long. **Raceme:** 2″–6″ long, very dense. **Flowers:** nearly ¾″ across; dorsal sepal elliptic-ovate, cucullate, blunt; lateral sepals obliquely semi-ovate, concave, blunt; petals very broadly ovate or orbicular-ovate, blunt, as long as the sepals, at times broader than long; lip linear-oblong, very succulent, blunt, with revolute margins; spur, slender, 1¼″ long. *December to February.*

A handsome plant well worthy of cultivation, with long racemes of green or green and white blossoms on stout stems clothed with many rich green leaves. It is a common plant over the whole of Eastern South Africa from Cape Colony to the Northern Transvaal, in damp or wet places. Near Oliviers Hoek in Natal at 5000 feet it is exposed to over 15° of frost for short periods during its winter rest. It should be grown in a rich soil beside a pond or stream, in full sun.

463. HABENARIA FORCEPS, Schltr.

Herminium forceps, Schltr. *Peristylis forceps*, Finet

Root: of 2 ovate, unequal tubers. **Stem:** 4″–8″ tall, erect, slender, leafy. **Leaves:** cauline, lanceolate, pointed, decreasing upwards into bracts, 2″–2½″ long. **Raceme:** 1½″–3″ long, fairly dense, many-flowered. **Flowers:** about ¼″ across; dorsal sepal broadly ovate, erect, blunt; lateral sepals narrowly ovate, blunt, spreading; petals obliquely triangular, 3-nerved, blunt; lip ligulate or trowel-shaped with a blunt thickened tip; spur reduced to a blunt sac. *July to October.*

A slender spire-like plant with rather short narrow leaves and a long slender raceme of from twenty to thirty pale green fragrant blossoms. It is of no great decorative value and is found in stony mountain pastures, usually in damp spots, on the mountains of Western Yunnan at 11,000–12,000 feet. It should be quite hardy in Great Britain in damp stony loam, in an open spot.

464. HABENARIA FORRESTII, Schltr.

Root: of narrowly oblong tubers. **Stem:** 9″–12″ tall, clothed at its base with 2–3 leaves and a few narrow bracts upwards. **Leaves:** linear, sub-erect, ¾″–2½″ long. **Spike:** 3″–5″ long, rather lax, many-flowered. **Flowers:**

about $\frac{1}{4}''$ across; dorsal sepal ovate, erect; lateral sepals narrowly oblong-ligulate, falcate at the tip, blunt, spreading; petals ovate-lanceolate, blunt, spreading; lip simple, ligulate, blunt; spur cylindrical, incurved, $\frac{1}{4}''$ long. *July to September.*

A very slender grass-like species with small pale green fragrant blossoms; it is of botanical interest only and is found in dry mountain meadows in North-Western Yunnan at from 11,000–12,000 feet above sea-level. It should be quite hardy in Great Britain in an open well-drained spot in the rock garden in good fibrous loam. It should, of course, be well supplied with water during its vegetative season.

465. HABENARIA GALPINII, Bolus

Root: of fairly large oblong tubers. **Stem:** 6″–9″ tall, fairly stout and leafy. **Leaves:** lanceolate, sessile, 3″–4″ long, gradually degenerating into bracts upwards. **Raceme:** 4″–6″ long, rather lax, many-flowered. **Flowers:** about $\frac{3}{8}''$ across; dorsal sepal ovate-elliptic, concave, rather pointed; lateral sepal semiobovate-oblong with an oblique point; petals cleft at the tip; upper lobe linear; lower lobe lanceolate-linear, longer than the upper lobe; lip divided into 3 linear or bristle-shaped lobes, the centre lobe being half as long again as the side ones; spur slender, $\frac{3}{4}''$ long. *March.*

The pale green blossoms of this plant, although they cannot lay claim to much decorative value, are sufficiently interesting to warrant its culture in a pan in the alpine house; they are produced in a long raceme on a stout stem clothed with from six to nine rich green leaves. It grows in moist rocky places in the Transvaal and reaches its greatest altitude near Johannesburg at 6000 feet, where it is exposed to 25° of frost during the winter. A gritty loam in a damp spot in the rock garden is indicated.

466. HABENARIA GLAUCIFOLIA, Franch.

Root: of oblong tubers. **Leaves:** 2 in number, opposite, transversely elliptic, pointed, $1\frac{1}{2}''$–$2\frac{1}{2}''$ long. **Scape:** about 12″ long, naked, covered with minute down. **Spike:** 3″–4″ long, lax, few-flowered. **Flowers:** about 1″ across; dorsal sepal oblong, blunt; lateral sepals semiovate; petals bifid, segments linear or triangular; lip unguiculate, 3-lobed, lobes linear; centre lobe longer than outer lobes; spur filiform, pendulous, inflated at the apex. *July.*

The two large leaves of this species are of a pretty grey-green colour. The blossoms vary from white to green, or white with a green lip and spur. It is quite a pretty species and is found in dry clearings in pine woods in Western Szechuan, Western China, at elevations of from 9000–13,500 feet above sea-level and should be perfectly hardy in Great Britain in the rock garden in soil collected from beneath conifers.

467. HABENARIA GRIFFITHII, Hook. f.

H. decipiens, Hook f. *Dithrix decipiens*, Hook f. *Herminium decipiens*, Griff.

Root: a small oblong tuber. **Stem:** 5″–8″ tall, rather slender, erect or flexuous, somewhat leafy. **Leaves:** lower leaves elliptic, pointed or blunt, shortly stalked, 1″–2½″ long; upper leaves linear-oblong, sessile, membranous. **Spike:** 1″–2″ long, furnished with close-set decurved blossoms. **Flowers:** about $\frac{3}{16}$″ across; dorsal sepal ovate-lanceolate, blunt; lateral sepals linear-oblong, rounded at the tip; petals equalling the sepals in length, narrowly lanceolate; lip oblong, deeply divided into 3 narrow segments. *July and August.*

A species of little decorative value with short one-sided spikes of very small green and white blossoms on a leafy flower-stem. It is found in damp grassy places in the highlands of Afghanistan and North-Western India and should prove sufficiently hardy for cultivation outdoors in the Southern and Western districts of Great Britain. It may be planted in a sunny spot in the rock garden in a cool moist loam.

468. HABENARIA HOCHSTETTERIANA, Kränzl.

H. replicata, Hochst.

Root: a medium sized ovoid tuber. **Stem:** ¾′–1¼′ tall, fairly stout, leafy. **Leaves:** cauline, linear, blunt, 2¼″–4″ long. **Raceme:** 2½″–4½″ long, lax. **Flowers:** about ½″ across; dorsal sepal oblong-lanceolate, rather blunt; lateral sepals cuneate-obovate, pointed at the end; petals very deeply 2-lobed; upper lobe linear, pointed, inner lobe lanceolate, pointed; lip 3-lobed; outer lobes linear; centre lobe broadly linear, slightly longer than the outer ones; spur filiform, ¾″ long. *October.*

A fairly dwarf plant with rather small green blossoms of very little garden value. It is a native of the highlands of Abyssinia where it is found in wet and boggy places frequently on lofty mountains, reaching sufficient elevation to ensure its hardiness in Southern Britain in the bog garden, or on the banks of a stream or pond, etc., in peat and fibrous loam.

469. HABENARIA HUMILIOR, Reichb. f.

Root: a rather small ovoid tuber. **Stem:** 6″–9″ tall, sparely leafy. **Leaves:** cauline, linear-lanceolate, pointed, somewhat recurved, 2″–4″ long. **Raceme:** 2″–3″ long, few or many-blossomed. **Flowers:** about ⅝″ across; dorsal sepal elliptic-oblong, blunt; lateral sepals obliquely cuneate-oblong or obovate-oblong; petals very deeply 2-lobed; upper lobe linear-filiform, curved; inner lobe oblong-lanceolate, rather blunt, with an obscure tooth on either side below the apex; lip 3-lobed, with linear-filiform lobes, the centre one longest; spur, filiform, clavate above, $\frac{3}{4}''$ long.

August and September.

A very low growing little plant with a fairly stout stem clothed with a few narrow leaves and a raceme of from three to twenty green blossoms. It should make a desirable addition to the alpine house or rock garden in peat and loam in a damp spot. It grows in damp places on the highlands of Abyssinia, reaching an elevation of over 8000 feet where it is exposed to over 15° of frost for short periods.

470. HABENARIA INCOMPTA, Kränzl.

Root: of several oblong obtuse tubers, $1\frac{1}{2}''$ long. **Stem:** 9″–12″ tall, rather stout and leafy. **Leaves:** mainly cauline, oblong, blunt, very thin, decreasing upwards into bracts. **Spike:** 3″–4″ long, many-flowered. **Flowers:** about $\frac{5}{8}''$ across; dorsal sepal small, cucullate, pointed; lateral sepals obovate-oblong, from a cuneate base, reflexed, veined laterally, pointed; petals very deeply 2-lobed, lobes linear-spathulate, blunt, densely fimbriate, appressed to the margin of the dorsal sepal, forming a galea; anterior lobe attenuate from a transversely oblong base, falcate-triangular; lip 3-lobed; lobes linear; centre lobe long; spur filiform, clavate at the apex, $\frac{3}{4}''$ long. *October.*

A very quaint species with green and white blossoms in long spikes. It should make a pretty addition to the rock garden in damp loam and peat. It is found in damp places on the mountains of Abyssinia, reaching an elevation of 7500 feet near Debra Eski. For culture in Western Britain only.

471. HABENARIA INCURVA, Rolfe

Root: of oval tubers. **Stem:** $\frac{1}{2}'$ tall, fairly stout, leafy. **Leaves:** cauline, lanceolate-linear, pointed, about $2\frac{1}{2}'$ long, decreasing upwards into bracts. **Raceme:** $2\frac{1}{2}''$ long, rather lax, many-flowered. **Flowers:** $\frac{1}{4}''$ across; dorsal sepal broadly elliptic, blunt; lateral sepals obliquely semiobovate; petals 2-lobed at the tip; upper lobe narrowly falcate-linear, blunt; lower lobe linear, blunt, longer than the upper lobe; lip divided into 3 filiform lobes; spur much curved, narrow below, thickened above, $\frac{3}{4}''$ long.

November to January.

The quaint long-spurred greenish-white blossoms of this little species are too small to render the plant of much decorative value for the garden. It should make an interesting addition to the alpine house. In a state of nature it grows on rock-strewn hillsides in the eastern parts of the Transvaal, where it reaches an elevation of about 6000 feet and is exposed to over 20° of frost during its resting period in the winter. In cultivation it should be grown in a moist gritty loam in full sun.

472. HABENARIA INGRATA, Rendle

Root: an oblong tuber. **Stem:** $1\frac{1}{4}'$–$1\frac{1}{2}'$ tall, leafy below. **Leaves:** cauline, linear, degenerating into sheaths above, $1\frac{1}{4}''$ long. **Raceme:** 4″ long, many-flowered. **Flowers:** about $\frac{3}{8}''$ across; dorsal sepal elliptic-oblong, rather blunt; lateral sepals obliquely cuneate-oblong; petals very deeply 2-lobed; upper lobe linear-filiform; inner lobe linear-lanceolate, pointed; lip divided into 3 linear lobes; centre lobe longer than the others; spur cylindrical, nearly 1″ long. *May.*

The small green and white blossoms of this species are of but little decorative value, they are produced in a dense four-inch spike on sparely leafy stems. It grows on wet soil amongst dwarf herbage and shrubs on Mount Ruwenzori in British East Africa at 9000 feet and should therefore be hardy in all but the most exposed parts of Great Britain. It should be grown in a raised part of the bog garden in peat, loam and moss.

473. HABENARIA INTACTA, Benth.

Aceras densiflora, Boiss. *A. intacta,* Reichb. f. *A. secundiflora,* Lindl. *Orchis intacta,* Link. *O. sagittata,* Mumby; *Tinea intacta,* Boiss.

Root: of 2 sessile, oblong tubers about 1″ long. **Stem:** $\frac{1}{2}'$–$1\frac{1}{4}'$ tall, fairly stout, leafy, frequently flexuous. **Leaves:** few in number, ovate-oblong near the base of the stem, degenerating into sheathing bracts upwards. **Spike:** 1″–$1\frac{1}{2}''$ long, fairly dense. **Flowers:** about $\frac{3}{16}''$ long, subunilateral; dorsal sepal lanceolate, pointed; lateral sepals lanceolate, curved towards the tip, larger than the dorsal sepal; petals linear, pointed, all forming a galea over the column; lip variable in shape, 3-lobed; outer lobes usually triangular; centre lobe large, oblong, entire or bifid. *March to May.*

This plant produces a fairly stout stem clothed with a few deep green leaves which are sometimes decorated with numerous small dark spots, and a spike of small pink or greenish-white blossoms with red spots on the lip. The plant is of no garden value; there are two varieties, *bifida* and *tridentata.* The type and its forms are found in Western and Southern Europe, North Africa, Madeira and Canary Isles in open pastures. It may be grown in a damp spot in calcareous loam.

474. HABENARIA INTERMEDIA, Don

Root: a rather large ovoid or oblong tuber. **Stem:** 8″–10″ tall, fairly stout. **Leaves:** ovate or oblong, rounded or cordate at the base, scattered up the stem, pointed. **Raceme:** of few flowers. **Flowers:** 2″ across; dorsal sepal lanceolate; lateral sepals ovate-oblong, pointed, downy; petals linear-falcate, entire or serrulate; lip deeply divided into 3 narrow segments; outer segments toothed to the middle of inner margin; centre segment linear; spur stout, about 1½″ long. *August.*

A handsome plant well worth cultivating, with leafy stems bearing a few very large greenish-white blossoms. It is sufficiently short for alpine house culture. In a state of nature it grows in damp places on open grassy mountain sides in the Himalaya from Kashmir to Sikkim, attaining an altitude of over 8000 feet above sea-level, and may be tried outdoors in Great Britain in sheltered localities. A damp part of the rock garden in an open sunny spot with good fibrous loam and leaf-soil is indicated.

475. HABENARIA LÆVIGATA, Lindl.

H. ornithopoda, Reichb. f. *H. anguiceps*, Schltr.

Root: of globose tubers. **Stem:** ¾′–1½′ tall, stout, leafy. **Leaves:** cauline, oblong or oblong-lanceolate, sessile, pointed, rather fleshy, 1″–2″ long. **Raceme:** about 3″ long, dense. **Flowers:** about ½″ across;. dorsal sepal ovate-oblong, blunt; lateral sepals obliquely semiovate-oblong, blunt; petals semiovate-oblong, blunt; lip fleshy, 3-lobed; side lobes diverging, oblong, shorter than the oblong centre lobe; spur very slender, 1¼″ long. *February.*

This species has green or greenish-yellow blossoms in fairly long racemes. Although they are of fair size they are too dull in colour to be of much garden value. It grows in damp grassy places in the mountainous districts of Eastern Cape Colony, Griqualand East, the Transvaal and the Orange Free State, where near Harrismith at 7500 feet above sea-level it probably attains its greatest altitude, and should therefore be perfectly hardy in Great Britain if it can be induced to rest during our winter. A good loam in a damp spot in full sun is indicated.

476. HABENARIA LATILABRIS, Hook. f.

Platanthera acuminata, Lindl. *P. latilabris*, Lindl. *P. Orchidis*, Wall.

Root: an irregular tuber emitting fleshy fibres. **Stem:** ½′–1½′ tall, leafy. **Leaves:** sessile and sheathing, ovate or oblong, pointed, 3″–5″ long. **Spike:** 3″–10″ tall, lax, many-flowered. **Flowers:** about ½″ in diameter; dorsal sepal orbicular, concave; lateral sepals broadly ovate, spreading or deflexed; petals variable in shape, usually broadly ovate; lip linear or lanceolate; spur short and slender, often upcurved. *August.*

The small yellowish-green blossoms of this plant are of no decorative value; they are produced in long, many-flowered spikes on rather slender leafy stems. It grows in marshy places in woods and open grassy mountain sides in the Himalaya, reaching an altitude of 12,000 feet, so should be perfectly hardy in Great Britain in a damp spot in the rock garden in good loam and peat or on the banks of a pond or stream, in full sun.

477. HABENARIA LEPTOCAULON, Hook. f.

Root: a cluster of thick fleshy fibres. **Stem:** $\frac{3}{4}$′–1′ tall, slender, clothed with 2–3 narrow sheaths above. **Leaf:** solitary, linear-oblong, below the middle of the stem, 1$\frac{1}{2}$″–4″ long. **Spike:** 1″–2″ long, of 3–8 blossoms, slender. **Flowers:** about $\frac{3}{8}$″ across; sepals lanceolate, 1-nerved, pointed; petals triangular-lanceolate from a broad swollen base; lip entire, linear; spur slender, about $\frac{1}{2}$″ long. *September.*

This species has rather small pale green blossoms in short few-flowered spikes; they are of but little decorative value. It grows in damp grassy places in the Lachen Valley in the Sikkim Himalaya at an elevation of about 11,000 feet and should be hardy enough for general cultivation outdoors in Great Britain in a moist sunny spot in the rock garden in loam and peat or in soil collected from beneath the shade of pines.

478. HABENARIA LIMPRICHTII, Schltr.

Root: of 2 oblong tubers. **Stem:** 9″–12″ tall, erect, stout, rather densely leafy, with a few sheaths at the base. **Leaves:** cauline, suberect, 3–6 in number, oblong-lanceolate, blunt or pointed, about 3$\frac{1}{2}$″ long. **Raceme:** about 2$\frac{1}{2}$″ long, somewhat dense, of 6–8 blossoms. **Flowers:** about 1$\frac{1}{4}$″ across; dorsal sepal ovate or ovate-lanceolate, rather pointed; lateral sepals spreading, ovate-lanceolate, slightly hooked at the tip; petals falcate-oblong, blunt, narrowed somewhat towards the base, fringed with hairs on the outer margin; lip divided into 3 segments, linear, outer margins fringed; centre segment narrow, blunt; spur cylindrical, dilated at the tip, 1″ long. *July and August.*

A pretty species with a stout leafy stem and a short dense spike of fringed white and green blossoms resembling those of *H. pectinata.* It is found in damp grassy places on the mountains of Yunnan, Western China, at 9500 feet and should be nearly hardy in Great Britain in a very damp spot in the rock garden in fibrous peat and loam.

479. HABENARIA LONGIFOLIA, Ham.

Gymnadenia longifolia, Lindl.

Root: a fair-sized ovoid tuber. **Stem:** $\frac{3}{4}$′–1$\frac{1}{2}$′ tall, slender, leafy. **Leaves:** scattered, erect, linear, pointed, 3″–5″ long. **Spike:** 2″–3″ long, lax and few-flowered. **Flowers:** about $\frac{3}{4}$″ long; dorsal sepal narrowly oblong-lanceolate; lateral sepals larger than the dorsal one, oblong-lanceolate; petals ovate, concave at the base; lip about three times as long as the sepals, very broadly oblong, divided into 3 deep segments; outer segments semicircular, quite entire; centre segment linear; spur slender, nearly 1$\frac{1}{2}$″ long. *July and August.*

A rather attractive plant with curious long and narrow pure white blossoms having a large lip and small sepals and petals. It is found in grassy places in the Western Himalaya, reaching an elevation above sea-level that ensures its hardiness in all but the most exposed parts of Great Britain in an open sunny spot in the rock garden in fairly damp, heavy loam.

480. HABENARIA MACOWANIANA Kränzl.

H. arachnoidea, MacOwan

Root: of globose tubers. **Stem:** ½′–1′ tall, sheath-clothed. **Leaves:** radical, orbicular or broadly cordate-orbicular, fleshy, 1″–2″ long. **Raceme:** 1½″–6″ long, dense. **Flowers:** nearly ½″ across; dorsal sepal broadly ovate; lateral sepals obliquely semiovate-oblong; petals 2-lobed at the tip; outer lobe narrowly falcate-oblong, pointed, fringed; inner lobe filiform, pointed, bristly, longer than the outer lobe; lip divided into 3 linear or filiform bristly lobes, the outer ones diverging and shorter than the centre one; spur clavate, ¼″ long. *November to January.*

A species of but little decorative value, with long racemes of green flowers on sheath-clothed flower-stems furnished at the base with two stemless, fleshy, rounded, deep green leaves. It grows in exposed grassy places on the tops of hills in Eastern Cape Colony and probably attains its greatest elevation above sea-level on the Bosch Berg in the Somerset Division at 4200 feet and is exposed to over 12° of frost during its winter rest. A good fibrous loam in a moist sunny spot is indicated. Suitable for mild localities only.

481. HABENARIA MACRANTHA, Hochst.

Root: an oblong tuber. **Stem:** 1′–2½′ tall, leafy. **Leaves:** cauline, ovate or ovate-lanceolate, pointed, 2″–6″ long. **Raceme:** 3″–7″ long, many-flowered. **Flowers:** over 1½″ across; dorsal sepal ovate, pointed; lateral sepals subobliquely ovate-oblong, pointed; petals lanceolate-oblong, rather pointed; lip 3-lobed, narrow at its base; outer lobes broad, cut into from 8–10 filiform segments; centre lobe linear, rather pointed; spur cylindrical, curved, 1½″ long. *September and October.*

A very beautiful plant with quaintly-shaped white and green blossoms in a long raceme; they measure over 1½″ across when fully expanded. It grows in bogs and marshes on the highlands of Abyssinia and Arabia. It probably attains its greatest altitude above sea-level in Abyssinia on Debra Tabor at 8400 feet and is there exposed to over 20° of frost for short periods when deciduous. A compost of peat, sphagnum-moss and a little light loam in the bog garden is indicated.

482. HABENARIA MAIREI, Schltr.

Root: of 2 small, oblong tubers. **Stem:** 12″–15″ tall, erect or slightly flexuous, leafy. **Leaves:** usually 5 or 6 in number, narrowly elliptic, pointed, suberect, cauline, about 3″ long. **Raceme:** 3″–5″ long, lax, few-flowered. **Flowers:** about $\frac{3}{4}$″ across; dorsal sepal erect, narrowly ovate; lateral sepals spreading, narrowly ovate, falcate at the tip; petals narrowly oblong, blunt, margins fringed; lip divided almost to the base into 3 narrow lobes; outer lobes fringed; centre lobe linear, blunt; spur cylindrical, pendent, incurved, $\frac{3}{4}$″ long. *August.*

A quaint yet somewhat pretty species with a spike of rather large fringed blossoms on a leafy stem; they are of a pale green colour throughout. The plant is found in damp open pastures on the plateau of Ta-hai, Yunnan, Western China, up to about 10,000 feet above sea-level and should therefore be quite hardy in Britain in a good damp fibrous loam in full sun.

483. HABENARIA MALACOPHYLLA, Reichb. f.

Root: of ovoid tubers. **Stem:** 1′–1$\frac{1}{2}$′ tall, fairly stout, leafy. **Leaves:** cauline, elliptic-lanceolate, membranous, 2″–6″ long. **Racemes:** 3″–9″ tall, loose. **Flowers:** about $\frac{3}{8}$″ across; dorsal sepal galeate, ovate, blunt; lateral sepals obliquely ovate-oblong, blunt and spreading; petals 2-lobed at the tip; upper lobe linear-oblong, rather pointed; lower lobe subfiliform, curved, longer than the upper one; lip divided into 3 subfiliform lobes, the centre one being the longest; spur curved, fairly stout, $\frac{1}{2}$″ long. *May to December.*

The long racemes of rather small green blossoms of this species, although freely produced, are of more interest to the specialist than to lovers of decorative gardens. It grows most frequently in damp shady woods and mountain ravines and is scattered over a vast tract of wooded country from Nigeria to British East Africa and from thence to Eastern Cape Colony, reaching its greatest altitude on Woodbush Mountains in the Transvaal at 6600 feet, where it is exposed to 15° or 20° of frost during the winter for short periods. A compost of leaf soil and loam in half shade is indicated.

484. HABENARIA MANNII, Hook. f.

Root: a rather small ovoid tuber. **Stem:** $\frac{1}{2}$′–1′ tall, leafy. **Leaves:** cauline, oblong lanceolate, pointed, 2″–4$\frac{1}{2}$″ long. **Raceme:** 2″–6″ long, usually many-flowered. **Flowers:** over 1″ across; dorsal sepal ovate, cucullate, rather blunt; lateral sepals oblong or semiovate-oblong, blunt; petals oblong, blunt, forming a galea with the dorsal sepal; lip 3-lobed, narrowly unguiculate; outer lobes filiform, with their tips cut into 8–10 fine threads; centre lobe linear, rather pointed; spur slender, subclavate at the apex, $\frac{1}{2}$″ long. *June and July.*

The large pale green blossoms of this species have some claim to beauty and are borne in a raceme of from two to twenty on a dwarf leafy stem. It should make an interesting addition to the alpine house. It grows in wet places on the Cameroon Mountains in the Cameroons, West Africa at 9000 feet, where it is at times exposed to 10° or 15° of frost. It should be grown on the edge of the bog garden in peat and sphagnum-moss.

485. HABENARIA MARGINATA, Coleb.

H. promensis, Wall. *Orchis clavata*, Heyne. *O. mysorensis*, Heyne. *Platanthera marginata*, Lindl.

Root: an ovoid tuber about 1″ long. **Stem:** 4″–10″ long, clothed with many lanceolate sheaths. **Leaves:** subradical, sessile, oblong, lanceolate or linear-oblong, few, ½″–5″ long. **Spike:** 2″–6″ long, cylindrical, many-flowered. **Flowers:** ½″ across; dorsal sepal broadly ovate, equalling in length the lateral sepals which are oblong-lanceolate in shape; petals ovate-falcate; lip divided into 3 linear segments, centre one shorter and broader than the others; spur stout, curved, inflated below, about ½″ long. *July and August.*

This species has rather pretty rich green leaves with a yellow border. The blossoms are small and of a pale green colour. It grows in moist grassy places and in clefts in rocks on the high mountains of India, reaching an elevation of 7000 feet in Western Himalaya and is sufficiently hardy for outdoor culture in Western and Southern Britain under the same conditions as other damp-loving species.

486. HABENARIA MAXILLARIS, Lindl.

Platanthera foliosa, Ad. *Habenaria Germainii*, Phil.

Root: of small oblong tubers. **Stem:** 18″–20″ tall, rather slender, leafy. **Leaves:** linear or linear-oblong, pointed or blunt, 3″–4″ long, decreasing upwards into bracts. **Raceme:** 3″–6″ long, cylindrical, somewhat densely flowered. **Flowers:** about ½″ across; dorsal sepal ovate, sharply pointed; lateral sepals oblong, pointed, deflexed; petals deeply bilobed; lobes linear-lanceolate, hooked; lip deeply 3-lobed; lateral lobes very narrowly linear; centre lobe linear; spur filiform, blunt, about ½″ long.

October to December.

This South American species produces a tall, slender, leafy stem bearing a fairly long raceme of rather small white and green blossoms of but little decorative value. It inhabits marshy open country in elevated districts in Guatemala, Peru and Chile as far south as Valdivia. Plants collected from the latter locality may be tried outdoors in the Western counties of Great Britain on the banks of a stream or pond, in good soil.

487. HABENARIA MICROCERAS, Hook. f.

Root: an oblong tuber. **Stem:** 1′–2½′ tall, leafy. **Leaves:** cauline, elliptical, rather pointed, 1½″–4″ long. **Racemes:** 4″–10″ long, rather dense. **Flowers:** $\frac{3}{16}$″ across; dorsal sepal and lateral sepals ovate-oblong, blunt; petals oblong, blunt; lip 3-lobed, fleshy; outer lobes oblong, slightly curved; centre lobe triangular, keeled in front; spur linear-oblong, slightly curved, blunt, very short. *July.*

Like the following species this plant has tiny green blossoms of no decorative value; they are borne in very long narrow spikes on the leafy flower-stems. It grows in wet boggy places in the alpine region of the Cameroon Mountains in the Cameroons, West Africa at an elevation of 10,000 feet above sea-level and is therefore quite hardy in Great Britain. It may be grown on the edge of the bog garden in fibrous peat and living sphagnum-moss.

488. HABENARIA MICRORHYNCHOS, Schltr.

Root: of small globose tubers. **Stem:** ¾′–1¼′ tall, leafy, slender. **Leaves:** cauline, elliptic-oblong, sessile, membranous, 1½″–2½″ long, degenerating into sheaths below. **Raceme:** 2″–3″ long, rather dense. **Flowers:** about ⅛″ across; dorsal sepal broadly ovate-oblong, blunt; lateral sepals broadly ovate, a little longer than the dorsal one; petals ovate-oblong, blunt; lip deeply divided into 3 lobes; side lobes triangular-linear, diverging; centre lobe linear-oblong, blunt, shorter than the side lobes; spur ellipsoid-oblong, blunt and minute. *November to January.*

This species has tiny green blossoms of no decorative value. It is a woodland plant and is confined, so far as is at present known, to the wooded portion of Woodbush Mountains in the Transvaal at various elevations up to 6000 feet and is exposed to over 12° of frost during its resting period in the winter. In cultivation it may be grown in a damp half-shady spot in leaf-soil and sand. It is only suitable for culture in warm localities.

489. HABENARIA MIERSIANA, Champ.

H. radiata, Miq.

Root: of oblong or ovoid tubers. **Stem:** up to 2′ tall, clothed with a few distant leaves and with narrow bracts above. **Leaves:** ovate-lanceolate or lanceolate, pointed, 3″–5″ long. **Spike:** 3″–6″ long, many-flowered. **Flowers:** about ⅝″ across; dorsal sepal and lateral sepals ovate-triangular, minutely fringed with fine hairs; petals narrowly lanceolate, forming a galea with the sepals; lip cuneate at the base, dilated, 3-lobed; outer lobes cuneately triangular, outer margins toothed; centre lobe linear or narrowly triangular; spur filiform, club-shaped at the tip, 1¼″ long. *July and August.*

A pretty species with sparely leafy stems bearing a long many-flowered raceme of creamy white blossoms with a green spur. It is found in damp or dry places in many parts of China and Japan. It should be quite hardy in Great Britain in an open spot in the bog or rock garden in peat, loam and sphagnum-moss and must not be allowed to get dry in the summer. In most specimens the leaves have pale margins.

490. HABENARIA MODESTISSIMA, Reichb. f.

Root: of small ovoid tubers. **Stem:** 4″–6″ tall, slender. **Leaves:** ovate-oblong, pointed below, lanceolate and stem clasping above. **Raceme:** 1″–2″ long, lax, few-flowered. **Flowers:** about $\frac{1}{4}$″ across; dorsal sepal ovate, pointed; lateral sepals oblong-ovate, slightly deflexed; petals very deeply bilobed; lobes lanceolate, outer one falcate; lip 3-lobed; outer lobes very narrowly linear, diverging; centre lobe linear, blunt; spur cylindrical, pointed, about $\frac{1}{2}$″ long. *January.*

A very dwarf species with a short raceme of small pale green blossoms of no decorative value. It is found in wet clearings in thin evergreen forests in South Brazil and in the Island of Chiloe. Plants collected in the latter locality should succeed in the open air in the damp Western counties of Britain in the bog garden in peat and sphagnum-moss, where it is never allowed to become dry.

491. HABENARIA MONTOLIVŒA, Kränzl.

Montolivœa elegans, Reichb. f.

Root: a small oval or oblong tuber. **Stem:** $\frac{1}{2}$′–1′ tall, sparely leafy. **Leaves:** cauline, ovate-oblong, gradually degenerating into bracts upwards, $\frac{3}{4}$″–1$\frac{1}{4}$″ long. **Raceme:** 1$\frac{1}{2}$″–2$\frac{1}{2}$″ long, somewhat dense. **Flowers:** under $\frac{3}{16}$″ across; dorsal sepal and lateral sepals ovate, pointed; petals ovate-oblong, rather blunt; lip shortly 3-lobed; outer lobes falcate-oblong, rather blunt; centre lobe triangular, blunt, longer than the outer lobes; spur oblong-globose, very short. *September to November.*

A plant with minute pale green blossoms in dense racemes on short stems clothed with less than half a dozen leaves. It has no horticultural value. In its native country which is Abyssinia it grows in marshes on the highlands, reaching its greatest altitude above sea-level on Debra Tabor at 8500 feet and is at times exposed to 15° or 20° of frost. A rich soil on the banks of a stream or pond is indicated.

492. HABENARIA NATALENSIS, Reichb. f.

H. Wilmsiana, Kränzl.

Root: of ovoid tubers. **Stem:** 1$\frac{1}{4}$′–2′ tall, leafy, slender. **Leaves:** sub-radical linear or linear-lanceolate, 2″–6″ long, degenerating into narrow sheaths above. **Raceme:** 2″–6″ long, lax, many-flowered. **Flowers:** about $\frac{3}{16}$″ across; dorsal sepal ovate, blunt; lateral sepals obliquely oblong, blunt; petals linear-oblong, subfalcate, rather pointed; lip divided into 3 subequal lobes, thickened at the tip; spur cylindrical, rather curved, about $\frac{3}{4}$″ long. *November to January.*

The small pale green or white blossoms of this slender species are of but little value to decorative gardening. It is a marsh plant, being found in such situations in open woodlands as well as in more exposed places on the mountains in Natal, Zululand and the Transvaal where in marshes on Woodbush Mountains at 6500 feet it is exposed to nearly 20° of frost for short periods during its winter rest. It may be grown in rich soil on the banks of a pond or stream.

493. HABENARIA OLIGANTHA, Hook. f.

Root: a branched rhizome emitting thick fleshy fibres. **Stem:** 6″–10″ tall, slender, naked above. **Leaf:** solitary, sessile, oblong, rather blunt, 2″–4″ long. **Spike:** 1$\frac{1}{2}$″–4″ long, lax-flowered. **Flowers:** about $\frac{3}{8}$″ across; dorsal sepal and lateral sepals subequal, oblong or oblong-lanceolate, pointed; petals as long as the sepals, triangular-lanceolate, pointed, fringed with fine hairs; lip linear-lanceolate, fleshy; spur stout, incurved, clavate, about $\frac{1}{2}$″ long. *August and September.*

A dwarf species of little or no garden value, the small green blossoms being half hidden by the large leafy bracts. It grows in damp rocky places on the banks of streams, etc., in the Sikkim Himalaya, reaching an elevation of 12,000 feet and should therefore be quite hardy in Great Britain in a damp spot in the rock garden in sphagnum-moss, peat and fibrous loam, in full sun but should always be kept cool and moist at the root.

494. HABENARIA ORANGANA, Reichb. f.

Root: of ovoid tubers. **Stem:** $\frac{3}{4}$′–1′ tall, stout, leafy. **Leaves:** cauline, oblong-lanceolate, sessile, 2″–3″ long, degenerating into sheaths below and decreasing upwards. **Racemes:** 2″–6″ long, dense. **Flowers:** nearly $\frac{1}{2}$″ across; dorsal sepal elliptic or obovate-elliptic, blunt; lateral sepals obliquely and broadly ovate, blunt; petals 2-lobed at the tip; outer lobe oblong, blunt; inner lobe oblong, blunt, shorter than the outer one; lip 3-lobed; outer lobes lanceolate-oblong, blunt; centre lobe linear, blunt, longer than the outer lobes; spur slightly curved, slender, $\frac{1}{2}$″ long. *October to January.*

This is a rather pretty species with long racemes of medium-sized white blossoms borne on a slender stem clothed with bright green somewhat fleshy leaves. It grows in wet places and marshes, frequently in mountainous districts, in Natal, the Transvaal and the Orange Free State where, near

Harrismith, it probably attains its greatest altitude above sea-level and is exposed to 25° or 30° of frost during the winter. A rich soil in a open sunny spot beside a pond or stream is indicated.

495. HABENARIA PACHYCAULON, Hook. f.

Root: a branched rhizome emitting thick fleshy fibres. **Stem:** 4″–6″ tall, very stout, with a few large sheaths above the solitary leaf. **Leaf:** sub-radical, oblong, thick, blunt, 2½″–3½″ long. **Spike:** 1½″–2″ long, very slender, lax-flowered. **Flowers:** about ¼″ across; sepals thick, linear-oblong; petals ovate-oblong, as long as the sepals; lip ovate-lanceolate, thick, fleshy; spur short, clavate. *August and September.*

A very dwarf, delicate little plant with loose spikes of small purple blossoms. It should make a pretty addition to the alpine house in a pan of leaf soil, peat and living sphagnum-moss. In its natural habitat in the Lachen Valley in the Sikkim Himalaya it is found at an elevation of 12,000 feet and is exposed to over 20° of frost for considerable periods. It may be grown outdoors in Great Britain in a damp spot in the rock garden in the above compost.

496. HABENARIA PAUCIFOLIA, Lindl.

Root: of small oblong tubers. **Stem:** 12″–14″ tall, slender, leafy. **Leaves:** lanceolate, pointed, 3–4 in number, 2″–3″ long, becoming smaller upwards. **Raceme:** about 4″ long, of 3–6 blossoms. **Flowers:** about ½″ across; dorsal sepal ovate, pointed; lateral sepals oblong-ovate, pointed, deflexed; petals deeply divided into 2 linear lobes; lip deeply 3-lobed; outer lobes linear; centre lobe linear, shorter than the outer lobes; spur filiform, pointed, pendulous, ⅝″ long. *November to January.*

A slender species clothed with a few narrow leaves; a few small pale green and white blossoms are produced in a very loose raceme and are of little or no decorative value. The plant is found on the banks of rivers near Valdivia in Central Chile and should succeed in the Western and Southern counties of Great Britain under the same conditions as it is subjected to in a state of nature.

497. HABENARIA PECTINATA, Don

H. ensifolia, Lindl. *H. Gerardiana,* Wall. *Orchis pectinata,* Smith

Root: a fair-sized ovoid tuber. **Stem:** 1′–2′ tall, robust, very leafy. **Leaves:** 4″–6″ long, ovate-lanceolate, most of them sheathing. **Spike:** 3″–8″ long, densely flowered. **Flowers:** about 2″ across; dorsal sepal lanceolate, erect; lateral sepals ovate-lanceolate, spreading; petals linear-falcate, smooth, somewhat dilated on the outer margin; lip 3-lobed, cut and toothed on the inner margin; centre lobe linear; spur slender, subclavate, $\frac{3}{4}''$ long. *August.*

A beautiful and desirable plant with very large creamy-white, green-tinted blossoms in dense spikes on leafy stems. It is found in damp or boggy, grassy and rocky places in the Sikkim Himalaya (where it attains an altitude of 9000 feet), Western China, and the Khasia Hills. It may be grown outdoors in Great Britain in all but the bleakest parts in a damp part of the rock garden in good loam and peat. It may also be grown in the bog garden or on the banks of a stream.

498. HABENARIA PRÆSTANS, Rendle

Root: a fair sized oval tuber. **Leaves:** cauline, ovate-lanceolate or oblong, rather blunt, degenerating upwards into bracts, 2″–6″ long. **Raceme:** 5″–6″ long, dense. **Flowers:** nearly $1\frac{1}{4}''$ across; dorsal sepal ovate, rather blunt; lateral sepals ovate-lanceolate, blunt; petals lanceolate-oblong, subfalcate, rather blunt; lip 3-lobed, very narrow at its base; outer lobes nearly 1″ long, divided into about 12 thread-like segments; centre lobe linear, rather blunt; spur cylindrical, slightly thickened above, over $\frac{3}{4}''$ long. *May to July.*

A handsome large-flowered species, with beautiful pale green and white blossoms in which the outer lobes of the lip are cut into long segments like a combe. It should prove a welcome addition to the bog garden in an open sunny spot. It grows on the sunny sides of mountains in wet or boggy places in British East Africa and British Central Africa where on the top of Mount Zomba it reaches an elevation of 7000 feet and is at times exposed to 15° or more of frost.

499. HABENARIA PUBESCENS, Lindl.

Root: a large ovoid tuber. **Stem:** $1'$–$1\frac{1}{2}'$ tall, stout, leafy towards the base, sheathed above. **Leaves:** elliptic-lanceolate, narrow towards the base, 4″–6″ long. **Raceme:** 4″–8″ long, many-flowered. **Flowers:** about $\frac{3}{8}''$ across; dorsal sepal hemispheric; lateral sepals narrowly ovate, blunt; petals linear; lip much longer than the sepals, deeply divided into 3 linear segments, centre one the broadest; spur slender, $\frac{1}{2}''$ long. *July and August.*

A leafy species with long racemes of rather small white blossoms tinted pale green towards the base. It is quite a pretty plant. It grows in damp grassy places in the Western Himalaya from Kumaon to Garwhal at 7000 feet above sea-level and should therefore be hardy in Great Britain in all but the bleakest localities. It may be planted in a damp spot in the rock garden in a good loamy soil.

500. HABENARIA REHMANNII, Bolus

Root: of large ovoid tubers. **Stem:** 1¼′–1¾′ tall, stout, leafy. **Leaves:** cauline, lanceolate-linear, rather pointed, fleshy, 2″–4″ long. **Raceme:** 3″–6″ long, rather lax, many-flowered. **Flowers:** about ⅜″ across; dorsal sepal ovate-oblong, rather blunt; lateral sepals obliquely ovate-oblong; petals 2-lobed; outer lobe linear, pointed; inner lobe linear, falcately incurved, downy, twice as long as the outer lobe; lip 3-lobed; side lobes linear, diverging, curved; centre lobe linear, diverging, longer than the side lobes; spur slender, curved, about ½″ long. *November to January.*

The long leafy racemes of this plant bear numerous green blossoms which are too small to render the plant of any garden value. It is a swamp loving species and is found in such spots in the Transvaal, where it probably attains its greatest altitude above sea-level on Woodbush Mountains at 6500 feet and is exposed to over 15° of frost during the winter. A rich soil on the banks of a pond is indicated. It is only suitable for outdoor culture in warm localities.

501. HABENARIA RICHARDIANA, Wight

Root: a large ovoid tuber. **Stem:** 6′–8′ tall, stout, clothed with many slender sheaths above, leafy below. **Leaves:** oblong-lanceolate, subradical, 4″–6″ long. **Spike:** of 8–10 blossoms, lax. **Flowers:** about ¾″ across; dorsal sepal ovate; lateral sepals similar but larger; petals triangular, very concave, rather pointed; lip very deeply 3-lobed; side lobes deeply toothed; spur stout, about 1½″ long. *June and July.*

Quite a desirable species from a garden point of view; it has large green and white blossoms on rather short stems and is suitable for alpine house culture. It grows in damp rocky places among short herbage on the Nilghiri and Travancore Hills at elevations up to 8000 feet and should therefore be quite hardy in the Southern and Western parts of Great Britain in a damp but sunny part of the rock garden in a compost of sandy loam and peat.

502. HABENARIA SAGITTIFERA, Reichb. f.

H. linearifolia, Maxim.

Root: of 2 small ovoid tubers. **Stem:** 2′–2½′ tall, rather slender. **Leaves:** few in number, narrowly linear, pointed, 3″–4″ long. **Raceme:** of 8–12 blossoms, lax. **Flowers:** about ½″ across; dorsal sepal ovate, pointed; lateral sepals semiovate, deflexed, suboblique; petals simple, ovate, blunt; lip 3-lobed; lateral lobes linear, toothed at the apex; centre lobe linear, blunt; spur cylindrical, blunt, ⅝″ long. *July and August.*

The blossoms of this species are purple, an unusual colour amongst this genus of Orchids; they are produced in few-flowered racemes on tall, rather slender stems. It is found on the banks of streams and pools over the greater part of Northern China, Manchuria and Japan. It should be quite hardy in Great Britain under the same cultural conditions as the other moisture-loving members of the genus.

503. HABENARIA SCHIMPERIANA, Hochst.

H. anomala, Lindl.

Root: an oblong tuber about $\frac{3}{4}''$ long. **Stem:** $1\frac{1}{4}'$–$1\frac{1}{2}'$ tall, leafy. **Leaves:** cauline, linear or oblong-linear, pointed, 3″–6″ long. **Raceme:** about 6″ long, lax. **Flowers:** over $\frac{1}{2}''$ across; dorsal sepal elliptic-oblong, rather blunt; lateral sepals obliquely cuneate-oblong, pointed above the middle; petals very deeply 2-lobed; upper lobe linear-filiform; inner lobe linear-subulate, longer and broader than the upper lobe; lip 3-lobed; outer lobes linear-filiform; centre lobe linear, longer than the outer lobes; spur clavate above, $\frac{1}{2}''$ long. *August to October.*

Not a very attractive plant, the blossoms being too small to have much garden value, they are white and green in colour and are freely produced in long spikes. It grows in marshes on the highlands of Abyssinia, where it is at times exposed to 15° or more of frost. It should be grown on the edge of the bog garden or on the banks of a pond or stream in good soil.

504. HABENARIA SCHLECHTERI, Kränzl.

Root: of large ovoid tubers. **Stem:** $1\frac{1}{2}'$–2′ tall, stout, leafy. **Leaves:** narrowly linear-oblong, sheathing the stem, 3″–4″ long, degenerating into bracts upwards. **Raceme:** 4″ long, many-flowered. **Flowers:** nearly 1″ across; dorsal sepal broadly elliptic-ovate; lateral sepals oblong-lanceolate; petals oblong-lanceolate, about as long as the dorsal sepal; lip deeply 3-lobed; outer lobes oblong, strongly pectinate; centre lobe oblong-lanceolate, rather pointed; spur very slender, nearly 6″ long. *October to January.*

A very beautiful species with rather fleshy pure white blossoms, remarkable for the great length of the slender spur which curls and twists about in all directions. The racemes consist of from six to eight blossoms, and are borne upon erect sheath-clothed flower-stems. It grows in damp grassy places and on the borders of woods in the Transvaal, where at Belfast it attains an altitude of 6500 feet and is exposed to over 20° of frost during the winter. A rich soil on the banks of a pond is indicated.

505. HABENARIA SECUNDIFLORA, Hook. f.

Root: a globular tuber about $\frac{1}{2}''$ across. **Stem:** 3″–5″ tall, erect, slender. **Leaves:** linear, base sheathing, pointed, 2″–5″ long. **Spike:** 1″–2″ long, more or less recurved, flowers secund, dense. **Flowers:** about $\frac{3}{8}''$ across; sepals lanceolate; petals narrowly lanceolate, pointed; lip oblong, saccate at the base, deeply divided into 3-segments to about the middle; lobes lanceolate; all the segments of the flower are joined together at the base; spur inflated, about $\frac{1}{4}''$ long. *August.*

A dainty little pink flowered species with slender stems clothed with a few narrow leaves. It is found in damp rocky places in sub-alpine situations in the Himalaya from Kumaon to Sikkim, reaching an elevation of 14,000 feet and should be quite hardy in Great Britain in a damp spot in the rock garden in moist sandy loam and peat.

506. HABENARIA SIMENSIS, Reichb. f.

Root: an ovoid tuber $\frac{3}{4}''$ long. **Stem:** $\frac{1}{2}'$–$1\frac{1}{4}'$ tall, leafy below. **Leaves:** cauline, few, oblong, pointed, sheathing below and degenerating into bracts above, about $3\frac{1}{2}''$ long. **Raceme:** 2″–4″ long, dense. **Flowers:** $\frac{3}{8}''$ across; dorsal sepal oblong, cucullate, pointed, small; lateral sepals deflexed, sub-orbicular-ovate, pointed; petals very deeply 2-lobed; upper lobe lanceolate, pointed, with a downy margin; inner lobe short, retuse, 2-lobed, lobes minute, pointed; lip 3-lobed; outer lobes short, lanceolate, pointed; centre lobe lanceolate, blunt, slightly thickened; spur very blunt, about $\frac{3}{8}''$ long. *September and October.*

The small green blossoms of this species are curious but have little or no decorative value; they are borne in dense racemes on stems clothed with about half a dozen oblong leaves. It grows in damp places on the highlands of Abyssinia, where it reaches an elevation of 8500 feet on Jan Meda and is exposed at times to nearly 20° of frost. A damp fibrous peat and loam in full sun is indicated.

507. HABENARIA SPLENDENS, Rendle

Root: a fairly large, oblong tuber. **Stem:** $1'$–$1\frac{1}{4}'$ tall, leafy. **Leaves:** cauline, ovate or ovate-lanceolate, pointed, degenerating upwards into bracts, 2″–4″ long. **Raceme:** 3″–6″ long, many-flowered. **Flowers:** nearly 2″ across; dorsal sepal ovate, rather pointed; lateral sepals ovate-oblong, pointed; petals lanceolate-oblong, rather blunt, $1\frac{1}{8}''$ long; lip 3-lobed, narrow at its base; outer lobes linear, divided into about 12 filiform segments; centre lobe linear, rather blunt; spur cylindrical, short. *July.*

An exceeding beautiful species with huge white, green-tinted blossoms nearly two inches across and two and a quarter inches long, they are freely borne on rather long leafy stems. It should prove a very welcome addition to our gardens. It is confined, so far as is at present known, to Mount Kilimanjaro (where it grows in wet soil) in Tanganyika, East Africa at elevations up to 10,000 feet and is exposed at times to 15° or 20° of frost. A mixture of fibrous peat and good fat loam in a wet, sunny spot is indicated.

508. HABENARIA STENANTHA, Hook. f.

Root: a rather large ovoid tuber. **Stem:** $\frac{1}{2}'$–$1\frac{1}{2}'$ tall, rather slender, leafy upwards. **Leaves:** sessile, oblong, usually sheathing, 3″–5″ long. **Spike:** 3″–10″ long, lax, few-flowered. **Flowers:** about $\frac{3}{8}''$ across; dorsal sepal oblong; lateral sepals linear, sharply deflexed; petals linear, erect; lip linear, blunt; spur slender, flexuous, $\frac{3}{4}''$ long. *August.*

The rather small yellowish-green blossoms of this species are of little or no decorative value; they are borne in long loose spikes on leafy stems. It grows in open grassy places on the Sikkim Himalaya at altitudes of 12,000 feet or more, and is exposed to over 20° of frost for long periods during the winter. It may be grown in a damp sunny spot in the rock garden in a good fibrous loam with the addition of plenty of sharp sand.

509. HABENARIA STENORHYNCHOS, Schltr.

Root: of small ovoid tubers. **Stem:** about $\frac{3}{4}'$ tall, slender, clothed with a few leaves. **Leaves:** cauline, linear-lanceolate, submembranous, pointed, $1\frac{1}{2}''$ long, reduced upwards into bracts. **Raceme:** $\frac{3}{4}''$–1″ long, few-flowered. **Flowers:** about $\frac{5}{8}''$ across; dorsal sepal elliptic-lanceolate, rather blunt; lateral sepals obliquely ovate-oblong, rather blunt; petals 2-lobed at the tip; upper lobe very narrowly linear; lower lobe narrowly linear, longer than the upper lobe; lip divided at the tip into 3 filiform, pointed, lobes, the centre lobe longer than the others; spur $\frac{1}{4}''$ long. *November to January.*

A delicate, dwarf species with fair-sized pure white blossoms, two to six in number, on a slender stem clothed with a few narrow rich green leaves. It is a desirable plant for the alpine house. It is a marsh species and grows in such situations on Woodbush Mountains in the Transvaal, at 6400 feet, where it is exposed to over 15° of frost during the winter for short periods. A good soil on the banks of a pond is indicated. It is only suitable for outdoor culture in warm localities.

510. HABENARIA TENUISPICA, Rendle

Root: a small ovoid tuber. **Stem:** slender, $1\frac{1}{2}'$–$2\frac{1}{2}'$ tall, leafy. **Leaves:** cauline, scattered, elongate linear, pointed, the lower one sheathing, the upper ones stem-clasping, 4″–7″ long. **Raceme:** 4″–6″ long, loose. **Flowers:** under $\frac{3}{16}''$ across; dorsal sepal broadly ovate, blunt, concave; lateral sepals ovate-oblong, blunt, reflexed; petals ovate-oblong, concave; lip 3-lobed, outer lobes narrowly linear-oblong; centre lobe linear-oblong, blunt; spur cylindrical, thickened above, $\frac{1}{4}''$ long. *July.*

This species has a very narrow rod-like raceme of very small green and white blossoms on a slender stem clothed with distant leaves. It is of no horticultural value and is confined, in a state of nature, to boggy ground in open spots on Mount Ruwenzori in British East Africa at 9000 feet above sea-level, where it is exposed for short periods to over 12° of frost. It may be grown on the edge of the bog garden or on the banks of a pond in peat and loam. This species is only suitable for outdoor culture in Western Britain.

511. HABENARIA TETRAPETALA, Kränzl.

Bonatea tetrapetala, Kräuss

Root: of large oblong tubers. **Stem:** 1′–3′ tall, stout, leafy. **Leaves:** cauline, linear-oblong, rather leathery, 3″–6″ long, decreasing upwards into bracts or imbricating sheaths. **Raceme:** 3″–8″ long, dense. **Flowers:** about ⅝″ across; dorsal sepal elliptic oblong, blunt; lateral sepals broadly and obliquely semiovate; petals 2-lobed at the tip; lobes subequal, oblong-lanceolate, pointed; lip 3-lobed at the tip; outer lobes oblong, blunt, diverging; centre lobe narrower, quite blunt; spur linear, curved, 1½″ long.

March and April.

This is quite a decorative species and bears fairly large green and white or pure white blossoms in long narrow racemes on tall stems clothed with long, rather narrow rich green leaves. It is a damp loving species and is found in marshes and damp spots on the mountains of Natal, Griqualand East and the Transvaal, where on the Woodbush Range it attains an altitude of 6000 feet above sea-level and is there exposed to over 12° of frost during the winter for short periods. A good soil on the banks of a pond or stream is indicated. For warm localities only. *See Plate 12 facing page 183.*

512. HABENARIA TOSAËNSIS, Makino

Root: of 2 small globular tubers. **Stem:** slender, up to 20″ tall, sparely leafy. **Leaves:** narrowly linear, pointed, rigid, 4″–5″ long, degenerating into bracts upwards. **Spike:** few or many-flowered, short, congested. **Flowers:** about 1″ long; dorsal sepal cordate-ovate, pointed; lateral sepals semi-obovate, pointed, reflexed, larger than the dorsal sepal; petals simple, triangular, pointed, small; lip 3-lobed; lobes linear; spur filiform, dilated and bullate at the tip, ¾″ long. *July and August.*

An interesting species with a tall, slender stem bearing a short congested spike of quaint green or green and white blossoms. It inhabits marshy country in many parts of Japan and should prove generally hardy in Great Britain in a damp or marshy spot in the rock garden or on the banks of a stream or pond, in good rich soil.

513. HABENARIA TRANSVAALENSIS, Schltr.

Root: of ovoid tubers. **Stem:** 1′–1¾′ tall, stout, leafy. **Leaves:** cauline, oblong or ovate-oblong, membranous, pointed, 2″–4″ long. **Racemes:** 4″–5″

long, rather lax. **Flowers:** about $\frac{3}{4}''$ across; dorsal sepal ovate-oblong, rather blunt; lateral sepals oblique, semiovate, pointed; petals 2-lobed; outer lobe linear, pointed; inner lobe linear, longer than the outer one; lip divided into 3 linear lobes; outer lobes diverging, longer than the centre one; spur curved, narrow at the base, thickened upwards, $\frac{3}{4}''$ long.

November and December.

A pretty and desirable plant with fairly large green and white blossoms borne in a long oblong raceme on a stout stem clothed with pale green leaves. It grows in damp or wet spots amongst shrubs in the Transvaal and probably attains its greatest elevation above sea-level on Woodbush Mountains at 6200 feet, and is there exposed to over 12° of frost for short periods during its winter rest. It should be grown in good loam and leaf soil in a damp spot in the rock garden. It is only suitable for outdoor culture in Western Britain.

514. HABENARIA TRICRURIS, Reichb. f.

Platanthera tricruris, A. Rich.

Root: a small ovoid tuber. **Stem:** $\frac{3}{4}'$–1′ tall, leafy above, sheath-clothed below. **Leaves:** ovate or ovate-oblong, pointed, $2\frac{3}{4}''$–$4\frac{1}{2}''$ long. **Raceme:** short, few-flowered. **Flowers:** nearly $\frac{3}{4}''$ across; dorsal sepal and lateral sepals ovate-oblong; petals oblong, connivent with the dorsal sepal and with the margins covered with minute hairs; lip 3-lobed, downy; outer lobes pectinate on their outer margins; centre lobe subspathulate-linear, blunt, broader than the side lobes, with an elevated line down its centre; spur cylindrical, curved, $\frac{3}{4}''$ long. *September to November.*

Quite a handsome somewhat dwarf species with fairly large green and white blossoms on a stem which is leafy above and clothed with open sheaths below. It is a native of the Abyssinian highlands, where it grows in wet soil on the exposed mountain sides at elevations up to 8000 feet, and is therefore quite hardy in Southern Britain in the bog garden in a sunny spot in peat and loam.

515. HABENARIA TRIDACTYLITES, Lindl.

Root: of 2 fair-sized oblong tubers. **Stem:** 3″–9″ tall, slender, bearing 2 leaves at the base, naked upwards. **Leaves:** oblong or oblong-lanceolate, 3″–4″ long, sub-opposite. **Raceme:** of 6 rather widely separated blossoms. **Flowers:** about $\frac{1}{2}''$ across; dorsal sepal ovate, pointed; lateral sepals linear-oblong, deflexed; petals narrowly triangular, falcate, pointed, forming a galea over the column; lip deeply divided into 3 linear lobes; spur filiform, incurved, about $\frac{3}{4}''$ long. *June and July.*

A dwarf, slender plant, producing but two leaves at the base of the flower-stem, which is naked and bears a raceme of fair-sized, rather pretty green and white blossoms. The plant inhabits damp or marshy spots on high ground in the Canary Islands and should thrive in Britain under the same conditions as *Orchis foliosa.*

516. HABENARIA TRIFLORA, Don.

Platanthera candida, Lindl.

Root: an ovoid tuber. **Stem:** ¾′–1′ tall, rather slender, leafy. **Leaves:** oblong, pointed, 1″–3″ long. **Flowers:** about 2″ long, 1–2 in number, on short stalks; dorsal sepal oblong-ovate; lateral sepals ovate-lanceolate; petals linear-subulate; lip 3-lobed, very large; outer lobes hatchet-shaped, crenulate; centre lobe shorter than the outer lobes, linear; spur very slender, straight, 1½″ long. *August.*

Were its blossoms more numerous, this species would be a most attractive garden plant. From one to two in number, they are borne on slender leafy stems and are remarkable for the length of the lip; they are white, tinted green. It is found in damp grassy places in the highlands of India, attaining its greatest altitude in the Kumaon Himalaya at 5000 feet. It may be grown outdoors in Great Britain in the warm western counties in a damp part of the rock garden in good fibrous loam and peat, in a sunny spot.

517. HABENARIA TYSONII, Bolus

Root: of ovoid tubers. **Stem:** ¾′–1′ tall, clothed with narrowly lanceolate, pointed sheaths. **Leaves:** radical, suborbicular or broader than long, sessile, rather fleshy, 1″–1½″ long. **Raceme:** 3″–5″ long, lax, many-flowered. **Flowers:** about ⅝″ across; dorsal sepal ovate, pointed; lateral sepals obliquely semiovate; petals 2-lobed; outer lobe falcate-linear, hairy on its margin; inner lobe filiform, curved bristly, longer than the outer one; lip 3-lobed, hairy; outer lobes narrowly linear, diverging; centre lobe linear, curved, longer than the side lobes; spur slender, about ½″ long.

October to February.

The pale green blossoms of this species are of fair size and are interesting although by no means showy; they are borne in a loose raceme of about two dozen on a sheath-clad flower-stem, clothed at its base by two pale green, somewhat fleshy leaves. It grows on high mountains in damp grassy places in Natal and Griqualand East where on Mount Currie at 6000 feet it is exposed to over 20° of frost during the winter. A good fibrous loam on the banks of a pond is indicated.

518. HABENARIA ULIGINOSA, Reichb. f.

Root: of narrowly oblong tubers about ½″ long. **Stem:** 18″–20″ tall, leafy. **Leaves:** linear-lanceolate, pointed, 3″–4″ long, degenerating upwards into spatha-like sheaths. **Raceme:** 3″–6″ long, densely many-flowered. **Flowers:** about ½″ across; sepals all similar, ovate-triangular, pointed; petals bilobed; lobes linear-falcate; lip deeply 3-lobed; outer lobes subfalcately lanceolate; centre lobe lanceolate, pointed; spur cylindrical, pendulous, clavate at the tip, about ⅝″ long. *October to January.*

A fairly robust plant, with a long dense raceme of rather pretty pale green and white blossoms on a tall leafy stem. This species is found on the borders of swamps and marshes both in the open and in clearings in forest, in Southern Brazil and the Island of Chiloe in Southern Chile. Plants collected from the latter locality should be at home in the damp western counties of Great Britain under the same cultural conditions as the other damp-loving species.

519. HABENARIA URCEOLATA, Clark

Diphylax urceolata, Hook. f.

Root: a small globose tuber. **Stem:** slender, recurved, 4″–6″ tall. **Leaves:** few, the radical leaf much larger than the others, elliptic-lanceolate, all membranous, pointed, 2″–4″ long. **Raceme:** 2″–3″ long, decurved. **Flowers:** about ½″ across, secund; sepals and petals narrowly lanceolate, pointed; lip entire, lanceolate, recurved, terminal half terete, pointed; spur fusiform, inflated, ⅜″ long. *August.*

A dainty little plant very suitable for alpine house culture. It has drooping racemes of fair-sized blossoms with white and pink sepals and petals and a green lip. It grows in damp places in rocky soil on the Sikkim Himalaya and Naga Hills. It reaches an elevation of 10,000 feet in the Himalaya and is exposed to about 15° of frost for considerable periods during the winter. It may be grown in the rockery in a damp place at the foot of a sandstone rock in full sun.

520. HABENARIA VAGINATA, A. Rich.

Root: a small ovoid tuber. **Stem:** about 8″ tall, clothed with a few lanceolate sheaths. **Leaves:** radical, broadly ovate, spreading, 1¾″–2¼″ long. **Raceme:** 2½″ long, many-flowered. **Flowers:** about ⅜″ long; dorsal sepal ovate, subobtuse; lateral sepals deflexed, falcate-oblong, rather blunt; petals subfalcate-oblong; lip 3-lobed; lobes subequal, linear-oblong, blunt; spur slender, slightly thickened towards the tip, nearly 1″ long.

September to November.

A very dwarf species producing a many-flowered raceme of green blossoms, interesting in the alpine house but of little decorative value. It grows in mountain bogs on the highlands of Abyssinia, where it attains an elevation of over 8000 feet and is exposed to 15° or more of frost for considerable periods. It may be grown in the bog garden or alpine house in fibrous peat mixed with a little loam and growing sphagnum-moss.

521. HABENARIA VARIABILIS, Ridl.

Root: an ovoid tuber $\frac{3}{4}''$ across. **Stem:** $1'$–$1\frac{1}{2}'$ tall, stout, leafy. **Leaves:** varying from oblong to lanceolate, pointed or blunt, appressed to the stem, degenerating into bracts upwards, 4″–5″ long. **Raceme:** 2″–7″ long, dense. **Flowers:** from $\frac{1}{8}''$–$\frac{1}{4}''$ across; dorsal sepal ovate, blunt, downy inside; lateral sepals deflexed, oblong, blunt, downy within; petals ovate, blunt, forming a hood with the dorsal sepal, more or less downy within; lip cuneate at the base, 3-lobed, subequal, oblong-obtuse; spur filiform, incurved, $\frac{3}{4}''$ long.

August to October.

This variable plant is of little decorative value, it produces rather long racemes of small green and white blossoms on fairly tall leafy stems. It is a plant of the alpine bogs in the mountains of Abyssinia, reaching its greatest altitude above sea-level on Mount Guna at 10,000 feet, and is therefore quite hardy in Great Britain in an open sunny spot in the bog garden in peat and living sphagnum-moss.

HEMIPILIA, Lindley

Dwarf, deciduous, terrestrial plants, numbering 15 species, with the habit of some of the smaller members of the genus *Habenaria*. Their root systems consist of two or more oblong tubers attached to the base of the stem, with a few stout fleshy roots above them. As soon as the seed capsules are perfected the largest tuber shrivels and the smaller ones persist and eventually produce flower-stems. The solitary leaf is frequently of large size and is, in some species, very prettily blotched and spotted with purple and silvery-white. The blossoms although pretty are rarely large enough to be termed decorative. The few known species are found in thinly-wooded country, frequently in clefts in rock, outcrops in vegetable debris, and moss. All are confined to Eastern India, China and Malaya. Propagation by imported tubers and by seeds.

522. HEMIPILIA CORDIFOLIA, Lindl.

Platanthera cordifolia, Lindl.

Root: an oblong tuber. **Leaf:** solitary, radical, amplexicaul, pointed, ovate-cordate, 2″–4″ long. **Scape:** 4″–10″ tall, slender. **Raceme:** few or many-flowered. **Flowers:** about $\frac{3}{4}''$ across; dorsal sepal oblong, blunt; lateral sepals falcately oblong; petals lanceolate, rather pointed; lip slightly 3-lobed; outer lobes rounded, small; centre lobe broad, subcrenate; spur recurved, small.

August.

A pretty little plant suitable for alpine house culture in a pan of loam, peat and sphagnum-moss. It produces a slender stem bearing a raceme of fairly large blossoms with pale pink sepals and petals and a deep pink lip. The plant grows in thinly wooded country and in ravines in rocky soil in the Himalaya from Nepal to Simla at altitudes from 5000–8000 feet, and may be tried outdoors in the warm moist western counties of Great Britain in the rock garden in the same compost as recommended for alpine house culture.

523. HEMIPILIA FLABELLATA, Bur & Franch.

Root: of ovoid or oblong tubers. **Leaf:** 3″–4″ long, solitary, radical, ovate-cordate, sheathing at the base, and with a thorn-like point. **Scape:** about 12″ tall, fairly stout, clothed with one or two small bracts. **Raceme:** 3″–4″ long, few-flowered. **Flowers:** about ½″ across; dorsal sepal small, oblong-elliptic; lateral sepals elliptic, suboblique, pointed; petals oblong, forming a galea with the dorsal sepal; lip narrow at the base, flabellate, slightly dilated at the tip, where it is toothed, the margins are smooth; spur cylindrical, pendulous. *August.*

A decorative species with loose racemes of pretty fringed blossoms varying from light rose to purplish-rose, with a deeply coloured lip. The plant is found in moist shady places among dwarf shrubs and on the margins of woods in Yunnan, Western China, at over 10,000 feet above sea-level. It should be quite hardy in Western and Southern Britain in a damp shady spot in the rock garden in good leaf-soil and loam.

524. HEMIPILIA HENRYI, Reichb. f.

Root: of oblong tubers. **Stem:** ¾′–1′ tall, fairly stout, smooth. **Leaf:** solitary, subradical, cordate, ovate, sessile, shortly pointed, 1½″–4″ long. **Raceme:** about 4″ long, many-flowered. **Flowers:** about ¾″ across; sepals ovate-oblong, blunt, lateral ones suboblique and spreading; petals oblong, rather blunt; lip obovate or square; lobes rounded or blunt; spur thickened at the base, gradually becoming narrower to the tip.

August and September.

A very beautiful species with large rose-pink blossoms with a deep pink lip. It is found in shady places on the mountains of Hupeh, Tchang, etc., China, at from 7000–9000 feet, and may be tried outdoors in Great Britain in warm sheltered localities, in the rock garden in peat and leaf-soil.

525. HEMIPILIA YUNNANENSIS, Schltr.

H. Bulleyi, Rolfe. *H. cordifolia* var. *yunnanensis*, Finet

Root: of oblong or ovoid tubers on slender fibres. **Leaf:** solitary, radical, ovate or orbicular, pointed, cordate at the base, about 1¼″ long. **Scape:** 4″–6″ tall, round, smooth, with a solitary sheath about the middle. **Raceme:** about 1½″ long, cylindrical, lax, few-flowered. **Flowers:** about ½″ across;

dorsal sepal ovate, blunt, concave, erect; lateral sepals ovate, blunt, reflexed and oblique; petals rhomboid-ovate, erect or oblique; lip cuneate at the base, 3-lobed; outer lobes ligulate-triangular; centre lobe nearly square or rhomboid, crenate; spur cylindrical, blunt, $\frac{1}{2}''$ long. *June to August.*

A dainty little species with few-flowered spikes of pretty rose-coloured blossoms with deep rose or crimson markings on the lip. The bright green leaves are spotted with purple and their under-surface is entirely purple. The plant is found in stony places on dry open banks amongst thin scrub in Western Yunnan, Western China, at elevations of from 7000–10,000 feet above sea-level. It should prove hardy in the rock garden in a sunny spot in fibrous loam.

HERMINIUM, Linnæus

Thirty-four species of deciduous terrestrial plants, known as Musk Orchids. They have short root stocks emitting long or short somewhat fleshy fibres; on the tips of several of the largest fibres an almost globular tuber is formed which eventually produces a flowering stem. The stem is usually erect and slender and is clothed with a few linear, lanceolate or oblong leaves. The blossoms are produced in fairly dense spikes which are secund in most of the species; they are too small to have any garden value. In a state of nature they are found in open hilly or mountainous country, frequently on limestone formations, and are true alpine plants in the Himalaya, where they are found in the short turf beyond the elfinwood but a few thousand feet from the snow-line. All the species are scattered over northern parts of the Old World and are most numerous in the mountains of Asia. Propagation by separation of the young tubers and by seeds.

526. HERMINIUM ALASCHANICUM, Maxim.

Root: of 2 oblong or ovoid tubers. **Stem:** 6″–12″ tall, slender, leafy. **Leaves:** oblong, narrower upwards, 1″–$1\frac{1}{2}''$ long. **Spike:** 2″–3″ long, dense, secund. **Flowers:** about $\frac{1}{8}''$ across; dorsal sepal ovate-lanceolate; lateral sepals lanceolate; petal narrow, with 3 teeth at the tip; lip concave, cuneate at the base, 3-lobed; lobes parallel, linear, pointed; spur, saccate, distinct. *September.*

This species is allied to *H. Monorchis* and has small pale yellowish-green blossoms, of botanical interest only. It is found in open pasture land in Southern Mongolia and should be quite hardy in Britain in an open sunny position in the rock garden in sandy loam.

527. HERMINIUM ALPINUM, Lindl.

Aceras alpinum, Pers. *Chamærepis alpina*, Spreng. *Chamæorchis alpina*, Rich. *Orchis alpina*, Schk. *O. graminea*, Crantz

Root: of 2 ovoid or oblong tubers about ½″ long. **Leaves:** mainly basal, numerous, linear, 1″–2½″ long, erect or slightly spreading. **Scape:** 2″–4″ tall, fairly stout, erect. **Spike:** ½″–2″ long, cylindrical, rather dense. **Flowers:** ¼″ long; dorsal sepal oblong, rounded at the tip; lateral sepals oblong-lanceolate, slightly curved; petals very narrowly oblong, all conniving and forming a hood over the column; lip variable, usually 3-lobed, with small outer lobes and a large rounded centre one. It is sometimes entire and lanceolate.
June to August.

A tiny alpine Orchid of no decorative value, with small green or purple blossoms in a short spike. It grows amongst short herbage in the alpine pastures of the Alps of Switzerland, France and Austria and is also found on the mountains of Scandinavia. It may be grown in an open spot in the rock garden in damp loam and peat.

528. HERMINIUM ANGUSTIFOLIUM, Benth.

H. longicruris, Wright; *Aceras angustifolia*, Lindl.

Root: a fair-sized oblong tuber. **Stem:** stout or slender, 1′–3′ tall, bearing but few leaves. **Leaves:** scattered, linear, 2″–8″ long. **Spike:** 2″–10″ long, slender, subsecund, very many-flowered. **Flowers:** decurved, ⅛″ across; sepals oblong, blunt; petals very narrowly linear, membranous, pointed; lip usually divided into 3 narrow lobes, the centre one being the shortest.
August.

A very tall spire-like Orchid, interesting but of no garden value. Numbers of very small pale green blossoms are borne in a long spike on a slender flower-stem clothed with one or several leaves. It grows in a variety of situations, but chiefly in open grassy places such as the flat grassy tops of cliffs in mountainous districts of India, Burma, China, Manchuria and Japan. In the Himalaya it attains an altitude of 15,000 feet, so is perfectly hardy in Britain in an open spot in the rock garden in fibrous loam and leaf-soil; the addition of a little calcareous matter would be beneficial.

529. HERMINIUM ANGUSTILABRE, King

Root: of oblong or fusiform tubers. **Stem:** about 4″ tall, clothed at its base with a solitary leaf and 2–3 sheaths above. **Leaf:** basal, oblong or elliptic, blunt, slightly stem-clasping. **Spike:** about 1″ long, few-flowered. **Flowers:** about ⅛″ across; dorsal sepal oblong or orbicular, concave, shortly pointed; lateral sepals narrowly pointed, deflexed; petals similar, but somewhat narrower; lip linear, pointed, deflexed. *July.*

A dwarf plant producing a slender stem bearing a short spike of very small green blossoms, of botanical interest only. It is found in open rocky places in damp situations in the Sikkim Himalaya at an elevation of 10,000 feet above sea-level. It should be quite hardy in the rock garden in a damp spot in peat and leaf-soil.

530. HERMINIUM BIPOROSUM, Maxim.

Root: of thickened fleshy fibres. **Leaf:** radical, oblong, blunt, 3-nerved, about 1″ long. **Scape:** slender, naked, about 4″ long. **Flower:** solitary, rarely more, $\frac{1}{8}$″ across; dorsal sepal short, ovate; lateral sepals and petals ovate-elliptic, suboblique; lip linear-oblong. *July.*

This plant is in stature similar to the preceding species and has the same type of tiny, pale green blossoms. It is found in sparely grassy country in the vicinity of Kuku-nor, Tangut, North-Eastern Tibet. It should be quite hardy in Great Britain in a fairly dry, open spot in the rock garden in sandy peat and leaf-soil.

531. HERMINIUM CŒLOCERAS, Schltr.

H. unicorne, Kränzl. *Peristylus cœloceras*, Finet

Root: an ovate-oblong tuber about $\frac{5}{8}$″ long. **Stem:** 3″–9″ tall. **Leaves:** 2 or rarely 3 in number, oblong, pointed, 3″–4″ long. **Spike:** 1″–2″ long, rather dense. **Flowers:** about $\frac{1}{8}$″ across; dorsal sepal broadly ovate, blunt; lateral sepals ovate, blunt; petals broadly ovate or suborbicular, blunt; lip 3-lobed; lateral lobes rather triangular, parallel; centre lobe similar but longer. *July and August.*

This little species is very like *H. Monorchis* in habit and has a rather short, slender stem clothed with a few pretty leaves. The blossoms which are rose-purple and white and sweetly fragrant, are borne in rather dense spikes. It should make a pretty little specimen in the alpine house in a pan of fibrous loam with plenty of sand. In Western Yunnan, Western China, it inhabits dry mountain pastures, at an elevation of from 9000–10,000 feet.

532. HERMINIUM CONGESTUM, Lindl.

Habenaria unalaschcense, Reichb. f. *H. Schischmareffiana*, Chamiss. *Neottia macrophylla*, Don; *Platanthera Schischmareffiana*, Lindl. *Spiranthes macrophylla*, Spreng. *S. unalaschcensis*, Spreng.

Root: a small oblong tuber. **Stem:** $\frac{1}{2}$′–1$\frac{1}{2}$′ tall, leafy. **Leaves:** 1–3 in number, oblong-lanceolate, 3″–6″ long. **Spike:** 2″–4″ long, many-flowered. **Flowers:** about $\frac{1}{6}$″ across; dorsal sepal broadly ovate; lateral sepals oblong;

petals ovate, as long as the sepals ; lip ovate or triangular-ovate, fleshy, pointed, pouched at its base, at times almost dilated into lobes. *July and August.*

The small green blossoms of this species are of no decorative value. It grows in very elevated alpine pastures and in the arctic regions in grassy, rocky places. It is found in the Himalaya at 16,000 feet above sea-level, North-Western America and the Aleutian Islands near Alaska. It may be grown in cool moist localities in Great Britain in the rock garden under the same conditions as the preceding species.

533. HERMINIUM DUTHIEI, Hook. f.

Root: a small oblong tuber. **Stem:** 4″–6″ tall, slender. **Leaves:** 2 in number, towards the middle or base of the stem, linear or oblong-lanceolate, 1″–2½″ long. **Spike:** curved, 2″–4″ long, many-flowered. **Flowers:** about ⅛″ across, subsecund; dorsal sepal broadly oblong; lateral sepals oblong; petals ovate-lanceolate, subfalcate, fleshy; lip triangular or orbicular-ovate but variable, pouched at the base. *August.*

A very dwarf and delicate plant with curved spikes of very small pale green blossoms. It is of botanical interest only. In a state of nature it grows on grassy cliffs near the Khasi Pass at Garwhal in the Western Himalaya at an altitude above sea-level of 12,000 feet, and is therefore quite hardy in Great Britain in an open sunny part of the rock garden in good fibrous loam and sharp sand.

534. HERMINIUM ECALCARATUM, Schltr.

Peristylus ecalcaratus, Finet

Root: of irregular, globular tubers. **Stem:** 6″–9″ tall, slender, usually naked. **Leaves:** usually 2 in number, rarely more, basal, oblong or lanceolate, 1″–3″ long. **Spike:** 1″–2″ long, many-flowered. **Flowers:** about $\frac{3}{16}$″ across; sepals oblong, blunt; petals ovate, blunt, forming a hood over the column with the sepals; lip narrow at the base, spoon-shaped towards the tip, obscurely 3-lobed, lobes rounded. *July and August.*

A slender Chinese plant with spikes of very small pale green flowers of no decorative value. It is found in open grassy places on the mountains of Yunnan, Western China, at 10,000–12,000 feet above sea-level, and should be quite hardy in Great Britain in an open spot in the rock garden in calcareous, fibrous loam.

535. HERMINIUM FALLAX, Hook. f.

Cybele alpina, Falc.

Root: a small oblong tuber. **Stem:** ½′–1½′ tall, slender, clothed with 1 or 2 leaves about the middle of the stem, and lanceolate sheaths above and below.

Leaves: linear or linear lanceolate, pointed, 2″–5″ long. **Spike:** 2″–5″ long, lax or densely-flowered. **Flowers:** nearly $\frac{1}{4}$″ across; sepals oblong or ovate-lanceolate, spreading; petals narrowly lanceolate, erect, falcate; lip shorter than the sepals, obscurely 3-lobed, oblong or linear. *July and August.*

A slender plant with a long narrow spike of small pale yellowish-green blossoms of no decorative value. It grows in open places in short herbage in the alpine and sub-alpine districts of the Himalaya, attaining an elevation of 12,000 feet above sea-level and is subjected to more than 25° of frost for short periods during the winter. It may be grown in a cool spot in the rock garden in fibrous loam and sand.

536. HERMINIUM FORRESTII, Schltr.

H. Josephii, Finet

Root: of oblong tubers and a few filiform rootlets. **Leaves:** 2 in number, basal, elliptic or oblong-elliptic, pointed, opposite, sheathing below. **Scape:** 3″–6″ tall, slender, naked. **Spike:** 1″–2″ long, of 6–12 blossoms. **Flowers:** about $\frac{1}{8}$″ across; dorsal sepal ovate, pointed; lateral sepals oblong-ligulate, blunt, equalling the dorsal sepal in length, spreading; petals lanceolate-ligulate, blunt, oblique; lip suborbicular-ovate, with 2 rows of lamellæ on its upper surface. *July.*

A plant of botanical interest only; it has slender spikes of tiny pale green blossoms and is very closely allied to *H. Josephii* (Reichb. f.), an Indian species. It is found in open mountain meadows in Yunnan, Western China, at from 11,000–12,000 feet above sea-level. It should prove quite hardy in Great Britain in an open position in the rock garden in good fibrous loam.

537. HERMINIUM GRACILE, King

Root: of fusiform tubers on thickened fibres. **Stem:** 4″–6″ tall, bearing a solitary leaf at its base. **Scape:** naked. **Leaf:** obovate or oblong, shortly pointed, about 1$\frac{1}{2}$″ long. **Spike:** 1$\frac{1}{2}$″–2$\frac{1}{2}$″ long, flowers few, distant. **Flowers:** about $\frac{1}{8}$″ across; dorsal sepal elliptic or orbicular, forming an elliptic galea with the petals; lateral sepals elliptic, deflexed, concave, blunt; lip narrowly ovate, tip blunt, deflexed. *July.*

A dwarf slender species with a solitary leaf and naked scape bearing a few widely separated tiny pale green blossoms of no decorative value. It is found in open rocky places amongst spare herbage in the Lachen valley, Sikkim Himalaya, at about 10,000 feet above sea-level, and should be quite hardy in cultivation in Great Britain under the same conditions as the preceding species.

538. HERMINIUM GRAMINEUM, Lindl.

Neottia monophylla, Don; *Spiranthes monophylla*, Spreng.

Root: a very small oblong tuber. **Stem:** 2″–6″ tall, very slender. **Leaf:** solitary, linear, pointed, 2″–6″ long. **Spike:** 1″–3½″ long, stem with rough ridges, many-flowered. **Flowers:** about ⅛″ across, secund, suberect; dorsal sepal oblong or broadly ovate; lateral sepals ovate, blunt, spreading; petals erect, linear, subfalcate; lip flat, with a concave base, ovate, pointed, variable in breadth. *August.*

A very tiny species with a solitary grassy leaf and spikes of small greenish-yellow blossoms. It is of botanical interest only, but might prove attractive in the alpine house as its flowers are probably scented. It inhabits open grassy places in the Himalaya from Kumaon to Nepal reaching an altitude of 8000 feet. It may be grown outdoors in Great Britain in all but the bleakest localities, in the rock garden in calcareous fibrous loam.

539. HERMINIUM JAFFREYANUM, King

Root: of oblong tubers about ⅜″ long. **Stem:** 3″–4″ tall, clothed near the base with 2 leaves, and a few sheaths above. **Leaves:** linear-lanceolate, 4″–5″ long. **Spike:** 1½″–2½″ long, dense, many-flowered. **Flowers:** about ⅛″ across; sepals elliptic, blunt, tip concave; petals ligulate, ringent; lip triangular, blunt. *August.*

Usually a more dwarf plant than the preceding species, with a slender scape bearing two leaves at its base and a dense many-flowered spike of very small green blossoms, of no decorative value. It is found on open grassy cliffs in the Sikkim Himalaya at elevations of from 8000–10,000 feet above sea-level and should therefore be quite hardy in Great Britain, in an open sunny spot in the rock garden in fibrous sandy loam.

540. HERMINIUM JOSEPHII, Reichb. f.

H. grandiflorum, Lindl.

Root: a rather small oblong tuber. **Stem:** ½′–1′ tall, stout, usually bearing 2 leaves, rarely 3. **Leaves:** lanceolate or oblong, 3″–5″ long. **Spike:** 1″–4″ long, lax-flowered. **Flowers:** over ⅜″ across; sepals ovate, lateral ones falcate, all erect; petals ovate, with narrowed, thickened, blunt tips; lip entire, broadly ovate, pointed, flat, with a thickened point.

July and August.

This species has larger blossoms than any other member of the genus, they are borne in a loose spike and are of the same pale yellowish-green colour as most of the other species; they are of little decorative value. The plant grows in open spots among short herbage in the Sikkim Himalaya, reaching an altitude of 14,000 feet, where it is exposed to over 20° of frost for considerable periods. It may be grown in the rock garden in a cool spot in a good calcareous loam and leaf-soil.

541. HERMINIUM LIMPRICHTII, Schltr.

Root: of 2 oblong tubers. **Leaf:** solitary, basal, strap-shaped or linear, rather pointed, suberect, 2″–2½″ long. **Scape:** 4″–6″ tall, slender, naked. **Raceme:** 1½″–2″ long, slender, many-flowered. **Flowers:** about ⅛″ across; dorsal sepal oblong, blunt; lateral sepals similar, oblique; petals subfalcate-lanceolate, oblique, about as long as the sepals; lip ovate, 3-lobed; lobes linear-oblong, blunt, of equal length. *August.*

A rather dwarf plant with a slender stem clothed at its base with a grassy leaf, and terminating in a rather dense spike of minute green blossoms of no decorative value. It is found on the wooded sides of mountains in Yunnan, Western China, attaining an elevation of 10,500 feet above sea-level and should therefore be quite hardy in Great Britain in a damp shady part of the rock garden, in fibrous peat and leaf-soil

542. HERMINIUM MONORCHIS, Br.

Ophrys Monorchis, Linn.

Root: an almost globular tuber. **Stem:** 4″–10″ tall, naked, or rarely with 1 sheath. **Leaves:** 2, rarely 3 in number, oblong or lanceolate, radical, 1″–4″ long. **Spike:** 1″–2″ long, many-flowered. **Flowers:** about ⅙″ across, secund; sepals and petals subconnivent; sepals oblong, blunt; petals ovate, with unequal sides towards the base; lip concave at the base, divided into 3 narrow, entire lobes. *May to August.*

This is our native Musk Orchis, so named on account of the musky odour emitted by its blossoms at night. The small green blossoms are of no decorative value. It is remarkable for its extremely wide habitat, being found all over Europe in hilly districts and the greater part of temperate Asia, reaching an elevation of 13,000 feet in the Himalaya. It usually grows in hilly calcareous pastures, and may be grown in the rock garden in fibrous calcareous loam and leaf-soil.

543. HERMINIUM NEOTINEOIDES, Ames and Schltr.

Root: of 2 small oblong tubers. **Stem:** 6″–9″ tall, slender, naked, erect. **Leaves:** usually 3 in number, suberect, strap-shaped, rather pointed, tapering to a short stalk, 1½″–2½″ long. **Raceme:** about 3″ long, dense, cylindrical, many-flowered. **Flowers:** about $\frac{3}{16}$″ across; dorsal sepal elliptic, blunt; lateral sepals elliptic or ovate-lanceolate, oblique; lip ovate, concave, 3-lobed;

outer lobes subfalcate-lanceolate, blunt; centre lobe ovate-lanceolate, blunt, longer than the lateral lobes. *July and August.*

This species, like the majority of its brethren, is only of botanical interest; it has dense, slender, cylindrical racemes or spikes of very small pale yellowish-green blossoms on a grass-like stem, clothed at its base with a few narrow leaves. The plant is found in damp shady places amongst rocks at 12,000 feet above sea-level in Western Szechuan, China, and may be given the same cultural treatment as *H. Limprichtii.*

544. HERMINIUM OPHIOGLOSSOIDES, Schltr.

Root: of oblong tubers. **Leaf:** solitary, basal, elliptic-ligulate, or oblanceolate-elliptic, sheathing at the base, 2″–3″ long. **Scape:** 3″–9″ tall, naked, slender, usually curved. **Spike:** 2″–4″ long, few or many-flowered, usually secund. **Flowers:** about $\frac{3}{16}$″ across; dorsal sepal ovate, blunt; lateral sepals lanceolate-ligulate, blunt, oblique, as long as the dorsal sepal; petals narrowly lanceolate-linear blunt; lip oblong, 3-lobed, segments narrowly linear, rather pointed, centre one the longest; spur saccate, conical blunt. *June.*

A quaint little species of no decorative value, with small greenish-yellow blossoms like those of *H. Monorchis.* It is found in moist grassy places on the banks of streams in Western Yunnan, Western China, at from 10,000–11,000 feet above sea-level. It should prove quite hardy in Great Britain in the bog garden or in a very damp place in the rock garden in peat, loam and sphagnum-moss.

545. HERMINIUM ORBICULARE, Hook. f.

Root: an oblong or ovoid tuber. **Stem:** 4″–6″ tall, very slender, clothed with minute subulate sheaths. **Leaves:** 2 in number, near the base of the stem, orbicular or oblong-lanceolate, 1″–1½″ long. **Spike:** 2″–3″ long, many-flowered. **Flowers:** about $\frac{1}{16}$″ across, secund; dorsal sepal ovate-oblong, small; lateral sepals orbicular-oblong, blunt, membranous; petals broadly oblong, membranous; lip orbicular, pouched at its base.

July and August.

This tiny species has the most minute blossoms of the genus; they are of a yellowish-green colour and of botanical interest only. It is found in grassy and rocky places in the Chumbi Valley of Sikkim Himalaya at sufficient elevation to ensure its hardiness in all but the bleakest parts of Great Britain. It may be grown in the alpine house or rock garden in good fibrous loam and peat.

546. HERMINIUM PUGIONIFORME, Lindl.

Root: a very small oblong or orbicular tuber. **Stem:** 2″–5″ tall, very slender or quite stout, clothed with a few sheaths or bracts. **Leaf:** solitary, basal, elongate-spathulate, blunt, 1″–3″ long. **Spike:** short, few-flowered. **Flowers:** about $\frac{1}{12}$″ across; dorsal sepal orbicular; lateral sepals very broadly ovate, blunt; petals oblong-ovate; lip dagger-shaped, dilated or pouched at its base, about as long as the sepals. *July to September.*

A dwarf species with rather short spikes of few, erect, pale green blossoms on a fairly stout stem clothed at its base with a solitary rounded leaf. It is of no horticultural value. It grows on exposed grassy cliffs and stony places in the Himalaya from Kashmir to Sikkim, where it reaches an elevation of 16,000 feet above sea-level. It should be perfectly hardy in Great Britain in the alpine house or rock garden in good calcareous loam and leaf-soil, with plenty of sharp sand.

547. HERMINIUM QUINQUELOBUM, King

Root: of oblong or globose tubers about $\frac{3}{4}$″ long. **Stem:** about 9″ tall. **Leaves:** usually 2, linear-lanceolate, pointed, about 7″ long. **Scape:** with 2 or 3 linear-lanceolate sheaths or bracts. **Spike:** 3″–4″ long, slender, flowers scattered. **Flowers:** about $\frac{1}{8}$″ across; dorsal sepal and lateral sepals ovate-oblong, blunt, ringent; petals linear, pointed, 3-lobed, lobes blunt, outer ones spreading. *August.*

A fairly robust species with a long slender spike of very small green blossoms of no decorative value. It is found on open grassy cliffs and in mountain pastures in the Sikkim Himalaya at an elevation of 9500 feet above sea-level. It should be hardy in all but the bleakest parts of Great Britain in an open sunny spot in the rock garden in fibrous loam and sand.

548. HERMINIUM SOULIEI, Schltr.

Root: of thick fusiform tubers on short thick fibres. **Stem:** 12″–16″ tall, thick and fleshy. **Leaves:** cauline and basal, suberect, lanceolate, pointed, sheathing at the base, 3″–4″ long. **Spike:** about 7″ long, densely many-flowered. **Flowers:** about $\frac{3}{16}$″ across; dorsal sepal ovate, smooth; lateral sepals obliquely oblong, spreading; petals linear-oblong, spreading; lip suborbicular, divided into 3 segments, outer ones linear-subulate, falcate and pointed, centre one lanceolate. *June and July.*

This rather tall species has the same yellowish-green coloured blossoms as most of the other members of the genus. It is of botanical interest only and is found in grassy openings in pine forests in Western Yunnan, Western China, at from 8,000–9,000 feet above sea-level. It is also found in Eastern Tibet. It should be hardy in the warmer parts of the Kingdom in a well drained part of the rock garden in loam and leaf-soil.

549. HERMINIUM TANGUITICUM, Rolfe

Herminium alaschanicum var. *tangutica*, Maxim.

Root: of ovoid-globose tubers, about $\frac{1}{2}''$ long. **Stem:** $2''$–$6''$ tall, clothed at its base with 2 or 3 leaves. **Leaves:** ovate-oblong, rather pointed, $\frac{3}{4}''$–$2''$ long. **Raceme:** $\frac{1}{2}''$–$1''$ long, densely many-flowered. **Flowers:** about $\frac{1}{4}''$ across; sepals ovate-oblong, rather blunt; petals obscurely 3-lobed, broad at the base, caudate and pointed at the tip; lip 3-lobed; outer lobes oblong, blunt, divaricate; centre lobe caudate, pointed. *August and September.*

A small fragile species suitable for alpine house cultivation; it produces a dense raceme of comparatively large green and purple blossoms, on a very slender stem, clothed at its base with two or three small rounded leaves. It is found in rocky places at Tangut, Kansu, in Tibet, and Western China, at elevations up to 11,000 feet above sea-level. It should be perfectly hardy in Great Britain in the rock garden, in an open sunny position in calcareous loam.

550. HERMINIUM YUNNANENSE, Rolfe

Root: an ovoid or ovoid-oblong tuber about $\frac{1}{2}''$ long. **Leaf:** 1, oblong or linear-oblong, pointed, suberect, leathery, $1\frac{1}{2}''$–$2\frac{1}{2}''$ long. **Scape:** $6''$–$12''$ tall, clothed with a few ovate-lanceolate sheaths. **Raceme:** about $2''$ long, oblong, dense, many-flowered. **Flowers:** about $\frac{1}{8}''$ across; sepals ovate, equal, rather blunt, concave; petals similar but smaller; lip oblong, concave at the base, with 3 teeth or small lobes at the apex. *September.*

The tiny greenish-yellow blossoms of this species are of botanical interest only. The plant is found in damp barren moorland in Western Yunnan at elevations up to 10,000 feet and should be quite hardy in Great Britain in the rock garden fully exposed to the sun in damp sandy peat.

HERSCHELIA, Lindley

These exquisitely beautiful plants are known in South Africa as Blue Disas, to which genus they are very closely allied and in which they were formally included. They are slender stemmed, deciduous terrestrial plants with oblong or oval, somewhat irregular tubers, of considerable size; they are usually sessile on the base of the stem with a few short fleshy roots above them. Each tuber perishes after it has produced a flower-stem and seed capsules, fresh ones are formed each season to take the place of those that have supplied the nourishment for the flowers and seeds. The narrow grassy leaves which are produced at the base of the stem are frequently shrivelled up before the plants are in blossom. The wiry flower-stem is clothed with a few sheaths and terminates in few-flowered spikes of beautiful blossoms. The plants, about 16 in number, are confined to Africa, south of the equator. They should have the same culture and may be propagated in the same manner as *Disas*.

551. HERSCHELIA BAURII, Kränzl.

Disa Baurii, Bolus

Root: an irregular tuber. **Stem:** slender. **Leaves:** radical, linear-filiform, ½′–1′ long. **Scape:** ¾′–1¾′ long, sheath-clothed. **Spike:** 4″–6″ long, lax, of about 12 blossoms. **Flowers:** about ¾″ across; dorsal sepal galeate, broadly ovate; spur narrow, thickened upwards, ⅜″ long; lateral sepals elliptic-oblong; petals dilated at the base in front, then narrow and again dilated at the tip, falcately bent; lip broadly elliptic, deeply lacerated.

September to February.

A very beautiful and desirable plant with large blue or blue-purple blossoms in long spikes on slender stems springing from a tuft of grassy leaves, which wither before the flowers are in perfection. It grows on hill and mountain slopes in fairly long grass, which its flower-stems over-top, in Tembuland and the Transvaal, where it probably attains its greatest elevation near Verrers Poort, Middleberg, at 5000 feet, and is there subjected to 15° of frost during the winter for short periods. It should be given a damp fibrous loam in a sunny spot.

552. HERSCHELIA CHARPENTIERIANA, Kränzl.

Disa Charpentieriana, Reichb. f. *Disa macroglottis*, Sond.

Root: an irregular tuber. **Stem:** rather slender. **Leaves:** elongate-linear or subfiliform, ¾′–1¼′ long, about 9 in number. **Scape:** 1¼′–1½′ tall, sheath-clothed. **Spike:** 3″–5″ long, of about 6 blossoms. **Flowers:** over ¾″ across; dorsal sepal galeate, ovate; spur slender, curved at the apex, ½″ long; lateral sepals ovate, spreading or deflexed; petals falcate-oblong, dilated at the base, oblique and deeply fringed at the tip, ascending; lip long-unguiculate, broken up into narrow, somewhat fleshy filaments.

November to January.

This is a handsome species with large greenish blossoms suffused with dull violet-blue; the tinting has a resemblance to the colouring of some of the *Helleborus* species. It grows in damp places on the hills and mountains amongst fairly tall grass and reeds in South-Western Cape Colony, and probably reaches its greatest elevation on the summit of the Zwartberg Pass near Prince Albert at 5300 feet, where it is exposed to over 20° of frost during the winter. A moist fibrous loam in full sun is indicated.

553. HERSCHELIA MULTIFIDA, Rolfe

Disa multifida, Lindl. *Disa lacera*, Kränzl.

Root: an irregular tuber. **Stem:** rather slender. **Leaves:** filiform, about $5\frac{1}{2}''$ long, few. **Scape:** about $1\frac{1}{2}'$ tall, sheath-clothed. **Spike:** about 3″ long, bearing about 4 flowers. **Flowers:** nearly $\frac{3}{4}''$ across; dorsal sepal galeate, ovate, with reflexed apex; spur narrowly conical, $\frac{3}{8}''$ long; lateral sepals narrowly ovate or triangular-ovate, very pointed; petals 2-lobed; lower lobe broadly rounded-oblong; upper lobe broadly oblong at the base, dilated, crenulate, obliquely apiculate at the tip; lip dilated and cut into several branched filaments. *October to January.*

This is also a large-flowered plant with much the same colouring as the previous species. It is a desirable garden plant and grows in a state of nature on grassy mountain slopes, and is confined, so far as is known, to the Blue Berg in the Clanwilliam Division of Western Cape Colony, where at 5000 feet above sea-level it is exposed to 20° or more of frost for short periods during the winter. It should be grown in a damp spot, fully exposed to the sun, in good fibrous loam.

554. HERSCHELIA SPATHULATA, Rolfe

Orchis spathulata, Linn. *Satyrium spathulatum*, Thunb. *Disa propinqua* var. *trifida*, Sond. *D. spathulata*, Sw.

Root: an irregular tuber. **Stem:** rather slender. **Leaves:** narrowly-linear, slightly arching, 3″–5″ long. **Scape:** $\frac{3}{4}'$–1′ tall, sheath-clothed. **Spike:** about 3″ long. **Flowers:** over $\frac{3}{4}''$ across; dorsal sepal galeate, broadly ovate; spur broadly conical, blunt, $\frac{1}{4}''$ long; lateral sepals ovate, with shortly falcate apex; petals falcate, obliquely dilated at the base in front, constricted in the middle, 2-lobed at the apex; lip broadly cordate, crenulate, frequently 3-lobed. *November to February.*

A dwarf species with from one to five large lilac-pink or purple blossoms borne on a slender stem from amidst about a dozen arching, grassy, bright green leaves. A very beautiful and desirable plant. It grows in moist grassy places in the highlands and on the banks of streams in valleys in South-Western Cape Colony and probably reaches its greatest elevation near Zwartbosch Kraal at 5000 feet, where it experiences 20° or more of frost during its winter rest. It should be given a raised position in the bog garden or on the banks of a pond in peat and loam, in the sun.

HEXALECTRIS, Rafin.

This genus contains but one species, it is an erect, leafless herb having much the appearance of a *Corallorhiza* and, like all the members of that genus, it is a saprophyte, living upon decaying leaves and twigs in the shady woods which it inhabits. The root is a mass of scaly, coral-like, fleshy fibres, buried but a few inches beneath the surface of the rotting vegetation in which it grows. The stout, erect, scale-clad, lurid stem bears a loose raceme of rather small soberly tinted blossoms. The plant is confined to the South-Eastern United States and Mexico and is only suitable for culture outdoors in Great Britain in very sheltered and mild districts. As with members of the genus above mentioned, this plant should be removed from its native habitat with as much of the soil in which it is growing as can be conveniently taken, and transported to the rock garden. Propagation by imported rhizomes or roots.

555. HEXALECTRIS APHYLLUS, Raf.

Root: scaly, coral-like. **Leaves:** none, their place being taken by sheathing or sessile scales. **Scape:** 4″–18″ tall, stout, usually erect. **Raceme:** 2″–12″ long, lax, many-flowered, interrupted. **Flowers:** $\frac{1}{2}$″ across; sepals linear-oblong or elliptic, more or less curved, rather pointed; petals similar to the sepals only shorter; lip 3-lobed, lobes rounded, centre one orbicular, crisped. *May to August.*

A quaint leafless plant with an erect greenish-purple sheath-clothed stem and a long loose raceme of smallish blossoms with brownish-purple segments striped with light purple. The plant is of no great horticultural value, and is found in shady woods growing in decaying leaves and other vegetable debris from Virginia and Missouri to Mexico. It may be grown outdoors in the warmer parts of Great Britain in a damp shady spot in the rock garden in pure vegetable soil and decaying oak and beech leaves.

HOLOTHRIX, L. C. Richard

The 57 deciduous, terrestrial Orchids which constitute this genus contain but few species of horticultural merit. They are usually dwarf plants with two or more oval tubers at the base of the short root stock, one tuber, after having supplied the nourishment for the growing plant, perishes, whilst the others persist and eventually give rise to flowering plants. One or two sessile rounded leaves are produced near the base of the slender hairy flower-stems, which terminate in one-sided spikes of small blossoms, mostly some shade of yellow. The various species are scattered over Africa from Abyssinia to the Cape, being more numerous in species in the south of the continent; they inhabit open rocky country and are frequently found at considerable elevations above sea-level. A considerable number are sufficiently hardy for culture outdoors in the warmer parts of Britain. Propagation by imported tubers and by seeds.

556. HOLOTHRIX ARACHNOIDEA, Reichb. f.

Root: an ovoid tuber. **Leaves:** radical, ovate, transverse, rather pointed, subcordate at the base, $\frac{3}{4}''$–$1\frac{1}{2}''$ long. **Scape:** 6″–9″ tall, hairy. **Spike:** 1″–$1\frac{1}{2}''$ long, bearing from 6–10 blossoms. **Flowers:** $\frac{3}{16}''$ across; dorsal sepal and lateral sepals lanceolate, pointed; petals oblong, abruptly cuspidate, with a much exserted apex; lip cuneate-flabellate, 5-lobed, lobes ligulate, pointed, disc papillose; spur conical, small. *September and October.*

A neat little plant with a short spike of tiny yellow blossoms on a slender stem clothed at its base with two oval leaves. It should prove attractive in a pan of fibrous peat and rich loam in the alpine house. It grows in damp places amongst short herbage on the mountains of Abyssinia; on Debra Erki it attains an elevation of 7000 feet above sea-level and may therefore be grown outdoors in the warmer parts of Great Britain.

557. HOLOTHRIX BRONGNIARTIANA, Reichb. f.

Root: a small ovoid tuber. **Leaves:** broadly ovate, radical, rather pointed, 1″–$1\frac{1}{2}''$ long. **Scape:** about 2″ tall, very slender, very hairy. **Spike:** short, rather secund. **Flowers:** about $\frac{1}{8}''$ across; sepals oblong, pointed, at times slightly velvety outside; petals ovate-falcate, pointed; lip cuneate-oblong, blunt, with the apex at times toothed; spur slender, very minute. *August to October.*

A very tiny plant consisting of two small, oval, deep green leaves pressed flat on the soil surface, and short spikes of tiny yellowish-green blossoms all facing the same way on the stem. It is of little decorative value but should prove interesting in the alpine house. It grows in damp rocky places on the mountains of Abyssinia, reaching an elevation of 7500 feet above sea-level on those in the Begemeder district and is exposed at times to 12° or 15° of frost. It should be grown in damp sandy peat and loam in a sunny spot.

558. HOLOTHRIX BURCHELLII, Reichb. f.

Scopularia Burchellii, Lindl. *Orchidea pectinata*, Burchell

Root: of large ovoid tubers. **Leaves:** radical, broadly ovate, orbicular or reniform, unequal, somewhat fleshy, $\frac{3}{4}''$–3″ broad. **Scape:** $\frac{1}{2}''$–$1\frac{1}{2}''$ tall, hairy, clothed with lanceolate sheaths. **Raceme:** 3″–6″ long, dense, rather one-sided. **Flowers:** $\frac{1}{4}''$–$\frac{1}{2}''$ long; sepals ovate or ovate-oblong, 1-nerved; petals oblong, divided into 7–9 filiform lobes; lip, oblong, divided into 11–13 curved, narrow lobes; spur narrowly conical, curved, slender. *September to November.*

This yellowish-white flowered species is not of any decorative value, but is remarkable on account of the difference in size of the upper and lower blossoms in the raceme, the former being twice the size of the latter; the yellowish-green leaves are two in number. It is found amongst herbage and short grass on mountain sides in Transkei and Cape Colony, where on mountain sides near Queenstown at 4000 feet it is exposed to over 12° of frost for short periods during the winter. It should be grown in a sunny spot in damp fibrous loam and is only suitable for outdoor culture in the warmest localities.

559. HOLOTHRIX INCURVA, Lindl.

Root: of ovoid tubers. **Leaves:** 2, unequal, ovate-orbicular, rather fleshy. **Scape:** about 6″ tall, covered with long hairs. **Racemes:** about $1\frac{1}{2}$″ long, lax, secund. **Flowers:** about $\frac{1}{4}$″ across; sepals ovate, rather blunt, 1-nerved, hairy at their tips; petals narrowly linear, twice as long as the sepals; lip 5-lobed to about the middle, shorter than the petals; lobes linear or filiform, blunt; spur broadly conical, very blunt, curved, minute.

October to January.

This species is of no horticultural value; the tiny greenish-white blossoms are borne in a one-sided raceme on the densely hairy flower-stem, clothed at the base by two rounded yellow-green leaves. It grows near the summits of high mountains amongst stones and dwarf herbage, and also amongst grass on mountain plains, in Cape Colony, Natal and the Orange Free State, where it probably reaches its greatest altitude on the Quaqua Mountains at 7500 feet and should therefore be quite hardy in Great Britain. A gritty loam in full sun is indicated.

560. HOLOTHRIX JOHNSTONII, Rolfe

Root: an ovoid tuber. **Leaves:** radical, ovate, very shortly petioled, opposite or nearly so, sparingly pilose, very ciliate, $1\frac{1}{4}$″–$2\frac{1}{4}$″ long. **Scape:** 5″–10″ long, covered with long hairs. **Spike:** 1″–2″ long of 6–10 flowers, secund. **Flowers:** about $\frac{3}{4}$″ across; sepals oblong, concave, connivent, blunt, hairy at the apex; petals linear, blunt; lip broadly oblong, divided at the tip into 5 spreading, oblong, blunt lobes; spur conical, blunt, very short.

June and July.

This species has larger blossoms than many other members of the genus; they are curiously constructed and are yellow and white in colour. Although it cannot lay claim to any great decorative value it is well worth cultivating. It is confined to open grassy spots on mountains in British Central Africa at 6000–7000 feet, and should be quite hardy in Southern Britain in a good moist fibrous loam in the rock garden.

561. HOLOTHRIX LINDLEYANA, Reichb. f.

H. secunda, Reichb. f. *Tryphia nivea*, Zeyh. *T. secunda*, Lindl.

Root: of 2 large ovoid tubers. **Leaves:** radical, ovate, subequal, smooth, membranous, $\frac{3}{4}''$–2″ long. **Scape:** $\frac{1}{3}''$–$\frac{3}{4}''$ long, slender, flexuous, sparely pubescent. **Raceme:** 1″–4″ long, dense or at times lax. **Flowers:** $\frac{1}{3}''$ long; sepals ovate, 1-nerved; petals linear-oblong, twice as long as the sepals, 1-nerved; lip flabellate, unequally 5-lobed, lobes oblong, blunt; spur conical, curved. *September to November.*

A delicate little species with long racemes of rather small white blossoms on slender flower-stems, clothed at the base with two oval leaves. It should make a pretty addition to the alpine house, planted in a deep pan. It grows in wooded country mostly in mountainous districts, and is scattered throughout the whole of Cape Colony in suitable localities, probably reaching its greatest elevation on the Zwanepoels Poort Mountains in the Willowmore Division at 4000 feet, where it is exposed to 12° of frost for short periods during the winter. A compost of leaf-soil and loam in half shade is indicated. It is only suitable for outdoor culture in the western counties.

562. HOLOTHRIX MICRANTHA, Schltr.

Root: of 2 large ovoid tubers. **Leaves:** radical, unequal, fleshy, somewhat concave, suborbicular, hairy, $\frac{1}{2}''$–$\frac{3}{4}''$ long. **Scape:** about $\frac{3}{4}'$ tall, rather stout, hairy. **Raceme:** 3″–4″ long, somewhat secund, dense. **Flowers:** $\frac{3}{16}''$ across; sepals broadly ovate, fringed with hairs at the apex, 1-nerved; petals lanceolate-linear, rather fleshy, 1-nerved; lip 5-lobed; lobes filiform, subequal, blunt; spur broadly conical, blunt. *October.*

This species is of no horticultural value; the tiny greenish-white blossoms are produced in a long one-sided raceme on a hairy flower-stem, clothed at its base by two rounded concave leaves. It is found on grassy cliffs on the mountains above Heidelberg in the Transvaal at 5400 feet, and is exposed to 15° or more of frost during its winter rest for short periods. It may be grown in gritty fibrous loam in a fairly damp spot in full sun.

563. HOLOTHRIX MULTISECTA, Bolus

H. multisecta, Durand and Schinz. *H. scopularia*, Schltr.

Root: of large ovoid tubers. **Leaves:** radical, unequal, rather fleshy, orbicular, hairy and fringed on their margins, $\frac{1}{2}''$–$\frac{3}{4}''$ long. **Scape:** $\frac{3}{4}'$–1′ tall, rather stout, very downy. **Raceme:** 2″–3$\frac{1}{2}''$ long, secund, dense. **Flowers:** about $\frac{1}{4}''$ long; sepals ovate, rather pointed, fringed, 1-nerved; petals linear-oblong below, 3-fid to about the middle, segments diverging; lip flabellate, divided to the middle into 5–7 linear, diverging lobes; spur narrowly conical, curved, blunt. *October to January.*

A species of no decorative value, with small greenish-yellow blossoms on a stout downy flower-stem from the base of which two unequal, rounded, fleshy, dull green leaves spring. It grows in rocky places on mountains in Natal, Griqualand East and Cape Colony, where on the summit of the Elandsberg in the Stockenstrom Division at 6000 feet it is exposed to over 25° of frost for considerable periods during the winter. A gritty fibrous loam in full sun is indicated.

564. HOLOTHRIX ORTHOCERAS, Reichb. f.

Tryphia orthoceras, Harv.

Root: of 2 ovoid tubers. **Leaves:** radical, broadly ovate or elliptic-ovate, rather pointed, submembranous, smooth, 1″–2″ long. **Scape:** ½′–¾′ tall, rather slender, downy. **Raceme:** 1″–3″ long, secund, dense or at times lax. **Flowers:** nearly ½″ long; sepals ovate, smooth, pointed, 1-nerved; petals oblong-lanceolate, 1-nerved; lip cuneate, unequally lobed; outer lobes linear; middle lobe divided into 3–5 broadly triangular teeth; spur narrowly conical, nearly straight. *March.*

Although the white blossoms of this species are not large, the plant is of some decorative value on account of the beautiful white veining on the green semi-transparent leaves. It is dwarf enough for alpine house culture. In a state of nature it grows in thin mountain woods, usually in damp moss-covered rocky ground, in Cape Colony, Transvaal and Natal where near the sources of the Polela River it reaches an altitude of 7000 feet and should be quite hardy in Great Britain if it can be induced to rest during our winter. A gritty leaf-soil in half shade is indicated.

565. HOLOTHRIX PARVIFOLIA, Lindl.

H. hispidula, Durand and Schiz. *Habenaria hispida*, Spreng. *Orchis hispida*, Thunb.

Root: of 2 ovoid tubers. **Leaves:** subradical, ovate or orbicular, thick and fleshy, blunt, coarsely hairy, about ½″ long, upper ones much smaller. **Scape:** ⅓′–½′ long, very hairy. **Raceme:** 1″–3″ long, somewhat lax, many-flowered. **Flowers:** about ⅛″ long; sepals ovate, blunt, downy, 1-nerved; petals falcate-linear, blunt, somewhat fleshy; lip shortly 5-lobed, fleshy; lobes oblong, blunt, centre ones long; spur stoutly cylindrical, curved. *November to January.*

The tiny, dull, ochreous-yellow blossoms of this little species are of no decorative value; they are borne in a comparatively long slender raceme on a

PLATE 13.

HOLOTHRIX ORTHOCERAS.

PLATE 14.

LIPARIS LILIIFOLIA.

hairy flower-stem, clothed near its base with two rounded leaves. It inhabits moist rocky places in the mountains of the coastal region of Cape Colony and parts of Natal, where at Van Reenen at 5000 feet it attains its greatest altitude above sea-level and is there exposed to over 15° of frost for short periods during its winter rest. A damp gritty fibrous loam in full sun is indicated, with protection from severe frost.

566. HOLOTHRIX PLEISTODACTYLA, Kränzl.

Root: an ovoid tuber. **Leaves:** radical, reniformly orbicular, with a subcordate base, crenulate, rather ciliate, with strong reticulate veins, $\frac{1}{4}''$–$\frac{3}{4}''$ long. **Scape:** 6″–7″ long, covered with rough hairs. **Raceme:** about 1″ long, secund, of many flowers. **Flowers:** nearly $\frac{3}{8}''$ across; sepals ovate, pointed, hairy; petals cuneate, pentadactylous in front; lip flabellate, polydactylous, segments about 12, linear, diverging; spur curved, short. *November.*

A quaint little plant with small blossoms varying from yellowish-white to brown; they are borne in short one-sided racemes on slender stems, clothed at the base with two spreading leaves of very unequal dimensions. It grows in grassy, rocky places on Kilimanjaro in Tanganyika, East Africa, at an elevation of 8800 feet, and should therefore be quite hardy in Southern Britain in the rock garden in good fibrous loam kept fairly moist.

567. HOLOTHRIX RUPICOLA, Schltr.

Root: of 2 small, ovoid tubers. **Leaves:** subradical, suborbicular or reniformly orbicular, rather blunt, fleshy, slightly ciliate on the margins, 1″ long. **Scape:** 3″–5″ tall, rather stout, hairy. **Raceme:** 2″–$2\frac{1}{2}''$ long, rather lax, secund. **Flowers:** nearly $\frac{1}{2}''$ across; sepals ovate, ciliate, pointed, 1-nerved; petals linear-lanceolate, pointed, 1-nerved; lip with a broad limb divided into 5-lobes to the middle; side lobes narrowly linear, diverging; spur broadly conical, much curved. *December to March.*

This species has somewhat larger blossoms than many of the other members of its genus, but their pale green and yellow tinting gives them very little garden value. It should prove interesting in the alpine house. In its native habitats it grows in rock fissures and reaches its greatest elevation on Mont aux-Sources at 9000 feet, in the Orange Free State. It is also found in Western Cape Colony and should be quite hardy in Great Britain if it can be induced to rest during our winter. A gritty loam in a moist sunny place is indicated.

568. HOLOTHRIX SCOPULARIA, Reichb. f.

H. Burchellii, Kränzl. *Scopularia secunda*, Lindl.

Root: of large ovoid tubers. **Leaves:** subradical, unequal, orbicular, rather fleshy, covered with fine hairs, $\frac{3}{4}''$–$1\frac{1}{4}''$ long. **Scape:** $\frac{3}{4}'$ tall, rather stout, very hairy. **Raceme:** 2″–3½″ long, dense, secund. **Flowers:** ⅜″ long; sepals ovate or ovate-oblong, rather pointed, fringed, 1-nerved; petals 3-fid to about the middle, linear-oblong below, 1-nerved; lip flabellate, with a narrow base, divided to about the middle into 8–9 linear, diverging lobes; spur narrowly conical, curved, blunt. *September to January.*

A species of no decorative value, with small pale greenish blossoms in a dense one-sided raceme on a stout hairy flower-stem, clothed with two hairy rounded leaves. It grows in the fissures of rocks on the highest mountains of South Africa, being found in Cape Colony, the Transvaal and the Orange Free State, where on Mont aux-Sources it attains an elevation of 9000 feet above sea-level, and should be perfectly hardy in this country. A gritty, moist loam in full sun is indicated.

569. HOLOTHRIX THODEI, Rolfe

Root: of 2 small ovoid tubers. **Leaves:** subradical, suborbicular, somewhat fleshy, hairy, ¼″–⅝″ long. **Scape:** 3″–5″ tall, rather stout, densely hairy. **Raceme:** 1½″ long, somewhat lax, many-flowered. **Flowers:** $\frac{3}{16}$″ long; sepals ovate oblong, rather blunt, margins hairy, 1-nerved; petals ovate-lanceolate, narrowed upwards, fleshy, 1-nerved; lip very broad, shortly 3-lobed, fleshy; centre lobe twice as long as the others; spur conical, straight.

October to December.

A very dwarf species with tiny green blossoms of no horticultural value; the whole plant is densely hairy. It inhabits stony and grassy places on the summits of the Quaqua Mountains in the Orange Free State at 7500 feet, and should therefore be quite hardy in Britain if it could be induced to rest during our winter months. It may be tried in a mixture of fibrous loam and sand in a damp spot fully exposed to the sun.

570. HOLOTHRIX TRIDENTATA, Reichb. f.

Peristylus tridentatus, Hook. f. *Platanthera tridentata*, Engl.

Root: of small, ovoid-globose tubers. **Leaves:** radical, orbicular, ciliate, about ½″ long. **Scape:** 2½″–5″ long, hairy. **Raceme:** ½″–1″ long, of from 4–12 blossoms. **Flowers:** about $\frac{3}{16}$″ across; sepals ovate, apex unequally tricuspidate; outer lobes short and blunt; inner lobe subulate, longer than the side lobes; petals broadly elliptic-oblong, apex very unequally tridentate, similar to the sepal; lip oblong, divided toward the apex into 7 unequal, oblong lobes; spur broadly conical, horizontal, rather curved, minute.

September.

Usually a very tiny plant with a short spike or raceme of small green and white, curiously constructed blossoms, it is, however, somewhat variable in height. The blossoms are of no decorative value. It is found in the alpine regions of the Cameroon Mountains, Cameroons, West Africa, at 11,000 feet, in rocky places amongst short grasses, and should be perfectly hardy throughout Great Britain. A sandy fibrous loam in full sun is indicated.

571. HOLOTHRIX VATKEANA, Reichb. f.

Root: a small ovoid or rounded tuber. **Leaves:** radical, ovate, or ovate-oblong, spreading, 1″–1¼″ long. **Scape:** ¾′–1¼′ tall, slender, slightly downy. **Raceme:** about 3″ long, lax, secund. **Flowers:** about ¼″ across; sepals triangular, pointed; petals lanceolate, apex caudate-acuminate; lip divided to the middle into 3 linear lobes; spur conical, oblong, incurved at its apex, minute. *August to October.*

This species is somewhat taller than most of the others; it bears a long slender flower-stem, clothed at its base with two spreading, nearly opposite, leaves and terminating in a fairly long spike of small yellow and white blossoms with but little claim to decorative value. It grows in grassy places, frequently in a limy soil, on the mountains of Arabia, Somaliland and Abyssinia, where on the plateau of Kohaito it attains an elevation of 8400 feet above sea-level and is exposed at times to nearly 20° of frost. A good loamy soil, well supplied with calcareous matter, is indicated.

572. HOLOTHRIX VILLOSA, Lindl.

H. parvifolia, Lindl. *H. gracilis,* Lindl. *Orchis hispida,* Thunb. *Habenaria hispida,* Spreng.

Root: of 2 ovoid tubers. **Leaves:** subradical, unequal, broadly ovate or ovate-orbicular, blunt, at times heart-shaped at the base, covered with very long hairs, ¾″–1½″ long. **Scape:** ⅓′–1′ tall, fairly stout, clothed with long hairs. **Raceme:** ¾″–4″ long, dense. **Flowers:** about 3/16″ across; sepals ovate, rather blunt, smooth, 1-nerved; petals ovate-lanceolate, narrow at the apex, rather blunt; lip 3-lobed to about the middle, with linear, rather blunt lobes; spur conical, somewhat curved, rather blunt. *November.*

A species of no decorative value, with very small ochreous-yellow blossoms in a long raceme on a stout hairy flower-stem, clothed at its base with two rather fleshy, very hairy leaves. It grows in a variety of situations, but is most commonly found in open grassy places on the mountains of Cape Colony, where on the summit of Cave Mountain in the Graaff Reinet Division it attains an elevation of 4300 feet above sea-level and is exposed to 18° of frost during the winter, for short periods. It may be grown in damp fibrous loam in a sunny spot.

HUTTONÆA, Harvey

Hallackia, Harv.

Terrestrial, deciduous herbs numbering 6 species; their underground portion consists of one, or two or more rounded tubers attached to the base of the stem, with a few stout white fibres above them. The rather stout stems are sparely leafy and the leaves are usually ovate and decrease in size towards the top of the stem, where they merge into floral bracts. The blossoms, which are medium-sized, are produced in fairly dense racemes and although pretty are of no great decorative value. All the species are confined to the eastern portion of South Africa and ascend to considerable elevations above sea-level, in some cases to nearly 9000 feet, and must experience sufficient frost when at rest in their native habitat to ensure their hardiness in sheltered parts of this country. Propagation by imported tubers and also by seeds when procurable.

573. HUTTONÆA FIMBRIATA, Reichb. f.

H. Hallackii, Bolus. *Hallackia fimbriata*, Harv.

Root: a globose tuber. **Leaves:** cauline, broadly cordate, membranous, very smooth, the lower one stalked, 2″–2¾″ long. **Scape:** erect or slightly flexuous, ¾′–1¼′ tall. **Raceme:** 2″–4″ long, rather loose, many-flowered. **Flowers:** about ⅜″ across; dorsal sepal ovate, fimbriate, reflexed; lateral sepals obliquely and broadly ovate, blunt, fimbriate; petals flabellate at the tip, shortly and irregularly fimbriate, deeply concave at the base; lip broadly flabellate, margins strongly fimbriate. *January and February.*

A very dainty plant with long, loose racemes of pretty fringed white blossoms with, at times, purple shadings. The flower-stem is clothed at its base with two heart-shaped leaves. It grows in damp grassy places in the mountainous districts of Natal and Griqualand East, where on Kwenkwe Mountain at 5500 feet it is exposed to nearly 20° of frost during the winter for short periods when it is at rest. A damp fibrous loam in full sun is indicated.

574. HUTTONÆA GRANDIFLORA, Rolfe

H. oreophila var. *grandiflora*, Schltr.

Root: a globose tuber. **Leaves:** cauline, distant, ovate or cordate-ovate, pointed, smooth, rather thin, ½″–1¼″ long. **Scape:** 6″–8″ tall, somewhat flexuous, slender. **Raceme:** very short. **Flowers:** about ⅝″ across; dorsal sepal ovate-oblong, fimbriate; lateral sepals oblique and very broadly ovate, much fimbriate; petals unguiculate, somewhat diverging, broadly dilated above, deeply and compoundly fimbriate; lip with a short broad claw and a much dilated fimbriated limb. *December to February.*

This little species should make a delightful addition to the alpine house, for it is dwarf of growth, with from two to four pale green, lilac and white blossoms of fair size on a slender flower-stem clothed with two oval leaves placed some distance apart. It grows on rocky, grassy ledges near the summit of Mapedis Peak, Mont aux-Sources, in the Orange Free State, at 8600 feet and should be perfectly hardy in Great Britain. It may be grown in good fibrous loam in a damp spot.

575. HUTTONÆA OREOPHILA, Schltr.

Root: a globose tuber. **Leaves:** cauline, sessile, broadly ovate, very smooth, $\frac{3}{4}''$–$2\frac{1}{2}''$ long. **Scape:** $\frac{1}{2}'$–$1'$ tall, somewhat flexuous. **Raceme:** $\frac{3}{4}''$–$2\frac{1}{2}''$ long. **Flowers:** about $\frac{3}{8}''$ across; dorsal sepal elliptic-lanceolate, denticulate, spreading or reflexed; lateral sepals obliquely and broadly ovate, closely fringed at the margins; petals long-unguiculate, somewhat diverging, broadly dilated and flabellate at the apex, concave at the base and fimbriate to the middle; lip broadly flabellate; limb irregularly fimbriate to nearly the middle, with narrow subcapitate lobes. *December and January.*

Although the blossoms of this species are rather small they are freely produced and have some claim to decorative value on account of their pretty colouring; the sepals are pale green, the petals mauve-purple and the lip is white. It grows in rocky, grassy places in Natal and probably reaches its greatest altitude at Oliviers Hoek at 5000 feet where it is exposed to 15° of frost for short periods during the winter. A good rather damp fibrous loam in full sun is indicated.

576. HUTTONÆA PULCHRA, Harv.

Root: a globose tuber. **Leaves:** cauline, sessile or the lowest subsessile, broadly ovate or subcordate-ovate, membranous, very smooth, $1''$–$6''$ long. **Scape:** $\frac{3}{4}'$–$1\frac{1}{2}'$ tall, rather stout. **Raceme:** $1''$–$6''$ long, usually lax, few- or many-flowered. **Flowers:** about $\frac{3}{8}''$ across; dorsal sepal subsessile, elliptic-ovate, reflexed above the middle; lateral sepals oblique and broadly ovate, recurved at the apex; petals long-unguiculate, somewhat diverging, dilated at the apex into a rounded limb with a deep sac in the centre, margin deeply fimbriate; lip suborbicular, irregularly fimbriate. *January to March.*

This is a rather more robust plant than many of the other members of the genus; it bears long loose racemes of rather small purple and white blossoms on a somewhat stout flower-stem clothed with two large, oval leaves. It grows in shady places in Eastern Cape Colony, Orange Free State and Natal, where at Byrne it reaches an elevation of 4500 feet and is exposed to 18° of frost during the winter for short periods. A compost of fibrous loam and leaf-soil in a damp half-shady spot is indicated.

577. HUTTONÆA WOODII, Schltr.

Root: a globose tuber. **Leaves:** cauline, sessile, elliptic-ovate, smooth, rather fleshy, $1\frac{1}{4}''$–$2''$. **Scape:** $\frac{3}{4}'$–$1'$ tall, rather stout, straight. **Raceme:** oblong, $2''$–$3\frac{1}{2}''$ long, somewhat dense. **Flowers:** nearly $\frac{1}{2}''$ across; dorsal sepal reflexed, elliptic-oblong, with a recurved, pointed apex; lateral sepals obliquely and broadly ovate, with the outer margin subcordate; petals unguiculate, somewhat diverging, dilated above, with rather long capitate appendages; lip with an obcordately dilated limb, irregularly fimbriate, with subcapitate appendages. *November to January.*

A somewhat dwarf species with fairly long racemes of fair-sized mauve-purple and white blossoms of some decorative value. The rather stout stem is clothed with two widely separated, oval, fleshy, dull green leaves. It is found in open grassy places in Natal and reaches its greatest elevation at Seven Fontein near Boston at 5000 feet where it is exposed to 15° of frost for short periods during the winter. A good fibrous loam in full sun is indicated. This species is only suitable for outdoor culture in warm localities.

LIMODORUM, Linnæus

About six species of handsome deciduous herbs, natives of South Europe, North Africa and North America. Their roots consist of a solid bulb or tuber which is at times thickened into a rhizome. In those species with a tuberous rootstock a fresh tuber is produced each year beside the old one which perishes. The American forms produce a large leaf one year and a leafless flower-stem the next; the European forms are leafless throughout the entire period of their existence. The blossoms are borne in loose terminal racemes and are usually some shade of purple or red; all are of decorative value. Propagation by imported roots and by seeds when available.

578. LIMODORUM ABORTIVUM, Sw.

L. austriacum, Seg. *Epipactis abortiva*, All. *Neottia abortiva*, Clairv. *Orchis abortiva*, Linn. *Serapias abortiva*, Scop.

Root: a short stout rhizome emitting several very thick clavate fibres $1''$ or $2''$ long. **Stem:** $\frac{3}{4}'$–$2'$ tall, stout, clothed with numerous spatha-like sheaths which take the place of leaves, they are ovate in shape, pointed, $\frac{1}{2}''$–$1''$ long. **Spike:** $3''$–$9''$ long, lax, few- or many-flowered. **Flowers:** $1\frac{1}{4}''$ across; dorsal sepal oblong, blunt, bent over at the tip; lateral sepals lanceolate, falcate at the tip, spreading; petals similar to the lateral sepals but very much smaller, suberect; lip, variable, oblong or orbicular, narrowing near the base, crenulate; spur stout, tapering, slightly curved, pointing downwards, $1''$ long. *May to July.*

This beautiful plant is in all probability a saprophyte. It has erect, purple, or rarely green, stems and a loose spike of from four to twenty blossoms, with purple or lilac sepals and petals and a rich violet-purple lip with a large white or pale yellow patch near its tip. The blossoms are yellowish-green in the form *viridi-lutescens* (G. Cam.). Other forms are *abbreviatum* and *brevicornu*. The plant is found in dry thickets in Middle and Southern Europe and North Africa. It may be grown in the rock garden in pure leaf-soil, in shade.

579. LIMODORUM TRABUTIANUM, Batt.

Root: a stout rhizome emitting thick, blunt, fleshy fibres. **Stem:** $\frac{3}{4}'$–$1\frac{3}{4}'$ tall, stout, clothed with several spatha-like sheaths. **Leaves:** obsolete. **Spike:** 3″–7″ long, usually lax, few- or many-flowered. **Flowers:** about $1\frac{1}{4}''$ across; dorsal sepal oblong-lanceloate, curved over the column; lateral sepals lanceolate, falcate at the tip, spreading; petals narrowly lanceolate, suberect; lip spathulate; spur almost obsolete. *April and May.*

This species is closely allied to *L. abortivum* (Sw.) but may be readily separated from that species by the almost total absence of the spur, and by the shape of the lip. The blossoms are lilac or rich purple in colour and have a pale coloured patch near the tip of the lip on the disc. It is found in dry thickets near Zaccar de Milianah, Algeria. It should prove sufficiently hardy for culture outdoors in the warmer parts of Great Britain in a well-drained half-shady spot, in leaf-soil and loam.

580. LIMODORUM TUBEROSUM, Linn.

Calapogon pulchellus, R. Br. *Cymbidium pulchellum*, Pursh.

Root: a corm which is annual in duration, a new one is produced from beside the old one each year. **Leaf:** appearing one year, followed the next year by the scape, solitary, basal, linear to narrowly-oblong, pointed, 4″–14″ long. **Scape:** solitary, $\frac{1}{2}'$–$2\frac{1}{2}'$ tall, straight or curved. **Spike:** 4″–16″ long, bearing from 3–22 blossoms. **Flowers:** nearly $1\frac{1}{2}''$ across, fairly regular; sepals ovate-oblong, obliquely pointed; petals lanceolate or oblong, rather longer than the sepals; lip fan-shaped, slightly toothed or crenulate on the margins, crested with hairs on its surface near the base. *June and July.*

A well-grown specimen of this plant is a handsome addition to any rock garden. The tall naked stems bear numbers of beautiful pinkish-purple blossoms, with a crest of pink, orange or yellow coloured hairs in the throat; the flowers are large and of good substance. It grows in peat bogs and mossy swamps, also in wet meadows, from Newfoundland to Florida. It is quite hardy in Great Britain and should be grown in the bog-garden, in peat and sphagnum-moss.

LIPARIS, Richard

This genus contains about 400 species, few of which are of any horticultural merit. Most of them are terrestrial plants, very few are epiphytes. The underground portion consists of a short rhizome furnished with short, somewhat thick fibrous roots. In some species the stems are thickened into large, cylindrical pseudo-bulbs, in others they are fairly slender. The leaves, one or more in number, are produced near the base of the stem and frequently sheath the pseudo-bulbs or are jointed to the top of them. The blossoms are usually small or medium-sized and some shade of green or purple; they are borne in racemes, the ovary is so twisted that the blossoms are usually reversed, the lip being uppermost. They are widely distributed over the temperate and tropical regions of the world in a variety of habitats, usually in contact with moisture. Propagation by division when at rest and by seeds.

581. LIPARIS CATHCARTII, Hook. f.

Root: a short rhizome. **Pseudo-bulbs:** $\frac{1}{2}''$–$\frac{3}{4}''$ tall, tufted, broadly ovoid. **Stem:** stout, erect, 1″–3″ tall. **Leaves:** 2 in number, opposite, oblong-ovate or subcordate, shortly stalked, $\frac{1}{2}''$–3″ long. **Scape:** stout, 2″–6″ long. **Raceme:** many-flowered. **Flowers:** about $\frac{5}{8}''$ across; sepals lanceolate, 3-nerved; petals narrowly linear; lip very broadly oblong-cordate, flat, crenulate, pointed, with 2 basal calli. *July and August.*

This is not a very decorative plant; it is dwarf and produces a short, many-flowered raceme of rather small yellowish-green blossoms with a pale-purple or straw-coloured lip. It grows on moist rocks covered with vegetable debris and also on the branches of large trees in the Sikkim Himalaya, where it attains an elevation of 10,000 feet, and should be perfectly hardy in all but the bleakest parts of Great Britain in a moist bank of living sphagnum-moss and peat in a half-shady humid spot.

582. LIPARIS GLOSSULA, Reichb. f.

Root: a stout creeping rhizome. **Pseudo-bulbs:** about 2″ tall, stout, rounded. **Stem:** short, stout. **Leaf:** solitary, sessile or shortly stalked, oblong or linear-oblong, blunt or pointed, 2″–4″ long. **Scape:** 4″–7″ long, stout. **Raceme:** fairly long, many-flowered. **Flowers:** about $\frac{5}{8}''$ across; sepals lanceolate, pointed, 3-nerved, lateral ones overlaid by the lip; petals narrowly linear-lanceolate; lip broadly ovate, large, flat, cuspidate and crenulate. *July.*

Like the preceding species this plant has rather dull green and purple blossoms of little decorative value, they are borne in fairly long, many-flowered racemes. It grows on trees and on damp rocks by the side of streams in the Himalaya from Kumaon to Chumbi, reaching an altitude of 9500 feet, where it is exposed to over 15° of frost for short periods. It may be grown outdoors in this country in mild humid localities under the same conditions as the preceding species to which it is very closely allied.

583. LIPARIS KRAMERI, Franch

Leptorchis Krameri, O. Ktze.

Root: a creeping rhizome. **Stem:** 3″–6″ tall, very slender, erect or flexuous. **Leaves:** 2 in number, subopposite, orbicular-ovate, blunt, ¾″–1″ long. **Raceme:** ¾″–2″ long, of 4–12 blossoms. **Flowers:** about ¼″ long; dorsal sepal broadly lanceolate, erect; lateral sepals similar but spreading; petals linear-lanceolate, blunt; lip unguiculate, obscurely 2-lobed, lobes rounded, usually with a tooth in the sinus. *April to June.*

A fragile little plant suitable for alpine house culture, with pale green, purple tinted, slightly fragrant blossoms. It is found in shady places and in thin woods in many parts of Japan and Korea. The plant should be quite hardy in Great Britain in a damp shady spot in the rock garden in almost pure leaf-soil and sand.

584. LIPARIS LILIIFOLIA, Linn.

Leptorchis lilifolia, Kuntze.

Root: a short corm. **Leaves:** basal, from 2–6 in number, broadly ovate or oblong-ovate, usually blunt, narrowing into short sheaths at the base, concave in section, 2″–6″ long. **Scape:** 4″–12″ tall, fairly stout. **Raceme:** 1½″–6″ long, lax, many-flowered. **Flowers:** about ¾″ across; sepals linear, spreading; petals linear-filiform or filiform, spreading, at times longer than the sepals; lip erect, cuneate or obovate-cuneate, pointed, about ½″ across. *May to July.*

A quaint species with large deep green leaves and a long, many-flowered raceme of green and purple blossoms; the ovary is twisted and most of the blossoms are inverted. Although the plant is by no means showy, it is worth growing in the rock garden in a shady spot in leaf-soil and sand. It is found in thickets and open woods in Eastern North America, from Maine to Minnesota and southward to Georgia and Missouri. *See Plate 14 facing page 251.*

585. LIPARIS LOESELII, Rich.

Leptorchis Loeselii, Mac M. *Sturmia Loeselii*, Reichb.

Root: a small corm. **Leaves:** basal, 2 in number, elliptic or elliptic-lanceolate, sometimes narrowly oblong, blunt, with a short outer sheath, 2″–6″ long. **Scape:** 2″–9″ tall, rather slender, erect, strongly ribbed. **Raceme:** ¾″–4″ long, few-flowered. **Flowers:** about ¼″ long; sepals narrowly lanceolate, spreading; petals linear, usually somewhat reflexed; lip broadly ovate, erect at the base, turned back at the tip. *May to August.*

A delicate little native plant with two broad basal leaves and a loose spike of small pale green or greenish-yellow blossoms; they are not of any decorative value. The plant has a wide range of habitat, being found over the greater part of Central Europe, parts of Asia and Eastern North America, in the raised parts of peat bogs, hummocks in swamps, moist places in woods and boggy meadows. It may be grown in a raised part of the bog garden in peat, leaf-soil and living sphagnum-moss.

586. LIPARIS MAKINOANA, Schltr.

L. liliifolia, A. Gr.

Root: of few, somewhat fleshy fibres from an oval, underground pseudo-bulb, about 1″ long. **Leaves:** 2–3 in number, springing from the apex of the pseudo-bulb, elliptic, rounded at the base, shortly stalked, 3″–6″ long. **Scape:** 8″–10″ tall, rather stout, angled, erect. **Raceme:** about 5″ long, rather laxly many-flowered. **Flowers:** about $\frac{5}{8}$″ across and $\frac{3}{4}$″ long; dorsal sepal lanceolate, reflexed; lateral sepals lanceolate, slightly eared at the base, spreading; petals narrowly linear, blunt, spreading; lip cuneate-obovate, rounded at middle, margin irregular. *June and July.*

This species is allied to the North American *L. liliifolia* and closely resembles it in habit and in the shape and tinting of its blossoms; they are quaint, but of little garden value. The plant is found in shady places at Hokkaida in Japan and should succeed in cultivation under the same conditions as *L. liliifolia.*

587. LIPARIS PARADOXA, Reichb. f.

L. odorata, Lindl. *Empusa paradoxa,* Lindl. *Malaxis lancifolia,* Smith. *Malaxis odorata.* Wild.

Root: a stout rhizome emitting numerous fleshy fibres. **Stems:** $\frac{1}{2}$′–1$\frac{1}{2}$′ tall, tufted, at times swollen at the base into pseudo-bulbs. **Leaves:** 1–5 in number, lanceolate to elliptic-lanceolate, narrowed into a broad stalk, pointed, and with strong nerves. **Scape:** 4″–10″ tall, stout, naked or clothed with 1 or 2 bracts. **Raceme:** many-flowered. **Flowers:** dorsal sepal narrowly oblong, blunt, 5-nerved, spreading; lateral sepals falcately oblong, recurved, at times spreading; petals linear; lip recurved, cuneately obovate, or obcordate, with 2 tubercles at its base. *July.*

A tall robust species, producing a tuft of stems from the rhizome, well furnished with sheathing, rich green leaves and a long many-flowered raceme of yellowish-brown blossoms three-eighths of an inch across the sepals. It is a handsome but not showy plant and grows in vegetable soil in woodlands and rocky places from Java, Siam, India to China and Japan. It may be grown outdoors in the warmer parts of Great Britain in damp leaf-soil and fibrous loam in a half-shady spot.

588. LIPARIS PAUCIFLORA, Rolfe

Root: of a few fleshy fibres. **Pseudo-bulbs:** ovoid, about 1″ long. **Leaves:** 2 in number, elliptic, shortly stalked, thin, 3″–4″ long. **Scape:** 7″–10″ tall, slender, few-flowered. **Flowers:** about $\frac{5}{8}$″ across; dorsal sepal linear-lanceolate, blunt; lateral sepals similar but hooked at the tip; petals very narrowly linear; lip ovate, blunt, undulate. *July.*

A quaint little Chinese species with few-flowered spikes of green and purple blossoms of little or no decorative value; it is found in shady places on rocks in Szechuan, Western China, at sufficient elevation above sea-level to ensure its hardiness outdoors in the milder parts of Great Britain, in the rock garden on a moss-covered rock or in a bed of fibrous peat and sphagnum-moss, where shelter can be had from direct sunshine.

589. LIPARIS PERPUSILLA, Hook. f.

Root: a small, short rhizome. **Pseudo-bulbs:** about $\frac{1}{4}$″ long, ovoid or oblong, tufted. **Leaves:** 4–5 in number, recurved, linear, pointed, leathery, with a strong midrib and recurved margins, $\frac{1}{2}$″–1″ long. **Scape:** 2″–4″ long, curved, obscurely margined, naked. **Raceme:** short, many-flowered. **Flowers:** under $\frac{1}{8}$″ long; sepals very broadly elliptic-oblong, blunt, 1-nerved; petals linear; lip minute, quadrate, 3-lobed; side lobes rounded; centre lobe broad and short, with 2 tubercles at the base. *July and August.*

A very tiny species suitable for a pan of chopped sphagnum-moss and peat in the alpine house. It has short racemes of tiny yellow flowers and small, narrow, leathery leaves. It grows on the branches of trees in the Sikkim Himalaya and reaches an altitude of 8000 feet above sea-level, where it is exposed to over 16° of frost during the winter months. Outdoors in Great Britain it may be tried on an apple-stump sunk in a sheltered part of the bog garden.

590. LIPARIS ROSTRATA, Reichb. f.

Root: a short, stout rhizome. **Pseudo-bulbs:** about $\frac{3}{4}$″ long, broadly ovoid. **Stem:** 1″–3″ tall, stout, erect. **Leaves:** 2 in number, elliptic-ovate or oblong, narrow at the base, $\frac{1}{2}$″–3″ long. **Scape:** 2″–6″ long, stout. **Raceme:** many-flowered. **Flowers:** about $\frac{5}{8}$″ across; sepals lanceolate, pointed, 3-nerved; petals very narrow; lip very broadly cordate, flat, crenulate, pointed, contracted at the base. *July.*

This species is of dwarf tufted habit and bears many-flowered racemes of small blossoms with pale green or purplish sepals and a yellowish-green lip; they are of small decorative value. It inhabits rocky places and grows in moss and vegetable debris in the North-Western Himalaya up to elevations of 8000 feet. It may be grown outdoors in mild sheltered localities in the rock garden on a bank of moist peat, loam and sphagnum-moss.

591. LIPARIS RUWENZORIENSIS, Rolfe

L. guineensis, Rendle

Root: of thick fleshy fibres. **Leaves:** subradical, elliptical-oblong, attenuate into a short petiole, 1″–1½″ long, blades 2½″–4″ long. **Scape:** 8″–9″ tall. **Raceme:** 3″–4″ long. **Flowers:** about ½″ across; dorsal sepal oblong, blunt; lateral sepals falcate oblong, blunt; petals linear, rather blunt; lip broadly orbicular-obovate, blunt, or nearly truncate, very shortly unguiculate, with 2 tubercules at its base. *August.*

This speces has medium-sized purple and green blossoms of no decorative value; they are fairly numerous and are borne in a raceme from 3–4 inches in length, clothed at its base with a few membranous leaves. It is found in damp, half shady spots on Mount Ruwenzori in British East Africa at an elevation above sea-level of 9000 feet, so is therefore quite hardy in Southern Britain, in loam and leaf-soil, in a damp half-shady spot.

LISSOCHILUS, R. Brown

Hypodematium, A. Rich.

Robust, handsome, deciduous terrestrial plants numbering about 160 species, with creeping rhizomes which in many species are thickened into large tubers bearing a few fleshy roots. The stout stems, which sometimes reach a height of ten feet, are well furnished at the base with linear or lanceolate leaves which shrivel in some species before the flowers are perfected; the flower-stems are sparely clothed with bracts which continue upwards and mingle with the blossoms which are borne in loose racemes and are usually large and very decorative. Very few of these strikingly handsome plants are found at sufficient elevation in their tropical and subtropical homes to give any hope that they may prove hardy in any part of Britain. They are closely related to the *Eulophia's*, and are confined to Africa and its Islands where they inhabit open grassy country. Propagation by imported tubers and by seeds. They may be grown in rich fibrous loam and leaf-soil, in full sun.

592. LISSOCHILUS ERYTHRÆ, Rolfe

L. graniticus, Schweinf.

Root: a stout, slowly extending rhizome. **Pseudo-bulbs:** oblong, clothed with loose membranous sheaths, 3″–4″ long. **Leaves:** lanceolate or elongate-lanceolate, pointed, ¾′–1¼′ long. **Scape:** over 3′ tall, stout, clothed with a few sheaths below. **Raceme:** a foot or more long, many-flowered. **Flowers:** about 1¼″ across; sepals elliptic-oblong, blunt; petals ovate-orbicular, blunt; lip pandurate-oblong; outer lobes eared, rounded; centre lobe broadly elliptical, blunt; disc with 3 crenulate keels; spur conical, blunt, short.

September to November.

A handsome species well worthy of cultivation, with long lance-shaped leaves and a robust stem bearing a long spike of large blossoms with dusky grey-green sepals, bright yellow petals and a yellow lip striped with purple at its base. It grows amongst vegetable debris and decayed granite on very elevated plateaus in Abyssinia, attaining its greatest elevation on that of Kohaito at 9000 feet and is therefore quite hardy in Britain. Cultivation, a close imitation of nature.

593. LISSOCHILUS KREBSII, Reichb. f.

L. Krebsii var. *purpurata*, Ridl. *L. Græfei*, Kränzl. *Eulophia Krebsii*, Bolus

Root: a stout, creeping rhizome. **Leaves:** lanceolate, pointed, attenuate at the base into a petiole. **Scape:** 2′–4′ tall, stout, with several sheaths on its lower part. **Raceme:** $\frac{3}{4}$′–1′ long, laxly many-flowered. **Flowers:** nearly 1$\frac{1}{4}$″ across; sepals elliptic-oblong, rather pointed; petals suborbicular; lip 3-lobed; outer lobes broadly oblong, blunt, divaricate; centre lobe broadly elliptical, blunt, deflexed at the sides; disc with a thickened keel; spur oblong, curved. *October.*

A beautiful and desirable plant with handsome membranous leaves and a tall stout stem bearing a long raceme of large flowers with brown sepals, yellow petals and a 3-lobed lip in which the outer lobes are red-purple and the centre one is bright yellow. It grows in open grassy places on the mountains of British Central Africa, reaching an elevation of 7000 feet, where it is exposed to 12° or 15° of frost for short periods. A rich fibrous sandy loam in a damp sunny spot is indicated.

594. LISSOCHILUS RUEPPELII, Reichb. f.

L. abyssinicus, Durand et Schinz. *Hypodematium abyssinicum,* A. Rich.

Root: of thick, creeping, underground stems. **Pseudo-bulbs:** in the form of a swollen stem, 3$\frac{1}{2}$″ long. **Leaves:** subradical, lanceolate or linear-lanceolate, pointed, $\frac{1}{2}$′–1$\frac{1}{4}$′ long. **Scape:** 1′–1$\frac{1}{2}$′ long, clothed with several short sheaths below. **Raceme:** 6″–8″ long, loosely many-flowered. **Flowers:** over 1″ across; sepals elliptic oblong or ovate-oblong, blunt; petals ovate-orbicular; lip 3-lobed; outer lobes suborbicular-oblong, blunt; centre lobe suborbicular, blunt; disc with 3 fleshy, obscurely crenulate keels; spur conical, blunt, short. *August to November.*

A somewhat dwarf species with long, narrow, bright green leaves and a short flower-stem bearing a long loose spike of large yellow blossoms marked with purple. It is found in open grassy places on the highlands of Abyssinia, where it reaches sufficient elevation to ensure its hardiness in Southern Britain in a sheltered but sunny spot in the rock garden in a good " fat " loam.

LISTERA, R. Brown

Diphryllum, Raf.

Sixty species of rather dwarf, deciduous, terrestrial plants, known as Tway-blade Orchids; they have short rhizomes bearing fibrous or very fleshy, almost tuberous roots. The leaves are invariably produced in a pair, opposite one another, frequently some distance up the stem, which terminates in a slender raceme of small curious-shaped, green blossoms of no decorative value. They are found in thin woods, pastures in moist places, and on mountain heaths, and frequently attain nearly alpine altitudes. With regard to distribution, they are widely scattered over both the Old and New Worlds in the northern hemisphere. All the species are hardy in Britain and may be grown in damp places in the rock garden in peat and leaf-soil. Some are found beneath the shade of conifers and should be grown in soil collected from such localities. Propagation by division of the roots and by seeds which are freely produced.

595. LISTERA AURICULATA, Wiegand

Root: clustered fleshy fibres. **Stem:** 4″–6″ tall, slender, smooth below, glandular pubescent above the leaves. **Leaves:** 2 in number, borne above the middle of the stem, ovate or elliptic ovate, 1″–2″ long. **Raceme:** $\frac{3}{4}$″–1$\frac{1}{2}$″ long, many-flowered. **Flowers:** about $\frac{1}{4}$″ long; sepals lanceolate-ovate; petals oblong-linear, blunt, spreading; lip oblong, broadening at the eared base, its margins are slightly downy and it is cleft in the centre to about $\frac{1}{3}$ of its length. *July.*

This fragile little plant bears a raceme of yellowish-green, purple-tinted blossoms far too small to be of any decorative value; they are borne on a slender stem with two oval leaves above the middle, placed opposite each other. It is found in cedar swamps in sphagnum-moss in Quebec, New Hampshire and Maine and is very local. It should be quite hardy in Great Britain, in a shady part of the bog garden in peat, pine-soil and sphagnum-moss.

596. LISTERA AUSTRALIS, Lindl.

Root: of thickened fibres. **Stem:** 3″–12″ tall, smooth below the raceme, slender. **Leaves:** 2 in number, opposite, below the centre of the stem, ovate or triangular-ovate, truncate or slightly cordate at the base, pointed, about 1$\frac{1}{4}$″ long. **Raceme:** 2″–3″ long, slender, many-flowered. **Flowers:** about $\frac{3}{8}$″ long; sepals broadly ovate, blunt; petals narrowly ovate; lip oblong, divided almost to the base into 2 narrowly linear segments with a small tooth between. *May to August.*

A plant, of but little horticultural value, of dwarf habit with racemes of small yellowish-green blossoms with some purple markings on the petals; the lip is many times larger than the sepals and petals. The plant is found in damp or swampy places in the open or on the borders of woods in the Eastern United States from New York to South Carolina and Florida. It should be quite hardy in a damp place in sandy loam in the rock garden or on the margin of the bog garden.

597. LISTERA CAURINA, Piper

Root: a cluster of many white, fleshy fibres. **Stem:** very slender, 4″–8″ tall, covered with minute glandular hairs above the foliage. **Leaves:** 2 in number, opposite, oblong-elliptic, blunt or pointed, about 1″ long. **Spike:** 2″–3″ long, slender, cylindrical, loosely many-flowered. **Flowers:** about $\frac{1}{4}$″ long; dorsal sepal broadly ovate, blunt; lateral sepals ovate; petals ovate-lanceolate, hooked, smaller than the sepals; lip 3-lobed; outer lobes small, linear; centre lobe bifid at the tip; lobes diverging, linear, pointed.

June to August.

This slender, fragile species has small pale green blossoms of botanical interest only; they are borne in a narrow spike on a slender flower-stem, clothed below its middle with two yellow-green, rounded leaves. The plant is found in cool, deciduous woods, and also at times in pine woods, in British Columbia. It may be grown in a shady spot in the rock garden in damp leaf-soil and sharp sand.

598. LISTERA CONVALLARIOIDES, Nutt.

L. Eschscholziana, Cham. *Epipactis convallarioides*, Pursh.

Root: of succulent, clustered, white fibres. **Stem:** 4″–8″ tall, slender, glandular-pubescent. **Leaves:** 2 in number, below the middle of the stem, ovate or suborbicular, at times rounded at the base, smooth, with from 3–9 nerves, about $1\frac{1}{4}$″ long. **Raceme:** $1\frac{1}{4}$″–$2\frac{3}{4}$″ long, loose. **Flowers:** about $\frac{1}{2}$″ long; sepals and petals linear-lanceolate, much shorter than the lip; lip wedge-shaped, broad at the apex and retuse, base usually with a short tooth on either side.

June to August.

A delicate little plant with small quaint blossoms of a greenish-yellow colour; they are borne in slender, three to twelve-flowered racemes, on short flower-stems clothed with a pair of yellow-green, opposite, rounded leaves. It is of botanical interest only and is found over the whole of Canada and as far south in the United States as Vermont and California; it is also found in Japan and Eastern Asia. It is perfectly hardy and may be grown in a damp spot in the rock garden in peat, decaying leaves and moss. It is found in damp woods in its habitat.

599. LISTERA CORDATA, R. Br.

Ophrys cordata, Michx.

Root: of fleshy, white fibres. **Stem:** 3″–8″ tall, very slender, smooth. **Leaves:** 2 in number, situated below the middle of the stem, sessile, opposite, broadly ovate, slightly cordate at the base, about $\frac{3}{4}$″ long. **Raceme:** rather loose, $\frac{1}{2}$″–2″ long, of from 2–20 blossoms. **Flowers:** under $\frac{1}{4}$″ long; sepals ovate, pointed, small; petals oblong, small; lip linear, 2-cleft, often with a small tooth on each side of the base, segments linear, frequently delicately hairy on the margin. *June to August.*

A small, slender native species with tiny purple and green blossoms of no decorative value. It is remarkable for the very extended range of its habitat for it is found in cool damp woods and on mountain heath over the whole of northern Europe as far south as the Alps and Caucasus, Northern Asia as far south as the Himalaya, Japan, the whole of Canada and as far south in the United States as New York. It extends far into the Arctic regions in Europe, Asia and America. It may be tried in the rock garden in a very cool damp spot in peat leaf-soil and moss.

600. LISTERA GRANDIFLORA, Rolfe

Root: of few fleshy fibres. **Leaves:** basal, cordate or ovate-cordate, rather pointed, about $1\frac{1}{4}$″ long. **Scape:** 9″–10″ tall, slender. **Raceme:** about 3″ long, few-flowered, downy. **Flowers:** about $\frac{3}{4}$″ across; sepals ovate-oblong, concave, rather pointed; petals linear, pointed; lip large, obcordate, with a thickened centre nerve. *July and August.*

A quaint little species with a loose, few-flowered raceme of fairly large green and purple blossoms with a comparatively large lip. It grows in damp dark rocky places on the mountains of Hupeh and Szechuan, Western China, and should be quite hardy in all but the most exposed parts of Great Britain, in a damp shady spot in the rock garden in peat and oak leaf-soil.

601. LISTERA MICRANTHA, Lindl.

Root: a short rhizome, emitting rather fleshy roots. **Leaves:** 2 in number, subradical, broadly ovate, $\frac{1}{2}$″ long. **Scape:** 3″–5″ tall, filiform, lax-flowered. **Flowers:** about $\frac{1}{8}$″ long; sepals and petals lanceolate, spreading; lip very much shorter than the sepals and divided in 3 short lobes.

July and August.

This is a very fragile little species and should prove quite interesting in a pan in the alpine house. The tiny pale green blossoms are of no decorative value. It is found in damp woods and bushy places in the Lachoong valley in the Sikkim Himalaya at 11,000 feet above sea-level and is exposed to 15° or 20° of frost for considerable periods during the winter. It may be grown in the alpine house or in a shady spot in the rock garden in loam and leaf-soil.

602. LISTERA NEPHROPHYLLA, Rydb.

Root: a cluster of thick fleshy fibres. **Stem:** 4″–6″ tall, very slender, smooth except just above the leaves. **Leaves:** 2 in number, opposite, usually reniform in shape, shining, blunt, with a sharp tooth at the apex, $\frac{3}{4}$″–1″ long. **Spike:** 1″–2″ long, loosely many-flowered. **Flowers:** about $\frac{3}{16}$″ long; dorsal sepal oblong, blunt; lateral sepals ovate; petals narrowly ovate, smaller than the sepals, all forming a loose hood or galea; lip 2-cleft into long linear, pointed lobes, with 2 similar tooth-like lobes near its base. *May to August.*

This plant is very closely related to *C. cordata* and is perhaps a Western American form of it. The spikes of minute green blossoms have no decorative value. It is found in damp shady woods frequently beneath the shade of conifers, in North-Western America from Alaska to Victoria, British Columbia. It may be grown in a damp shady spot in the rock garden in rich leaf-soil and sharp sand.

603. LISTERA NIPPONICA, Makino.

Root: a short rhizome, with filiform roots. **Stem:** 4½″–8½″ tall, erect, slender, smooth below, downy above. **Leaves:** 2 in number, placed about the middle of the stem, opposite, ovate-orbicular or subreniform-orbicular, about 1″ long. **Raceme:** 1″–2″ long, lax, of 3–9 blossoms. **Flowers:** about $\frac{3}{8}$″ long; dorsal sepal and lateral sepals oblong-lanceolate; petals oblong, slightly broader than the sepals; lip very broadly wedge-shaped, narrow at the base, where there are 2 small ovate ears, very broad toward the tip, 2-lobed, slightly dentate, crenulate; sinus with a broad tooth in its centre. *July and August.*

The quaint blossoms of this species are olive-green in colour tinted with purple. It inhabits the sub-alpine regions of shady parts of mountains in the provinces of Shimotsuke, Shinano, Kai and Iwashiro, Japan, and should prove quite hardy in the rock garden in this country. A compost of loam and leaf-soil in a shady spot is indicated.

604. LISTERA OVATA, Br.

Epipactis ovata, Crantz. *Ophrys ovata,* Linn.

Root: a short rhizome emitting fleshy fibres. **Stem:** 2″–6″ tall, round. **Leaves:** cauline, broadly ovate, 2 in number, sessile, pointed, nearly opposite, 2″–4″ long. **Scape:** with raceme 6″–12″ long, clothed with 1–2 small sheaths. **Raceme:** 3″–6″ long, downy, laxly many-flowered. **Flowers:** about $\frac{3}{8}$″ long; sepals ovate; petals linear; lip twice as long as the sepals, divided into 2 very narrow linear lobes. *May and June.*

This species is a fairly common native plant and is known as the common Twayblade. The long racemes of small green blossoms are quaint but have no decorative value. It is a rather robust species, reaching a total height of eighteen inches under good conditions. It is found in damp places in woods, thickets and pastures throughout Northern and Central Europe to the Ural Mountains and southward to the Caucasus, and is also reported from the North-Western Himalaya. It may be grown in a damp shady spot in the rockery in loam and peat.

605. LISTERA PINETORUM, Lindl.

Root: a bundle of fleshy fibres on a short stock. **Stem:** 4″–8″ tall, clothed above the middle with 2 leaves. **Leaves:** orbicular-cordate or very shallowly cordate, with 5–7 nerves. **Scape:** rather stout, very short, bearing a few-flowered pubescent raceme. **Flowers:** about $\frac{1}{2}$″ long, decurved; sepals and petals ovate-lanceolate; lip about 3 times as long as the sepals, deeply divided into 2 narrow lobes. *June to August.*

A quaint little plant with small brownish-green blossoms; interesting but of no decorative value. It should prove of some little value for the alpine house. It grows in damp places in the pine woods of the Lachen Valley in the Sikkim Himalaya at an altitude of 11,000 feet and is exposed to 20° or more of frost for considerable periods during the winter. It may be grown outdoors in most parts of Great Britain in a damp shady part of the rock garden in fibrous peat and leaf-soil.

606. LISTERA PUBERULA, Maxim.

Root: a cluster of fusiform roots on a short rhizome. **Stem:** 3″–8″ tall, very slender, sparely leafy. **Leaves:** rounded, cordate at the base, $\frac{3}{4}$″–1″ long. **Scape:** very slender. **Raceme:** of 4–8 blossoms. **Flowers:** about $\frac{3}{8}$″ long; sepals and petals broadly lanceolate; lip wedge-shaped, 2-lobed, lobes blunt, much longer than the sepals. *July to September.*

A delicate and fragile Chinese and Tibetian plant with small pale green, purple-tinted blossoms, of no decorative value. It is closely related to *L. pinetorum* and *L. Savateri* but may be distinguished by its much more hairy stem and smaller flowers. It is found in conifer forests at Kansu in China, and Tibet at 10,000 to 12,000 feet above sea-level and should be quite hardy in this country under the same conditions as *L. pinetorum.*

607. LISTERA SAVATIERI, Maxim.

Listera Eschscholtziana, Cham. *Listera japonica*, Franch

Root: a long creeping rhizome. **Stem:** erect, slender, 5″–10″ tall. **Leaves:** 2, opposite, elliptic-ovate or orbicular-ovate, blunt or pointed, $\frac{3}{4}$″–$1\frac{1}{4}$″ long. **Raceme:** 1″–3″ long, lax, of 6–21 blossoms. **Flowers:** about $\frac{3}{8}$″ long; dorsal sepal oblong-lanceolate, usually blunt; lateral sepals similar but oblique;

petals linear, very blunt; lip narrowly obovate-cuneate, gradually attenuate below, obcordate or ovate above, with rounded lobes; with or without a tooth in the sinus. *July and August.*

A slender species with a many-flowered raceme of small pale green blossoms of no garden value; it is found beneath the shade of trees in mixed deciduous forests on the mountains in the provinces of Tosa, Hitachi, Shimotsuke, Ino, and Iwashiro in Japan. It should prove quite hardy in Great Britain in a shady spot in beech leaf-soil.

608. LISTERA SHIKOKIANA, Makino

Root: a creeping rhizome with filiform roots. **Stem:** 2″–7″ tall, erect, smooth below, minutely hairy above. **Leaves:** 2 in number, opposite, ovate-triangular or triangular, pointed, broadly truncate or subcordate below, $\frac{1}{2}$″–$\frac{7}{8}$″ long. **Raceme:** erect, lax, 2–5 flowered. **Flowers:** about $\frac{1}{2}$″ long; dorsal sepal oblong-lanceolate or oblong-ovate; lateral sepals slightly oblique, oblong or oblong-lanceolate; petals spathulate-oblong or linear-oblong, quite blunt, revolute on the margins; lip sagittate, with a tooth on each side at the base; lobes blunt and irregularly toothed at the tip; tooth in sinus broad. *May to July.*

A somewhat dwarf plant with small bright green, oval leaves and a short, few-flowered spike of rather large olive-green and purple blossoms, large considering the size of the plant. It is found in damp spots in thin forest lands on mountains in the provinces of Tosa, Uzen and Yamito, Japan, and should prove quite hardy in Great Britain in the rock garden in a damp half-shady spot in a compost of leaf-soil and peat.

609. LISTERA SMALLII, Weigand

L. reniformis, Small

Root: of fleshy fibres. **Stem:** 3″–12″ tall, slender, smooth below, downy above. **Leaves:** 2 in number, opposite, placed about the middle of the stem, reniform or ovate-reniform, pointed, smooth above, downy beneath, about 1$\frac{1}{2}$″ across, sessile. **Raceme:** 2″–4″ long, rather loose. **Flowers:** about $\frac{1}{4}$″ long; sepals oblong or linear-oblong, rather blunt; petals similar but not reflexed; lip broadly oblong at the apex narrowing towards the base and with 2 prominent teeth at the sides near base, deeply cleft in the centre into 2 rounded lobes. *June to August.*

The small, pale green blossoms of this species are of no decorative value, they are borne in fairly long spikes or racemes on slender stems, clothed with two deep green leaves below the middle. It is a mountain plant and is usually found in damp thickets, it is a native of the Eastern United States from Pennsylvania to North Carolina and Tennessee. It should be quite hardy in Great Britain in a damp shady part of the rock garden in leaf-soil and loam.

610. LISTERA TENUIS, Lindl.

Root: a small bundle of fleshy fibres. **Stem:** 4″–5″ long, very slender, clothed with two leaves above the middle. **Leaves:** ovate, pointed, sessile, $\frac{1}{2}$″–1″ long. **Scape:** almost filiform, bearing a few-flowered raceme. **Flowers:** about $\frac{3}{8}$″ long; sepals and petals ovate-lanceolate, small; lip cuneately obcordate, lobes rounded, twice as long as the other segments.

July and August.

A very fragile little species with a slender stem clothed about the middle with two oval leaves; the flower-stem bears a few-flowered raceme of large blossoms in comparison to the size of the plant, they are of a pale greenish-yellow colour. It grows in moist pine woods in the Lachen Valley in the Sikkim Himalaya at an elevation of 11,500 feet and is exposed to over 20° of frost for considerable periods during the winter. It may be grown outdoors in leaf-soil and peat in a damp half-shady part of the rock garden.

611. LISTERA WARDII, Rolfe

Root: a cluster of thick, fleshy fibres from a short rootstock. **Stem:** 4″–9″ tall, rather slender, smooth. **Leaves:** 2 in number, sessile, opposite, ovate, shortly pointed, 1″–1$\frac{3}{4}$″ long. **Spike:** 2″–4$\frac{1}{2}$″ long, of 5–10 flowers. **Flowers:** about $\frac{3}{8}$″ long; sepals spreading, oblong, rather blunt; petals linear, blunt; lip cuneate at the base then obcordate, shortly 2-lobed at the tip.

June.

The pale green blossoms of this Chinese plant are too small to have any decorative value. It is closely allied to *L. grandiflora* and is found in very dense mountain forest in North-West Yunnan, Western China, at 10,000 feet above sea-level. It should be quite hardy in Great Britain in a damp shady spot in the rock garden in a calcareous leaf-soil.

612. LISTERA YATABEI, Makino

L. convallarioides, Finet

Root: a slender, creeping rhizome. **Stem:** about 7$\frac{1}{2}$″ tall, erect, smooth below, downy above, clothed with 2 appressed sheaths. **Leaves:** 2 in number, placed about the middle of the stem, orbicular or subreniform, sessile at the base, about $\frac{3}{4}$″ long. **Raceme:** 1$\frac{1}{2}$″–2″ long, of 9–11 blossoms, loose. **Flowers:** about $\frac{3}{16}$″ long; dorsal sepal ovate-lanceolate; lateral sepals lanceolate-oblong; petals linear; lip broadly linear below, divergent, with 2 shortly oblong, blunt, slightly oblique lobes above; with a minute tooth in the sinus.

July.

This species closely resembles *L. puberula* (Maxim) from Western China. It is very dwarf and has fairly long racemes of small yellowish-green blossoms which are of no decorative value. It is found beneath the shade of deciduous trees in forests on mountains in the provinces of Shinano and Shimotsuke, Japan, and should be quite hardy in Britain under the same cultural conditions as *L. Savatieri* (Maxim).

LYPERANTHUS, R. Brown

Eleven species of dwarf, deciduous, terrestrial plants with a root system consisting of two or more oblong tubers attached to the base of the underground portion of the stem, with a few white fleshy roots above them. The rather stout stems are clothed at the base with a solitary leaf, oblong or lanceolate in shape; above this leaf are several large leaf-like bracts which diminish in size until they merge into the floral bracts. The blossoms, which though quaint and interesting are too sombrely coloured to be of any decorative value, are borne in few-flowered spikes. They are found in open grassy country in moist places in Eastern Australia, Tasmania, New Zealand and many of the islands in the Antarctic Ocean. They may be tried outdoors in Britain in humid localities in fibrous peat, fibrous loam and grit, in a damp but sunny spot. Propagation by imported tubers and by seed when available.

613. LYPERANTHUS ANTARCTICUS, Hook. f.

Root: of oblong tubers. **Stem:** 4″–6″ tall, stout, leafy. **Leaves:** radical and cauline, linear-oblong or oblong-lanceolate, 1″–2″ long, decreasing in length upwards. **Spike:** short. **Flowers:** ½″ long, carried horizontally; dorsal sepal galeate, helmet-shaped, pointed; lateral sepals linear-subulate, pointed; petals falcate-linear, pointed; lip broadly ovate-oblong, blunt, with 5 slender ridges on the disc. *December and January.*

A quaint little plant with 2 or 3 dull lurid purple and green blossoms perched on a leaf-clothed stem like some weird insects. It should prove an interesting addition to the alpine house. It grows in open, damp, grassy spots in the Auckland Islands and the South Island of New Zealand, where at Waipori Creek it attains an altitude of 2,500 feet above sea-level and is exposed to 20° of frost for considerable periods during its winter rest. It should be grown in a good fibrous loam in a damp spot in full sun.

614. LYPERANTHUS NIGRICANS, R. Br.

Caladenia nigricans, Reichb. f. *Leptoceras pectinata*, Endl.

Root: of small ovoid tubers. **Stem:** 3″–12″ tall, stout and leafy. **Leaves:** radical and cauline, lower leaf broadly ovate-cordate, others lanceolate, sheath-like. **Spike:** of 4 distant blossoms. **Flowers:** about ¾″ long; dorsal sepal broad, galeate; lateral sepals narrowly linear, spreading; petals narrowly linear, rather shorter than the lateral sepals, incurved; lip 3-lobed; outer lobes small, erect; centre lobe recurved or revolute with a deeply fringed margin; disc with prominent, broad, lateral line. *December.*

A curious but dull-flowered species with a stout stem clothed with very large yellowish-green, purple-tipped sheaths or degenerate leaves. It bears from 2 to 4, sombre reddish or lurid purple blossoms of no decorative value. It is found in damp woods and forest lands in New South Wales, Victoria, Western Australia and Tasmania and seems to be very thinly scattered and local. It should be sufficiently hardy for culture out of doors over the greater portion of the British Isles. A compost of leaf soil and loam in a damp half-shady spot should suit it.

MALAXIS, Swartz

Formerly this genus contained but one species; the number has now been brought up to 26, most of which come from the East Indies, New Guinea and the Philippine Island. The solitary European species has a solid tuber placed on the surface of the soil, resembling a pseudo-bulb; a few weak roots spring from its base and anchor it to the sphagnum-moss in the bogs on which it grows. In strong specimens tiny tubers form at the base of the large tuber and so perpetuate the species. The majority of the species produce but one leaf and a spike of yellow or green blossom, of interest to the botanist only. Propagation by separation of the tubers and by seeds when procurable.

615. MALAXIS PALUDOSA, Sw.

Epipactis paludosa, Linn. *Limnas paludosa,* Ehrh. *Ophrys paludosa,* Linn. *Orchis paludosa,* Pallas. *Sturmia paludosa,* Reichb. f.

Root: short, slender, fleshy, with a small bulb-like body above the ground, about ½″ long. **Leaves:** 2 in number, with 1 or 2 scale-like leaves below in robust specimens, ovate-lanceolate, ½″–1″ long. **Scape:** 2″–5″ tall, very slender, erect, naked. **Spike:** 1″–2″ long, lax, of about 12 blossoms. **Flowers:** about ⅛″ across; dorsal sepal ovate, pointed; lateral sepals lanceolate, spreading; petals narrowly lanceolate, small; lip linear-lanceolate, entire, slightly longer than the other segments. *June and July.*

A tiny native plant of no horticultural value, with minute pale green blossoms in a loose spike. It is found in spongy bogs growing in sphagnum-moss; these conditions must be closely copied for its successful culture in the garden or alpine house. The plant ranges over nearly the whole of Northern Europe from Britain to Russia and Siberia and is also found on some of the mountains of Central Europe.

MICROSTYLIS, Nuttall

Achroanthes, Raf. **Crepidium**, Blume. **Pterochilus**, Hook.

Dwarf, deciduous or evergreen terrestrial plants, many of which have comparatively large, rich green leaves marked with purple and brown spots and blotches, some are wholely purple with silvery spots and margins. The blossoms are interesting and in some species beautiful and decorative; they are borne in slender few-flowered racemes from the centre of the leaves; they are reversed on their stalks, the lip being uppermost. In a few of the tropical species the stems are swollen into pseudo-bulbs; these are epiphytal. Unfortunately the species which are hardy enough for culture outdoors in Britain are among the least attractive of the genus, which numbers about 300 species; the great majority of them are found in Tropical Asia in a variety of situations. The species enumerated in the following pages may be tried outdoors in the more humid counties of Britain, in a shady part of the rock garden with protection in winter. Propagation by imported roots and by seeds.

616. MICROSTYLIS CYLINDROSTACHYA, Reichb. f.

Dienia cylindrostachya, Lindl.

Root: of numerous fleshy fibres from a short rhizome. **Stem:** tuberous at the base, sheathed-clothed. **Leaf:** solitary, 3″–4″ long, oblong or rounded, blunt. **Scape:** 4″–18″ tall, slender. **Raceme:** 1″–6″ long, many-flowered. **Flowers:** under $\frac{1}{8}$″ across; sepals narrowly oblong, spreading; petals linear, very narrow; lip ovate, pointed, margins thickened. *August.*

A tall, slender Orchid with long cylindrical spikes of very small pale yellowish-green blossoms of no decorative value. It grows in damp stony soil, among dwarf herbage in the Himalaya from Kashmir to Sikkim and attains an altitude of 12,000 feet above the sea; it should therefore be perfectly hardy over the whole of Great Britain as far as cold is concerned. It may be grown in the rock garden in a sunny spot in damp leaf-soil, peat and fibrous loam.

617. MICROSTYLIS MONOPHYLLOS, Lindley

M. brachypoda, Gray. *Achroanthes monophylla*, Greive. *Tipularia discolor*, Beck.

Root: a short corm. **Leaf:** solitary, ovate, oblong or elliptic, blunt, narrowed into a long sheathing stalk, $1\frac{1}{4}$″–$2\frac{1}{2}$″ long. **Scape:** 4″–8″ tall, slender. **Raceme:** 1″–4″ long, slender. **Flowers:** about $\frac{1}{8}$″ across, numerous, on erect stalks; sepals and petals linear or linear-lanceolate; lip ovate or nearly triangular, pointed, irregularly toothed on the margins.

July and August.

A slender fragile species, with an erect stem clothed with a solitary yellowish green leaf and a slender spike of tiny, pale green or greenish-white blossoms of no decorative value. It is found in moist or swampy places in shady woods, mostly in rich leaf-soil, and ranges in Eastern North America from Nova Scotia to Manitoba and southward to Texas. It is perfectly hardy in Great Britain and may be grown in the rock garden or alpine house in a shady spot, in good leaf-soil and sand.

618. MICROSTYLIS MUSCIFERA, Ridley

Root: of numerous fleshy fibres from a short rhizome. **Stem:** 6″–18″ tall, swollen at the base into a tuber. **Leaves:** 2 in number, oblong or rounded, sessile, or on a short stalk, blunt, 2″–4″ long. **Raceme:** 1″–5″ long, many-flowered. **Flowers:** under $\frac{1}{8}$″ across; sepals oblong; petals linear; lip ovate, pointed, with thickened margins. *August.*

This species is very closely allied to *M. cylindrostachya* and, like it, has minute yellowish-green blossoms of no garden value. It grows in damp soil in rocky places in the Himalaya from Kashmir to Sikkim, attaining an altitude of 12,000 feet above sea-level. It should be perfectly hardy in Great Britain in a damp spot in the rock garden in leaf-soil, peat and loam.

619. MICROSTYLIS OPHIOGLOSSOIDES, Nutt

Achroanthes unifolia, Raf. *Malaxis unifolia,* Michx. *M. ophioglossoides,* Pursh.

Root: a short corm. **Leaf:** solitary, rarely 2, oblong-ovate, sheathing, placed about the middle of the stem, $\frac{3}{4}$″–1$\frac{1}{2}$″ long. **Scape:** 4″–12″ tall, slender, usually with a small sheath at the base. **Raceme:** 1″–4″ long, erect. **Flowers:** about $\frac{1}{8}$″ across; sepals and petals oblong, pointed; lip oblong, with 3 long teeth at its apex. *July and August.*

A dwarf Orchid, usually with a solitary leaf about the middle of the slender stem which bears a rather loose raceme of tiny pale green or yellowish-green blossoms of no decorative value. It grows in a variety of situations, such as shady or open woods, on banks in moist rich soil, dry sandstone hills, and wet meadows, ranging in Eastern North America from Newfoundland to Saskatchewan and southward to Florida and Missouri. It is quite hardy in Great Britain in sandy loam and leaf-soil in a half-shady part of the rock garden.

620. MICROSTYLIS YUNNANENSIS, Schltr.

Root: a short rhizome with several ovoid tubers on slender roots. **Stem:** erect, 4″–9″ tall, clothed near the base with 2 leaves. **Leaves:** oblong or elliptic, with sheathing stalks, 1″–2″ long. **Raceme:** long, rather dense, many-flowered. **Flowers:** about $\frac{3}{8}''$ across; dorsal sepal lanceolate, drawn out into a long point; lateral sepals similar only spreading; petals obliquely linear-lanceolate, narrowly pointed; lip cordate-ovate and eared at the base, narrowly lanceolate at the tip, with 2 calli at the base and thickened nerves on the disc. *July.*

The small greenish-yellow blossoms of this species are faintly fragrant; they are too small to be of any decorative value. The plant inhabits mountain meadows on the eastern flanks of the Lichang Range in Yunnan, Western China, at altitudes of from 11,000–12,000 feet above sea-level. It should be quite hardy in Great Britain in the rock garden in an open sunny spot in fibrous loam.

MICROTIS, R. Brown

Very slender deciduous, terrestrial plants of no garden value, with small green, globular blossoms in loose or dense spikes, on tall, frequently stout, erect stems clothed with a solitary grassy leaf with but a short free point and a closed or open sheath that clothes one-half and at times two-thirds of the stem. The root system consists of two or more globular tubers, either sessile or on short stalks at the base of the underground portion of the stem, with a few fleshy fibres above them. In some species the spikes of blossoms, which greatly resemble those of the Grape Hyacinths, are pleasantly fragrant. The thirteen species are found in damp sandy soil in open spots in Eastern India, Southern China, Australia, New Caledonia and New Zealand. The more hardy species may be grown in damp sandy soil in a sunny spot in the rock garden with protection to their roots in winter. Propagation by imported tubers and by seeds when procurable.

621. MICROTIS ARATA, Lindl.

M. minutiflora, F. Muell.

Root: of small globular tubers. **Leaf:** solitary, subradical, $1\frac{1}{2}''$–$3''$ long, very narrow. **Scape:** $3''$–$6''$ tall, fairly stout, terete, smooth. **Spike:** $\frac{1}{2}''$–$2''$ long, fairly dense. **Flowers:** about $\frac{3}{16}''$ across; dorsal sepal rounded, very concave, blunt; lateral sepals and petals oblong, very blunt, spreading; lip broadly oblong, blunt, convex, marked with 2 longitudinal lines. *November and December.*

The smallest member of the genus. It has a very bright green stem and leaf and a short spike of tiny yellowish-green blossoms with greenish-white lips. The plant is of no garden value and is found in a state of nature in damp spots, usually in poor soils amongst dwarf herbage and low bushes in Victoria and Western Australia. It ascends the Grampions to a considerable elevation above sea-level in Victoria and should be quite at home in a damp spot in sandy soil in Great Britain.

622. MICROTIS PARVIFLORA, R. Br.

M. Benthamiana, Reichb. f.

Root: of globose tubers emitting short fibres. **Leaf:** solitary, subradical, rounded, very narrow, with a very long sheath, 6″–12″ long. **Scape:** ½′–1½′ tall, fairly slender, round, smooth. **Spike:** 2″–5″ long, dense, or loose in various specimens. **Flowers:** about ⅛″ long; dorsal sepal broad, concave, blunt; lateral sepals ovate, smaller than the dorsal sepal; petals oval, very minute; lip blunt, oblong; disc with a papillose protuberance near the tip. *December*.

This species is rather more slender than many of the others. It has a bright green stem clothed with a very narrow grassy leaf with a long sheath, and a dense or loose spike of tiny bright green blossoms of no garden value. There is a variety named *densiflora* with a very dense spike, the blossoms have a very broad dorsal sepal. The plant is found in similar situations as *M. porrifolia*, in Queensland, New South Wales, Victoria, Western Australia and Tasmania and is sufficiently hardy for general culture outdoors in Great Britain. A damp fibrous loam in full sun should prove suitable.

623. MICROTIS PORRIFOLIA, Sprengel

M. Banksii, A. Cunn. *Epipactis porrifolia*, Swartz. *Ophrys unifolia*, Forst.

Root: of oblong tubers. **Leaf:** solitary, basal, terete, tubular, 9″–15″ long. **Scape:** ½′–2′ tall, rather stout, terete, smooth. **Spike:** 1″–6″ long, dense, many-flowered. **Flowers:** about ⅛″ long; dorsal sepal broadly ovate, joined to the petals, forming a hood; lateral sepals narrowly oval, placed beneath the lip; lip oblong, wavy at the margins, obscurely 2-lobed at the tip, with 2 glandular appendages at its base and one at the tip. *December*.

The small, green, somewhat fleshy blossoms of this species are of no horticultural value; they are borne in long narrow spikes of from twenty to eighty. It is a common plant in damp spots throughout the whole of Eastern Australia and the North and South Islands of New Zealand, ascending the mountains to sufficient elevations to ensure its hardiness in all but the coldest parts of Great Britain. A good soil on the banks of a pond or stream should prove suitable.

MONADENIA, Lindley

This genus contains a number of ornamental plants few of which reach sufficient altitude above sea-level in their native country to justify an attempt to cultivate them in the open air in Britain; they are deciduous and terrestrial;

their root systems consist of two or more sessile tubers on the base of the underground portion of the stem; each tuber perishes when it has supplied the nourishment for the perfection of a flower-spike and is replaced by young tubers if the plant is in a healthy condition. The stems are clothed with a few ovate-oblong or lanceolate leaves near the base; these are reduced upwards into bracts and those that subtend the flowers are narrow. The blossoms are borne in many-flowered spikes and are frequently very decorative. The plants, which number about thirty species, are confined to South Africa; they may be tried outdoors in the milder parts of Britain in an open but sheltered part of the rock garden and should be protected in winter. Propagation by imported tubers and by seeds where these are available.

624. MONADENIA BASUTORUM, Rolfe

Disa Basutorum, Schltr.

Root: a sessile tuber. **Stem:** rather slender. **Leaves:** radical, ovate, $\frac{3}{4}''$–1″ long, 2 in number. **Scape:** 3″–5″ tall, sheath-clothed. **Spike:** 1″ long, lax, many-flowered. **Flowers:** $\frac{3}{8}''$ across, dorsal sepal galeate, ovate or ovate-oblong, somewhat incurved; spur spreading or reflexed, oblong, $\frac{1}{4}''$ long; lateral sepals obliquely ovate, blunt; petals erect, broadly ovate, apex inflexed; lip linear-oblong, dilated slightly at its apex. *October.*

This little plant with its small greenish or brownish-green blossoms is of no garden value. It is almost an alpine plant, for it grows on the heath-covered summits of the Drakensberg Range in Basutoland at an elevation of 10,000 feet and should therefore be perfectly hardy in Great Britain if it could be induced to blossom in our summer· It should be grown in fibrous peat in a fairly moist open spot fully exposed to the sun.

625. MONADENIA BREVICORNIS, Lindl.

Disa brevicornis, Bolus

Root: a sessile tuber. **Stem:** stout. **Leaves:** cauline, lanceolate or linear-lanceolate, rather fleshy, 2″–4″ long. **Scape:** 1′–$1\frac{1}{2}'$ tall. **Spike:** 3″–7″ long, dense. **Flowers:** $\frac{5}{8}''$ across; dorsal sepal broadly elliptic-oblong, concave; spur oblong, blunt, $\frac{5}{8}''$ long; lateral sepals obliquely oblong, spreading; petals obliquely ovate-oblong, blunt and fleshy; lip linear-oblong, blunt. *February and March.*

The sober tinted blossoms of this species, although of fair size, have but little decorative value; the sepals are yellowish-green and the petals and lip reddish-purple or purple. It grows on moist grassy mountain slopes in the Transvaal, Eastern Cape Colony, Tembuland, Natal and Griqualand East, where at 5000 feet it is exposed to over 20° of frost for considerable periods when at rest. It requires a moist fibrous loam in a spot fully exposed to the sun.

626. MONADENIA COMOSA, Reichb. f.

M. rufescens, Lindl. *Disa affinis*, N. E. Br. *D. comosa*, Schltr.

Root: a sessile tuber. **Stem:** stout. **Leaves:** basal, lanceolate-oblong to elliptic-oblong, 3″–8″ long, rather thin. **Scape:** ½′–1½′ tall, sheath-clothed. **Spike:** 2″–7″ long, usually lax, many-flowered. **Flowers:** over ¾″ in diameter; dorsal sepal galeate, oblong, blunt, rather thin; spur slender, curved, 1″ long; lateral sepals oblong, rather thin; petals obliquely ovate at the base, falcate-oblong above, rather fleshy; lip broadly oblong or elliptic-oblong, fleshy. *September to November.*

This is a handsome plant with large blossoms and should prove an acquisition to our gardens. It has sulphur-yellow sepals and deep yellow petals and lip. The two or three rich green leaves soon wither. It grows in moist grassy places on the mountains in South-Western Cape Colony and attains its greatest elevation on the Drakenstein Mountains in the Paarl Division at 5000 feet and is there exposed to 20° of frost in the winter for short periods. It should be grown in moist fibrous peat and loam in a sunny spot.

627. MONADENIA OPHRYDEA, Lindl.

M. lancifolia, Sond. *Disa ophrydea*, Bolus

Root: a sessile tuber. **Stem:** stout. **Leaves:** mostly basal, linear-oblong, acute, curled in at the margins, rather fleshy, 2″–4″ long. **Scape:** ½′–1½′ tall, sheath-clothed. **Spike:** 3″–6″ long, lax. **Flowers:** nearly ¾″ across; dorsal sepal galeate, oblong, blunt; spur filiform, slightly curved, ¾″ long; lateral sepals ovate-oblong; petals obliquely ovate-oblong, emarginate or shortly bidentate, fleshy; lip oblong, blunt. *September and October.*

This is a striking and handsome plant with deep red sepals and almost crimson-black petals and lip; the blossoms are sufficiently large to make it a desirable garden plant. It inhabits marshes and moist grassy spots on the mountains of South-Western Cape Colony and attains an elevation of 4000 feet on the Outeniqua Mountain above Montague Pass in the George Division and is there subjected to over 12° of frost for short periods during the winter. It should be grown beside a pond or in the bog garden in a good loamy soil. This species is only suitable for warm localities.

MYRMECHIS, Blume

Three species of terrestrial herbs with very slender stems which are frequently procumbent or ascending; they spring from horizontally creeping rhizomes and are clothed with rounded leaves with short stalks. The quaint blossoms are borne in very few-flowered spikes, terminal on the tips of the flexuous stems; they are interesting but too few in number to render the plants of much garden value. In a state of nature they are found in shady, rocky places among fairly dwarf herbage, frequently in thin or open woods, where their slender stems are supported by the more sturdy plants amidst which they grow. One species in confined to the Malay Islands, another to Western China and a third species is found only in Japan. Two are sufficiently hardy for outdoor culture in Great Britain. Propagation by imported roots.

628. MYRMECHIS CHINENSIS, Rolfe

Root: a slender, creeping rhizome. **Stem:** 1′–1¼′ tall, slender, smooth. **Leaves:** orbicular, blunt or pointed, 1½″–2″ across, on a very short stalk. **Spike:** 1″–1½″ long, sparely downy, bearing 1–3 blossoms. **Flowers** about ⅜″ across; sepals and petals ovate-oblong, pointed; lip saccate at the base, then linear-oblong, and slightly dilated at the tip; disc with several oblong, blunt calli. *May to July.*

A slender, sparely leafy plant with rather tall stems bearing a few small white or pink blossoms of little decorative value. The plant is found in stony, shady spots on the mountains of Western China at from 7000–9000 feet above sea-level, and should be sufficiently hardy for outdoor culture in the warmer parts of the Kingdom in a damp half-shady spot in the rock garden in leaf-soil and peat.

629. MYRMECHIS JAPONICA, Rolfe

Rhamphidia japonica, Reichb. f.

Root: a slender, creeping rhizome furnished with numerous fibres. **Stem:** 1′–1½′ tall, slender, flexuous, ascending. **Leaves:** orbicular, blunt or pointed, 1″–2½″ long, shortly stalked. **Spike:** of 1–3 blossoms. **Flowers:** about ⅝″ across; sepals and petals ovate-oblong, pointed; lip narrowly oblong, saccate at the base, broadly dilated at the tip, with several oblong calli on the disc. *May to July.*

This species is closely related to the preceding one, but may be distinguished by the greater dilation of the tip of the lip. It has the same tintings in the blossoms, but being larger they are more decorative. The plant is found in shady places, usually in mountainous country, in Central and Southern Japan and should be quite hardy in Great Britain in a shady spot in the rock garden in leaf-soil and loam.

MYSTACIDIUM, Lindley

Æranthus, Reichb. f.

The members of this genus, which number about 90 species and are all epiphytic, have dense or few-flowered spikes of small or medium-sized, pale tinted blossoms, of little or no decorative value, they are borne on long or short stems, clothed with linear or lanceolate, leathery or fleshy leaves which spring from a cluster of thick, fleshy fibres. With the exception of a solitary species in Ceylon they are all confined to Africa and the adjacent Islands. They are found on moss and fern-clad trees and rocks, mainly in the dense, moist, tropical and subtropical rain forests; the following species are both mountain plants and may be tried outdoors in the warm, humid western counties, in a sheltered, shady spot on a moss-covered, rough-barked tree such as an oak or an apple, and should be protected from frost as much as possible. They may also be tried on a damp moss- and fern-clad rock in peat and sphagnum-moss. Propagation by division and by seeds.

630. MYSTACIDIUM CAFFRUM, Bolus

Angræcum caffrum, Bolus

Roots: numerous, slender, white. **Stem:** short, stout, about ½″ long. **Leaves:** cauline, linear-oblong or strap-shaped, obliquely 2-lobed, blunt, somewhat narrowed at the base, leathery, 2″–2½″ long. **Scape:** 1¾″–2″ long, flexuous, spreading. **Spike:** rather dense, many-flowered. **Flowers:** about ½″ across; dorsal sepal very broadly elliptic; lateral sepals broadly elliptic, blunt; petals very broadly elliptic; lip ovate-orbicular, blunt, smaller than the petals; spur funnel-shaped, thickened at the apex. *June and July.*

A dainty little plant for the alpine house, not more than three or four inches tall with several flower-stems springing from the base of the leaves; the white blossoms are freely produced and are well set off by the leathery deep green leaves. It grows on moss-grown trees and at times on damp rocks in woodlands in Pondoland, Natal and Griqualand East, where at Fort Donald it reaches an elevation of 4500 feet and is there exposed to 12° of frost. It may be tried on a moss-covered tree outdoors in the warmest parts of Great Britain.

631. MYSTACIDIUM GRACILE, Harv.

Aëranthus gracilis, Reichb. f.

Roots: numerous, slender, flexuous. **Leaves:** obsolete. **Scape:** very slender, arching, 1″–1¾″ long. **Raceme:** lax, one-sided. **Flowers:** about $\frac{3}{16}$″ long; sepals and petals subconnivent, ovate-lanceolate; lip ovate-oblong, about as long as the petals, with very short side lobes at the mouth of the spur; spur funnel-shaped at the mouth, narrow and curved above, $\frac{3}{4}''$ long.

May and June.

An interesting little species with small, white, half-closed blossoms, about half-a-dozen in number, in a one-sided raceme on slender, flexuous flower-stems springing from a short leafless stem. It should make an attractive addition to the alpine house and is remarkable for the length of its spurs on the base of the lip of the blossoms. It grows on large, moss-covered trees in woodlands and primæval forests in Natal and Eastern Cape Colony, where on the Kaga Berg Range it reaches an elevation of 4500 feet and is there subjected to over 15° of frost during the winter. It may be tried in the open in a warm humid locality on a moss tree trunk in the shade.

NEOBOLUSIA, Schlechter

A genus containing 3 species of erect, terrestrial Orchids closely allied to the genus *Brachycorythis*. Their roots consist of one or two ovoid tubers, at times on the ends of stout fibres; the stem is fairly slender and sparely leafy, in one species the leaf is solitary. The blossoms are borne in a long or short raceme, mingled with leafy bracts, and are generally of decorative value. The three species are marsh plants and are found at considerable elevations on the mountains of their native homes; all are confined to South Africa; two are found at sufficient altitude to warrant an attempt to cultivate them in the open in this country, in the bog garden or on the banks of a stream or pond in good rich soil. Propagation by imported tubers and by seeds when available.

632. NEOBOLUSIA TYSONII, Schltr.

Brachycorythis Tysonii, Bolus

Root: of 2 ovoid tubers. **Stem:** $\frac{3}{4}'$–$1\frac{1}{4}'$ tall, sparely leafy, slender and smooth. **Leaves:** basal, lanceolate-oblong, attenuate at the base, $1\frac{1}{2}''$–$5''$ long. **Raceme:** 2″–6″ long, few to many-flowered. **Flowers:** about $\frac{3}{8}''$ across; dorsal sepal ovate; lateral sepals ovate-lanceolate, oblique, somewhat spreading; petals obliquely ovate, shorter than the dorsal sepal, incurved; lip with a broadly dilated suborbicular, minutely crenulate limb; disc with a slender keel extending to the apex of the lip. *December to February.*

A dainty slender species with a sheath-clothed flower-stem furnished near its base with two or three oblong, deep green leaves, and terminating in a fairly long raceme of pale green blossoms with brownish markings on the sepals and a lilac-coloured band at the base at the white lip. It is a high mountain plant and grows in marshy spots near their summits in Eastern Cape Colony, Griqualand East, Natal, Orange Free State and the Transvaal, where on Woodbush Mountains at 8800 feet it is exposed at times to the zero point F. of frost. A rich soil beside a pond or stream is indicated.

633. NEOBOLUSIA VIRGINEA, Schltr.

Platanthera virginea, Bolus. *Brachycorythis virginea*, Rolfe

Root: an ovoid tuber. **Leaf:** solitary, broadly ovate, shortly petiolate, submembranous, $\frac{3}{4}''$–1″ long. **Scape:** slender, flexuous, about 6″ tall, with 1 lanceolate sheath about the middle. **Raceme:** rather short. **Flowers:** about $\frac{3}{8}''$ across; dorsal sepal ovate-oblong, rather pointed; lateral sepals oblique, ovate-oblong, somewhat spreading; petals broadly ovate, rather blunt, somewhat oblique at the base; lip broadly ovate, subentire, rather blunt; disc with a blunt keel near its base. *December and January.*

A delightfully dainty, almost alpine species with a slender stem bearing from three to five delicate blossoms with white sepals, pink petals and a bright pink lip with a green central nerve and base. It is found on the summits and sides of a few of the highest mountains in Natal and the Orange Free State, where it attains its greatest altitude on Mont aux-Sources at 9000 feet and should therefore be perfectly hardy in Great Britain if it could be induced to rest during our winter. It should be grown in a gritty fibrous loam in a moist open spot.

NEOTTIA, Linnæus

Neottidium, Schlechter

A very small genus numbering but 16 species of curious leafless, deciduous, terrestrial plants known as Birds-Nest Orchids, from the thick masses of fleshy fibres which form their root systems being likened to a very miniature rooks' nest. The tinted stems are clothed with a few brownish or purple scales or sheaths and the quaint hooded blossoms with their prominent two-lobed lips are borne in loose or dense many-flowered spikes; they are by no means decorative but are quite interesting and should appeal to the lover of curious plants. All the known species are found in woods, growing as saprophytes in decaying vegetable matter in the northern temperate regions of the Old World. They are all hardy and should be transplanted to the rock garden in a damp shady spot with as large a portion as possible of the soil in which they are growing in a state of nature. Propagation by careful division of the rootstock and also by seeds.

634. NEOTTIA CAMTSCHATEA, Rich.

N. camtschatica, Sprge. *N. kamtchatica*, L. *Ophrys camtschatea*, Linn.

Root: a cluster of fleshy, fusiform roots. **Stem:** $\frac{1}{2}'$–$1\frac{1}{4}'$ tall, fairly stout, clothed with a few scales. **Leaves:** obsolete. **Raceme:** 2″–5″ long, loose, few-flowered. **Flowers:** about $\frac{1}{4}''$ long; sepals subequal, ovate, blunt, spreading; petals linear, smaller than the sepals; lip wedge-shaped, bilobed, lobes rounded; lip very concave. *June and July.*

This species is of little or no decorative value. It produces loose racemes of rather small brownish-green blossoms on tall scaly stems. It is found in spruce forests, growing in decaying leaves over the roots of trees in the peninsula of Kamchatka. It should be perfectly hardy in Great Britain in a damp shady spot in the rock garden, in soil collected from beneath the shade of spruce or pine trees.

635. NEOTTIA GRANDIFLORA, Schltr.

Root: of numerous fleshy fibres. **Stem:** $9''$–$14''$ tall, stout, fleshy, clothed with a few sheaths. **Leaves:** obsolete. **Raceme:** $5''$–$7''$ long, erect, densely many-flowered. **Flowers:** about $\frac{3}{4}''$ long; dorsal sepal oblong, rather pointed; lateral sepals falcately elliptic, pointed, dilated on the outer margin; petals linear or linear-ligulate, oblique, with a revolute margin; lip cuneate, obovate, bilobed; lobes obliquely oblong, blunt, outer margins crenulate. *August.*

This handsome plant is a saprophyte, living on half-decayed leaves and twigs in the damp forests which it inhabits. It very much resembles in habit and appearance our native *Cotyledon Umbilicus*. The blossoms have their segments rich olive-green in colour bordered by a paler tint; the stem and bracts are greenish-brown. It is a native of Western China, reaching elevations of over 10,000 feet. It may be tried outdoors under the same cultural conditions as our native species.

636. NEOTTIA LISTEROIDES, Lindl.

N. Lindleyana, Deene.

Root: a thick cluster of numerous, rather fleshy fibres. **Stem:** $\frac{3}{4}'$–$1\frac{1}{4}'$ tall, clothed with 3–4 sheaths. **Leaves:** obsolete. **Raceme:** $\frac{1}{2}'$–$1'$ long, downy, lax-flowered. **Flowers:** $\frac{1}{2}''$ long; sepals lanceolate, truncate, concave, spreading, the lateral ones falcate; petals almost linear with convolute margins; lip nearly 3 times as long as the sepals, linear-oblong, divided into 2 ovate or linear-subacute parallel lobes. *July and August.*

A curious leafless species with tall sheath-clothed stems of a brownish-purple colour and rather small red-brown blossoms borne in a long loose spike or raceme. It is of very little decorative value and is found in damp wooded ravines and thin thickets in the Himalaya from Kashmir to Sikkim, reaching an elevation of 11,000 feet, and is therefore quite hardy in Great Britain, in a damp half-shady spot in leaf-soil and peat.

637. NEOTTIA MICRANTHA, Lindl.

Nidus micranthus, O. Ktze.

Root: a cluster of fleshy fibres. **Stem:** $\frac{1}{2}'$–$1\frac{1}{2}'$ tall, clothed with a few scales in the place of leaves. **Raceme:** 2″–6″ long, narrow, flowers few and distant. **Flowers:** about $\frac{1}{4}''$ long; sepals lanceolate, pointed, spreading; petals smaller, but similar in shape; lip concave at the base, ovate, short, pointed.

June.

A rather tall, slender plant with a long, narrow raceme of small blossoms, with greenish-brown sepals and petals and a pale green lip. It is of no decorative value and is found in calcareous soil in dense shady pine forests, in Western Yunnan, Western China, at from 10,500–11,000 feet above sea-level. It should be quite hardy in Great Britain in the rock garden, in calcareous leaf-soil in a damp shady spot.

638. NEOTTIA NIDUS-AVIS, Rich.

Helleborine nidus-avis, Schm. *Listera nidus-avis*, Hook. *Ophrys nidus-avis*, Linn.

Root: a dense mass of small, fleshy, fusiform fibres. **Stem:** 12″–15″ tall, clothed with a few sheathing scales in the place of leaves. **Spike:** 2″–3″ long, rather densely many-flowered. **Flowers:** about $\frac{3}{8}''$ long; sepals broadly ovate, pointed; petals similar only more rounded; lip oblong or cuneate, deeply cleft at the tip into 2 oblong diverging lobes with blunt tips.

April to June.

A curious native plant known as the Birds-Nest Orchis from the fancied resemblance of its cluster of matted roots to a bird's nest. The stem and scales are of a pale brown colour whilst the blossoms are dingy brown throughout. It is found in woods over the greater part of Europe and Western Siberia, and like all the other members of the genus should be dug up with as much as possible of the soil in which it is growing and transferred to a shady part of the rock garden.

NERVILIA, Gaudin

This genus comprises over 60 species of deciduous, terrestrial herbs of dwarf habit, somewhat closely allied to the genus *Pogonia*; their root systems are composed of rounded tubers of annual duration, with a few short, fleshy roots above them springing from where the tubers join the stem. Small tubers are produced from the sides of the parent tuber; these eventually become large enough to produce flowering stems after the large one has perished, which takes place after the seed capsules have ripened. The major portion of the species produce a solitary, somewhat rounded leaf and a short flower-stem bearing one or two small or medium-sized blossoms of curious construction; with few exceptions they are not showy and are only of interest to botanists and those gardeners who love plants for their own sake and not for the display of colour they give. Propagation by imported roots.

639. NERVILIA NIPPONICA, Makino

N. punctata, Makino. *Pogonia punctata*, Makino

Root: an ovoid or globose tuber. **Leaf:** solitary, cordate-orbicular, about $1\frac{3}{4}''$ across, on a fairly long stalk. **Scape:** about $3\frac{1}{2}''$ tall, smooth, clothed with a few small sheaths. **Flower:** solitary, terminal, nodding, about $\frac{5}{8}''$ long; sepals narrowly lanceolate, dorsal sepal erect, lateral sepals slightly spreading; petals similar only shorter; lip 3-lobed; outer lobes very small and blunt; centre lobe elliptical, blunt, crisped. *June and July.*

A tiny plant, suitable for alpine house decoration, with purple blossoms with a white, purple-spotted lip. The leaf and stem are also tinted with purple. It is found in damp shady places in many parts of Japan, usually in woods, growing in decaying leaves. It may be grown in the rock garden under the same conditions as members of the genus *Epipogum*.

NIGRITELLA, Richard

This genus contains but 1 species, it is a delightful little alpine herb with a rootstock of rounded tubers buried just below the surface of the soil. After having produced the nourishment for the flower-stem and seed capsules the tuber perishes; young tubers are produced on the ends of the larger roots and form one of the methods by which the plant increases. Many of the smaller Orchids are plentiful one season and nearly absent the next on account of the young tubers requiring more than a season to become strong enough to produce flower-stems. The plant and its forms may be increased by separation of the tubers and, in the case of the type, by seeds when available.

640. NIGRITELLA ANGUSTIFOLIA, Rich.

Gymnadenia nigra, Reichb. f. *Habenaria nigra*, R. Br. *Orchis minata*, Crantz. *O. nigra*, Scop. *O. suaveolens*, Steud. *Satyrium nigrum*, Linn.

Root: of 2 oblong tubers about $1\frac{1}{4}''$ long, ending in 2 or 3 finger-like lobes. **Leaves:** mainly basal, clustered, linear, channelled, $1''$–$3''$ long. **Scape:** slender, $4''$–$12''$ tall, clothed with a few bract-like leaves, erect. **Spike:** $\frac{3}{4}''$–$1\frac{1}{2}''$ long, pyramidal, very densely many-flowered. **Flowers:** about $\frac{3}{8}''$ long and the same in breadth; dorsal sepal broadly lanceolate, erect; lateral sepals lanceolate, spreading; petals narrowly lanceolate; lip lanceolate, entire, similar to the petals. *June to August.*

A delightful little plant with neat, deep green, grassy foliage and a slender stem bearing a clover-like head of small wine-red, pink or white blossoms. There is a pretty form known as subspecies *rubra* (Richter) and several varieties, such as *flava, longibracteata, pallida* and *rosea*. It also produces several interesting hybrids with members of the genus *Platanthera*. The plant and its forms are found in alpine pastures on most of the higher mountains of Europe. They may be grown in the rock garden in fairly moist calcareous loam.

OBERONIA, Lindley

Tufted, epiphytic, evergreen plants with minute blossoms of no decorative value. The roots are fairly numerous, somewhat stout and fleshy and spring from a very short, stout stem which bears a tuft of narrow, sword-shaped, distichous leaves, frequently hooked at their tips. The flower-stems are usually very short and spring from among the leaves; the blossoms are borne in dense round spikes or racemes. The following species are very tiny plants and although they are of no garden value should prove very attractive in the alpine house for they are neat and compact and their tiny blossoms are curiously constructed. A shallow pan well crocked and filled with osmunda-fibre or peat, with sphagnum-moss and some small pieces of charcoal is suitable and the same compost on a damp sandstone rock outdoors may be tried. The genus numbers about 230 species and is scattered over tropical Asia, Australia, and the islands of the Pacific. Propagation by imported plants and seeds.

641. OBERONIA OBCORDATA, Lindl.

Malaxis obcordata, Reichb. f.

Root: of stout fibres. **Stem:** 1″–2″ long, flat and flexuous. **Leaves:** cauline, distichous, linear-falcate, 1″–1½″ long. **Scape:** 1″–1½″ long. **Spike:** about 1″ long, very dense. **Flowers:** about $\frac{1}{16}$″ across; sepals broadly ovate, subequal; petals linear-oblong; lip oblong, from a narrow base, 3-lobed; outer lobes short, falcate; centre lobe large, obcordately 2-lobed.

July and August.

A very dwarf epiphytic of tufted habit, with narrow sickle-shaped bright green leaves and short spikes of minute yellow blossoms in densely clustered whorls. It should prove interesting in a pan of sphagnum-moss and osmunda-fibre in the alpine house. It grows on damp moss-covered rocks and trees in the Khasia Hills and Sikkim Himalaya at altitudes of from 5000–9000 feet and is exposed during the winter to 15° or 20° of frost for considerable periods.

642. OBERONIA TREUTLERI, Hook. f.

Root: of stout, fleshy fibres. **Stem:** rather stout, with a tendency to elongate. **Leaves:** subalternate, distichous, oblong or oblong-lanceolate, rather thin, 1″–2½″ long. **Scape:** 2½″ tall, slender. **Spike:** about 1″ long, with the blossoms in dense whorls. **Flowers:** under $\frac{1}{16}$″ across, sepals broadly ovate; petals linear-oblong; lip 3-lobed, lobes subequal; outer lobes oblong or rounded; centre lobe very shortly obcordate, all crenate and fleshy.

August.

This species is not quite so dwarf as that previously described, the stem having a tendency to increase in length with age. It is of no horticultural value and produces short, whorled spikes of tiny pale yellowish-green blossoms. It grows on damp mossy rocks and trees in the Sikkim Himalaya at an elevation of 8000 feet and is there subjected to 10° or 15° of frost during the winter. It may be tried outdoors in mild sheltered localities under the same cultural conditions as the foregoing species.

ODONTOCHILUS, Blume

Attractive little plants with quaint blossoms and large rich green leaves which are frequently veined and blotched with red, purple or gold. All are well worth growing for their foliage alone. They number about 20 species and two are found at sufficient elevations in their mountain homes to ensure their hardiness outdoors in the mild and sheltered parts of this country. They are terrestrial plants with a creeping rhizome bearing a few stout whitish fibres. The leaves are few in number, broad and large for the size of the plants and taper to a sheathing stalk. The blossoms are borne in a rather short, many-flowered spike and are frequently reversed, the lip being uppermost; they are quaint and usually have a conspicuous lip. They are scattered over Eastern India, Malaya and the islands of the Pacific and are usually found in wooded country. The following species may be tried outdoors in the rock garden in very mild localities in a shady spot in peat, decaying oak and beech leaves mixed with sphagnum-moss. Propagation by division of the rhizomes and by imported seeds.

643. ODONTOCHILUS ELWESII, Clarke

Root: a rather fleshy, creeping rhizome. **Stem:** stout below, 6″–8″ high. **Leaves:** ovate-lanceolate, rather crowded, 1½″–2½″ long. **Spike:** of 2 to 4 blossoms, hairy. **Flowers:** about ½″ across; dorsal sepal narrowly ovate, small; lateral sepals ovate, larger than the dorsal sepal, all hairy; petals semicircular, usually with long points; lip 2-lobed, lobes subquadrate.

July.

A pretty little species suitable for alpine house culture, with stout stems clothed with numerous oval, deep green leaves decorated with three bright red veins, and short stems bearing a few pretty blossoms of pale green or white sepals and petals with purple tips and a white and purple lip. It is found in the same habitat and under the same conditions as the following species but is perhaps a trifle less hardy. It may be tried outdoors in the warm western counties of Great Britain in a sheltered part of the rock garden in fibrous peat, a little loam and sphagnum-moss.

644. ODONTOCHILUS PUMILUS, Hook. f.

Cheirostylis pusilla, Lindl.

Root: a slender, creeping, underground stem. **Stem:** 2″–3″ tall, ascending from a prostrate base, stout for the size of the plant. **Leaves:** ovate, pointed, stalked, $\frac{1}{3}$″–$\frac{1}{2}$″ long. **Scape:** short, with one membranous fringed sheath, bearing from 1–3 blossoms. **Flowers:** $\frac{1}{4}$″ across, subglobose; dorsal sepal broadly ovate, with a blunt, recurved tip; lateral sepals obliquely triangular-ovate; petals lanceolate; lip oblong, terminal lobes subquadrate, crenulate.

June and July.

A very tiny prostrate species with short ascending stems clothed with oval, rich green leaves and short scapes bearing a few rather heath-like white blossoms. It is very suitable for alpine-house cultivation. It grows on damp mossy rocks usually in shade in the Sikkim Himalaya, ascending to 10,000 feet above sea-level and is exposed to over 25° of frost for short periods during the winter. It may be grown in the rock garden in a half-shady spot in fibrous peat, and sphagnum-moss.

OPHRYS, Linnæus

This genus, which numbers about 15 species, contains many of the most beautiful of the more dwarf terrestrial Orchids; they are deciduous plants; their root systems consist of rather small, rounded tubers, either sessile or shortly stalked; in most species these are annual, one or more young tubers are produced annually, the old one shrivels and perishes as soon as the seed capsules have ripened. In many species the fresh tubers given off as offsets from the parent tuber take more than one year to grow to flowering size, thus accounting for the plentifulness one year and paucity the next which may be observed with many species. The leaves are usually somewhat narrow and the beautiful blossoms are produced in few-flowered spikes in many species, they have a remarkable likeness to bees, wasps and flies. The various species, with but few exceptions, are scattered over the countries bordered by the Mediterranean. Propagation by separation of the tubers and by seeds.

645. OPHRYS APIFERA, Huds.

O. rostrata, Ten.

Root: of 2 ovoid tubers about 1″ long. **Leaves:** few, but with more on the stem than in most species, ovate or oblong-ovate below, lanceolate and pointed on the stem, 3″–4″ long. **Scape:** 6″–18″ tall, rather slender, flexuous. **Spike:** 3″–5″ long, of 3–6 widely separated blossoms. **Flowers:** about $1\frac{1}{8}$″ long by the same measurement in breadth; dorsal sepal ovate-oblong, hooked at the tip; lateral sepals ovate-lanceolate, curved slightly downwards; petals triangular or ovate, very small, hairy; lip very variable in shape, more or less wedge-shaped, with 2 pendent, lanceolate, pointed lateral lobes and with a small tooth in the indentation at its tip. *June.*

This quaint species has a remarkably large column and is curiously constructed; the sepals are pale pink or purple; the petals are green and the velvety crimson-purple lip has yellow lines and markings near its base and two white spots near the tip. It is found in open grassy places on hills in Western and Central Europe and is rare. It may be grown in the rock garden in an open sunny spot in sandy fibrous loam. The varieties *aurita, austrica, chlorantha, intermedia* and the hybrid *friburgensis* are desirable.

646. OPHRYS ARANIFERA, Huds.

Root: of 2 ovoid tubers about 1″ long. **Leaves:** basal, about 6 in number, reflexed, oblong, usually blunt, 1″–$2\frac{1}{2}$″ long. **Scape:** 4″–15″ tall, rather stout, usually flexuous, clothed with 1 or more bracts. **Spike:** 2″–6″ long, lax, few-flowered, usually flexuous. **Flowers:** about $\frac{7}{8}$″ long; dorsal sepal oblong, blunt, erect; lateral sepals oblong or ovate, spreading; petals oblong, much smaller than the sepals; lip very variable in shape, usually about as broad as long, rounded, with a shallow cleft at its apex. *April and May.*

This species, although pretty and delicate, is not so desirable as some of the other members of the genus; it has pale green blossoms with a brown, green-margined lip with some variable pale markings near its base. The plant is found over most of Europe and Western Asia in dry pastures and runs into numerous forms and subspecies, such as *ambigua, arachnitiformis, arata, elongata, euchlora, exaltata, fissa, latipetala, litigiosa, lumilata, parallela, rotula, specularia, subfucifera, taurica, Tommasinii* and *viridiflora.* It may be cultivated in the rock garden in a well-drained sunny spot in sandy loam of a calcareous nature.

647. OPHRYS BERTOLONII, Moretti

O. grassensis, Jaivy. *Arachnite Bertolonii*, Tod.

Root: of 2 ovoid, somewhat irregular tubers about 1″ long. **Leaves:** basal and cauline, oblong-lanceolate, degenerating into long pointed sheaths on the stem, 2″–2½″ long. **Scape:** fairly stout, 4″–12″ long, frequently slightly curved or zigzag in the spike. **Spike:** 3″–4″ long, of 4–5 widely separated blossoms. **Flowers:** 1¼″ long by 1″ wide; dorsal sepal ovate, nearly erect; lateral sepals oblong-falcate, pointed; petals linear or triangular; lip oblong, broadening towards the tip, where it is divided into 2 rounded lobes; there is a small tooth in the sinus and the whole lip projects forward.

April and May.

A very charming plant with large, brightly coloured blossoms. The sepals are pale pink or lilac; the petals are rich rose-pink and the lip is of a rich deep velvety crimson with a more or less oblong pale violet or purple spot in its centre, this is rather variable in shape. It inhabits thickets and grassy places on hill sides from the Balearic Isles to Greece. The varieties *parviflora, dalmatica, flavicans, Inzengæ,* and *Landaueri* differ but little from the type; the hybrid *Barlæ* is quite pretty. It may be grown outdoors in a sheltered sunny spot in the rock garden in sandy loam.

648. OPHRYS BOMBYLIFERA, Link

O. caniculata, Viv. *O. distoma,* Biv. *O. hiulca,* Mauri. *O. labiofossa,* Bront. *O. pulla,* Cyr. *O. Tabinifera,* Will. *Arachnites bombyliflora,* Tod.

Root: of 3 or more tubers, ovoid, at times stalked, ½″–¾″ long. **Leaves:** subradical, oblong-lanceolate, rather pointed, undulate, recurved, 1″–2″ long. **Scape:** about 6″ tall, slender, slightly sinuous, clothed with a solitary thin sheath. **Spike:** of 2–3 widely separated blossoms. **Flower:** over ¾″ across; sepals oblong, concave; petals oblong, recurved, short, downy; lip deeply 3-lobed; lobes concave, prolonged below; the centre lobe subglobular, cleft horizontally at the tip. *March to May.*

A delicate little plant with very pretty "baggy" blossoms with pale green sepals and petals and a hairy brown lip very like the body of a small Humble Bee. Like all the other members of the genus it is a gem for alpine-house decoration. It is found on open chalky hills from Portugal to Greece, North Africa and the Canary Isles. It may be grown in a sunny sheltered spot in the rock garden in sandy calcareous loam.

649. OPHRYS FERRUM-EQUINUM, Desf.

Root: of 2 oblong tubers about 1¼″ long. **Leaves:** basal, about 4 in number, oblong-lanceolate, the uppermost very pointed, 1½″–2″ long. **Scape:** 4″–9″ tall, fairly stout and at times curved. **Spike:** 2″–3″ long, of 3–4 widely separated blossoms. **Flowers:** about ¾″ long by ½″ wide; dorsal sepal ovate-lateral; lateral sepals lanceolate or triangular; petals triangular; lip entire, oblong, concave, with a slight notch and tooth at the tip.

March and April.

A dainty, rather small-flowered species with bright pink or pale purple sepals, deep pink petals and purple-violet or purple-crimson lip with a few pale markings on it. It grows in sandy and calcareous soils in rather hilly country amongst short herbage in Greece, Turkey, Western Asia and Transcaucasia. The sub-species *Sprunneri* from Syria has white or pale blue markings on the lip. The type and the subspecies may be grown outdoors in the rock garden in mild sunny localities in light calcareous loam in a sunny well-drained spot.

650. OPHRYS FUCIFLORA, Hall

O. adrachnites, Bertol. *O. discors*, Bianca. *O. truncata*, Dulac. *Orchis arachnites*, Linn.

Root: of 2 oblong potato-like tubers 1″ long. **Leaves:** mostly basal, 4–5 in number, ovate-oblong, those on the upper part of the stem sheathing and small, 2″–2½″ long. **Scape:** ½′–1¼′ tall, rather slender and sometimes zig-zag. **Spike:** 3″–4″ long, of 4–6 blossoms, slightly more crowded than in many of the other species. **Flowers:** about 1⅛″ long by 1″ wide, secund; dorsal sepal oblong, curved over the column; lateral sepals ovate or oblong, frequently curving downwards; petals linear-lanceolate, minute; lip variable in shape, nearly as broad as it is long, with a small process in the sinus at its tip.

March to May.

A very quaint and handsome species with lilac or pale purple sepals and petals and dull purplish-crimson or brownish-crimson lip with some variable markings in yellow near its base. The plant is found in calcareous soils in pastures and on open sunny hill sides in Middle and Southern Europe. The varieties and subspecies *albescens*, *attica*, *biancæ*, *brachyotus coronifera*, *cornigera*, *latissima*, *linearis*, *panormitana*, *pseudapifera*, *orgyifera*, *oxyrhynchos* and *Untchjii* are worth growing. The plant may be grown in the rock garden in a sunny spot in sandy calcareous loam.

651. OPHRYS FUSCA, Link.

Root: of ovoid tubers ½″ long. **Leaves:** basal, few in number, broadly oblong, rather blunt, tapering towards the base, recurved, 1″–1½″ long. **Scape:** 4″–8″ tall, fairly stout, sheath-clothed. **Spike:** of 3–6 widely separated blossoms. **Flowers:** 1″ long by 1″ across; dorsal sepal ovate, hooded; lateral sepals ovate or broadly lanceolate, spreading; petals linear, suberect, small; lip wedge-shaped, nearly flat, lobed, swollen at the base.

February in Africa, March and April in Europe.

An attractive little plant with quaint but very pretty blossoms with pale green sepals, yellowish-green or brown petals and a rich purple, hairy lip with a smooth yellow margin and some yellow markings near its base.

It is widely distributed over the whole of the Mediterranean both in Africa and Europe, inhabiting open sunny places amongst short herbage, mostly on calcareous soils. It may be grown in sheltered districts in the rock garden in sandy calcareous loam. The varieties or subspecies *atlantica*, from the mountains of Algeria, and *funerea*, from Corsica, etc., are very pretty. Culture as for the other lime-loving species.

652. OPHRYS LUTEA, Cav.

Root: of irregular ovoid tubers. **Leaves:** basal, 3–4 in number, oblong or broadly lanceolate, recurved, sheathing, 2″–3″ long. **Scape:** 6″–9″ tall, fairly stout, clothed with a solitary sheath. **Spike:** lax, of few blossoms. **Flowers:** about $\frac{7}{8}$″ long and 1″ across; dorsal sepal ovoid, blunt, projecting over the column; lateral sepals ovate, spreading; petals linear, erect; lip very broadly 3-lobed; outer lobes broad, pointed; centre lobe very broad, truncate, cleft, margin wide and smooth. *March and April.*

A pretty and desirable species with a sinuous flower-stem bearing three or four "baggy" blossoms with green and pink sepals, yellow petals and a hairy purple and blue lip with a broad, smooth yellow margin. There are several pretty varieties such as, *minor*, *pallida*, and *obœsa*. The type and its forms are found in rocky and sandy places among short herbage from Portugal to Persia and in North Africa; they may be grown in a sheltered, sunny, well-drained spot in the rock garden in sandy loam.

653. OPHRYS MUSCIFERA, Huds.

Root: of two ovoid tubers $\frac{3}{4}$″ long. **Leaves:** mainly basal, about 5 in number, lanceolate or ovate-lanceolate, sheathing at the base, uppermost stem-sheathing, 2″–3″ long. **Scape:** $\frac{1}{2}$′–1$\frac{1}{4}$′ tall, rather slender. **Spike:** 2″–4″ long, lax, of 4–8 blossoms. **Flowers:** $\frac{3}{4}$″ long by $\frac{1}{2}$″ across; dorsal sepal ovate, more or less erect; lateral sepals ovate or ovate-lanceolate, spreading, longer than the dorsal sepal; petals linear or filiform, suberect; lip 3-lobed; outer lobes linear or lanceolate, pointed, diverging; centre lobe wedge-shaped, rounded and notched at its tip. *March to May.*

This species is perhaps not so attractive as many of the others. The blossoms, which are borne in a one-sided spike, have pale green sepals, pale purple petals and a purple, green-tipped lip with a greenish triangular mark in its centre. It is found in meadows, clearings in woods and on sandy and calcareous hills over most of Northern Europe. The varieties *bomibifera*, *parviflora*, *ochroleuca*, *peloria* and the hybrids *hybrida*, *apicula* and *Reichenbachiana* are in some cases preferable to the type. Culture as for the other lime-loving species.

654. OPHRYS ŒSTRIFERA, Marsch.

O. scolopax œstrifera, Reichb. f.

Root: of 2 oblong or ovoid tubers about 3/4″ long. **Leaves:** radical and cauline, those on the stem bract-like, oblong-lanceolate to lanceolate, 1½″–2″ long. **Scape:** ½′–1¼′ tall, rather stout, clothed with a few sheath-like leaves. **Spike:** 2″–4″ long, lax, bearing 4–6 blossoms. **Flowers:** about 7/8″ long and 3/4″ broad; dorsal sepal oblong, nearly erect; lateral sepals ovate-oblong, spreading; petals linear, suberect, very small; lip oblong-obovate, 3-lobed; outer lobes triangular; centre lobe 3-lobed with a cleft at the apex in which there is a blunt tooth. *May.*

A very quaint species with flowers resembling a Botfly, as its scientific name implies. The sepals are rose-purple with green veins; the petals are pale purple and the lip is covered with dense, dark brown, velvety hairs and there are frequently obscure markings at the base. This species is found on the sides of calcareous hills, etc., from Sardinia to Asia Minor and Algeria. The variety *bremifera* is quite desirable. The plant may be grown outdoors in warm sheltered localities in a sunny spot in sandy calcareous loam.

655. OPHRYS PECTUS, Mutel.

Root: of globose tubers about 3/4″ across. **Leaves:** basal, 3–5 in number, oblong, blunt or rather pointed, 1½″–2″ long. **Scape:** about 6″ tall, clothed with a few sheaths. **Spike:** of 2–4 blossoms. **Flowers:** about ½″ across and 5/8″ long; dorsal sepal obovate, cucullate, blunt, incurved at the tip; lateral sepals oblong, blunt, spreading; petals linear, blunt, much smaller than the sepals; lip fiddle-shaped, lobes obsolete, disc swollen, tip retuse, subemarginate. *February and March.*

A quaint little African species with spikes of small flowers with whitish-yellow or greenish-yellow sepals and petals and a brownish-purple lip. It is found on sunny hill-sides near Bona, Algeria, and may be tried outdoors in the warmest parts of Great Britain in a very sunny part of the rock garden in sandy loam perfectly drained. Its tubers should be protected from frost during the winter.

656. OPHRYS SCOLOPAX, Cav.

O. corniculata, Brot. *O. bombyliflora*, Reichb. f. *O. picta*, Link. *O. sphegifera*, Willd.

Root: of 2 ovoid tubers about 3/4″ long. **Leaves:** mainly basal, 3–6 in number, oblong-lanceolate, pointed, 1½″–2½″ long. **Scape:** ½′–1′ tall, rather stout, and usually naked. **Spike:** 3″–6″ long, secund or cylindrical, of 4 to 6 blossoms. **Flowers:** about 1″ long by 3/4″ wide; dorsal sepal ovate, curved over the column; lateral sepals ovate, usually curved downwards; petals linear, suberect, minute; lip variously shaped, usually oblong and rounded, at times larger at the top than the bottom, slightly cleft, with a small process in the sinus. *May and June.*

An exquisitely beautiful species with pale purple sepals and petals and crimson-purple velvety lip marked with golden rings and lines forming intricate patterns: the lateral lobes of the lip frequently project like two horns. The plant inhabits pastures and open spots on hill sides usually on a calcareous formation and is found over the greater part of Europe, North Africa and Western Asia. The varieties and subspecies *atropos, asilifera, cornuta, araneola* and *honckensis* are all very beautiful. Culture as for the other lime-loving species.

657. OPHRYS SPECULUM, Link.

O. hirsuta, Duf. *O. vernixia*, Bort. *Arachnite speculum*, Tod. *Orchis ciliata*, Biv.

Root: of 2 or 3 ovoid tubers about $\frac{1}{2}''$ long. **Leaves:** subradical, oblong or lanceolate, 3 to 5 in number, undulate, recurved, 2″–3″ long. **Scape:** 6″–8″ tall, slender, curved, clothed with 1–2 sheaths. **Spike:** of from 2 to 5 blossoms. **Flowers:** $\frac{3}{4}''$ across and $\frac{3}{4}''$ long; dorsal sepal ovate, hooded; lateral sepals broadly lanceolate, concave at their tips, spreading or reflexed; petals small, narrowly triangular; lip 3-lobed; outer lobes triangular; centre lobe broad, rounded at the tip, hairy except in the centre.

March and April.

A delightful little plant with most exquisitely coloured blossoms. The sepals are green striped with rich purple-brown; the petals which are of a velvety texture are pink, and the lip is brown with a yellow border and there is a large heart-shaped spot of shining lapis lazuli blue in its centre. The varieties *Di Stefanii, incubracea, lacætæ* and *oxyrhynchos* are desirable. The plant grows on grassy hillsides in all the countries bordering the Mediterranean. It may be grown in a sunny sheltered spot in the rock garden in sandy calcareous loam.

658. OPHRYS TENTHREDINIFERA, Willd.

O. arachnites, Link. *O. grandiflora*, Ten. *O. episcopalis*, Poi. *O. Tenoreana*, Lindl. *O. villosa*, Desf.

Root: of 2 oblong tubers about 1″ long. **Leaves:** subradical, ovate or ovate-oblong, reduced upwards into 3 leaf-like bracts on the stem, 2″–$2\frac{1}{2}''$ long. **Scape:** $\frac{1}{2}'$–1′ tall, rather stout. **Spike:** 2″–4″ long, of 4–8 blossoms. **Flowers:** nearly 1″ long by the same breadth; dorsal sepal ovate, concave, curved over the column; lateral sepals ovate, spreading, or slightly twisted at the tip;

PLATE 15.

OPHRYS SPECULUM.

PLATE 16.

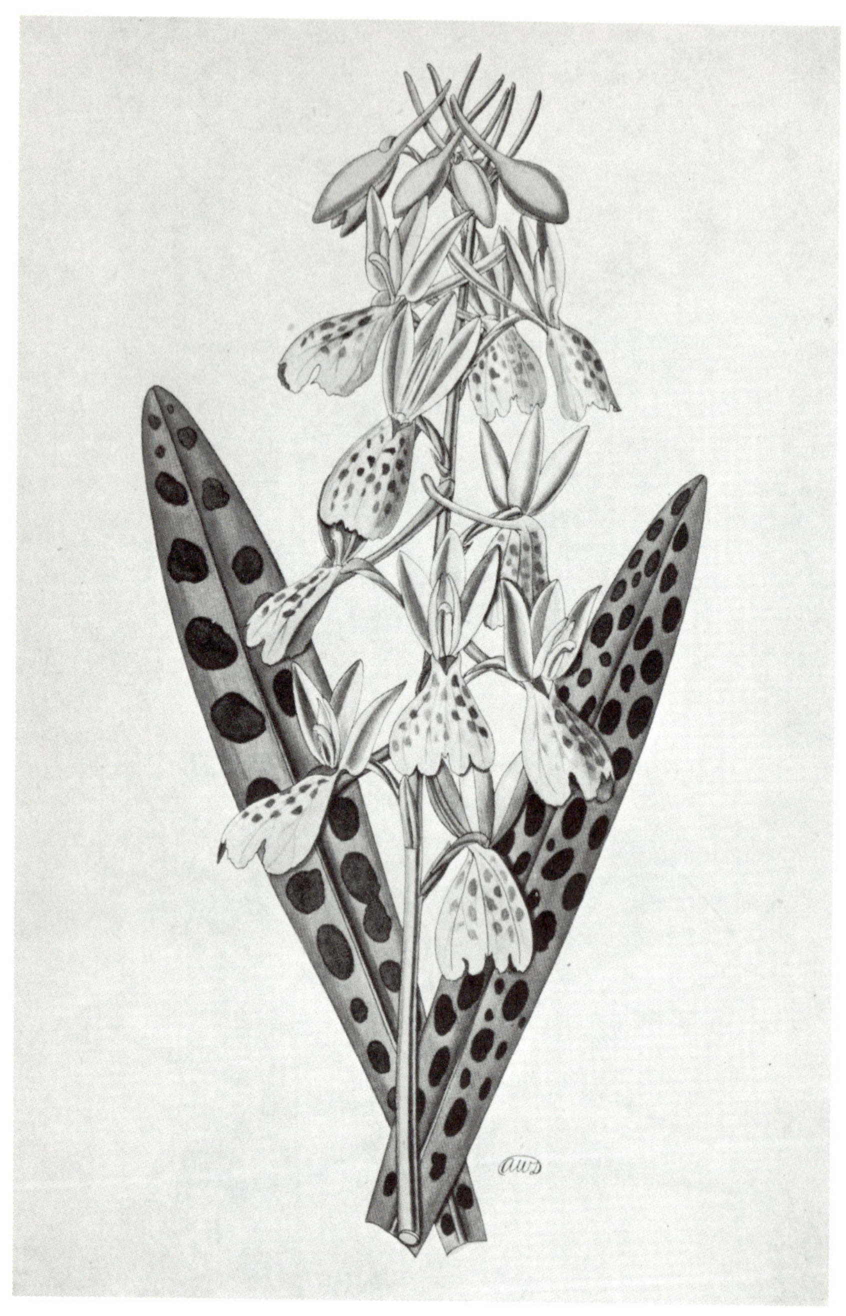

ORCHIS PROVINCIALIS.

petals linear, minute; lip very slightly 3-lobed, very broadly wedge-shaped, slightly cleft at the tip, with a small tooth in the sinus. *March to May.*

An extremely beautiful Orchid with a loose one-sided spike of large blossoms. The sepals are rose-pink, lilac, or pale purple; the petals are tinted in the same manner, whilst the lip is rich velvety crimson-purple with a yellow or cream-coloured border and a square yellow marking at its base with yellow spots on each side of it. It is found in sandy and calcareous pastures and on open sunny hill sides from Portugal to Greece, and Algeria. The variety *Davei* has a rich crimson lip and is very beautiful. *Choffatii* has cream-coloured blossoms with a small lunar mark on the lip; other varieties are *præcox*, *serotina* and *Ficalheana*; there is a subspecies called *neglecta*. Culture as for the other lime-loving species.

ORCHIS, Linnæus

A genus numbering about 70 species of very handsome terrestrial herbs, containing a number of species of very considerable garden value. Their roots consist of two or more rounded or palmately lobed tubers, rarely more than an inch or so long; fresh tubers are produced yearly to replace that which has supplied most of the nourishment for the growing plant. The stems are generally stout for the size of the plant and are more or less leafy. The leaves are lanceolate or oblong and are frequently decorated with purple spots or blotches. The pretty, spurred blossoms are borne in long or short, few- or many-flowered spikes, some are sweetly fragrant. The various species are scattered over most of the northern hemisphere, their headquarters being no doubt Central and Southern Europe; most of them are lovers of damp, sunny situations. Propagation by separation of the tubers when at rest and also by seeds which are freely produced by many species.

659. ORCHIS ANATOLICA, Boiss

Root: of 2 ovoid tubers about $\frac{1}{2}''$ long. **Stem:** fairly stout, at times slightly curved, 6″–12″ tall, leafy below. **Leaves:** sheathing, oblong or oblong-lanceolate, narrower upwards, 1″–2″ long. **Spike:** 2″–4″ long, loose, many-flowered. **Flowers:** about $\frac{5}{8}''$ long exclusive of the spur; sepals and petals lanceolate, at times slightly curved towards the tip, erect; petals smaller than the sepals, conniving, forming a galea over the column; lip ovate, slightly 3-lobed; centre lobe very small, either triangular or nearly square, with a slight notch. *May and June.*

A dainty little species with purple-violet blossoms of fair size considering the height of the plant. The lip has a pale centre but is quite unspotted. This species is found in open pastures, most frequently in hilly places, from the Greek Archipelago to Mesopotamia. The plant may be grown in an open spot in the rock garden in damp calcareous loam and sand. There is a dwarf variety named *Kochii* (*rariflora*).

660. ORCHIS ANGUSTIFOLIA, M.B.

O. incarnata var. *angustifolia*, Wilk. *O. latifolia* var. *angustifolia*, Lindl.

Root: of 2 palmately lobed tubers, one sessile and the other stalked. **Stem:** $\frac{3}{4}'$–$2\frac{1}{2}'$ tall, more or less hollow, leafy. **Leaves:** few in number, cauline, linear-lanceolate, 3″–7″ long. **Spike:** 2″–6″ long, usually lax, many-flowered. **Flowers:** about $\frac{5}{8}''$ long; dorsal sepal narrowly ovate; lateral sepals lanceolate, curved at the tip; petals similar only smaller, conniving over the column; lip rounded, slightly 3-lobed, lobes rounded, centre one reduced to a small triangular point; spur curved, rather slender, $\frac{3}{8}''$ long. *May and June.*

A very slender species with a narrow spike of about a dozen pretty blossoms of a crimson-purple colour; the lip has a white base and some semicircular purple lines on its disc. The plant is found in moist pastures usually in rich soils. There are numerous pretty forms such as *Blyttii*, *caucasica*, *filiformis*, *Grisebachii*, *Haussknechtii*, *Mylandrii*, *Reichenbaachii*, *Russowii*, *sanionis* and *Traunstrineri*, which range over most of Northern and Central Europe as far as the Caucasus. In cultivation it may be treated like *O. latifolia.*

661. ORCHIS ARISTATA, Fisch.

Root: of 2 ovoid or oblong tubers. **Stem:** 6″–18″ tall, erect, leafy. **Leaves:** ovate-lanceolate, pointed, $2\frac{1}{2}''$–5″ long. **Spike:** 2″–3″ long, dense, many-flowered. **Flowers:** $\frac{1}{2}''$ across; dorsal sepal ovate-lanceolate, pointed; lateral sepals lanceolate, spreading; petals narrowly lanceolate, incurved; lip ovate, 3-lobed; lateral lobes rounded, deflexed; centre lobe ovate, pointed; spur cylindrical, fleshy, pendulous, about $\frac{5}{8}''$ long. *June.*

This species is very closely allied to *O. latifolia* and is well worth cultivating. It has dense spikes of blossom varying from white to purple. In a state of nature it is found in wet pasture land, the edges of swamps and marshes, ranging from Western China to Korea, Japan, and the Aleutian Islands. It should be perfectly hardy in Great Britain under the same cultural conditions as other moisture-loving species.

662. ORCHIS BEESIANA, W. W. Sm.

Root: of 2 small globose or oblong tubers. **Stem:** 9″–20″ tall, slender, erect, clothed with 3 remote leaves. **Leaves:** suberect, oblong-lanceolate or linear-lanceolate, pointed, $2\frac{1}{2}''$–$4\frac{1}{2}''$ long. **Spike:** 2″–4″ long, of 12–20 blossoms. **Flowers:** about $\frac{1}{2}''$ across; dorsal sepal oblong, erect; lateral sepals oblong, pointed, reflexed; petals ovate-elliptic, blunt; lip large, deeply 3-lobed;

outer lobes oblong, toothed; centre lobe bilobed; spur cylindrical, almost erect, blunt, $\frac{1}{2}''$ long. *August.*

A pretty slender species with numerous rose-coloured flowers in a fairly dense compact spike. The plant is found in stony mountain meadows in Western Yunnan, Western China, at elevations of from 10,000–12,000 feet above sea-level and should prove quite hardy in Great Britain, in the rock garden in damp stony calcareous loam, fully exposed to the sun.

663. ORCHIS BREVICALCARATA, Schltr.

Hemipilia brevicalcarata, Finet. *Gymnadenia brevicalcarata*, Finet.

Root: of 2 ovoid tubers. **Stem:** 3″–6″ long, fairly stout, hollow. **Leaf:** solitary, membraneous, suborbicular, contracted into a short stalk. **Scape:** sheathed at the base, slender, bearing 4–8 blossoms. **Flowers:** $\frac{3}{8}''$ long, erect; dorsal sepal ovate, blunt, or pointed; lateral sepals similar in shape but larger and somewhat oblique; petals ovate, oblique, forming a loose galea with the dorsal sepal; lip narrowly cuneate, 3-lobed, lobes suborbicular; spur reduced to a small sac. *June.*

A very dwarf species with a solitary rounded leaf and a few-flowered spike of purplish-rose blossoms. It is found in boggy soil near the banks of streams in Western Yunnan, Western China, at an elevation of from 8000–9000 feet above sea-level and should succeed outdoors in the milder parts of Great Britain, in the bog garden or on the banks of a stream in peat, loam and moss.

664. ORCHIS CARIOPHORA, Linn.

Root: of 2 or more, sessile, oblong tubers, 1″ long. **Stem:** $\frac{1}{2}'$–$1\frac{1}{2}'$ tall, leafy to the top. **Leaves:** suberect on the lower part of the stem, sheathing above, lanceolate, pointed, 1″–3″ long. **Spike:** $1\frac{1}{2}''$–$4\frac{1}{2}''$ long, densely many-flowered. **Flowers:** about $\frac{5}{8}''$ long; sepals united to the middle forming a galea, ovate-lanceolate; petals lanceolate, much smaller than the sepals; lip 3-lobed; outer lobes rhombic, rather crenate, centre lobe larger than the outer ones, oblong, entire; spur conical, curved, $\frac{1}{4}''$ long. *May and June.*

A very quaint, somewhat slender plant with a cylindrical spike of rather small blossoms like a monk's cowl. The sepals and petals are decorated alternately with red and green stripes, and the lip is green, with a pink disc spotted with crimson; the variety *major* from North Africa is an exceedingly beautiful plant with a long dense spike of crimson and green blossoms; other forms are *albiflora, apricorum, brevibracteata, carpetana, cimicina* and *latifolia.* The plant is found in meadows and pastures in Southern and Eastern Europe and North Africa. Culture as for *O. laxiflora.*

665. ORCHIS CHAMPAGNEUXII, Barn.

O. morio var. *picta alba*. *O. morio* var. *picta rosea*.

Root: of 2 or 3 oblong, somewhat irregular tubers, one sessile and the others on long or short stalks. **Stem:** 6″–12″ tall, stout, frequently slightly zig-zag. **Leaves:** basal and cauline, reflexed below, sheathing the stem and decreasing into bracts upwards, lanceolate, 1½″–2″ long. **Spike:** 1″–3″ long, loose, cylindrical, of 6–12 blossoms. **Flowers:** about ½″ long exclusive of the spur; dorsal sepal ovate; lateral sepals lanceolate, conniving with the dorsal sepal and forming a galea; petals ovate, shorter than the sepals; lip as broad as long, 3-lobed; outer lobes broad, crenate; centre lobe very small, rounded; spur very stout, thickened towards the apex, ½″ long. *March and April.*

A delightful plant, very closely allied to *O. morio* and *O. longicornu*. It has green, pink-tipped sepals and petals and a pure white lip dotted with crimson, and a white spur. It is found on sandy hillsides in the South of France and Western Italy and may be grown in a sunny spot in the rock garden in warm sheltered spots in well-drained sandy loam; the roots should be protected in winter.

666. ORCHIS CHONDRADENIA, Makino

O. Fauriei, Finet. *Chondradenia Yatabei*, Maxim.

Root: of small ovoid or globose tubers with a few fleshy roots above them. **Stem:** 4″–8″ tall, fairly stout, smooth. **Leaf:** solitary, broadly ovate, pointed, sessile, 1″–3″ long. **Scape:** stout, bearing but few blossoms. **Flowers:** about ½″ across; dorsal sepal and lateral sepals nearly similar, broadly ovate; petals lanceolate-oblong, pointed; lip 3-lobed; outer lobes rounded; centre lobe spathulate oblong; spur short, blunt. *April to June.*

This little species reaches alpine situations on the mountains of Japan. It has a fairly stout stem and a few-flowered raceme or spike of small but pretty rosy-lilac, pale pink or at times white blossoms. It is found both in open and shady situations, usually in wet boggy places. It should be quite hardy in Great Britain in the bog garden in sphagnum-moss and peat in full sun.

667. ORCHIS CHUSUA, Don

Gymnadenia Chusua, Lindl.

Root: of oblong entire tubers. **Stem:** ¼′–1½′ tall, stout or flexuous. **Leaves:** mostly basal, few, linear or linear-lanceolate, pointed, almost filiform from plants growing at great elevations, 3″–6″ long. **Spike:** 2″–4″ long, of from 2–18 blossoms. **Flowers:** about ¾″ across; dorsal sepal orbicular, small; lateral sepals oblong-lanceolate, suberect; petals oblong, blunt, spreading;

lip broadly obovate, 3-lobed but variable; lobes broad, rounded, spreading, toothed or crenate with the middle lobe retuse; spur stout, cylindrical, blunt, ½″ long. *June.*

This species is very variable in height and robustness; specimens from alpine elevations are short and bear very few blossoms, these vary from pale purple to white and are sufficiently large to be called decorative. It grows in damp rocky places in short grass in the alpine Himalaya from Kumaon to Sikkim, reaching an altitude of 13,000 feet. It may be grown in the bog garden in fibrous peat and sphagnum-moss. The variety *nana* (King) is smaller in all its parts than the type.

668. ORCHIS COMPERIANA, Stev.

Comperia taurica, Linn.

Root: of 2 oblong tubers about ¾″ long. **Stem:** 1′–1½′ tall, stout, leafy below. **Leaves:** several, ovate or oblong, degenerating upwards into bracts, 1½″–2½″ long. **Spike:** 2″–4″ long, oblong, many-flowered. **Flowers:** about 1½″ long; dorsal sepal and lateral sepals narrowly oblong or lanceolate; petals oblong, with a long sharp tooth at the tip and two smaller teeth on each side of it; sepals and petals forming a galea; lip long, ovate, divided at the tip into 4 very narrow ribbon-like segments; spur stout, curved, ⅜″ long. *May and June.*

An extremely quaint and at the same time pretty plant. It somewhat resembles our Lizard Orchid and has pale rose-coloured or white sepals and petals, and a rose or white lip spotted on the disc with deep pink. The plant is found on wooded mountain sides from Southern Turkey to Smyrna and Lydia. It may be grown in the rock garden in a damp spot in loam and leaf-soil.

669. ORCHIS CORDIGERA, Fries.

O. cruenta, Willd. *O. angustifolia,* Reichb. f.

Root: of 2 irregular tubers, divided at the tip into from 2 to 4 horn-like lobes. **Stem:** 4″–12″ tall, hollow, clothed with but few leaves. **Leaves:** lanceolate above, ovate-elliptic at the base of the stem, 2″–4″ long. **Spike:** 1″–3″ long, lax, many-flowered. **Flowers:** about ⅝″ long; dorsal sepal narrowly ovate; lateral sepals falcately lanceolate, erect; petals similar but smaller, conniving over the column; lip as broad as long, 3-lobed; outer lobes large, rounded; centre lobe narrow, lanceolate; spur conical, curved, pointing downwards, ¼″ long. *May to July.*

A pretty slender species with rich purplish-red blossoms with some deep crimson semicircular markings on the lip. The leaves are spotted with purple. There are several pretty forms such as *Blyttii, bosnica, Klingii, rivularis,* and *rocheliana.* The type and its forms are found in damp pastures in Northern and Eastern Europe; they may be grown in the rock garden in damp loam and peat.

670. ORCHIS CYCLOCHILA, Maxim.

Habenaria cyclochila, Franch. *Gymnadenia cyclochila*, Korsh.

Root: of palmately lobed tubers with long fibrous roots above. **Stem:** 3″–6″ tall, erect, clothed at the base by a solitary leaf. **Leaf:** subbasal, obovate or orbicular, on a short stalk, reticulate. **Spike:** of 3–4 lax blossoms. **Flowers:** about ½″ long; sepals lanceolate, erect, incurved; petals oblong, erect, incurved; lip obovate or rounded, margins irregularly toothed and undulate; spur cylindrical, blunt, pendulous, ⅝″ long. *May and June.*

A pretty little species with rather small white or pale lilac blossoms on a slender rounded stem, clothed at its base by a prettily reticulated and tessellated leaf. It is very closely allied to *O. spathulata* and *O. Stracheyi* from the Himalaya. It is found in moist grass-lands usually in elevated localities in Japan. In cultivation it should succeed under the same treatment as the above-mentioned species.

671. ORCHIS DELAVAYI, Schltr.

Root: of 2 oblong tubers. **Stem:** 3″–5″ tall, erect, smooth, clothed with one leaf at the base and 1 or 2 pointed sheaths upwards. **Leaf:** spreading, oblong-ligulate, pointed, about 1″ long. **Raceme:** erect, lax, of 2–5 blossoms. **Flowers:** about ⅜″ long excluding the spur; dorsal sepal ovate-oblong, erect; lateral sepals ovate-oblong, spreading; petals obliquely ovate-oblong, suberect; lip cuneate below, 3-lobed above the middle, obliquely ovate-oblong; outer lobes nearly square, rounded at the tip; centre lobe square, tip emarginate; spur cylindrical, blunt, usually ascending, ½″ long. *June.*

A dainty little species, very suitable for alpine-house cultivation. It produces a few small white or pale purple blossoms with some dark markings on the lip, on a short stem clothed with one or two sheaths. The plant inhabits grassy mountain pastures in Western Yunnan at 10,500 feet above sea-level and should be generally hardy in Britain in the rock garden in sandy calcareous loam.

672. ORCHIS EXILIS, Ames and Schltr.

Root: of oblong tubers. **Stem:** 10″–14″ tall, slender, leafy. **Leaves:** 2–3 in number, linear or linear-lanceolate, degenerating upwards into sheaths, pointed, 2″–4″ long. **Spike:** 2″–4″ long, few-flowered, loose. **Flowers:** about ½″ across; dorsal sepal elliptic, erect, blunt; lateral sepals elliptic-oblong, oblique, reflexed; petals ovate-oblong, blunt, margins hairy; lip cuneate at the base, 3-lobed; outer lobes rhomboidal, blunt; centre lobe ovate-triangular, blunt; spur suberect, cylindrical, curved, about $\frac{1}{4}''$ long. *June.*

This species is closely allied to *O. Chusa* and has a slender stem clothed with a few narrow grassy leaves, and a loose few-flowered spike of rather pretty, deep or pale purple blossoms which are too small to be of much decorative value. The plant is found in damp grassy places in Yunnan, Western China. It may be tried outdoors in the rock garden in a damp sunny spot in good fibrous loam. Its roots should be protected in the winter.

673. ORCHIS FOLIOSA, Soland

O. incarnata var. *foliosa*, Kränzl.

Root: of rather large palmate tubers. **Stem:** up to 3′ tall, very robust, leafy. **Leaves:** radical and cauline, ovate, sheathing below, 10″–12″ long. **Spike:** 3″–8″ long and as much as $3\frac{1}{2}''$ through, densely many-flowered. **Flowers:** about $\frac{3}{4}''$ across and 1″ long; dorsal sepal ovate-lanceolate, blunt; lateral sepals broadly lanceolate, blunt; petals lanceolate, blunt, shorter than the sepals, converging; lip large, broader than long, 3-lobed; outer lobes very broad and blunt; centre lobe small, triangular, blunt. *July and August.*

This strikingly handsome plant is the most desirable of all the members of the genus *Orchis*. It produces robust, shining, rich green foliage and massive spikes of lilac and purple blossoms; there is also a very beautiful white form. The plant is probably only a form of the widely-spread *O. incarnata*, and is found in marshy places and on the banks of streams in the Madeira Islands. It has proved perfectly hardy in Great Britain planted in rich fibrous loam in a damp sunny spot in the border or rock garden.

674. ORCHIS FRAGRANS, Poll.

O. coriophora var. *fragrans*, Gr. and Goch. *O. coriophora* var. *pollinaria*, Poll. *O. cassidea*, Man.

Root: of 2 ovoid tubers about $\frac{3}{4}''$ long, one slightly stalked, the other sessile. **Stem:** $\frac{1}{2}'$–$1\frac{1}{4}'$ tall, rather slender, leafy, sinuous or straight. **Leaves:** mainly basal, narrowly lanceolate, very pointed, concave, degenerating into bracts up the stem. **Spike:** about 3″ long, cylindrical, flowers numerous. **Flowers:** $\frac{1}{2}''$ long; dorsal sepal lanceolate; lateral sepals narrowly lanceolate, conniving with the dorsal sepal and forming a pointed galea; petals linear, pointed; lip 3-lobed; outer lobes crenate, dentate; centre lobes small and pointed; spur stout or rather slender, curved, $\frac{1}{4}''$ long. *April to June.*

This species is closely allied to *O. coriophora* but although it is sweetly scented it is not so desirable a plant; it has purplish-red blossoms with a green tip to the lip and some crimson spots on the disc. It is found in meadows and pastures in Southern Europe, Western Asia and North Africa. Some desirable forms are *alba, inodora, Martinii, pallescens, purpurata* and *virscens*. They may be grown in a sunny sheltered spot in the rock garden in sandy loam.

675. ORCHIS GIRALDIANA, Kränzl.

Root: of irregular tubers. **Stem:** 6″–8″ tall, rather slender, leafy. **Leaves:** cauline, few, lanceolate, pointed, 2″–4″ long. **Spike:** 2″–3″ long, usually many-flowered. **Flowers:** about $\frac{5}{8}$″ long; dorsal sepal ovate, pointed, erect; lateral sepals narrowly ovate, blunt, suberect; petals lanceolate, arching over the column; lip orbicular ovate, 3-lobed; outer lobes oblong, blunt; centre lobe broad, blunt; spur cylindrical, rather slender, blunt. *June.*

A pretty Chinese species with a somewhat slender stem and a short spike of fair-sized blossoms varying from rich rosy-purple to deep rosy-red. It is found in damp grassy places and in stony meadows on the mountains of North-West Yunnan, Western China, at from 10,000–11,000 feet above sea-level. It should be perfectly hardy in Great Britain in a damp sunny spot in the rock garden in good calcareous loam.

676. ORCHIS GLOBOSA, Linn.

O. Halleri, Crantz. *Nigritella globosa*, Reichb. f. *Traunsteinera globosa*, Reichb. f.

Root: of 2 oblong, lobed tubers, about 1$\frac{1}{4}$″ long. **Stem:** $\frac{3}{4}$′–1$\frac{1}{2}$′ tall, fairly stout, sparely leafy, usually flexuous. **Leaves:** few, lanceolate or oblong, erect and more or less sheathing the stem, 2″–6″ long. **Spike:** pyramid-shaped or subglobose, dense, many-flowered, 1″–2″ long. **Flowers:** about $\frac{3}{8}$″ long; dorsal sepal lanceolate, narrowing towards the tip which is frequently club-shaped; lateral sepals similar but obliquely twisted near the tip; petals resembling the dorsal sepal but smaller, all suberect; lip 3-lobed, wedge-shaped; lobes subequal, centre one with a slender tooth at the apex; spur slender, $\frac{1}{8}$″ long. *May and June.*

The blossoms of this species are too small to be of much decorative value, but they are most exquisitely formed and the crowded spike looks like a head of clover. They usually have pale pinkish-purple sepals and petals and a pale but bright crimson lip with some dark spots on it. The plant is found in mountain meadows over the greater part of Europe. It may be grown in the rock garden in an open sunny spot in damp fibrous sandy loam. The forms and varieties *albiflora, gracilis, major* and *sphærica* are all very pretty.

677. ORCHIS HIRCINA, Crantz.

Loroglossum hircinum, C. L. Rich.

Root: of 2 oblong tubers about 1¼″ long. **Stem:** 1′–2′ tall, robust, leafy to the top. **Leaves:** oblong-lanceolate or ovate-lanceolate, 4″–8″ long, becoming smaller and sheathing the stem upwards. **Spike:** 4″–6″ long, dense or rather lax, oblong or cylindrical. **Flowers:** about 3″ long and ⅜″ across; dorsal sepal ovate; lateral sepals ovate, slightly falcate; petals oblong, much smaller than the sepals, all forming a galea; lip 3-lobed; outer lobes almost filiform, sinuate, pointed; centre lobe 2″ long, narrow, ribbon-like, bifid at the tip; spur stout, conical, ¼″ long. *May to July.*

An extremely curious native plant known as the Goat or Lizard Orchis. The weird blossoms have green sepals and petals striped and bordered with red, and a white disc on the pale green lip bordered and spotted with bright red. There are numerous curious forms and subspecies, such as *affinis*, *anomala*, *calamistrata*, *carprinum*, *divergens*, *floribunda*, *forcipula*, *formosum*, *heteroglossa*, *platyglossa*, *thuringiaca*, and *tipuloides*. The plant is found in open and half-shady places frequently on calcareous soils, in Middle and Southern Europe, North Africa and the Canary Isles. It may be grown in the rock garden or border in good fairly moist calcareous loam.

678. ORCHIS IBERICA, Desf.

O. leptophylla, C. Koch. *O. natolica*, F. & N.

Root: of 2 fusiform, lobed tubers about ¾″ long. **Stem:** slender, often sinuous, sparely leafy, ½′–1¼′ tall. **Leaves:** few, linear, erect, decreasing into bracts upwards, 2″–6″ long. **Spike:** 2″–4″ long, lax, few or sometimes many-flowered, very slender. **Flowers:** under ½″ long; dorsal and lateral sepals lanceolate, the latter slightly hooked at the tip; petals linear or narrowly lanceolate, much smaller than the sepals; sepals and petals forming a galea over the column; lip ovate, 3-lobed; outer lobes rounded, crenate; centre lobe very small, lanceolate, pointed; spur rather stout, curved, pointing downwards. *May and June.*

A very slender plant, with usually a few-flowered spike of rather small pale purple blossoms with almost white centres to their lips. It is of no great horticultural value. There are several forms such as *Fraasii*, *leptophylla*, *longifolia*, *Stevinii*, etc. The type and its forms are found in mountain marshes and on the banks of pools from Greece to Transcaucasia. They may have the same culture as the other moisture-loving species.

679. ORCHIS INCARNATA, Linn.

O. angustifolia, Wim. and Grab. *O. comosa* var. *angustifolia*, Ambros. *O. divaricata*, Reichb. f. *O. latifolia* var. *angustifolia*. *O. lanceolata*, Dictr.

Root: of 2 palmately lobed tubers. **Stem:** 1′–3′ tall, stout, hollow, leafy to the top. **Leaves:** cauline, lanceolate, slightly sheathing the stem, 3″–12″ long. **Spike:** 2″–6″ long, dense, many-flowered. **Flowers:** about $\frac{7}{8}$″ long; dorsal sepal broadly lanceolate, pointed; lateral sepals falcately lanceolate, suberect; petals similar, slightly smaller, forming a galea over the column; lip about as broad as long, 3-lobed; outer lobes rounded, crenate; centre lobe very small, tooth-like; spur stout, curved, pointing downwards.

May to July.

A robust leafy native plant with handsome spikes of purple blossoms with pale centres to their lips. There are numerous beautiful forms, such as *brevicalcarata*, *cruenta*, *cilicia*, *Durandii*, *integrata*, *lanceata*, *Munbyana*, *ochroleuca*, *osmanica*, *praetermissia*, *purpurella*, *rhombeilabia*, *sesquipedalis*, *trifurca* and *triloba retusa*. The type and its forms are found in marshes and wet pastures in most parts of Europe and North Africa. It may be grown in the bog garden or on the banks of a pond in rich calcareous loam.

680. ORCHIS ITALICA, Pioret

O. undulatifolia, Biv. *O. Simia* var. *undulatifolia*, Well. *O. tephrosanthos*, B. R. *O. tephrosanthos* var. *undulatifolia*, B. R.

Root: of 2 oblong tubers, one shortly stalked, $\frac{3}{4}$″ long. **Stem:** very stout, leafy, 4″–12″ tall. **Leaves:** numerous, oblong-lanceolate, with much undulated margins, the uppermost sheathing the stem and at times imbricate. **Spikes:** about 2″ long, oblong or pyramidal, rather loose, of 12–18 blossoms. **Flowers:** over 1″ long; dorsal sepal broadly lanceolate; lateral sepals lanceolate, very pointed, oblique at the tip, forming a galea with the dorsal sepal; petals oblong, small; lip deeply 3-lobed; outer lobes linear, pointed, diverging; centre lobe deeply bifid, lobes linear, incurved, with a point in the sinus.

February to May.

This species very much resembles *O. Simia* but is not quite so beautiful though quite worth cultivating. The blossoms are bright reddish-purple throughout, the sepals and petals being of a deeper tint, with a few dark spots on the lip. It grows in grassy spots on hillsides throughout the Mediterranean region. The subspecies *Bovanæ* is quite desirable. The type and its form may be grown in a warm sheltered spot in the rock garden in calcareous loam.

681. ORCHIS LACTEA, Poiret

O. acuminata, Desf. *O. corsica*, Viv. *O. Henriei*, Henon. *O. Ricasiolina*, Parl. *O. Tenoreana*, Guss. *O. variegata*, Bert.

Root: of 2 ovoid or oblong tubers. **Stem:** 6″–15″ tall, stout, leafy, at times zig-zag. **Leaves:** mostly cauline, lanceolate, deeply channelled, $1\frac{1}{2}$″–4″ long. **Spike:** $1\frac{1}{2}$″–3″ long, cylindrical, many-flowered. **Flowers:** about $\frac{1}{2}$″ long, narrow; sepals conniving forming a galea, all lanceolate; petals lanceolate, very small; lip 3-lobed; outer lobes ribbon-like, truncate, toothed; centre lobe broadly or narrowly wedge-shaped, rounded and notched at the tip, with a sharp tooth in the sinus; spur clavate, curved, $\frac{3}{16}$″ long.

February to April.

A plant of but little decorative value with a rather dense spike of small pale purple or pinkish-purple blossoms with a few deep spots on the lip. The plant is found in sandy places on hills among short herbs and thin woods in the countries bordering the Mediterranean both north and south. The forms *acuminata, Hanrii* and *Tenoreana* are preferable to the type; *corsica* and *denticulata* are other forms. The plants may be grown in the rock garden in sandy loam and leaf-soil.

682. ORCHIS LATIFOLIA, Linn.

O. affinis, Koch. *O. fistulosa*, Moench. *O. comosa*, Scop. *O. Hatagirea*, Don. *O. majalis*, Reichb. f. *O. triphylla*, Koch.

Root: of lobed tubers. **Stem:** 1′–3′ tall, frequently hollow, leafy upwards. **Leaves:** erect, oblong, linear-oblong or lanceolate, spotted or unspotted. **Spike:** 1″–6″ long, cylindrical, many-flowered. **Flowers:** about $\frac{3}{4}$″ long; sepals ovate, reflexed; petals ovate-lanceolate, usually arched over the column; lip oblong or rhomboid, crenate, entire or very obscurely 3-lobed; outer lobes or sides deflexed; spur stout, pendulous. *May to July.*

A very handsome native plant with tall upright stems clothed with rich green leaves and dense spikes of rather large pink, purple or white blossoms. There are several desirable forms such as *alba* (very beautiful), *affinis, baltica, dunensis, corsica, elata, indica, lapponica* and *pinguis*. The type and its forms grow in meadows and pastures in damp rich soils from Britain to Western China. In the Himalaya it reaches an elevation of 16,000 feet above sea-level. In cultivation it should be grown in an open sunny spot in rich heavy loam abundantly supplied with moisture.

683. ORCHIS LAXIFLORA, Lam.

O. caspia, Trautv. *O. ensifolia*, Vill. *O. laxiflora* var. *Lamarkii*, Franch. *O. palustris* var. *laxiflora*, Rom. *O. platychila*, C. Koch. *O. Tabermœmontanii*, Ginel.

Root: of 2, somewhat irregular, ovoid or oblong tubers, about 1″ long. **Stem:** $\frac{3}{4}$′–2′ tall, erect, stout, leafy. **Leaves:** cauline, suberect, numerous, linear-lanceolate, longest near the middle of the stem, 3″–9″ long. **Spike:** 4″–6″ long, loose, more or less cylindrical. **Flowers:** $\frac{3}{4}$″–1″ long; dorsal sepal lanceolate; lateral sepals lanceolate, slightly falcate towards the tip; petals similar only smaller; lip broadly wedge-shaped, suddenly narrowing near the base, 3-lobed; outer lobes broad, rounded, crenate; centre lobe very small, rounded, slightly cleft; spur stout, cylindrical, slightly curved, suberect, $\frac{3}{4}$″ long; the petals form a loose galea over the column. *May and June.*

A rather handsome native plant of usually robust habit with loose spikes of reddish-purple or crimson-purple blossoms with a pale centre to the lip; the upper part of the stem and bracts have purple tintings. There are two forms, *longibracteata* and *plaudosa.* The plant and its forms are found in sandy meadows not far from the sea over the greater part of Middle and Southern Europe and Northern Africa, including the Channel Islands. It may be grown in a fairly damp spot in sandy loam.

684. ORCHIS LONGIBRACTEATA, Biv.

Aceras longibracteata, Reichb. f. *Barlia longibracteata,* Parlat. *Loroglossum longibracteatum,* Moris.

Root: of large, irregular, ovoid tubers, stalked and sessile. **Leaves:** cauline and basal, oblong, pointed, undulate, degenerating upwards into broad lanceolate sheaths, 6″–9″ long. **Scape:** rather slender, in fine specimens nearly 2′ tall. **Spike:** 4″–6″ long, dense. **Flowers:** 1″–$1\frac{1}{4}$″ long; sepals lanceolate, forming a galea; petals lanceolate, enclosed within the galea formed by the sepals; lip oblong, 3-lobed; outer lobes irregular; centre lobe always emarginate; spur, stout. *January to May.*

A quaint yet beautiful plant with handsome, robust foliage and long spikes of from twenty to fifty large blossoms of a pale purple colour deepening to purplish-brown on the margins of the large undulated lip. It is a very decorative species and is found on shady hillsides and in thin woods along the shores of the Mediterranean from Spain to Greece and Algeria. It is also found in the Canary Isles. It may be grown in the rock garden in a fairly damp shady spot in a good rich loam.

685. ORCHIS LONGICORNU, Poiret

Root: of 2 oblong, somewhat irregular tubers, one stalked and the other sessile. **Stem:** 6″–9″ tall, rather slender, leafy. **Leaves:** broadly lanceolate or broadly linear, spreading below, degenerating into sheaths above, 1″–2½″ long. **Spike:** 1″–3″ long, very loose, of 4–8 blossoms. **Flowers:** about ⅝″ long, exclusive of the spur; dorsal sepal ovoid, conniving with the lanceolate lateral sepals forming a galea; petals ovate, smaller than the sepals; lip nearly as broad as long, 3-lobed; outer lobes crenate, much larger than the square centre lobe; spur very stout, upcurved, cylindrical, ¾″ long.
February to April.

An exceedingly quaint and at the same time attractive little species with pale reddish-purple blossoms having a very deep red-purple lip, with a broad white patch spotted with crimson down its centre; the bracts and upper parts of the stem are usually pale purple. It is a native of the countries bordering the Mediterranean and is found in damp bushy places. It may be grown in a sheltered part of the rock garden in very moist sandy loam.

686. ORCHIS MACULATA, Linn.

O. Gervasiana, Tod. *O. Bonanniana*, Tod. *O. longibracteata*, Schm. *O. mixta*, Swartz. *O. solida*, Moench.

Root: of 2 palmately-lobed tubers. **Stem:** ¾′–2′ tall, fairly stout, leafy to the top. **Leaves:** oblong-lanceolate or lanceolate, sheathing the stem slightly, 3″–6″ long. **Spike:** 2″–5″ long, densely many-flowered. **Flowers:** about ¾″ long; dorsal sepal ovate; lateral sepals falcately lanceolate, erect; petals similar but slightly smaller, forming a galea over the column; lip longer than wide, 3-lobed; lobes variable; centre one usually narrow and pointed; spur stout, slightly curved, pendulous, ⅜″ long. *May and June.*

A pretty native plant with dense spikes of pale lilac or purple blossoms with semicircular crimson markings on the lip. There are numerous forms and subspecies such as *alpina, Brotheri, Cartalinæ, Cavellii, curvifolia, elodes, ericetorum Fuchsii immaculata, lusitanica, media, Meyeri, obtusifolia, O. Kellyi, palustris, saccifera, trannsilvanica*, and *triloba*, many of which are well worth growing. The type and its forms are found in moist meadows, pastures and thin woodlands throughout Europe, Siberia and North Africa. They may be grown in a damp spot in the rock garden in fibrous loam and leaf-soil. Plants collected from chalky districts should have some calcareous matter in their compost.

687. ORCHIS MASCULA, Linn.

O. cariophora, Gen. *O. glaucophylla*, A. Kern. *O. Morio* var. *masculus*, Linn. *O. ovalis*, Schm. *O. vernalis*, Salisb.

Root: of 2 ovoid tubers about ¾″ long, one frequently on a very short stalk. **Stem:** ¾′–2′ tall, stout, leafy below. **Leaves:** usually tufted at the base, sheathing the stem upwards, oblong-lanceolate, suberect, 3″–6″ long. **Spike:** 3″–5″ long, oblong, many-flowered. **Flowers:** 1″ long; dorsal sepal lanceolate; lateral sepals lanceolate, slightly falcate; petals similar only smaller, forming a loose galea; lip much longer than wide, 3-lobed; outer lobes large, slightly crenate; centre lobe obovate, bifid at the tip with a sharp tooth in the sinus; spur stout, cylindrical, about ¾″ long. *April to June.*

A beautiful native plant with handsome blue-green foliage, usually sprinkled with crimson-purple spots near the base, and long spikes of rosy-purple blossoms with a white or pinkish-purple spotted disc to the lip. There are several pretty forms such as *brevicalcarata*, *fallax*, *Marizii*, *obtusiflora*, *olbiensis* (*olivetorum*), *pinetorum*, *speciosa*, *stabina* and *stenoloba*. They are found in moist woods, pastures and shady places from England to Siberia and North Africa. The type and its forms may be grown in a damp shady spot in the rock garden in loam and leaf-soil.

688. ORCHIS MATSUMURANA, Schltr.

Root: of 2 subglobose tubers. **Stem:** 4″–8″ tall, fairly stout, leafy. **Leaves:** cauline, few in number, narrowly oblong below, lanceolate on the upper part of the stem and degenerating into bracts amongst the blossoms, 1½″–2″ long. **Spike:** about 1½″ long, usually of 5 blossoms, secund. **Flowers:** about ⅝″ across; dorsal sepal ovate-oblong, concave, blunt; lateral sepals elliptic-oblong, oblique; petals narrowly oblong; lip cuneate at the base, 3-lobed; outer lobes oblong, somewhat dilated at the tip; centre lobe oblong, shortly 2-lobed at the tip, with a small tooth in the sinus; spur cylindrical, ¾″ long. *July.*

A very dwarf leafy species producing a few-flowered spike of rather large pale purple blossoms resembling those of *O. pauciflora* (Fisch). It is found in damp grassy places at Nikko, Japan. It should be sufficiently hardy for cultivation outdoors in most parts of Great Britain in a damp or wet sunny spot in good fibrous loam and sandy peat. The roots should be protected during the winter.

689. ORCHIS MILITARIS, Linn.

O. galeata, Poiret. *O. mimusops*, Thunb. *O. nervata*, Manch. *O. signifera*, Ved.

Root: of 2, somewhat irregular, potato-like tubers, 1″ long. **Stem:** rather slender, leafy, frequently sinuous, $\frac{3}{4}'$–$1\frac{1}{2}'$ tall. **Leaves:** few, oblong-lanceolate, concave, 2″–4″ long. **Spike:** 3″–5″ long, many-flowered, oblong or pyramidal. **Flowers:** about $\frac{3}{4}''$ long; dorsal sepal lanceolate; lateral sepals falcate-lanceolate, forming an open galea with the dorsal sepal; petals very narrowly lanceolate, curved; lip 3-lobed; outer lobes narrowly linear, slightly diverging; centre lobe wedge-shaped, divided into two large diverging lobes at the tip with a point between them; spur stout, curved, $\frac{1}{4}''$ long.

May and June.

A very handsome species well worthy of cultivation. It is a native plant and produces many-flowered spikes of quaint blossoms with pale purple or lilac-crimson, striped sepals and petals and a crimson-purple lip with a white disc spotted with crimson. The plant is found throughout the greater part of Europe, Western Asia and Siberia in hilly, open situations. The forms *Albiflora, acuminata, arenaria, longibracteata, nervata, Raddeana* and *spathulata* are worth growing. The type and its forms may be grown in the rock garden in fairly moist calcareous loam and leaf-soil.

690. ORCHIS MORIO, Linn.

O. crenulata, Gilib.

Root: of 2 oblong tubers about 1″ long, with a few thick, short roots above them. **Stem:** 6″–15″ tall, fairly stout, leafy. **Leaves:** basal and cauline, oblong or oblong-lanceolate, sheathing the stem upwards, 1″–$2\frac{1}{2}''$ long. **Spike:** 2″–4″ long, rather densely many-flowered. **Flowers:** about $\frac{3}{4}''$ long, horizontal or suberect; sepals and petals ovate or lanceolate, forming a galea over the column; lip variable, usually broader than it is long, more or less 3-lobed; centre lobe small, notched at the tip; spur horizontal or ascending, cylindrical, thickened at the end, $\frac{1}{2}''$ long.

May and June.

A pretty native species with slightly tapering spikes of from six to twelve blossoms varying in colour from red-violet to reddish-purple or flesh pink, and very rarely to white; the centre of the lip is usually paler than the other parts and is generally spotted. The bracts are tinted purple as is the stem at times. It is found over nearly the whole of Europe and parts of Western Asia in fields, meadows, etc. The forms *caucasica, Nicodemii, Skorpilii, syrica* and *tlemcensis* are desirable; the subspecies *picta* (Loisel) is not so pretty as the type. All may be grown in the rock garden in fairly moist fibrous loam.

691. ORCHIS PALCZEWSKII, Kränzl.

Root: of stout cylindrical fibres. **Stem:** $2\frac{1}{2}''$–$3\frac{1}{2}''$ tall, leafy, sheathed at the base. **Leaves:** mainly basal, narrowly elliptic, blunt, about $2\frac{1}{2}''$ long. **Spike:** of 2–3 blossoms. **Flowers:** about $\frac{1}{2}''$ across; sepals ovate, blunt; petals linear, tip very minutely denticulate or erose, as long as the sepals; lip shortly unguiculate, subquadrate, 3-lobed; lateral lobes rounded; centre lobe square, bilobed and retuse at the tip, margins crenulate; disc smooth or covered with minute down. *May.*

A dwarf few-flowered species suitable for alpine-house culture, with quaint lilac-pink or purple blossoms and ample foliage. It is found in damp situations in open country in Eastern Siberia and should be quite hardy in Great Britain in a damp sunny spot in the rock garden in loam and peat.

692. ORCHIS PALLENS, Linn.

O. sulphurea, Linn.

Root: of 2, somewhat irregular, oblong tubers about $1''$ long. **Stem:** $1'$–$1\frac{1}{2}'$ tall, stout, sparely leafy. **Leaves:** about 3 or 4 in number, oblong-lanceolate rather blunt, sheathing the stem above, degenerating into bracts, $3''$–$6''$ long. **Spike:** $2''$–$5''$ long, somewhat dense, pyramidal or more rarely oblong. **Flowers:** about $\frac{3}{4}''$ long; dorsal sepal oblong or ovate; lateral sepals and petals lanceolate, the latter smaller than the former, conniving in a loose galea over the column; lip about as broad as long, 3-lobed; outer lobes rounded; centre lobe smaller than the outer lobes, rounded or nearly square, notched, whole lip fringed with minute hairs; spur stout, cylindrical, suberect, $\frac{1}{2}''$ long. *May to July.*

A pretty species with rather close spikes of rich yellow or cream coloured fragrant blossoms. The variety *pseudo-pallens* is also desirable. The type and its forms are found in mountain meadows over Central and Southern Europe as far east as the Caucasus. It may be grown in the rock garden in calcareous, fibrous loam.

693. ORCHIS PALUSTRIS, Jacq.

O. elegans, Heuf. *O. germanorum*, Mor. *O. Heuffeliana*, Schur.

Root: of 2 oblong or egg-shaped tubers about $1\frac{1}{4}''$ long. **Stem:** $\frac{3}{4}'$–$2'$ tall, stout, leafy. **Leaves:** rather numerous, linear-lanceolate, suberect, sheathing below, narrower and smaller above, $3''$–$6''$ long. **Spike:** $3''$–$9''$ long, lax, many-flowered. **Flowers:** about $1''$ in length; dorsal sepal ovate; lateral sepals lanceolate, slightly falcate; petals similar, equalling the sepals in length, slightly incurved, forming a loose galea; sepals erect; lip as broad as long,

3-lobed; outer lobes rounded; centre lobe smaller than the outer lobes, rounded, slightly toothed and with a shallow notch in the centre; spur stout, cylindrical, $\frac{1}{2}''$ long, horizontal or suberect. *May to July.*

An exceedingly handsome marsh plant with unspotted foliage and long spikes of bright purple blossoms with dark spots on the lip which has its outer lobes somewhat darker than the remainder of its surface. The forms *elegans*, *intermedia*, *minor* and *quadrifida* are desirable. The plant and its forms are found in bogs and marshes from Central and Southern Europe to Persia and North Africa. An open spot in the bog garden in rich loam is suitable.

694. ORCHIS PAPILIONACEA, Linn.

Root: of 2 irregular, ovoid tubers, one sessile and the other shortly stalked, $\frac{3}{4}''$ across. **Leaves:** cauline, linear-lanceolate, usually deeply channelled, $2''$–$3''$ long. **Scape:** $4''$–$8''$ tall, fairly stout, leafy, and slightly curved. **Spike:** lax, bearing from 2–6 blossoms. **Flowers:** nearly $1\frac{1}{4}''$ long and $\frac{5}{8}''$ across; sepals lanceolate, pointed, connivent below, spreading above; petals lanceolate, smaller and shorter than the sepals, connivent, forming a galea over the column; lip varying from fan-shaped and rhomboid to suborbicular, crenately toothed, shallowly lobed; side lobes incurved somewhat; spur straight, $\frac{3}{8}''$ long. *April to June.*

A very beautiful little species with pale green unspotted foliage and spikes of about half-a-dozen very large blossoms, pale purple, lilac or pale pink in ground colour with beautiful crimson veinings on the lip. It grows in warm, sunny pastures and grassy places from Portugal to Turkey and Algeria along the shores of the Mediterranean. It may be grown outdoors in a good light loam in a sunny spot in the rock garden.

695. ORCHIS PATENS, Desf.

O. brevicornis, Viv. *O. panormitana*, Tin. *O. patens* var. *Fontanesii*, Reichb. f.

Root: of 2 ovoid tubers $\frac{3}{4}''$ long. **Stem:** $\frac{3}{4}'$–$1\frac{1}{2}'$ tall, rather slender. **Leaves:** few, mainly basal, oblong or lanceolate, sheathing, $2''$–$4''$ long. **Spike:** $2''$–$6''$ long, cylindrical, many-flowered and fairly dense. **Flowers:** $\frac{1}{2}''$ long; dorsal and lateral sepals lanceolate, more or less erect; petals narrowly lanceolate, about the same length as the sepals, erect; lip 3-lobed, longer than broad; outer lobes narrowly wedge-shaped; centre lobe very broadly wedge-shaped, rounded and slightly cleft at the tip, much larger than the outer lobes; spur stout, rather conical, $\frac{3}{8}''$ long. *May and June.*

A species with somewhat glaucous foliage, frequently ornamented with brown spots, and long cylindrical spikes of blossoms, with pale purple and green sepals and petals and a pale purple lip with darker red-purple outer lobes and spots on the disc; *brevicornis*, *canariensis* and *orientalis* are desirable forms. The plant and its forms are found on grassy and rocky hill sides throughout most of the Mediterranean region including the Canary Isles. It may be grown in a sheltered part of the rock garden in fibrous, calcareous loam and sand.

696. ORCHIS PAUCIFLORA, Fisch.

O. Joo-lokiana, Makino. *O. Morio*, Makino. *Gymnadenia pauciflora*, Lindl.

Root: of 2 oblong or ovoid tubers about ¾″ long. **Stem:** 4″–9″ tall, fairly stout, bearing 2 distant leaves. **Leaves:** linear-lanceolate, pointed, 2″–3″ long. **Spike:** ¾″–2″ long, fairly dense, few-flowered. **Flowers:** about ⅝″ across; dorsal sepal ovate-lanceolate, pointed; lateral sepals lanceolate, pointed, reflexed; petals linear-lanceolate, pointed, conniving over the column; lip cuneate, nearly square, pubescent; spur cylindrical, carried horizontally, rather short. *May and June.*

Quite a dainty species with short spikes of rich violet-coloured blossoms on fairly stout stems. It is found in damp pasture-land in Dahuria, Manchuria, Korea and temperate Japan. It should be quite hardy in Great Britain in the bog garden or near the waters edge on the banks of a stream or pond in loam and peat.

697. ORCHIS PERSICA, Schltr.

Root: of oblong or ovoid tubers. **Stem:** 7″–9″ tall, leafy below. **Leaves:** about 3 in number, lanceolate-ligulate, usually blunt, erect or spreading, 3½″–4½″ long. **Spike:** about 3½″ long, cylindrical, densely many-flowered. **Flowers:** about ¾″ long; dorsal sepal oblong, concave, blunt; lateral sepals obliquely oblong, erect and recurved; petals narrowly oblong, blunt; lip ovate, shortly 3-lobed, densely hairy at the base; outer lobes obliquely oblong, blunt; centre lobe similar but longer and narrower; spur cylindrical, pendulous, blunt, about ½″ long. *April to June.*

A delightful species allied to *O. laxiflora* (Lam.) with dense spikes of bright rose-coloured blossoms. It is found in damp pastures and on the borders of marshes in Western Persia, ascending the mountains to a considerable elevation. It should be quite hardy in this country under the same conditions as the other moisture-loving species.

698. ORCHIS PROVINCIALIS, Balb.

O. Cyrillii, Ten. *O. Morio* var. *provincialis*, Als. *O. leucostachys*, Griesb.

Root: of 2 irregular, ovoid, almost sessile tubers, ½″–¾″ long. **Leaves:** sub-basal, few, broadly linear or oblong-lanceolate, rather blunt, degenerating into 1 or 2 leaf-like bracts upwards, 3″–6″ long. **Scape:** ¾′–1½′ tall, slender.

Spike: lax, many-flowered. **Flowers:** about 1″ long; dorsal sepal wedge-shaped, blunt; lateral sepals ovate, pointed; petals lanceolate, conniving, forming a galea over the column; lip deeply 3-lobed; outer lobes somewhat irregular in shape, usually pointed; centre lobe emarginate, generally with a tooth at the notch; spur carried horizontally, stout, thickened at the tip, $\frac{5}{8}$″ long. *April and May.*

A very beautiful plant with handsome, rich green foliage, thickly blotched with purple, and a long loose spike of about twenty large pale yellow blossoms, with a purple-spotted lip. It grows in rather damp, grassy places on wooded hill-sides in the Mediterranean region from Spain to Asia Minor, and may be grown outdoors over the greater part of Britain in a damp, half-shady spot in a good fibrous loam. The two forms *calabra* and *pauciflora* are desirable plants. *See Plate 16 facing page 295.*

699. ORCHIS PUNCTULATA, Stev.

O. Steveniana, Comp.

Root: of 2 oblong tubers about $\frac{3}{4}$″ long. **Stem:** $\frac{1}{2}$′–1$\frac{1}{4}$′ tall, fairly stout. **Leaves:** few in number, oblong or ovate-oblong, blunt, 2″–6″ long. **Spike:** 2″–5″ long, loose, cylindrical. **Flowers:** about $\frac{5}{8}$″ long; dorsal sepal narrowly ovate; lateral sepals lanceolate, curved somewhat at the tip; petals lanceolate, conniving with the sepals and forming a galea over the column; lip 3-lobed; outer lobes ovate, rounded; centre lobe narrow, pointed, much smaller than the outer lobes; spur cylindrical, blunt, curved downwards.

March and April.

A pretty and desirable plant with slender spikes of white or rosy-white blossoms spotted with deep rose. It is found in open grassy places on the mountains of Asiatic Turkey and Mesopotamia and should prove quite hardy in Great Britain in the rock garden in fairly moist fibrous loam in an open sunny situation.

700. ORCHIS PURPUREA, Huds.

O. brachitata, Gilib. *O. fuscata*, Pall. *O. militaris* var. *purpurea*, Huds.

Root: of 2 ovoid or subglobose tubers 1$\frac{1}{4}$″ long. **Stem:** rather stout, leafy below, $\frac{3}{4}$′–2$\frac{1}{2}$′ tall. **Leaves:** mainly basal, oblong or oblong-lanceolate, 6″–12″ long. **Spike:** 3″–6″ long, oblong or slightly tapering upwards, many-flowered. **Flowers:** over $\frac{3}{4}$″ long; dorsal sepal ovate-oblong; lateral sepals lanceolate, conniving with the dorsal sepal in an open galea; petals oblong; lip 3-lobed; outer lobes linear; centre lobe broadly wedge-shaped, widely cleft at the tip, with a small point in the sinus; spur stout, conical or cylindrical, $\frac{1}{4}$″ long. *March to May.*

A very handsome native species of robust habit with large spikes of pale purple or pinkish-purple blossoms, with green tips to the sepals and crimson spots on the white disc of the lip. It grows in hilly pastures and clearings in woods over nearly the whole of Europe from Britain to Asia Minor. There are many handsome forms such as *albida, amediastima, breviloba, convergens, confusa, expansa, incisiloba, latiloba, longidentata, longimediastima, minima, moravica, parallela, rotundiloba* and *spathulata.* The type and its forms may be grown in the rock garden in fairly moist fibrous loam with or without chalky matter in it.

701. ORCHIS PYRAMIDALIS, Linn.

O. bicornis, Gilib. *O. condensata,* Desf. *Anacamptis pyramidalis,* Reichb. *A. pyramidata,* Rubani.

Root: of 2 ovoid tubers, one sessile and one shortly stalked. **Stem:** fairly stout or quite slender, $\frac{3}{4}'$–$2'$ tall, sinuous, leafy to the top. **Leaves:** linear-lanceolate, sheathing upward, suberect below, $3''$–$6''$ long. **Spike:** $2''$–$3''$ long, pyramid-shaped, rather dense. **Flowers:** $\frac{3}{8}''$ long exclusive of the spur; dorsal sepal lanceolate, erect; lateral sepals lanceolate, slightly falcate at the tip, spreading; petals narrowly falcate-lanceolate, erect; lip as broad as long, 3-lobed; lobes nearly square in shape, spreading, the centre one smaller than the others; spur slender, curved, $\frac{1}{2}''$ long. *May to July.*

The blossoms of this plant very much resemble those of *Orchis quadripunctata* and are of no great decorative value; they are of a pale pink or pale purple throughout and have remarkably long spurs. The plant is found on dry banks and in pastures, chiefly in limestone districts, over the greater part of Central and Southern Europe including Great Britain. There are several interesting forms such as *angustiloba, albiflora, brachystachys, tanayensis* and *vallesiaca.* Hybrids with *Orchis* and *Gymnadenia* are *Ashersonii, Durandii, fallax, simarrensis* and *Weberi.* The plants may be grown in the rock garden in calcareous loam, peat and sand.

702. ORCHIS QUADRIPUNCTATA, Biv.

O. Hostii, Fratt. *Anacamptis quadripunctata,* Lindl. *Gymnadenia humilis,* Lindl.

Root: of 2, somewhat irregular, oblong tubers about $\frac{3}{4}''$ long. **Stem:** sparely leafy, rather slender, $\frac{1}{2}'$–$1\frac{1}{4}'$ tall, erect. **Leaves:** cauline, few, oblong or oblong-lanceolate, $1''$–$3''$ long, uppermost stem-clasping. **Spike:** slender, cylindrical, lax, many-flowered, $3''$–$6''$ long. **Flowers:** $\frac{3}{4}''$ long; dorsal sepal oblong or narrowly oval; lateral sepals lanceolate, slightly falcate at the tip; petals similar, only smaller, curving over the column; lip 3-lobed; outer lobes large, rounded; centre lobe almost square or oblong, minutely toothed, or notched; spur slender, curved, cylindrical, $\frac{1}{2}''$ long. *April and May.*

A quaint little plant of but little decorative value, with a slender spike of very small pale reddish-purple blossoms, with a white centre to the spotted lip. The long, slender spur is very conspicuous. There are several forms such as *albiflora*, *Cupanii* and *macrochila* and a subspecies *Brancifortii*. The plant and its forms are found on hill and mountain sides from Italy to Crete. It may be grown in the rock gardens in an open but sheltered spot in good fibrous loam of a sandy nature.

703. ORCHIS ROBOROWSKYI, Maxim.

Root: of oblong tubers. **Stem:** $\frac{1}{4}'$–$\frac{3}{4}'$ tall, fairly stout. **Leaves:** few in number, linear or linear-lanceolate, mostly basal, degenerating upwards into bracts, 3″–6″ long, very narrow in stunted plants. **Spike:** loose, of 2–3 blossoms. **Flowers:** about $\frac{1}{2}''$ across; dorsal sepal ovate; lateral sepals narrowly ovate or lanceolate; petals lanceolate or elliptic-lanceolate, blunt; lip obscurely 3-lobed or entire, cuneate-obovate; spur cylindrical, blunt. *June.*

A pretty plant with a fairly stout stem bearing a few rose-red blossoms with some purple markings on the lip. It is suitable for alpine house culture in a pan of peat, loam and sphagnum-moss. It is found in grassy places on hill and mountain sides in Siberia, Tibet and Western China. It should prove quite hardy in Great Britain in a fairly damp open spot in the rock garden, in peat and loam.

704. ORCHIS ROMANA, Sebast.

O. bracteata, Ten. *O. lucana*, Spreng. *O. mediterranea*, Klinge. *O. pseudo-sambucina*, Ten. *O. sulphurea*, Spreng.

Roots: of 2 palmately lobed tubers about $1\frac{1}{4}''$ long. **Stem:** fairly stout, leafy, erect or sinuous, $\frac{3}{4}'$–$1\frac{1}{2}'$ tall. **Leaves:** numerous, basal and cauline, varying from ovate to lanceolate, sheathing at the base, at times forming a basal tuft, 3″–6″ long, gradually reduced upwards into bracts amongst the blossoms. **Spike:** 2″–4″ long, congested into a head, or loose, and few-flowered. **Flowers:** about $\frac{5}{8}''$ long, exclusive of the spur; dorsal sepal oblong, pointed; lateral sepals lanceolate, all erect, petals narrowly lanceolate or linear, smaller than the sepals, erect; lip as broad as long, 3-lobed; outer lobes short and broad; centre lobe small, rounded or truncate; spur cylindrical, horizontal, $\frac{5}{8}''$ long. *March to June.*

A leafy species with a spike of rather pretty purplish-red blossoms with a pale centre to the lip. Pretty forms are *insularis*, *Markusii*, *ochroleuca* and *sicula*. All are found in marshes, bog and wet mountain pastures from Portugal to Western Asia, but are absent from Southern France. The plants may be grown in a sheltered part of the bog garden or on the banks of a stream or pond in good rich loam. The tubers should be protected from severe frost by rather deep planting.

705. ORCHIS ROTUNDIFOLIA, Gray.

Habenaria rotundifolia, Rich. *Platanthera rotundifolia*, Lindl.

Root: of rather thick, fleshy, fibres. **Stem:** 6″–10″ tall, slender, naked, usually quite erect. **Leaf:** solitary, varying from orbicular to oval, with one or two small sheathing scales below, $1\frac{1}{4}$″–$2\frac{3}{4}$″ long. **Spike:** rather loose, of 2–10 blossoms. **Flowers:** about $\frac{5}{8}$″ long, usually more or less secund; sepals and petals oval, dorsal sepal and petals forming a galea over the column; lateral sepals spreading; lip longer than the petals, 3-lobed; centre lobe longer than the others, dilated, 2-lobed or notched at the apex; spur slender, shorter than the lip. *June and July.*

An exquisite little plant with a solitary, rounded, rich green leaf and slender, pink and green flower-stems bearing a loose spike of rose coloured blossoms with a white lip spotted with purple or deep pink. It inhabits peat bogs and swampy places in woods where there are open spaces, and ranges from Greenland and the whole of Canada southward to New York and Minnesota. The plant is quite hardy and may be grown in the bog garden in peat and living sphagnum-moss.

706. ORCHIS RUPESTRIS, Schltr.

Gymnadenia rupestris, Miq. *Platanthera rupestris*, Schltr.

Root: of narrowly oblong tubers. **Stem:** about 9″ tall. **Leaves:** cauline, linear or linear-lanceolate, 2″–3″ long. **Spike:** short, few-flowered. **Flowers:** about $\frac{1}{2}$″ across; dorsal sepal oblong, cucullate, blunt; lateral sepals oblong, blunt, reflexed; petals obovate, emarginate; lip 3-lobed; outer lobes obliquely rhomboid; centre lobe obovate, retuse, emarginate; spur cylindrical, blunt, curved, about $\frac{3}{4}$″ long. *June and July.*

A delicate and pretty species, sufficiently dwarf in stature for alpine-house cultivation. Its blossoms are of a delicate rose-purple hue and are produced in a short few-flowered spike on an erect stem. It inhabits damp places on some of the lesser elevated mountains of Japan and should be hardy in most parts of Great Britain in a damp spot, fully exposed to the sun, in a compost of peat and chopped sphagnum-moss.

707. ORCHIS SACCATA, Ten.

O. collina, Ban. *O. sparsiflora*, Ten.

Root: of 2, sessile, oblong tubers, about $\frac{3}{4}$″ long. **Stem:** 4″–8″ tall, stout, sparely leafy. **Leaves:** basal and cauline, ovate or ovate-oblong, pointed spatha-like, 1″–2″ long. **Spike:** rather narrow, of about 6 blossoms, 2″–3″ long. **Flowers:** about $\frac{5}{8}$″ long; dorsal and lateral sepals oblong or lanceolate, conniving to form a galea; petals narrowly oblong or linear, very much smaller than the sepals ; lip entire, ovate or suborbicular, strongly veined near the margin ; spur cylindrical, fairly stout, curved, $\frac{1}{2}''$ long. *February to April.*

This little species, although pretty, is perhaps not so desirable as some of the other species, for its blossoms are of a rather dull purplish-red, pale on the spur and down the centre of the lip. The plant is found in grassy places on hills, usually at no great distance from the sea, in Southern Europe, Western Asia and North Africa from Spain to Persia. It may be grown in the rock garden in warm and sheltered districts in fairly moist, fibrous loam and sand.

708. ORCHIS SALINA, Turcz.

Root: of 2 oblong tubers about $\frac{3}{4}''$ long. **Stem:** 1′–2′ tall, erect, fairly stout, leafy. **Leaves:** linear-lanceolate, erect, pointed, 3″–4″ long. **Spike:** 3″–5″ long, lax, few-flowered. **Flowers:** about $\frac{1}{2}''$ across ; dorsal sepal lanceolate, blunt ; lateral sepals similar but longer, spreading ; petals narrowly lanceolate, incurved ; lip rhomboid, crenate, slightly 3-lobed, lobes pointed, downy ; spur cylindrical, pendulous, pointed, rather short. *May to July.*

An erect species with a loose spike of fair-sized blossoms varying from white to pale purple. It is quite worth cultivating and is found in the spare herbage growing near the borders of saline lakes in South-Western Siberia, Persia, Tibet and parts of Western China. It should be quite hardy in Britain and would probably require a soil richer in sodium than is requisite for other members of the genus.

709. ORCHIS SAMBUCINA, Linn.

O. bipalmata, Pour. *O. incarnata* var. *sambucina,* Lapeyr. *O. lutea,* Dulac. *O. pallens,* Mor. *O. Schleicheri,* Sweet. *O. salina,* Fries.

Root: of 2 palmately lobed tubers, 1″–$1\frac{1}{2}''$ long. **Stem:** 6″–9″ tall, stout, erect, leafy. **Spike:** 2″–4″ long, oblong, compact, many-flowered. **Flowers:** about $\frac{3}{4}''$ long ; dorsal sepal lanceolate ; lateral sepals lanceolate, slightly falcate ; petals similar but smaller and incurved ; lip ovate or ovate-oblong, slightly 3-lobed ; centre lobe very small, triangular, tooth-like ; spur very stout, curved, pendulous ; outer lobes of lip toothed. *May to July.*

A very beautiful plant of dwarf, robust habit with compact spikes of well-formed blossoms with cream-coloured sepals and petals and a yellow lip decorated with a double ridge of red hairs on its upper surface. The numerous beautiful forms differ very much in colour from the type ; the most desirable are *candida, bracteata, incarnata* and *sambucino-lingua.* The plant is found in marshes and damp pastures on most of the mountain ranges of Central and Southern Europe. The type and its forms may be grown in the bog garden or on the banks of a stream or pond in good loam and peat.

710. ORCHIS SANCTA, Linn.

O. cariophora var. *sancta*, Reichb. f. *O. Urvilleana*, Steud.

Root: of 2 sessile, somewhat irregular, potato-like tubers, about 1¼″ long. **Stem:** ½′–1¼′ tall, fairly stout, frequently sinuous. **Leaves:** mainly basal, lanceolate or linear-lanceolate, those on the stem narrow, bract-like, 1″–2½″ long. **Spike:** 1½″–2½″ long, fairly dense, many-flowered. **Flowers:** about ¾″ long, erect; dorsal and lateral sepals lanceolate, conniving and forming an erect, pointed galea; petals narrowly lanceolate, not much shorter than the sepals; lip cuneate at the base, divided into 3 lobes; side lobes cut to the base of the lobes into 3 sharp teeth; centre lobe lanceolate, rather large; spur cylindrical, curved, ½″ long. *April to June.*

A dwarf species with rather curious blossoms, too dull in colour to be of much decorative value; they are dull purplish-red throughout with the exception of the centre of the lip, which is pale purplish-pink. The plant is found in mountain meadows from Greece to Syria and Palestine. It may be grown in an open sunny spot in the rock garden in fairly moist sandy loam.

711. ORCHIS SIMIA, Lam.

O. cercopitheca, Poiret; *O. zoophora*, Engl.

Root: of 2 oblong, potato-like tubers about 1″ long. **Stem:** rather slender, erect or slightly zig-zag, ¾′–1½′ tall, leafy below. **Leaves:** mainly basal, reduced upwards into sheaths, lanceolate, deeply channelled, 2″–4″ long. **Spike:** 2″–3″ long, oblong or subglobose, fairly dense, many-flowered. **Flowers:** about 1¼″ long; dorsal sepal oblong, erect; lateral sepals lanceolate, very pointed, forming a loose galea with the dorsal sepal; petals very narrowly lanceolate or linear; lip 3-lobed; outer lobes very narrow, linear; centre lobe again divided into 2 narrowly linear lobes equalling the outer lobes in length with a tooth in the sinus; spur stout, blunt, ¼″ long. *April to June.*

An exceedingly quaint yet beautiful species with quite large "spidery" blossoms of lilac or pale purple sepals and petals and a white, crimson-spotted lip with crimson-purple lobes. It is found on open hillsides and also in thin woods on mountains, usually in calcareous soils, over nearly the whole of Middle and Southern Asia and Asia Minor. The subspecies *Stevenii* and *macrophylla* are desirable. The type and its forms may be grown in the rock garden in a fairly damp spot, in calcareous loam.

712. ORCHIS SPATHULATA, Reichb. f.

Gymnadenia spathulata, Lindl.

Root: an elongate underground stem branching into thick fibres. **Stem:** 2″–5″ tall, sheathed, stout or flexuous. **Leaf:** solitary, radical, elliptic, sessile or shortly stalked, blunt, fleshy, narrowed at the base. **Scape:** stout, bearing from 2–4 blossoms. **Flowers:** about ½″ across and ⅝″ long; dorsal sepal ovate, blunt; lateral sepals oblong, rather pointed, spreading or suberect; petals elliptic, blunt, ascending; lip varying from elliptic to cuneate-obovate, crenulate, obscurely 3-lobed or entire; spur stout and blunt.

May and June.

A pretty little species with fairly large rosy-purple blossoms on stout stems. It is found in damp grassy places in poor sandy soils in the Alpine Himalaya from Kumaon to Sikkim, reaching an altitude of 13,000 feet above sea-level. It should be perfectly hardy in Great Britain in the rock garden in a damp but sunny spot, in sandy fibrous loam and sphagnum-moss. The plant is also found in Yunnan, Western China.

713. ORCHIS SPECTABILIS, Linn.

Galeorchis spectabilis, Ryd. *Orchis humilis*, Michx.

Root: a cluster of thick, fleshy fibres. **Leaves:** usually 2 in number, oblong-elliptic, blunt, narrowed towards the base, fleshy, 2″–4″ long. **Scape:** 4″–12″ tall, terminating in a spike of from 3–12 blossoms. **Flowers:** about ¾″ across and 2″ long; sepals and petals ovate or oblong, conniving, forming a galea; lip diverging, oblong or ovate, entire, petal-like; spur about ⅝″ long, blunt.

April to June.

A very beautiful Orchid of dwarf habit with a thick, fleshy, five-angled stem and a spike of large violet, purple and white blossoms; the fleshy leaves are dull green and are clammy to the touch. The plant is a native of rich woodlands and forests, delighting in rich vegetable soil, from New Brunswick to Minnesota and southward to Georgia and Arkansas. It is quite hardy in this country in a damp shady spot in the rock garden, in pure leaf-soil and sand.

714. ORCHIS SPITZELII, Saut.

O. brevicornis, Marc.

Root: of 2 oblong or ovoid tubers about 1″ long. **Stem:** ¾′–1½′ tall, slender, at times sinuous. **Leaves:** mainly basal, about 6 in number, ovate or oblong, tapering at the base, uppermost sheathing the stem, 2″–3″ long. **Spike:** 3″–6″ long, narrow, many-flowered, rather dense. **Flowers:** about ⅝″ long; dorsal sepal oblong; lateral sepals lanceolate, forming a loose galea with the dorsal sepal; petals lanceolate, nearly as long as the sepals; lip as broad as long, 3-lobed; outer lobes broad, truncate, larger than the almost square centre lobe; spur stout, slightly curved, ¼″ long. *April to June.*

This species has a long slender spike of somewhat darkly-tinted blossoms; they have green and purple sepals and petals and a dull purple lip with a pale centre, spotted with crimson-purple. There is a still darker form from Bosnia named *Sendtneri* (Reichb. f.). The type and its form are found in grassy places on mountains from the South of France to Austria, Hungary and Yugo-Slavia; they may be grown in the rock garden in fairly moist calcareous loam.

715. ORCHIS STRACHEYI, Hook. f.

Root: of branched, thick fibres. **Stem:** 3″–9″ tall, stout, sheathed. **Leaf:** solitary, radical, elliptic or obovate, 1″–3″ long. **Scape:** stout, few-flowered. **Flowers:** about $\frac{5}{8}$″ across; sepals subequal, oblong-lanceolate, lateral ones suberect; petals elliptic, blunt, ascending; lip longer than the sepals, broadly cuneate, 3-lobed to the middle; lobes blunt; spur stout, incurved, blunt. *May to July.*

This little plant is possibly a hybrid between *O. chusua* and *O. spathulata*; it has the flowers of the former and the habit and leaf of the latter. The blossoms vary from white to pale purple and are borne in stout, few-flowered spikes. It grows in damp grassy places in rocky soil in the western Himalaya, reaching an elevation of about 11,000 feet above sea-level and is exposed to over 15° of frost for considerable periods during the winter. A damp sunny spot in a good, sandy, fibrous loam is indicated

716. ORCHIS SZECHENYIANA, Reichb. f.

Root: of 2 small ovoid or oblong tubers. **Stem:** erect, 3″–6″ tall, smooth, fairly stout. **Leaf:** solitary, basal, suberect, oblong-lanceolate, pointed, 2″–3″ long. **Raceme:** lax, of 5–10 blossoms. **Flowers:** about $\frac{1}{2}$″ long, excluding the spur; dorsal sepal narrowly ovate, erect; lateral sepals similar but spreading; petals obliquely ovate-oblong, incurved; lip narrow below, 3-lobed; lobes very blunt; spur cylindrical, blunt, $\frac{1}{2}$″ long. *June.*

A dainty little plant with a single pale green leaf and a short raceme of fair-sized pink and lilac blossoms. It should prove attractive in a pan of fibrous loam in the alpine house. The plant inhabits open mountain meadows in Szechuan, Western China, and should be sufficiently hardy for outdoor culture over the greater part of the Kingdom, in the rock garden in fibrous loam, preferably of a calcareous nature.

717. ORCHIS TRIDENTATA, Scop.

O. aetensis, Tin. *O. cercopitheca,* Lamk. *O. conica,* Guss. *O. brevilabris,* Fisch. *O. Gussonii,* Tod. *O. parlatoris,* Tin. *O. Scopolii,* Timb. *O. taurica,* Lindl. *O. variegata,* All.

Root: of 2 sessile, oblong tubers about $\frac{3}{4}$″ long. **Stem:** $\frac{3}{4}$′–$1\frac{1}{2}$′ tall, fairly stout, leafy. **Leaves:** oblong-lanceolate below, lanceolate above, uppermost pointed, degenerating into bracts, $1\frac{1}{2}''$–$2\frac{1}{2}''$ long. **Spike:** about 2″ long, dense, many-flowered, subglobose. **Flowers:** about $\frac{5}{8}''$ long; sepals and petals conniving, forming a galea, both lanceolate; lip very deeply 3-lobed; side lobes ribbon-like, truncate and toothed at the apex; centre lobe wedge-shaped, toothed at the tip; spur conical, curved, $\frac{3}{8}''$ long. *April and May.*

A quaint little species with a ragged looking head of rather small blossoms remarkable for their deeply three-lobed, much toothed lip. It has pale reddish-purple petals and sepals, which are frequently tinted green at the base, and a white or pale purple lip, spotted rich crimson. The plant is found among short herbage on hill and mountain sides in Middle and Southern Europe and also in Western Asia. There is a pretty form (*commutata*) from Eastern Europe and Western Asia. The type and its form may be grown in an open position in the rock garden in fairly moist calcareous loam and sand.

718. ORCHIS USTULATA, Linn.

O. amoena, Crantz. *O. columnæ*, Schm. *O. hyemalis*, Raf. *O. imbricata*, Vest. *Himnatoglossum parviflorum*, Spreng.

Root: of 2, sessile, oblong tubers, about $\frac{3}{4}''$ long. **Stem:** 3″–12″ tall, rather stout, leafy or bract-clothed. **Leaves:** oblong-lanceolate, degenerating upwards into bracts which are frequently imbricate, 1″–2″ long. **Spike:** oblong or slightly tapering upwards, dense, many-flowered, about 2″ long. **Flowers:** about $\frac{1}{2}''$ long, narrow; dorsal sepal ovate, conniving with the lanceolate lateral sepals, forming a hood; petals oblong, small; lip 3-lobed; outer lobes linear, truncate, diverging; centre lobe broadly wedge-shaped or divided into 2 broad, blunt lobes with a minute tooth in the centre; spur thick, cylindrical, curved, $\frac{1}{8}''$ long.

March and April. (*June to August in the north.*)

A queer little plant with a spike of blossom resembling *Ajuga reptans*, only considerably larger. The flowers have green, pink-tipped sepals and petals and a white lip with crimson spots. It grows in open woods, meadows and pastures, usually in dry situations, over nearly the whole of Central and Southern Europe, including England, and ascends the mountains to a height of 6000 feet. There are several forms such as *albiflora*, *daphneolens*, *grandiflora* and *virescens*. The type and its varieties may be grown in the rock garden in a well-drained, open spot, in good fibrous loam and leaf-soil.

OREORCHIS, Lindley

Fourteen species of deciduous or subevergreen terrestrial plants with stout stems which are frequently swollen at the base into tubers resembling pseudo-bulbs; these are produced on the surface of the soil from a few fibrous roots;

one or two have lobed tubers buried in the compost. From one to two long, narrow leaves are produced from the swollen stem and from between them slender, flexuous flower-stems rise bearing few-flowered racemes of small or medium-sized, quaintly constructed blossoms, mixed with minute bracts. The various species, which are scattered over Northern Asia, are usually found in thin forest land, frequently attaining considerable elevations above sea-level in the Himalaya and neighbouring ranges. They may be grown outdoors in most parts of Britain in a damp, half-shady spot in the rock garden in osmunda fibre or peat, leaf-soil, sphagnum-moss and sand. Propagation by imported plants and seeds when available.

719. OREORCHIS FOLIOSA, Lindl.

Root: a tuber resembling a pseudo-bulb. **Leaf:** radical, linear-lanceolate, strongly nerved, 3″–6″ long. **Scape:** 6″–12″ tall, slender, sheathed. **Raceme:** few-flowered. **Flowers:** ½″ long; dorsal sepal linear-oblong, rather pointed; lateral sepals falcately-oblong, pointed; petals broadly-oblong, blunt; lip 3-lobed, produced at the base into a sac; outer lobes rounded; centre lobe twice the size of the lateral ones, rounded. *July.*

A quaint plant, suitable for cultivation in the alpine house. The curious red-brown blossoms are widely scattered up the slender flower-stem, which is clothed at its base with a solitary, narrow, deep green leaf, at times tinted with red. It cannot claim to have any decorative value. In a state of nature it grows in thinly-wooded country, usually at the base of large trees, in the Himalaya from Simla to the Lachen Valley, where it reaches an altitude of 12,000 feet above sea-level. It should therefore be perfectly hardy in this country in a shady spot in leaf-soil and loam. This species is also found in Western China.

720. OREORCHIS INDICA, Hook. f.

Corallorhiza indica, Lindl.

Root: a lobed tuber. **Leaf:** radical, lanceolate, strongly nerved, 4″–8″ long. **Scape:** ¾′–1¾′ tall, rather stout, sheath-clothed. **Raceme:** few-flowered. **Flowers:** about ¾″ across; dorsal sepal linear-lanceolate; lateral sepals subfalcately lanceolate; petals narrowly subfalcately oblong, blunt; lip 3-lobed; outer lobes ear-shaped, incurved, blunt; centre lobe rounded, entire or sub-2-lobed; disc ridged between the side lobes. *August.*

A much more robust plant than the preceding species, quaint and well worth growing in a shady part of the rock garden in vegetable soil and loam. It produces a very tall, erect, red or yellowish-brown stem clothed with two or three sheaths and a loose raceme of fairly large yellowish-brown or reddish-brown blossoms. It grows in thin forest lands and in rocky places beneath the shade of trees in the Western Himalaya, reaching an altitude of 10,000 feet and should be quite hardy in all but the most exposed parts of Britain. The plant may be protected from frost during the winter.

721. OREORCHIS MICRANTHA, Lindl.

Root: an ovoid or globose, tuber-like pseudo-bulb. **Leaves:** 2 in number, narrowly-linear, 3″–8″ long. **Scape:** 1′–1½′ tall, fairly stout, clothed with 2–3 tubular sheaths. **Raceme:** few-flowered. **Flowers:** ¼″ long; dorsal sepal oblong, blunt; lateral sepals falcately oblong; petals lanceolate; lip with small lanceolate, falcate, basal lobes; centre lobe large, with a 2-lobed crumpled tip; disc with a tall, linear, grooved, fleshy callus. *June.*

This species, which is of no garden value, has much smaller blossoms than the foregoing plants; they are of the same dull yellowish-brown or reddish brown colour and are borne in a loose raceme on the tall brown-tinted stem which is clothed with a few tubular yellowish-brown sheaths. It is found in thin forest lands and woods in moist mossy places in the Kumaon Himalaya up to 10,000 feet and should have the same treatment in cultivation as *O. foliosa.*

722. OREORCHIS PARVULA, Schltr.

Root: a fleshy corm-like tuber or rhizome, jointed and with several fibrous rootlets. **Leaf:** solitary, lanceolate-elliptic, blunt, tapering to a short stalk, about 5″ long. **Scape:** about 6½″ tall, clothed with 3 or 4 narrow sheaths. **Raceme:** of 8–15 blossoms, rather lax. **Flowers:** about ½″ across; dorsal sepal ligulate, blunt; lateral sepals ligulate, subfalcate; petals similar to lateral sepals; lip shortly unguiculate, oblong, 3-lobed; outer lobes short, ligulate, falcate; centre lobe ovate-spathulate with 2 parallel lamellæ down its centre. *June.*

A Chinese plant with racemes of rather small yellowish-green blossoms; quaint but of little decorative value. It is found on thinly wooded mountains in Yunnan, Western China, at 10,000 feet above sea-level and should therefore be hardy in all but the most exposed parts of the Kingdom in a shady, somewhat damp spot in the rock garden in leaf-soil and peat.

723. OREORCHIS PATENS, Lindl.

O. lancifolia, A. Gr. *Corallorhiza patens*, Lindl.

Root: a rhizome, shortly jointed and covered with loose scales. **Stem:** 6″–9″ tall, clothed with a few loose, membranous sheaths. **Leaf:** solitary, basal, sword-shaped, plicate. **Raceme:** lax, of 7–8 blossoms. **Flowers:** about ⅜″ across; dorsal sepal oblong, blunt; lateral sepals falcately oblong, blunt; petals narrowly oblong; lip 3-lobed; outer lobes linear, blunt; centre lobe oblong or rounded, crisped, with 2 lamellæ on the disc. *June.*

Like the other members of the genus this species is of but little garden value. It has rather small blossoms with brownish-green sepals and petals and a yellowish-green lip spotted with red; they are fragrant. It is found in open pine woods and in half-shady, stony places in Siberia, Tibet, China and Japan, reaching an elevation of 11,000 feet in Yunnan. It should be quite hardy in Great Britain in a half-shady spot, in soil collected from beneath the shade of conifers.

724. OREORCHIS SETSCHUANICA, Ames and Schltr.

Root: of 2 ovoid tubers on a short stock. **Leaf:** solitary, basal, erect, narrowly lanceolate, stalked, 6″–9″ long. **Scape:** 1′–$1\frac{1}{2}$′ tall, slender, erect, round, clothed with 3 or 4 narrow sheaths. **Raceme:** about 6″ long, laxly many-flowered. **Flowers:** about $\frac{3}{8}$″ across; dorsal sepal narrowly oblong, pointed; lateral sepals spreading, narrowly falcate-oblong, pointed; petals similar to the lateral sepals, oblique; lip shortly unguiculate, 3-lobed; lateral lobes subfalcate-linear, blunt; centre lobe suborbicular or rounded-triangular, margins undulate. *June.*

A curious Chinese species with a loose, many-flowered raceme of yellowish-brown or reddish-brown blossoms of no real decorative value. It is found in thickets and thin woodlands in Western Szechuan at from 7000–11,500 feet above sea-level, so should therefore be quite hardy in Britain in a damp shady spot in the rock garden, in sandy leaf-soil.

ORTHOCERAS, R. Brown

This genus contains but 1 species, it is a deciduous, terrestrial plant of erect habit. The root system consists of several fair-sized, oval tubers, the largest of which supplies the nourishment for the growing plant and after this has perfected its seeds the tuber withers away, meanwhile the smaller tubers gradually reach flowering size and so the species is preserved and increased. The flower-stems are erect and fairly stout; they are clothed with a few narrow sheathing leaves and lance-shaped sheaths. The blossoms are borne in loose spikes, and although they are by no means showy they are quaint and interesting and the plant is well worth growing in the rock garden, in an open sunny spot in good, somewhat heavy soil; it is advisable to protect the tubers from prolonged frost by means of a covering of dry bracken or leaves. Propagation by imported tubers and by seeds when procurable.

725. ORTHOCERAS STRICTUM, R. Br.

O. Solandrii, Lindl. *Diuris Novæ-Zelandiæ*, A. Rich.

Root: an ovoid tuber emitting a few fleshy fibres. **Leaves:** subradical, linear, 3″–6″ long. **Scape:** 1′–1½′ tall, clothed with a few lanceolate sheaths. **Spike:** 6″ or more long, blossoms rather distant. **Flowers:** about 1¼″ long; dorsal sepal almost galeate, blunt; lateral sepals antennæ-like, slight clavate, nearly 1″ long; petals narrow, very short, toothed at the tip; lip 3-lobed; outer lobes broad and oblique; centre lobe ovate, twice as long as the outer lobes; there is a callus between the lateral lobes, broad and prominent.

December and January.

An interesting but by no means showy plant with long spikes of curiously constructed blossoms, green and white outside, brownish-purple or brownish-yellow within. It is found in open districts, usually on dry soil, frequently in clay, in hilly localities in New South Wales, Victoria, South Australia and over the whole of New Zealand, where it ascends to an elevation of over 4000 feet above sea-level and is therefore quite hardy in Great Britain. A heavy loam in an open sunny spot should meet its requirements.

ORTHOPENTHEA, Rolfe

Delightful, dwarf, deciduous, terrestrial plants with sessile, rounded tubers and a few fleshy roots above them. The narrow grassy leaves are rather numerous and are reduced in length upwards until they degenerate into bracts on the upper part of the stem and amongst the blossoms which are inverted and are produced in few or many-flowered spikes; the flowers are quite large considering the size of the plant. The few that are sufficiently hardy for outdoor culture in Britain should make delightful additions to the alpine house in deep pans of moist, fibrous peat, fibrous loam and sand. The genus numbers 10 species and is confined to Africa, the greater majority are natives of Cape Colony. They may be tried outdoors in warm sheltered localities in the rock garden in a damp sunny spot in fibrous peat and fibrous, gritty loam; their tubers should be protected from severe frost in the winter by a hand-light or covering of dry leaves. Propagation by imported tubers and by seeds which are freely produced in a state of nature.

726. ORTHOPENTHEA BIVALVATA, Rolfe

Ophrys bivalvata, Linn. *Serapias melaleuca*, Thunb. *Disa melaleuca*, Sw. *Disa bivalvata*, Durand and Schinz. *Penthea melaleuca*, Lindl.

Root: a sessile tuber. **Stem:** moderately stout. **Leaves:** radical and cauline, numerous, rigid, 1″–3″ long, linear or lanceolate-linear, reduced upwards into bracts. **Scape:** ⅓″–1″ tall, sheath-clothed. **Spike:** subcorymbose,

1″–2″ broad, many-flowered. **Flowers:** nearly $\frac{3}{4}$″ across; dorsal sepal galeate, obovate, subsaccate above the middle; lateral sepals ovate-oblong, oblique; petals broadly oblong, oblique; lip rhomboid-oblong. *November.*

This pretty plant is almost a study in black and white, for the petals and lip are of so deep a brown tint that they appear black in some lights; the sepals are white with slight green veinings on the dorsal one. It is usually found in moist, light soils amongst short herbage, on the mountains of the well-watered districts of Cape Colony, reaching its greatest elevation at 5000 feet on the Blue Berg in the Clanwilliam Division, where 20° of frost are registered during the winter. A gritty loam in full sun is indicated.

727. ORTHOPENTHEA ELEGANS, Rolfe

Penthea elegans, Sond. *Disa elegans,* Reichb. f.

Root: a sessile tuber. **Stem:** moderately stout. **Leaves:** cauline, lanceolate or linear-lanceolate, 3″–5″ long, fairly numerous, reduced upwards into bracts. **Scape:** $\frac{1}{2}$′–1$\frac{1}{2}$′ tall, sheath-clothed. **Spike:** subcorymbose or shortly racemose, few-flowered. **Flowers:** 1$\frac{1}{4}$″ across; dorsal sepal galeate, broadly elliptic, somewhat curved; lateral sepals broadly elliptic, blunt; petals spathulate-oblong, falcately curved; lip rhomboid or rhomboid-lanceolate. *October to December.*

A very beautiful, large-flowered species of considerable garden value; it has pure white sepals and purple, yellow-tipped petals and lip, and differs from the other species in not having its blossoms upside down on their stems. It grows on grassy mountain slopes in Western Cape Colony and probably reaches its greatest elevation on the summit of the Zwartberg Range at 5300 feet and should be quite hardy in all but the coldest parts of Great Britain if it can be induced to rest during our winter. A moist, fibrous loam in full sun is indicated.

728. ORTHOPENTHEA MINOR, Rolfe

Penthea minor, Sond. *Disa minor,* Reichb. f.

Root: a sessile tuber. **Stem:** rather slender. **Leaves:** radical, linear-spathulate, attenuated at the base, $\frac{3}{4}$″–1″ long. **Scape:** 3″–5″ tall, with one or two sheaths. **Spike:** very short, few-flowered. **Flowers:** under $\frac{1}{2}$″ in diameter; dorsal sepal galeate, subglobose, subsaccate behind; lateral sepals broadly ovate-elliptic, concave; petals oblong, suberect, concave; lip linear-spathulate, very blunt. *December and January.*

A dwarf, compact little plant with a slender flower-stem springing from the tufted foliage, and bearing about half-a-dozen pretty little golden-yellow blossoms carried upside down on their stems. It should prove a welcome addition to the rock garden or alpine house. It grows in fairly open rocky places amongst short herbage at 4000–5000 feet elevation on Great Winterhoek Mountains in the Tulbagh Division of Cape Colony and is there subjected to as much as 25° of frost during its resting period. It should be given a moist sandy peat and loam in sun or shade.

729. ORTHOPENTHEA RICHARDIANA, Rolfe

Disa Richardiana, Lehm. *Penthea obtusa*, Lindl.

Root: a sessile tuber. **Stem:** rather slender. **Leaves:** radical, spathulate-lanceolate, attenuate below, $\frac{3}{4}''$–$1\frac{1}{4}''$ long. **Scape:** 3″–6″ high, sheath-clothed. **Spike:** short, subcorymbose, $\frac{3}{4}''$–1″ broad. **Flowers:** over $\frac{1}{2}''$ across; dorsal sepal galeate, subglobose, very blunt, margins inflexed; lateral sepals broadly ovate, spreading, very blunt; petals obovate-oblong, denticulate; lip oblong or obovate, blunt. *November.*

Like the preceding species, this little plant with its dainty blossoms and neat, compact tuft of suberect leaves should prove a useful addition to the rock garden or alpine house; it has white sepals and golden-yellow petals and lip. It grows on moss-covered rocks and moist banks on mountains in Western Cape Colony and reaches its greatest elevation of 5000 feet at Genadendal in the Caledon Division, where it is exposed to over 20° of frost during the winter for short periods. It should be given a half-shady spot in the rock garden in moist, fibrous peat and loam.

PACHITES, Lindley

This genus is limited to 2 species; they are slender, erect, deciduous, terrestrial plants; their slender, wiry stems are clothed with rather narrow, grassy leaves, smooth and sharply pointed, these are rather long near the base of the stem but gradually diminish upwards into bracts, being small when they mingle with the flowers which are borne in cylindrical spikes and are inverted, the lip being uppermost owing to the twisted ovary. The plants have delicately tinted blossoms and are well worth growing. They are found on the shelving sides of hills and mountains amongst dwarf heaths and low-growing grasses in South-Western Cape Colony. But one species is sufficiently hardy for culture outdoors in the warmer parts of this country; it may be tried in a damp sunny part of the rock garden and should have its fleshy roots protected in winter. Propagation by root division and by seeds.

730. PACHITES APPRESSA, Lindl.

Root: of finger-like tubers. **Stem:** rather stout. **Leaves:** cauline, fairly numerous, erect, linear, 3″–5″ long, degenerating into bracts upwards. **Scape:** $\frac{3}{4}'$–$1\frac{1}{2}'$ tall. **Spike:** oblong, 3″–6″ long, rather dense. **Flowers:** over

$\frac{1}{2}''$ across; sepals suberect, elliptic-oblong, blunt, margins incurved; petals elliptic-oblong, blunt, margins incurved; lip elliptic-lanceolate, erect, with two horn-like processes near its base. *January and February.*

The blossoms of this plant, although of small size, are decorative on account of their delicate tinting; they are lilac in ground colour with two yellow stripes on the lip; the column is yellow, margined with red at the top. It grows on mountain slopes in short herbage in Western Cape Colony, reaching its greatest elevation on the Zuurbraak Range in the Swellendam Division at 4000 feet, where it is exposed to over 12° of frost during the winter for short periods. It should be grown in moist, fibrous loam and peat in full sun.

PANISEA, Lindley

Six dwarf, tufted epiphytes very closely allied to the *Cœlogynes*; only one species is found at sufficient altitude in its native habitat to justify inclusion in this work. It has a small rhizome which produces a few fleshy roots. The leaves are borne in pairs from the apex of narrow and much-crowded pseudo-bulbs; they are fairly broad and diminish below into fairly long stalks. The flower-stalks spring from the rhizome at the base of the pseudo-bulbs; they are short and bear a spike composed of a few medium-sized, pretty blossoms. The plant is found on evergreen and deciduous trees and also on moss and fern clad rocks in the Himalaya and reaches sufficient elevation to give reasonable hope that it may prove hardy in many parts of Britain in humid localities. Propagation by imported plants and by seed when procurable.

731. PANISEA PARVIFLORA, Lindl.

Dendrobium demissum, Don. *Cœlogyne parviflora*, Lindl.

Root: a small rhizome emitting a few fleshy fibres. **Pseudo-bulbs:** narrowly ovoid, crowded, $\frac{1}{2}''$–1″ long. **Leaves:** 2 in number, from the apex of the pseudo-bulb, plaited, elliptic-lanceolate, pointed, shortly stalked, 2″–3″ long. **Scape:** filiform, lateral, 2″–4″ tall, bearing from 3–5 blossoms. **Flowers:** $\frac{3}{4}''$ long; dorsal sepal linear-oblong; lateral sepals lanceolate, pointed, 5-nerved, membranous; petals ovate-lanceolate, 3-nerved, swollen at the base; lip narrowly lanceolate, entire or toothed. *July and August.*

A small tufted Orchid of epiphytic habit with fair-sized white blossoms with a pale brown column. It is a pretty little plant and should make a pleasing addition to the alpine house in a pan of sphagnum-moss and peat, or on a damp sandstone rock or tree-fern stump outdoors in the same compost. It is found on the branches of trees in the Khasia Hills and in the Sikkim Himalaya at altitudes up to 10,000 feet and should be hardy outdoors in Great Britain in all but the most exposed localities.

PECTEILIS, Rafin

About half a dozen species of somewhat handsome, leafy terrestrial Orchids of erect, deciduous habit. They are closely related to some members of the genus *Platanthera* and some of the species were formerly included in that genus and in *Habenaria*. Their roots consist of fair-sized oblong or irregular tubers nearly sessile on the base of the underground part of the stem, which is usually leafy and frequently stout in the most robust species; the flowers are borne in few-flowered racemes and are frequently of large size with beautifully fringed lips; they are usually white or pale green in colour. All are interesting and worthy of a place in the garden or glasshouse. The various species range from Japan to China, India and the East Indian Islands and are lovers of moisture at the root. Propagation by imported tubers and by seeds when available.

732. PECTEILIS RADIATA, Raf.

Orchis Susannæ, Thunb. *O. radiata*, Sprgl. *Platanthera radiata*, Lindl. *Hemihabenaria radiata*, Finet.

Root: of ovoid or globose tubers with fibrous roots above. **Stem:** 6″–12″ tall, slender, leafy, zig-zag. **Leaves:** cauline, linear, pointed, 3″–6″ long, slightly twisted. **Raceme:** of 2 or rarely 3 blossoms. **Flowers:** about 1″ across; dorsal sepal erect, narrowly ovate or lanceolate, pointed; lateral sepals similar but larger, spreading; petals ovate, pointed, erect; lip unguiculate at the base, 3-lobed; outer lobes wedge-shaped, deeply cut into narrow, linear segments; centre lobe ligulate, pointed; spur slender, cylindrical, pendulous, curved, over 1″ long. *July and August.*

Quite a desirable little plant for alpine-house decoration although by no manner of means showy. The blossoms are yellowish-green and white, tinted with purple; the lip is frequently yellow. It is found in damp shady places on mountains in various parts of Japan and Korea and should be quite hardy in Britain in the rock garden in damp fibrous loam and peat.

733. PECTEILIS SUSANNÆ, Raf.

Platanthera Susannæ, Lindl. *Habenaria gigantea*, D. Don.

Root: of 2 oblong, irregular tubers, 3″–4″ long. **Stem:** 2′–4′ tall, leafy, stout, erect. **Leaves:** numerous, imbricate, clothing the stem to the first flower, ovate-oblong, the last few cucullate. **Raceme:** lax, short, of 3–5 blossoms. **Flowers:** 3″–4″ across; dorsal sepal rhomboid, very broad, spreading; lateral sepals subquadrately-oblong, ascending; petals linear, pointed, small; lip 3-lobed; outer lobes very broad, truncate, pectinate; centre lobe linear or dilated downwards; spur slender, long. *August and September.*

This robust species is probably the most handsome of the genus. It produces a few huge snow-white or greenish-white fragrant blossoms on the top of the leaf-clothed stem. It inhabits marshes, frequently at considerable elevations on the mountains, and is native in the Malay Islands, Eastern India and China, where on the mountains of Yunnan it reaches an elevation of 9000 feet. Plants collected from such altitudes should succeed in Britain on the banks of a pond or stream.

PENTHEA, Lindley

A genus limited to 11 species of slender, deciduous, terrestrial plants; their root systems consist of two or more oval or oblong tubers of small size; they are sessile at the base of the underground portion of the stem and there are several fleshy pale-coloured fibres above. Like so many of the other tuberous-rooted Orchids their tubers shrivel and perish after producing flowers, fresh tubers being formed each growing season; these with the help of seeds maintain the species. Their slender stems are clothed with narrow leaves which gradually diminish in length upwards and degenerate into bracts amongst the flowers which are produced in corymbose spikes. Both species are found in moist open places in South-Western Cape Colony and may be tried outdoors in Britain in sheltered localities but should have protection from severe frost in the winter. Propagation by imported tubers and by seed which are freely produced in their native habitats.

734. PENTHEA FILICORNIS, Lindl.

P. reflexa, Lindl. *Orchis filicornis*, Linn. *Disa filicornis*, Thunb. *D. patens*, Sw. *D. reflexa*, Reichb. f.

Root: of oblong-ovoid tubers. **Stem:** rather stout. **Leaves:** radical and cauline, linear or narrowly lanceolate-linear, $\frac{1}{2}''$–$1\frac{1}{2}''$ long, narrowing upwards into bracts. **Scape:** 4″–10″ long, clothed with narrow sheaths. **Spike:** short, loosely subcorymbose. **Flowers:** $\frac{5}{8}''$ across; dorsal sepal galeate, obovate-spathulate; spur reduced to a nearly obsolete sac; lateral sepals oblong; petals falcate oblong; lip narrowly linear. *November and December.*

A pretty species with fairly large pink blossoms in which the lateral sepals are suffused with purple and the remainder of the segments sprinkled with purple spots. It grows in moist grassy places and on the banks of streams in South-Western Cape Colony and probably reaches its greatest altitude on the Bosch River in the Knysna Division at 4500 feet, where it experiences during the winter months as much as 12° of frost for short periods. It should be given a moist, fibrous loam in full sun and is only suitable for outdoor culture in Western Britain.

735. PENTHEA PATENS, Lindl.

Ophrys patens, Thunb. *Serapias patens*, Thunb. *Disa patens*, Sw. *Disa tenuifolia*, Sw.

Root: of ovoid-oblong tubers. **Stem:** somewhat slender. **Leaves:** radical, linear or narrowly lanceolate-linear, numerous, $\frac{1}{2}''$–1″ long. **Scape:** 3″–10″ long, clothed with numerous sheaths. **Spikes:** short, loosely corymbose. **Flowers:** over 1″ across; dorsal sepal broadly ovate or cordate-ovate, nearly flat; spur obsolete; lateral sepals narrowly ovate from a broad oblique base, tip narrowly falcate; petals falcate-oblong; lip narrowly linear.

October to December.

A very beautiful plant with slender, leafy spikes of about half-a-dozen large bright yellow blossoms of considerable decorative value. It grows on grassy mountain slopes amongst fairly short herbage in South-Western Cape Colony and probably reaches its greatest elevation near Pikeniers Kloof in the Piquetberg Division at 5000 feet, where the thermometer falls to 15° for short periods during the winter months. It should be grown in a moist but open spot in good fibrous loam.

PERISTYLUS, Blume

Slender, leafy, deciduous, terrestrial plants closely allied to the genus *Herminium*. They have a root system of globular or oval tubers, sessile at the base of the underground portion of the stem, their slender, erect stems are usually clothed with rather broad, short leaves and the blossoms are produced in loose or dense spikes. The flowers are small, green or white in colour and of but little decorative value. The plants are found in damp grassy places on the margins of swamps and in bogs in various parts of the northern temperate regions, and near the tops of some of the higher mountains of the tropics. They number about 30 species; many seem to be very closely allied and will probably be reduced to varieties when better known; the majority are quite hardy in this country and may be grown in moist or wet spots, such as the bog garden or banks of a stream or pond in sandy loam, mixed with peat if possible. Propagation by imported tubers.

736. PERISTYLUS LEFEBUREANUS, A. Rich.

Habenaria Lefeburiana, Durand et Schinz. *Platanthera Lefeburiana*, Engl.

Root: of ovoid or globose tubers. **Stem:** 3″–6″ tall, leafy in the middle with several sheaths below. **Leaves:** broadly ovate-oblong, blunt, $\frac{3}{4}''$–$1\frac{1}{2}''$ long. **Spike:** $\frac{1}{2}''$–$1\frac{1}{2}''$ long, dense. **Flowers:** $\frac{3}{16}''$ across; sepals ovate-oblong, very blunt; petals broadly obovate, very blunt; lip as broad as long, shortly

3-lobed at its apex; outer lobes very broadly triangular-ovate, very blunt; centre lobe triangular-ovate with a fleshy disc; spur saccate, very minute. *May to August.*

A very dwarf species with tiny pale green blossoms in short oblong spikes, on stems clothed with a few oval leaves towards the middle. It is of no decorative value and grows in damp, grassy places amongst stones on the mountains of Abyssinia, where on Mount Guna it attains an elevation of 10,000 feet above sea-level and is therefore quite hardy in Great Britain. A damp sandy loam in full sun should suit it.

737. PERISTYLUS PETITIANUS, A. Rich.

Habenaria Petitiana, Durand et Schinz. *Platanthera Petitiana*, Engl.

Root: an ovoid-oblong or globose tuber. **Stem:** $\frac{1}{2}'$–$1\frac{3}{4}'$ tall, leafy, clothed with several sheaths near its base. **Leaves:** ovate or broadly elliptic-oblong. **Raceme:** $\frac{3}{4}''$–$5\frac{1}{2}''$ long, dense or somewhat lax. **Flowers:** about $\frac{3}{16}''$ across; sepals ovate-oblong, blunt; petals falcate-oblong, blunt; lip deeply 3-lobed; outer lobes linear, falcate, slightly longer than the centre lobe which is linear; spur oblong, minute. *July to September.*

Like all its brethren this plant is of no horticultural value; it bears a long raceme of pale green blossoms on a rather slender, sparely leafy stem. It is found in open grassy places on the highlands of Abyssinia and attains sufficient altitude above sea-level to ensure its hardiness in all but the bleakest parts of Great Britain in the rock garden or border in damp fibrous loam, in an open sunny spot.

738. PERISTYLUS QUARTINIANUS, A. Rich.

Habenaria rœmeriana, Durand et Schinz. *Platanthera Quartiniana*, Engl.

Root: an ovoid or globose tuber. **Stem:** about $1\frac{1}{4}'$ tall, clothed with a few sheaths towards its base, and bearing 2–3 leaves above. **Leaves:** oblong or lanceolate-oblong, pointed, 2″–3″ long. **Spike:** 4″–5″ long, lax. **Flowers:** about $\frac{1}{4}''$ across; sepals ovate, with hairy margins, carinate near the apex; petals broadly ovate, blunt, carinate; lip 3-lobed; outer lobes linear, blunt; centre lobes linear, incurved, blunt, slightly longer than the outer lobes; spur cylindrical, $\frac{1}{2}''$ long. *August and September.*

A species of but little decorative value, with loose, cylindrical spikes of rather small green and white blossoms. The yellowish-green leaves are produced near the base of the stems. It grows in damp, open, grassy places on the mountains of Abyssinia, where it reaches an elevation of nearly 9000 feet above sea-level and is exposed to over 20° of frost for short periods when at rest. A damp, fibrous loam in a sunny spot is indicated.

739. PERISTYLUS STEUDNERI, Rolfe

Herminium Steudneri, Reichb. f.

Root: of small tubers on fleshy fibres. **Stem:** $\frac{3}{4}'$–$1\frac{1}{4}'$ tall, leafy above, clothed with narrow black-spotted sheaths below. **Leaves:** few, oblong, pointed, distant, decreasing upwards into bracts, $\frac{1}{2}''$–$1\frac{1}{4}''$ long. **Raceme:** cylindrical, $1\frac{1}{2}''$–$3''$ long, dense. **Flowers:** $\frac{3}{16}''$ across; sepals ligulate-triangular, blunt; petals lanceolate, pointed; lip 3-lobed; outer lobes triangular; centre lobe narrower, with a longitudinal keel; spur subglobose, obscurely 2-lobed at its apex. *May to July.*

A slender species producing stems clothed with from six to eight small leaves, and spikes of small green and white flowers of no decorative value. It is a local plant in grassy hollows on the highlands of Abyssinia, where it reaches an altitude of 8500 feet above sea-level and is subjected to over 15° of frost for short periods. In cultivation it requires a mixture of peat and fibrous loam in a damp but sunny spot.

740. PERISTYLUS VOLKENSIANUS, Rolfe

Platanthera Volkensiana, Kränzl.

Root: an ovoid or oblong tuber about $\frac{3}{4}''$ long. **Stem:** $2'$–$3'$ tall, very slender, leafy in the centre, clothed with a few sheaths below. **Leaves:** oblong, pointed, attenuate at the base, $5''$–$6''$ long. **Spike:** up to $10''$ in length, dense. **Flowers:** under $\frac{3}{16}''$ across; sepals ovate, blunt; petals oblong, blunt, as long as the sepals; lip 3-lobed; outer lobes linear, diverging, from a broad base; centre lobe linear, pointed; disc with an elevated keel; spur curved, slightly flattened, blunt. *August.*

A very tall slender species with stems clothed with a few oblong leaves and long cylindrical spikes of tiny greenish-yellow flowers of no horticultural merit. It is found in grassy places amongst rocks on Kilimanjaro in Tanganyika, East Africa at 9500 feet and should therefore prove quite hardy in Great Britain in a sheltered sunny spot in the rock garden in damp peat and loam.

PERULARIA, Lindley

About 8 species of marsh-loving, deciduous, terrestrial herbs included by some authors in the genus *Platanthera* or *Habenaria*. They have roots of oblong or ovoid tubers with a few white fleshy roots from the crown. The tubers are annual, fresh ones are produced yearly to perpetuate the species. The stems reach a moderate height and are clothed at the base with large rounded leaves; the blossoms are borne in long, many-flowered spikes, they are comparatively small and of little decorative value, being tinted with various shades of green and purple. The species range from China and Japan to North America. Propagation by imported tubers and by seeds.

741. PERULARIA FUSCESCENS, Lindl.

P. flava, Rydb. *Habenaria flava*, Linn. *H. herbiola*, R. Br. *Platanthera fuscescens*, Kränzl. *Orchis fuscescens*, Linn.

Root: of palmately lobed tubers. **Stem:** 12″–15″ tall. **Leaves:** 2 in number, obovate-oblong, ovate-lanceolate or lanceolate, blunt or pointed, 6″–9″ long. **Spike:** 2″–4″ long, densely many-flowered. **Flowers:** about $\frac{3}{8}$″ across; dorsal sepal oblong, blunt; lateral sepals similar, crenulate; petals narrowly oblong with minute teeth at the tip; lip triangular below, linear towards the tip; disc with elevated lines; spur filiform, thickened at the tip, $\frac{1}{4}$″ long. *June to August.*

A rather robust species with a dense spike of small yellow and green blossoms shaded with brown. It is of no great decorative value and is found over the greater part of North America, Northern Asia and the Azores in swamps and wet pastures. It should be perfectly hardy in Great Britain in good heavy loam on the banks of a pond or stream.

742. PERULARIA SOULIEI, Schltr.

Platanthera Souliei, Kränzl.

Root: of oblong or ovoid tubers. **Stem:** about 15″ tall, clothed at the base with 2 leaves. **Leaves:** broadly oblong, blunt or pointed, sheathing at the base, 4″–6″ long. **Spike:** 4″–5″ long, many-flowered. **Flowers:** about $\frac{1}{4}$″ across; dorsal sepal suborbicular, concave; lateral sepals oblong, rounded at the tip and slightly toothed on the margins; petals narrowly oblong or narrowly ovate-oblong, blunt; lip 3-lobed; lateral lobes small, somewhat triangular, diverging; centre lobe linear, blunt; spur curved, slightly flattened, $\frac{1}{4}$″ long. *July and August.*

The small white and green blossoms of this species are produced in long slender spikes on fairly tall stout stems; the spikes of blossom are sufficiently dense to be quite decorative. It is found in wet grass lands and swamps in Eastern Tibet and should be quite hardy in cultivation in this country in the bog-garden or on the banks of a stream or pond in good loam.

743. PERULARIA USSURIENSIS, Schltr.

Platanthera ussuriensis, Maxim.

Root: of narrowly oblong or fusiform tubers. **Stem:** about 12″ tall, rather slender. **Leaves:** 2 in number, oblong or ovate-cuneate, blunt, 3″–4″ long. **Spike:** short, few- or many-flowered. **Flowers:** about $\frac{3}{16}$″ across;

dorsal sepal ovate or orbicular, blunt; lateral sepals usually ligulate, deflexed; petals oblong, blunt, minute; lip divided into 3 triangular lobes; centre lobe blunt, the longest; spur filiform, incurved, $\frac{1}{4}''$ long. *June and July.*

A rather dwarf, slender plant with minute pale yellowish-green blossoms of no decorative value. It inhabits damp spots in open country in Japan and Manchuria, and should be perfectly hardy in Great Britain in the bog garden or on the banks of a stream or pond in good loam and peat.

PLATANTHERA, Lindley

Deciduous terrestrial plants numbering about 250 species with small or medium-sized blossoms borne in dense spikes or racemes. Few have blossoms of any decorative value though many are very curiously constructed and should appeal to lovers of quaint and interesting plants. Their root system consists of rounded or at times lobed tubers, sessile on the underground portion of the stem; their flower-stems are usually stout and are clothed with variously shaped leaves which are more numerous towards the basal part of the stem. The plants are scattered throughout much of the temperate and sub-tropical regions of the northern hemisphere, a few being found in South America and Africa; they usually inhabit damp, grassy places in open situations, frequently attaining considerable elevations above sea-level. Many are perfectly hardy in Britain and may be grown in a sunny spot in damp fibrous loam. Propagation by imported tubers and seeds.

744. PLATANTHERA ALBO-MARGINATA, Kränzl.

Habenaria albo-marginata, King

Root: of globular, depressed tubers about $\frac{3}{4}''$ in diameter. **Stem:** 6″ tall, fleshy. **Leaves:** 2 in number, oblong-lanceolate, about $1\frac{1}{2}''$ long. **Spike:** of 8–10 blossoms. **Flowers:** about $\frac{1}{2}''$ across; dorsal sepal and lateral sepals ovate-elliptic, blunt; petals ovate, spreading; lip subrotund and deeply 3-lobed; outer lobes oblong, blunt; centre lobe oblong, longer than the outer lobes; spur cylindrical, upcurved, $\frac{5}{8}''$ long. *June.*

A pretty little species, sufficiently dwarf for alpine house culture. The blossoms, which are comparatively large for the size of the plant, have green sepals with a white margin, white petals and lip and a bright green spur. It is found in damp rocky places in the Sikkim Himalaya near Jongi at over 12,000 feet above sea-level. It should succeed outdoors in Great Britain in a damp position in the rock garden in good sandy loam and leaf-soil.

745. PLATANTHERA ALGERIENSIS, Batt.

Root: of 2 fusiform tubers $1''$–$1\frac{1}{4}''$ long. **Leaves:** basal, 2 or rarely 3 in number, opposite, oblong-lanceolate, 6″–12″ long. **Scape:** $1'$–$2\frac{3}{4}'$ tall, stout, clothed with a few lanceolate bracts which are large and leaf-like. **Spike:** 4″–9″ long, erect, cylindrical, very densely many-flowered. **Flowers:** about 1″ long exclusive of the spur; dorsal sepal ovate; lateral sepals broadly lanceolate, curved, spreading; petals narrowly oblong, forming with the dorsal sepal a galea over the column; lip entire, oblong-lanceolate; spur curved, slender, clavate towards the tip, 1¼″ long. *March to May.*

A robust species with large leaves and a long dense spike of medium-sized yellowish-green blossoms; despite its dull tints it is well worth cultivating. It is found in damp spots in grassy country near Algiers and may be grown in the rock garden in very mild localities in damp, somewhat heavy loam.

746. PLATANTHERA ARCUATA, Lindl.

Habenaria arcuata, Hook. f.

Root: a cluster of branched, thick, tuberous fibres. **Stem:** ¾′–1¼′ tall, very stout and leafy. **Leaves:** oblong or lanceolate, pointed, narrowing towards the top of the stem, sheathing at the base, 3″–4″ long. **Spike:** stout, many-flowered. **Flowers:** about ¾″ across; dorsal sepal cucullate, beaked; lateral sepals oblong, blunt, deflexed; petals linear, small, membranous; lip linear, large, twice as long as the sepals, with incurved margins; spur incurved pointed, 2½″ long. *May and June.*

An attractive robust species with large green and white blossoms with very long incurved spurs. It grows in marshy places in open sunny spots in the Western Himalaya at sufficient elevation above sea-level to ensure its hardiness in Western and Southern Britain in a sunny position in the bog garden in loam and peat or on the banks of a pond in fairly rich soil

747. PLATANTHERA BAKERIANA, Kränzl.

Habenaria Bakeriana, King

Root: of oblong or ovoid tubers. **Stem:** about 12″ tall, slender. **Leaf:** usually solitary, rarely 2, oblong-lanceolate, pointed, 2″–3″ long. **Spike:** about 4″ long, many-flowered. **Flowers:** about ¼″ across; dorsal sepal oblong; lateral sepals oblong-lanceolate, subfalcate, pointed; petals ovate, suboblique, forming a galea over the column with the dorsal sepal; lip simple, narrowly linear, as long as the sepals; spur filiform, incurved, about ⅜″ long.

July.

A dwarf, green-flowered species of little or no decorative value. It is found in fairly damp places in thin woods in the Lachen Valley in the Sikkim Himalaya at 9000 feet above sea-level, and should be quite hardy in all but the bleakest parts of Great Britain in the rock garden in a half-shady spot in damp peat and leaf-soil.

748. PLATANTHERA BIERMANNIANA, Kränzl.

Habenaria Biermanniana, King

Root: of 2 oblong or narrowly ovoid tubers. **Stem:** 10″–14″ tall. **Leaves:** cauline, 3–4 in number, oblong-lanceolate, pointed, sheathing at the base, about 3″ long. **Spike:** 2″–4″ long, many-flowered. **Flowers:** about $\frac{1}{4}$″ across; sepals and petals ovate, forming a galea over the column; lip linear, toothed; spur oblong, deflexed, blunt, $\frac{1}{4}$″ long. *July.*

A slender species of somewhat dwarf habit with fairly long spikes of rather small green and white blossoms of but little decorative value. It is found in damp, rocky, half-shady places near Sinchal in the Sikkim Himalaya at an elevation of about 8000 feet above sea-level. It should be quite hardy in the Western and Southern counties of Great Britain in a damp half-shady position on the rock garden in leaf-soil and loam.

749. PLATANTHERA BIFOLIA, Rich.

P. schuriana, Fuss. *P. solstitialis*, Bom. *Gymnadenia bifolia*, Mey. *Habenaria bifolia*, Sw. *Lysias bifolia*, Sabisb. *Orchis alba*, Lamk.

Root: of 2 fusiform tubers 1″ or 2″ long with several thick fibres above them. **Leaves:** basal, 2 in number, rarely more, usually opposite, ovate-lanceolate, blunt or pointed. **Scape:** $\frac{3}{4}$′–1$\frac{3}{4}$′ tall, clothed with several bracts, stout, erect or slightly curved. **Spike:** 4″–8″ long, loosely many-flowered. **Flowers:** about $\frac{3}{4}$″ long exclusive of the spurs; dorsal sepal ovate, drawn to a blunt point; lateral sepals lanceolate, curved towards the tip; petals narrowly oblong, curved and conniving to form a galea over the column; lip entire, linear, tongue-like; spur slender, cylindrical, curved, about 1″ long. *April to June.*

A pretty native plant known as the Butterfly Orchis with long spikes of rather large white blossoms tinted with green on the lip and spur. There are several forms such as *carducciana*, *densiflora*, *laxiflora*, *nudicaulis*, *patula*, *pervia*, *quadrifolia*, *robusta*, *subalpina*, and *trifolia*. There are also a few interesting hybrids with members of the genus *Orchis*. The type and its forms are found in open woods and grassy places on mountain sides throughout Europe and temperate Asia to China; they may be grown in the rock garden in a damp open spot in leaf-soil and loam.

750. PLATANTHERA BLEPHARIGLOTTIS, Hook. f.

Platanthera holopetala, Lindl. *Blephariglottis Blephariglottis*, Willd. *Habenaria Blephariglottis*, Lindl. *Orchis Blephariglottis*, Pursh.

Root: a cluster of thick fleshy fibres. **Stem:** 1′–2$\frac{3}{4}$′ tall, leafy, fairly stout. **Leaves:** mostly cauline, linear-oblong or oblong-lanceolate, rather pointed, smaller upwards, 3″–7″ long. **Spike:** 1¼″–4″ long, rather lax, usually many-flowered. **Flowers:** about ½″ across; sepals suborbicular to orbicular-ovate, blunt; petals similar to the sepals only smaller, toothed or fringed at the apex; lip oblong, entire, usually cut into many narrow segments.

July and August.

A pretty wand-like plant with a spike of many pure white, fringed flowers. It grows in peat bogs, swamps, and damp woods from Newfoundland to Ontario and southward to Florida. It is perfectly hardy in Great Britain in the bog garden or on the banks of a stream or pond in good loam and leaf-soil.

751. PLATANTHERA BOREALIS, Reichb. f.

Habenaria borealis, Cham.

Root: of 2 ovoid tubers about 1″ long with a few roots above them. **Stem:** 1½′–2½′ tall, stout, leafy. **Leaves:** cauline, numerous, lowermost oblong-lanceolate, blunt, uppermost lanceolate, pointed, degenerating into bracts among the blossoms, 2″–6″ long. **Spike:** 4″–8″ long, rather dense, many-flowered. **Flowers:** about ⅝″ across, by ⅝″ long; dorsal sepal ovate, blunt; lateral sepals and petals lanceolate; lip ovate-oblong, dilated at its base; spur usually clavate, about ⅜″ long. *June and July.*

This is a robust leafy plant with a long spike of white or greenish-white blossoms, resembling those of *P. dilatata*, of which it is probably the Western representative. The plant is well worth growing in a boggy part of the rock garden in peat and sand. It is found in boggy places on a rocky subsoil on the mountains from Alaska to Washington in North-Western America.

752. PLATANTHERA BRACTEATA, Torr.

Habenaria bracteata, R. Br. *H. viridis* var. *bracteata*, Reichb. f. *Peristylis bracteatus*, Lindl. *Orchis bracteata*, Pursh. *Coeloglossum bracteata*, Parl.

Root: of very thick fibres, sometimes almost tuberous. **Stem:** ¾′–2′ tall, stout, leafy. **Leaves:** very variable, elliptic, ovate, oblong or oblong-lanceolate, 4″–6″ long. **Spike:** 2″–4″ long, loose, many-flowered. **Flowers:** about ⅜″ across; sepals ovate or lanceolate; petals very narrowly linear, almost filiform; lip oblong-spathulate, with 2 or 3 large rounded tooth-like lobes at its apex; spur club-shaped, about ¼″ long. *May and June.*

A tall leafy Orchid of little or no garden value. It has rather short loose spikes of small pale green blossoms and is found in moist meadows, damp grassy places in woods, mostly in clearings, over nearly the whole of Canada and the Eastern United States as far south as North Carolina. It is perfectly hardy in Great Britain and may be grown in good loam and leaf-soil, in a damp spot in the rock garden, and kept moist the whole year round.

753. PLATANTHERA CHORISIANA, Reichb. f.

P. Matsudai, Makino; *Peristylis Chorisianus*, Lindl. *Habenaria Chrosiana*, Reichb. f.

Root: of 2 ovoid or oblong tubers. **Stem:** $\frac{3}{4}$′–2′ tall, fairly stout, bearing 2 leaves. **Leaves:** cauline, ovate or ovate-lanceolate, pointed, 2″–4″ long. **Spike:** 3″–5″ long, lax, few-flowered. **Flowers:** about $\frac{3}{8}$″ across; sepals ovate, pointed or blunt, membranous, spreading; petals rounded-ovate, conniving over the column, somewhat fleshy; lip ovate, hooded towards the tip; spur cylindrical, rather short. *June to August.*

The rather small pale green blossoms of this species are not of any great decorative value. The plant grows in wet marshy places and on the banks of streams in Northern Japan and the Aleutian Islands, and should, of course, be quite at home in Great Britain on the banks of a stream or pond in good sound loam. The variety *elata* (Finet) is larger in all its parts.

754. PLATANTHERA CILIARIS, Lindl.

Habenaria ciliaris, R. Br. *Blephariglottis ciliaris*, Rydb. *Orchis ciliaris*, Pursh.

Root: of thick cord-like fibres, at times almost tuberous. **Stem:** $\frac{3}{4}$′–2$\frac{1}{2}$′ tall, leafy, fairly stout. **Leaves:** mostly cauline, oblong or lanceolate, pointed, smaller towards the top of the stem, 4″–8″ long. **Spike:** 1$\frac{1}{2}$″–4$\frac{1}{2}$″ long, oblong, many-flowered. **Flowers:** about $\frac{1}{2}$″ across by nearly 1″ in length; sepals orbicular or obovate, entire; petals smaller than the sepals, linear or oblong-linear, usually toothed; lip oblong, cut from below the middle into numerous very narrow spreading segments; spur slender, about $\frac{1}{8}$″ long.
July and August.

A beautiful species with feathery spikes of bright orange-coloured flowers. It is a decorative and desirable plant for the rock garden. In a state of nature it is found in woods and meadows frequently on light soils from Ontario to Florida. It may be grown in good light fibrous loam and leaf-soil in a rather damp, half-shady spot, and is quite hardy in Great Britain.

755. PLATANTHERA CRISTATA, Michx.

Blephariglottis cristata, Raf.

Root: a cluster of thick, narrowly fusiform fibres. **Stem:** $\frac{1}{2}$′–2′ tall, fairly stout, leafy. **Leaves:** numerous or few, linear or linear-lanceolate, degenerating upwards into bracts, 2″–8″ long. **Spike:** 2″–4″ long, rather dense and stout. **Flowers:** about $\frac{1}{4}$″ across; sepals orbicular-ovate; petals similar in shape to the sepals but fringed or cut on their margins like a comb; lip oblong, very deeply cut into narrow segments; spur about $\frac{1}{4}''$ long. *July and August.*

A tall, slender plant, leafy below and terminating in a long close spike of small, deeply fringed and cut, white or greenish-white blossoms; the whole spike has a pretty feathery appearance. It is found in open places in low swampy woods in the Eastern and South-Eastern United States and should be perfectly hardy in Great Britain in the bog garden, or on the banks of a pond or stream. A rather rich soil is indicated.

756. PLATANTHERA DENSA, Lindl.

P. clavigera, Lindl. *Habernaria densa*, Wall.

Root: a large ovoid tuber. **Stem:** $1'$–$3'$ tall, very stout, leafy upwards. **Leaves:** many, ovate or oblong, pointed, sheathing at the base, $3''$–$5''$ long. **Spike:** $\frac{3}{4}'$–$1\frac{1}{4}'$ long, narrow, densely-flowered. **Flowers:** $\frac{1}{4}''$ across, erect; sepals subequal, ovate, blunt, puberulous; petals nearly as long as the sepals, obliquely ovate, blunt, fleshy; lip linear, blunt, as long as the spur which is clavate and about $\frac{1}{8}''$ long. *June and July.*

A very robust species with small greenish-white blossoms of but little decorative value. It may perhaps prove of use for furnishing the banks of a pond or stream and should be given a rich soil. It grows in swampy grassy places in the open on the Himalaya, reaching an elevation of 9000 feet, and is therefore suitable for culture outdoors over the greater part of Britain.

757. PLATANTHERA DILATATA, Lindl.

Habenaria dilatata, Gray; *Limnorchis dilatata*, Rydb. *Orchis dilatata*, Pursh.

Root: of thick, fleshy fibres. **Stem:** $1'$–$2'$ tall, fairly stout and fleshy, leafy. **Leaves:** cauline, linear-lanceolate, blunt or pointed, $3''$–$8''$ long. **Spike:** $2''$–$9''$ long, narrow, many-flowered. **Flowers:** about $\frac{1}{2}''$ across; sepals ovate, blunt; petals lanceolate, blunt; lip entire or obscurely 3-lobed, dilated at the base, blunt at the tip; spur blunt, clavate, incurved, about $\frac{3}{8}''$ long. *June to September.*

Although the snowy-white blossoms of this plant are not large, they are produced in long many-flowered spikes and are delicately fragrant; it is worthy of cultivation for this fact alone. The plant grows in wet meadows, swamps, mossy bogs, etc., in Iceland and over nearly the whole of Canada, extending far into the Arctic regions and southward in the United States to New York and Nebraska. It is, of course, perfectly hardy in Great Britain and may be grown in the bog garden, in peat and sphagnum-moss. The form *viridiflora* has green blossoms.

758. PLATANTHERA DIPHYLLA, Reichb. f.

Cœloglossum coradum, Nym. *C. diphyllum*, Fiori. *Gymnadenia diphylla*, Link. *Habenaria cordata*, R. Br.

Root: a potato-like tuber about 1″ long, with a few fibrous roots above it. **Stem:** slender, usually curved, ½′–1′ tall. **Leaves:** 2 in number, elliptic-cordate at the base, covered with reticulated veins, 1″–2″ long, usually some distance up the stem and widely separated. **Spike:** 2″–4″ long, rather lax, many-flowered, secund. **Flowers:** about ¼″ long, sepals and petals lanceolate, suberect; lip divided into 3 subequal lanceolate lobes as far as the middle; spur minute. *February to May.*

A slender, translucent plant with pretty rich green leaves covered with dark veinings, and one-sided spikes of small pale green blossoms, of no decorative value. The plant is found in damp, somewhat shady places among dwarf herbage in Southern Europe, North Africa and the Canary and Madeira Islands. It may be grown in the rock garden in sheltered localities in fairly damp leaf-soil and loam.

759. PLATANTHERA DITMARIANA, Kom.

Root: of elongated subcylindric tubers. **Stem:** 6″–9″ tall, slender. **Leaves:** cauline, 2 in number, rounded-ovate or orbicular-ovate, blunt, 3″–4″ long. **Spike:** 1″–2″ long, densely many-flowered. **Flowers:** about $\frac{3}{16}$″ across; dorsal sepal broadly ovate; lateral sepals oblong, dilated at the tip, spreading; petals narrowly oblong, slightly hooked; lip entire, broadly oblong, blunt; spur slender, curved, blunt, ⅜″ long. *June to August.*

A slender plant closely allied to *P. obtusata* (Rich.) from North America. It has dense many-flowered spikes of small green and white blossoms which prove interesting in the alpine house. The plant is found in wet grassland, swamps, and on the banks of rivers in the peninsula of Kamchatka, and is, of course, quite hardy with regard to cold in this country. An open situation in the bog garden or on the banks of a stream in fibrous peat, loam and sphagnum-moss is indicated.

760. PLATANTHERA DYERIANA, Kränzl.

Habenaria Dyeriana, King

Root: of 2 oblong tubers. **Stem:** about 10″ tall, very leafy. **Leaves:** basal and cauline, numerous, oblong, blunt, 1″–1½″ long, becoming smaller upwards. **Spike:** 1″–2½″ long, few- or many-flowered. **Flowers:** about ½″ across; dorsal sepal ovate-triangular, blunt; lateral sepals similar, crenulate; petals narrowly ovate-triangular, tip minutely toothed; lip triangular and linear towards the tip, with thickened lines on the disc; spur filiform, thickened at the tip, about ¼″ long. *August.*

A dwarf species with comparatively large green and white, fragrant blossoms. It is found in rather damp, rocky places in pine woods in the Lachen Valley, Sikkim Himalaya at an elevation of 12,000 feet above sea-level and should be quite hardy in Great Britain in damp leaf-soil and loam in a half-shady spot in the rock garden.

761. PLATANTHERA ELEGANS, Lindl.

Habenaria elegans, Bolander

Root: of 2 oblong or ovoid potato-like tubers. **Stem:** ¾′–2½′ tall, rather slender, almost naked. **Leaves:** usually 2 in number, basal, ovate or oblong, 3″–7″ long, withering as soon as the flower-spike is perfected. **Spike:** 4″–12″ long, loosely many-flowered. **Flowers:** about ½″ across; dorsal sepal ovate-lanceolate; lateral sepals lanceolate; petals narrowly lanceolate; lip oblong-lanceolate with 2 small recurved, spreading lobes at the base; spur filiform, ½″–¾″ long. *July and August.*

This species closely resembles *Habenaria unalaschensis*, but may be separated from that species by the much longer and more thread-like spur; it has the same greenish-white flowers. There is a form known as *multiflora* (Rydb.) with a more dense spike of blossoms with long spurs. Both are rather pretty plants and are found in grassy places on gravelly soils in thin deciduous woods in British Columbia. It may be grown in the rock garden in decayed oak leaves and gritty loam.

762. PLATANTHERA FIMBRIATA, Lindl.

Habenaria fimbriata, R. Br. *Blephariglottis grandiflora*, Rydb.

Root: of thick coarse fibres, tufted. **Stem:** 1′–4′ tall, stout, leafy. **Leaves:** mostly cauline, lanceolate or oblong-obovate, usually erect, becoming smaller towards the top of the stem, 4″–12″ long. **Spike:** 4″–16″ long, many-flowered. **Flowers:** about ¾″ across and 1¼″ long; sepals ovate, blunt; petals oblong, usually toothed at the tip; lip deeply divided into 3 broad, fan-shaped lobes, cut and deeply fringed on their margins; spur slender, about 1¼″ long. *June to August.*

Under good conditions this beautiful plant reaches a height of four feet; the robust stems are clothed with numerous rich green leaves and end in long, many-flowered spikes of large, deeply fringed, lilac purple or white blossoms. It grows in moist woods, meadows and on the borders of swamps, usually in rich soils, in Eastern North America from Nova Scotia to North Carolina. It is quite hardy in this country in rich heavy loam on the banks of a pond or stream and should prove a great addition to the water garden.

763. PLATANTHERA FINETIANA, Schltr.

Hemihabenaria stenantha, Finet, var. *auriculata*, Finet

Root: elongated, filiform and probably tuberous. **Stem:** up to 24″ tall, sparely leafy. **Leaves:** 3–4 in number, oblong-elliptic or elliptic-lanceolate, 4″–6″ long. **Spike:** 4″–6″ long of 15–20 flowers, rather dense. **Flowers:** about $\frac{3}{8}$″ across; dorsal sepal oblong-elliptic, blunt, concave, erect; lateral sepals obliquely broadly ovate, blunt, deflexed; petals obliquely ligulate, erect; lip linear-subulate, with reflexed margins; spur filiform, incurved, $\frac{5}{8}$″ long. *July and August.*

A tall, slender, sparely leafy species with quaint green and white blossoms produced in long dense many-flowered spikes. It is quite a decorative plant and is allied to *P. japonica.* In a state of nature it is found in damp grassy places on the mountains of Szechuan, Western China, at 9000–10,000 feet above sea-level. It should be hardy in all but the bleakest parts of the Kingdom in the bog garden or on the banks of a stream or pond in peat and loam.

764. PLATANTHERA FRAGRANS, Schltr.

Limnorchis fragrans, Rydb.

Root: of thick fleshy fibres. **Stem:** 8″–12″ tall, very slender, leafy above. **Leaves:** cauline, linear, pointed, about 4″ long. **Spike:** $1\frac{1}{2}$″–3″ long, slender, lax. **Flowers:** about $\frac{3}{8}$″ long; sepals lanceolate, pointed, strongly striate; petals similar only narrower; lip narrowly linear, dilated at the base, shorter than the spur, which is filiform in shape and somewhat curved and about $\frac{1}{4}$″ long. *July.*

A delicate and fragile little plant closely allied to *P. dilatata.* It has slender, few-flowered spikes of small, pure white, very fragrant flowers, and is worth growing in the alpine house for its scent alone. It is found in bogs and swamps in the Willoughby Mountains of Vermont, U.S.A. It should be quite hardy in this country and may be tried in the rock or bog garden, in wet fibrous peat and sphagnum-moss.

765. PLATANTHERA FREYNII, Kränzl.

P. densa, Freyn

Root: of ovate or fusiform shortly 2-lobed tubers. **Stem:** 8″–10″ tall, sheathed at the base. **Leaves:** 2 in number, near the base of the stem, elliptic, sheathing below, about 3″ long. **Spike:** 2″–3″ long, densely many-flowered. **Flowers:** about $\frac{1}{2}$″ across; dorsal sepal cordate; lateral sepals obliquely elliptic, blunt, as long as the dorsal sepal; petals obliquely lanceolate, shorter than the sepals; lip broadly linear, slightly ascending, about ½″ long. *June.*

A Siberian species of some garden value, with dense spikes of rather small white or greenish-white blossoms and two rounded leaves near the base of the stem. It is found in damp mountain meadows near Lake Baikal in Eastern Siberia and should prove perfectly hardly in Great Britain in a damp spot in the rock garden in good fibrous loam and peat.

766. PLATANTHERA GALEANDRA, Reichb. f.

Platanthera Championii, Lindl. *P. obcordata*, Lindl. *Gymnadenia galeandra*, Reichb. f. *G. obcordata*, Reichb. f. *Habenaria galeandra*, Benth. *Orchis obcordata*, Don; *O. Susannæ*, Heyne

Root: a small, globose or oblong tuber. **Stem:** 6″–8″ tall, stout or rather-slender, smooth or downy. **Leaves:** sessile, ovate-oblong, contracted at the base, 1″–2″ long. **Spike:** 2″–4″ long, many-flowered. **Flowers:** ½″ across; dorsal sepal ovate; lateral sepals falcately-lanceolate; petals narrowly lanceolate; lip broadly cuneiformly obovate or obcordate, downy at the base; spur a short conical sac. *June and July.*

This species produces comparatively long spikes of rather small pale purple blossoms, half hidden by the large leafy bracts. It is not of much decorative value. It is a marsh plant and is found in the Western Himalaya (where it attains an altitude of 8000 feet), and from thence to China. It may be grown outdoors in this country on the banks of a pond or stream in an open sunny spot in a good rich loam.

767. PLATANTHERA GRAMINIFOLIA, Schltr.

Habenaria graminifolia, Rydb.

Root: of 2 ovoid or oblong tubers with a few fleshy roots above them. **Stem:** 1′–1¾′ tall, slender, leafy. **Leaves:** cauline, numerous, linear or linear-lanceolate, decreasing in size upwards, 4″–12″ long. **Spike:** 2″–4″ long, fairly dense, many-flowered. **Flowers:** about ⅜″ across and ½″ long; dorsal sepal ovate, blunt; lateral sepals ovate, longer than the dorsal sepal; petals linear or narrowly lanceolate; lip ovate, obscurely 3-lobed, lobes rounded; spur clavate, about ¼″ long. *June and July.*

This species usually has very narrow, grass-like leaves; the blossoms are borne in a short spike and are pure white. It is a pretty plant and should succeed outdoors in a damp or wet part of the rock garden, or on the edge of the bog garden, in peat and sphagnum-moss. In a state of nature it grows in bogs and swamps in North-Western America from Alaska to British Columbia.

768. PLATANTHERA HENRYI, Rolfe

Habenaria Henryi, Rolfe

Root: of 2 oblong or ovoid tubers and numerous fibres. **Stem:** 1′–2′ tall, leafy. **Leaves:** cauline, oblong or elliptic-oblong, pointed or rather blunt, 1½″–4″ long. **Raceme:** 4″–9″ long, lax, usually few-flowered. **Flowers:** about ½″ across; dorsal sepal erect, ovate, concave, rather blunt; lateral sepals spreading, oblong, blunt; petals obliquely ovate-lanceolate, pointed, forming a galea with the dorsal sepal; lip entire, oblong-linear, blunt, fleshy; spur slender, cylindrical, curved, ⅝″ long. *June to August.*

A species with rather small pale green, faintly fragrant blossoms in long loose racemes. It is found on open grassy places on the sides of mountains in Shingkiang, Kiangsi, Hupeh, Szechuan and Yunnan, Western China, reaching an altitude of nearly 12,000 feet above sea-level. It should be perfectly hardy in Great Britain in an open sunny spot in the rock garden in fibrous loam and sand.

769. PLATANTHERA HEYNEANA, Lindl.

Habenaria glabra, A. Rich. *H. Heyneana*, Lindl.

Root: an oblong or ovoid tuber. **Stem:** ½′–1′ tall, stout, leafy upwards. **Leaves:** ovate, erect or recurved, subimbricate, shortly sheathing, pointed. **Spike:** 2″–4″ long, secund, many-flowered. **Flowers:** about ½″ across; dorsal sepal ovate-oblong; lateral sepals oblong-lanceolate, petals linear-oblong; lip divided into 3 linear segments almost to the base, the centre one broader than the others; spur subclavate, ⅜″ long. *July.*

This plant has rather small greenish-yellow blossoms of little or no decorative value; they are borne in rather long, one-sided spikes on leafy stems. It grows in open, damp, grassy places in Southern India, reaching an elevation of 7500 feet on the Nilghiris Mountains and should be sufficiently hardy for culture outdoors in England south of the Trent, and in Western Scotland. It may be planted on the banks of a stream or pond or in the rock garden in a moist sunny soil in good loam and a little peat.

770. PLATANTHERA HOLOGLOTTIS, Maxim.

P. neuropetala, Franch. *Habenaria neuropetala*, Miq.

Root: of 2 oblong or fusiform tubers. **Stem:** 1½′–3½′ tall, stout, leafy. **Leaves:** lanceolate or linear-lanceolate, pointed, 6″–9″ long, decreasing in length upwards. **Spike:** 6″–12″ tall, densely many-flowered. **Flowers:** about ⅜″ across; dorsal sepal oblong, blunt; lateral sepals similar, deflexed;

petals ovate, blunt, shorter than the sepals; lip linear, blunt, fleshy; spur filiform, incurved, $\frac{5}{8}''$ long. *May to July.*

A very robust plant with long dense spikes of green blossoms. It is an interesting though not very showy species and is found in rich soil on the banks of rivers and lakes in Eastern Siberia, Northern China and Japan, and should prove quite hardy in Great Britain, planted in similar situations to those in which it is found in nature.

771. PLATANTHERA HOOKERI, Lindl.

Habenaria Hookeri, Torr. *Lysias Hookeriana*, Rydb.

Root: of rather thick fleshy fibres. **Stem:** 8″–16″ tall, fairly stout, leafy. **Leaves:** cauline, spreading or ascending, oval, orbicular or obovate, fleshy, shining, 3″–6″ long. **Raceme:** 4″–8″ long, rather loose, many-flowered. **Flowers:** over $\frac{1}{2}''$ across; sepals lanceolate, pointed, spreading; petals narrowly linear or awl-shaped, pointed; lip entire, linear-lanceolate, pointed, about $\frac{3}{8}''$ long; spur slender, about $\frac{3}{4}''$ long. *June to September.*

The yellowish-green blossoms of this species are of botanical interest only; they are borne in a long loose spike or raceme, on tall leafy stems. It is found in damp woodlands and usually grows on the edges of swamps in clearings. It ranges from Nova Scotia to Ontario and southward to Pennsylvania and Iowa. It is quite hardy in Great Britain and may be grown in a cool spot in the bog or water garden, in wet peat and sphagnum-moss.

772. PLATANTHERA HURONENSIS, Schltr.

Orchis Huronensis, Michx. *Habenaria Huronensis*, Spreng. *Limnorchis Huronensis*, Rydb.

Root: of thick fleshy fibres. **Stem:** 8″–12″ tall, slender, leafy. **Leaves:** cauline, oblanceolate, blunt below, lanceolate and pointed on the upper part of the stem. **Spike:** 2″–5″ long, rather lax, few-flowered. **Flowers:** about $\frac{3}{16}''$ across, carried almost erect; sepals oblong, pointed; petals narrowly lanceolate, pointed; lip linear-lanceolate, entire; spur cylindrical, curved, slightly thickened at the tip, $\frac{1}{8}''$ long. *June and July.*

This delicate and slender plant has few-flowered spikes of tiny light green blossoms of no decorative value. It might prove of interest in the alpine house or in the rock garden in peat and sphagnum-moss. It is scattered over Eastern Canada and is found in the United States as far south as New York and Dacota in peat bogs, swamp and the boggy margins of pools.

773. PLATANTHERA HYPERBOREA, Lindl.

P. Königii, Lindl. *Habenaria hyperborea*, R. Br. *Limnorchis hyperborea*, Rydb. *Orchis hyperborea*, Pursh.

Root: a cluster of thick fleshy fibres. **Stem:** $\frac{3}{4}'$–2′ tall, rather stout. **Leaves:** cauline, lanceolate, usually pointed, 2″–12″ long. **Spike:** 2″–8″ long, narrow and cylindrical, many-flowered. **Flowers:** about $\frac{1}{2}''$ across, divaricate; sepals and petals ovate, blunt; lip lanceolate, entire, blunt, about $\frac{3}{8}''$ long; spur clavate, slightly incurved, about $\frac{1}{4}''$ long. *May to August.*

An erect, somewhat leafy plant, with a long narrow spike of pale green or yellowish-green blossoms with narrow segments. It is of no decorative value and is found in bogs, swamps, moist spots in openings in woods and swampy alpine lakes, reaching great elevations on the mountains. Its range extends from Iceland and Greenland southward, throughout Canada and Eastern United States, as far south as New Jersey. It is, of course, perfectly hardy in Great Britain and may be grown in the bog-garden or on the banks of a pond in peat and sphagnum-moss.

774. PLATANTHERA INTEGRA, Schltr.

Gymnadenia flava, Lindl. *Gymnadeniopsis integra*, Rydb. *Habenaria integra*, Spreng.

Root: of thickened fibres, almost tuberous. **Stem:** 1′–2′ tall, fairly stout, leafy below. **Leaves:** broadly linear or linear-lanceolate, becoming smaller upwards, 2″–8″ long. **Spike:** 1″–3″ long, oblong, many-flowered. **Flowers:** about $\frac{3}{8}''$ across; sepals oval or obovate, blunt; petals ovate, usually larger than the sepals; lip oblong or ovate-oblong, irregularly toothed or crenulate, longer than the petals; spur straight, about $\frac{3}{8}''$ long. *July to September.*

Although the orange-coloured blossoms are small they are bright enough to render this plant of some decorative value. The stems are clothed below with narrow grassy leaves and are nearly naked above. The plant grows in swampy pine woods, from New Jersey to Florida and should be quite hardy in Great Britain in the rock garden, in a damp shady spot in good leaf-soil and loam.

775. PLATANTHERA JAPONICA, Lindl.

P. manubriata, Kränzl. *P. setchuanica*, Kränzl. *Habenaria japonica*, A. Gray

Root: of narrowly oblong or fusiform tubers. **Stem:** 18″–20″ tall, fairly stout. **Leaves:** few, variable, cuneate, rotund or oblong, about 4″ long, degenerating upwards into bracts. **Spike:** 3″–6″ long, few- or many-flowered, lax or dense. **Flowers:** about $\frac{5}{8}$″ across; dorsal sepal cucullate, pointed; lateral sepals obliquely-oblong, pointed, deflexed; petals linear, blunt, straight; lip simple, linear, margins reflexed, base almost saccate; spur filiform, 2″ long. *July.*

A pretty plant with pale green, long-spurred, highly fragrant blossoms on fairly tall stems. It grows in damp places on the margins of woods over nearly the whole of temperate Japan and the mountains of China, reaching an elevation of 11,000 feet in Western Yunnan, Western China. It is perfectly hardy in Great Britain in a damp spot in the rock garden or on the banks of a stream or pond in good loam and peat.

776. PLATANTHERA JUNCEA, Kränzl.

Habenaria juncea, King

Root: of small, oblong or ovoid tubers. **Stem:** 12″–15″ tall, slender. **Leaf:** solitary, basal, oblong-lanceolate, pointed, shortly stalked, 2″–3″ long. **Scape:** with 2 linear-lanceolate distant bracts. **Spike:** slender, with a few remote blossoms. **Flowers:** $\frac{3}{16}$″ across; dorsal sepal and lateral sepals ovate-triangular; petals narrowly oblong, blunt; lip simple, ovate-lanceolate, pointed; spur cylindrical, incurved, $\frac{1}{8}$″ long. *July.*

A slender species with minute green blossoms of no decorative value. It is found in rocky places in pine woods in the Lachen Valley, Sikkim Himalaya, at 10,000 feet above sea-level and should be quite hardy over nearly the whole of Great Britain. It may be planted in a fairly damp, half-shady spot in the rock garden in soil collected from beneath the shade of conifers.

777. PLATANTHERA LACERA, A. Gray

P. psycodes, Lindl. *Habenaria lacera*, R. Br. *Orchis lacera*, Michx. *O. psycodes*, Pursh. *Blephariglottis lacera*, Rydb.

Root: of thick fleshy fibres on slender fusiform tubers. **Stem:** 1′–2$\frac{3}{4}$′ tall, fairly stout, erect. **Leaves:** mostly cauline, oblong or oblong-lanceolate, shorter above, 3″–8″ long. **Spike:** rather narrow, 3″–12″ long. **Flowers:** about $\frac{3}{8}$″ across; sepals ovate or suborbicular, blunt; petals linear, about as long as the sepals, blunt; lip divided to below the middle into 3 very deeply fringed lobes; spur clavate, about $\frac{5}{8}$″ long. *June and July.*

This is quite a decorative species despite the fact that the blossoms are rather small; they have some green in their yellow colouring. It grows in damp woods, in rich vegetable soil in eastern North America from Nova Scotia to Georgia and Missouri. It is quite hardy in Great Britain and may be grown in a damp shady spot in the rock garden, in good loam and leaf-soil.

778. PLATANTHERA LEPTOCERATITIS, Schltr.

Habenaria leptoceratitis, Rydb.

Root: of 2 ovoid or oblong, potato-like tubers. **Stem:** 8″–16″ tall, slender, leafy. **Leaves:** cauline and basal, linear or linear-lanceolate, decreasing in size upwards, 2″–3″ long. **Spike:** 2″–3″ long, fairly dense, many-flowered. **Flowers:** about ⅜″ across; dorsal sepal broadly lanceolate, pointed; lateral sepals lanceolate, spreading; petals linear-lanceolate, all about the same length; lip lanceolate, somewhat dilated at the base; spur filiform, strongly curved, about ¼″ long. *June and July.*

A pretty slender species with rather dense spikes of pure white blossoms mingled with long pointed bracts. It is found in damp openings in woods, margins of swamps and bogs in North-Western America from Alaska to Washington. It should be quite hardy in Great Britain in the bog garden or in a damp sunny spot in the rock garden in peat and loam.

779. PLATANTHERA LEUCOPHÆA, A. Gray

Orchis leucophæa, Nutt. *Blephariglottis leucophæa*, Rydb.

Root: of stout fibres. **Stem:** 1′–3′ tall, stout, erect, leafy. **Leaves:** cauline, elliptic, ovate or oblong-lanceolate, becoming smaller towards the top of the stem, 2″–10″ long. **Spike:** 2″–8″ long, comparatively few-flowered. **Flowers:** about ¾″ across; sepals broadly ovate, almost membranous; petals obovate or spathulate, irregularly toothed on tip and margins; lip very deeply divided into 3 crenate lobes cut into fine segments forming a spreading fringe; spur about ¼″ long. *July.*

A handsome plant with very tall leafy stems bearing loose spikes of large, pure white blossoms, with deeply cut and fringed segments; they are very fragrant. The plant grows in open, swampy places in woods and on moist prairie land from Nova Scotia to Arkansas and is perfectly hardy in Great Britain in an open spot in the rock garden in damp fibrous loom and leaf-soil.

780. PLATANTHERA LEUCOSTACHYS, Lindl.

Habenaria leucostachys, Wats.

Root: of 2 oblong tubers about 1½″ long with a few stout roots above them. **Stem:** 2′–4′ tall, very robust, stout, leafy. **Leaves:** cauline, numerous, linear or linear-lanceolate, gradually reduced upwards into bracts among the blossoms, 4″–12″ long. **Spike:** 4″–12″ long, fairly dense, many-flowered. **Flowers:** about ¾″ across; dorsal sepal ovate, blunt; lateral sepals lanceolate, rather pointed; petals similar only somewhat smaller; lip oblong, dilated above the middle into a broad rhombic base; spur swollen in the middle, pointed, about ¼″ long. *May to August.*

An exceedingly robust plant with long spikes of fairly large pure white blossoms which are very fragrant. It is a very beautiful species and is well worthy of cultivation. The form *robusta* (Rydb.) is an even more desirable plant and frequently reaches five feet in height; both are found in damp soil and swamps from Alaska to Washington. A damp spot in full sun, in peat and sandy loam, is indicated.

781. PLATANTHERA MAKINOI, Yatbe

Root: of oblong tubers. **Stem:** about 12″ tall, stout, leafy. **Leaves:** basal and cauline, ovate-oblong or elliptic, about 2½″ long. **Spike:** about 2½″ long, dense, many-flowered. **Flowers:** about ⅜″ across; dorsal sepal ovate or oblong, blunt; lateral sepals subobliquely ovate, blunt; petals falcate-ovate or narrowly triangular, small; lip oblong-ovate, dilated in the middle, short; spur cylindrical, incurved, $\frac{3}{16}$″ long. *July and August.*

This species is closely allied to *Habenaria* or *Platanthera hyperborea* (Lindl.); it has dense spikes of small yellowish-green or white flowers of but little decorative value. It is found in damp or wet situations in various parts of Japan and should prove hardy in Great Britain in the bog garden or on the banks of a pond or stream in a good heavy loam.

782. PLATANTHERA MANDARINORUM, Reichb. f.

P. Keiskei, Franch. *P. oreades*, Franch. *Habenaria Keiskei*, Miq.

Root: of 2 ovoid tubers about ¾″ long. **Stem:** 9″–15″ tall, slender. **Leaves:** usually 1–6 in number, oblong or linear-lanceolate, pointed, 2″–3″ long, becoming narrower and smaller upwards. **Spike:** 2″–3″ long, lax, few- or many-flowered. **Flowers:** about ¾″ across; dorsal sepal small, oblong; lateral sepals narrowly-oblong, blunt, reflexed; petals falcately ovate-lanceolate, blunt; lip narrowly linear, blunt; spur filiform, 1¼″ long. *June and July.*

A pretty and desirable plant with spikes of comparatively large white and green blossoms on leafy stems. It inhabits woods of *Cryptomeria japonica* and other conifers in China and Japan and should be quite hardy in Great Britain in a half-shady spot in the rock garden, in soil collected from beneath the shade of spruces or cryptomerias.

783. PLATANTHERA MAXIMOWICZIANA, Schltr.

Root: of 2 small rounded tubers. **Stem:** 5″–10″ tall, slender. **Leaves:** cauline, few in number, oblong-lanceolate, pointed, 2″–3″ long, becoming smaller and narrower upwards. **Spike:** short, few-flowered. **Flowers:** about

$\frac{3}{8}''$ across; dorsal sepal ovate, pointed; lateral sepals narrowly ovate, frequently slightly hooked at the tip, all erect; petals narrowly ovate, pointed; lip entire, broadly linear, blunt; spur cylindrical, fleshy, about $\frac{1}{2}''$ long. *July and August.*

This species produces short racemes of small yellowish-green fragrant blossoms of no decorative value. The plant is found in moist grassy places in the open over the greater part of Japan and Korea. It should be quite hardy in this country in the bog garden or in a damp open spot in the rock garden in loam and peat.

784. PLATANTHERA MEDIA, Schltr.

Limnorchis media, Rydb.

Root: a number of stout, fleshy fibres. **Stem:** $1\frac{1}{4}'$–$2\frac{1}{2}'$ tall, stout, leafy. **Leaves:** cauline, lanceolate, pointed, 4″–8″ long. **Spike:** 6″ to 15″ long, slender, densely-flowered; flowers divaricate. **Flowers:** about $\frac{3}{8}''$ across; sepals ovate-oblong, rather pointed; petals lanceolate, blunt; lip lanceolate, entire, blunt, slightly dilated near the base, about $\frac{1}{2}''$ long; spur curved, blunt, about $\frac{3}{8}''$ long. *June to August.*

A very tall and slender leafy Orchid, with a long, narrow, densely-flowered spike of pale green and purple blossoms. It is an interesting but by no means showy plant and inhabits mossy bogs and the margins of swamps and pools, in North America from Eastern Canada southward to New York and Minnesota. It is quite hardy in Great Britain and may be grown in good soil, on the margin of a pond or stream with its roots nearly in the water.

785. PLATANTHERA MICHÆLII, Schltr.

Habenaria Michælii, Greene

Root: of 2 fair-sized potato-like tubers with several fleshy roots above them. **Stem:** about 2′ tall, rather stout, bract-clothed. **Leaves:** basal, withering before the flowers are produced, ovate or oblong, very few, 4″–6″ long. **Spike:** 4″–7″ long, densely many-flowered. **Flowers:** about $\frac{3}{8}''$ across; dorsal sepal oblong or ovate, blunt; lateral sepals oblong, rather blunt; petals lanceolate, blunt; lip larger than the other segments, ovate, rather blunt; spur filiform, about $\frac{1}{8}''$ long. *June to August.*

A delicate species with dense spikes of small but pretty flowers with white, green-veined petals and sepals and a pure white lip. It is found in grassy places in clearings in oak woods and beneath the shade of other deciduous trees in British Columbia. In this country it may be grown in the rock garden in sheltered districts, in a half-shady spot in damp, oak leaf-soil and loam, with plenty of sharp sand.

786. PLATANTHERA MINOR, Reichb. f.

P. interrupta, Maxim. *P. japonica* var. *minor*, Miq.

Root: of 2 small globular tubers. **Stem:** 6″–9″ tall, slender. **Leaves:** 2–3 in number, oblong, blunt, or oblong-lanceolate and pointed, 2″–3″ long, decreasing in size upwards. **Spike:** rather short, few- or many-flowered. **Flowers:** about $\frac{3}{8}$″ across; dorsal sepal ovate, pointed; lateral sepals semi-ovate, falcate, erect; petals narrowly ovate, pointed; lip simple, linear, as long as the sepals; spur cylindrical, fleshy, $\frac{3}{8}$″ long. *June and July.*

The small green and white blossoms of this little plant would make no show in the open rockery but should prove interesting in the alpine house, where they would not be overlooked. The plant is a native of China, Korea and Japan and may be grown in damp peat and chopped sphagnum-moss in full sun.

787. PLATANTHERA MONTANA, Sch.

P. chlorantha, Custer. *P. bifolia* var. *montana*, Bach. *Habenaria chloroleuca*, Rid. *H. chlorantha*, Bab. *H. virescens*, Zollik.

Root: of 2 oblong or fusiform tubers about 1″ long. **Leaves:** usually 2 in number, basal, oblong, blunt, 3″–4″ long. **Scape:** $\frac{3}{4}$′–2′ tall, rather slender, clothed with a few narrow bracts. **Spike:** 4″–6″ long, lax, many-flowered. **Flowers:** about $\frac{3}{4}$″ long exclusive of the spur; dorsal sepal almost triangular; lateral sepals obliquely lanceolate, spreading; petals linear, forming a galea over the column with the dorsal sepal; lip lanceolate, tongue-like; spur fairly stout, cylindrical, curved, about 1$\frac{1}{8}$″ long. *May and June.*

This native plant very closely resembles *P. bifolia* but is perhaps more desirable; it has white, green-tinted blossoms in a loose spike. There are several desirable forms such as *grandiflora*, *lancifolia*, *Schulzei* and *Wankelii*. The type and its forms are found in damp places on the mountains of Central and Southern Europe and North Africa; they may be grown in the bog garden or on the banks of a stream or pond in peat and loam.

788. PLATANTHERA NEGLECTA, Schltr.

Root: of 2 oblong tubers. **Stem:** 1″–1$\frac{1}{4}$″ tall, 1 leaf below the middle, with leaf-like sheaths above, slender, smooth. **Leaf:** solitary, suberect, oblong, blunt, cuneate at the base, 3$\frac{1}{2}$″–4$\frac{1}{2}$″ long. **Raceme:** 4″–5″ long, lax, of 6–12 blossoms. **Flowers:** about $\frac{3}{8}$″ long; dorsal sepal suborbicular, blunt, concave, erect; lateral sepals deflexed, oblong, blunt; petals narrowly strap-shaped, pointed, oblique, spreading; lip linear, blunt, decurved, somewhat dilated at the base; spur slender, dilated in the middle, pointed, $\frac{3}{8}$″ long. *July and August.*

This species produces a slender flower-stem clothed below with an oblong leaf and several leaf-like sheaths; it terminates in a long slender spike of small reddish-purple blossoms of no great decorative value. The plant is found in moist mountain woods in Korea and Schantung, North-Eastern China. It should be quite hardy in Great Britain, in a damp shady spot in the rock garden in fibrous loam and leaf-soil.

789. PLATANTHERA NEMATOCAULON, Hook. f.

Habenaria nematocaulon, Hook. f.

Root: a branched stock of thick fleshy fibres. **Stem:** 3″–8″ tall, naked or with one or two sheaths above. **Leaf:** solitary, near the base of the stem, oblong, rather pointed, 1″–1½″ long. **Spike:** 2″–4″ long, very slender, lax-flowered. **Flowers:** about $\frac{1}{16}$″ long; dorsal sepal ovate-lanceolate, pointed; lateral sepals similar only broader; petals triangular-ovate; lip oblong-lanceolate, blunt; spur clavate, very short. *June to August.*

The minute pale green blossoms of this species are of no horticultural value. It is a very delicate little plant and grows in a state of nature in moist rocky places in the Sikkim Himalaya at an altitude of 12,000 feet. Plants collected from such an elevation should be perfectly hardy in Great Britain in a sunny part of the bog garden in growing sphagnum-moss and peat.

790. PLATANTHERA NIPPONICA, Makino

P. Matsumurana, Schltr.

Root: of 2 ovoid or oblong tubers. **Stem:** 12″–15″ tall, slender, smooth, clothed at its base with a solitary leaf and above with 4–6 lanceolate sheaths. **Leaf:** ligulate, blunt or pointed, erect, slightly narrowed towards the base, 1″–2″ long. **Raceme:** 1½″–2½″ long, lax, of 3–8 blossoms. **Flower:** about ¼″ across; dorsal sepal oblong, blunt, concave, smooth, erect; lateral sepals oblong-ligulate, blunt, oblique and deflexed; petals oblong, subfalcate, blunt, erect; lip ligulate, blunt, dilated at the base; spur filiform, ascending, ⅝″ long. *June and July.*

A smooth, slender species with a few-flowered raceme of pale green blossoms of little decorative value. It is found in damp grassy places, frequently on mountains, in the province of Yetsu, Japan. It should prove quite hardy in Britain, under the same cultural conditions as the other damp-loving species.

791. PLATANTHERA NIVEA, Lindl.

Gymnadenia nivea, Nutt. *Gymnadeniopsis nivea*, Rydb. *Habenaria nivea*, Lindl.

Root: stout, almost tuberous. **Stem:** ¾′–1¾′ tall, usually slender, leafy. **Leaves:** mainly basal, much reduced in size upwards, linear or linear-oblong,

2″–8″ long. **Spike:** $\frac{3}{4}$″–4″ long, cylindric, rather dense. **Flowers:** about $\frac{3}{8}$″ across; dorsal sepal ovate, concave; lateral sepals ovate, much dilated on the inner side of the base; petals broadly-linear or linear-oblong, smaller than the sepals; lip linear, at times dilated towards the tip, and with 2 teeth at its base; spur filiform, $\frac{3}{8}$″ long. *July and August.*

The blossoms of this species, although daintily coloured, are rather too small to have much decorative value; they are borne on leafy stems and vary from white to pink in colour. It grows in pine woods and on wooded hillsides in Eastern North America from Delaware to Florida. It should be quite hardy in Great Britain in a damp shady place in the rock garden, in good leaf-soil and fibrous loam.

792. PLATANTHERA OBTUSATA, Lindl.

Habenaria obtusata, Rich. *Lysiella obtusata*, Rydb. *Orchis obtusata*, Pursh.

Root: of rather long fibres. **Stem:** 3″–8″ tall, slender, naked, 4-angled. **Leaf:** solitary, basal, obovate, tapering below, 2″–4″ long. **Raceme:** 1$\frac{1}{2}$″–2$\frac{1}{2}$″ long, loose. **Flowers:** about $\frac{1}{4}$″ long; sepals oblong, the dorsal one elliptic-ovate, erect, lateral ones spreading, dilated or obtusely 2-lobed at the base; lip entire, linear-lanceolate, blunt, deflexed; spur slender, curved, blunt, about $\frac{3}{16}$″ long. *July to September.*

A delicate and fragile little plant with a solitary shining green leaf and a spike of about a dozen small pale green and white blossoms. It might prove attractive in the alpine house. It is found in damp mossy woods, mossy bogs and swamps, ascending to great elevations in the mountains, ranging over the whole of the forest regions of Canada and the Eastern United States, from the Arctic regions southward to New York and Colorado. The plant is also found in Northern Sweden. It is of course quite hardy in Great Britain and may be grown in the bog garden, in peat and moss.

793. PLATANTHERA OKUBOI, Makino

Root: an elongate, narrowly fusiform tuber. **Stem:** 9″–18″ tall, erect, stout. **Leaves:** cauline, 5–8 in number, 4″–9″ long, varying from elliptic to narrowly oblong, blunt. **Raceme:** erect, 2″–4″ long, densely many-flowered. **Flowers:** about $\frac{1}{2}$″ across; dorsal sepal ovate, erect; lateral sepals ovate-lanceolate or oblong-lanceolate, longer than the dorsal sepal; petals subfalcately ovate-linear or oblong-linear, blunt; lip lanceolate-ligulate, blunt, entire; spur cylindrical, falcate towards the tip. *May.*

The two lowermost leaves of this species are very much larger than those above them. The plant produces a dense raceme of greenish-white blossoms which are quite decorative. It is closely allied to the North American *P.*

orbiculata, and is confined to the Island of Hachijo off the province of Mishiyama, Japan, where it inhabits the margins of swamps. It should be hardy in all but the bleakest parts of the Kingdom in the bog garden or on the banks of a stream or pond in rich soil.

794. PLATANTHERA OMEIENSIS, Schltr.

Habenaria omeiensis, Rolfe

Root: of 2 rounded or oblong tubers. **Stem:** about $1\frac{3}{4}'$ tall, fairly stout, leafy. **Leaves:** cauline, oblong-lanceolate or oblong, shortly pointed. **Raceme:** about 4″ long, lax, few-flowered. **Flowers:** about $\frac{3}{4}''$ across; dorsal sepal ovate, rather pointed, concave; lateral sepals oblong, blunt; petals linear-oblong, blunt; lip linear, incurved, pointed; spur long, flexuous. *June and July.*

A quaint flowered species allied to *P. stenantha* (Hook. f.). It produces tall stems well clothed with rather narrow foliage and short, few-flowered racemes of fairly large green and white blossoms of no great decorative value. The plant is found in damp shady places on Mount Omei in Szechuan, Western China, at an elevation of 8000 feet and should prove hardy in the warmer parts of Great Britain in the rock garden in damp fibrous peat and loam, in a shady spot.

795. PLATANTHERA OPHRYDIOIDES, F. Schmidt

P. Reinii, Franch.

Root: of narrowly oblong tubers. **Stem:** 8″–10″ tall, slender. **Leaves:** 1–2 in number, ovate or elliptic, blunt or pointed, about 2″ long, degenerating upwards into linear-lanceolate bracts. **Spike:** of 5–10 blossoms, loose. **Flowers:** about $\frac{1}{2}''$ across; dorsal sepal ovate, pointed; lateral sepals similar, somewhat narrower, reflexed; petals ovate, pointed, erect; lip simple, narrowly oblong; spur filiform, about $\frac{1}{2}''$ long. *August.*

A dwarf, slender species of but little garden value, with loose spikes of rather small pale green blossoms. It inhabits damp situations, usually in the open, over nearly the whole of Japan and the island of Sakhalin. It should, of course, be quite hardy in Great Britain in the bog garden or on the banks of a stream in peat and good loam.

796. PLATANTHERA ORBICULATA, Lindl.

Habenaria orbiculata, Torr. *H. macrophylla*, Goldie. *Lysias orbiculata*, Rydb. *Orchis orbiculata*, Pursh.

Root: of thick fleshy fibres. **Stem:** $1'$–$2\frac{1}{4}'$ tall, stout, erect, nearly naked. **Leaves:** basal, usually 2 in number, with their blades flat upon the ground, orbicular or oval, undulate on their margins, silvery beneath, 4″–9″ long, degenerating into narrow scales on the stem. **Raceme:** 4″–9″ long, many-flowered. **Flowers:** about $\frac{3}{4}$″ across; dorsal sepal suborbicular or reniform; lateral sepals oblong, falcate; petals smaller than the sepals, falcate; lip linear, narrow, entire, curved; spur slender, about $\frac{1}{4}$″ long.

July and August.

A tall species with two large leaves at the base of an erect flower-stem, terminating in a rather loose raceme of fairly large greenish-white blossoms. It is quite a decorative plant and grows in shady woods, usually in rich soils, throughout the greater part of Canada and the Eastern United States, as far south as Georgia; it is quite hardy and may be grown in rich loam and leaf-soil in a damp shady spot.

797. PLATANTHERA PERAMŒNA, A. Gray

Blephariglottis peramœna, Rydb.

Root: a cluster of narrow, tapering tubers. **Stem:** $\frac{3}{4}$′–2$\frac{1}{2}$′ tall, erect, leafy. **Leaves:** mainly cauline, oblong or lanceolate, small towards the top of the stem, 3″–8″ long. **Spike:** 1$\frac{1}{2}$″–6″ long, oblong, many-flowered. **Flowers:** about $\frac{1}{2}$″ across; sepals suborbicular or orbicular-ovate, the dorsal one sometimes smaller than the lateral sepals; petals orbicular-ovate, contracted into a stem at the base, entire or toothed, smaller than the sepals; lip deeply divided into 3 cuneate lobes; outer lobes sharply toothed; centre lobe deeply notched at its apex; spur slender. *July and August.*

A pretty species remarkable for its deeply coloured blossoms; they are of a rich purple-violet colour and are borne in rather long spikes on tall leafy stems. The plant grows in damp meadows in Eastern North America from New Jersey to North Carolina and Tennessee and should be quite hardy in Great Britain in a damp, sheltered spot in the rock garden, in good fibrous loam.

798. PLATANTHERA PLATYCORYS, Schltr.

Root: of 2 ovoid or oblong tubers. **Stem:** about 15″ tall, clothed with a few slender sheaths above the middle. **Leaf:** solitary, subradical, ovate or elliptic, blunt, 2$\frac{1}{2}$″–3$\frac{1}{2}$″ long. **Raceme:** 3″–5″ long, erect, lax, of 10–17 blossoms. **Flowers:** about $\frac{5}{8}$″ across, suberect; dorsal sepal ovate, concave, suberect; lateral sepals deflexed, narrowly oblong, slightly hooked at the tip; petals oblong-lanceolate or linear-lanceolate, blunt; lip narrowly strap-shaped, blunt, somewhat dilated at the base; spur subfiliform, incurved, pointed, about $\frac{1}{2}$″ long. *July.*

An erect, slender species with a fairly long raceme of medium-sized green and white blossoms of some decorative value. It is found in deciduous mountain woods on Mount Yudono-San, Nippon, Japan, and should be quite hardy in Great Britain in the rock garden under the same conditions as *P. neglecta*.

799. PLATANTHERA PSYCODES, A. Gray

Habenaria psycodes, Gray; *Blephariglottis psycodes*, Rydb. *P. incisa*, Lindl. *Orchis fimbriata*, Pursh. *O. incisa*, Pursh.

Root: of thick fibres. **Stem:** $\frac{3}{4}'$–$2\frac{3}{4}'$ tall, stout, leafy. **Leaves:** ovate, elliptic or oblong-lanceolate, becoming small upwards, 2″–10″ long. **Spike:** 2″–6″ long, usually many-flowered. **Flowers:** about $\frac{5}{8}''$ across; sepals ovate, blunt, dorsal one narrower than the others; petals oblong or oblong-lanceolate, with a few teeth on the outer margins; lip very deeply divided into 3 fan-shaped lobes, deeply fringed or cut on their margins; spur slender, clavate at the apex, about $\frac{5}{8}''$ long. *July and August.*

This species produces very tall leafy stems terminating in a spike of fair-sized lilac, or rarely white, delightfully fragrant blossoms. It should make a pretty addition to the bog garden and is found in a state of nature in wet meadows, swamps, moist woods, etc., in Eastern North America from Newfoundland to North Carolina. It should be quite hardy in Great Britain in good loam and leaf-soil on the banks of a pond or stream.

800. PLATANTHERA SACHALINENSIS, F. Schmidt

Root: of 2 small ovoid tubers. **Stem:** up to 24″ tall, rather stout. **Leaves:** 2–3 in number, distant, oblong or ovate, blunt, about 6″ long. **Spike:** 4″–8″ long, densely many-flowered. **Flowers:** about $\frac{1}{4}''$ across; dorsal sepal oblong, blunt; lateral sepals subfalcate; petals ovate, blunt, spreading; lip simple, linear; spur filiform, curved, about $\frac{3}{8}''$ long. *July and August.*

This species is worth growing on account of its sweetly-scented blossoms, they are too small to have much decorative value; the petals, sepals and lip are white and the spur is green. It should prove perfectly hardy in Great Britain, in the bog garden or on the banks of a stream or pond in good soil, as it is native in the island of Sakhalin and Northern Japan where it is exposed to more degrees of frost than is usual in this country.

801. PLATANTHERA SATYRIOIDES, Reichb. f.

Cœloglossum Satyrioides, Nym. *Himantoglossum Satyrioides*, Spreng. *Orchis Satyrioides*, Steve. *Peristylis Satyrioides*, Reichb. f.

Root: of 2 oval or oblong tubers about 1″ long. **Leaves:** basal, 2, rarely more in number, elliptic or ovate-oblong, 2″–4″ long. **Scape:** about 12″ tall, slender, clothed with a few sheaths. **Spike:** 2″–4″ long, lax, few-flowered. **Flowers:** $\frac{1}{2}''$ long exclusive of the spur; dorsal sepal oblong, blunt; lateral sepals lanceolate, blunt, curved; petals narrowly lanceolate, curved, forming an open galea with the dorsal sepal; lip 3-lobed; outer lobes oblong; centre lobe spathulate, recurved, all finely toothed; spur slender, curved, about 1″ long. *April and May.*

This species has a loose spike of rather small blossoms with green and dull purple sepals and petals and a green lip shaded with brown and covered with very fine hairs. The plant is of no garden value and is a native of Turkey and Persia, where it is found in marshes and wet pastures. It may be planted on the banks of a stream or pond in good heavy loam, and should prove quite hardy.

802. PLATANTHERA SIKKIMENSIS, Hook. f.

Habenaria sikkimensis, Hook. f.

Root: a branched rhizome with thick, fleshy fibres. **Stem:** 10″–12″ tall, stout and leafy. **Leaves:** narrowly oblong, 3″–4″ long. **Spike:** 3″–4″ long, few-flowered. **Flowers:** about 1¼″ across; dorsal sepal broadly ovate, blunt; lateral sepals oblong-lanceolate, spreading, pointed; petals triangular-lanceolate; lip linear; spur very stout, blunt, incurved, ¾″ long. *June and July.*

The large pale green blossoms of this species are quite attractive; they are borne on tall, stout, leafy stems in a loose spike. It is found in open grassy places on the Sikkim Himalaya at various elevations up to 9000 feet, where it is subjected to over 15° of frost for long periods during the winter. It may be grown outdoors in Great Britain in a moist sunny spot in the rock garden in a compost of loam and peat with plenty of rough sand. It is only suitable for outdoor culture in warm sheltered localities.

803. PLATANTHERA SORORIA, Schltr.

Root: of ovoid or oblong tubers. **Stem:** 6″–9″ tall, erect, slender, sheath-clothed. **Leaves:** oblong-elliptic, blunt, sheathing at the base. **Raceme:** 1″–1½″ long, rather lax, of 5–10 blossoms. **Flowers:** about ⅜″ across; dorsal sepal erect, ovate, blunt, concave, smooth; lateral sepals obliquely lanceolate, blunt, smooth; petals obliquely ovate-lanceolate, subfalcate, erect; lip linear, blunt, dilated in the middle; spur filiform, pendulous, ⅝″ long. *June.*

A delicate, slender little plant with a few broad leaves at the base of the stem and a short raceme of a few small greenish blossoms. It is of little or no decorative value and is found in damp places on Mount Yidesan in the province of Iwasiro, Japan. In Great Britain it should be quite hardy in the open in a damp half-shady spot in rough peat and loam.

804. PLATANTHERA STENOSTACHYA, Lindl.

Habenaria peristyloides, Wight. *H. stenostachya*, Benth. *Cœloglossum densum*, Lindl. *C. cernuum*, Rof. *C. peristyloides*, Reichb. f.

Root: an irregular tuber. **Stem:** $\frac{1}{2}'$–$2\frac{1}{2}'$ tall, usually slender, with numerous small sheaths above the leaves. **Leaves:** nearly all subradical, erect, lanceolate, sheathing at the base, 1″–4″ long. **Spike:** 3″–5″ long, of few or many blossoms. **Flowers:** under $\frac{3}{8}''$ across; sepals subequal, linear, concave, pointed; petals triangular, ovate or oblong, fleshy; lip divided into 3 long and narrow lobes, base almost saccate; spur straight, stout. *May to July.*

A plant of little or no decorative value, with long spikes of small yellowish-green or white blossoms on slender flower-stems. It grows in damp or swampy places in elevated districts in India, Burma, and China and is sufficiently hardy for culture outdoors in the warmer parts of Great Britain in a damp spot in the rock garden or on the banks of a pond or stream in a good rich loam.

805. PLATANTHERA STRICTA, Lindl.

P. gracilis, Lindl. *Habenaria gracilis*, Lindl. *H. stricta*, Wats.

Root: of 2 ovoid or oblong tubers about 1″ long. **Stem:** $\frac{3}{4}'$–$2\frac{1}{4}'$ tall, fairly stout, leafy. **Leaves:** cauline and basal, linear-oblong, blunt below, lanceolate and pointed on the upper part of the stem, gradually degenerating into bracts among the flowers, 3″–9″ long. **Spike:** 6″–12″ long, loosely many-flowered. **Flowers:** about $\frac{3}{8}''$ across; dorsal sepal broadly ovate; lateral sepals ovate, blunt, spreading; petals narrowly lanceolate; lip linear-lanceolate, pointed; spur clavate, about $\frac{1}{4}''$ long. *May to August.*

A species of little or no horticultural value, with long spikes of pale yellowish-green blossoms on fairly stout leafy stems. It is a common plant in hilly districts in North-Western America in swamps and bogs, ranging from Alaska to Washington. It may be grown in this country on the banks of a pool or in the bog garden in a rich loamy soil.

806. PLATANTHERA TAKEDAI, Makino

Root: of 2 fusiform tubers. **Stem:** 7″–10″ tall, erect, smooth, with 2 sheaths at the base and 2 remote leaves on the upper part. **Leaves:** ovate-oblong to ovate-linear or linear-lanceolate, pointed, sessile, 2″–3″ long. **Raceme:** 1″–$2\frac{1}{2}''$ long, lax, of 8–10 blossoms. **Flowers:** about $\frac{3}{8}''$ across; dorsal sepal broadly ovate, blunt; lateral sepals broadly linear, turned downwards; petals narrowly ovate, pointed, nearly as long as the sepals; lip simple, broadly linear, narrow above; spur very short, conical.
July and August.

This species is closely allied to *Platanthera ophrydioides* (Fr.) and may be only a variety of it. The small green blossoms are of little or no decorative value and are produced in lax racemes. It is found in damp places on Mount Myoko, Shimotsuke, Japan, and should therefore be quite hardy in Great Britain in a damp or wet place in fibrous peat and loam.

807. PLATANTHERA TENUIOR, Schltr.

Brachycorythis tenuior, Reichb. f. *Habenaria tenuior*, N. E. Br.

Root: of ovoid tubers. **Stem:** leafy, $\frac{1}{2}'$–$1\frac{1}{4}'$ tall, rather slender. **Leaves:** ovate or ovate-lanceolate, $\frac{3}{4}''$–$1\frac{1}{2}''$ long, decreasing into sheaths below and bracts above. **Racemes:** $1\frac{1}{4}''$–$4\frac{1}{4}''$ long, rather dense, many-flowered. **Flowers:** about $\frac{3}{8}''$ across; dorsal sepal elliptic-oblong, concave, blunt; lateral sepals obliquely semiovate-oblong, rather blunt and spreading; petals oblong, blunt, oblique; lip oblong or ovate-oblong, entire, minutely crenulate; disc with a fleshy central nerve. *November to January.*

This is a pretty species with long racemes of rather small lilac or purple blossoms on a slender stem clothed with many deep green leaves. It inhabits open, damp, grassy places in the Orange Free State, Natal and the Transvaal and probably reaches its greatest elevation above sea-level at Marabastad (4700 feet) in the Transvaal, where it is exposed to 12° of frost for short periods during its winter rest. It should be grown in a damp gritty fibrous loam in full sun and is only suitable for outdoor culture in Western Britain.

808. PLATANTHERA TIPULOIDES, Lindl.

Orchis Tipuloides, Linn. *Habenaria tridentata*, Hook. f.

Root: of 2 oblong or fusiform tubers about 1″ long. **Leaves:** 2, rarely more in number, lanceolate-oblong, suberect. **Scape:** $\frac{3}{4}'$–$1\frac{1}{4}'$ tall, rather slender, clothed with a few narrow bracts. **Spike:** 2″–6″ long, lax, of 5–11 blossoms. **Flowers:** $\frac{1}{2}''$ across excluding the spur; dorsal sepal very broadly oblong, rounded at the tip; lateral sepals oblong, contracted in the middle, blunt, spreading; petals linear, sinuous, forming a loose galea with the dorsal sepal; lip tongue-like; spur slender, curved, $1\frac{1}{4}''$ long. *May to July.*

A plant of no decorative value, with a slender spike of rather small greenish blossoms with long, slender, curved spurs. It is found in bogs and swamps in high northern latitudes, ranging from North America to Northern Europe and Asia, extending well into the Arctic regions. The plant may be grown in the bog garden or on the banks of a stream or pond in rich fibrous loam and peat.

809. PLATANTHERA VIRIDIFLORA, Schltr.

Habenaria viridiflora, Rydb.

Root: of 2 ovoid tubers about $1\frac{1}{4}''$ long. **Stem:** $\frac{3}{4}'$–2′ tall, stout, leafy, erect. **Leaves:** cauline, lower ones linear-oblong or oblong-lanceolate, blunt, uppermost lanceolate, pointed, 3″–6″ long. **Spike:** 4″–6″ long, rather dense, many-flowered. **Flowers:** about ½″ across; dorsal sepal ovate, blunt; lateral sepals oblong; petals lanceolate, smaller than the sepals; lip lanceolate, about ¼″ long; spur club-shaped, about ¼″ long. *May to July.*

A plant of no garden value, with greenish-yellow, unpleasantly-scented blossoms, in a rather dense raceme or spike. It is found in boggy or swampy places, in woods, mostly composed of deciduous trees, ranging from Alaska to British Columbia and is the Western representative of *P. hyperborea.* It should be perfectly hardy in Great Britain, in a half-shady spot in the rock garden, in peat and sphagnum-moss kept moist.

810. PLATANTHERA VIRIDIS, Lindl.

Cœloglossum viride, Hartm. *Habenaria viridis,* R. Br. *Gymnadenia viridis,* Reich. *Himantoglossum viride,* Reichb. f. *Orchis viridis,* Crantz.

Root: of several lobed tubers about 1½″ long. **Stem:** 3″–9″ tall, slender, sparely leafy. **Leaves:** basal and cauline, ovate below, and lanceolate and bract-like on the upper part of the stem, 1″–2″ long. **Spike:** 2″–3″ long, rather loose, many-flowered. **Flowers:** from ⅜″–½″ long; dorsal sepal ovate; lateral sepals falcately lanceolate; petals falcately linear, small, all forming a hood over the column; lip wedge-shaped, bifid at the tip with a tooth in the sinus; spur minute, conical, blunt. *May to July.*

A quaint little native plant with a loose spike of rather small pale green blossoms of no decorative value. There are several forms such as *bracteatum, islandicum, gracillimum* and *labellifidum,* and the plant forms several curious hybrids with members of the genus *Orchis.* The type and its forms are found in damp or marshy places in many parts of Europe, Siberia, China and North America; they may be grown in the bog garden in good loamy soil.

811. PLATANTHERA VOLCANICA, Lindl.

Root: of oblong or ovoid tubers. **Stem:** 2′–2½′ tall, stout, leafy. **Leaves:** linear-lanceolate, pointed, sheathing at the base. **Spike:** 9″–12″ long, very densely many-flowered. **Flowers:** about 3/16″ across; dorsal sepal ovate, blunt; lateral sepals oblong, blunt, deflexed; petals ovate, slightly hooked at the tip; lip oblong-linear, deflexed, with a thickened nerve; spur filiform, about ⅜″ long. *October.*

The extremely small pale green blossoms of this species are of no decorative value; they are borne in long dense spikes on tall leafy stems. The plant is found in rather dry situations in Mexico on the volcanoes of Guajalate and Orizaba, where it reaches an elevation of 10,000 feet; it is also found on the Cordilleras of Oaxaca. From such elevations it should prove quite hardy in Great Britain in an open sunny spot in the rock garden in loam and peat.

PLEIONE, Don

Exceedingly beautiful deciduous Orchids numbering about 20 species; they are included in the genus *Cœlogyne* by many authors but may be distinguished from that genus by their deciduous habit and, with the exception of one species, by the leaves appearing before the blossoms. The root is a short rhizome usually crowded with pseudo-bulbs; the leaves are usually solitary and spring from the tip of the pseudo-bulbs. The blossoms are borne on short scapes which usually spring from the base of the pseudo-bulbs; they are generally solitary and terminal, though occasionally two are produced. In size and shape many of them resemble the blossoms of a *Cattleya*; most of the species are terrestrial plants and are found growing on the surface of moss- and humus-covered rocks and boulders and a few are at home on moss-grown trees. The plants are found in various parts of India and China and may be propagated by separation of the pseudo-bulbs.

812. PLEIONE DELAVAYI, Rolfe

Cœlogyne Delavayi, Rolfe

Root: of few fleshy fibres. **Pseudo-bulbs:** globular or slightly flattened. **Leaves:** appearing after the blossoms, elliptic-oblong or elliptic lanceolate, pointed, 3″–6″ long. **Scape:** 3″–3½″ long, sheath-clothed. **Flower:** solitary, about 3″ across; dorsal sepal, lateral sepals, and petals all narrowly lanceolate; lip rhomboid, obscurely 3-lobed; centre lobe fimbriate, with 3 rows of teeth down the centre of the disc. *May to July.*

This beautiful plant is allied to *C. bulbocodioides* (Franch.) but has larger and more handsome blossoms of a bright rose-purple colour with deeper markings on the lip. It is found in mossy soil and on moss-covered rocks in open pastures, on the mountains of North-Western Yunnan, Western China, at elevations of from 7500–9000 feet. The plant may be tried outdoors in the warmer parts of Great Britain in a sheltered but open part of the rock garden in peat and moss.

813. PLEIONE FORRESTII, Schltr.

Root: a short rhizome with several filiform rootlets. **Pseudo-bulbs:** pear-shaped, with several ridges near the apex, about 1″ long. **Leaves:** absent at flowering time, probably ovate-lanceolate. **Scape:** about 6″ tall, erect, bearing a solitary blossom. **Flower:** about 3″ across; sepals and petals oblong-ligulate, blunt, smooth; lip rhomboid, obscurely 3-lobed; lateral lobes rounded, short, margins toothed; centre lobe much larger, nearly square, margin toothed or fringed, nerves thickened, and toothed at the base down its centre. *April and May.*

A beautiful species with very large bright orange coloured blossoms with brown markings. It is found on moss-covered boulders and cliffs in shady valleys on the eastern flanks of the Tali Range, Western Yunnan, Western China, at elevations of from 9000–10,000 feet above sea-level. It should succeed outdoors in the milder parts of Great Britain. The conditions under which it is found in a state of nature should be copied as far as possible.

814. PLEIONE GRANDIFLORA, Rolfe

Root: a fairly slender rhizome. **Pseudo-bulbs:** ovoid or ovoid-oblong, about 1½″ long. **Leaves:** wanting at flowering time, probably oblong-lanceolate. **Scape:** 4″–5″ long, sheathed at the base. **Flower:** solitary, about 4″ across; sepals and petals nearly similar, lanceolate-oblong, blunt; lip obscurely 3-lobed, broadly elliptic-oblong, deeply fringed; disc with 5 rows of fringe-like teeth. *April and May.*

The huge white blossoms of this very beautiful species are probably larger than those of any other member of the genus, in some specimens there are some crimson-purple markings on the lip. The plant is found on moss-covered cliffs and boulders, in shady mountain valleys in Western Yunnan, Western China, at from 8000–10,000 feet above sea-level. It should be possible to cultivate it in the open air in warm sheltered localities in Great Britain, on a moss- and fern-clad rock, in leaf-soil and a little loam.

815. PLEIONE HENRYI, Rolfe

P. pogonioides, Rolfe; *Cœlogyne Henryi*, Rolfe; *C. pogonioides*, Rolfe

Root: of few fleshy fibres from the base of the pseudo-bulbs. **Pseudo-bulbs:** narrowly ovoid, about ¾″ long. **Leaf:** solitary, produced with the blossoms, elliptic-lanceolate, rather blunt, 4″–7½″ long. **Scape:** 3″–6″ long, sheath-clothed at the base, bearing 1–2 blossoms. **Flowers:** about 3″ across; dorsal sepal, lateral sepals, and petals narrowly lanceolate and pointed; lip obscurely 3-lobed; outer lobes rounded; centre lobe orbicular-oblong, fringed on the margins, with 3 rows of sharp teeth down its centre. *June.*

This is one of the largest of the Chinese species; it has very handsome blossoms of a rich magenta-rose colour with magenta markings on the lip. It grows in crevices in rocks and in dry stony places on the mountains of North-Western Yunnan, Western China, at elevations of from 9000–10,000 feet; it is also found in Hupeh and Szechuan. It may be tried outdoors in the rock garden in sandy loam, peat and moss.

816. PLEIONE HOOKERIANA, Don

Cœlogyne Hookeriana, Lindl.

Root: a slender, creeping rhizome. **Pseudo-bulbs:** narrowly ovoid, ¾″–1″ long. **Leaf:** elliptic-lanceolate, pointed, 2″–4″ long, springing from the centre of the scape. **Scape:** 1″–2½″ long, slender, sheath-clothed, springing from the apex of the pseudo-bulb and bearing a solitary blossom. **Flower:** about 2″ across; sepals and petals nearly similar, oblong-lanceolate, pointed; lip large, concave, very obscurely 3-lobed, margin toothed or undulate; disc with 5 ciliate ridges. *April to June.*

This species is quite a little gem; it is dwarf and has large blossoms with pale rose-purple sepals and petals and a white lip with pale reddish-brown blotches; the disc has five yellow, fringed ridges on its surface. The plant grows on moss-covered rocks and banks, usually in the sun, in the Sikkim Himalaya up to 10,000 feet above sea-level and should be sufficiently hardy for outdoor culture in the warmer parts of Great Britain on a bank of peat and loam surfaced with moss. The form *brachyglossa* (Reichb. f.) is probably too tender for outdoor culture in Britain. *See Plate 17 facing page 366.*

817. PLEIONE HUMILIS, Don

Cœlogyne humilis, Lindl. *Cymbidium humile*, Sm. *Epidendrum humile*, Sm.

Root: a slender rhizome. **Pseudo-bulbs:** flagon-shaped, 1″–1½″ long. **Leaves:** elliptic or lanceolate, sheathed at the base and springing from the top of the pseudo-bulbs, 2″–6″ long. **Scape:** 2″–3″ tall, sheath-clothed, springing from the base of a pseudo-bulb. **Flower:** usually solitary, rarely 2, from 1″–2″ across; sepals and petals subequal, lanceolate and rather narrow; lip obovate, fringed; disc with fringed lamellæ. *September to November.*

A delightful little species with large blossoms varying from white to pale purple with some reddish-purple, orange or brown markings on the lip. It is found in moss on the trunks of large trees and on moss banks in the Himalaya from Nepal to Sikkim, reaching an altitude of 8000–9000 feet above sea-level. It should succeed outdoors in warm humid localities in the rock garden on a bank of peat and sphagnum-moss.

818. PLEIONE PRÆCOX, Don

P. birmanica, Reichb. f. *Cœlogyne præcox*, Lindl. *Cymbidium præcox*, Smith; *Epidendrum præcox*, Smith

Root: a small, creeping rhizome. **Pseudo-bulbs:** very variable, usually bottle-shaped or very shortly cylindric, depressed at the top. **Leaves:** 1–2 in number, elliptic or lanceolate, pointed, sheathed at the base, 2″–9″ long. **Scape:** 3″–4″ long, sheath-clothed, bearing 1, rarely 2, blossoms. **Flower:** 2½″–4″ across; sepals and petals narrowly lanceolate, recurved, pointed; lip bifid, deeply fimbriate in specimens from Eastern India and Burma; disc with 3–5 crested lamellæ. *September and October.*

A very beautiful plant with large pseudo-bulbs blotched with red-purple on a rich green ground. The huge rose-purple blossoms are fragrant and are produced at a different season to the leaves. The form *Wallichiana* (Lindl.) has very richly-coloured blossoms. The plant is found on mossy banks in dense shady forests on the Himalaya, the mountains of Burma as far south as Tenasserim, and in Yunnan, Western China, where it reaches an elevation of over 9000 feet. Plants collected from such an altitude should be hardy in warm sheltered localities under the same cultural conditions as *P. humilis* (Don).

819. PLEIONE YUNNANENSIS, Rolfe

Root: a slender rhizome. **Pseudo-bulbs:** spherical, much flattened, pumpkin-like, small. **Leaves:** wanting at flowering time, lanceolate, pointed. **Scape:** 4″–5″ tall, slender, clothed with several sheaths. **Flower:** solitary, about 3″ across; sepals and petals nearly similar, oblong-lanceolate, pointed; lip obovate-orbicular, at times obscurely 3-lobed, blunt, fringed towards the tip; disc with 5 lamellæ. *April.*

A very charming and seemingly variable species with large, solitary blossoms of a rosy-lilac, pink or reddish-purple colour. It is found growing in rocky places among short herbage and dwarf grasses, on mountain slopes in Western Yunnan, Western China. It may be tried outdoors in the warm Western and Southern counties of Great Britain in an open well-drained spot, in fibrous peat and good fibrous loam.

POGONIA, Jussieu

The majority of the 120 species which constitute this genus are beautiful plants with comparatively large blossoms for plants so dwarf in habit. Some have a rounded, tuberous rootstock, whilst in others it is slender with fibrous roots; their stems are usually erect and fairly stout and are either leafy or clothed with a few scales; some have a tuft of leaves or leaf-like bracts at the top of the stem and resemble a *Trillum*, others produce a large rounded leaf from near the base of the flower-stems after the capsules have ripened. The blossoms are usually produced in few-flowered racemes and are frequently ornamental. They are found in thin woods and in open grassy places scattered over Asia, North America and Australia with a solitary species in Africa, and are most numerous with regard to species in the tropics. Propagation by separation of the tubers and by division of the rhizome and also by seeds, which are freely produced in nature.

820. POGONIA AFFINIS, Austin

Isotria affinis, Rydb.

Root: of rather long, fleshy fibres. **Leaves:** produced at a different season to the flowers, elliptic or ovate, 1″–2″ long. **Scape:** 6″–10″ long, almost naked except for a whorl of 5 sessile, leaf-like bracts at the top. **Flower:** about 1½″ across; solitary or 2 in number, on a short stalk from the top of the scape; sepals linear, spreading; petals linear, erect, shorter than the sepals; lip 3-lobed, rounded, nearly erect, and crested over nearly the whole of its upper surface. *June.*

This species very much resembles the following species but is smaller in all its parts; the quaint greenish-yellow blossoms are of but little decorative value, they are however rather sweetly scented. It is found in damp woods, growing in moss and vegetable debris, in Eastern North America from Connecticut to Southern New York, Pennsylvania and New Jersey and is both rare and local. It may be grown outdoors in a damp spot in the rock garden, or on a raised bank in the bog garden, in peat leaf-soil and sphagnum-moss.

821. POGONIA DIVARICATA, R. Br.

Root: of cord-like fibres. **Stem:** ¾′–2′ tall, erect, rather stout. **Leaves:** mainly basal, narrowly oblong or oblong-lanceolate, rather blunt, sessile, 2″–6″ long. **Flower:** usually solitary at the top of the stem, subtended by a bract, nearly 3½″ across the sepals; sepals linear, pointed; petals narrowly elliptic, pointed, shorter than the sepals; lip 3-lobed; lobes rounded, very concave, almost tubular, about as long as the petals. *June and July.*

This handsome species produces a tall, stout stem clothed at its base with large glaucous green leaves, and bears a very large pale pink or lilac blossom at the top accompanied by one or two leaf-like bracts. The plant inhabits marshy meadows, the margins of swamps, etc., in the Eastern United States from New Jersey to Florida. It should be quite hardy in Great Britain in a damp part of the rock garden or on the banks of a pond in good loam.

822. POGONIA JAPONICA, Reichb. f.

P. ophioglossoides, A. Gr. *P. similis*, Bl.

Root: of thickened fibres. **Stem:** ¾′–1½′ tall, stout, erect. **Leaves:** varying from elliptic to linear, narrowing upwards, 3″–4″ long. **Flower:** solitary or rarely 2 or 3, terminal, about 1½″ across; sepals oblong, blunt; petals narrowly oblong, blunt; lip obscurely 3-lobed; outer lobes deeply fringed; centre lobe crested. *June and July.*

This species is very closely allied to the North American *P. ophioglossoides* (Ker.) and has the same type of handsome pink or purple, deeply fringed blossoms. It is found in damp grassy places, in bogs and on the margins of streams in open country in various parts of Japan. It should prove perfectly hardy in this country in a sunny position in the bog garden or on the banks of a stream or pond in peat and a small portion of leaf-soil.

PLATE 17.

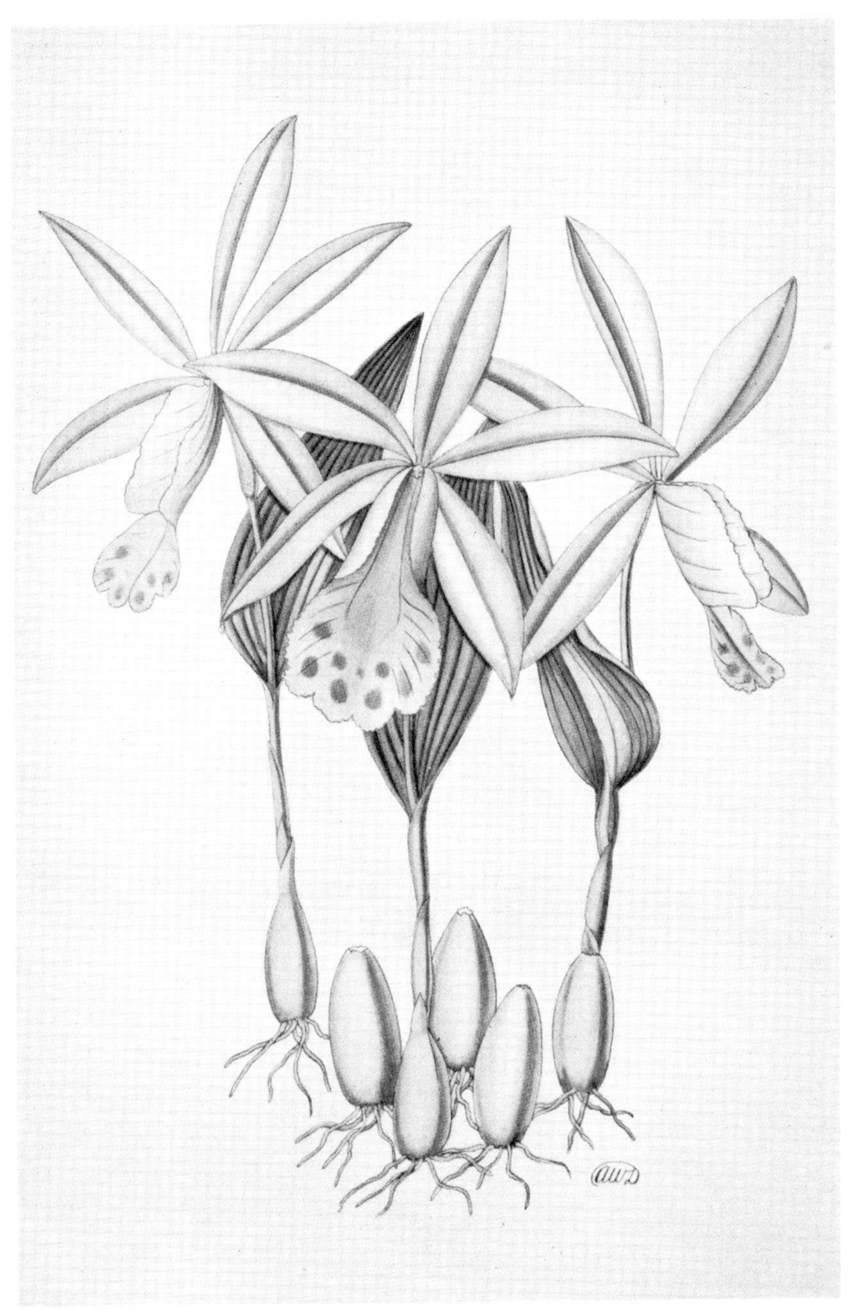

PLEIONE HOOKERIANA.

PLATE 18.

POGONIA OPHIOGLOSSOIDES.

823. POGONIA OPHIOGLOSSOIDES, Ker.

Arethusa ophioglossoides, Pursh.

Root: of thick, cord-like fibres. **Stem:** $\frac{3}{4}'$–$1\frac{1}{2}'$ tall, fairly stout, erect. **Leaves:** mainly basal, lowermost linear, oblong or elliptic, tapering to a slender stalk, longer than the blade, 3″–5″ long; uppermost oblong-lanceolate to elliptic, clasping, $1\frac{1}{2}''$–3″ long. **Flowers:** solitary or several at the top of the stem, about $1\frac{3}{4}''$ across; sepals linear, elliptic or oblong, pointed; petals elliptic, about as long as the sepals; lip spathulate or linear-spathulate, fimbriate, crested. *June and July.*

A beautiful plant with fairly stout stems clothed at their base with light green foliage and from one to three large rose-pink blossoms at the apex. It should prove a welcome addition to the rock garden in a damp spot in good fibrous loam. It grows in peat bogs, mossy swamps, marshes, margins of lakes, wet meadows, etc., in Eastern North America from Newfoundland to Florida.

824. POGONIA PENDULA, Lindl.

Arethusa pendula, Pursh. *A. parviflora*, Michx. *Triphora pendula*, Nutt. *T. trianthophora*, Rydb.

Root: fleshy, tuberous. **Stem:** 3″–12″ tall, rather slender. **Leaves:** 2–10 in number, suborbicular to ovate in shape, stem clasping, $\frac{1}{2}''$–1″ long. **Flowers:** about $\frac{1}{2}''$ long, axillary; sepals and petals elliptic, blunt, of nearly equal length, bending over the column; lip divided into 3-rounded lobes, narrow towards the base. *August and September.*

This little plant has numerous, rather small, pale purple blossoms in a drooping cluster at the top of the stems which sometimes spring in a cluster from the same root. It cannot be said to be of much decorative value but should prove interesting in the alpine house. It grows in rich soils in damp woods from Ontario to Florida and should be perfectly hardy in Great Britain in a shady part of the rock garden in good fibrous loam and leaf-soil, kept fairly moist in the summer.

825. POGONIA PURPURATA, Reichb. f.

Root: of spherical or ovoid tubers each about $\frac{3}{4}''$ in diameter. **Stem:** obsolete. **Leaf:** radical, elliptic-ovate, pointed, plicate, petiolate, about 3″ long. **Scape:** 6″–9″ tall, clothed with 2 or 3 distant sheaths. **Raceme:** loose. **Flowers:** about 1″ across; sepals narrowly lanceolate, spreading; petals broadly lanceolate; lip strongly 3-lobed; outer lobes generally rounded at the apex, erect; centre lobe subulate-oblong, pointed, longer than the side-lobes, recurved somewhat. *November.*

Although this plant cannot lay claim to any great decorative value its pale green, purple veined blossoms, about half a dozen in number in a loose raceme on the erect flower-stem, should appeal to lovers of interesting plants. It is quite leafless when in blossom and grows in a state of nature in stony places, covered with short herbage, in the Transvaal and probably reaches its greatest altitude on the Magaliesberg Range at 4800 feet, where it is exposed to over 12° of frost when deciduous. It should be grown in a good gritty loam in full sun.

826. POGONIA VERTICILLATA, Nutt.

Isotria verticillata, Raf. *Arethusa verticillata,* Pursh. *A. medeoloides,* Pursh.

Root: of long, fleshy fibres. **Leaves:** produced at a separate time of year to the flowers, elliptic or oval, smooth, 1″–2″ long. **Scape:** 8″–16″ tall, clothed with several basal sheaths and with a whorl of 4 or 5 elliptic or oval, pointed, sessile bracts at its apex. **Flowers:** terminal, on short ascending stalks, nearly 3″ across the segments; sepals linear or linear-filiform, spreading; petals linear, erect; lip 3-lobed; lobes rounded, crested, nearly erect. *May and June.*

A very quaint plant with a fairly stout stem bearing a whorl or tuft of thick green bracts at the top, and very large dusky purple and green blossoms. It is an interesting but not showy species and grows in damp or marshy woods, usually on rich soils, in Eastern North America from Ontario to Florida. It should be quite hardy in Great Britain in a damp shady spot in the rock garden, in rich loam and leaf-soil.

827. POGONIA YUNNANENSIS, Finet

Root: of small tubers. **Stem:** 3″–6″ tall, sheath-clothed at the base, slender, erect. **Leaf:** solitary, membranous, lanceolate, pointed. **Flower:** solitary, about ⅝″ across, erect, subtended by a leafy bract; sepals and petals subequal, narrowly lanceolate, blunt or pointed; lateral sepals oblique and blunt; lip erect, 3-lobed; lateral lobes rectangular, front margins denticulate; centre lobe subrotund, very short. *June.*

A very delicate little species of dwarf habit with a slender stem clothed at its base by a solitary leaf, large in proportion to the size of the plant; the solitary rose-purple blossom is carried erect and is accompanied by a leaf-like bract. The plants are found in moist, mountain meadows in North-West Yunnan at 9000 feet above sea-level. It should succeed outdoors in the bog garden in the milder parts of the Kingdom, or in a pan of loam, peat and sphagnum-moss in the alpine house.

POLYSTACHYA, Hooker fils

A genus of over 230 epiphytal species with small or medium-sized blossoms which in the majority of the plants are of no great decorative value; their short stems are usually leafy and are sometimes thickened at the base into pseudo-bulbs; the oblong or narrow, leathery, distichous leaves are contracted at the base into sheaths. The root system is composed of a few fleshy fibres which anchor the plants to the trees and rocks of their native habitats. The blossoms are borne in few- or many-flowered racemes, rarely panicles, and are frequently interesting if not showy. They are woodland plants and are widely scattered throughout the tropics, the greater majority are African. The few that are found at sufficient elevation in their native habitat to justify inclusion in this book may be tried outdoors in the warm humid Western counties in sheltered localities on the branches of a tree or on a damp rock in peat and sphagnum-moss. Propagation by division of the pseudo-bulbs and by seeds.

828. POLYSTACHYA CADUCA, Reichb. f.

Root: of creeping fleshy fibres. **Pseudo-bulbs:** ovoid, usually under ½″ long, bearing from 2 to 3 leaves. **Leaves:** linear, or oblong-linear, rather pointed, 1″–3″ long. **Scape:** 1½″–2″ long, bearing a few blossoms, covered with minute hairs. **Flowers:** about ⅜″ across; dorsal sepal ovate-oblong, concave; lateral sepals obliquely triangular, pointed; petals lanceolate-oblong, pointed; lip unguiculate, slightly undulate, downy, with a transverse callus near its base. *July to September.*

A very dwarf and compact little plant, producing several spikes of small yellow and white blossoms from the tips of the pseudo-bulbs. It is of little or no horticultural value but should prove interesting in the alpine house. In a state of nature it is found on the trunks and branches of trees in various parts of the Abyssinian highlands at elevations up to 8200 feet and is exposed to 12° or 15° of frost for short periods. It may be tried outdoors in Great Britain in a humid sheltered half-shady spot in growing moss on a rough barked tree.

829. POLYSTACHYA CONFUSA, Rolfe

Root: of slender, creeping, fleshy fibres. **Pseudo-bulbs:** ovoid, about ⅓″ long, bearing 1–2 leaves and clothed below with a few sheaths. **Leaves:** oblong, spreading, rather blunt, 1¼″–1½″ long, narrowing at the base. **Scape:** 1″–1½″ long, downy, bearing from 1–3 blossoms. **Flowers:** about ⅜″ across; dorsal sepal ovate-oblong, pointed; lateral sepals broadly triangular-ovate, pointed; petals linear-oblong, pointed; lip broadly unguiculate, 3-lobed; outer lobes rounded; centre lobe broadly ovate, somewhat concave, blunt; with a downy disc. *September.*

A very tiny species with small pseudo-bulbs bearing one or two deep green, oblong leaves and terminal spikes of a few greenish-yellow blossoms of little or no garden value. It is found on damp moss- and lichen-covered rocks at over 9000 feet above sea-level on Kilimanjaro in Tanganyika, East Africa and is exposed to 12° of frost for short periods. It may be tried in the open ground on a damp limestone rock in sphagnum-moss and peat in a half-shady humid spot.

830. POLYSTACHYA CULTRATA, Lindl.

P. cultriformis, Spreng. *Dendrobium cultriforme*, Thou.

Root: of numerous creeping, fleshy fibres. **Pseudo-bulbs:** linear-oblong or ovoid, ½″–4″ long, bearing a solitary leaf. **Leaf:** oblong, blunt, 2½″–6″ long. **Scape:** 3″–6″ long, bearing a more or less branched panicle of blossoms, ¾″–3″ long. **Flowers:** over ⅜″ across; dorsal sepal triangular-ovate, pointed; lateral sepals triangular-ovate, pointed, carinate; petals subspathulate-elliptic, pointed; lip cuneate-unguiculate, 3-lobed; outer lobes semiovate, blunt, short; centre lobe ovate, pointed; disc furfuraceous, with a thick fleshy callus between the side lobes. *June to December.*

This species is somewhat more robust than most of the other hardy members of the genus. The small yellow and white blossoms are borne in a loose panicle and are rather more decorative than those of most of the other species. It grows on rocks and trees in the Mauritius, Madagascar, Tanganyika, West and East Africa where on Kilimanjaro at 10,000 feet it is subjected to over 25° of frost for short periods. Culture as for the other species.

831. POLYSTACHYA GLABERRIMA, Schltr.

Root: of fleshy, creeping fibres. **Pseudo-bulbs:** ovoid, about ⅝″ long. **Leaves:** linear, shortly emarginate, 1¼″–2½″ long. **Scape:** terminal, erect, smooth, about 2″ long, bearing 1 or 2 blossoms, with a small membranous sheath below the middle. **Flowers:** about ½″ across; dorsal sepal ovate, very pointed; lateral sepals obliquely falcate-ovate, attenuated and very pointed at the apex, with the front margin much broadened at the base; petals linear, dilated above the middle, pointed; lip erect, rhomboid, elongate towards the apex, smooth, with a thickened centre nerve. *September to November.*

This little plant is not of any great garden value but should prove attractive for alpine house decoration. The slender stem which bears one or two white blossoms does not overtop the deep green leaves which spring in twos and threes from the top of the pseudo-bulbs. It grows on moist, mossy rocks on the Saddleback Mountains near Barberton in the Transvaal at 5000 feet, where it is exposed to 12° of frost for short periods during the winter. It should be tried in loam and growing moss on a moist rock in the bog garden.

832. POLYSTACHYA JOHNSTONII, Rolfe

Root: of fleshy, creeping fibres. **Pseudo-bulbs:** subglobose, nearly ¾″ long, bearing 3–4 leaves. **Leaves:** oblong, blunt or emarginate, recurved,

$1\frac{1}{2}'-2\frac{1}{2}'$ long. **Scape:** subcompressed or ancipitous, villous, 2″–3″ long. **Raceme:** 1″–$1\frac{1}{4}$″ long, many-flowered. **Flowers:** over $\frac{1}{2}$″ across, villous; dorsal sepal ovate-lanceolate, pointed; lateral sepals triangular-ovate, carinate; petals falcate-lanceolate, pointed; lip 3-lobed, reflexed; outer lobes reniform-orbicular; centre lobe elliptic-ovate, pointed; disc villous with a transverse fleshy tubercle at the base of the centre lobe.

August to November.

This little plant has a total height of from three to four inches and bears somewhat larger blossoms than most of the other species; they are greenish-yellow in colour and are not very attractive. It grows on the trunks of trees and rocks in open unshaded places on the mountains of British Central Africa, where it reaches an altitude of 7500 feet and is exposed to over 12° of frost for short periods. It may be tried in the milder parts of Great Britain on a damp rock in peat and moss.

833. POLYSTACHYA NIGRESCENS, Rendle

Root: of creeping, fleshy fibres. **Stem:** 7″–9″ tall, slender, not pseudo-bulbous, bearing from 3–5 leaves. **Leaves:** linear or oblong-linear, rather blunt, 3″–5″ long. **Scape:** slender, 2″–3″ long, bearing 2–5 blossoms. **Flowers:** about $\frac{3}{8}$″ across; dorsal sepal ovate-oblong, pointed; lateral sepals triangular, pointed; petals subspathulate-lanceolate, pointed; lip cuneate-unguiculate, blade ovate or sub-trilobed; outer lobes broadly rounded; centre lobe ovate, undulate, recurved, rather pointed; disc with 2 linear-oblong calli in the centre. *September to December.*

A rather robust species producing slender stems clothed with a few narrow leaves and terminating in a loose spike of under half-a-dozen yellow, green and purple blossoms of very little decorative value. It grows amongst tree-ferns, and at 10,000 feet (its greatest altitude) amongst heather on Mount Ruwenzori in British East Africa. It should be quite hardy in all but the bleakest parts of Great Britain in moist peat and loam, in half shade.

834. POLYSTACHYA OTTONIANA, Reichb. f.

P. capensis, Sond.

Root: a stout, woody rhizome. **Pseudo-bulbs:** ovoid, about $\frac{3}{4}$″ long, covered with imbricate sheaths. **Leaves:** linear or linear-oblong, coriaceous, $1\frac{1}{2}$″–6″ long. **Scape:** 1″–4″ long, erect, downy. **Raceme:** at times reduced to a solitary blossom, simple. **Flowers:** nearly $\frac{3}{4}$″ across; sepals triangular-ovate or triangular oblong, somewhat spreading; petals oblong, blunt; lip 3-lobed, much shorter than the petals; side lobes small and blunt; centre lobe broadly oblong, blunt, revolute; disc pubescent, keeled. *October and November.*

A pretty, delicate plant with rather large white blossoms with a yellow line on the centre lobe of the lip; two or three leathery bright green leaves spring from the apex of each pseudo-bulb. It grows on moss-covered trees and rocks in shady forests and ravines on the mountains in Eastern Cape Colony, Natal and the Transvaal, where in wooded ravines near Barberton it probably reaches its greatest elevation of 5000 feet and is exposed to 10° of frost during the winter. It may be tried on a damp moss-covered rock in a shady part of the bog garden in very warm localities.

835. POLYSTACHYA PREUSSII, Kränzl.

Root: of fairly stout, creeping fibres. **Pseudo-bulbs:** ovoid or ovoid-oblong, ½″–1″ long, bearing 2–4 leaves. **Leaves:** oblong-linear, bluntly bidentate, 1″–3″ long. **Scape:** 3″–6″ tall. **Raceme:** simple, ¾″–1¾″ long. **Flowers:** about ⅜″ across; dorsal sepal ovate-oblong, pointed; lateral sepals broadly triangular-ovate, pointed; petals lanceolate, pointed; lip spathulate, with a long downy stalk; blade suborbicular, pointed; disc with a long 4-lobed callus at the base of its blade. *August to October.*

An interesting little species though of no great decorative value. It is of tufted habit and bears a small panicle of yellow and purple blossoms. It is found in the temperate regions of the Cameroon Mountains in the Cameroons, West Africa, at an altitude of from 6800–8200 feet, growing as an epiphytic on the stems of *Hypericum*, *Leucothöe*, etc. It may be tried outdoors in Great Britain in mild, damp localities on the branches of trees and shrubs with rough loose barks.

836. POLYSTACHYA PUBESCENS, Reichb. f.

P. Lindleyana, Harv. *Epiphora pubescens*, Lindl. *Lissochilus sylvaticus*, Eckl.

Root: a stout, woody rhizome. **Pseudo-bulbs:** ovate or thickened at the base, narrowed above, 1″–1½″ long, with several broad imbricate sheaths below. **Leaves:** elliptic-oblong to linear-oblong, coriaceous, 1½″–6″ long. **Scape:** 3″–8″ tall, downy, with a few lanceolate sheaths below. **Raceme:** elongate, many-flowered. **Flowers:** about ⅝″ across; sepals ovate or ovate-oblong, spreading, dorsal sepal narrower than the others; petals spathulate-oblong, blunt, shorter than the dorsal sepal; lip 3-lobed; side lobes ovate, blunt; centre lobe ovate, larger and longer than the side lobes; disc pubescent or villous. *November.*

A pretty species with medium-sized deep yellow blossoms with the lateral sepals barred with brown. Each pseudo-bulb bears two or three bright green leaves. This species grows on moss-covered trees and rocks in forests and ravines in Eastern Cape Colony, Natal and the Transvaal, where on Woodbush Mountains it reaches its greatest elevation at 6000 feet and is exposed to over

15° of frost for short periods during winter. Plant on a moss-covered rock in the bog garden in half-shade with a little peat placed over the rhizome.

837. POLYSTACHYA RENDLEI, Rolfe

Root: of few fleshy fibres. **Stem:** $\frac{1}{2}'$–3′ tall, cylindrical, bearing from 1–5 leaves. **Leaves:** linear-oblong, blunt, 2″–$2\frac{3}{4}''$ long. **Panicles:** $1\frac{1}{2}''$–2″ long, many-flowered. **Flowers:** about $\frac{3}{8}''$ across; dorsal sepal triangular-ovate; lateral sepals broadly triangular, pointed; petals subspathulate-lanceolate, pointed, narrow at the base; lip unguiculate, with an obscurely 3-lobed blade; outer lobes very broadly rounded; centre lobe oblong, small, blunt; disc puberulous with a central crest with raised margins.

October to December.

A tall straggling species with rounded stems clothed with a few narrow leaves, and panicles of small yellow and purple flowers. It is found on moss-covered rocks in half-shady places in British Central Africa reaching its greatest altitude above sea-level on the top of Mount Zomba at 7000 feet, and is at times exposed to over 12° of frost. It may be tried in the warmer parts of Great Britain on a moss-covered limestone rock in a damp half-shady spot.

838. POLYSTACHYA RIVÆ, Schweinf.

Root: of thick, fleshy, creeping fibres. **Pseudo-bulbs:** aggregated, subcompressed, bicarinate, not thickened below. **Leaves:** oblong-oval or oblong-linear, 4″–6″ long. **Scape:** $\frac{1}{2}'$–$1\frac{1}{4}'$ tall, clothed with a few convolute sheaths. **Raceme:** of many flowers. **Flowers:** nearly $\frac{5}{8}''$ across and nearly as long; dorsal sepal oblong-ovate, pointed, connivent; lateral sepals triangular-ovate, gibbous at the base, connivent; petals spathulate; lip shortly unguiculate, 3-lobed; outer lobes connivent, broadly ovate, pointed; centre lobe broadly ovate, thickened, recurved; disc convex, inside of flower pubescent.

July and August.

A species with blossoms of a decidedly decorative nature; they are pale yellow in ground colour with a brighter yellow lip. It is of tufted habit and grows on mossy cliffs in Northern Abyssinia reaching its greatest altitude in Eritrea at 6500 feet and is exposed for short periods to 12° or 15° of frost. It may be grown outdoors in mild districts in Great Britain on a damp limestone rock in moss and peat.

839. POLYSTACHYA RUWENZORIENSIS, Rendle

Root: of thin, creeping fibres. **Pseudo-bulbs:** subcylindric, superposed, 1″–$1\frac{1}{4}''$ long, bearing 2 leaves. **Leaves:** linear or linear-lanceolate, blunt, 1″–$1\frac{1}{4}''$ long. **Scape:** slender, 1″ long, puberulous. **Raceme:** very short, few-flowered. **Flowers:** about $\frac{1}{4}''$ across; dorsal sepal ovate-oblong, pointed;

lateral sepals triangular-ovate, pointed; petals linear-lanceolate, pointed; lip unguiculate, 3-lobed; outer lobes broadly semiovate, blunt; centre lobe ovate, pointed; disc smooth, with a transverse, crenulate, membranous callus between the lobes. *September and October.*

This species reaches a total height of about six inches and forms clusters of pseudo-bulbs bearing two leaves and few-flowered racemes of small yellow and white blossoms. It is found among heather and dwarf herbage on Mount Ruwenzori in British East Africa at 9000 feet and is therefore quite hardy in the warmer parts of Great Britain. It should be tried in sandy fibrous peat and a little loam in the rock garden.

840. POLYSTACHYA TRANSVAALENSIS, Schltr.

Root: a rhizome with short internodes. **Pseudo-bulbs:** cylindric, narrowed towards the apex, $1\frac{1}{4}''$–$4\frac{3}{4}''$ long, with 2 acuminate sheaths below. **Leaves:** narrowly oblong, unequally 2-lobed at the apex, $1''$–$3\frac{1}{2}''$ long. **Scape:** up to 6″ long. **Raceme:** simple, usually many-flowered. **Flowers:** about $\frac{5}{8}''$ across; dorsal sepal triangular-lanceolate, very pointed; lateral sepals obliquely falcate-ovate, broader than the dorsal sepal; petals linear, dilated into a rhomboid limb at the apex; lip cuneate at the base, dilated into a transversely rhomboid limb; disc velvety, with an obscure callus in the centre. *November.*

A delicately coloured species with racemes of many fair-sized blossoms with green sepals and white petals and lip, the latter has a green boss in the centre; two or three leathery bright green leaves rise from the apex of each pseudo-bulb. It grows on the moss-covered branches of large trees in the mountain forests of the Transvaal where it reaches its greatest elevation on Woodbush Mountains at 6500 feet and is there exposed to over 15° of frost during winter. It may be tried on a moss-covered rock in the bog garden.

PRASOPHYLLUM, R. Brown

This genus contains about 62 deciduous, terrestrial plants with fairly large tubers, globular or oval in shape with a few thick roots springing from the upper part where stem and tuber meet; they are like those of many other tuberous-rooted species, annual, a fresh tuber being formed beside the old one each season and the plant increases by the formation of several small tubers, which form on the tips of the fleshy roots. The leaves are solitary, grass-like and sheath the stem, which is usually rather stout and terminates in a long or rather short cylindrical spike of small or medium-sized reversed flowers, the lip being above and the dorsal sepal below; they are pretty but would be of greater garden value if they were more brightly tinted. The plants are found in light moist soils in open situations in Australia and New Zealand, a number being sufficiently hardy for outdoor culture in Britain in such moist spots as the banks of ponds and streams. Several are highly fragrant. Propagation by imported tubers and by seeds.

841. PRASOPHYLLUM ARCHERI, Hook. f.

Root: of ovoid tubers emitting short fibres. **Leaf:** solitary, cauline, almost subulate, clothing the stem with its long sheath, leaving 1″ or so of blade free. **Scape:** 6″–12″ tall, stout, rounded. **Spike:** $\frac{1}{2}$″–1″ long, rather lax. **Flowers:** about $\frac{1}{4}$″ long; dorsal sepal lanceolate, concave, ciliate; lateral sepals linear-falcate, dilated at the base; petals lanceolate, ciliate, about as long as the dorsal sepal; lip oblong-linear, fringed with long hairs and tapering to a point. *November and December.*

A plant of no decorative value, with a stout, pale green stem clothed by the long leaf-sheath with about one inch of free bristle-like blade just beneath the first flower, and a loose spike of green and red blossoms. It grows in moist sandy ground in several parts of Tasmania and should be sufficiently hardy for culture outdoors over the greater portion of the British Isles. A sandy loam in a damp sunny spot should suit it.

842. PRASOPHYLLUM AUSTRALE, R. Br.

P. lutescens, Lindl.

Root: of ovoid tubers emitting short, stout fibres. **Leaf:** solitary, cauline, narrowly linear, with a long sheath clothing the flower-stem, blade 3″–6″ long. **Scape:** 2′–3′ tall, stout. **Spike:** 3″–7″ long, fairly dense. **Flowers:** about $\frac{3}{8}$″ across; dorsal sepal broadly ovate, concave, very pointed; lateral sepals lanceolate, united to the middle, base dilated, recurved, fleshy; petals broadly lanceolate, very pointed; lip lanceolate, with a broad, fleshy, erect base abruptly recurved, frequently undulate; blossoms upside-down. *November.*

A tall reed-like species with a long sheathing grass-green leaf and a long rather dense spike of yellowish-green blossoms striped with reddish-brown. It cannot lay much claim to decorative value. In its native habitat it grows in swamps and pools, rooting in the rich mud of vegetable debris at the bottom, in Victoria and Tasmania. It should prove quite hardy in all but the bleakest parts of Great Britain. A very rich soil on the banks of, or in, a pond should suit it.

843. PRASOPHYLLUM BRACHYSTACHYUM, Lindl.

Root: of nearly globular tubers. **Leaf:** solitary, in the form of a long sheathing bract with a free subulate blade about $\frac{3}{4}$″ long. **Scape:** 5″–8″ tall, slender, rounded. **Spike:** $\frac{1}{2}$″–1″ long, dense. **Flowers:** about $\frac{3}{8}$″ across; dorsal sepal galeate; lateral sepals lanceolate, shortly pointed; petals narrowly triangular-lanceolate; lip lanceolate, joined to the base of the column by an articulation; blossoms upside-down on the stem. *December and January.*

A quaint little species with an articulate joint to the lip where it is attached to the column; this allows it to move up and down like a tongue. The blossoms have pale green sepals and petals and a pale red lip; it is of no decorative value but the construction of its blossoms is interesting. In nature it grows in damp, grassy places in the highlands of Tasmania and should prove quite hardy in sheltered localities in Great Britain. A damp fibrous loam in full sun should prove suitable for its cultivation.

844. PRASOPHYLLUM BREVILABRE, Hook. f.

Root: of ovoid, irregular tubers. **Leaf:** solitary, cauline, with a very long sheath, blade almost subulate, 1″–3″ long. **Scape:** 1′–1¼′ tall, rather stout. **Spike:** 2″–4″ long, rather dense. **Flowers:** ⅜″ across; dorsal sepal lanceolate, pointed; lateral sepals broadly lanceolate; petals narrowly lanceolate; lip oblong, erect then reflexed, small, with undulate margins; blossoms upside-down. *December.*

A moderately slender species with fairly crowded spikes of small yellowish-green blossoms of no decorative value. The leaf and stem are of a very vivid green. It is found on the borders of swamps and in wet grassy places in Queensland, New South Wales, Victoria and Tasmania and is exposed to over 12° of frost in its most elevated stations for short periods during the winter. In cultivation it may be grown on the banks of a pond or stream in a rich soil in the full sun of mild sheltered localities.

845. PRASOPHYLLUM COLENSOI, Hook. f.

Root: of ovoid tubers with rough coats. **Leaf:** solitary, cauline, linear, sheathing the lower part of the stem, free part 3″–8″ long. **Scape:** 4″–10″ long, stout. **Spike:** 1″–3″ long, many-flowered. **Flowers:** ¼″ across; sepals spreading, ovate-oblong, rather pointed; petals linear-oblong, spreading; lip trowel-shaped, rather pointed, fleshy, tip thickened; blossoms upside-down. *November to January.*

The rather small, greenish-yellow, sweet-scented blossoms of this species are of but little decorative value; they are borne in an elongated spike of many blossoms on a stout stem which is clothed with one sheathing, grass-like, pale green leaf. It is abundant in open grassy places in rather moist situations in both the North and South islands of New Zealand, where it is found as far south at Otago at sufficient altitudes to ensure its complete hardiness in Great Britain. It may be cultivated in a good, damp, loamy soil in an open sunny spot in the rock garden.

846. PRASOPHYLLUM DESPECTANS, Hook. f.

Root: of small ovoid, somewhat irregular tubers. **Leaf:** reduced to a small sheathing bract below the blossoms. **Scape:** 4″–8″ tall, very slender. **Spike:** ½″–1″ long, fairly dense. **Flowers:** $\frac{3}{16}$″ across; dorsal sepal broadly lanceolate, very concave, pointed; lateral sepal lanceolate, pointed, oblique at the base; petals broadly lanceolate, half as long as the lateral sepals; lip lanceolate, recurved, channelled, articulate on the base of the column, movable; blossoms upside-down. *September.*

A very slender plant with tiny green and red blossoms with pointed segments. It is of no decorative value and grows in damp sandy soil in open spots in several parts of Tasmania, where it is exposed to 10° or 12° of frost for short periods during its winter rest. It may be grown in a damp sunny spot in the rock garden in sandy soil and is only suitable for outdoor culture in warm localities.

847. PRASOPHYLLUM ELATUM, R. Br.

P. australe, Lindl.

Root: of rather large irregular tubers. **Leaf:** solitary, cauline, with the sheath covering the greater part of the stem, free blade narrow, linear, 2″–6″ long. **Scape:** 1½′–3′ tall, very robust. **Spike:** 4″–12″ long, many-flowered. **Flowers:** about ⅝″ across; dorsal sepal lanceolate, very pointed; lateral sepals broadly lanceolate, connate from the middle upwards, points free; petals, lanceolate, very pointed; lip ovate-oblong, sessile, with undulate margins; blossoms upside-down. *October.*

Probably the most robust species; its stout stems are at times three feet tall and bear a very long spike of green blossoms, frequently tinted with red. The flowers are too dull in colour to render it of much decorative value. It inhabits damp or wet sandy soils in New South Wales, Victoria, South Australia, Western Australia and Tasmania, where it is exposed to over 12° of frost for considerable periods during the winter in its most elevated stations. A sandy loam on the banks of a pond or stream should meet its requirements.

848. PRASOPHYLLUM FLAVUM, R. Br.

Root: of large irregular tubers. **Leaf:** solitary, cauline, forming a loose sheath around the stem, blade ½″–1″ long, narrowly linear, pointed. **Scape:** 2′–3′ tall, stout. **Spike:** 4″–9″ long; many-flowered. **Flowers:** about ⅝″ across; dorsal sepal lanceolate, pointed; lateral sepals lanceolate, connate for the greater part of their length with free tips; petals narrowly lanceolate, nearly as long as the sepals; lip ovate-oblong, sessile, almost gibbose, concave, erect at the base, recurved towards the tip; blossoms upside-down.

September to December.

A very robust species with a stout stem clothed with a long leaf-sheath and a many-flowered spike of rather small yellowish-green blossoms on very short stems. It is of but little decorative value and is found in damp grassland or edges of swamps in New South Wales and Tasmania where in its more elevated habitats it is exposed to 12° or more of frost for considerable periods during its winter rest. Suitable for outdoor culture in mild localities only. A good fibrous loam on the banks of a pond in full sun is indicated.

849. PRASOPHYLLUM FUSCUM, R. Br.

P. alpinum, R. Br. *P. affine*, Lindl. *P. rostratum*, Lindl.

Root: of fair-sized ovoid tubers. **Leaf:** solitary, cauline, with a long sheath enclosing the stem, free blade 2″–9″ long, narrowly linear. **Scape:** 1½′–2½′ tall, stout or slender. **Spike:** 3″–6″ long, dense or lax. **Flowers:** about ⅝″ across; dorsal sepal lanceolate, concave, very pointed; lateral sepals narrowly lanceolate, at times connate near the base; petals linear, shorter than the sepals; lip narrowly lanceolate, very concave, erect then recurved; blossoms upside-down. *November and December.*

A most variable species both in height and colouring; it produces a long or short spike of rather small blossoms varying from pale green, shaded with lilac to olive-green suffused reddish-brown. The alpine form known as *alpinum* is dwarf and pale coloured and is sweetly scented. The plant is generally found in damp grassy places and edges of marshes, usually in elevated regions, throughout Eastern Australia and reaches an elevation of nearly 6000 feet in the Grampians of Victoria and is therefore quite hardy in Great Britain in a damp spot in a good fibrous loam.

850. PRASOPHYLLUM INTRICATUM, C. Stuart

Root: of small ovoid tubers. **Leaf:** solitary, cauline, reduced to a short linear bract about the middle of the stem. **Stem:** 6″–9″ tall, slender. **Spike:** 1″–2″ long, many-flowered. **Flowers:** about ¼″ across; dorsal sepal broadly lanceolate, very concave, pointed; lateral sepals lanceolate, longer than the dorsal sepal; petals narrowly lanceolate, slightly shorter than the lateral sepals; lip broadly obovate, recurved, convex, ciliate on the edges; blossoms upside-down. *December and January.*

A dwarf slender-stemmed plant, with a small leaf-like bract near its middle and a short many-flowered spike of blossoms with brown or pale yellow sepals and petals and a dull purple lip. It is of but little decorative value. In a state of nature it grows in damp grassy places, usually in sandy soils, in various parts of Tasmania and is exposed to 12° of frost for short periods during the winter in its most elevated stations. A damp spot in the rock garden in a sandy loam should meet its requirements. The plant is only suitable for outdoor culture in warm sheltered districts.

851. PRASOPHYLLUM NIGRICANS, R. Br.

Root: of small ovoid tubers. **Leaf:** solitary, cauline, narrowly linear, bract-like, just beneath the spike. **Scape:** 3″–6″ tall, very slender. **Spike:** ½″–1″ long, loose. **Flowers:** ⅜″ across; dorsal sepal broadly galeate, very pointed; lateral sepals broadly lanceolate, gland-tipped; petals triangular-lanceolate, pointed; lip ovate or ovate-oblong, pointed, joined by a movable joint to the base of the column; blossoms upside-down.

October to December.

This deeply-tinted little species has a slender bract-clothed flower-stem bearing a short spike of a few very small blossoms, of no decorative value, with green and brown sepals and petals and a brownish-purple lip. It grows in damp, grassy places, usually in the open, in New South Wales, South Australia and Tasmania at sufficient elevation above sea-level to ensure its hardiness in the warmer parts of Great Britain. A good fibrous loam in a damp sunny spot in the rock garden is indicated.

852. PRASOPHYLLUM PATENS, R. Br.

Root: of large irregular tubers. **Leaf:** solitary, cauline, sheathing the greater part of the stem, free blade 2″–6″ long, grass-like, pointed. **Scape:** 2′–3′ tall, very robust. **Spike:** 3″–9″ long, flowers scattered. **Flowers:** ½″ across; dorsal sepal and lateral sepals lanceolate, quite free; petals broadly lanceolate, very blunt; lip ovate or oblong, erect then reflexed, margins undulate; blossoms upside-down on the stems.

November and December.

A tall robust plant with a stout stem sheathed by a solitary bright green leaf. The blossoms which are rather small are borne in a long rather loose spike; the sepals are yellowish-green, the lip is paler in tint and is bordered with white. The plant is of but little garden value and is found in a state of nature in moist sandy places in open country over the whole of Eastern Australia from Queensland to Tasmania, and is common. It should be quite hardy outdoors in all but the bleakest parts of Great Britain. A damp sunny spot in sandy loam is indicated.

853. PRASOPHYLLUM RUFUM, R. Br.

P. nudum, Hook. f.

Root: of small irregular tubers. **Leaf:** solitary, cauline, reduced to a sheathing bract with about ¾″ of free blade. **Scape:** 6″–8″ tall, slender. **Spike:** ½″–¾″ long, rather dense. **Flowers:** ⅛″ across; dorsal sepal, ovate, concave, with a sharp point; lateral sepals lanceolate, pointed; petals also lanceolate, as long as the dorsal sepal; lip narrowly lanceolate or at times lanceolate, recurved, articulate to the base of the column.

December and January.

A very slender species with smaller blossoms than any other of its brethren. They are borne in a rather dense spike and are dull reddish-brown throughout except for some green tintings on the backs of the sepals. It is of no decorative value and like all members of the genus its flowers are upside-down. In nature it is found in damp grassy country in Eastern Australia and also in New Zealand, and is hardy enough for outdoor culture in the warmer parts of Great Britain. A moist sandy loam in full sun is indicated.

854. PRASOPHYLLUM WOOLLSII, F. Muell.

Root: of very small ovoid tubers. **Leaf:** solitary, cauline, reduced to a very short, linear, leafy bract. **Scape:** very slender, about 6″ long. **Spike:** about $\frac{3}{4}$″ long, few-flowered. **Flowers:** about $\frac{1}{4}$″ across; dorsal sepal lanceolate, rather pointed; lateral sepals lanceolate-subulate, slightly gibbous at the base; petals narrowly lanceolate, pointed, minutely ciliate, shorter than the sepals; lip ovate-oblong, blunt, minutely ciliate, articulate to the column by a movable joint; blossoms upside-down on stem. *October to January.*

A very dwarf and extremely slender plant with a short, loose spike of very small green and dull red blossoms of no decorative value. It is found in damp stony places on the Blue Mountains of New South Wales and reaches sufficient elevation to ensure its hardiness in the warmer parts of Great Britain. It may be grown in an open sunny spot in the rock garden in a damp sandy loam.

PTEROSTYLIS, R. Brown

Exceedingly quaint deciduous, terrestrial Orchids with large, pale-coloured blossoms which bear a remarkable resemblance to the closed mandibles of an eagle in miniature, and were they more brightly coloured they would no doubt be very popular. Their root systems consist of rounded tubers which, when fully developed, are the size of hazel nuts; the plants increase by means of small tubers formed on the ends of fairly long roots which spring from the base of the stem where it joins the parent tuber. The root leaves are usually produced in the form of a loose rosette and are frequently found at a different season from the flowers; they are generally very pale or glaucous in colour and somewhat thick. The blossoms are at times solitary and at others in loose many-flowered spikes. The genus numbers about 70 species and is found in Australia, Tasmania, New Caledonia and New Zealand; many are hardy enough for culture outdoors in Britain. Propagation by imported tubers and by seeds when available.

855. PTEROSTYLIS APHYLLA, Lindl.

Root: of small ovoid tubers. **Leaves:** basal, in a spreading tuft, ovate, ¼″–½″ long, withering away before the flowers are perfected. **Scape:** 3″–5″ tall, bearing 1–2 sheaths. **Flowers:** ¾″ long, 1–3 in number; dorsal sepal and petals together forming a broad, blunt hood; lateral sepals united forming an oval lip tapering into 2 long incurving points, shorter than the galea; true lip very short and blunt with a blunt undivided appendage.

November and December.

A very quaint little plant with a rosette of pale green leaves and a fairly stout bract-clothed stem bearing from one to three blossoms, nearly white in ground colour with a bright green tip to the hood and a crimson stain near its base; the tip of the lip just shows from between the hood and the lateral sepals and is emerald green. It is found in damp, open, grassy places in Tasmania and is there exposed to 12° of frost for short periods during the winter. A damp fibrous loam in a warm sheltered spot is indicated.

856. PTEROSTYLIS BANKSII, R. Br.

P. australis, Lindl.

Root: of small tubers on slender fleshy fibres. **Stem:** 6″–18″ tall, fairly stout, leafy. **Leaves:** cauline, linear-lanceolate, alternate, sheathing the whole stem, 6″–12″ long. **Flower:** solitary, terminal, 3″ long; dorsal sepal and petals conniving and forming a beaked hood; lateral sepals long, filiform, ascending; lip linear with its tip exserted; appendage linear, curved, downy at the top.

October and November.

A species of fairly robust habit and upright growth with a very large green blossom resembling the crossed mandibles of a bird. The leaves are of a bright but pale green. It is common in moist grassy places throughout the North Island of New Zealand and as far south in the South Island as Otogo. It attains an elevation on the mountains of its native habitat to ensure its complete hardiness in all but the coldest parts of Great Britain. It may be grown in a damp, sandy, fibrous loam in the rock garden.

857. PTEROSTYLIS BARBATA, Lindl.

P. squamata, R. Br.

Root: of small oblong tubers on long fibres. **Stem:** 3″–8″ tall, stout, smooth, erect. **Leaves:** radical, ovate-lanceolate, numerous, erect, sessile, ½″–1″ long, sometimes degenerating into sheaths up the stem. **Flower:** solitary, erect, about 1″ long; dorsal sepal hooded; lateral sepals deflexed, with narrowly linear tips; petals linear-subulate; lip filiform, exserted, pendulous, plumose; appendage curved, downy at the tip. *November.*

A very quaint species consisting of a stout stem springing from a close rosette of tiny pale green leaves, and a solitary terminal blossom of a pale green and white colour with a pendulous bottle-brush-like lip of long golden hairs terminating in a purple gland. It is found in bogs and damp grassy places on sandy soils in New South Wales, Victoria, Western Australia, Southern Australia, Tasmania and throughout New Zealand at elevations which ensure its hardiness in England. It may be grown in the bog garden or in a damp sandy sunny spot in the rock garden.

858. PTEROSTYLIS CONCINNA, R. Br.

P. acuminata, Sieb.

Root: of oblong tubers. **Leaves:** radical, in a spreading rosette, ovate or broadly oblong, ½″–¾″ long, on a short stalk. **Scape:** 4″–6″ tall, with a bract below the middle. **Flower:** solitary, about ¾″ long; dorsal sepal and petals together forming a beaked hood; lateral sepals joined at the base with diverging horn-like tips embracing the galea; true lip oblong-linear, ending in 2 broad lobes; appendage linear-subulate, curved upwards, with a terminal tuft of setæ. *November and December.*

The pale green and white beak-like blossom of this species is carried quite erect on the tip of the flower-stem which is quite straight and rises from a tuft of tiny pale green leaves. It is an interesting though not showy plant. In a state of nature it grows in bushy places on rather poor, somewhat moist soil in New South Wales and Victoria. It should be quite hardy in the warmer parts of Great Britain in the open ground. A compost of sandy loam in a damp half-shady spot should suit it.

859. PTEROSTYLIS CUCULLATA, R. Br.

P. dubia, R. Br. *P. scabrida*, Lindl.

Root: of rather large oblong tubers. **Leaves:** basal, in a crowded tuft, ovate or oblong-elliptical, 1″–3″ long, degenerating upwards into 1–3 leaf-like bracts. **Scape:** 4″–7″ tall, fairly stout. **Flower:** solitary, erect, 1½″ long; galea formed by dorsal sepal and petals, erect, incurved, covered with minute down; lower lip formed by the two lateral sepals narrowly cuneate, the two lobes tapering to a fine point embracing the galea but not attaining its length; true lip oblong-linear, concealed within the blossom; appendage linear, dilated and tufted at the tip. *October and November.*

An interesting species with a large pale green blossom, very like the beak of a vulture in shape, carried quite erect on its stout stem. The foliage is of a pale whitish-green colour and is larger than that of any of the other species. It grows in shady spots such as thin woods and ravines, mostly on poor soils, in Victoria, South Australia and Tasmania and is exposed to over 15° of frost for considerable periods when at rest. A compost of sandy leaf-soil in a damp half-shady spot is indicated.

860. PTEROSTYLIS CURTA, R. Br.

Root: of fair-sized ovoid tubers. **Leaves:** radical, in a compact rosette, ovate or ovate-elliptic, $\frac{3}{4}''$–$1\frac{1}{2}''$ long, usually on rather long stalks. **Scape:** about 6″ tall, clothed with 1–3 sheathing bracts. **Flower:** solitary, erect, about $1\frac{1}{4}''$ long; dorsal sepal and petals converging, forming a galea, broad and pointed; lateral sepals united at the base, cuneate, with 2 broadly lanceolate lobes, not so long as the galea; true lip concealed within the galea, linear, blunt; appendage linear, curved, tufted at the tip. *October.*

An interesting and quite handsome species with a large and broad, beak-like blossom of a pale green and white colour with some brown shading at its base. The foliage forms a compact rosette of a bright but pale green colour. The plant grows in shady places over the whole of Eastern Australia from Queensland to Tasmania, where it is common. It should be quite hardy in all but the most exposed parts of Great Britain. A compost of leaf-soil and sand in a damp half-shady spot should suit it. Var. *grandiflora* has blossoms over two inches long.

861. PTEROSTYLIS FOLIATA, Hook. f.

Root: of oblong tubers on the ends of stout, fleshy fibres. **Stem:** 2″–10″ tall, rather stout. **Leaves:** radical and cauline, oblong or elliptic-oblong, lower ones petioled, upper ones degenerating into sheaths, $\frac{3}{4}''$–$2\frac{1}{2}''$ long. **Flower:** solitary, erect, terminal, about $\frac{5}{8}''$ long; dorsal sepal and petals joined in a hood with a much curved tip; lateral sepals linear, filiform towards their tips; lip narrow, tip a little exserted, appendage narrow, downy at the apex. *December and January.*

The rather small pale green blossoms of this species are more curious than beautiful; the leaves are broader than those of most of the other species and its habit is more tufted. It inhabits bogs both on high and low ground in the North Island of New Zealand and probably attains its greatest altitude above sea-level in bogs on the summits of the Ruahine Range at an elevation of 3000 feet and should therefore be quite hardy in Great Britain. It may be grown in the bog garden in peat and sphagnum-moss.

862. PTEROSTYLIS FURCATA, Lindl.

Root: of small ovoid tubers. **Leaves:** basal, fairly crowded but not in a rosette, ovate-oblong, elliptical, decreasing upwards into bracts, 1″–2″ long. **Scape:** about 6″ tall, bract-clothed. **Flower:** solitary, erect, $1\frac{1}{2}''$ long, encircled by a large bract; dorsal sepals and petals conniving, forming a beaked galea; lateral sepals joined at the base, forming a narrowly cuneate lower lip with 2 almost linear lobes tapering into a fine point, shorter than the galea; lip oblong-linear, concealed within the galea; appendage linear, curved, dilated, tufted at the tip. *October.*

This species is very closely allied to *P. cucullata*, and has the same shaped pale blossom perched on a stout stem; the leaves are more scattered and somewhat shorter. It is not showy but is quite interesting. In a state of nature it is found in shady places such as thin woods, mountain ravines, etc., in Tasmania at sufficient elevation to ensure its complete hardiness in all but the most exposed parts of Great Britain. A compost of leaf-soil and sand in a half-shady spot in the rock garden is indicated.

863. PTEROSTYLIS GRAMINEA, Hook. f.

Root: of very small tubers on the ends of slender fibres. **Stem:** 6″–10″ tall, leafy, slender. **Leaves:** cauline, sheathing, narrowly linear-lanceolate, 1″–3″ long. **Flower:** solitary, terminal, erect, ¾″–1″ long; dorsal sepal and petals forming a beaked hook; lateral sepals filiform, erect; lip linear, with a linear, curved appendage, with a downy tip. *September to November.*

This species is considered to be a somewhat starved form of *P. Banksii* by some botanists. The solitary green and white blossom is borne on the tip of the slender stem which is clothed with narrow, very pale green leaves, these are at times tinted with brown on the margin near the tip. It grows in moist grassy places mostly in elevated districts in the North Island and the greater part of the South Island of New Zealand and should prove quite hardy in the warmer parts of Great Britain. It may be cultivated in the bog garden or in a damp sandy soil in the rock garden.

864. PTEROSTYLIS LONGIFOLIA, R. Br.

Root: of elongate tubers. **Leaves:** cauline, linear-lanceolate, degenerating into bracts or sheathing scales below, ¾″–2″ long, shortly sheathing at the base. **Scape:** 9″–15″ tall, slender. **Flowers:** ⅝″ long, in a terminal raceme; dorsal sepal and petals conniving, forming a galea very much curved, the narrow tip pointing directly downwards; lower lip oblong, reflexed, divided into 2 narrowly lanceolate lobes; true lip oblong, downy on its surface, tufted at the tip; appendage very short, blunt, erect. *October.*

A very variable plant with a raceme of from three to seven pale green, curious-looking blossoms with their " beaks " tinted with olive-green and brown. It should make an interesting addition to the alpine house. It is a common plant in dry soils in the thin forests of New South Wales, Victoria, South Australia and Tasmania, ascending the mountains to sufficiently high altitudes to ensure its hardiness in Great Britain. A sandy leaf-soil in a shady part of the rock garden is indicated.

865. PTEROSTYLIS MUTICA, R. Br.

Root: of small ovoid tubers. **Leaves:** radical, in a rosette, ovate, almost sessile, ½″–¾″ long. **Scape:** 4″–8″ tall, slender, with a few sheaths. **Flowers:** in a spiral spike, 5 to 10 in number, ⅜″ long; dorsal sepal and petals converging into a broad much incurved hood or galea; lateral sepals joined at the base and prolonged into 2 short broad lobes; lip within the galea, oblong, very blunt; appendage narrowly oblong, thick, blunt. *October and November.*

A quaint little plant suitable for a pot or pan in the alpine house. It produces a little rosette of leaves like some of the *Sedura* species, and a slender spike of about nine pale green, rather globular blossoms. It is fairly common in open spots both in rich and poor soils over the whole of Eastern Australia from Queensland to Tasmania and is exposed to as much as 15° of frost for considerable periods in the winter on its highest stations. In cultivation it may be grown in a good fibrous loam in full sun in a warm sheltered spot.

866. PTEROSTYLIS NANA, R. Br.

Root: of small ovoid tubers. **Leaves:** radical, in a rosette, ovate, from ¼″–½″ long. **Scape:** 5″–8″ tall, very slender, clothed with a solitary bract about the middle. **Flower:** about ½″ long, solitary; dorsal sepal and petals together forming a hood with a very hooked tip; lateral sepals forming a lower lip, broadly cuneate, divided into 2 linear-subulate lobes; true lip linear, blunt, smooth; appendage linear, curved, with a few thick hairs at the tip. *October.*

A very delicate and slender plant with a rather small blossom perched on the top of a slender stem, it is pale green and is frequently tipped with purple. It is interesting but of no decorative value and is found in shady places in Victoria, Southern and Western Australia and Tasmania. It should be quite hardy in the warmer parts of Great Britain in a half-shady spot in the rock garden in a compost of sandy leaf-soil.

867. PTEROSTYLIS NUTANS, R. Br.

Root: of ovoid tubers. **Leaves:** radical, in a rosette, ovate, or elliptic, ½″–1½″ long, on short stalks. **Scape:** 6″–12″ tall, with a solitary sheathing bract. **Flower:** about 1″ long; dorsal sepal and petals forming a galea curved near the base and again towards the end; lateral sepals joined at the base, forming a lower lip, divided into 2 lobes which are narrow and taper to sharp points embracing the galea; true lip oblong-linear, blunt; appendage narrowly linear, penicillate. *September to November.*

This species has the galea formed by the connivence of the dorsal sepal and petals so curved that the blossoms appear to be nodding; they are large and are white, green-veined at the base and tinted bright green at the tip. It is frequent over the whole of Eastern Australia from Queensland to Tasmania, in shady places, usually in a poor soil, and is exposed to over 12° of frost for short periods in some of its habitats. A sandy leaf-soil in a damp half-shady spot is indicated. The plant is only suitable for outdoor culture in warm localities.

868. PTEROSTYLIS OBTUSA, R. Br.

Root: of small ovoid tubers. **Leaves:** in a rosette from a bud, separate from the flower-stem, ovate, $\frac{1}{2}''$–$\frac{3}{4}''$ long. **Scape:** about 6″ tall, sheath-clothed. **Flower:** solitary, about $1\frac{1}{2}''$ long, erect; dorsal sepal and petals conniving, forming an incurved galea; lateral sepals joined, forming a lower lip, very broadly cuneate, almost truncate, lobes very attenuate, subulate, embracing the galea; true lip oblong-linear, blunt; appendage linear, curved, penicillate. *November and December.*

A very quaint species with a long beak to its hood and long spreading bristle-like points to the lateral sepals. The blossom is white and green in colour and is borne on a sheath-clothed stem having no basal rosette of leaves which are produced at a separate time of year from the blossoms. It is frequent in shady places in New South Wales and Tasmania and should be quite hardy in the warmer parts of Great Britain in a sheltered half-shady spot in leaf-soil and sand.

869. PTEROSTYLIS OLIVERI, Petrie

Root: of 2 small oblong or ovoid tubers. **Stem:** 6″–12″ tall, leafy. **Leaves:** variable, lowermost elliptic-oblong or oblong-lanceolate, uppermost oblong-lanceolate or lanceolate, lowermost narrowed into a broad stalk, $1\frac{1}{2}''$–$3\frac{1}{2}''$ long. **Flower:** solitary, very rarely 2 in number, 1″–$1\frac{1}{2}''$ long; dorsal sepal ovate below, tapering to a long narrow point which is curved and nearly reaches the ovary; lateral sepals united to the middle, cuneate below, gradually narrowed into 2 filiform lobes which embrace the dorsal sepal; petals narrow, falcate; lip narrowly linear, blunt; appendage short, curved, penicillate.

December and January.

This little species is found in damp half-shady places in the South Island of New Zealand up to elevations of 4000 feet. It has the usual pale green and white blossoms so common to most species of the genus. It should be quite hardy in most parts of the Kingdom, in the rockery in a half-shady place in damp leaf-soil and fibrous peat.

870. PTEROSTYLIS PARVIFLORA, R. Br.

Root: of small oblong tubers. **Leaves:** ovate, $\frac{1}{4}''$–$\frac{1}{2}''$ long, produced in a rosette from a separate bud to the flower-stem. **Scape:** 4″–8″ tall, clothed

PLATE 19.

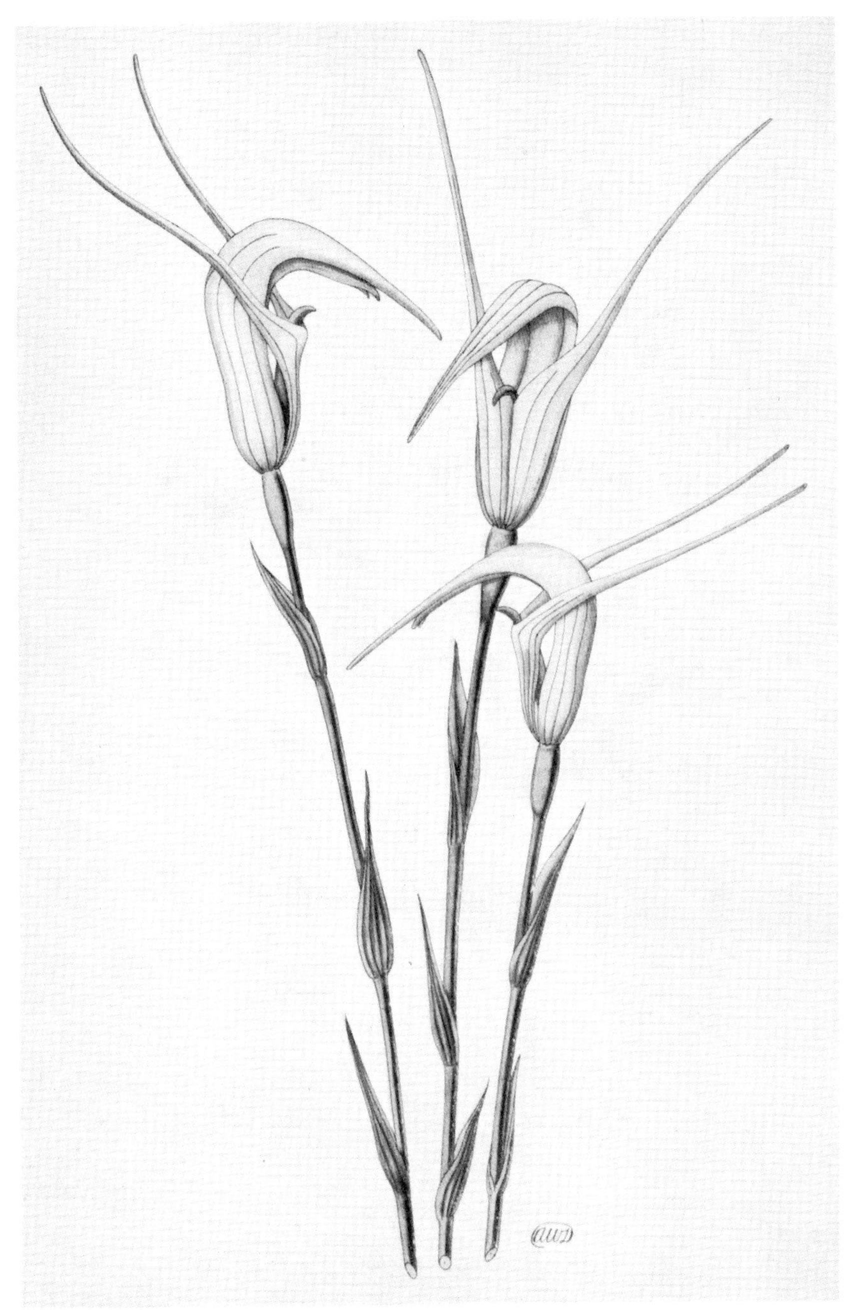

PTEROSTYLIS OBTUSA.

PLATE 20.

SATYRIUM MEMBRANACEUM.

with 2–3 sheathing bracts. **Flowers:** $\frac{3}{8}''$ long, in a raceme of 2–5; dorsal sepal and petals forming a much incurved galea; lateral sepals joined, forming a lower lip, cuneate, 2-lobed, lobes tapering to a fine point, shorter than the galea; true lip very short and blunt; appendage short and slender, tufted at the tip. *October.*

This little species produces a fairly long raceme of small pale green, brown-tinted blossoms on a slender bract-clothed stem. The rosette of tiny pale green leaves is usually produced at a separate season from the blossoms. It grows in shady places, usually in sandy soils, over the whole of Eastern Australia from Queensland to Tasmania and should be quite hardy in Southern and Western Britain in a fairly damp half-shady spot in a sandy leaf-soil.

871. PTEROSTYLIS PEDUNCULATA, R. Br.

Root: of ovoid or oblong tubers. **Leaves:** in a radical rosette, ovate or broadly oblong, $\frac{1}{2}''$–1″ long, on fairly long stalks. **Scape:** rather slender, about 6″ tall, clothed with 2–4 loose sheaths. **Flower:** solitary, about $\frac{5}{8}''$ long, erect; dorsal sepal and petals conniving, forming a fairly broad galea with a very hooked tip; lateral sepals joined, forming a broadly cuneate lower lip with 2 lanceolate, very pointed lobes, abruptly bent up and embracing the galea; true lip oblong, very blunt, pubescent on the surface; appendage long, linear, dilate at the tip, slightly penicillate. *September to November.*

A plant with a rather long stem and an insignificant blossom of a pale green colour perched erect on the top of it. The basal rosette is rather spare and soon withers away. The plant is a native of New South Wales and Tasmania, where it is found in thin woods on light soils. It should prove quite hardy in the warmer parts of Great Britain in a half-shady spot in sandy leaf-soil.

872. PTEROSTYLIS PRÆCOX, Lindl.

P. alata, Reichb. f. *Disperis alata*, Labill.

Root: of small oblong tubers. **Leaves:** in a basal rosette, narrowly linear or linear-lanceolate, $\frac{3}{4}''$–$1\frac{1}{2}''$ long. **Scape:** about 6″ tall, slender, clothed with a few bracts. **Flower:** solitary, erect, 1″ long; dorsal sepal and petals conniving, forming an incurved galea; lateral sepals joined, forming a cuneate lower lip divided to the middle into 2 lanceolate sharply pointed lobes embracing the galea; true lip linear, tapering above the middle, hidden within the galea; appendage linear, curved, penicillate. *May to July.*

This species resembles *P. obtusa* in the blossoms, which are pale green, but may be easily distinguished by its longer leaves. It is interesting, but, like all its brethren, not showy. It grows in shady places in Victoria and Tasmania and should be quite hardy in the warmer parts of Great Britain in a half-shady position in the rock garden in sandy leaf-soil.

873. PTEROSTYLIS REFLEXA, R. Br.

P. revoluta, R. Br. *P. scabra*, Lindl. *P. pyramidalis*, Endl.

Root: of small ovoid tubers. **Leaves:** in a rosette, produced on a separate bud at an earlier season of the year to the flower, ovate-oblong, ¾″–1″ long. **Scape:** 6″–9″ tall, clothed with leaf-like sheaths. **Flower:** solitary, erect, about 1½″ long; dorsal sepal and petals joined, forming a galea tapering to a fine point; lateral sepals forming a lower lip, cuneate at the base, tapering to fine points, embracing the galea; true lip lanceolate, tapering at the end into a fine point; appendage linear, curved, penicillate at the tip. *November to January.*

A very variable species both with regard to height and size of the blossom. The stem is somewhat downy, fairly stout, terminating in a large beak-like pale green blossom with long curved points. It is common in New South Wales, Victoria, South Australia and Western Australia in shady places in the mountains and lowlands, reaching sufficient elevation in the former to ensure its hardiness in Great Britain. A sandy leaf-soil in a half-shady spot is indicated.

874. PTEROSTYLIS RUFA, R. Br.

P. gibbosa, R. Br. *P. squamata*, R. Br. *P. Mitchellii*, Lindl.

Root: of ovoid tubers. **Leaves:** in a radical rosette at the base of the stem, ovate, ½″–1″ long. **Scape:** 6″–10″ tall, with 2–4 sheathing bracts. **Flowers:** about ½″ long, 3–4 in a short raceme; dorsal sepal and petals together forming a galea with a long fine point; lateral sepals joined into a lower lip, broadly cuneate, divided to the middle into 2 narrow, pointed lobes; true lip ovate-oblong, concave, bordered with cilia; appendage short, thick, rugose, often ciliate. *November.*

An extremely variable plant with a sheath-clothed stem bearing from three to four pale green, brown tinted blossoms with very long curved points to their segments. It is found in thin forest land over nearly the whole of Australia in one or other of its forms, and grows at sufficient elevations on the mountains to ensure its hardiness in the warmer parts of Great Britain. It may be cultivated in a half-shady spot in the rock garden in sandy leaf-soil.

PTERYGODIUM, Swartz

The greater number of the 36 species which make up this genus are very beautiful plants with dense or sometimes loose spikes of white or yellow blossoms. They have short rootstocks, terminating in a fair-sized rounded tuber with a smaller tuber developing beside it, and if the plant is in a robust healthy state several very small tubers on the ends of short, somewhat fleshy roots which spring from the base of the stem, where it joins the large tuber. The fairly stout and at times flexuous stems are clothed with oblong or lanceolate suberect leaves which diminish in size towards the top of the stem and subtend each blossom in the form of bracts. The plants are found in open, moist, grassy places frequently on the sides of hills and mountains with a rocky subsoil. Several are found at sufficient elevation in their native country to give some hope that they may prove hardy enough for culture outdoors in the Southern and Western counties of Britain. All the species are South African. Propagation by division and by seeds.

875. PTERYGODIUM ACUTIFOLIUM, Lindl.

Root: a sessile tuber. **Stem:** stout and flexuous. **Leaves:** cauline, oblong-lanceolate, 3″–7″ long. **Scape:** $\frac{1}{2}$′–2′ tall. **Spike:** 1$\frac{1}{2}$″–4″ long, rather dense and often many-flowered. **Flowers:** nearly 1″ across; dorsal sepal ovate-lanceolate, subconcave, with a rounded sac behind the sharply reflexed apex; lateral sepals obliquely ovate, widely spreading, petals cohering with the dorsal sepal into a spreading, broadly semiobovate, very oblique limb; lip broadly triangular-ovate, sharply reflexed, undulate; appendage triangular-oblong, erect, with a recurved apex. *November and December.*

A beautiful species with deep golden-yellow blossoms in fairly long dense spikes on stout leafy stems. It grows on moist mountain slopes amongst reeds and grasses in Cape Colony, where it reaches its greatest altitude in Du Toits Kloof in the Worcester Division at 4000 feet and is there subjected to over 12° of frost for short periods during its winter rest. It should be grown in fibrous peat and good loam in a raised part of the bog garden or on the banks of a pond or stream and is only suitable for outdoor culture in warm spots.

876. PTERYGODIUM ALATUM, Sw.

Ophrys alata, Thunb.

Root: a small sessile tuber. **Stem:** moderately stout. **Leaves:** radical and cauline, oblong-lanceolate, $\frac{3}{4}$″–1$\frac{3}{4}$″ long, gradually degenerating into bracts upwards. **Scape:** 3″–6″ tall. **Spike:** 1″–2$\frac{1}{2}$″ long, rather dense, many-flowered. **Flowers:** about $\frac{1}{2}$″ across; dorsal sepal lanceolate-oblong; lateral sepals lanceolate-oblong, spreading; petals cohering with the dorsal sepal into an obovate-orbicular limb, outer margin crisped and crenulate; lip 3-lobed, front lobe broadly triangular; side lobes rounded, crenulate; appendage somewhat 3-lobed, clavate, erect. *September.*

The pale sulphur-yellow blossoms of this little species are on the small side and it is more suited to the alpine house than the garden. It grows on moist, grassy mountain slopes and summits in South-Western Cape Colony, where it reaches its greatest elevation on the Klein Drakenstein Mountains in the Paarl Division at 6000 feet and should be quite hardy in Great Britain. A moist, fibrous peat and loam is indicated.

877. PTERYGODIUM CARNOSUM, Lindl.

Corycium carnosum, Rolfe

Root: of oblong tubers. **Stem:** moderately stout, flexuous. **Leaves:** cauline, linear, sessile, 2″–5″ long, reduced upwards into bracts. **Scape:** $1\frac{1}{4}$′ tall. **Spike:** 4″–6″ long, dense. **Flowers:** $\frac{3}{8}$″ long; dorsal sepal narrowly ovate, concave; lateral sepals broadly and obliquely ovate, sub-connivent; petals broadly and obliquely ovate, deeply concave, curved at the apex; lip broadly flabellate, broadly unguiculate; appendage erect, galeate, rounded in the middle, curved at the apex. *October to December.*

A pretty species with globular, pale or deep purple blossoms with a white lip; they are contracted at the mouth and are borne in fairly long spikes on stout stems, clothed with about half-a-dozen spreading grey-green leaves. It grows in fairly moist, grassy places in hilly districts in Natal and Cape Colony, probably reaching its greatest elevation at Du Toits Kloof in the Worcester Division at 4000 feet, where it is subjected to 12° of frost for short periods during the winter. A moist fibrous loam is indicated in a warm sheltered spot.

878. PTERYGODIUM CATHOLICUM, Sw.

Ophrys catholica, Linn. *Ophrys alaris*, Linn. *Arethusa alaris*, Thunb.

Root: a small sessile tuber. **Stem:** moderately stout, somewhat flexuous. **Leaves:** cauline, distant, oblong or elliptic-oblong, sessile, sheathing at the base, 1″–5″ long. **Scape:** $\frac{1}{2}$′–1′ tall. **Spike:** 3–8 flowered. **Flowers:** $\frac{3}{4}$″ across; dorsal sepal ovate-lanceolate, subconcave; lateral sepals ovate, curved at the apex, spreading; petals broadly elliptic-oblong, very oblique, cohering with the dorsal sepal into an expanded limb; lip broadly rhomboid-orbicular, very undulate, reflexed; appendage ovate-oblong, obscurely 3-lobed, blunt, recurved at the tip. *August to October.*

A beautiful species with large pale sulphur-yellow blossoms which sometimes have orange-red petals and lip, they are produced on rather stout stems clothed with two or three distant leaves. It is found in moist grassy places in Cape Colony, where it reaches its greatest elevation in the Caledon Division at Genadendal, 4000 feet, where it is subject to 12° of frost during the winter. A moist fibrous peat and loam is indicated. The plant is only suitable for a warm, sheltered spot.

879. PTERYGODIUM HASTATUM, Bolus

Root: a small sessile tuber. **Stem:** slender, flexuous. **Leaves:** cauline, elliptic-oblong or lanceolate-oblong, $1\frac{1}{2}$″–$4\frac{1}{2}$″ long, 2 in number. **Scape:** $\frac{1}{2}$′–1′ tall. **Spike:** 2″–3″ long, lax, many-flowered. **Flowers:** about $\frac{1}{2}$″ across; dorsal sepal elliptic-oblong, very concave; lateral sepals elliptic-ovate, concave, spreading; petals obliquely quadrate-orbicular with a crenulate outer-margin, they cohere with the dorsal sepal into an expanded limb; lip 3-lobed; front lobe oblong; side lobes auriculate, crenulate; appendage 3-lobed, erect; front lobe broadly rhomboid; side lobes smaller. *February and March.*

This is not a very decorative species but should prove interesting in a deep pan in the alpine-house. The blossoms have green sepals and white petals and lip. It grows in rocky ground amidst dwarf herbage in Natal, the Transvaal and the Orange Free State, where it attains its greatest elevation on Mont aux-Sources at 7400 feet and should be quite hardy in Great Britain could it be induced to rest during our winter. A compost of fibrous peat, loam and sand in a moist open sunny spot is indicated.

880. PTERYGODIUM LEUCANTHUM, Bolus

Root: a sessile tuber. **Stem:** moderately slender. **Leaves:** lanceolate or oblong-lanceolate, ½″–3″ long, cauline. **Scape:** ½′–1¼′ tall. **Spike:** 1″–2″ long, of about 9 blossoms. **Flowers:** about ½″ across; dorsal sepal elliptic-oblong, concave; lateral sepals obliquely ovate-oblong, concave, spreading; petals semiorbicular, cohering with the dorsal sepal into an expanded limb; lip transversely-oblong, emarginate or bilobed, very small, broader than long; appendage oblong, bilobed, incurved. *January and February.*

A pretty plant for alpine-house decoration though by no means showy. The sepals are green and the lip and petals white. It grows in rocky, grassy places on very high mountains in Eastern Cape Colony and the Orange Free State, where it probably reaches its greatest elevation on Mopedis Peak, Mont aux-Sources at 8400 feet and, like the previous species, should be perfectly hardy in Great Britain if it could be induced to rest during our winter. A gritty peat and loam is indicated.

881. PTERYGODIUM MAGNUM, Reichb. f.

Corycium magnum, Rolfe

Root: of elongated, stalked tubers. **Stem:** stout, leafy, with short basal sheaths. **Leaves:** cauline, oblong-lanceolate, sessile, sheathing at the base, 4″–9″ long. **Scape:** 2′–2½′ tall. **Spike:** 6″–18″ long, cylindrical, dense. **Flowers:** about ½″ long; dorsal sepal oblong-lanceolate, concave; lateral sepals ovate-lanceolate, subconcave, spreading; petals obliquely suborbicular-oblong, with the outer margin strongly fringed; lip cuneate-obovate or flabellate, fringed at the apex; appendage subtrilobed. *November to January.*

A robust species with very long spikes of green, red-striped blossoms, borne on very stout stems clothed with about half-a-dozen suberect leaves. It grows in moist places amongst grasses on high mountains in Cape Colony,

Griqualand East, Natal, Orange Free State and the Transvaal, where it probably reaches its greatest elevation on Woodbush Mountains at 6500 feet, and is exposed to over 20° of frost during the winter. It should be given a rich fibrous loam in a moist spot in full sun.

882. PTERYGODIUM NIGRESCENS, Schltr.

Corycium nigrescens, Sond.

Root: of oblong, stalked tubers. **Stem:** moderately stout. **Leaves:** cauline, lanceolate, pointed, sheathing at the base, 2″–6″ long, reduced upwards into bracts. **Scape:** $\frac{1}{2}$′–2′ tall. **Spike:** 2″–6″ long, cylindrical, dense. **Flowers:** about $\frac{1}{4}$″ long; dorsal sepal suborbicular, concave, blunt; lateral sepals joined, forming a very concave suborbicular limb; petals obliquely orbicular, deeply saccate, with the outer margin broadly dilated; lip pandurate-oblong, concave; appendage spur-like, on claw of lip.

December and January.

A quaint species with very globular dark brown or dark purple blossoms of but little decorative value; they are rather small and are borne in many-flowered spikes, on stout stems clothed with spreading leaves. It grows in open grassy places, frequently in rocky ground, on high mountains in Cape Colony, Orange Free State, the Transvaal and Natal, where it reaches its greatest elevation on Satsannas Peak at 9200 feet and should therefore be perfectly hardy in Great Britain if it can be induced to rest during the winter. A gritty, fibrous loam in full sun is indicated.

883. PTERYGODIUM TRICUSPIDATUM, Schltr.

Corycium tricuspidatum, Bolus

Root: of oblong, stalked tubers. **Stem:** stout, erect, leafy. **Leaves:** cauline, lanceolate, 2″–3$\frac{1}{2}$″ long. **Scape:** 1$\frac{1}{4}$′ tall. **Spike:** 4″–6″ long, dense. **Flowers:** nearly $\frac{1}{4}$″ long; dorsal sepal broadly ovate, concave; lateral sepals broadly elliptic-oblong, blunt, concave; petals obliquely ovate or suborbicular, very concave, forming with the dorsal sepal a globose galea; lip broadly unguiculate, cuneately 3-lobed; centre lobe narrowly subulate; side lobes oblong-lanceolate, diverging; appendage oblong, small. *February to May.*

This species is of no decorative value; it has very globular, green and brown blossoms in a long dense spike on a stout stem clothed with spreading, dull green leaves. It grows in open grassy places on mountain slopes in Eastern Cape Colony, Griqualand East and Natal, where at Charlestown it probably reaches its greatest elevation of 5000 feet and is subjected to over 15° of frost during its resting period. It should be given a sunny spot in a good moist fibrous loam and is only suitable for outdoor culture in warm localities.

RŒPEROCHARIS, Reichenbach, fils

A small genus numbering 12 species of leafy, deciduous, terrestrial Orchids very closely allied to the *Habenarias*, differing but little from them except in the remarkable construction of the column. Their root-systems are composed of several fairly large fleshy tubers attached to the base of the underground portion of the stem, with some white, thick fibres springing from the stem just above them. They have slender leafy stems clothed with narrow, frequently grass-like, leaves and bear loose or dense many-flowered racemes of small green or white, curiously constructed blossoms, quite interesting but of little or no decorative value. All the species are natives of Africa, the greater number being found in the highlands of Abyssinia, usually in moist or wet places with a subsoil of rock. The following species may be safely tried outdoors in the milder parts of Britain on the banks of streams or ponds. Propagation by imported tubers and by seeds when procurable.

884. RŒPEROCHARIS ALCICORNIS, Kränzl.

Root: an ovoid or globose tuber over ½″ long. **Stem:** about 1′ tall, slender, leafy, clothed with blunt sheaths below. **Leaves:** cauline, linear-lanceolate, pointed, 2″–4″ long. **Spike:** 3½″ long, lax, many-flowered. **Flowers:** about ¼″ across; dorsal sepal very broadly ovate, contracting suddenly to a sharp point; lateral sepals suboblique, semiovate, reflexed, pointed, larger than the dorsal sepal; petals very oblique, cuneate-obovate, pointed, with the outer margins irregularly dentate and undulate; lip narrowly linear, dilated at its base; spur slender, inflated, blunt, recurved at the apex. *August to October.*

A slender leafy plant with narrow leaves and short loose spikes of small yellow blossoms with brown markings. It is found in damp, rocky, grassy places on Mount Guna in Abyssinia at elevations up to 8000 or 9000 feet and should therefore be quite hardy in all but the bleakest parts of Great Britain, in a damp, sandy loam in a sunny spot in the rock garden.

885. RŒPEROCHARIS BENNETTIANA, Reichb. f.

Root: an ovoid-oblong or globose tuber about 1″ long. **Stem:** 1¼′–1½′ long, leafy, sheathed below. **Leaves:** cauline, lanceolate-oblong, suberect, decreasing in length upwards, 3″–4″ long. **Raceme:** about 5″ long, very dense. **Flowers:** about ⅜″ across; dorsal sepal ovate, pointed; lateral sepals oblique semiovate, pointed, suberect; petals broadly ovate, suddenly narrowing near the apex into a falcate-linear appendage; lip 3-lobed; outer lobes narrowly falcate-linear, diverging; centre lobe narrowly elongate-linear; spur subclavate with a bidentate apex, ¼″ long. *October.*

An erect leafy plant with a slender flower-stem and a dense cylindrical raceme of rather small yellowish-green blossoms of no decorative value. It grows in moist grassy places on the mountains of Abyssinia, reaching its greatest elevation on San Meda at 8500 feet, where it is exposed to 15° or more of frost for short periods. It may be tried outdoors in a damp sunny spot in fibrous peat and loam in mild sheltered spots.

886. RŒPEROCHARIS PLATYANTHERA, Reichb. f.

Root: a globose tuber, ½″ long. **Stem:** 1¼′ tall, slender, leafy. **Leaves:** squamiform at the base, linear-lanceolate above, pointed, pressed to the stem, 2″–5″ long. **Spike:** 2″–4″ long, congested. **Flowers:** about ¼″ across; dorsal sepal broadly ovate, rather blunt; lateral sepals obliquely ovate with a contracted apex; petals ovate, narrower than the sepals; lip 3-lobed, with a narrow base; side lobes narrowly linear; diverging centre lobe narrowly linear, slightly curved and bidentate; spur slender, clavate and bidentate at the apex. *July.*

A slender leafy plant bearing a congested, erect spike of small yellowish-green blossoms of but little decorative value. It grows on the banks of streams and other such wet places in the elevated parts of Abyssinia, attaining an elevation of over 8000 feet above sea-level in some of its habitats and is exposed to 12° or 15° of frost. It should be sufficiently hardy for outdoor culture in the more sheltered parts of Great Britain in rich soil on the banks of a stream or pond.

887. RŒPEROCHARIS URBANIANA, Kränzl.

Root: a broadly ovate or subglobose tuber. **Stem:** ½′–1′ tall, slender, with a few leaves about the middle. **Leaves:** oblong or oblong-lanceolate, rather pointed, 1¼″–3″ long. **Raceme:** 1½″–3″ long, lax, many-flowered. **Flowers:** about ⅜″ across; dorsal sepal ovate or ovate-lanceolate, pointed; lateral sepals obliquely ovate, pointed; petals obliquely ovate, rather blunt; lip 3-lobed; outer lobes linear, diverging; centre lobe linear, longer than the outer lobes; spur cylindrical, ½″ long. *August to October.*

An alpine species from an elevation of 10,000 feet on Mount Guna in Abyssinia. It bears long spikes of from eight to fifteen white and green blossoms on a slender flower-stem clothed with from two to four oblong leaves. Although of but little decorative value it should prove attractive in the alpine house. It is quite hardy in Great Britain and should be given a damp sunny spot in fibrous peat and loam.

SACCOLABIUM, Blume

Schænorchis, Blume; **Acampe,** Lindl. **Uncifera,** Lindl.

Dwarf evergreen epiphytes or rarely terrestrial plants with small blossoms which are often beautifully tinted and highly fragrant. The root-system consists of numerous thick fleshy roots from a short, stout stock which bears a tuft of rather narrow leaves either flat or rounded in section. The flower-stems are lateral and bear short, very dense spikes or racemes of small blossoms. The various species are confined to Eastern Asia and the majority of the 230 odd species are found on trees and rocks in the tropical rain-forests of that part of the world. The solitary species which is hardy enough for culture outdoors in the British Isles is a terrestrial plant. Propagation by imported plants and by seeds when procurable.

888. SACCOLABIUM DISTICHUM, Lindl.

Root: of long fleshy fibres. **Stem:** 4″–8″ long, filiform. **Leaves:** lanceolate, pointed, very fleshy, about 1″ long. **Scape:** about as long as the leaves, bearing 2–3 blossoms. **Flowers:** ½″ across; sepals and petals obovate-oblong; lip semicircular with a saccate subhemispherical spur.

May to October.

A dwarf plant of no great decorative value. The slender tufted pendulous or prostrate stems are clothed with dull green, fleshy leaves; the flower-stem bears a few fair-sized blossoms of a pale green colour spotted with purple; they are at times greenish-white. The plant is found on damp moss and fern-clad rocks in Eastern India, Burma and Yunnan, Western China, where it reaches an elevation of 11,000 feet above sea-level. It should be quite hardy in the British Isles in a sheltered shady spot in the rock garden on a moss-covered rock with peat and leaf-soil about its roots.

SARCOCHILUS, R. Brown

Gunnia, Lindl. **Thrixspermum,** Lour.

The majority of the members of this genus of some 140 species are interesting if not very decorative plants; the 3 species which are found sufficiently far south in their range to be included in this work are delightful little plants for alpine-house decoration; they are evergreen epiphytes with long straggling and frequently wiry roots from which springs a tuft of delicate narrow leaves, these are sometimes hooked at the tip. The pretty blossoms are borne in racemes from lateral flower-stems which are often produced in a horizontal manner; each blossom is subtended by a small bract. The members of the genus are spread over the East Indies, New Guinea, Australia and New Zealand, and are found in rain-forests, on the moss-covered branches of trees. They may be tried outdoors in Britain in very mild damp localities on the branches of a moss- or fern-clad tree or on a sandstone rock in peat and sphagnum-moss. Propagation by imported plants and by seeds.

889. SARCOCHILUS ADVERSUS, Hook. f.

Root: wiry, straggling and very long. **Stem:** short. **Leaves:** tufted, linear-oblong, 1″–2″ long, few. **Scape:** 1″–2″ tall, terminal, very slender. **Flowers:** $\frac{1}{10}$″ in diameter, fleshy; sepals ovate-oblong, of about equal length; petals nearly as long as the sepals, linear-oblong, blunt; lip subquadrate, obscurely lobed. *October and November.*

A very tiny leathery-leaved epiphytic with a spike about one inch long, packed with ten or twenty minute yellow-green flowers of no decorative value but interesting on a block of moss-covered wood in the alpine house. It grows on the moss-covered branches of trees in dense humid forests in the North Island of New Zealand and is barely hardy enough for outdoor culture in Great Britain except in the warmest districts such as the humid valleys open to the sea in South Devon and Cornwall, where no doubt it would succeed on moss-grown trees in shade.

890. SARCOCHILUS FITZGERALDII, F. Muell.

Root: of long, fairly stout fibres. **Stem:** from 2″–3″ tall, rather stout, covered with the imbricate base of the leaves. **Leaves:** oblong or falcate, 3″–6″ long. **Raceme:** 6″–12″ long, bearing from 3–4 blossoms. **Flowers:** $\frac{1}{2}$″ across; dorsal sepal and lateral sepals oblong; petals oblong-lanceolate, about the same length as the sepals; lip 3-lobed; side lobes broadly ovate, large; centre lobe very short, broad and almost scale like, with a short, thick, solid spur; disc with a 2-lobed callus between the lateral lobes.

October to December.

A pretty little species with leathery leaves of a rich green colour and short racemes of comparatively large pure white blossoms, spotted with rich crimson or maroon. It grows on the mossy branches of trees in dense forests in New South Wales, reaching its greatest altitude on Mount Warning, where it is exposed to over 12° of frost for short periods during its winter rest. It should be grown on a mossy tree or damp moss-covered rock in a humid shady spot and is only suitable for outdoor culture in the warm Western counties of Britain.

891. SARCOCHILUS PARVIFLORUS, Lindl.

S. Barklyanus, F. Muell. *S. australis*, Lindl. *S. Gunnii*, F. Muell. *Gunnia australis*, Lindl. *Thrixspermum australe*, Reichb. f. *T. parviflorum*, Reichb. f.

Root: of long, fairly stout fibres. **Stem:** very short, under 1″ long, clothed with the bases of fallen foliage. **Leaves:** narrowly-oblong or falcate, thin, 2″–4″ long. **Raceme:** 3″–6″ long, slender, bearing 3–6 blossoms. **Flowers:** about $\frac{1}{2}$″ across; sepals narrowly oblong; petals narrowly oblong, shorter than the sepals; lip 3-lobed; side lobes ovate-oblong, nearly as long as the sepals; centre lobe very small with a thick conical spur $\frac{1}{4}$″ long. *November and December.*

A daintily coloured little species with deep green, rather thin leaves and short racemes of yellowish-green blossoms; the lip is white, tinted with yellow and spotted and streaked with red. It grows in thick forest lands on damp, moss-covered trees and bushes and in dense ravines in the mountains in New South Wales, Victoria and Tasmania and should prove sufficiently hardy for culture outdoor in the warm humid valleys of South-Western Britain on a moss-covered rock or tree in a damp shady spot.

SATYRIDIUM, Lindley

This genus contains but a solitary species, it is a pretty slender plant and is well worth a trial in a damp spot in the rock garden or on the banks of a stream or pond in the milder parts of Britain. Like the majority of the South African Orchids, it has thickened tuberous roots of considerable size, mixed with white fleshy fibres. The flower-stem has a few thin, fairly narrow leaves at its base; the upper part is clothed with several narrow sheaths that take the form of membranous bracts amongst the blossoms which are produced in a dense, many-flowered spike and are delicate and quite pretty. The plant should be grown in a good fibrous soil and should have its roots protected from severe frost during the winter by a covering of bracken or dry leaves. Propagation by imported tubers and by seeds, which are freely produced in its native habitat, as is the case with so many of the tuberous rooted Orchids.

892. SATYRIDIUM ROSTRATUM, Lindl.

Satyrium rhynchanthum, Bolus

Root: of elongate thickened fibres. **Leaves:** basal or sub-basal, oblong or lanceolate, submembranous, rather spreading, 1″–2$\frac{1}{2}$″ long. **Scape:** $\frac{3}{4}$′–1$\frac{3}{4}$′ tall, clothed with numerous lanceolate sheaths. **Spike:** 1″–6″ long, rather dense, many-flowered. **Flowers:** about $\frac{3}{8}$″ across; dorsal sepal oblong, blunt; lateral sepals falcate-oblong, spreading; petals elliptic-oblong, at times minutely toothed at the apex; lip slightly hooded, ovate, beaked at the apex; spur oblong, very stout, blunt, $\frac{1}{4}$″ long. *October to January.*

This plant is very closely related to some members of the genus *Satyrium*. It has rather small blossoms, lilac in ground colour, with a purple spotted lip and a conspicuous carmine anther; they are borne in long spikes on a slender sheath-clothed flower-stem furnished at its base with two or four deep green leaves. It grows in damp or marshy spots in South-Western Cape Colony and probably reaches its greatest altitude above sea-level in Du Toits Kloof in the Worcester Division, where it is exposed to over 12° of frost for short periods during the winter. A good fibrous loam on the banks of a pond is indicated.

SATYRIUM, Swartz

Robust deciduous terrestrial plants with stout crowded spikes of pretty and interesting blossoms. The root system consists of several ovoid or globular tubers with numerous fleshy roots where the stem and tubers join. The larger tuber perishes when it has produced a flower-stem and seed capsules, whilst the smaller tubers gradually increase in size and produce flower-stems. In some species the stout stems are clothed at the base with a few large leaves which frequently lie flat upon the surface of the soil; in other species the leaves are cauline and decrease upwards into bracts which subtend each blossom. The flowers, which are small or medium-sized, are borne in dense many-flowered cylindrical spikes. The various species, which number about 156, are scattered over Southern China, India, Africa and its islands; the greater number of the species are found in South Africa. Many of these robust, strong-growing plants may be tried in damp spots in the rock garden or pond side in the British Isles. Propagation by imported tubers and by seed if available.

893. SATYRIUM APHYLLUM, Schltr.

Root: of globose tubers. **Leaves:** produced on lateral buds at the base of the scape, ovate-oblong, rather pointed, 2″–2½″ long. **Scape:** ¾′–2′ tall, clothed with several imbricate sheaths. **Spike:** 4″–8″ long, lax, many-flowered. **Flowers:** about ⅜″ across; dorsal sepal linear-oblong, blunt; lateral sepals oblong-lanceolate, longer than the dorsal sepal; petals elliptic-oblong, blunt, crenulate, shorter than the dorsal sepal; lip helmet-shaped with a narrow reflexed margin; spur curved, stout, about ¼″ long.

October to January.

The rather small pale yellowish-green blossoms of this species are of no decorative value; they are borne in a long loose spike on a sheath-clothed flower-stem; the leaves, two in number, shrivel before the flowers are perfected. It inhabits marshy spots in Eastern Cape Colony, Tembuland, Griqualand East, Natal and the Transvaal. It probably attains its greatest altitude above sea-level on the Shepstone Berg in the Queenstown Division at 5500 feet and is there exposed to over 20° of frost during the winter when at rest. A good soil on the banks of a pond or stream is indicated.

894. SATYRIUM ATHERSTONEI, Reichb. f.

S. monopelatum, Kränzl. *S. trinerve*, Schltr. *S. triphyllum*, Kränzl.

Root: of ovoid tubers. **Leaves:** cauline, oblong or linear-oblong, rather fleshy, 3″–6″ long. **Scape:** 1′–2′ tall, clothed with 2–3 narrow sheaths. **Spike:** 1″–4½″ long, very dense. **Flowers:** about $\frac{3}{16}$″ across; sepals and petals united to the middle; dorsal sepal oblong, blunt; lateral sepals broadly oblong, blunt, somewhat spreading; petals oblong, blunt; lip ovoid-globose, helmet-shaped, slightly reflexed at the tip; spurs rather stout, curved, ⅛″ long. *October to February.*

A plant of no decorative value with very small white or white and yellow blossoms in fairly long, densely-packed racemes on a tall, slender, sheath-clothed flower-stem furnished with long, deep green foliage. It grows in swamps and damp grassy places in Eastern Cape Colony, Natal and the Transvaal, where at Woodbush Mountains it attains its greatest altitude of 6300 feet and is there exposed to over 12° of frost for fairly long periods during its winter rest. A rich compost on the banks of a pond or a damp spot in the rock garden in full sun is indicated. The plant is only suitable for outdoor culture in warm localities.

895. SATYRIUM BICALLOSUM, Thunb.

Root: of ovoid tubers. **Leaves:** cauline, ovate or ovate-oblong, decreasing upwards into bracts, ¾″–1½″ long. **Scape:** 3″–10″ tall, stout, leafy. **Spike:** 1″–4″ long, dense. **Flowers:** about ¼″ across; dorsal sepal ovate-oblong, blunt; lateral sepals obliquely ovate-oblong, blunt; petals ovate-oblong, blunt; lip galeate with a broadly oblong, blunt, deflexed apex; spurs broadly saccate, minute. *September to January.*

This is a rather dwarf species with dense spikes of small white or yellowish-white blossoms of little or no decorative value. It grows in damp stony places on the mountains of South-Western Cape Colony and probably reaches its greatest altitude above sea-level on the Drakenstein Mountains in the Paarl Division at 4000 feet, where it is subjected to over 12° of frost for short periods during its winter rest. It may be grown in a good moist gritty loam in full sun in a warm sheltered spot.

896. SATYRIUM BIFOLIUM, A. Rich.

Root: of ovoid-oblong tubers up to 1″ long. **Leaves:** basal, 2 in number, suborbicular, horizontal, 2″–4″ across; cauline, 5–7 in number, oblong-lanceolate, sheath-like. **Scape:** 1¼′–1¾′ tall. **Raceme:** 2½″–4½″ long, rather dense. **Flowers:** 1¼″ across; dorsal sepal cuneate-oblong, blunt; lateral sepals broadly-oblong; petals narrowly oblong, united to the sepals at their base; lip galeate, margin reflex, apex broad, blunt, crenulate, erect; spurs linear, $\frac{3}{4}''$ long. *August and September.*

A robust plant with a stout sheath-clothed stem bearing an oblong raceme of rather large hooded blossoms of a greenish-yellow colour. It is found in marshes on the mountains of Abyssinia, where it attains an elevation of over 7000 feet above sea-level and is therefore sufficiently hardy for outdoor culture in Southern Britain on the banks of a pond or stream in a rich, somewhat heavy soil.

897. SATYRIUM BRACHYPETALUM, A. Rich.

Root: an ovoid-oblong tuber, $\frac{1}{2}''$–$\frac{3}{4}''$ long. **Leaves:** cauline, numerous, oblong-lanceolate, rather pointed, degenerating into bracts above and sheaths below, $1\frac{1}{2}''$–3″ long. **Scape:** 1′–$1\frac{1}{2}'$ tall, stout, leafy. **Raceme:** 3″–6″ long, rather dense. **Flowers:** about $\frac{3}{8}''$ across; dorsal sepal linear-oblong, blunt; lateral sepals very broadly oblong; petals linear-oblong, united for about half their length to the sepals; lip galeate, oblong, margin and apex reflexed, base united to the lateral sepals; spurs linear, curved, $\frac{1}{2}''$ long.
August to October.

A rather stout species with long racemes of small half-closed yellowish-green blossoms of little or no decorative value. It grows on mountain sides amongst dwarf herbage in Abyssinia and probably reaches its greatest elevation on Mount Heja at 9000 feet and is therefore quite hardy in Great Britain. It should be grown in a damp spot in the rock garden in sandy loam and peat.

898. SATYRIUM CHLOROCORYS, Reichb. f.

Root: an ovoid or oblong tuber $\frac{3}{4}''$ long. **Leaves:** basal, elliptic or ovate-oblong, rather pointed, $2\frac{1}{2}''$–$4\frac{1}{2}''$ long. **Scape:** $\frac{3}{4}'$–$1\frac{1}{2}'$ tall, clothed near the top with 2–3 lanceolate sheaths. **Raceme:** 3″–5″ long, rather lax. **Flowers:** about $\frac{3}{8}''$ across; dorsal sepal oblong, blunt; lateral sepals broadly oblong; petals spathulate, united for about half their length to the sepals; lip galeate, keeled, sides inflexed near the base, mouth suborbicular above, nearly closed below, apex very broad, slightly reflexed; spurs linear, slightly curved, $\frac{1}{2}''$ long. *August to October.*

The small green blossoms of this species are of but little garden value. It is found in damp places amongst rocks and dwarf herbage on Mount Kilimanjaro in Tanganyika, East Africa, at an elevation of 10,000 feet, so is quite hardy in Great Britain in all but the most exposed localities. It may be grown in damp sandy loam in a sunny spot in the rock garden.

899. SATYRIUM CORDIFOLIUM, Lindl.

Root: an ovoid tuber. **Leaves:** basal, ovate or cordate-orbicular, blunt, 2″–2½″ long. **Scape:** 4″–6″ tall, stout, with at times a few small leaves on it. **Spike:** 1¼″–3″ long, dense. **Flowers:** about ⅝″ long; dorsal sepal, lateral sepals and petals united to the middle almost like a corolla; dorsal sepal, oblong, blunt; lateral sepals falcate-oblong, blunt, much larger than the dorsal sepal; petals oblong, rather blunt, short; lip broadly ovate, cucullate, with a blunt reflexed apex; spur minute. *November to January.*

A very dwarf species suitable for alpine-house culture with dull yellow Lachenalia-like blossoms in a long dense spike on a dwarf, stout flower-stem furnished at its base with two spreading yellowish-green leaves. It grows in damp rocky places on mountains amongst short herbage in Transkei and Eastern Cape Colony, where on the Kat Berg, near its summit, at 5000 feet it probably attains its greatest altitude above sea-level and is exposed to 20° of frost for considerable periods during the winter. A good loam and fibrous peat in an open damp spot is indicated.

900. SATYRIUM CORIOPHOROIDES, A. Rich.

S. macrostachyum, Hochst.

Root: an ovoid-oblong tuber, 1½″ long. **Leaves:** cauline, numerous, oblong-lanceolate, sheathing at the base, decreasing in length upwards, 2″–4″ long. **Scape:** 1½′–2¾′ tall, stout, clothed with 2 or 3 loose sheaths below, very leafy above. **Raceme:** 4″–8″ long, very dense. **Flowers:** about ⅜″ across; dorsal sepal linear-oblong, blunt; lateral sepals broadly oblong; petals linear-oblong, united for about half their length to the lateral sepals; lip galeate, as broad as long, mouth broad with a narrow reflexed margin, apex blunt, basal angle united to the lateral sepals; spurs linear, curved, ½″ long. *July to October.*

Like *S. brachypetalum* this species produces barren leafy shoots beside the flowering ones. It has rather small pale purple blossoms of little decorative value. It grows on the mountains of Abyssinia in damp rocky places at elevations up to 8500 feet and is exposed to 15° or 20° of frost at times, when deciduous. It may be grown in damp loam and peat in a sunny spot in the rock garden.

901. SATYRIUM CRASSICAULE, Rendle

Root: an ovoid-oblong tuber, 1″–1½″ long. **Leaves:** cauline, lanceolate or oblong-lanceolate, ⅓′–1¼′ long. **Scape:** very stout, 2′–3′ tall, clothed with a few leaves. **Raceme:** 4″–9″ long, dense. **Flowers:** about ⅜″ across; dorsal sepal elliptic-oblong, blunt; lateral sepals broadly oblong, spreading;

petals elliptic-oblong, united for a quarter of their length to the sepals; lip galeate, broader than long, mouth broad, apex broadly triangular, somewhat reflexed, the basal third of the lip is united to the lateral sepals; spurs narrow, curved, ½″ long. *June and July.*

A robust plant clothed with a few long leaves and bearing dense spikes of small white and yellow blossoms of little decorative value. It grows in wet sunny places in the open and in marshes on the mountains of the Ruwenzori Range in British East Africa at elevations of from 6000–10,000 feet, so should be quite hardy in all but the bleakest parts of Great Britain, in the rock garden or on the banks of a pond in good loam and peat, with moisture and sunshine.

902. SATYRIUM CRISTATUM, Sond.

S. pentadactylum, Kränzl.

Root: of ovoid tubers. **Leaves:** sub-radical, ovate oblong to broadly elliptic, rather pointed, fleshy, 3″–6″ long. **Scape:** ¾′–1½′ tall, clothed with several sheaths. **Spike:** 2″–6″ long, dense. **Flowers:** about ½″ across; dorsal sepal oblong or elliptic-oblong, blunt; lateral sepals broadly elliptic-oblong; petals oblong or elliptic-oblong, blunt; lip helmet-shaped, broadly elliptic oblong, with a crenulate, reflexed apex; spur stout, curved, about ½″ long. *February and March.*

This species is quite a desirable garden plant with medium-sized white blossoms streaked on their segments with bright red; they are borne in a long narrow spike on a stout sheath-clothed stem, furnished near its base with two or three dull green, fleshy leaves. It is a common, rather variable plant, widely distributed throughout the Eastern part of South Africa in swamps on high ground, and probably attains its greatest altitude above sea-level on the Elands Berg in the Stockenstrom Division at 6000 feet, and should therefore be quite hardy in Britain. A good soil on the banks of a pond in full sun is indicated.

903. SATYRIUM DENSUM, Rolfe

Root: an oblong tuber. **Leaves:** cauline, 2 in number, oblong-lanceolate or obovate-oblong, rather blunt, 6″–7″ long. **Scape:** 2′–2¼′ tall, stout, sheath-clothed. **Raceme:** 7″–9″ long, dense. **Flowers:** about ⅝″ across; dorsal sepal narrowly oblong, reflexed; lateral sepals broadly oblong, spreading; petals narrowly oblong, reflexed, united for about a third of their length to the sepals; lip galeate, subcompressed, broad, mouth rather narrow, apex broadly triangular-ovate, pointed, reflexed; spurs elongate-linear, slightly curved, ¾″ long. *October and November.*

This species bears a very dense spike of fair-sized blossoms of a yellowish-green colour; they are of no great decorative value. It grows in wet places amongst rocks and dwarf herbage on the top of Mount Zomea in British Central Africa at 7000 feet above sea-level and is exposed to over 12° of frost at times during its resting period. A good fibrous loam in a damp sunny spot is indicated.

904. SATYRIUM GOETZENIANUM, Kränzl.

Root: of several rounded or oblong tubers. **Leaves:** few, oblong or lanceolate, decreasing in size upwards, 3″–6″ long. **Scape:** 1′–2½′ tall, stout, sparely leafy. **Spike:** 4″–7″ long, many-flowered. **Flowers:** about ½″ across; sepals and petals obovate-oblong, subequal, fringed with minute hairs on the margin; lip broadly ovate, cucullate, pointed at the apex with a large opening, smooth inside; spurs very slender, small. *August.*

A dainty species with rather small pink and pale yellow flowers in long spikes. It grows in damp rocky soil in open places amongst dwarf shrubs and herbage on the volcano of Kirunga, north of Lake Kivu in the Congo Free State at 9850 feet and should therefore be sufficiently hardy for culture outdoors in the warmer parts of Britain in a damp open spot in the rock garden in peat and fibrous loam with some lumps of sandstone.

905. SATYRIUM HUMILE, Lindl.

Root: of small rounded tubers. **Leaves:** radical, ovate or suborbicular, somewhat blunt, sessile, rather fleshy, 1¼″ long. **Scape:** ½′–¾′ tall, sheath-clothed. **Spike:** 1½″–2½″ long, lax, many-flowered. **Flowers:** about ⅜″ across; dorsal sepal linear-oblong, blunt; lateral sepals oblong or lanceolate, rather spreading; petals linear-oblong, blunt; lip helmet-shaped, ovate-oblong, with a very broad, blunt, reflexed apex; spurs slender, curved, about ⅝″ long. *October to December.*

A dwarf, somewhat stout-stemmed plant with fairly long spikes of rather large yellow or yellowish-green blossoms of no great decorative value. The two spreading, fleshy leaves at the base of the stem are dull green in colour. It grows in moist spots in elevated valleys in South-Western Cape Colony and probably attains its greatest altitude in Du Toits Kloof in the Worcester Division, where it experiences over 12° of frost during its winter rest for short periods. In cultivation it should be grown in a compost of loam and peat in a damp spot fully exposed to the sun. It is only suitable for outdoor culture in warm localities.

906. SATYRIUM LIGULATUM, Lindl.

Root: of fair-sized ovoid tubers. **Leaves:** basal, oblong or ovate-oblong, rather blunt, submembranous, subsessile, 2″–6″ long. **Scape:** 1′–1¾′ tall, stout, clothed with numerous imbricate sheaths. **Spike:** 2″–6″ long, rather dense. **Flowers:** about $\frac{3}{8}''$ across; dorsal sepal lanceolate-oblong, rather blunt; lateral sepals lanceolate with a long, obliquely twisted apex; petals resembling the lateral sepals; lip helmet-shaped, elliptic-ovate, with a broadly triangular reflexed apex; spurs stout, curved, $\frac{1}{4}''$ long.

November and December.

A plant with quaint, curiously constructed pure white blossoms, too small to have any decorative value but sufficiently interesting to justify its culture in a pan in the alpine house. The thin pale green leaves at the base of the stem are two in number. It is found on the edges of swamps, river banks, etc., in Western and Southern Cape Colony and probably reaches its greatest elevation on the Kat Berg in the Stockenstrom Division at 5300 feet and is exposed to 20° or more of frost during the winter. A rich soil on the banks of a pond or stream in full sun is indicated.

907. SATYRIUM LINDLEYANUM, Bolus

S. bracteatum, Lindl.

Root: of ovoid tubers. **Leaves:** cauline, few, ovate or ovate-oblong, pointed, $\frac{3}{4}''$–2″ long, degenerating upwards into bracts. **Scape:** 3″–10″ tall. **Spike:** 1″–4″ long, dense, many-flowered. **Flowers:** about $\frac{1}{4}''$ across; dorsal sepal ovate-oblong, rather blunt; lateral sepals oblong, spreading, blunt; petals ovate-oblong, rather pointed; lip galeate, broadly oval with a reflexed margin; spurs saccate, very minute. *November to January.*

A dwarf species with small but pretty yellowish-white blossoms with brown tips to their lips; they are borne in a long spike on stout stems clothed with a few dull green leaves. The plant is found in damp rocky soil on the mountains in Kloofs in South-Western Cape Colony and probably reaches its greatest elevation above sea-level in Du Toits Kloof in the Worcester Division at 4000 feet, where it is exposed to over 12° of frost for short periods during the winter. A good gritty loam in a damp half-shady spot is indicated. The plant is only suitable for outdoor culture in South-Western Britain.

908. SATYRIUM LONGICAUDA, Lindl.

Root: of ovoid or oblong tubers. **Leaves:** radical, oblong or elliptic-oblong, at times lanceolate, pointed, 3″–8″ long. **Scape:** 1′–1$\frac{3}{4}'$ tall, clothed with numerous imbricate sheaths. **Spike:** $\frac{3}{4}''$–1$\frac{1}{4}''$ long, dense. **Flowers:** about $\frac{1}{2}''$ across; dorsal sepal oblong or linear-oblong, blunt; lateral sepals oblong, spreading; petals oblong or elliptic-oblong, blunt; lip helmet-shaped, elliptic-ovate, tip suborbicular, dentate, reflexed; spurs filiform, curved, short. *January to March.*

A pretty fragrant species with medium-sized white or white pink-tinted blossoms in rather short crowded spikes on stout sheath-clothed flower-stems furnished with a few dull green basal leaves which are at times also produced on short shoots near the base of the flower-stem. It is very widely scattered over the whole of Eastern Cape Colony and probably attains its greatest elevation above sea-level on the moist rocky summits of the Mawahqui Mountain in Natal at 7000 feet and, could it be induced to rest during our winter, should be quite hardy in Great Britain. A good gritty loam in a wet spot in the rock garden is indicated.

909. SATYRIUM LUPULINUM, Lindl.

S. pallidiflorum, Schltr.

Root: of large ovoid tubers. **Leaves:** cauline, ovate or ovate-oblong, subsessile, rather pointed, fleshy, 1″–2¼″ long. **Scape:** ½′–1½′ tall, stout, clothed with several imbricate sheaths. **Spike:** 3″–6″ long, dense. **Flowers:** ⅜″ across; dorsal sepal linear-oblong, blunt; lateral sepals linear-lanceolate, spreading; petals oblong, falcate above the middle, crenulate, blunt; lip helmet-shaped, broadly elliptic-ovate with a broadly triangular, blunt, reflexed tip; spurs slender, curved, ½″ long. *September and October.*

This species is remarkable for the depth of the tint of its rather small blossoms, they vary from tawny yellow to dark brown and are produced in long narrow spikes on sheath-clothed flower-stems furnished near the base with a few fleshy leaves. It grows in damp grassy places both on the mountains and plains of South-Western Cape Colony and reaches its greatest altitude in the Outeniqua Mountains in the George Division at 4000 feet and is exposed to over 12° of frost for short periods during the winter. A good fibrous loam in a damp spot is indicated.

910. SATYRIUM MACROPHYLLUM, Lindl.

Root: of large oblong or ovoid tubers. **Leaves:** subradical, ovate-oblong to broadly elliptic, blunt, rather fleshy, subsessile, 4″–12″ long. **Scape:** 1¼′–2¼′ tall, very stout. **Spike:** 4″–10″ long, somewhat dense. **Flowers:** about ½″ across; dorsal sepal linear, blunt; lateral sepals oblong, shorter than the dorsal sepal; petals linear, blunt; lip helmet-shaped, broadly ovate, with a reflexed tip; spurs slender, curved, 1″ long. *February to May.*

A very robust species with long spikes of pretty pale or deep pink blossoms on a tall sheath-clothed flower-stem with from two to four large deep green leaves near its base. It grows in wet and marshy places both on the mountains and lowlands of Eastern Cape Colony and probably reaches its greatest elevation near Kokstad in Griqualand East at 6000 feet and is there exposed to over 20° of frost during winter for considerable periods; it is also found in Transkei and Natal. It should be grown in a good fibrous loam on the banks of a pond or stream.

911. SATYRIUM MACULATUM, Burch

S. longicolle, Lindl. *S. longicollum*, Drège

Root: of ovoid tubers. **Leaves:** radical, ovate or ovate-orbicular, blunt, sessile, rather fleshy, $1\frac{1}{4}''$–$3''$ long. **Scape:** $\frac{1}{2}'$–$1\frac{1}{2}'$ tall, clothed with numerous imbricate sheaths. **Spike:** $2''$–$6''$ long, dense, or at times lax. **Flowers:** about $\frac{5}{8}''$ across; dorsal sepal oblong, blunt; lateral sepals broadly oblong, blunt, somewhat spreading; petals narrowly oblong, shorter than the sepals; lip helmet-shaped, oblong or ovate-oblong, reflexed at the tip; spurs slender, curved, $1\frac{1}{4}''$ long. *October and November.*

A pretty and desirable plant with medium-sized white or pale pink, purple-spotted blossoms in long spikes on a tall sheath-clothed flower-stem at the base of which two thick, dull green leaves are produced. It grows in damp grassy spots on the mountains and kloofs of Southern Cape Colony and probably attains its greatest elevation above sea-level at Lange Kloof near George in the George Division at 5300 feet and is there subjected to 20° of frost for short periods during the winter. It should be grown in a good loam in a damp spot in full sun.

912. SATYRIUM MAIREI, Schltr.

Root: of ovoid or oblong tubers. **Stem:** $8''$–$10''$ tall, stout, clothed with 2 clasping, lanceolate sheaths. **Leaves:** basal, 2 in number, spreading, oblong or oblong-lanceolate, usually opposite, blunt, smooth, $4''$–$5''$ long. **Raceme:** about $4''$ long, densely many-flowered. **Flowers:** about $\frac{3}{8}''$ across; dorsal sepal narrowly oblong, blunt; lateral sepals oblong, somewhat dilated below on the outer margin; petals narrowly oblong, blunt, oblique, connivent with the sepals forming a galea over the column; lip subglobular and helmet-shaped; spurs cylindrical, pointed, $\frac{3}{16}''$ long. *October.*

A dwarf species with a pair of large leaves at the base of the stout-stem which terminates in a dense cylindrical spike or raceme of small helmet-shaped pink and white blossoms. It is of no great decorative value and is found in a state of nature in mountain meadows in Yunnan, Western China, and should prove hardy in most parts of Great Britain in an open sunny spot in the rock garden, in peat and sandy loam.

913. SATYRIUM MEMBRANACEUM, Sw.

S. cucullatum, Thunb.

Root: a large ovoid tuber. **Leaves:** radical, orbicular, blunt, rather fleshy, $1\frac{1}{2}''$–$4''$ long. **Scape:** $\frac{3}{4}'$–$1\frac{1}{2}'$ tall, stout, clothed with numerous lanceolate sheaths. **Spike:** $3''$–$8''$ long, dense. **Flowers:** about $\frac{5}{8}''$ across; dorsal sepal oblong, pointed; lateral sepals broadly oblong, spreading; petals oblong, blunt, margin fringed; lip broadly helmet-shaped with a reflexed, fringed apex; spurs slender, curved, 1″ long. *September to December.*

A delightful species with fringed, pink blossoms of fair size in a crowded spike on a stout flower-stem; the flowers are thin in texture. The plant is a native of Eastern Cape Colony, where it grows in damp shady places amongst rocks; it probably attains its greatest altitude on the northern slopes of the Kat Berg in the Queenstown Division at 5300 feet, where it is exposed to over 20° of frost for short periods when deciduous. A moist gritty peat with some fibrous loam, in half-shade, is indicated. *See Plate 20 facing page 387.*

914. SATYRIUM MICRORRHYNCHUM, Schltr.

Root: of rather small ovoid tubers. **Leaves:** radical, broadly ovate, nearly opposite, 2″–3″ long. **Scape:** about 9″ tall, clothed with a few lanceolate sheaths near the base. **Spike:** about 3″ long, dense. **Flowers:** about $\frac{3}{16}$″ across; dorsal sepal linear-oblong, blunt; lateral sepals linear-lanceolate; petals linear-oblong, shorter than the sepals; lip galeate, with a somewhat reflexed, blunt tip; spurs very short, minute. *February.*

An alpine plant with very small, half-closed white or greenish-white blossoms of no decorative value; they are borne in a long spike on a slender stem clothed towards its base with a few spatha-like sheaths. It is confined to the summit of Mont aux-Sources in the Orange Free State at 11,000 feet, where it grows in damp spots amongst short grass and heaths, it is exposed to a zero F. temperature for considerable periods in its native habitat during its resting period and may be grown in fibrous loam and peat with plenty of grit in a damp sunny spot.

915. SATYRIUM MYSTACIUM, Kränzl.

Root: of several subglobular or ovoid tubers. **Leaves:** few in number, scattered up the stem, lanceolate, pointed, decreasing upwards into bracts, 2″–5″ long. **Scape:** 1′–2½′ tall, stout, leafy. **Spike:** 3″–7″ long, many-flowered, somewhat lax. **Flowers:** $\frac{3}{8}$″ across; dorsal sepal ligulate, blunt; lateral sepals ovate-oblong with cartilaginous apex and minutely hairy margins; petals nearly similar to the lateral sepals only smaller; lip deeply cucullate, narrowed into the spurs and keeled, margins minutely hairy; spur ½″ long.
August and September.

A pretty though small-flowered plant of rose-coloured blossoms with brown-tinted lateral sepals and petals. It is found in damp rocky places on Mount Ruwenzori in British East Africa at 8500 feet above sea-level and may be tried outdoors in the warmer parts of Britain in a damp open spot in the rock garden in moist loam and peat.

916. SATYRIUM NEGLECTUM, Schltr.

Root: of large ovoid or globose tubers. **Leaves:** on short branches at the base of the flowering stem, elliptic-oblong, rather pointed, blunt, with 2–3 short sheaths below, 6″–12″ long. **Scape:** $1\frac{1}{4}'$–$2\frac{1}{2}'$ tall, very stout, clothed with numerous imbricate sheaths. **Spike:** 6″–12″ long, dense. **Flowers:** about $\frac{3}{8}''$ across; dorsal sepal linear-oblong, blunt; lateral sepals broadly oblong, spreading; petals elliptic-oblong, blunt; lip helmet-shaped, broadly elliptic-ovate, with a broadly orbicular-oblong, crenulate, reflexed apex; spurs slender, curved, $\frac{3}{4}''$ long. *January.*

A very robust species with a long, narrow spike of small, rather pretty pink or carmine-rose blossoms on an unusually stout fleshy stem; the leaves which are two in number are of a deep green colour. It is found on moist mountain slopes in grass and short herbage in Griqualand East, Natal, Orange Free State and the Transvaal, where it attains its greatest altitude on Woodbush Mountains at 6400 feet and is there exposed to 20° of frost for short periods in the winter. A moist fibrous loam in full sun is indicated.

917. SATYRIUM NEPALENSE, Don

S. albiflorum, A. Rich. *S. pallidum,* A. Rich. *S. Perrottetianum,* A. Rich.

Root: an ovoid tuber, frequently large. **Stem:** $\frac{1}{2}'$–$2\frac{1}{2}'$ tall, usually very stout, sheathed above. **Leaves:** few, from oblong to linear-oblong, rather fleshy, sessile, sheathing at the base, $\frac{1}{4}'$–$\frac{3}{4}'$ long. **Spike:** 3″–6″ long, dense, many-flowered. **Flowers:** about $\frac{5}{8}''$ across; dorsal sepal narrowly oblong, recurved; lateral sepals linear-oblong, spreading; petals almost linear; lip broadly oblong, concave, with a pronounced keel on the back; spurs usually stout, about $\frac{3}{4}''$ long. *September.*

A variable species with fairly long spikes of pretty fragrant blossoms varying in colour from deep pink to white. In a large clump it is very decorative. It grows in a variety of situations, usually in moist grassy spots in fairly open country, in the highlands of India, China, and Burma, reaching an elevation of 14,000 feet in the Himalaya; plants collected from such an altitude are quite hardy in Great Britain in a good rich moist soil in the rock garden. Var. *ciliata,* Lindl., is a small form with short spurs.

918. SATYRIUM OCELLATUM, Bolus

S. rostratum, Krauss. *S. nutans,* Kränzl.

Root: of fair-sized ovoid tubers. **Leaves:** basal, oblong-lanceolate, pointed, rather fleshy, 3″–6″ long. **Scape:** $1'$–$2\frac{1}{2}'$ tall, clothed with several lanceolate sheaths. **Spike:** 3″–6″ long, many-flowered. **Flowers:** about

$\frac{3}{8}$″ across; dorsal sepal oblong or linear oblong, blunt; lateral sepals broadly oblong, spreading at the tip; petals linear-oblong, blunt, united to the sepals for about half their length; lip helmet-shaped, obovate-elliptic, with a narrow, pointed apex; spurs 1″ long. *August to February.*

A strong-growing species with a long spike of medium-sized white or pale pink blossoms borne on a stout, fleshy, sheath-clothed stem furnished with three or four dull green leaves at its base. It is very widely scattered in mountain marshes and lowland swamps in Eastern South Africa, probably attaining its greatest altitude on Woodbush Mountains in the Transvaal at 6500 feet, where it is exposed to over 20° of frost during the winter. A rich soil on the banks of a pond or stream is indicated.

919. SATYRIUM PARVIFLORUM, Sw.

S. cassideum, Lindl. *S. densiflorum*, Lindl. *S. eriostomum*, Lindl. *S. lydenburgense*, Reichb. f. *S. parviflorum* var. *Schimperi*, Schltr. *S. tenuifolium*, Kränzl. *Diplecthrum parviflorum*, Pers.

Root: of ovoid tubers. **Leaves:** subradical, broadly ovate or elliptic-oblong, rather fleshy, 3″–8″ long. **Scape:** 1′–2$\frac{1}{2}$′ tall, stout, sheath-clothed, the lower ones leaf-like. **Spike:** 4″–8″ long, dense. **Flowers:** about $\frac{1}{4}$″ across; dorsal sepal spathulate-oblong, blunt; lateral sepals falcate-oblong, blunt; petals spathulate-oblong, united to the middle with the sepals; lip helmet-shaped, broadly ovoid or obovate globose, margin and apex reflexed and crenulate; spurs curved, at times diverging, about $\frac{1}{2}$″ long. *September to November.*

A species of no decorative value, with small green or yellowish-green blossoms in long spikes on a sheath-clothed flower-stem furnished at its base with two to four spreading, dull green leaves. It is a common plant in moist situations over nearly the whole of South Africa, reaching its greatest altitude on Woodbush Mountains in the Transvaal at 7000 feet and should be quite hardy in Britain. A rich soil on the banks of a pond is indicated.

920. SATYRIUM PLAUDICOLA, Schltr.

Root: of ovoid tubers. **Leaves:** radical, broadly ovate or orbicular, rather pointed, 1$\frac{1}{4}$″–3″ long. **Scape:** about 6″ tall, slender. **Spike:** 2″–2$\frac{3}{4}$″ long, dense. **Flowers:** about $\frac{1}{4}$″ across; dorsal sepal lanceolate, blunt; lateral sepals oblique, falcate-ovate, rather pointed; petals oblong, rather pointed, united to the sepals for about half their length; lip helmet-shaped, ovate, with a keel beneath, and a revolute, blunt apex; spurs saccate, short. *December.*

A dwarf and slender plant with a fairly long, dense spike of small white or pink blossoms. The two bright green leaves are borne at the base of the stem. It should make an interesting little plant in a pan in the alpine house. It grows on the marshy banks of rivers in the Transvaal and probably reaches its greatest elevation above sea-level on the banks of the Little Olifant River at 5000 feet, where it is exposed to over 15° of frost during the winter. A rich soil on the banks of a stream or pond is indicated, in a warm, sheltered spot.

921. SATYRIUM PYGMÆUM, Sond.

Root: of small globose tubers. **Leaves:** radical, ovate, sessile, rather pointed, somewhat membranous, $\frac{3}{4}''$–$1\frac{3}{4}''$ long. **Scape:** 3″–7″ tall, clothed with numerous ovate, amplexicaul, acute sheaths. **Spike:** 1″–3″ long, lax, many-flowered. **Flowers:** about $\frac{1}{4}''$ across; dorsal sepal oblong, blunt; lateral sepals very broadly oblong; petals ovate-oblong, blunt; lip helmet-shaped, broadly ovate, blunt, slightly crenulate; spurs stout, curved, $\frac{1}{4}''$ long. *October and November.*

This little species cannot lay claim to any great decorative value but should prove interesting in the alpine house; it has small greenish-yellow blossoms with the segments and spurs tipped red. The two leaves are bright green in colour. It is confined to moist mountain slopes and kloofs in Southern and Western Cape Colony and probably reaches its greatest elevation above sea-level on the Winterhoek Mountains in the Tulbagh Division at 4000 feet and is there exposed to over 12° of frost for short periods during the winter. A fibrous loam in a damp spot is indicated. Suitable for culture outdoors in mild localities only.

922. SATYRIUM SACCULATUM, Rolfe

S. coriophoroides var. *sacculata*, Rendle

Root: an ovoid or oblong tuber. **Leaves:** basal, broadly oblong, blunt, 3″–5″ long. **Scape:** about $2\frac{1}{2}'$ tall, clothed with numerous ovate-lanceolate sheaths. **Raceme:** about 3″ long, many-flowered. **Flowers:** about $\frac{1}{4}''$ across; dorsal sepal linear-oblong; lateral sepals broadly oblong; petals linear-oblong, united to the sepals for about half their length; lip galeate, as broad as long, with a narrow mouth, inflexed margins and incurved apex; spurs linear-oblong, nearly straight; basal angle of the galea with a pair of additional spurs in front of the normal ones. *July to September.*

A robust species with a long narrow spike of small green and yellow blossoms of no horticultural value. It is found in bogs and wet places in moss on the Ruwenzori Range in British East Africa at 10,000 feet, and is therefore quite hardy in this country in a sunny spot in the bog garden in peat and sphagnum-moss.

923. SATYRIUM SCHIMPERI, Hochst.

Root: of oblong or ovoid-globose tubers nearly 1″ long. **Leaves:** cauline, 2 in number, ovate-oblong, rather blunt, 2″–3″ long. **Scape:** ½′–1′ tall, sheath-clothed above and below. **Raceme:** 2″–3″ long, lax. **Flowers:** about ⅜″ across; dorsal sepal oblong, blunt; lateral sepals broadly oblong, blunt; petals oblong, united to the sepals for about half their length; lip galeate, subcompressed, keeled, basal half united to the lateral sepals, mouth oblong, apex with a very short broad blade, reflexed; spurs linear, curved, ¼″ long. *October and November.*

A dwarf species with a fairly long raceme of small yellowish-green blossoms of little or no horticultural value. It grows in damp and marshy places on the mountains of Abyssinia, reaching an elevation of 8500 feet on Debra Tabor and is there exposed to over 15° of frost for considerable periods. It may be grown in a damp or boggy spot in the rock garden in peat and loam.

924. SATYRIUM SETCHUENICUM, Kränzl.

Root: of ovoid tubers. **Stem:** 15″–20″ tall, stout. **Leaves:** ovate-oblong, pointed, erect, 6″–8″ long. **Scape:** clothed with large sheaths. **Spike:** 3″–4″ long, densely many-flowered. **Flowers:** about ⅜″ long; dorsal sepal oblong, blunt; lateral sepals oblong, suboblique; petals ovate-oblong, blunt; lip cucullate, almost closed at the mouth; spurs minute. *August and September.*

A tall, somewhat stout species with pretty rose-pink fragrant blossoms in long dense spikes. It is a decorative and desirable species and inhabits dry elevated grassland and grows on humus-covered boulders and mountain slopes in Szechuan and Yunnan at elevations up to 11,000 feet above sea-level. It should therefore be quite hardy in Great Britain in a well-drained spot in the rock garden in leaf-soil, loam and sand.

925. SATYRIUM SPECIOSUM, Rolfe

S. Buchananii, Rolfe

Root: an oblong tuber, ¾″–1″ long. **Leaves:** cauline, broadly elliptic-oblong or ovate-oblong, rather pointed, 3″–6″ long. **Scape:** 1¾′–2′ tall, clothed with 2–3 leaves near the middle, sheath-clothed above and below. **Raceme:** 4″–7″ long, usually many-flowered. **Flowers:** about ¾″ across; dorsal sepal oblong-lanceolate, blunt; lateral sepals broadly lanceolate, spreading; petals oblong-lanceolate, united for half their length to the sepals; lip galeate, subcompressed, mouth rather narrow, tip broadly ovate, reflexed, the base is united to the lateral sepals for a quarter of its length; spurs narrow, curved, ½″ long. *September to November.*

A tall plant with a long raceme of deep red blossoms of considerable decorative value. It is found in wet places and on the banks of rivulets in the highlands of British Central Africa and reaches its greatest elevation above sea-level on the top of Mount Zomba at 7000 feet, and is sufficiently hardy for culture outdoors in the warmer parts of Great Britain in good soil on the banks of a stream or pond.

926. SATYRIUM SPHÆROCARPUM, Lindl.

S. militare, Lindl. *S. beyrichianum*, Kränzl.

Root: of ovoid tubers. **Leaves:** subradical, ovate oblong or elliptic-oblong, rather pointed, 2″–6″ long. **Scape:** 1′–1¾′ tall, clothed with a few large sheaths. **Spike:** 2″–8″ long, dense. **Flowers:** nearly ¾″ long; sepals united to nearly the middle; dorsal sepal lanceolate-oblong; lateral sepals broadly oblong; petals lanceolate-oblong; lip helmet-shaped, broadly elliptic-ovate, apex reflexed; spurs, stout, curved, ½″ long. *November to February.*

A handsome, comparatively large-flowered species bearing, on a rather stout sheath-clothed flower-stem, a long, closely packed spike of white blossoms blotched and suffused with bright red. The leaves are rather fleshy, two to four in number, dull green in colour. It is usually found in moist places in open situations in Eastern Cape Colony, Natal and Griqualand East, where, near Kokstad, at 4800 feet it probably reaches its greatest elevation and is exposed to over 15° of frost for considerable periods. A good fibrous loam in a damp sunny spot is indicated.

927. SATYRIUM WILMSIANUM, Kränzl.

Root: of small ovoid tubers. **Leaves:** radical, elliptic-oblong, rather pointed, 1½″–2″ long. **Scape:** 4″–6″ tall, clothed with 2 membranous sheaths. **Spike:** 1″–1½″ long, lax, few-flowered. **Flowers:** about ⅜″ across; dorsal sepal spathulate-oblong, blunt; lateral sepals oblong, blunt, twice as large as the dorsal sepal; petals spathulate-oblong, united to the sepals for about half their length; lip helmet-shaped, broadly ovoid or obovate-globose, with the apex and margin reflexed and crenulate; spurs slender, curved, about ¾″ long. *April.*

A very dwarf species of little or no decorative value, with small yellowish-green blossoms from four to eight in number in a loose spike on a slender flower-stem with two rounded, membranous leaves at its base. It is found in damp rocky soil near Lydenburg in the Transvaal at 5600 feet and is exposed to over 15° of frost during the winter for considerable periods. A good gritty loam in full sun is indicated.

928. SATYRIUM WOODII, Schltr.

Root: of large ovoid tubers. **Leaves:** radical or on short lateral stems at the base of the flowering stem, oblong or elliptic, rather blunt, 4″–6″ long. **Scape:** $1\frac{1}{4}'$–$1\frac{3}{4}'$ tall, clothed with numerous imbricate sheaths. **Spike:** 3″–6″ long, dense. **Flowers:** about $\frac{5}{8}''$ across; dorsal sepal linear-oblong, blunt; lateral sepals broadly oblong, blunt, rather spreading; petals elliptic-oblong, blunt; lip helmet-shaped, broadly elliptic-ovate with a reflexed, pointed apex; spurs slender, curved, about $\frac{3}{4}''$ long. *October to December.*

A showy desirable species with medium-sized pink or orange-red blossoms in a long somewhat crowded spike on a sheath-clothed flower-stem. It inhabits marshes in the open, and in open spots in woods in Natal and the Orange Free State, where, in the Harrismith district, it attains an elevation of 6500 feet above sea-level and is there exposed to over 20° of frost for short periods during its winter rest. A good rich soil on the banks of a stream or pond is indicated.

929. SATYRIUM YUNNANENSE, Rolfe

Root: of 2 ovoid-oblong tubers about $\frac{3}{4}''$ long. **Stem:** 6″–10″ tall, fairly stout, sheath-clothed. **Leaves:** 2, basal, ovate or ovate-oblong, blunt, spreading, opposite, sessile, 2″–4″ long. **Raceme:** $1\frac{1}{2}''$–$2\frac{1}{2}''$ long, ovoid-oblong, densely many-flowered. **Flowers:** about $\frac{1}{2}''$ across; dorsal sepal oblong, blunt; lateral sepals ovate-oblong, blunt, rather spreading; petals elliptic-oblong, blunt; lip hood-like, rounded; spurs linear-oblong, rather blunt, $\frac{3}{16}''$ long. *September.*

A pretty and desirable species having a stoutish sheath-clothed stem with two large leaves at its base and an oblong spike of numerous bright orange-coloured blossoms. It is found in moist rocky places in Yunnan, Western China, at elevations of from 7000–10,000 feet above sea-level and should prove quite hardy in Great Britain in all but the most exposed spots, in a damp stony loam in full sun.

930. SATYRIUM ZOMBENSE, Rolfe

Root: an oblong tuber about 1″ long. **Leaves:** cauline, 4 in number, oblong-lanceolate, pointed. **Scape:** $1\frac{1}{4}'$–$1\frac{1}{2}'$ tall, sheath-clothed. **Raceme:** 2″–4″ long, many-flowered. **Flowers:** nearly $\frac{1}{2}''$ across; dorsal sepal narrowly oblong, blunt; lateral sepals broadly oblong, spreading, blunt; petals narrowly oblong, united for about half their length to the sepals; lip galeate, mouth broad and open, apex very broad and truncate, slightly reflexed; spurs linear-oblong, $\frac{1}{4}''$ long. *September to November.*

This species has fairly stout stems clothed with a few sheaths and four leaves below. The blossoms, which are purple and yellow in colour, are produced in oblong racemes and are rather pretty. It grows in marshes and bogs on the top of Mount Zomba in British Central Africa at an elevation of 7000 feet above sea-level and is sufficiently hardy for culture outdoors in the warmer parts of Great Britain in the bog garden in peat and sphagnum-moss.

SCHIZOCHILUS, Rolfe

This genus of deciduous, terrestrial plants numbers about 14 species, with small blossoms in one-sided racemes. They are pretty and worth growing although by no means showy. Their roots are composed of several oblong or ovoid tubers on the base of the underground portion of the stem, with a few short, fleshy fibres above them; they are annual inasmuch as they perish after flowering. The flower-stems are usually sheath-clothed, although they are at times well furnished with narrow leaves which gradually diminish in size until they mingle with the blossoms in the form of bracts. The flowers are delicately perfumed in some of the species. The members of the genus are confined to Rhodesia, Transvaal, Orange Free State, Natal and Cape Colony; several are hardy enough for experimental culture outdoors in many parts of Britain in the rock-garden in a light moist soil. Propagation by imported tubers and by seeds from their native habitat.

931. SCHIZOCHILUS ANGUSTIFOLIUS, Rolfe

Root: of ovoid tubers. **Leaves:** radical, narrowly linear, $1\frac{1}{2}''$–$3''$ long, pointed. **Scape:** about 6″ tall, clothed with 3–5 narrow sheaths. **Raceme:** $\frac{1}{2}''$–$1''$ long, oblong or subcapitate, broad, dense. **Flowers:** about $\frac{3}{16}''$ across; sepals ovate or ovate-oblong, 3-nerved, rather blunt; petals broadly ovate, minute, 1-nerved; lip 3-lobed, rather downy; side lobes broadly rounded or rather ovate, blunt; centre lobe broadly oblong, blunt, twice as long as the side lobes; disc 3-nerved; spur broadly oblong, blunt, minute.

November to January.

The blossoms of this species are too small to have any decorative value, but it should prove interesting in a pan in the alpine house. The whole blossom is usually pure white, although at times the lip is bright yellow. It grows in open grassy spots on elevated plains near Harrismith in the Orange Free State at over 6000 feet and is subjected to over 20° of frost for short periods during its winter rest. It may be grown in a damp spot in full sun in a good fibrous loam.

932. SCHIZOCHILUS BULBINELLA, Bolus

S. Burchellii, Ind. Kew. *Brachycorythis Bulbinella*, Reichb. f. *Platanthera Bulbinella*, Schltr.

Root: of 2 ovoid tubers. **Leaves:** radical or subradical, linear or linear-oblong, rather pointed, 2″–3½″ long. **Scape:** ½′–1′ tall, clothed with about 6 lanceolate sheaths. **Raceme:** 1″–1¾″ long, oblong, rather broad. **Flowers:** about $\frac{3}{16}$″ across; sepals broadly ovate, rather blunt, 3-nerved; petals broadly ovate, rather blunt, 1-nerved; lip as long as the sepals, obscurely or shortly 3-lobed, slightly downy; side lobes rounded or very blunt and very short; centre lobe oblong or ovate-oblong, rather blunt; disc with 3 nerves or obscure keels at the base; spur saccate, very minute. *December and January.*

Although the blossoms of this little plant are very small, their bright golden-yellow colouring gives the species some decorative value. It grows in stony places on hills and mountains in the Transvaal, Transkei and Griqualand East, where it reaches its greatest altitude on Mount Currie at 6500 feet and is exposed to over 20° of frost during the winter. A gritty fibrous loam in half-shade is indicated.

933. SCHIZOCHILUS FLEXUOSUS, Harv.

Root: of 2 ovoid tubers. **Leaves:** radical or subradical, linear or linear-oblong, 1½″–3″ long, rather pointed. **Scape:** ¾′–1′ long, somewhat flexuous, clothed with 4–6 lanceolate sheaths. **Raceme:** ½″–1½″ long, oblong or sub-capitate, somewhat recurved, dense. **Flowers:** about ⅜″ across; sepals ovate or ovate-oblong, rather blunt, 3-nerved; petals broadly ovate, rather pointed, 1-nerved; lip 3-lobed, rather downy; outer lobes falcate-ovate, rather blunt; inner lobe linear-oblong, rather blunt, twice as long as the side lobes; disc with 3 minute tubercles at the base; spur cylindrical, blunt, about $\frac{3}{16}$″ long. *November.*

The blossoms of this plant are much larger than those of the preceding species; they are pure white but are not of sufficient size to give the plant much decorative value. It grows amongst short grasses on dry hillsides in Natal, and probably reaches its greatest elevation on hills near Liddesdale at 4000 feet, where it is exposed to 12° of frost during the winter for short periods. A gritty fibrous loam in full sun is indicated. The plant is only suitable for culture in warm spots.

934. SCHIZOCHILUS GERRARDII, Bolus

Brachycorythis Gerrardii, Reichb. f. *Platanthera Gerrardii*, Schltr.

Root: of ovoid tubers. **Leaves:** radical or subradical, narrowly linear, pointed, ¾″–2½″ long. **Scape:** ⅓′–¾′ tall, clothed with about 6 narrow sheaths.

Raceme: 1″–3″ long, elongate, narrow, dense. **Flowers:** about $\frac{3}{16}$″ across; sepals ovate, somewhat concave, rather blunt, 3-nerved; petals suborbicular or broadly ovate, 1-nerved; lip shortly 3-lobed, rather fleshy and somewhat downy; side lobes semiovate or broadly rounded, blunt; centre lobe ovate or ovate-oblong, twice as long as the side lobes; disc with 3 fleshy tubercles below the middle; spur oblong, minute. *December to March.*

The tiny white blossoms of this species have no decorative value. It is dwarf enough for culture in a pan in the alpine house. In its native habitat it grows in rather dry stony places on mountain slopes in Griqualand East and the Transvaal, where on the Devil's Knuckles, near Spitz Kop in the Lydenburg district, at 6000 feet it is exposed to 20° of frost for short periods during the winter. A gritty fibrous loam in full sun is indicated.

935. SCHIZOCHILUS REHMANNII, Rolfe

Root: of oblong tubers. **Leaves:** radical or subradical, linear or linear-oblong, rather pointed, 1½″–5″ long. **Scape:** 1′–1½′ tall, clothed with 3–5 narrow sheaths. **Raceme:** 1″–3″ long, oblong, rather lax. **Flowers:** about ⅜″ across; sepals oblong, blunt, 3-nerved; petals narrowly ovate-oblong, pointed, 1-nerved; lip 3-lobed, downy; outer lobes falcate-ovate, rather blunt; centre lobe oblong, twice as long as the side lobes; disc with 3 prominent tubercles at the base; spur cylindrical, blunt, ¼″ long.
November to March.

The wand-like racemes of orange-coloured blossoms of this species though small have some claim to decorative value. It grows in stony places amongst short herbage in the Transvaal and probably reaches its greatest altitude on Woodbush Mountains at 7000 feet and is exposed to over 20° of frost for short periods during the winter months when it is deciduous. It should be grown in a damp spot fully exposed to the sun in fibrous loam.

936. SCHIZOCHILUS STRICTUS, Rolfe

Platanthera Zeyheri, Schltr.

Root: of oblong tubers. **Leaves:** radical, linear-oblong, rather pointed, 2″–3″ long. **Scape:** about 12″ tall, clothed with about half-a-dozen narrow sheaths. **Raceme:** 1″–1½″ long, dense, recurved. **Flowers:** about ⅜″ across; sepals ovate-oblong or ovate-lanceolate, 3-nerved; petals ovate-oblong, pointed, half as long as the sepals; lip 3-lobed, downy; outer lobes falcate-oblong, rather pointed; centre lobe linear-oblong, rather blunt, longer than the outer lobes; disc with a narrowly oblong tubercle at its base; spur cylindrical. *December to February.*

A rather pretty species with small, bright yellow blossoms in a fairly long, dense raceme on a sheath-clothed flower-stem springing from a tuft of from five to eight bright green, grass-like leaves. It grows in damp and marshy spots in the Transvaal and probably reaches its greatest elevation near the Klein Olifants River at 6000 feet, where it is exposed to 20° or more of frost during its winter rest. It should be grown in moist fibrous loam and should do well beside a pond or stream.

937. SCHIZOCHILUS TRANSVAALENSIS, Rolfe

Root: of ovoid tubers. **Leaves:** radical, linear or linear-oblong, $1\frac{1}{4}''$–$3''$ long. **Scape:** $\frac{3}{4}'$–$1\frac{1}{2}'$ tall, somewhat flexuous, clothed with narrow sheaths which closely clasp the stem. **Raceme:** $1\frac{1}{2}''$–$3\frac{1}{2}''$ long, rather dense, elongate. **Flowers:** about $\frac{3}{8}''$ across; sepals ovate or ovate-oblong, rather blunt, 3-nerved; petals broadly ovate, 1-nerved, two-thirds as long as the sepals; lip shortly 3-lobed, rather fleshy and downy; outer lobes semiovate or broadly rounded, blunt; centre lobe ovate or triangular-ovate, three times as long as the outer lobes; disc with 3 fleshy tubercles at the base; spur conical, very minute.

December and January.

The long dense spikes of pure white blossoms although small are decidedly pretty on their flexuous sheath-clothed stems rising from the centre of a tuft of about half-a-dozen rich green, grassy leaves. It grows in marshy places in the Transvaal and probably reaches its greatest elevation near Lydenburg at 5000 feet, where it is exposed to over 15° of frost for short periods during the winter. A good soil beside a pond is indicated.

938. SCHIZOCHILUS ZEYHERI, Sond.

Brachycorythis Zeyheri, Reichb. f. *Platanthera Zeyheri*, Schltr.

Root: of ovoid tubers, 2 in number. **Leaves:** radical and subradical, linear or linear-oblong, $1''$–$4\frac{1}{2}''$ long. **Scape:** $\frac{1}{2}'$–$1\frac{1}{4}'$ tall, clothed with about half-a-dozen lanceolate sheaths. **Raceme:** $\frac{3}{4}''$–$2''$ long, rather dense, somewhat broad. **Flowers:** nearly $\frac{1}{2}''$ across; sepals ovate-oblong, prominently 3-nerved; petals narrowly ovate, half as long as the sepals, 1-nerved; lip 3-lobed, downy, as long as the sepals; outer lobes falcate-ovate, blunt; centre lobe linear-oblong, twice as long as the side lobes; disc with a small erect tubercle at its base; spur cylindrical or subcompressed, oblong.

December to March.

A pretty species with tall sheath-clothed flower-stems terminating in a dense, rather broad raceme of yellow blossoms which at times vary to porcelain-white with a yellow lip; the leaves, three to eight in number, are of a bright green colour. It grows in marshes on the summits of high mountains in the Transvaal, Orange Free State, Natal and Cape Colony, where on the Elands Berg at 6000 feet in the Stockenstrom Division it is exposed to a zero F. temperature during the winter for short periods. A good soil beside a pond is indicated.

SCHIZODIUM, Lindley

Dainty little deciduous, terrestrial Orchids numbering about 15 species, all of which are confined to the south-western corner of Cape Colony, where they are found in open spots amongst short herbage, frequently at considerable elevations in the mountains. The root system consists of oblong or ovoid, somewhat irregular tubers at the base of the underground portion of the stem, which is slender and frequently flexuous. The leaves are produced in a spreading tuft at the base of the stem and are mostly spathulate or elliptic-ovate. The floral bracts are generally ovate-lanceolate and the blossoms are borne in short, usually lax racemes and although they are on the small side the plants are well worth growing and should prove very attractive in the alpine house in pans of fibrous loam and peat with plenty of sand; they may also be tried in the rock garden in the same compost in a fairly damp sunny spot. Propagation by imported roots and also by seeds which are freely set in nature.

939. SCHIZODIUM CLAVIGERUM, Lindl.

S. bifidum var. *clavigerum*, Schltr. *Disa clavigera*, Bolus

Root: an oblong tuber. **Stem:** slender, flexuous. **Leaves:** radical, spathulate, about ½″ long. **Spike:** lax, of 4 or less blossoms. **Flowers:** ¼″ across; dorsal sepal elliptic-oblong, erect; spur clavate or subclavate, blunt, 3⁄16″ long; lateral sepals oblong; petals narrowly oblong, shortly bifid at the apex with a rounded basal lobe in front; lip pandurate-oblong, concave at the base. *September.*

This species is more suited to the alpine house than the garden, where its small, flesh-pink, carmine-spotted blossoms would make but little show. It grows in rocky ground amidst short herbage in South-Western Cape Colony and probably reaches its greatest elevation near Lowry's Pass in the Stellenbosch Division at 6000 feet, and should be perfectly hardy in Great Britain if it could be induced to change its resting period to our winter. It should be given a gritty loam in full sun in a damp spot.

940. SCHIZODIUM OBTUSATUM, Lindl.

S. bifidum, Schltr.

Root: an oblong tuber. **Stem:** slender, flexuous. **Leaves:** radical, spathulate, about ½″ long. **Scape:** 3″–5″ tall, clothed with 3 or 4 sheaths. **Spike:** composed of 1–4 lax flowers. **Flowers:** ¼″ across; dorsal sepal elliptic-oblong, concave, erect; spur clavate; lateral sepals oblong; petals narrowly oblong, with prominent rounded angles in front; lip sub-pandurate, somewhat curved at the base. *July to November.*

The small pink blossoms of this species and the neat spoon-shaped leaves should make it a desirable plant for the alpine house, where it would not be overlooked, as it would be in the rock garden. It is found on mountain slopes amongst short herbage in South-Western Cape Colony and reaches its greatest elevation on the Drakenstein Mountains in the Paarl Division at 4000 feet and is there subjected to 12° or more of frost during the winter. It should be grown in fibrous loam in a sunny spot and is only suitable for outdoor culture in warm localities.

SERAPIAS, Linnæus

A small genus of very delightful, deciduous, terrestrial plants numbering 5 species, which form natural hybrids among themselves and with several members of the genus *Orchis*, for which the generic name of *Orchiserapias* (G. Cam.) has been coined. In *Serapias* the root system is composed of two or more irregular potato-like tubers sessile at the base of the underground portion of the stem; there are a few fleshy roots where stem and tuber meet. The stout stems are clothed with a few narrow, pale green leaves which degenerate into bracts upwards and are usually large and finely coloured where they subtend and almost hide the blossoms. The blossoms are borne in dense, or at times loose, spikes and are generally very ornamental. The plants are found in all the countries bordering the Mediterranean from Spain to Asia Minor and Northern Africa, usually in open sunny spots in sandy and calcareous soils. They may be grown outdoors in sunny sheltered localities but should have their roots protected from severe frost. Propagation by separation of the tubers and by seeds.

941. SERAPIAS CORDIGERA, Linn.

Root: of 2 irregular potato-like, sessile tubers. **Stem:** $\frac{1}{2}'$–1′ tall, rather stout, sheath-clothed. **Leaves:** few, linear or linear-lanceolate, deeply channelled, undulate, degenerating into lanceolate sheaths upwards. **Spike:** 2″–4″ tall, bearing from 4–6 blossoms. **Flowers:** nearly $1\frac{1}{2}''$ long; sepals and petals lanceolate, connivent, forming a galea; lip large, 3-lobed; outer lobes small, rounded, erect; centre lobe pendulous, very broadly lance-shaped or heart-shaped; disc hairy. *April to June.*

A very quaint but at the same time beautiful Orchid with very large blossoms half hidden, with the exception of the lip, by the huge lilac or pink, red-veined floral bracts. The sepals and petals are lilac or pink with crimson nerves, and the lip is reddish-brown with dark outer lobes; the leaves are lined purple below. The plant is found in open places in sandy soils in the South of France and Italy, and also in Greece. It may be grown outdoors in a sunny spot in the rock garden in sandy fibrous loam. The form *leucantha* has a yellow lip and is very desirable.

942. SERAPIAS LINGUA, Linn.

Root: of a few small, ovoid tubers, one or two on long fibres and one sessile at the base of the stem. **Stem:** 6″–9″ tall, rather slender. **Leaves:** cauline, lanceolate, sheathing the stem, more or less erect, edges undulate, 3″–6″ long. **Spike:** about 2″ long, few-flowered. **Flowers:** $1\frac{1}{4}$″ long; sepals and petals connivent, forming a galea; petals subulate above, enlarged below into a broadly ovate base; lip variable in shape, usually 3-lobed; side lobes erect, rounded; centre lobe ovate, oblong-ovate or ovate-lanceolate, usually downy. *April to June.*

An extremely dainty Orchid with pale green unspotted foliage and very delicately tinted blossoms. The sepals and petals forming the hood over the column are lilac, veined crimson; the lip is salmon or rose-pink with dull crimson outer lobes; the floral bracts are lilac, veined crimson. The plant is found on dry chalky hillsides throughout the Mediterranean region and may be grown in a sunny spot in the rock garden in calcareous soil. The form *leucoglottis* (Welw.) is a very desirable plant.

943. SERAPIAS LONGIPETALA, Poll.

S. pseudo-cordigera, Moric.

Root: of 2 ovoid, irregular, sessile tubers. **Stem:** 9″–12″ tall, leafy, the upper part clothed with large leafy bracts. **Leaves:** cauline, linear-lanceolate, lower recurved, upper erect, all sheathing, 4″–7″ long. **Spike:** few-flowered, congested by the large leafy bracts. **Flowers:** over $1\frac{1}{2}$″ long; sepals and petals connivent, forming a galea, lanceolate; petals as in the previous species; lip 3-lobed; side lobes rounded, nearly hidden in the galea; centre lobe lanceolate or ovate-lanceolate; disc hairy. *May and June.*

A beautiful and desirable species with pale green foliage and quaint blossoms half hidden by the large, leafy, lilac-coloured floral bracts. The sepals and petals are lilac, veined violet, and the lip is pale salmon-pink, veined crimson, with deep crimson outer lobes. The plant is found on open grassy hillsides, usually not far from the sea, ranging from the South of France to the Caucasus. It may be grown outdoors in sheltered sunny localities under the same conditions as *S. lingua*. The forms *mauritanica* and *pallescens* are pretty plants.

944. SERAPIAS NEGLECTA, Dntrs.

Root: of 2 ovoid tubers about $\frac{3}{4}$″ long, one stalked and the other sessile. **Stem:** 4″–9″ tall, stout, leafy. **Leaves:** few, linear-lanceolate, degenerating into broadly lanceolate bracts, lower ones recurved, upper undulate and erect, 3″–6″ long. **Spike:** about 2″ long, few-flowered, congested. **Flowers:** over

$1\frac{1}{2}''$ long; sepals and petals forming a galea, lanceolate; petals subulate above, enlarged below; lip 3-lobed; side lobes rounded, protruding; centre lobe large, broadly cordate, sharply pointed, with a hairy disc. *May to July.*

A very handsome and desirable species with rich green foliage and very large floral bracts, yellow-green below shading to lilac at the tip and veined with crimson; the sepals and petals are of a delicate lilac colour and the lip is salmon-red, the outer lobes and margins being chestnut-brown. It grows in open grassy places in Southern France and Italy and may be cultivated in Great Britain in the same manner as *S. cordigera.* There are several forms with deeper coloured flowers than the type.

945. SERAPIAS OCCULTATA, Gray

S. laxiflora var. *parviflora,* Reichb. f. *S. parviflora,* Parl. *S. strictiflora,* Welw.

Root: of 2 ovoid tubers, one sessile and the other shortly stalked. **Stem:** $4''$–$7''$ long, erect, slender, leafy and sheath-clothed. **Leaves:** few, narrowly lanceolate, deeply channelled, sheathing, degenerating into bracts upwards. **Spike:** of few erect blossoms. **Flowers:** about $\frac{5}{8}''$ long; sepals and petals lanceolate, small, connivent, forming a galea; lip small, slightly longer than the sepals, 3-lobed; side lobes rounded, hidden within the galea; centre lobe ovate-lanceolate, reflexed, downy. *March to May.*

A slender, erect-growing species with small but pretty blossoms of pale purple sepals and petals with violet nerves; the lip is chestnut-brown with erect sepia-coloured side lobes. The floral bracts are pale purple, veined violet, and are large and very decorative. It is found on exposed hillsides, usually not far from the sea, from the South of France to Smyrna and may be grown under the same conditions as *S. lingua.* There are several forms with deeply tinted blossoms.

SPATHOGLOTTIS, Blume

This genus contains about 10 species of handsome terrestrial Orchids scattered over tropical Asia, Australia and some of the islands of the Pacific. Their root system consists of a creeping rhizome over which are scattered numerous pseudo-bulbs; these are usually broadly conic and bear from one to three leaves. The flower-stem springs from beside a pseudo-bulb and is usually erect and somewhat slender; the beautiful blossoms are borne in loose racemes on the top of the naked scape and are frequently of considerable size and decorative value. Only one species is sufficiently hardy for experimental culture outdoors in this country. Propagation by division of the rhizome with one or two pseudo-bulbs and also by seeds when procurable.

946. SPATHOGLOTTIS FORTUNEI, Lindl.

S. pubescens, Lindl.

Root: a creeping rhizome. **Pseudo-bulb:** ovoid, about 1″ long. **Leaves:** narrowly linear, usually 3 in number, 2″–12″ long. **Scape:** 1′–2′ tall, stout or slender. **Raceme:** short, of 6–8 blossoms. **Flowers:** about 1″ across; sepals subequal, ovate or lanceolate, 5–7-nerved; petals similar but much broader and very blunt, 9-nerved; lip 3-lobed; outer lobes ovate, erect, downy; centre lobe cuneately flabellate or obcordate; disc with 1–3 keeled nerves; lip saccate at the base. *August.*

A beautiful plant with rather large bright golden-yellow blossoms with some red or chocolate-brown markings at the base of the lip. It is found in open situations on limestone hills and in dry clay pastures in Burma and China, reaching an elevation of 9000 feet in Western Yunnan. Plants collected from such altitudes should be hardy in the warmer parts of Great Britain in a sunny spot in the rock garden in a good heavy, calcareous loam.

SPIRANTHES, Richard

A large genus numbering 260 species of deciduous terrestrial plants, few of which are of any horticultural value, although several are desirable on account of their fragrant blossoms. Their underground portions consist of a short stock and few or many oblong or fusiform tubers, sometimes of considerable size. The stems are usually leafy but are sometimes clothed with a few scales or sheaths, and a tuft of narrow leaves is produced beside them. In most species the blossoms are produced in a spirally-twisted spike and are rather small and pale in colour. The plants are usually found in open country in damp soils and are distributed over the greater part of the temperate and tropical regions of the world; some are found well within the Arctic regions. A few are hardy in Britain and may be grown in a damp spot in the rock garden or pond-side in good fibrous loam with some peat if possible. Propagation by division of the roots and by seeds.

947. SPIRANTHES ÆSTIVALIS, Rich.

Epipactis spiralis, Linn. *Gyrostachys æstivalis*, Dumort. *Neottia æstivalis*, D. C. *Ophrys æstiva*, Balb. *O. uliginosa*, Pour. *Orchiastrum æstivum*, Mich.

Root: of 2, rarely more, hairy, fusiform tubers about 1½″ long. **Stem:** 6″–12″ tall, leafy, fairly stout. **Leaves:** numerous, cauline and basal, linear-lanceolate, sheathing, almost distichous, 2″–4″ long. **Spike:** 3″–5″ long, spiral, lax, many-flowered. **Flowers:** about ¼″ across; dorsal sepal and lateral sepals equal, lanceolate, pointed; petals similar, slightly smaller, all spreading; lip oblong-ovate, with the edges near the tip slightly dentate.

June and July.

A delicate little native plant with grass-like pale green leaves and spirally twisted spikes of pure white blossoms; they are pretty but too small to be of much decorative value. The plant is found in bogs and marshes over nearly the whole of Europe except the extreme north. It may be grown in the bog garden in sphagnum-moss and peat.

948. SPIRANTHES AUSTRALIS, Lindl.

Neottia australis, R. Br.

Root: a short rhizome with a cluster of oblong tubers. **Stem:** fairly stout, leafy, 6″–15″ tall. **Leaves:** linear or narrowly lanceolate, 1¼″–4″ long, degenerating into sheathing scales upwards. **Spike:** 2″–4″ long, spiral, usually very dense, blossoms sessile. **Flowers:** about ½″ long; dorsal sepal and petals erect, forming a hood over the column with the tips spreading; lateral sepals ovate, spreading; lip unguiculate below, broadly ovate above, undulate, crisped or almost fringed. *August and September.*

This species has a very extensive habitat being native from New Zealand, Eastern Australia, the greater part of tropical and temperate Asia to Eastern Europe. It varies very much in habit and colour. The blossoms are usually pink with a white lip but are at times pure white; they are dainty and quite decorative. In its native countries it is found in damp, grassy places and should be perfectly hardy in Great Britain in a damp open spot in the rock garden in fibrous loam and sand. *S. sinensis* and *S. chinensis* from China and *S. amœna* and *S. stylites* from Japan differ from *S. australis* in only a few minute particulars.

949. SPIRANTHES CERNUA, Rich.

Gyrostachys cernua, Kuntze; *Neottia cernua*, Pursh.

Root: a cluster of thick fibres. **Stem:** ½′–2′ tall, rather stout, clothed with small sheaths. **Leaves:** mainly basal, linear or oblong, nearly sessile or narrowed into a stalk, 2″–12″ long. **Spike:** 2″–6″ long, cylindrical, slightly twisted. **Flowers:** about ⅜″ long, numerous; sepals oblong or ovate, pointed; petals oblong, pointed, conniving with the dorsal sepal; lip oblong, sometimes broadened at the base, crenulate at the tip and crenate at the base where there are 2 linear calli. *August to October.*

This is quite a pretty species with neat foliage and waxy white, fragrant blossoms in a somewhat dense spike. It is very closely allied to *Spiranthes Romanzoviana*, and is found in bogs, swamps and wet meadows, usually on sandy soils, in Eastern North America from Nova Scotia to Florida. It is quite hardy in Great Britain and may be grown in the bog garden or a wet spot in the rock garden, in sandy loam and peat.

950. SPIRANTHES EXIGUA, Rolfe

Hetæria exigua, Schltr.

Root: of oblong tubers or thickened fibres. **Leaves:** obsolete. **Scape:** about $2\frac{1}{2}''$ tall, very slender, clothed with a solitary imbricating sheath. **Raceme:** about 1″ long, lax, few-flowered. **Flowers:** over $\frac{1}{4}''$ across; sepals ovate, blunt, lateral ones oblique; petals narrowly oblong, rather blunt; lip oblong, rather pointed, with minute hastate lobes; base with 2 tubercles. *August.*

A quaint leafless species with a loose raceme of few pale green blossoms of no decorative value. It grows in open grassland on the mountains of Hupeh. It should succeed in most parts of Great Britain in an open sunny spot in the rock garden in good fibrous loam.

951. SPIRANTHES GRACILIS, Bigel.

Gyrostachys gracilis, Kuntze

Root: of thick, clustered fibres. **Stem:** $\frac{3}{4}'$–2′ tall, slender, clothed with a few clasping sheaths. **Leaves:** mainly basal, oblong-elliptic or ovate-lanceolate, shortly stalked, $\frac{1}{2}''$–2″ long. **Spike:** 1″–6″ long, slender, many-flowered. **Flowers:** about $\frac{3}{16}''$ long; sepals ovate, the lateral ones spreading; petals ovate or oblong, erect; lip oblong, crenate or undulate near the tip and with 2 erect calli near its base. *August to October.*

A pretty although by no means showy plant with long, almost naked, spikes of many small white blossoms with green centres to their lips. It is found in open woods, grassy hillsides, swamps, etc., usually on a sandy soil, from Arctic Canada down the eastern side of the United States to Florida. It should therefore be perfectly hardy in Great Britain in a damp part of the rock garden, in a light sandy loam.

952. SPIRANTHES LATIFOLIA, Torr.

Gyrostachys plantaginea, Britt. *Spiranthes plantaginea*, Torr.

Root: a cluster of thickened fibres. **Stem:** 4″–15″ tall, rather stout, clothed with sheathing scales above. **Leaves:** mainly basal, broadly linear or oblong, shortly stalked, 2″–6″ long. **Spike:** 1″–4″ long, oblong, many-flowered. **Flowers:** about $\frac{3}{16}''$ long; dorsal sepal oblong; lateral sepals narrowly lanceolate, free; petals oblong, united to the dorsal sepal, forming a hood over the column; lip oblong, undulate, tapering at the base into a short stalk where there are 2 small calli. *June and July.*

This little species should prove rather attractive in the alpine house, although its blossoms are too small to be of any decorative value; they are borne in stout spikes and have white sepals and petals and a yellow lip. It is found in woods and on shady banks from Nova Scotia to North Carolina and is perfectly hardy in Great Britain, in a damp shady spot in the rock garden, in loam and leaf-soil.

953. SPIRANTHES LINEARIS, Rydb.

Gyrostachys linearis, Rydb.

Root: of several thick fibres. **Stem:** slender, 1′–1½′ tall, covered with glandular hairs above. **Leaves:** mainly basal, narrowly linear, 2″–4″ long. **Spike:** 2″–4″ long, slender, many-flowered. **Flowers:** about $\frac{5}{16}$″ across; sepals linear-lanceolate, lateral ones spreading, upper one broader, converging with the oblong petals; lip oblong, cordate at its base. *July and August.*

The yellow blossoms of this species are too small to be of any decorative value; they are borne in a slender spike on a stem which is clothed with bright green leaves below the middle. It is found on the borders of swamps, moist meadows, etc., in the Eastern United States from New York to Florida. It should be quite hardy in Great Britain on the edge of the bog garden or on the banks of a stream or pond in good loam.

954. SPIRANTHES OCHROLEUCA, Rydb.

Gyrostachys ochroleuca, Rydb.

Root: a cluster of thickened fibres. **Stem:** 1′–1½′ tall, rather stout, clothed with a few lanceolate scales, downy. **Leaves:** mainly basal, linear, pointed, tapering into a distinct stalk at the base, lower ones frequently sessile. **Spike:** 2″–6″ long, dense, usually tapering to a point. **Flowers:** about ⅜″ long; sepals ovate or oblong, rather pointed; petals oblong, conniving with the dorsal sepal over the lip; lip ovate or oblong, rounded at the tip and with 2 hairy linear calli near the base. *August and September.*

Although the rather small yellowish-green blossoms of this plant are of little or no decorative value, they are deliciously fragrant and it is well worth growing on this account. It is found on damp grassy hillsides in Eastern North America from New Hampshire to North Carolina. It should be perfectly hardy in this country in an open spot in the rock garden, in fairly damp, sandy loam.

955. SPIRANTHES ODORATA, Lindl.

Gyrostachys odorata, Kuntze

Root: a cluster of stout or tuberous fibres. **Stem:** $\frac{3}{4}$′–2′ tall, clothed with lanceolate scales above. **Leaves:** mainly basal, oblong or oblong-lanceolate, with fairly long stalks, 4″–12″ long. **Spike:** 4″–6″ long, rather stout, many-flowered. **Flowers:** about $\frac{3}{8}$″ across and $\frac{1}{2}$″ long; sepals ovate or oblong, pointed; petals similar in shape to the sepals; lip broadly ovate at the base, narrowing to oblong towards the tip, irregularly toothed or crisped; calli at the base slender, incurved, hairy below.

September and October.

The blossoms of this species are large for the genus, they are yellowish-white in colour and very fragrant. It is well worth growing and is found in a state of nature on the banks of rivers, frequently in the water, in Kentucky, North Carolina, Georgia, South Carolina, Florida and Texas. It is only suitable for outdoor culture in the warm Western and Southern districts of Great Britain, in good rich loam on the banks of a stream or pond.

956. SPIRANTHES PRÆCOX, Walt.

Gyrostachys præcox, Kuntze

Root: of several tuberous fibres. **Stem:** $\frac{3}{4}$′–2$\frac{1}{2}$′ tall, slender, leafy to the top. **Leaves:** mostly cauline, linear, sometimes dilated in the middle, narrow and sheathing at the base, 2$\frac{1}{2}$″–12″ long, degenerating into sheathing scales above. **Spike:** 1″–4″ long, many-flowered, spirally twisted. **Flowers:** nearly $\frac{3}{8}$″ long, curved or slightly nodding; sepals and petals ovate or oblong, pointed, subequal; lip cordate at the base, oblong, crisped above the middle, usually recurved at the tip, with 2 linear calli near the base.

July and August.

A leafy species with twisted spikes of numerous white or yellow downy blossoms; they are too small to be of much decorative value. The plant grows in damp spots on the borders of woods and meadows, in Eastern North America from New York to Florida. It should be perfectly hardy in Great Britain in a damp but sunny part of the rock garden, in fibrous loam and leaf-soil.

957. SPIRANTHES SIMPLEX, A. Gray

Gyrostachys simplex, Kuntze

Root: thickened, tuber-like. **Stem:** very slender, clothed with a few scales, or naked, 4″–12″ tall. **Leaves:** on a short stem, ovate or oblong, withering before the flower-stem is developed, about 1″ long. **Spike:** $\frac{1}{4}$″–2″

long, slender, many-flowered. **Flowers:** about $\frac{1}{8}''$ long, secund; sepals and petals similar in shape, ovate or oblong, erect or curving outwards at the tip; lip broadly oblong, crisped at the tip, narrowing into a stem at the base where there are 2 calli. *August and September.*

A delicate fragile plant with naked one-sided spikes of very small white blossoms. It is of little decorative value but might be useful for alpine-house culture. It grows in sandy meadows in Eastern North America from Massachusetts to Florida and should be perfectly hardy in Great Britain, in an open part of the rock garden in sandy loam.

958. SPIRANTHES SPIRALIS, C. Koch.

S. autumnalis, Rich. *Epipactis spiralis*, Crantz. *Gyrostachys autumnalis*, Dum. *Neottia spiralis*, Swartz; *Ophrys autumnalis*, Bab.

Root: of several oblong or fusiform hairy tubers, $\frac{3}{4}''$–$1\frac{1}{2}''$ long. **Leaves:** in a rosette or tuft springing from the root, numerous, ovate or ovate-oblong, tapering towards the base, 1″–2″ long. **Scape:** 6″–12″ tall, lateral, curved, rather slender, clothed with numerous sheath-like bracts. **Spike:** 2″–5″ long, spirally twisted. **Flowers:** about $\frac{1}{4}''$ across; sepals lanceolate-oblong, pointed; petals similar but smaller; lip wedge-shaped, usually entire at the tip. *August to October.*

This native species produces a slender bract-clothed stem from beside the tuft of dull green leaves, and a spirally twisted spike of small white blossoms in which the lip is sometimes tinted with green. The plant is of little garden value and is found in a state of nature in dry hilly pastures throughout Europe to Asia Minor and Northern Africa. It may be grown in the rock garden in a well-drained spot in sandy loam.

959. SPIRANTHES STRICTA, Rydb.

Gyrostachys stricta, Rydb.

Root: a cluster of fleshy fibres. **Stem:** 6″–14″ tall, smooth, leafy below. **Leaves:** lowermost linear or linear-oblanceolate, degenerating upwards into bracts, 3″–6″ long. **Spike:** 2″–4″ long, more or less cylindric, many-flowered. **Flowers:** about $\frac{3}{8}''$ long, widely expanded with a very open throat; dorsal and lateral sepals ovate, usually pointed; petals rather similar but narrower; lip oblong, broad at the base, dilated and crisped at the apex, with, at times, 2 small calli near its base. *July and August.*

This is probably the most desirable member of the genus. It has smooth juicy stems clothed with narrow semi-erect rich green leaves and a many-flowered spike of snowy white, highly fragrant blossoms, arranged in three rows. The plant grows in peat bogs and on the mossy margins of swamps, ascending the mountains to considerable elevations and ranges from Newfoundland to Idaho and southward to Pennsylvania and Colorado, and Western Ireland. It may be grown in the bog garden, in peat and sphagnum-moss.

STENOGLOTTIS, Lindley

This genus consists of 2 species of deciduous terrestrial Orchids only one of which is found at sufficient elevation in its native country to give reasonable hope that it may prove fairly hardy in Britain. The root system consists of a short stock and several finger-like tubers, frequently of considerable size; the flower-stems are usually short and are clothed at the base with a tuft of leaves which vary much in shape and size in the different species. The blossoms are borne in dense rather one-sided racemes and are rather too small to be termed decorative. At least one species has ornamental leaves. The plants are found in wooded country frequently at considerable elevations in the mountains in British Central Africa and southward to Eastern Cape Colony. Propagation by imported tubers and by seeds if obtainable as the plants form plump capsules in their native habitats.

960. STENOGLOTTIS FIMBRIATA, Lindl.

Root: of finger-like tubers. **Leaves:** in a dense rosette, oblong or lanceolate, pointed, slightly undulate at the margins, $1\frac{1}{2}''$–$3\frac{1}{2}''$ long. **Scape:** $\frac{1}{2}'$–$1'$ tall, slender, erect. **Raceme:** $1\frac{1}{2}''$–$6''$ long, lax, many-flowered. **Flowers:** $\frac{1}{2}''$ long; sepals broadly ovate; petals ovate, broader and shorter than the sepals; lip linear oblong, sharply 3-lobed at the tip. *August to April.*

This is a pretty little plant with a tuft of bright green oblong leaves which are at times spotted and barred purple-black. The blossoms, which are borne in long racemes on the slender stem, are light purple in ground colour with a few oblong, purple or violet blotches on the lip. It inhabits woods and mountain ravines in Eastern Cape Colony, Natal and the Transvaal, where on Spitz Kop near Lydenburg at 5500 feet it probably attains its greatest elevation above sea-level and is exposed to nearly 20° of frost during its resting period in the winter. Cultural indications are mixtures of leaf-soil and loam in half-shade.

STIGMATODACTYLUS, Maximowicz

This genus consists of but one species; it is a very dwarf terrestrial plant and is closely allied to the Tasmanian *Burnettia cuneata.* The root system consists of a brittle, fleshy underground stem, sparely branched, with small ovoid tubers on the ends of the larger roots; the fleshy stem bears a solitary leaf and terminates in a few-flowered raceme of small, erect blossoms.

It is found in shady places on the mountains in the Island of Shikoku, Japan, where it grows in decaying leaves. It is rare and local. Propagation by imported tubers.

961. STIGMATODACTYLUS SIKOKIANUS, Maxim.

Root: a soft, fleshy, somewhat curved rhizome with a small tuber at the end. **Stem:** $1\frac{1}{2}''$–$4''$ tall, slender, angulate, with a solitary leaf above the middle. **Leaf:** ovate, crisped on the margins, sessile, $\frac{1}{2}''$–$\frac{3}{4}''$ long. **Raceme:** terminal, loose, of 1–3 blossoms. **Flowers:** about $\frac{1}{4}''$ across; sepals linear, bearded with a few long hairs; petals similar but not bearded; lip shortly unguiculate, orbicular, entire, crenulate on the front margin; appendage directed to the front, 2-lobed, lobes bifid at the tip. *September.*

A very quaint little plant suitable for alpine-house cultivation. It produces a slender scape terminating in one or two flowers with the dorsal sepal and petals pale green shaded with purple, the lateral sepals are pale green and the lip is very pale purple. It is found on Mount Yokogura in the province of Yosa, Japan, growing in shady places among dead leaves. It should be sufficiently hardy for outdoor culture in the warmer parts of the Country, in a damp shady spot in the rock garden, in decaying oak and beech leaves.

THELYMITRA, Forster

A genus of about 60 most delightful deciduous, terrestrial Orchids strikingly Ixia-like in habit and flower. It may be safely said that all are worth growing, some are exquisitely beautiful and are remarkable for the regular segments of their blossoms; petals, sepals and lip are all about the same shape. Their underground portion consists of two or more sessile or stalked tubers on the base of the stem with a few fleshy roots above; the largest tuber after having supplied the nourishment for the flowers and seeds shrivels and the other tubers when of sufficient size produce flowering stems, so the species is maintained. The stems are usually slender and are clothed with solitary grass-like leaves; the blossoms are solitary or in many-flowered spikes and racemes; they are frequently large and some are of a beautiful cobalt-blue colour. The plants grow in open situations in New Zealand, New Caledonia, Tasmania, Australia and on the high mountains of the East Indies. Propagation by imported tubers and by seeds.

962. THELYMITRA ANTENNIFERA, Hook. f.

Macdonaldia antennifera, Lindl.

Root: of 2 oval or oblong tubers. **Leaf:** solitary, narrowly linear, rather thick, $3''$–$6''$ long. **Scape:** wiry, flexuous, clothed with 1–2 bract-like leaves. **Flowers:** $1\frac{1}{4}''$ across, 1–3 on stalks of varying length; sepals and petals ovate, usually rather blunt; lip similar to the sepals and petals; column with lobes erect and spathulate. *October and November.*

A beautiful species of very slender, delicate habit, bearing from one to three large yellow blossoms tinted with pink on their under surfaces; the column is deep crimson-purple and is quite conspicuous against the paler tint of the segments. It is a very desirable and decorative species and grows in moist, open spots, usually in light soils in Victoria, Southern Australia, Western Australia and Tasmania, ascending the mountains to sufficient elevation to ensure its hardiness in all but the bleaker parts of Great Britain. It may be given a damp sunny spot in the rock garden in a compost of sandy fibrous loam.

963. THELYMITRA ARISTATA, Lindl.

T. grandis, F. Muell. *T. angustifolia*, Hook. f.

Root: of 2 stout, oblong tubers. **Leaf:** basal, solitary, linear-lanceolate, 6″–18″ long. **Scape:** 1′–3′ tall, stout, clothed with 1 or 2 leaf-like bracts. **Spike:** about 4″ long, loose, bearing from 2–6 blossoms. **Flowers:** 1″–1½″ in diameter; sepals, petals and lip broadly oblong, pointed, of about equal length, forming a regular flower; column lobes produced in the form of a hood over the anther, usually forked and downy. *November.*

A very robust species with a tall, stout stem clothed with a long grass-like leaf and one or two leafy bracts; it terminates in a spike of large, pale blue or purple, Ixia-like blossoms. The plant should prove a welcome addition to gardens. It is found in a state of nature in open, moist situations usually on poor soils in Victoria, Southern Australia, Western Australia and Tasmania, and should be hardy enough for outdoor culture over the greater portion of the British Isles in sheltered, sunny spots in a compost of damp fibrous loam and sand.

964. THELYMITRA CARNEA, R. Br.

Root: of 2 small ovoid tubers. **Leaf:** narrowly linear, cauline, solitary, 1½″–3″ long. **Scape:** slender, flexuous, wiry, 6″–12″ long. **Flowers:** ½″–¾″ across, from 1–3 in number on stems of various lengths; sepals, petals and lip all ovate in shape, pointed, rather concave, forming a blossom regular in outline; column with truncate wings, fringed. *December.*

A slender graceful little species with small but brightly coloured blossoms resembling some species of Ixia; they vary from deep pink to blood-red and the stalks on which they are borne are frequently tinted with the same colour; the solitary grass-like leaf is of a very bright green colour. In its native habit it grows in moist grassy places, mostly in the open, in the lowlands and at a considerable elevation on the mountains. It is fairly frequent in New South

Wales, Victoria, South Australia and Tasmania, and should be quite hardy in all but the bleakest parts of Great Britain in a sheltered, sunny spot in damp fibrous loam.

965. THELYMITRA CYANEA, Lindl.

T. venosa, Hook. f. *Macdonaldia cyanea*, Lindl.

Root: of 2 ovoid tubers. **Leaf:** solitary, linear, narrow, deeply grooved, 4″–6″ long. **Scape:** 6″–12″ tall, slender, bearing 2 sheathing leaf-like bracts. **Spike:** loose, of from 1–6 blossoms. **Flowers:** about $\frac{3}{4}$″ across; sepals, petals and lip ovate, rather blunt, forming a flower with a regular outline; column with lobes oblong or lanceolate, thickened. *December.*

A delightful plant closely allied to *T. venosa*, with a slender, rich-tinted flower-stem bearing a few Ixia-like blossoms with regular segments of a beautiful rich deep blue colour; there is also an uncommon pure white form. It is found in moist soils, and soils which are subject to frequent inundation during the winter months. It appears to be confined to Tasmania, where it is fairly frequent. In cultivation in Great Britain it should prove quite hardy in the warmer parts of the Country in a sunny spot on the banks of a stream or pond.

966. THELYMITRA FLEXUOSA, Endl.

T. Smithiana, Hook. f. *Macdonaldia concolor*, Lindl. *M. Smithiana*, Gunn.

Root: of 2 small ovoid tubers. **Leaf:** solitary, cauline, narrowly linear, rather thick, 3″–4″ long. **Scape:** 6″–9″ tall, flexuous, clothed with 1–2 leaf-like bracts. **Flowers:** $\frac{1}{2}$″ across, 1–2 in number, sepals, petals and lip, ovate, blunt, of equal length, forming a regular blossom; column-wing broadly truncate, sinuate, lobes not prominent. *October and November.*

A dainty species with a crimson tinted wiry, flexuous stem bearing one or two bright yellow blossoms tinted orange on their backs and bearing a striking superficial resemblance to the flowers of a Cowslip. It is found in moist grassy places in open country both in mountainous districts and the lowlands in Victoria, Western Australia and Tasmania. In Great Britain it should be quite hardy in the warmer and more sheltered districts in a damp fibrous loam in full sun in the rock garden.

967. THELYMITRA IXIOIDES, Sw.

T. iridioides, Sieb. *T. juncifolia*, Lindl. *T. lilacina*, F. Muell.

Root: of 2 fair-sized, ovoid tubers. **Leaf:** cauline, solitary, linear or linear-lanceolate, 4″–6″ long. **Scape:** 1′–1$\frac{1}{2}$′ tall, rather slender, clothed with 1–2 leaf-like bracts. **Spike:** about 6″ long, of from 5–10 blossoms. **Flowers:** about 1″ across; sepals, petals and lip broadly oblong, rather pointed, forming a more or less regular saucer-shaped blossom; column-wing forming a broad hood over the anther with a crest on its back.

November and December.

A very beautiful plant of a highly decorative nature which in the best forms produces a long spike of large pale blue blossoms, very like those of the Ixia in outline; they are usually sprinkled with purple spots, some more than others. The foliage and stem are rich green. It is a common plant in Queensland, New South Wales, Victoria, Western Australia and Tasmania, on the mountains and in the lowlands in open spots usually in moist sandy soils. It should be quite hardy in a sheltered sunny spot in a moist light soil in all but the bleakest parts of Great Britain.

968. THELYMITRA LONGIFOLIA, Forst.

T. Forsteri, Swartz; *T. stenopetala*, Hook. f. *T. nuda*, R. Br. *T. arenaria*, Lindl. *T. graminea*, Lindl. *T. pauciflora*, R. Br. *T. versicolor*, Lindl. *Serapias regularis*, Forst.

Root: of ovoid tubers. **Leaf:** solitary, cauline, varying from narrowly linear to linear-lanceolate, channelled or flat, rather leathery, 4″–9″ long. **Scape:** fairly stout, 8″–16″ tall. **Spike:** from 1″–4″ long. **Flowers:** $\frac{1}{4}$″–$\frac{3}{4}$″ across; sepals and petals ovate-lanceolate, pointed, of nearly equal length; lip obovate; column-wing produced in a hood over the anther.

November to January.

This species is a very variable plant with regard to height, shape of the leaf and size of the blossoms. In its best forms it is a very beautiful plant of large flowers with spreading purple-blue sepals and lip and paler petals. The blossoms vary in number from two to ten and are very Ixia-like in shape. It grows in a variety of soils and situations, most frequently in open grassy places, throughout almost the whole of Australia and New Zealand and as far south as the Auckland Islands. Plants from the most southern portions of its range should be quite hardy in Great Britain. A good damp loam in full sun is indicated. *See Plate 22 facing page 433.*

969. THELYMITRA MACMILLANII, F. Muell.

Root: of 2 ovoid tubers. **Leaf:** solitary, cauline, narrowly linear, 3″–5″ long. **Scape:** slender, flexuous, zig-zag above, clothed with 1–2 bract-like leaves. **Flowers:** about $\frac{3}{4}$″ across, 1–3 in number on stalks of varying length; sepals, petals and lip ovate, usually somewhat blunt, of nearly equal length,

PLATE 21.

SERAPIAS CORDIGERA.

PLATE 22.

THELYMITRA LONGIFOLIA.

forming a regular, slightly concave blossom; column-wing produced into 2 lateral, diverging lobes, curved and slightly denticulate.

November and December.

A slender plant with rich deep red blossoms on stalks of varying lengths springing from the upper part of the main stem which is very deeply tinted red on yellowish-green. The plant is found in open moist spots on sandy soil at low elevations in Victoria and should be quite hardy in the warmer parts of Great Britain in the open ground in a sunny sheltered place in the rock garden in a moist sandy soil.

970. THELYMITRA PULCHELLA, Hook. f.

Root: of small ovoid tubers. **Leaf:** cauline, solitary, linear, deeply channelled, thick, 6″–9″ long. **Scape:** rather stout, $\frac{1}{2}$′–1$\frac{1}{4}$′ tall. **Spike:** about 3″ long, fairly dense. **Flowers:** 1″ across; sepals and petals ovate, rather pointed, of about equal length, forming a regular flower; lip obovate, pointed.

November and December.

A very lovely species with large blue-purple Ixia-like blossoms in spikes of nearly a dozen on fairly tall stems clothed with a solitary bright green leaf. It grows in open grassy country, generally in cool moist soil in both the North and South Islands of New Zealand and probably attains its greatest altitude above sea-level on the Montere hills in the South Island at 1500 feet above sea-level; specimens collected from this elevation should be perfectly hardy in England. It may be grown in a moist fibrous loam in full sun in the rock garden.

971. THELYMITRA UNIFLORA, Hook. f.

Root: of small ovoid tubers. **Leaf:** cauline, solitary, narrowly linear, deeply channelled, fleshy, blunt, 2″–6″ long. **Scape:** stout, 6″–8″ tall, bearing from 1–3 blossoms. **Flowers:** $\frac{1}{2}$″ across, sepals and petals linear-oblong, rather pointed, of nearly equal length; lip obovate-cuneate, pointed.

December and January.

A pretty little species with delicate pale blue blossoms on a fairly stout flower-stem clothed with a solitary bright green grassy leaf. It should prove a delightful subject for a pan in the alpine house. It grows in moist open grassy places in the lowlands of the South Island of New Zealand and the Auckland Islands, from which locality it should be perfectly hardy in Great Britain. In cultivation it may be tried in a good fibrous loam in a damp spot in the rock garden in full sun.

TIPULARIA, Nuttall

Quaint, terrestrial, deciduous plants numbering but 4 species, with long spikes of small greenish blossoms of no decorative value; they are, however, rather curiously constructed. The root system consists of several corms or rounded tubers which are frequently found on the surface of the soil like pseudo-bulbs. The solitary ovate or lanceolate leaf, with a short or long stalk, springs from the top of the tuber at the base of the flower-stem. The plants inhabit shady places such as thin woods and thickets and have a rather curious distribution, being confined to Northern India, Japan and North America; they should be quite hardy in this country in a damp half-shady spot in the rock garden in a rich light soil. Propagation by separation of the corms or tubers and also by seeds which are freely produced by plants in a state of nature.

972. TIPULARIA JAPONICA, Matsumura

Root: a pseudo-bulb-like tuber, usually above ground, about $\frac{5}{8}''$ long, with a few roots from the base. **Stem:** slender, 6″–12″ long, smooth. **Leaf:** solitary, ovate, pointed. **Raceme:** lax, of few flowers. **Flowers:** under $\frac{1}{8}''$ across; sepals oblong-spathulate, spreading; petals somewhat similar; lip rounded, 3-lobed; outer lobes rounded, toothed; centre lobe longer, blunt; spur slender, nearly $\frac{1}{4}''$ long. *June and July.*

A slender plant with a solitary, rounded leaf and a lax, few-flowered raceme of very small yellowish-green and brown blossoms of no decorative value. It is found in damp shady woods on the mountains in Eastern Nippon, Japan. It should be perfectly hardy in Great Britain in a shady part of the rock garden in leaf-soil, peat and loam.

973. TIPULARIA JOSEPHII, Reichb. f.

Root: a small tuber-like pseudo-bulb emitting a few fibres. **Leaf:** solitary, ovate, on a fairly long stalk, 5–7-nerved, 2″–3″ long. **Scape:** 8″–12″ tall, slender. **Raceme:** rather loose. **Flowers:** about $\frac{3}{8}''$ across; sepals linear, with revolute margins, 3-nerved; petals linear, blunt, 1-nerved; lip 3-lobed; outer lobes rounded; centre lobe flat, ovate or ovate-lanceolate, pointed; lip much smaller than the sepals; spur long and slender.
July and August.

This plant is interesting but of no garden value. The tall slender flower-stem springs from beside the oval leaf and terminates in a loose raceme of small yellowish-brown blossoms. It grows in woods and thin forests in vegetable soil and moss on the Sikkim Himalaya, reaching an elevation of 12,000 feet and should therefore be quite hardy in Great Britain in a shady part of the rock garden in leaf-soil, peat and loam kept reasonably moist.

974. TIPULARIA UNIFOLIA, Muhl.

T. discolor, Nutt.

Root: a number of corms or rounded tubers, often connected by offsets. **Leaf:** solitary, ovate or ovate lanceolate, pointed, truncate or subcordate at the base, plaited, $1\frac{1}{2}''$–$3\frac{1}{2}''$ long, developing in the autumn and lasting into the spring. **Scape:** 1′–2′ tall, erect, springing from beside the leaf. **Raceme:** 6″–12″ tall, many-flowered. **Flowers:** about $\frac{3}{8}''$ across; sepals linear or oblong-linear, rather blunt; petals somewhat similar; lip 3-lobed, oblong; outer lobes broader than the centre one; spur slender, about $\frac{3}{4}''$ long.

July and August.

This plant produces a tall naked stem from beside the rather large yellowish-green leaf and terminates in a long, lax, many-flowered raceme of rather small yellowish-green blossoms of no decorative value. It inhabits damp woods and shady banks in the Eastern United States from Vermont to Michigan and southward to Florida. It is quite hardy in Great Britain in a damp shady spot in the rock garden in leaf-soil and sand.

YOANIA, Maximowicz

The solitary species which constitutes this genus is a leafless, deciduous, terrestrial Orchid of little decorative value but well worth growing as a curiosity. In habit and appearance it somewhat resembles our native Coral-root and is no doubt either a saprophyte or a parasite and usually grows over the roots of trees in thin woods, generally in hilly or mountainous country. It should be possible to grow the plant in a damp half-shady spot in leaf-soil and grit over the roots of a birch, willow or poplar and it would probably be more conducive to success if a considerable portion of soil could be imported with the roots *in situ*; this method may be very successfully employed with British parasites such as *Monotropa Hypopithys* and *Lathræa squamaria.* Instructions for importing Orchids from abroad will be found in the forepart of the book.

975. YOANIA JAPONICA, Maxim.

Root: of stout, branched fibres. **Leaves:** obsolete. **Stem:** 3″–6″ tall, stout, erect or tortuous, clothed with helmet-shaped sheaths. **Raceme:** of from 4–6 blossoms. **Flowers:** about $\frac{3}{4}''$ long; sepals oblong, oblique, blunt, fleshy; petals broadly ovate; lip cymbiform, with a thickened tip at times.

July to September.

A quaint, leafless Orchid with brownish-white stems and blossoms, the latter being quite large in comparison to the size of the plant. It is interesting but not decorative. It grows in thin mountain woods and in thinly wooded ravines in Burma and Japan and is sufficiently hardy for culture outdoors in Great Britain in all but the bleakest parts, in the rock garden in fibrous loam and leaf-soil in a half-shady spot.

ZEUXINE, Lindley

Slender, deciduous, terrestrial plants numbering about 78 species, natives of tropical Asia and Africa, two of which are found at sufficient altitudes to justify their experimental culture outdoors in sheltered spots in Western and Southern Britain. They have creeping stems, for the most part above the mossy soil in which they grow; these produce numerous, rather stout, somewhat fleshy fibres. The leaves are radical, few in number, stalked, ovate or lanceolate and are frequently rather large and thin in texture; the blossoms are borne in few- or many-flowered spikes and are too small and usually too few in number to be of very much garden value; they should, however, appeal to lovers of beauty in miniature. The plants described below may be tried outdoors in the above-mentioned localities in a half-shady spot in leaf-soil and sandy loam; their roots should be protected in the winter. Propagation by imported roots and by seeds.

976. ZEUXINE GOODYEROIDES, Lindl.

Monochilus galeatus, Lindl.

Root: a creeping rhizome. **Leaves:** subradical, ovate, sessile or shortly stalked, 1″–1½″ long. **Scape:** 3″–9″ tall, slender, nearly smooth. **Spike:** short, few-flowered. **Flowers:** about ¼″ across; dorsal sepal ovate, pointed; lateral sepals lanceolate; petals falcate, very blunt; lip very small, cymbiform, terminal lobe orbicular or oblong, concave, membranous or thick, with 2 short spurs within near the base. *May and June.*

A dwarf species with pretty rich green leaves with a pale green or white centre stripe and short, few-flowered spikes of small white and green blossoms of no decorative value. It grows in thin forests and shady places among rocks in the Eastern Himalaya and Burma, reaching an elevation of 8000 feet above sea-level in its Himalayan habitat. It may be grown outdoors in Southern and Western Britain in a shady spot in the rock garden, in good fibrous loam and leaf-soil.

977. ZEUXINE SULCATA, Lindl.

Z. bracteata, Wight. *Z. brevifolia*, Wight. *Petrygodium sulcatum*, Roxb.

Root: a creeping rhizome. **Stem:** 2″–16″ tall, leafy to the top. **Leaves:** few or many, sessile, linear-lanceolate, margin usually recurved, 1″–2″ long. **Spike:** ½″–2″ long, dense-flowered. **Flowers:** about $\frac{3}{16}$″ long; sepals oblong, blunt, membranous; petals oblong, blunt; lip cymbiform, bearing a hammer-headed terminal lobe or two small lobes. *February.*

A plant of many synonyms, with leafy stems bearing a short dense spike of very small white, yellow or pale pink blossoms of but little decorative value. It grows in a variety of situations both on the plains and hills of Afghanistan, India, China and the East Indies. It may be grown outdoors in the warmer parts of Great Britain in a damp spot in the rock garden in good fibrous loam.

INDEX

OF

GENERA, SPECIES, VARIETIES AND SYNONYMS

Synonyms least used and somewhat obscure, not mentioned in the text, are included below, with page number omitted. These can be identified by the species number.